"The editors and contributors of this book are to be congratulated for producing a unique and invaluable volume, containing an enormous amount of essential, up-to-date information for the interpretation of the New Testament. Here students will not only learn of the history of the New Testament but also discover helpful paths through the dense thicket of contemporary hermeneutics—all excellently done and attractively presented."

— **Donald A. Hagner**
author of *The New Testament: A Historical and Theological Introduction*

"Mitternacht, Runesson, and their contributors have produced a magnificent introductory textbook on the earliest social, historical, and textual contexts of devotion to Jesus, with due attention given also to the intricacies of interpretation. This book is comprehensive and authoritative, but never at the expense of accessibility. I will be assigning this book to my students at the first opportunity."

— **Chris Keith**
St. Mary's University, Twickenham

"New Testament scholarship is and has always been international and multilingual. Consequently, for more than a decade now, one of the very best introductions to the New Testament has been available only in Swedish: Dieter Mitternacht and Anders Runesson's *Jesus och de första kristna* (2006). But now, thanks to Rebecca Runesson and Noah Runesson's deft translation, this revised and expanded edition of the book is accessible to those of us who speak English but not (yet) Swedish. The twenty-two contributors are a who's who of Scandinavian biblical scholarship, and the emphasis on hermeneutics as well as history is an especially inspired feature."

— **Matthew V. Novenson**
University of Edinburgh

"Whereas the vast majority of introductions to the New Testament are more than content simply to describe the contents and contexts of the twenty-seven documents that comprise the same, in *Jesus, the New Testament, and Christian Origins*, twenty-two skillful Scandinavian scholars, led by editors Dieter Mitternacht and Anders Runesson, not only orient students to the New Testament and its bewildering world but also illustrate how these fascinating texts can continue to be interpreted and appropriated in variegated ways. The upshot of this expansive, extensive edited volume is nothing less than a valuable, accessible reference resource for those who are wanting and willing to grapple with the meaning(s) of the New Testament."

— **Todd D. Still**
George W. Truett Theological Seminary, Baylor University

"This wonderful book expertly invites students into the academic study of the New Testament by not simply surveying the contents of the New Testament but also introducing the historical contexts that gave rise to these writings and their collection into a canon. Best of all, it will empower students to dive into New Testament interpretation by modeling various methodological approaches to its study."

— **Matthew Thiessen**
McMaster University

"Not a New Testament introduction in the usual sense, this impressive text nonetheless provides a well-paved, well-lit path into serious New Testament study. The authors cultivate historical, textual, and readerly interests, all in the service of equipping their own readers with competence and confidence for interpreting these canonical texts."

— **Joel B. Green**
Fuller Theological Seminary

"*Jesus, the New Testament, and Christian Origins* is an impressive multi-authored work that combines several discrete subdisciplines: the history of New Testament scholarship; the political, social, and literary milieux within which early Christianity originated and developed; New Testament introduction and theology; early church history; and methods of biblical interpretation. Although a collective effort, the work is clear and coherent, reflecting strong editorial leadership. Special strengths include comprehensive reviews of current scholarly thinking on major interpretative issues such as life-of-Jesus research, the 'new perspective' on Paul, the 'parting of the ways,' and the delineation of six identifiable streams of early Christian thought. Ample bibliographies, along with numerous diagrams, tables, and boxes of supplementary material, enhance its pedagogical value. A remarkable synthesis that deserves to become a 'pull-down' book for biblical scholars, theological students, and pastors."

— **Carl R. Holladay**
Emory University

JESUS, THE NEW TESTAMENT, AND CHRISTIAN ORIGINS

Perspectives, Methods, Meanings

Edited by Dieter Mitternacht and Anders Runesson

Translated by Rebecca Runesson and Noah Runesson

William B. Eerdmans Publishing Company
Grand Rapids, Michigan

Originally published in Swedish by Verbum AB, Stockholm, Sweden, under the title *Jesus och de första kristna*.

Wm. B. Eerdmans Publishing Co.
4035 Park East Court SE, Grand Rapids, Michigan 49546
www.eerdmans.com

Printed in the United States of America

27 26 25 24 23 22 21   1 2 3 4 5 6 7

ISBN 978-0-8028-6892-3

Library of Congress Cataloging-in-Publication Data

Names: Mitternacht, Dieter, editor. | Runesson, Anders, editor. | Runesson, Rebecca, translator. | Runesson, Noah, translator.
Title: Jesus, the New Testament, and Christian origins : perspectives, methods, meanings / edited by Dieter Mitternacht and Anders Runesson ; translated by Rebecca Runesson and Noah Runesson.
Other titles: Jesus och de första kristna. English
Description: Grand Rapids, Michigan : William B. Eerdmans Publishing Company, 2021. | "Originally published in Swedish under the title Jesus och de första kristna." | Includes bibliographical references and index. | Summary: "An introduction to the New Testament in its historical context, along with an overview of different interpretative approaches and exegetical exercises"—Provided by publisher.
Identifiers: LCCN 2020028360 | ISBN 9780802868923
Subjects: LCSH: Bible. New Testament—Criticism, interpretation, etc. | Jesus Christ—History of doctrines. | Church history—Primitive and early church, ca. 30–600.
Classification: LCC BS2361.3 .J4913 2020 | DDC 225.6—dc23
LC record available at https://lccn.loc.gov/2020028360

Unless otherwise noted, quotations from Scripture are taken from the New Revised Standard Version of the Bible.

Artwork at the beginning of chapters 1–6 is by Per Gyllenör.

For Birger Olsson—
mentor, colleague, friend

Contents

Foreword

The book that you are holding in your hands, *Jesus, the New Testament, and Christian Origins: Perspective, Methods, Meanings*, edited by Dieter Mitternacht and Anders Runesson, is an introduction to early Christianity that is very different from the typical New Testament introductions currently available. One of the courses focusing on Christianity most frequently offered by many colleges, universities, and theological seminaries is typically called "Introduction to the New Testament," and the kind of text designed to be used in such courses typically has that phrase as part or all of the title. Such texts typically focus on the twenty-seven individual documents that make up the canonical New Testament, discussing a range of issues, such as when and where each document was written; the identity of the individual authors or editors; the genre, content, structure, purpose, and key theological themes of each document; the sources of each document, including oral and written traditions; the possible relationships of particular documents to each other (e.g., the literary relationship between the four Gospels); the audience for which they were originally intended; and a bibliography on recent research on each book. Some introductions to the New Testament emphasize the historical background of the New Testament,[1] while others include a treatment of theological issues as well,[2] and yet others include

1. This is true of the widely used text by W. G. Kümmel, *Introduction to the New Testament* (Nashville: Abingdon, 1975, originally published in German).

2. E.g., Paul J. Achtemeier, Joel B. Green, and Marianne Meye Thompson, *Introducing the New Testament: Its Literature and Theology* (Grand Rapids: Eerdmans, 2001); Carl A. Holladay, *A Critical Introduction to the New Testament: Interpreting the Message and Meaning of Jesus Christ* (Nashville: Abingdon, 2005); Donald A. Hagner, *The New Testament: A Historical and Theological Introduction* (Grand Rapids: Baker Academic, 2012); M. Eugene Boring, *An Introduction to the New Testament: History, Literature, Theology* (Louisville: Westminster John Knox, 2012).

some early Christian noncanonical texts.[3] Often the historical process by which each text was eventually included in the canon of the New Testament is also surveyed. Introductions to the New Testament are typically arranged in one of two ways. The discussion of books of the New Testament can occur either in their canonical order, that is, beginning with the four Gospels and ending with Revelation, or in the historical order in which the books were written, that is, treating the Pauline letters first (the oldest documents in the New Testament), followed by the Gospels and Acts and then the rest of the epistolary literature and Revelation. Such introductory texts are written at various levels of sophistication; some are intended for college students at the beginning level and others are written for more advanced students at the graduate level. The purpose behind such introductory texts is, or ought to be, to teach students to read the New Testament in an informed and intelligent manner.

This text, which is intended for students at a relatively advanced level of study, that is, those in graduate schools or theological seminaries, is very different from these more conventional introductions to the New Testament. The primary overlap with more conventional introductions occurs in chapter 4, which focuses on the main features of the twenty-seven canonical New Testament texts, written from 50 to 130 CE (this time frame indicates that the authors use the historical-critical method). The central core of this introduction consists of three chronologically arranged chapters, chapters 3–5. (I will give a more detailed chapter-by-chapter analysis below, but here a brief summary will suffice.) Chapter 3, "The Historical Jesus," focuses on the sources for our knowledge of the historical Jesus, beginning with non-Christian texts, including Josephus and several second-century Roman authors, followed by a brief discussion of evidence for Jesus found in the Pauline letters and the apocryphal gospels, then a more lengthy consideration of the evidence for Jesus found in the Gospels, bearing in mind that the miraculous cannot be verified by the historical method. Chapter 4, "The Texts," begins with a short introduction to the textual criticism of the New Testament, that is, how to reconstruct the most original written form of the New Testament books, followed by a discussion of each of the twenty-seven books of the New Testament, discussed in canonical order. Chapter 5, "The Emergence of Early Christianity," examines the history of the Christ-believing Jews and the eventual separation of Christianity from Judaism, followed by a discussion of Paul, his congregations, and his successors, and the Johannine messianic faith and variety of Judaism and Gnosticism from the first and second centuries CE. The historical order of these three chapters emphasizes the fact that the New Testament texts contain traditions that stretch back to the historical Jesus himself and at the same time provide information about the early groupings within earliest Christianity, accentuating the various trajectories in the development of early Christianity.

3. Delbert Burkitt, *An Introduction to the New Testament and Origins of Christianity* (Cambridge: Cambridge University Press, 2002).

These three core chapters are framed by chapters 2 and 6. Chapter 2, "Historical Background and Setting," provides historical and cultural background, consisting of ancient Near Eastern history, Greco-Roman religion and culture, and the beliefs and practices of Second Temple Judaism, forming the broader historical and cultural context within which early Christianity arose and developed. Chapter 6, "Readings," provides a discussion of the principles of New Testament interpretation and a selection of nine different step-by-step approaches to interpreting nine different types of New Testament texts. Chapter 1, "Invitation to Study the New Testament," provides an introductory overview of the entire text and its arrangement.

The discussion in each of the six chapters is enhanced by the inclusion of twenty "text boxes," that is, helpful information to aid the reader (e.g., the temple in Jerusalem, Olympic gods and goddesses); four "tables," that is, various lists of information of interest to the reader (e.g., canon lists); twenty-two "figures," that is, helpful illustrations (e.g., the floor plan of the temple of Jerusalem, the two-source hypothesis); and twenty-five images or photos that illuminate aspects of the text (e.g., the Acropolis in Athens, tombs in the Holy Sepulcher).

As the preceding paragraph indicates, this text provides a much more comprehensive resource for structuring an introductory course in early Christianity than do the more typical introductions to the New Testament described at the outset. This text not only covers the kinds of largely literary topics focusing on the twenty-seven books of the New Testament mentioned above (dealt with in chapter 4), but also supplements the discussion of the individual books of the New Testament with important related areas of study. The overall arrangement of the book is therefore chronological, providing insight into the various developments of earliest Christianity from its origins in Jesus of Nazareth in the early first century to its development in various directions in various historical and social contexts from the later first century through the third century. While some introductions to Christianity occasionally include references to some early Christian texts later than the New Testament, such as the Gospel of Thomas, the present text emphasizes the canonical New Testament texts but also includes an overview of a variety of later Jewish-Christian and gnostic texts in chapter 5, which provide information about the various religious contexts of developing early Christianity.

This book contextualizes the New Testament texts in a variety of ways by providing historical and social contexts, emphasizing what came before and was presupposed by New Testament authors and their readers; that is, Hellenistic and Roman background material and particularly Hebrew and Jewish history and traditions. The books of the New Testament are intertextual, that is, they assume a knowledge of the Jewish scriptures, both Hebrew and Greek, and allude to them frequently both directly and indirectly. An introductory text should also deal with how early Christianity developed during the first century of its development and expansion. The present volume does this well, covering the historical and cultural background of early Christianity and its expansion and development throughout the Mediterranean world, including surveys of Near Eastern, Greco-Roman, and Jewish history and culture; the study of the historical Jesus; the emergence of early Christianity, including the separation of Christianity from Judaism; the growth and development of early Christianity, including a survey of Pauline and Johannine Christianity; and the influence of Gnosticism. One of the salutary things that this new text can encourage is the development of courses on the New Testament and early Christianity more comprehensively, dealing with these related areas of study in a more adequate and inclusive manner.

It should also be recognized that courses in New Testament introduction are most frequently offered in colleges and theological seminaries that reflect particular denominational and theological traditions that span the spectrum from conservative and uncritical to liberal and critical, with everything else in between. More conservative introductions tend to accept at face value the claims of authorship made in the New Testament texts; that is, the presence of pseudepigraphy in the New Testament is generally denied. All the letters attributed to Paul, such as the Pastorals, are assumed to have actually been written by Paul, just as the apostle Peter is assumed to have actually written 1 and 2 Peter. For conservative scholars, the canonical status of individual books of the New Testament is typically dependent on whether they were actually written by the author to whom they are attributed. The text by Mitternacht and Runesson, on the other hand, is written from the standpoint of the historical-critical method; that is, the historical method is used as the basic way of understanding the texts. That means that there are some prominent features of the New Testament, such as miracles, which the historical-critical method cannot treat. While more conservative introductions regard the Pastoral Letters (1–2 Timothy and Titus) as actually written by Paul, as each claims to be, and dated therefore within Paul's lifetime (ca. 50–64 CE), the Mitternacht and Runesson text, in line with mainline historical-critical scholarship, regards the Pastorals as pseudonymous, that is, probably written by a follower of Paul rather than the apostle himself in the early second century CE.

While most introductions to the New Testament are written by a single author (occasionally by two or three)—typically someone who has taught New Testament for many years and is intimately familiar with all of the issues mentioned above—this text, originally written in Swedish, was written by twenty-two Scandinavian New Testament scholars, most of whom are both Swedish and Lutheran, and edited by Dieter Mitternacht (professor of New Testament at the Lutheran Theological Seminary in Hong Kong) and Anders Runesson (professor of New Testament at the University of Oslo).

As mentioned above, this book consists of six chapters, the first of which, "Invitation to Study the New Testament," provides a brief historical overview of the key aspects of research done in the field of New Testament and early Christian studies and how it has developed over time. This chapter reveals just how distinctive this volume is from typical New Testament introductions. The chapter begins by summarizing what is known about the movement begun by Jesus of Nazareth, who founded what eventually became the largest religion in the world. (The historical Jesus is dealt with in detail in chapter 3, "The Historical Jesus.") The chapter then provides a brief overview of Palestinian Judaism (dealt with in detail in chapter 2, "Historical Background and Setting"). This first chapter then discusses the diversity and unity of the books of the New Testament, mentioning several gospels that never became part of the New Testament and examining how the canonical New Testament eventually emerged, with some variety, as the later Christian churches functioned as interpretive communities; the New Testament canon thus provided a means of unifying the diverse groups of Christians scattered throughout the Mediterranean world (dealt with in detail in chapter 4, "The Texts").

The third chapter, which focuses on the historical Jesus, is particularly important and treats a subject rarely discussed in typical introductions to the New Testament. The authors distinguish between the historical Jesus, that is, *the Jesus of history* (the person who lived in first-century Palestine and whose life is open to historical reconstruction, as is any other historical person's), *the historical Jesus* (the designation given to the reconstructed portrait of the Jesus of history), and *the real Jesus* (the actual person named Jesus who, like any other historical person, cannot be fully reconstructed using the methods of historical research). The Jesus who is the focus of this chapter is the Jesus who is accessible to historians. In general, the Gospels must be seen as primarily reflecting the life and faith of the early church rather than of the actual Jesus. Several methods have been formulated to provide access to the Jesus of history. One of the most important historical methods is the criterion of double dissimilarity: that is, only those traditions in the Gospels that are dissimilar from the Judaism of Jesus's time and from the Christian community are deemed authentic. Since this problematical method is not used generally by historians, it should be replaced with the criterion of plausibility: that is, gospel traditions that plausibly fit into a first-century Jewish context and plausibly explain the impact of Jesus on the Christian movement have a better claim to provide us with reliable historical information about Jesus. Historical research on Jesus, the authors argue, should be carried out (1) with less distrust of the historical sources, (2) with ordinary historical methods, and (3) with what historiography can and should achieve. Early stories about Jesus are therefore read with the historian's eye.

The central theme of the proclamation of Jesus was the kingdom of God, that is, the total transformation of God's creation and his chosen people, a transformation that was both present and future. Jesus was a charismatic who was surrounded by a group of disciples who memorized his teachings. The event of Jesus's crucifixion was preserved in a passion story older than the Gospels. Since the historical method cannot deal with the category of "miracle," all that can be claimed for stories of the resurrection of Jesus is that those who knew Jesus were convinced that he rose from the dead.

Another important chapter is chapter 4, which focuses on the twenty-seven canonical texts of the New Testament, examining how oral traditions were incorporated into written texts and how scholars today, using the surviving ancient manuscripts, attempt to reconstruct the earliest form of the texts (a discipline called textual criticism). The first section begins with a discussion of the textual criticism of the New Testament, then turns to the process of canonization. The discussion of the texts of the New Testament begins with the four Gospels and Acts. A discussion of the Pauline letters comes next, beginning with a focus on the seven letters that scholars agree were written by Paul, followed by a discussion of the three letters whose Pauline authorship is debated, then by a discussion of the three letters that most scholars agree were not written by Paul but rather by followers of Paul.

Chapter 5, entitled "The Emergence of Early Christianity," provides a reconstruction of how early Christianity gradually developed from a group within mid-first-century Palestinian Judaism, which can be characterized as Christ-believing Jews, through the early second century, when Christ-believing non-Jews increasingly achieved prominence within the Jesus movement, even forming their own congregations, some of which excluded various forms of Christ-centered Judaism. By the early second century CE, Ignatius of Antioch even argued that Christianity was the antithesis of Judaism; that is, they were separate religions. The gradual emergence of Christianity as a religion separate from Judaism (which was a religion accepted by the Romans) meant that non-Jewish Christ believers had to find ways to be accepted by the Roman authorities. They did this in two ways: (1) they maintained that Christianity was not a new development but was actually very old and in complete continuity with Judaism, and (2) they denied the right of Judaism to its own traditions, arguing that Christianity was the true Israel and had replaced Judaism. Christ-believing Jews became increasingly marginalized from the second century on as non-Jewish Christ believers steadily increased in numbers and Jewish Christ believers became increasingly marginalized. This complex analysis of the gradual emergence of Christianity from Judaism is an important subject never discussed in conventional introductions to the New Testament and rarely touched on even in histories of early Christianity.

Chapter 5 then continues by discussing Paul, his congregations, and his successors as reflected in the Pauline letters and the book of Acts. According to the genuine Pauline letters (Romans, 1–2 Corinthians, Galatians, Philippians, 1 Thessalonians, and Philemon), Paul was aware that he was entrusted with a mission to proclaim the gospel to the uncircumcised. Acts tells a slightly different story, in which Paul's target group was primarily Jews, and only when Jews in various cities rejected his message did he turn to gentiles. The chapter then provides a complex summary of Paul's central convictions and beliefs, focusing on such topics as the message of the crucified Christ;

the imminent expectation of the return of Christ; God's dealings with Israel and the gentiles; one body, many members; and Jewishness, circumcision, and the law.

In discussing the last cluster of interrelated themes, emphasis is placed on Paul's contextual theology. In letters such as Romans, Galatians, and 1 Corinthians, Paul provides advice to the churches he addresses in a variety of contexts. The differences between Paul's arguments on becoming a Jew, circumcision, and the law in these three letters are all dependent on the particular contexts in which these issues are discussed. Two other closely related themes center on justification by faith and participation in Christ. Here the authors indicate how thoroughly the traditional understanding of the Pauline understanding of justification by faith has changed over the last fifty years. The so-called new perspective on Paul maintains that Second Temple Judaism was not, as many have argued, a legalistic religion. When Paul referred to "the works of the Law," he did not understand them as earning salvation; rather, works were to be understood as the means of remaining "in" salvation. Paul opposed the works of the Law as they represented the national exclusivism of Judaism. Against his opponents who argued that only Jews could be full members of the people of God, Paul maintained that all who believed in Christ were also children of Abraham. Finally, in Paul's view, salvation was not something that had been accomplished, but rather something that is still happening and will be completed in the future. In discussing the successors of Paul, the authors trace the three trajectories of Pauline influence: (1) the Pastoral Letters (1–2 Timothy and Titus), almost certainly not written by Paul, (2) Luke-Acts, and (3) Colossians and Ephesians. The Pastoral Letters are of particular importance in reflecting the development of leadership in the churches originally founded by Paul, emphasizing leadership ideals intended to help congregations find their place in society as respectable associations.

In the section of chapter 5 entitled "Johannine Christ Followers," there is a discussion of Johannine literature, consisting of the Gospel of John and the three letters of John. These texts reflect a group of messianic Jews in the early church who adhered to the language and message of Jesus preserved in the Johannine literature. The text does not understand the Gospel of John as a historical source for the life of Jesus so much as a way of understanding the distinctive views and experiences of Jews who came to believe in Jesus as the Messiah and who produced the Johannine texts. The Johannine literature is in fact a type of crisis literature, reflecting the conflicts of some of those who returned to or remained in a Jewish sect that did not acknowledge Jesus as the Messiah; some of these Jews who came to believe in Jesus later abandoned the sect. It appears that the Johannine Christians remained within the public Jewish synagogue.

From here the authors briefly characterize various types of non-rabbinic Jews and Judaism, including the prophetic Jesus-oriented Judaism reflected in the Martyrdom and Ascension of Isaiah, and non-rabbinic Jewish communities that existed in the third and fourth centuries CE, represented by such texts as the pseudo-Clementine

Homilies and *Recognitions*, the *Didascalia Apostolorum*, and the *Apostolic Constitutions*. Very little is known of the groups who produced these texts, but at least in Syria it is clear that the boundary between Jews and Christians was blurred for centuries. Chapter 5 concludes with an examination of Gnosticism and a discussion of the diversity that existed at this time and the struggle to gain unity.

The sixth chapter is a practical introduction to interpretative methods, including examples of various types of scriptural exegesis on select New Testament passages.

This unique introduction to early Christianity provides a textual resource without parallel for academic courses concerned with a comprehensive, multidimensional treatment of the historical study of early Christianity in all its complexity.

David E. Aune

Preface

Back in 2010, when Allen Myers, then senior editor at Eerdmans, invited us to consider publishing an English translation of our Swedish introduction to the New Testament from 2006 (*Jesus och de första kristna*), we all thought that the process would be completed within a couple of years. As the project developed, however, we became increasingly convinced that we should take the opportunity not only to update and translate the book but also to expand it to include new material responding to this ever-expanding field where the New Testament, Christian origins, and early Jewish studies increasingly intersect.

Ten years later, we are happy that we made that decision. The book that you now hold in your hands not only describes and explains current historical research in the field but also takes seriously the task of encouraging students to become actively involved in interpretation, giving them the tools necessary to do so. This integrated approach to writing a textbook on the New Testament, which moves beyond traditional approaches and disciplinary barriers, is, we believe, uniquely positioned to drive the discussion forward and contribute to fostering a new generation of students of the New Testament, some continuing on to become teachers, others to become preachers, and yet others to become the scholars of tomorrow.

It goes without saying that in order for a book like this to communicate effectively the most recent developments in research, as well as chart a way forward in the many specialized areas that together make up the field of New Testament studies, it is necessary to put together a whole team of scholars. We are grateful to all of the authors of this volume for their willingness to contribute their time and expertise to this project in the midst of otherwise very busy schedules. It has been a pleasure to work with you all. We also want to thank those who read and commented on the whole or parts of the manuscript, especially Ryan Davies, Mark Nanos, and Hugo

Lundhaug. While some texts were submitted to us in English, most of the chapters were updated in Swedish by the authors and then translated into English by Rebecca Runesson and Noah Runesson. Without their work, this project would not have been possible; we are very grateful for the time and effort they invested in this book. The indexes have been prepared by Daniel M. Gurtner, and we are very grateful to him for his careful and excellent work. We also want to express our gratitude to the people at Eerdmans for their dedicated and patient work on this project. A special thanks to now-retired senior editor Allen Myers, who was an invaluable conversation partner as our plans took form; to New Testament editor Trevor Thompson, who oversaw the work as chapters were submitted and translated; and to senior project editor Jennifer Hoffman, whose outstanding work and efficiency made the final and most intensive stages of galley proofing and final editing so much easier and enjoyable.

Last but not least, we want to express our sincere gratitude to Birger Olsson, professor emeritus of New Testament at Lund University. In Lund, Birger was our mentor as we learned to become scholars, challenging us always to go further and deeper, seeking new meanings by approaching materials from a range of different methodological vantage points. Since then, Birger has been a generous, supportive, and trusted colleague and friend, setting an example for others to follow. It is a joy for us, as editors, to dedicate this book to him. Thank you, Birger!

October 2020

Abbreviations

General and Bibliographic

ANRW	*Aufstieg und Niedergang der römischen Welt*
AYBRL	Anchor Yale Bible Reference Library
AYBC	Anchor Yale Biblical Commentary
b.	born
BECNT	Baker Exegetical Commentary on the New Testament
BibInt	*Biblical Interpretation*
ca.	circa
ch(s).	chapter(s)
cf.	*confer*, compare
ConBNT	Coniectanea Biblica: New Testament Series
CRINT	Compendia Rerum Iudaicarum ad Novum Testamentum
d.	died
e.g.	*exempli gratia*, for example
EJL	Early Judaism and Its Literature
esp.	especially
FRLANT	Forschungen zur Religion und Literatur des Alten und Neuen Testaments
Gk.	Greek
Heb.	Hebrew
ICC	International Critical Commentary
i.e.	*id est*, that is
JBL	*Journal of Biblical Literature*
JECS	*Journal of Early Christian Studies*

JSHJ	*Journal for the Study of the Historical Jesus*
JSNTSup	Journal for the Study of the New Testament Supplement Series
Lat.	Latin
LEC	Library of Early Christianity
LNTS	The Library of New Testament Studies
LXX	Septuagint
MS(S)	manuscript(s)
NA^{28}	Nestle-Aland, *Novum Testamentum Graece*, 28th edition
NHC	Nag Hammadi codices
NICNT	New International Commentary on the New Testament
NIGTC	New International Greek Testament Commentary
NIV	New International Version
NRSV	New Revised Standard Version
NT	New Testament
NTS	*New Testament Studies*
OT	Old Testament
par(r).	parallel(s)
r.	reigned
RBS	Resources for Biblical Study
SBLDS	Society of Biblical Literature Dissertation Series
SNTSMS	Society for New Testament Studies Monograph Series
SP	Sacra Pagina
ST	*Studia Theologica*
WBC	Word Biblical Commentary
WUNT	Wissenschaftliche Untersuchungen zum Neuen Testament

Old Testament

Gen	Genesis	Neh	Nehemiah
Exod	Exodus	Esth	Esther
Lev	Leviticus	Job	Job
Num	Numbers	Ps(s)	Psalm(s)
Deut	Deuteronomy	Prov	Proverbs
Josh	Joshua	Eccl	Ecclesiastes
Judg	Judges	Song	Song of Songs
Ruth	Ruth	Isa	Isaiah
1–2 Sam	1–2 Samuel	Jer	Jeremiah
1–2 Kgs	1–2 Kings	Lam	Lamentations
1–2 Chr	1–2 Chronicles	Ezek	Ezekiel
Ezra	Ezra	Dan	Daniel

Hos	Hosea	Nah	Nahum
Joel	Joel	Hab	Habakkuk
Amos	Amos	Zeph	Zephaniah
Obad	Obadiah	Hag	Haggai
Jonah	Jonah	Zech	Zechariah
Mic	Micah	Mal	Malachi

New Testament

Matt	Matthew	1–2 Thess	1–2 Thessalonians
Mark	Mark	1–2 Tim	1–2 Timothy
Luke	Luke	Titus	Titus
John	John	Phlm	Philemon
Acts	Acts	Heb	Hebrews
Rom	Romans	Jas	James
1–2 Cor	1–2 Corinthians	1–2 Pet	1–2 Peter
Gal	Galatians	1–3 John	1–3 John
Eph	Ephesians	Jude	Jude
Phil	Philippians	Rev	Revelation
Col	Colossians		

Other Jewish and Christian Writings

Apoc. Pet.	Apocalypse of Peter	Gos. Thom.	Gospel of Thomas
Bar	Baruch	Herm.	Shepherd of Hermas
Barn.	Barnabas	Ign. *Magn.*	Ignatius, *To the Magnesians*
CD	Cairo Genizah copy of the Damascus Document	Ign. *Rom.*	Ignatius, *To the Romans*
1–2 Clem.	1–2 Clement	Jdt	Judith
DA	*Didascalia Apostolorum*	1–2 Macc	1–2 Maccabees
Did.	Didache	Pol. *Phil.*	Polycarp, *To the Philippians*
Gos. Jud.	Gospel of Judas		
Gos. Mary	Gospel of Mary	Pss. Sol.	Psalms of Solomon
Gos. Pet.	Gospel of Peter	Sir	Sirach

ΙϹ ΧϹ

1

Invitation to Study the New Testament

Beginnings

This book is dedicated to the study of one of the most intriguing peculiarities of human history: the story of how a lowly Jewish artisan from an insignificant Galilean village of about four hundred inhabitants was executed by Roman imperial forces on suspicion of subversive behavior—only to become the most influential individual ever to have set foot on this planet. Jesus is today, two thousand years after his death, the central figure in a great number of creeds that together make up Christianity, the largest religion in the world, with most of its adherents now living in the so-called Global South. In terms of convictions, the central force behind these two thousand years of expansion is the astonishing claim that the man executed was brought back to life by the God of Israel. This belief spread rapidly around the Mediterranean, also among non-Jews, in the first few centuries of the Common Era. The originally oral traditions about Jesus's life and teachings were eventually written down, and a number of the resulting texts came to be seen by the mainstream churches as Holy Scripture. Within three hundred years the belief in Jesus as the risen Lord (Gk. *kyrios*), who would return to pass judgment on humanity and establish the kingdom of God, had filtered through into the upper social strata and been designated the state religion of the Roman Empire, the very same empire that had crucified the one now worshiped. Indeed, a most remarkable journey from periphery to center.

This journey began sometime between the years 7 and 4 BCE, when Jesus was born. According to the Gospels of Matthew and Luke this event occurred in Bethlehem, in Judea. Jesus then grew up in the village of Nazareth in Galilee, in the highlands of the north, which at this time was ruled by the Jewish vassal tetrarch Herod Antipas (4 BCE–39 CE), son of Herod I, also called "the Great." Judea, the country's southern part where the capital Jerusalem was located, was from 6 CE ruled directly by Rome through prefects, of which Pontius Pilate, the man who condemned Jesus to death, undoubtedly is the most well known. The country that Jesus grew up in was a nation under Roman colonial control. The Roman imperial presence was felt by all, not least because of taxes and other burdens affecting the masses. The land that had been united under a Jewish king at the time of Jesus's birth was, when Jesus began his ministry, politically divided.

The Jewish elite in the Jerusalem temple, as well as the vassal rulers in Galilee and the northeastern regions of what was once Herod I's kingdom, had to carefully balance between Roman demands, on the one hand, and the needs and will of the people, on the other. Those who did not belong to the ruling elite reacted to this political situation in different ways. Tax collectors, for example, could further their own financial gain by charging more tax than the Romans required, thereby increasing their commission. In the New Testament we have an echo of this type of fraud in the story of the tax collector Zacchaeus, who, after he met Jesus, decided to return the money he had gained through illegal means to all his victims (Luke 19). Others chose the way of armed resistance and rebellion. This resulted in, for example, two major revolts, first between the years 66 and 70 CE and then once more between 132 and 135 CE. There were also those who did not choose violence but rather hoped that the God of Israel would intervene and in a miraculous manner reestablish Israel as a kingdom (cf. Acts 1:6–7).

The public, civic synagogue institution, where the local affairs of villages and cities were dealt with and Holy Scriptures were read and interpreted every Sabbath, constituted a sociopolitical and religious focal point where people gathered for deliberation on various matters. Religion and politics, the cultic and the common, were intertwined in ancient understandings of the world; the Sabbath's discussion of Holy Scripture concerned the entirety of human existence and the society in which people lived. Additionally, by publicly reading and interpreting texts from Israel's past, the people's history was kept alive and relevant. Passages from the Scriptures that spoke of the liberation of the Jewish people from Egypt, or the people's deliverance from the Babylonian exile, were read and interpreted in the context of contemporary situations. Luke 4 tells us, in a paradigmatic sort of way, of how Jesus makes use of the Sabbath's Scripture reading and discussion to this effect.

The use of ancient texts in interpreting the present and the future—in cities and in rural areas, in the homeland and in the diaspora—contributed to creating a distinct Jewish culture and identity. A great deal of the texts that have been preserved from the first century CE bear witness to the importance that was attributed to certain writings. Of course, different groups could, and would, have different ideas not only about how these special writings should be interpreted but also about what should be considered Holy Scriptures in the first place. For example, the group known as the Sadducees accepted, like the Samaritans, only the five books of Moses (Torah), while the Pharisees, like Jesus and his followers, considered the prophetic writings and some other texts, traditionally called "the Writings," to be authoritative texts too.

Box 1.1
Dating

When dating historical events, many are used to the terms "before Christ" (BC) and *Anno Domini* (AD = "the year of the Lord"). For Christians this usage is certainly appropriate, but for persons adhering to other systems of belief, or none, the terminology may seem inadequate. Many academic publications today use a terminology that does not presume Christian faith or worldview yet still adheres to the Western dating tradition. This book uses "before the Common Era" (BCE) and "Common Era" (CE). Such terms give the additional benefit of preventing the common misconception that Jesus was born in the year 1, which in all likelihood he was not (see chapter 3).

The New Testament and Its Texts

Jesus did not write any texts himself. Nor did the collection of texts we know as the New Testament exist in the early Jesus movement. Those who accepted Jesus as Messiah (Gk. *Christos*) read and found guidance in the same holy texts that were used by many other contemporary Jewish groups. Christians later came to call these texts the *Old Testament*. Jews came to call them *Tanak*. This latter word is an acronym that is derived from the first letters in *Torah* (the Law, the five books of Moses), *Nevi'im* (the Prophets), and *Ketuvim* (the Writings). In this book we will refer to this collection of texts as the *Hebrew Bible* and in some places, when we would like to point to the early Greek translation of these texts, as the *Septuagint* (LXX). The twenty-seven writings that were authored by Jesus's followers, and that eventually were included in the New Testament, represent different genres. The oldest are letters written by Paul to the assemblies he and others had founded around the Mediterranean. In these letters he motivates and admonishes Christ followers about how they, as he sees it, should best express their trust in Christ, in both theology and practice.

Occasional oral traditions about Jesus are found in the Pauline letters. The most well-known example of such is surely the story of Jesus's last supper with his friends: "on the night when he [Jesus] was betrayed . . ." (1 Cor 11:23–25). It is not until the Gospel of Mark, written more than a decade after Paul's last letter, that we find a coherent retelling of Jesus's life and teachings. Following this text, a kind of ancient biography, we have the Gospels of Matthew, Luke, and John, likely written in this order at some point between the years 80 and 100 CE, although a growing number of scholars now suggest that Luke may have been written in the early second century. Just like the Gospel of Mark, these gospels present Jesus's life in the form of a narrative, albeit in different, sometimes supplementing, sometimes contradicting, ways. How it came to be that these gospels display such similarities and differences will be further explored in chapter 4.

The New Testament also contains the earliest account of the expansion of the Jesus movement, the book of Acts. In this text we are offered a story of how the apostles spread traditions about and sayings of Jesus, claiming him to be the resurrected Messiah, the one promised by the Jewish sacred Scriptures. As the author vividly recounts the bravery of men and women, accompanied by divine miracles, the reader learns that the mission is first directed toward fellow Jews and then expanded to include Samaritans and finally other non-Jews around the Roman Empire. At first Peter, one of Jesus's closest disciples, is portrayed as the principal figure behind these developments, but this focus later shifts to Paul. Both Peter and Paul receive their instruction to spread the news about the resurrected Messiah to non-Jews through visions—Peter on a roof in the city of Joppa, Paul on the road to Damascus. Paul, a Jewish intellectual who had been a zealous persecutor of Jews who had joined the Jesus movement, is entirely transformed by his encounter with the risen Christ and becomes one of the most eager missionaries of the movement.

Among the remaining texts of the New Testament are those that are formulated as letters but are more similar to treatises meant for a wide and general audience. Here we find the so-called Pastoral Letters, three letters written in the name of Paul that carry forward and adapt his legacy to new situations. Furthermore, there are three letters associated with John, of which the first and longest can hardly have been meant as a letter in the strict sense of that word. These texts mirror the Johannine tradition's emphasis on true faith in Christ. The Letter of James and the Letter to the Hebrews—neither of which belongs to the proper genre of ancient letters—appear to be written with a Jewish audience in mind, although the texts never mention which communities they are writing to. Finally, we have Revelation, the only apocalyptic text in the New Testament. It describes, with colorful and complicated metaphorical language, what is to happen in the final days, when God will judge the evil and vindicate the righteous. While this is a text about the future, it is saturated with a critique of the society in which the author lived, being especially hostile toward Rome.

Diversity, Unity, and Continuity

Most scholars hold that the texts of the New Testament were written over a period of eighty years—that is, between approximately 50 and 130 CE. The individuals who wrote them could hardly have predicted that their texts would become part of a literary collection that would be preserved for millennia and considered as holy as the Jewish Bible. Neither could the gospel authors, who shaped their portraits of Jesus with great care, know that their accounts would be included side by side in a collection of four gospels, providing the reader with diverse descriptions of who Jesus was and what he accomplished. It is this diversity that makes this literary collection so intriguing and challenging. In fact, already in antiquity attempts were made to merge the four gospels into one, thereby neutralizing the differences between them. At the same time, there were also strong forces that rejected such a harmonization of the gospels. The decision to allow the four different accounts to represent the truth about Jesus was deliberate and accepted early on by most authorities.

There were also other gospels that were not included in the New Testament, all of them written later than the four. One of these has become rather well known: the Gospel of Thomas. This text is not a narrative like the other gospels but contains a compilation of Jesus's words. For whatever reasons, the early authorities in the movement considered this list of Jesus's words to depart too much from what they understood the other four gospels conveyed. It was never included in the canon, therefore, but shared the fate of a multitude of other writings about Jesus that were discarded.

The early centers of belief in Jesus as the Christ—Jerusalem, Alexandria, Antioch, Ephesus, and Rome—sought unity in all this diversity. Finally, in the fourth century, they agreed that twenty-seven books should be considered especially authoritative and thus be recognized by all Christians as part of a collection of holy writings. This meant that a visible sign of unity within the (majority) church was achieved, while still preserving a form of measured diversity. Different accounts of Jesus's life and teachings, and different rules for how a Christ follower should live, were allowed to stand side by side in the same literary collection. The basic (theological) position seems to have been that revealed truth allowed for, even required, diversity, although within certain limits, which, of course, were determined by those considered authorities.

The word "gospel" (Gk. *euangelion*) means "good news." This word was used early on to describe Jesus's teachings. With time, however, the term came to denote the texts that present accounts of Jesus (gospels). In a comparable manner, the descriptor "New Testament" began to be used for a single collection of texts in the second century. The word "testament" comes from Latin and translates the Greek *diathēkē* (covenant), which in turn is a translation of the Hebrew word *berit*. These designations indicate that the texts included in this collection, the New Testament, were thought to describe in a meaningful way God's covenant with his people and humankind, a covenant that has its center in Jesus, called the Christ.

The term "new covenant" is, however, older than this. It occurs as early as in Jer 31:31–34, where a promise is made that there will come a time when God will make a *new covenant* with his people Israel. Describing the covenant, the passage continues: "I will put my law within them, and I will write it on their hearts; and I will be their God, and they shall be my people." The Hebrew Bible tells of many covenants, which were made at different points in time during Israel's history (e.g., between God and Noah, Abraham, the people of Israel at Mount Sinai, and David). In all these cases, the new was not considered to be a replacement or annulment of the old, but rather seen as an addition to what already existed, as a sign of God's faithfulness. The covenants were complementary in nature, in other words. The term "new" could even carry a negative connotation, as "old" traditions were generally considered better and more trustworthy. An example of this way of thinking may be found in Gal 3:17; a new covenant cannot abolish or supersede an older one (compare 1 Cor 3:10–13).

The literary collection that came to be known as the New Testament was added to and combined with the more ancient Jewish Scriptures, which Jesus's followers had venerated since the very beginning: the Torah, the Prophets, and the Writings. This in turn eventually led to the Christians coining the term "Old Testament" as a descriptor for these more ancient texts. The definitive contents of both collections (Old and New Testaments), however, was decided long after these descriptive terms had come into use. In fact, not even today do we find absolute agreement between different church traditions as to exactly which texts should be included in the canon.

From the time when the texts included in the New Testament were written until the time when the collection as such was agreed on, Christianity grew and expanded its presence around and beyond the Mediterranean world. The formation of the canon may be interpreted as an attempt at unifying Christians in order to prevent schisms and to counteract the development of isolated Christian groups that had little in common with others. As a recognized literary collection, the New Testament later also became a tool for mediating and reaching agreements between various Christian groups.

Many groups of Christ followers were marginalized in this historical process. Some of them are named in, for example, the writings of the church fathers, while others will remain unknown to us. In striving to limit diversity, the majority church identified, for better or for worse, what it saw as heretical groups. During the 1900s several sensational finds of papyri in Egypt were made, which have contributed to the fact that we today have access to some of the texts owned and copied by these groups themselves. The latest in this line of discoveries is the Gospel of Judas. The text is mentioned by the church fathers and was published in 2006 after extensive restoration work. Such finds are extremely important, since they make possible a better understanding than ever before of the early Christian movement in all its diversity.

The historical Jesus interpreted in word and deed what were for him the holy texts of the Hebrew Bible. Later, the texts that were written about Jesus himself were at once a result of and an influence on the Jesus movement and emerging Christianity. Thus, text and history become intertwined in a fascinating development that results in the birth of a world religion—a religion that still holds sacred the texts that bear witness to the early centuries' view on what defines legitimate diversity within Christianity. Throughout history and today, these texts have been and are read and interpreted in a wide variety of ways.

To Read and Interpret

The diversity of textual interpretation corresponds to the diversity of readers and reading communities. In the past, just as in the present, humans have sought in different ways and for different reasons to understand. Reading and rereading is a hermeneutical process that in many ways is similar to the rereading of texts from Israel's history by Jesus and others during the first century. How one reads is dependent on one's identity and what one wants from the reading, the aim of the reading. The very same text can mean different things depending on how it is read. A good example of this is the early reception of the Gospel of Matthew. The text was in all likelihood written by Jewish Christ followers who were careful to interpret their trust (Gk. *pistis*) in Jesus within the frame of their Jewish identity. Very soon, however, Matthew came to be used by non-Jews, which resulted in a different understanding of the text. That which in the beginning had been Matthew's inner-Jewish criticism of other Jewish groups was later interpreted by non-Jewish Christian groups as a general critique of Jews and Judaism as such—an entirely different reading that facilitated the construction and strengthening of a Christian identity that located itself outside of, and aimed to be independent from, Judaism. The tragic aftermath of this type of shift in meaning has been the object of extended analyses by scholars aiming to understand the use of the Gospel of Matthew in Christian anti-Jewish rhetoric.

Another example of how communicative settings affect texts and readings may be found in the New Testament's Johannine literature. As early as among the church fathers, there were those who held that the First Letter of John was a form of reading manual, meant to guide the reader through the Gospel of John. The gospel strongly emphasizes that the Messiah is God's eternal and only Son and that his presence on earth is a revelation of God's glory. The purpose of such an emphasis could have been to overcome a tendency among certain Christ-following Jews that saw Jesus as solely human. This in turn led to the text's polemical prong being pointed toward "the Jews." Interestingly, the effect of the gospel's strong emphasis on Jesus's divinity led the Christ followers in Ephesus to instead deny Christ's *human* nature (1 John 4:2–3). Thus, the author's attempt at preventing what he believed was a faulty train of thought seems, from his perspective, to have led to more misunderstandings rather than clarity. It is possible, then, that this whole process led to the writing of the First Letter of John to serve as a kind of instruction into how the Gospel of John should be understood. To correct perceived misreading, the letter emphasizes that the word of life indeed was from the beginning, but that it also is "what we have looked at and touched with our hands" (1 John 1:1).

A third example is seen in the Letter of James, with its emphasis on the connection between faith and works, or deeds (cf. Jas 2:14–26). The letter has been interpreted by some as a reaction to a flawed reading of the letters of Paul. In Lutheran tradition, there have even been claims that the Letter of James polemicizes against Pauline theology. Luther called the letter an "Epistle of Straw," which would burn on the Lord's Day when everything is tried in fire, and only the gold, silver, and gemstones of the gospel remain (cf. 1 Cor 3:12–14). More likely, however, is that the Letter of James is a reaction to a misguided interpretation of Pauline texts that viewed Paul's emphasis on faith as more or less canceling the importance of good deeds, an idea foreign to the apostle (cf. Rom 2:6–11; 3:31; Gal 5:19–23).

When reading and interpreting any text, it is important to be aware of the role that the interpreter and the interpretative context play when understanding is formed. From the very first period of the Jesus movement, different groups of Christ followers constituted interpretative communities, not only regarding theological issues, but also on practical questions such as what Christian life ought to look like in terms of ritual, ethics, and everyday life. By uniting twenty-seven texts in one collection of authoritative books, the emerging mainstream Christian church was shaped into a larger interpretative community, although it still held a great deal of diversity.

For two thousand years Christians have continued to aim at forming their faith and their lives in agreement with their interpretations of the New Testament, and this has inevitably at times resulted in intolerance and violence directed against people expressing opinions differing from those of the (empowered) majority. Often in the history of Christianity, individuals and groups have claimed their interpretations to be absolute representations of truth, and on the basis of such claims some have even broken away from other groups and begun new churches, as if unity required absolute agreement on textual interpretation. Interpretative diversity, however, remains the original posture of the movement in this regard. It all begins with diverging oral traditions about Jesus, which are interpreted differently by groups with varying levels of access to those traditions. Diversity then continues as four gospels and a number of other texts are recognized as authoritative, despite their often-contradictory perspectives, and brought together into a single canonical collection. The result of this process is the "library" we call the New Testament, which together with the Hebrew Bible is still read and interpreted throughout the world, both within and beyond the churches.

This Book

This book moves from historical perspectives, chapters 2–5, to more reading- and interpretation-oriented subjects, chapter 6. In order to introduce the study of the New Testament and Christian origins, taking aim at a historical understanding of

Box 1.2
The Hebrew Bible

The canon of the Hebrew Bible is notoriously difficult to date, but most scholars would agree that it was established about a century after the birth of Jesus. The Jewish name for the literary collection, Tanak, is an acronym of the words Torah (the Law), Nevi'im (the Prophets), and Ketuvim (the Writings). The Tanak contains twenty-four books, while, for example, the Protestant Old Testament, owing to a different way of counting, contains thirty-nine books. The actual text in the two collections is, however, basically the same.

Tanak

Torah
Genesis, Exodus, Leviticus, Numbers, Deuteronomy

The Early Prophets
Joshua, Judges, Book of Samuel (one book), Book of Kings (one book)

The Later Prophets
Isaiah, Jeremiah, Ezekiel, the Twelve (one book: Hosea, Joel, Amos, Obadiah, Jonah, Micah, Nahum, Habakkuk, Zephaniah, Haggai, Zechariah, Malachi)

The Writings
Job, Psalms, Proverbs, Ruth, Song of Songs, Ecclesiastes, Lamentations, Esther, Daniel, Ezra-Nehemiah (one book), Chronicles (one book)

Old Testament

The Pentateuch
Genesis, Exodus, Leviticus, Numbers, Deuteronomy

Historical Books
Joshua, Judges, Ruth, First and Second Samuel, First and Second Kings, First and Second Chronicles, Ezra, Nehemiah, Esther

Poetic Books
Job, Psalms, Proverbs, Ecclesiastes, Song of Songs

The Major Prophets
Isaiah, Jeremiah, Lamentations, Ezekiel, Daniel

The Minor Prophets
Hosea, Joel, Amos, Obadiah, Jonah, Micah, Nahum, Habakkuk, Zephaniah, Haggai, Zechariah, Malachi

Many Bibles contain an "Additions to the Old Testament" section, which usually consists of the following books: Tobit, Judith, the Greek version of Esther, First and Second Maccabees, Wisdom of Solomon, Wisdom of Jesus Ben Sira (Sirach), Baruch, Epistle of Jeremiah, Additions to Daniel, and the Prayer of Manasseh. These texts are part of the Septuagint and are integrated into the Old Testament in Catholic and Orthodox editions of the Bible.

Jesus, his early followers, and the texts they wrote, the remainder of chapter 1 will present an overview of key aspects of research done within the field, demonstrating how the field has developed over time. In addition, we have included a section discussing more methodologically oriented questions about how historical knowledge may be obtained in the first place.

Chapter 2 aims to reconstruct the historical context in which Jesus and his followers lived, and in which the texts about him were written. The reader will be led through history, from Persian times to the period in which the Jesus movement begins to take shape. We will learn about the religious and cultural environment in the Roman Empire and about various forms of Jewish practice and belief around the first century CE. Within this larger context, we will then aim the spotlight at Jesus in order to attempt to understand who he was and what he wanted to achieve (chapter 3).

Chapter 4 is dedicated to the texts of the New Testament. The chapter begins with a discussion of how oral traditions were textualized; how scholars reconstruct the texts today on the basis of the ancient manuscript evidence; and how, when, and why certain texts came to be included in the New Testament. After these introductory discussions, the New Testament texts themselves will be presented one by one, along with their communicative settings, content, structure, and key theological thoughts. Chapter 5 moves on to provide a historical perspective depicting some of the diversity and struggles for unity that existed from the earliest period until the emergence of Christianity as we know it today—that is, the time during which the New Testament was written and canonized.

The first part of the book is thus structured chronologically. The reader is led step by step through history according to the principle that that which occurred first, historically, is presented first. In other words, the events occurred before the texts were written; therefore, the texts are presented after the events. At this point it is important, we believe, to distinguish between the *via inventionis* and the *via expositionis*. The first expression refers to the path (*via*) that is followed in the analytical process (*inventionis*), and the latter refers to the manner in which one presents (*expositionis*) the results to the reader. Why, then, have we chosen a chronological layout for a textbook? Let us explain briefly.

If someone wishes to know more about, for example, Alexander the Great, who lived between 356 and 323 BCE, he or she will have to study the texts written about Alexander. We know that there were authors already during Alexander's reign who recorded details about his life and exploits, but all these texts have been lost. The material accessible to the historian consists of texts that were written much later, which cite some of these earlier writings. Although debated, the most reliable of these texts is generally said to be the Greek historian Arrian of Nicomedia, who was active around 150 CE—several hundred years after Alexander's death. The historian is thus confined to later accounts, which he or she must search in order to retrieve reliable information about the historical Alexander. However, texts function only as *one among many* source types that can be used when reconstructing a portrait of Alexander. Information pulled from the texts is thus combined with other information from older, more indirect sources (such as inscriptions) that are closer to Alexander's actual lifetime, in order to gain an understanding of what may be considered reasonable for the 300s BCE. The reconstruction, then, ultimately consists of a mixture of types of information from different sources.

The texts from the mid-second century CE, however, contain information not only about Alexander but also about the time and context in which the text itself was authored. It is therefore possible to analyze the texts themselves, for example, as representations of an author's fascination with a hero. The texts, in this case, are thus studied for their own sake and as expressions of a later time's perception of events in the past. It is not Alexander as a historical figure but rather the text's own historical context, the author's perspective and purpose of writing, that is examined.

When conclusions about Alexander and the texts about him are then presented in book form, the historian may choose to first create a historical picture by describing Alexander's life in chronological order, from birth to death, and thereafter present the portraits painted of him by later texts. These portraits may then be compared to and contrasted with the historical picture that the historian has reconstructed. In other words, although the *via inventionis*, the research process, is multifaceted, making it impossible for the author to follow a strict chronological order, the presentation of the results of such a research process, the *via expositionis*, ought to be organized and chronological for the sake of clarity.

Another way to introduce Alexander and the texts surrounding him would be to imitate the research process and thus begin with the later texts and proceed backward in time. The difficulty with such an arrangement is that it risks misleading the reader into thinking that the texts are used *solely* as a window into Alexander's life and not as interesting and important artifacts in themselves, artifacts that have their own context, purpose, and historical value.

With an overall chronological presentation, then, the reconstruction of historical figures and events, which builds on a diverse body of sources, is separated from the aims and contexts of the later texts.

By choosing a chronological layout, we are joining a current pedagogical trajectory applied to textbooks. Several historical introductions to the early Christian period and its texts have recently prioritized chronology as a frame within which to present research results. Here we find, for example, Per Bilde's *En religion bliver til* (*The Origin of a Religion*; in Danish) and L. Michael White's *From Jesus to Christianity*. The difference between the present work and these two examples is that we have chosen to work with the New Testament as canon, rather than to include a larger variety of texts over a longer period of time. The main reason for this is the impact the canon has had, *as canon*, in culture, religion, and politics over the centuries. This means that while the book you are now reading does include discussion of both texts and movements beyond the canon and the majority church, the twenty-seven canonical texts are treated in greater depth than these other texts and groups. At the end of the book, there is a list (see appendix 1) that summarizes other texts that are roughly contemporary with the New Testament texts and that are important for our understanding of the latter.

We chose to place the chapter about the New Testament texts between the chapters "The Historical Jesus" (ch. 3) and "The Emergence of Early Christianity" (ch. 5) in order to mirror the fact that these texts originated at the same time that Christianity took shape as a religion, but they also preserve traditions that stretch back to Jesus himself. The texts therefore constitute a source of information on both the historical Jesus and the early Christ groups in which they were authored, much the same as the texts about Alexander the Great give us information about both the historical Alexander and the time at which those texts were written. Of course, if the reader so wishes, he or she may begin by reading chapters 2 and 4, and then continue with chapters 3 and 5, as this would imitate a research process that focuses on the historical Jesus.

An important aim of this book is to nurture in the reader a desire to study the New Testament texts and the history surrounding them outside of the context of this present work, inspiring him or her to become an informed independent interpreter. In order to contribute to and guide the reader along such a path, the book's second part (ch. 6) presents theories of interpretation, as well as examples of different types of interpretations that may emerge depending on the methods chosen. We have also included some concrete instructions for how work with historical texts may be carried out. One of the purposes of this is to illustrate the breadth and diversity of textual interpretation, and at the same time demonstrate how dependent all interpretation is on perspective, interests, and methods.

With a certain chronological overlap at the beginning and the end, this book covers the discipline called "New Testament studies," which usually, from a chronological perspective, inhabits the space between what in Christian scholarly traditions have been labeled "Old Testament studies" and "church history." It is our hope that this introduction to Jesus, the New Testament, and Christians origins will contribute to increased historical knowledge and understanding, and also serve as an invitation to the reader to engage in an academic, critical reading of New Testament texts, assisted by the diversity of perspectives and methods that are perhaps the most distinctive characteristic of New Testament research today.

A History of New Testament Research

The Origins of Biblical Research

Ever since the New Testament was read for the first time, people have been attempting to clarify the content and origins of this unique collection of books. The author of the Second Letter of Peter complained that some of Paul's letters could be difficult to understand (2 Pet 3:16), which should indicate to us that the desire to study and truly understand these texts began very early, perhaps around the beginning of the second century, even though the canon itself was not in place at that time.

As the early church began selecting which of the many texts should shape their official faith, this study of the texts grew in importance. According to the authorities of the time, an important criterion for a text to be regarded as authoritative was that it had been authored by an apostle or a disciple of an apostle. An early example of this idea of apostolic legitimacy can be found in the writings of Papias, bishop of Hierapolis in Phrygia in the second century. He referred to an old tradition he claimed he had access to, that the author of the Gospel of Mark was in fact the apostle Peter's interpreter, who decided to write down, though not in order, what he remembered of Peter's teachings. This tradition is found in Eusebius's book *Ecclesiastical History* 3.39.15, the oldest preserved history of the church. Eusebius lived circa 260–339 CE. We shall return to the selection process in more detail in chapter 4.

It was also important to determine the meaning of the texts. In Alexandria the texts were read allegorically, which is to say they were not read literally but rather read on the assumption that they had five (Clement of Alexandria) or three (Origen) levels of meaning. Christians in Antioch nurtured a different school of thought, in which the study of the New Testament focused more on linguistic and historical methodologies. In this way, already during the fourth and fifth centuries, it was possible to question certain texts (Theodore of Mopsuestia) and instead view biblical history through a more typological approach (John Chrysostom). From such perspectives, authorities could think of biblical history as if it were a model for the later church.

From the many ways to interpret the texts of the New Testament, a fourfold approach began to emerge during the early Middle Ages. This model consisted of the following interpretative methods: the *historical* (the literal meaning of the texts), the *allegorical* (the texts are about Christ and the church), the *tropological* (the texts speak of the individual human being), and the *anagogical* (the texts are about the heavenly world). There was much discussion about the relative value of these approaches as well as their interrelationship. Thomas Aquinas, the most prominent theologian of the thirteenth century, argued that the three latter models had to be grounded in the historical model, but there were others who interpreted the texts without consideration of their historical meaning.

With the Reformation came an emphasis on the idea that only Scripture should determine the formation of Christian life and worship. Consequently, Lutheran theologians wanted to attribute only one meaning to the text, a historical or literal one. They argued that such a goal could be reached if one used biblical texts to interpret other biblical texts, to interpret Scripture with Scripture. In reality, however, this led to a situation in which each person developed his or her own interpretative keys. For Martin Luther, the main figure of the Reformation during the first half of the 1500s, the hermeneutical key was Christ and the context of the Christian faith. At this time, a focus on close readings of the biblical texts developed. Jean Calvin, the reformer of Basel and Geneva during the 1500s, argued that the purpose of theology was limited to a replication of the factual content of the Bible. Using his deep knowledge of ancient Greek and Latin literature, he studied the Bible at length and produced commentaries for almost every book it contained.

The Breakthrough of Modern Biblical Scholarship

Modern biblical scholarship sprang from the French enlightenment of the eighteenth century. Instead of using the constitution of the heavenly realm as a point of departure, scholars now began establishing a coherent worldview based on human experience and knowledge, liberated from any constraining dogmas and authoritarian religious and political authorities.

Around this time, Johann David Michaelis (1717–1791) was active in Göttingen. Michaelis worked untiringly with exegetical problems from the point of view that the key to a sound understanding of the biblical texts was thorough knowledge of the biblical languages and historical facts. At the same time, Johann Salomo Semler (1725–1791) was active in Halle, where Michealis had studied and taught previously. Semler argued that religion was something personal that revolved around the concept of faith. Theology, on the other hand, was about rational reflection and scholarship. The study of the canon belonged to this latter category (see the section "Which Texts Belong to the New Testament? The Canonization Process," p. 211).

Biblical scholars had made use of linguistic and historical methodologies already a couple decades earlier—for example, the French monk Richard Simon (1638–1712). However, with Michaelis and Semler came a general consensus about what biblical scholarship was, and this consensus eventually developed into the historical-critical methodologies applied in the discipline. Michaelis and Semler had many students, including Johann Jakob Griesbach and Johann Gottfried Eichhorn. As professor in Jena, Griesbach contributed to the study of the original texts (text criticism) and the relationship between the first three gospels (the Synoptic problem). Eichhorn, active in Jena and Göttingen, is most known for his contribution to Old Testament scholarship, but he did introduce to our field ancient myth as a way for ancient societies to express their perceptions of reality and wrote an introduction to the New Testament. The concept of myth would later become crucial for the interpretation of the New Testament.

At this point, modern biblical scholarship had made a definite breakthrough. The time ahead was characterized by discussions about the consequences of the new approach. Hermann Samuel Reimarus (1694–1768) published a book in Hamburg in 1754 in which he denied both that Jesus had performed miracles and the existence of supernatural revelations. His radical view that Jesus's teaching was limited to moral instruction based on the Old Testament, and that his disciples in a deceptive way had tried to create a new religion after his death, triggered an intense debate. After Reimarus's death, Gotthold Ephraim Lessing (1729–1781) fueled the debate by publishing in 1774 an anonymous fragment of one of Reimarus's texts. It became difficult to separate historical and rationalistic approaches from reflections on the very validity of the Christian faith. Johann Gottfried Herder (1744–1803), a court preacher in Weimar, attempted to solve the conflict between faith and rational knowledge by seeing history as a successive revealing of God for humanity. The rationalistic point of departure of this type of biblical scholarship did not prevent people from trying to find solutions to the problem that historical claims about the biblical stories undeniably also make claims, in a society that is Christian, about the nature of ultimate reality and truth in a more religious sense.

A General Summary of Historical Jesus Research

The newfound freedom within the biblical field became especially obvious where the question of the historical Jesus was concerned. In 1835 something groundbreaking occurred. The young David Friedrich Strauss (1808–1874) in Tübingen, only twenty-seven years old, published a book about Jesus's life that was heavily influenced by the then radical philosophy of Georg Wilhelm Friedrich Hegel. He was not happy with the tendency of biblical scholars—especially his teacher Friedrich Schleiermacher—to reject the mythical strokes of the Gospels and yet assert that the historical Jesus and the Christ of contemporary faith was one and the same person. The myth as interpretative key returns with Strauss's research. In his work, myths stand for a type of abstract idea about the supernatural. The Gospels, he argued, present myths within a historical framework and thus embody Jesus as an idea. The person behind the myths is an ordinary human being, subjected to human limitations just as much as everybody else. Jesus may serve as a manifestation of the divine within the genuinely human, but it is the idea that is of enduring importance, not the actual historical person. Therefore, there is no historical connection between the Jesus of history and the Christ of faith (myth). Strauss's critical attitude toward the sources and his questioning of the notion that they were free of error, as well as his problematizing of their status as historically unique, still constitute important insights meriting consideration within historical Jesus research to this day.

The latest clearly defined phase within Jesus research is often called "the Third Quest." The first phase of the quest for the historical Jesus is defined as liberal (in the sense of "free from the church") attempts to sculpt the real Jesus from behind the Gospels as a teacher of timeless truths about God's fatherhood, the human soul, and love. The rationalism of the Enlightenment had created optimism about the possibility of reconstructing history as it actually had played out. German scholars still led the research, especially Berlin's famous church historian, Adolf von Harnack (1851–1930).

Early on, scholars realized that reconstructions of the historical Jesus were too optimistic. Albert Schweitzer (1875–1965), who in his youth was active as an exegete in Strasbourg, pointed out that the liberal Jesus portrayals actually portrayed the values that were relevant in Europe during the 1700s and 1800s. Schweitzer himself believed that Jesus's teaching and actions revolved around his eschatology. Jesus was convinced that the end of the ages was near. Schweitzer's view had been anticipated a couple decades previously when Johannes Weiss (1863–1914), son-in-law to the liberal theologian Albrecht Ritschl, had advocated that Jesus's teachings about the kingdom of God were based on Jewish beliefs about the immediate destruction of the world in the coming judgment. The historical dimensions of the Gospels were also beginning to be seriously questioned at that time. Conterminously with Weiss, Martin Kähler (1835–1912) argued that the historical Jesus (*der historische Jesus*) could only be reconstructed as a person interpreted via faith (*der geschichtliche Christus*). In his study of the Gospel of Mark a couple of years later, William Wrede (1859–1906) undermined the entire liberal Jesus research project by showing that the Markan narrative, the earliest of all the gospels, rather than getting us closer to the historical Jesus, is itself defined by an understanding of who the Christ of faith is.

It was around this time that the most influential exegete of the 1900s was schooled. Shortly after the First World War had destroyed much of liberal theology's optimism and belief in the abilities of humanity, and as systematic theologians (e.g., Karl Barth) began toning down the possibility of finding God in creation, Rudolf Bultmann (1884–1976) presented the approach that would in a very definite way end the liberal Jesus research. He suggested that there is very little we can actually know about Jesus. The gospels are put together from smaller entities, steeped in the activities and views of the assemblies from which they emerged. They consist of preaching, not historical reports. With the so-called form-critical program, Bultmann and a number of other scholars (e.g., Karl Ludwig Schmidt, Martin Dibelius) put a stop to the first phase within Jesus research.

The second phase was to a large degree a reaction against Bultmann by some of his former students. In the 1950s, Ernst Käsemann (1906–1998), at this point professor in Tübingen, pointed out the theological risks that come with separating the Christ of faith from its basis in the historical Jesus. His assertions initiated a new interest in Jesus. Among Bultmann's earlier students, now spread across Germany and parts of the United States, only Hans Conzelmann (1915–1989) in Göttingen defended the thesis that the historical Jesus had no place in the theology of the New Testament. The rest had taken on Käsemann's challenge to create theologically valid research about the historical Jesus. The quest for the historical Jesus had received new inspiration, but now the aim was not to play Jesus against the church but rather to ascertain what roots the preached Christ had in the historical Jesus.

The second phase was theologically motivated, but that does not mean that it was not based on academic standards. As historians, scholars tried to bring forth valid criteria for how one should reconstruct a historical portrait of Jesus. A basic pillar of these criteria was the idea that historical material that reflected Jewish piety contemporary with Jesus, or texts that mirrored the convictions of the earliest church, had to be taken out of the equation when the historical Jesus was to be reconstructed. This criterion was called the criterion of dissimilarity, but it functioned poorly as a scholarly tool, as it arguably reflected more than anything else a desire to paint Jesus as unique in history

Eventually, scholars realized that the historical Jesus could not be separated from his cultural and religious surroundings. In the beginning of the 1970s, the Hungarian-born Jewish scholar Geza Vermes (1924–2013), professor at Oxford University, emphasized in his book on Jesus that a strictly historical approach means that one has to understand Jesus in his immediate Jewish context in Galilee. Vermes became an important scholar in the transition from the second to the third phase of Jesus research, which began in the 1980s. The third phase was a reaction against the theological focus of the second phase, which ultimately, proponents argued, led to a limiting of the role played by the Jewish society in which Jesus lived, as well as confining the source material analyzed to the New Testament.

The third phase thus distances itself from the criterion of dissimilarity and argues that a historically likely reconstruction of Jesus has to be based on his own context, focusing on the Jewish setting and the emergence of the Jesus movement. This next step in the research trajectory, however, has not brought with it a consensus view of Jesus. The criteria provide certain frames but do not steer the individual aspects of the research process. There is also a difference in how scholars apply the criteria and which criteria are seen as more important than others. Among the many current portraits of Jesus today, we find a mysterious preacher of wisdom (Marcus J. Borg, John D. Crossan) as well as an eschatological prophet (compare the works of, for example, E. P. Sanders, Gerd Theissen/Anette Merz, John P. Meier, James D. G. Dunn, and Dale Allison; see also the discussion in chapter 3, "The Historical Jesus," especially the section "How to Find the Historical Jesus," p. 172). Today, important developments in historical Jesus research include taking into account social and collective memory research, as the criteria of authenticity, while still applied by many scholars, have come under increasing fire as misguided, and we might be moving toward a more hermeneutically sensitive phase of historical Jesus research.

A General Summary of Gospel Research

Parallel with the different phases of Jesus research, there have been attempts to clarify the role of the Gospels as historical sources about Jesus. The most important are the

Synoptic Gospels—that is, Matthew, Mark, and Luke. The Synoptic problem was observed early on by scholars and has its basis in the fact that the first three gospels exhibit great textual similarities. Since the beginning of the twentieth century, the most commonly accepted theory has been the two-source hypothesis. According to this theory, Matthew and Luke are independent of each other, but both use Mark. For the overlap between Matthew and Luke that does not come from Mark, it is assumed that these authors used a source scholars call "Q" (from the German *Quelle*, meaning "source"). The overlap consists mainly of Jesus sayings, and so Q is assumed to have been a so-called *sayings gospel*. In addition, the theory also assumes that Matthew and Luke had access to their own sources, which account for their unique materials, in the form of other texts or oral traditions. Scholars have tried and are still trying to reconstruct Q and comment on the different stages in its literary emergence (e.g., James M. Robinson, John S. Kloppenborg, and Harry T. Fleddermann).

The two-source hypothesis has seen criticism mainly from two perspectives. Some argue that the Q source never existed: after all, we have never found any actual physical evidence of its existence. The Synoptic problem is instead explained by asserting that Luke had access to both Matthew and Mark. This model is called the Farrer hypothesis, after the British scholar Austin Farrer, who published an article on the subject in the mid-1950s. Today, Mark Goodacre is the most vocal proponent of this theory, which is experiencing growing popularity among scholars.

Another model that dispenses with the Q hypothesis is the Griesbach hypothesis, after Griesbach, who toward the end of the 1700s asserted that Mark is the youngest gospel and Matthew the oldest, and that the author of Mark selected material from Luke and Matthew, which he then incorporated into his gospel. This hypothesis also assumes that Luke knew Matthew. There are other models too, each more complicated than the next, which attempt to explain the Synoptic Gospels without Q. There are scholars who argue that the order of the gospels in the two-source theory may be correct, but the textual relationship should not be determined by modern views of what a text is. What we call sources—even Q—may have actually consisted of oral traditions that circulated among the early Jesus followers. Scholars as early as Herder (see above) had suggested that there existed an original gospel that was transmitted orally. Although the Farrer hypothesis is gaining ground today, as noted, the majority of scholars still agree with some form of the two-source hypothesis, but often with modifications.

The gospels, including John, speak not only about its main character, Jesus, but also give away information about their authors and the context in which they lived. During the 1950s, some of Bultmann's students (Günther Bornkamm, Hans Conzelmann, Willi Marxsen) developed an approach known as redaction criticism. They argued that the authors put together the gospels using traditions and other textual materials—that is, they edited together their gospels rather than authored them. Their selective editorial process, especially the small additions they made themselves, illustrates their own special theology and the theology of the community in which it was produced. Thus, scholars applying this method are not primarily interested in the gospels as reports of Jesus's life but rather want to study them as a reflection of their authors and their respective context. Since the 1980s, this perspective has been further developed with the help of sociological perspectives; scholars sometimes speak of a socio-redactional methodology (Philip F. Esler). With the help of this method, scholars aim to give the gospel authors sharper contours. An important subject today involves establishing how the communities that produced the gospels understood themselves in the context of contemporary Jewish piety and the different Jewish groups. Scholars are divided in their opinions in this regard. Some suggest that the gospel authors were marking their independence, others that at least the group behind the Gospel of Matthew saw their messianic faith as a variant of Jewish piety.

The redaction-critical and socio-redactional methods stand in contrast to two other tendencies within gospel research. Since the early 1980s, many scholars, under the influence of the study of literature, have chosen to approach the gospels as stories or narratives. The American R. Alan Culpepper published a book in 1983 on the Gospel of John, which, for the first time, applied a consistent narrative methodology to a New Testament text. In the beginning, this method was not concerned with the relationships between the gospels, the text as a report of Jesus's life, or the group behind the text. Rather, it highlighted that all we have are the stories themselves. Today, however, scholars have discovered that narrative style may say something about how the group behind the texts thinks or works, and how the first recipients of the stories may have interpreted them.

Another group of scholars, under the leadership of the British scholar Richard Bauckham, argue that we can no longer assume that the groups behind the gospels had the sort of local basis that has previously been assumed within the redaction-critical and socio-editorial camps. They were written by people who wished to spread the message about Jesus to a larger audience, to a large number of communities, not just a local group of believers. Thus, according to this perspective, one cannot use the gospels to reconstruct the sociological reality of a certain place. Instead, one needs to be aware of the texts' patterns of openness.

A General Summary of Pauline Research

The year 1977 marks the beginning of a new age for modern research on Paul. The American E. P. Sanders, then a professor at McMaster University in Canada, reacted in an important book to the trend in New Testament scholarship of portraying Jewish piety at the time of Jesus in discriminating ways, which he found similar to the polemics of the Reformation. In this previous scholarship, Sanders noted, Jewish piety was described as revolving around the need to observe every aspect of the law in the most minute detail in order to reach salvation (legalism). Paul, these scholars argued, represented, like Luther, the idea of a gospel without the law.

A year before Sanders published his book, the Swedish scholar Krister Stendahl, then at Harvard University, published lectures and articles written since the 1960s where he aimed to critique one-sided readings of Paul based on Lutheran convictions regarding righteousness through faith alone. Sanders developed Stendahl's reaction further and in his own way. According to Sanders, Jewish piety is characterized by what he calls "covenantal nomism," not legalism. He bases this claim on the fact that the belief that the covenant between God and Israel is a free gift from God is reflected in the majority of Jewish texts from around the turn of the era. God chooses a people as his own. The law (Gk. *nomos*) should be obeyed not as a way to earn salvific righteousness but rather as a response to God's gift; God chose the people, and to show their gratefulness they follow his law. The sacrificial system provides an opportunity for forgiveness when the people have not managed to give their response fully. According to Sanders, Paul really only had one problem with the Jewish pattern of piety: it did not include Christ. Paul first received the solution, as he experienced Christ, and thereafter saw the problem with Jewish piety. According to Sanders, Paul's newfound belief in the participation in Christ and the decisive drama that Christ triggered led him to understand the problematic aspects of Jewish covenantal nomism. He changed one religious system for another.

Sanders's work generated what has been called "the new perspective on Paul," but research has been multifaceted and pointed in different directions. Some seek to nuance his image of Jewish piety by highlighting factors suggesting that Jewish groups in reality did not live up to the basic idea of the covenant and abused God's free gift to them. These scholars believe that Paul's discussions about the law illustrate that he himself was taking a position against a form of misdirected legalism (Stephen Westerholm) or nationalistic marking of their own identity (Dunn).

There are also questions about Paul's own religious identity. Those who accept Sanders's perspective on covenantal nomism can still be reluctant to accept his strong emphasis on Paul's experience of Christ and his change from one religious system to another. Instead, many scholars attempt to understand Paul's belief in Christ within the frame of Jewish covenantal nomism. His dissatisfaction had to do with other Jewish groups that had abused God's gift, rather than signifying his leaving the religion of his youth or having to do with the problems involved when non-Jews now were to share the covenantal promises. This leads to the wider question of the relationship between the early Jesus movement and Judaism. Scholars analyze the letters of Paul and other texts in order to understand in which way Paul was part of the development of the Jesus movement into a group whose identity would eventually separate from Judaism.

To a higher degree than before, it is today common to notice the tensions and contradictions in Paul's reasoning. Previously, it had been assumed that Paul progressively changes and develops his thought about, for example, eschatology and the law. A new forum for discussion was begun when scholars took the next step and argued that Paul did not have a thorough understanding of his Jewish heritage and, especially where the law is concerned, contradicts himself (Sanders, Heikki Räisänen). Only a minority of scholars agree that his contradictions are substantial, but the idea is affecting biblical scholarship. It has led to a new awareness of the tensions within Paul's letters, and attempts to explain them have followed. Some argue that Paul communicated using very complicated and sophisticated techniques that to the untrained eye may seem to be contradictions, and that the different communities he was writing for had different needs and thus merited different approaches. It has also become more difficult to present a general and overall harmonizing description of Paul's thinking. Attempts are still made especially in Germany (Peter Stuhlmacher, Udo Schnelle, Michael Wolter), but for the most part scholars limit themselves to descriptions of the theology of specific letters. To avoid simplification of Paul's complex thinking, scholars can choose to work with specific levels of and relationships between the coherence and contingency in his letters (J. Christiaan Beker). Another solution to the problem is to use Romans as a representative point of departure for the whole of Pauline theology, and then read the other letters from that perspective (Dunn).

While the debate after Sanders revolved around Jewish patterns of religion, there nonetheless exists an important branch of Pauline scholarship that analyzes the letters according to their Greco-Roman context. Two perspectives will be noted here. A very intensive research field, with its starting point in the lecture of the German-American Hans Dieter Betz in Sigtuna, Sweden, 1974, has focused on the heritage from the early rhetorical readings of the Pauline letters. With improved analytic tools stemming from a knowledge of how rhetoric was used in ancient texts to convince others of a cause, Paul's way of making points and convincing others of his beliefs are analyzed. This rhetorical-critical way of analyzing the letters is often combined with the Greco-Roman custom of writing letters (epistolography) and illustrates how the Pauline letters—and other New Testament texts—were authored with considerable literary finesse.

Another research field that today receives increasing attention combines a literary interest with an investigation of Greco-Roman elements in Paul's thinking. This type of approach springs from a desire to take seriously the fact that Paul was a Jew born and raised outside Israel with an education in Greek philosophy, in combination with the fact that his main aim is the conversion of non-Jews. Several studies suggest that his writings had indeed been influenced by the way Greek philosophy deals with moral questions (Abraham J. Malherbe, Stanley K. Stowers, and Troels Engberg-Pedersen).

A Hermeneutic Awareness

Exegetical research is a cultural phenomenon. The history of research illustrates, as we have seen, that throughout the centuries scholars have studied the texts on the basis of their contemporary context. Research today is no exception. Today, scholars use methodology and perspectives taken from modern historical research, literary studies, sociology, cultural anthropology, archaeology, and psychology. We carry out research according to the epistemological context and models that our Western culture views as means of acquiring knowledge. In other cultures, Western assumptions about what constitutes knowledge may not exist. In recent years, exegetes have, to a higher degree than in earlier periods, realized how bound they are to their own context, and have thus made the act of interpretation itself into an object of investigation and self-critical analysis.

This becomes especially noticeable within three fields. First, exegetes today are more interested than before in the reception history of the texts; that is, there is a focus on how the texts have been interpreted by people in different societies and churches through the centuries (Ulrich Luz, Robert Evans). Influenced by philosophical hermeneutics, scholars realize that every reading is an interpretation from a certain perspective, and every New Testament text carries within it an openness to different interpretations and interpretative effects. Exegetes now see themselves as standing within this constantly changing interpretative history, not outside as mere observers.

Second, there is today a larger awareness of the moral responsibilities that exegetes have for their interpretations. The realization that researchers are part of an ideological context in which they choose methods and perspectives has led to the raising of questions with regard to how the scholars' own contexts control the interpretations produced. Modern gender studies, especially, has revealed the power structures at work in the white, male-dominated Western scholarly culture (Elisabeth Schüssler Fiorenza). In recent years, the goal of gender studies has been aided by the emergence of postcolonial studies. This field studies how political and other power structures influence what is considered "acceptable research." Traditional Western belief in objectivity and the superiority of its interpretative paradigms is challenged by perspectives from the Two-Thirds World (Fernando Segovia).

Finally, the possibility of carrying out an overall New Testament theology has been problematized. In connection with the exegetes removing themselves from the constraints of church doctrines, there has emerged a tendency to describe the early Jesus movement using nonconfessional, religio-historical, sociological, and psychological research models (Räisänen, Theissen, Ekkehard W. Stegemann, and Wolfgang Stegemann). As an alternative, it has been pointed out that the hermeneutic awareness of the scholar's contextual limitations illustrates how these religio-historical, sociological, and psychological models actually constitute an example of how our context's epistemological norms determine our research, and that biblical scholarship needs to exercise a greater degree of openness when dealing with such a diversity of equally important interpretative traditions.

Further Reading

Baird, William. *History of New Testament Research.* 3 vols. Minneapolis: Fortress, 1992–2013.

Bauks, Michaela, Wayne Horowitz, and Armin Lange. *Between Text and Text: The Hermeneutics of Intertextuality in Ancient Cultures and Their Afterlife in Medieval and Modern Times.* Göttingen: Vandenhoeck & Ruprecht, 2013.

Gillingham, Susan E. *One Bible, Many Voices: Different Approaches to Biblical Studies.* Grand Rapids: Eerdmans, 1999.

McKim, Donald K., ed. *Dictionary of Major Biblical Interpreters.* 2nd ed. Downers Grove, IL: IVP Academic, 2007.

Moore, Stephen D. *The Bible in Theory: Critical and Postcritical Essays.* Atlanta: Society of Biblical Literature, 2010.

Reventlow, Henning Graf. *History of Biblical Interpretation.* 4 vols. Translated by Leo G. Perdue. Atlanta: Society of Biblical Literature, 2009–2010.

Sawyer, John F. A., ed. *The Blackwell Companion to the Bible and Culture.* Oxford: Blackwell, 2006.

Taylor, Marion Ann, and Agnes Choi, eds. *Handbook of Women Biblical Interpreters: A Historical and Biographical Guide.* Grand Rapids: Baker Academic, 2012.

Thiselton, Anthony C. *Hermeneutics: An Introduction.* Grand Rapids: Eerdmans, 2009.

The Peculiar Case of Pauline Scholarship and Judaism

As indicated in the previous section, Paul has often been assumed to stand at the very crossroads where Christianity departs from Judaism. Indeed, for many interpreters, Paul is *the* person responsible for inventing Christianity as a religion. This alone would suggest the need, in a book on the New Testament and Christian origins, for a separate section discussing more specifically Paul's relationship to Judaism in New Testament scholarship. In light of the use of Paul in anti-Jewish polemic, some interpreters would go further, arguing that it is a moral responsibility of the modern exegete to engage with and evaluate research histories of those parts of biblical scholarship that have with particular fervor fueled conflict, prejudice, and pain. In the history of Christianity and biblical scholarship, theological misrepresentations and historically questionable portrayals of Paul have all too often been used to both negatively caricature contemporary Jews *and* reconstruct a highly biased historical background with which to justify these caricatures. To understand why the Pauline letters in particular have been used as tools of oppression, we need to understand the research history of Paul's relationship with (and within) Judaism.

Paul's relation to Judaism has arguably been the dominant aspect determining the results of Pauline scholarship. Traditionally, Paul was considered to have left Judaism and converted to Christianity. Seen as the most prominent Christian theologian, Paul was believed to have invented the law-free gospel for all humans and created a sharp contradiction between Judaism and Christianity. This view is the result of a long development that began already in antiquity and culminated after the Enlightenment when normative Christian theology and New Testament scholarship merged together, creating a powerful hermeneutical key for Pauline scholars. The fundamental component in this view of Paul's relationship to Judaism is a negative perception of Jews and Judaism. The following presentation aims to explain the emergence of this research paradigm and the ways in which recent scholarship has challenged it.

Anti-Judaism and the Rise of Christianity

In the middle of the first century CE, non-Jews who believed in Jesus were most likely connected to Jesus-oriented Jewish communities. The early Jesus movement was one of many varieties of Judaism, characterized by the idea that the death of Jesus made it possible for non-Jews to enter into a covenant with the God of Israel. While some Jesus-oriented Jews believed this meant that non-Jews should convert to Judaism, Paul argued that adherents of the movement should retain their ethnic identities and that humanity would eventually be saved as both Jews and members of the nations, respectively. This idea, which has roots in the Hebrew Bible and subsequent Jewish apocalyptic literature, caused political problems since non-Jews were obliged to participate in the official cult whereas Jews normally were exempted from this requirement. In mixed communities, where Jesus-oriented Jews and non-Jews coexisted, non-Jewish followers of Jesus were most likely seen as Jews by outsiders, and no conflict with the society was salient. However, in connection with the Jewish war, anti-Jewish feelings arose. This made the situation complicated for non-Jews, and the idea to separate from the Jewish part of the Jesus movement seems to have been born in connection with this. Consequently, in the beginning of the second century we find the earliest evidence of non-Jews who claim to be followers of Jesus but who repudiate Judaism. Around 115, Ignatius, bishop in Antioch-ad-Orontes, states that it is an abomination to combine belief in Jesus with Judaism. Such anti-Jewish statements were probably not primarily theological but rather part of a discourse aimed at convincing the Roman authorities to allow non-Jewish followers of Jesus to become a legally recognized religion. Since Judaism was considered a potential threat to the civilized order in the aftermath of the Jewish war, such an enterprise could only succeed if repudiation of Judaism was a significant part of the rhetoric.

This originally political discourse soon turned into a theological discourse and became a powerful part of the consolidation process of emergent Christianity. Anti-Jewish ideology even developed into a literary genre of sorts, the so-called "against the Jews" literature. Thus, in the middle of the second century, Melito of Sardis claims that the Jews were collectively responsible not only for killing Jesus but for having murdered God. In Justin Martyr's fictional dialogue with the Jew Trypho from around the same period, Justin argues that the blessings once bestowed on the people of Israel had now been transferred to the Christians, who constitute the "true" Israel.

Augustine and the Pelagian Controversy

Changes in theology also affected the portrayal of Jews and Judaism. Whereas Paul seems to have been occupied with the question of how the *category* "non-Jew" could be brought into a covenantal relationship with the God of Israel, resulting in non-Jews' salvation, theologians during late antiquity became more interested in the salvation of the *individual*. The question at stake was whether a human being could please God by living righteously, thus affecting the prospect of that individual's salvation.

The monk Pelagius, who appeared in Rome shortly before 400 CE, argued that it was possible to live a sinless life since humanity is endowed with free will. Sin, according to Pelagius, should be considered single acts of volition, and the individual will be judged on the basis of whether evil or good deeds have dominated in his or her life. Against this view, Augustine (354–430 CE) argued that humans cannot do anything to affect the prospect of redemption since humanity, through the fall of Adam, is marred by original sin. This led him to the conclusion that God alone decides who is to be saved and who is predestined to perdition. The main issue at hand in the so-called Pelagian controversy and subsequent discussions on salvation was basically the relation between "grace" and "works." This became one of the main issues during the Reformation.

The Reformation—Grace and Works

Martin Luther (1483–1546) was originally inspired by ideas similar to those of Pelagius: God would infuse his grace as a reward, provided that a person first did what was in his or her power. For Luther, however, the experience of not being able to offer God enough repentance and love led to the logical conclusion that he was predestined to condemnation. During his personal crisis, he found a solution in a radical interpretation of Rom 1:17: "The one who is righteous will live by faith." In contrast to contemporary mainstream theology, Luther argued that Christians gain access to God's righteousness by faith *only*, without works, since no one can please God by trying to live a righteous life. Good deeds will follow faith, but only as a consequence of this ascribed righteousness. This is what Luther meant by "grace," and in Luther's theology "works" stand in stark contrast to the notion of grace.

Luther's theology created an unbridgeable gulf between Judaism and Christianity. According to Jewish theology, the torah is supposed to be observed. Although the majority of Jewish theologians would claim that perfect torah observance was never required (the torah does actually contain regulations for how to repair a broken relationship with God), there is indeed some kind of relation between torah observance and salvation in Judaism. The Reformation, however, created a sharp distinction between two opposing religious systems: Christianity, on the one hand, was based on "grace," and Judaism, on the other hand, was founded on "works." As a result of this (mis)representation, Jews became the personification of humans doomed to perdition because of their inability to understand that salvation comes only through faith in Christ, without works of the law. Judaism came to represent self-righteousness, the worst sin of all in a Lutheran world.

The Reformation therefore gave reasonable theological explanation as to why Judaism was inferior to Christianity, an ideology that had been developing since the beginning of the second century. According to this theological paradigm, Jews strive for righteousness in vain by trying to observe torah, while Christians receive the gift of righteousness by grace. This particular construction of Christian theology and its relation to Judaism would soon exert a strong influence on biblical scholarship.

Theology Becomes Science

Modern biblical scholarship is a product of the Enlightenment. Yet, in spite of the ambition to challenge the assumptions of normative theology, many scholars were, of course, influenced by the general cultural climate in which the opposition between Judaism and Christianity was an important aspect. Thus, the theological idea of the inferiority of Judaism soon became integrated into the emerging scholarly discourse. For instance, the extremely radical scholar Ferdinand Christian Baur (1792–1860) used Friedrich Hegel's philosophy when interpreting the development of early Christianity. Hegel envisioned history as a continuous process toward increasingly higher stages, where a *thesis* merged with its *antithesis*, producing a *synthesis* embodying elements from both the thesis and the antithesis.

Baur applied this idea to the history of early Christianity and found a conflict between a law-free, Pauline, universal type of Christianity and a Jewish-oriented, particularistic type, represented by Peter, still bound by the torah. In the Gospel of

John, Baur considered this conflict to have been resolved, as all threats against the universalism of Christianity—Judaism, Jewish Christianity, and Gnosticism—had been eliminated. Christianity had taken the place of Judaism as the highest form of religion, and the inferiority of Judaism received a scientific legitimation of sorts. Judaism therefore became Christianity's antithesis.

Another important factor in the process of integrating the idea of Judaism's inferiority into biblical scholarship was the publication of Ferdinand Weber's (1836–1879) *System der altsynagogalen palästinischen Theologie aus Targum, Midrasch und Talmud* (*The Theological System of the Ancient Palestinian Synagogue from Targum, Midrash and Talmud*) in 1880.Weber, who wanted to become a missionary to the Jewish people, studied the classical Jewish texts and tried to organize them in a form of Jewish systematic theology. Rabbinic literature is, however, hardly suited for such systematization, and Weber's reconstruction is heavily influenced by Protestant theology. The view presented is thus rather distorted. Judaism, according to Weber, was characterized by legalism and works-righteousness, meaning that Jews tried to earn their salvation by acquiring merits through observing the torah, with no inner commitment. Because of the incident of the golden calf (Exod 32:1–14), the Jewish people are separated from God and can hope for redemption only through perfect torah observance.

Weber's presentation of ancient Judaism soon became the standard work used by almost all New Testament scholars, and his ideas of the character of Judaism are reflected in several influential New Testament handbooks, theologies, studies, and commentaries well into the twentieth century. The idea of the inferiority of Judaism was thus firmly established and provided New Testament scholars with an appropriate ideological background against which the New Testament could be interpreted. From this perspective, the idea that Paul left Judaism and converted to Christianity seems quite reasonable. On the assumption that Weber's view of Judaism is correct, if Judaism really represented a particularistic, legalistic religious system, Paul's law-free, universalistic, and anti-Jewish theology appears to be the better choice and this portrayal is fully possible to harmonize with the apostle's letters.

Toward New Assumptions

In the middle of the twentieth century, almost all Pauline scholars saw Paul as a Jewish apostate who had realized the flaws of Judaism, especially the flaws inherent in torah observance. Even though there had been dissenting voices over the years challenging the established view of Judaism and individual scholars who had begun to reflect on the connection between the Protestant portrait of Paul and the atrocities committed against the Jewish people during World War II, it would not be until the 1970s that the scholarly community was prepared to accept an alternative view of ancient Judaism.

The publication of E. P. Sanders's *Paul and Palestinian Judaism* in 1977 would eventually result in a virtual revolution for New Testament scholarship. Sanders, who was interested in Paul's relation to Judaism but not satisfied with the dominant view based on the work of Ferdinand Weber, undertook a new investigation into the nature of ancient Judaism. Sanders's reading of the Jewish sources completely contradicts the picture painted by Weber. Ancient Judaism was, according to Sanders, characterized by love, grace, and forgiveness. Jews observed the torah not to earn their salvation but as an expression of their willingness to remain in a covenantal relationship with Israel's God. A broken relationship with God can be repaired through the sacrificial system described in the Torah. Sanders labeled this relation between torah observance and covenantal theology *covenantal nomism*, a pattern he found in most expressions of Judaism in the period between 200 BCE and 200 CE.

Even though Sanders's reconstruction of ancient Judaism was very radical, his interpretation of Paul was not, even though the traditional anti-Jewish aspects were significantly downplayed. Paul, Sanders states, did not embrace the pattern of covenantal nomism that Sanders found in other Second Temple Jewish texts, even though he found nothing particularly wrong with the torah. Paul does not deny that there is a righteousness coming from the law (Phil 3:9), but it is another kind of righteousness than the one that comes from faith in Jesus, which is the only one that leads to salvation. This is the reason why all other attempts to attain salvation were wrong. Paul's main objection to the torah, according to Sanders, is that it does not constitute the way to salvation staked out by God.

The fact that Sanders also believed that Paul broke with Judaism probably contributed to the success of his study. Scholars could embrace Sanders's reconstruction of Judaism, while still holding on to the traditional idea of a distinct opposition between Judaism and Christianity. However, Sanders's reconstruction of Judaism naturally led to new problems. Jewish "legalism" and "work-righteousness" had constituted a perfect background for explaining both Jesus and Paul, but the idea of covenantal nomism called in question virtually all previous scholarship, and some scholars started to formulate new questions: If Judaism provided means for reconciliation, what was really the point of Jesus's death on the cross? And if torah observance is an expression of the will to live in a covenantal relationship with God, why did Paul speak of the torah as a curse (Gal 3:10)? These and similar questions paved the way for quite new and radical perspectives on Paul.

New Perspectives on Paul

One of the first scholars who used Sanders for interpreting Paul was James D. G. Dunn. In a famous lecture, published in 1983 as "The New Perspective on Paul," Dunn suggests that Sanders's concept of covenantal nomism could indeed be applied to

Paul. Paul's way of reasoning, Dunn states, actually presupposes the notion of a covenant between God and the Jewish people and alludes to the view of "righteousness" found in, for example, the Psalms and Isaiah. Thus, the absolute majority of Jews, including Paul, would have agreed that Jews within the covenant were righteous, and that this righteousness, given by grace, comes from faith. Accordingly, Jews in general did not believe that they were automatically made righteous only by observing the torah. However, when Paul in Gal 2:16 states that "no one will be justified by the *works of the law*," this, according to Dunn, refers only to Jewish identity markers, such as food and purity regulations, circumcision, and Sabbath celebration. These identity markers are what Paul reacts against. The problem Paul discovered was that Jewish identity markers created a distinction between Jews and the non-Jews so that the covenant was too narrowly interpreted in Jewish tradition, excluding everyone but Jews. Dunn states that, according to Paul, God's actions toward a person, Jew or non-Jew, should not depend on specific *Jewish* observances but on faith in Jesus. In this way, the meaning of the covenant is not invalidated but expanded to include all believers, regardless of ethnicity. As the starting point for a scholarly tradition aiming at understanding Paul from *within* Judaism, not *outside*, *in contrast to*, or *apart from* Judaism, Dunn's interpretation must be regarded as a significant breakthrough. With the publication of Dunn's article, the so-called new perspective on Paul was born.

Dunn's "new perspective" involved many new insights, especially the idea that Paul did not repudiate the torah as such, but only Jewish identity markers. This means that the traditional opposition between Judaism and Christianity is significantly downplayed—but not obliterated. However, during the 1980s some scholars started arguing that Paul did not address humankind in general but predominantly non-Jews. This had been hinted at by other scholars before (notably Johannes Munck), but now this idea was inserted into a post-Sanders perspective. For example, in 1987 Lloyd Gaston published a collection of ten articles, *Paul and the Torah*, in which he takes on the anti-Jewish tendencies within Christianity. His starting point is the observation that it is common among Christians to consider Paul to have broken with Judaism, and that the church consequently has taken the place of the Jewish people in the history of salvation. In addition, according to most scholars at the time, Paul held the view that the torah had ceased to be a valid way for salvation even for Jews, and that the Christian church has replaced Israel as God's chosen people. Gaston, however, claims that Paul defended himself against such charges and rather emphasized that his mission was in accordance with the torah (Rom 3:31; 11:1).

The solution to the paradox that Paul, on the one hand, seems to be criticizing the torah and, on the other hand, stresses its continued validity is, according to Gaston, to be found in the question of *intended audience*. Gaston emphasizes that we should take seriously the fact that Paul presents himself as the apostle to the non-Jews, which means that he writes to non-Jews about matters that concern them. Therefore, when Paul writes about the torah in a negative manner, it concerns the torah in relation to non-Jews, not the role of the torah in a Jewish context. According to Gaston, Paul agreed with other Jews in believing that the torah undeniably leads to righteousness *within* the covenant, but that it becomes a curse for those *outside* the covenant. The only way for non-Jews to escape the curse of the torah is to be included in the covenant through Christ. According to Gaston, Christ is for non-Jews what the torah is for Jews, and humanity will thus be saved by two covenants running parallel to each other.

The combination of Sanders's reconstruction of ancient Judaism, especially the concept of covenantal nomism, and the focus on Paul as the apostle to non-Jews, addressing precisely non-Jews rather than the whole of humanity, has led to a new research paradigm that in fact is in total opposition to the traditional one. Whereas most pre-Sanders Pauline scholars understood Paul to be in *opposition* to Judaism, a growing number of scholars now aim at interpreting Paul as *representing* Judaism. Within this so-called *Paul-within-Judaism perspective*, the fundamental assumption is that Paul remained completely Jewish and that he understood his call to be part of Israel's mission to be "a light to the nations" (Isa 49:6). Some scholars adhering to this research paradigm even take for granted that Paul was torah observant as a result of the assumption that he never broke with Judaism (e.g., Mark D. Nanos). Rather than abandoning the torah himself, Paul argued that non-Jews should not observe the torah the way Jews did. Paul's vision was to bring non-Jews into a covenantal relationship with the God of Israel, through Jesus, which indeed called for a significant change of behavior but did not change their ethnic status. Jews were to remain Jewish and non-Jews were still members of the nations, but through Christ their soteriological status had changed.

From initially being without any salvific hope, non-Jews could now be saved, provided that they put their trust in Christ and changed their behavior accordingly. From a Paul-within-Judaism perspective, Paul's critique of the torah is explained by assuming that he addressed non-Jewish members of the Jesus movement who probably wanted to observe parts, or even all, of the torah. This would, according to Paul, compromise God's oneness, since God would only be the God of the Jews rather than the God of the whole world. From this perspective, it was not Jews who constituted the main problem within the early Jesus movement, but non-Jews. The main issue was how Jewish members of the early Jesus movement should relate to non-Jews, who through Jesus had been included in the covenant with Israel's God.

Conclusion

In contemporary Pauline scholarship, one can discern three major trajectories concerning Paul's relation to Judaism. Many scholars still adhere to a traditional Lutheran perspective that no doubt is heavily dependent on normative theology. Within this tradition, Paul is still seen as having broken with Judaism. Even though Sanders's view of Judaism is generally accepted, he is often—and sometimes correctly—criticized for having exaggerated the aspect of grace within Judaism.

Dunn's "new perspective on Paul" has proven to be a powerful compromise between a more traditional perspective and Sanders's new view of Judaism. Many contemporary scholars are, to various degrees, influenced by this paradigm. Another way of looking at Dunn's perspective is to regard it as a transition between a traditional perspective on Paul and the more recent Paul-within-Judaism perspective, which locates Paul fully within a Jewish context. Without claiming that this latter way of interpreting Paul is free from ideological constraints, scholars working from the hypothesis that Paul remained fully Jewish, and that his religion was Judaism, generally aim at understanding the apostle from the first-century context, without taking later developments into consideration.

Further Readings

Dunn, J. D. G. "The New Perspective on Paul." *Bulletin of the John Rylands University Library of Manchester* 65 (1983): 95–122.

Eisenbaum, P. *Paul Was Not a Christian: The Original Message of a Misunderstood Apostle.* New York: HarperOne, 2009.

Fredriksen, P. *Paul: The Pagans' Apostle.* New Haven: Yale University Press, 2017.

Gaston, L. *Paul and the Torah.* Vancouver: University of British Columbia Press, 1997.

Nanos, M. D. *The Mystery of Romans: The Jewish Context of Paul's Letter.* Minneapolis: Fortress, 1996.

Nanos, M. D., and M. Zetterholm. *Paul within Judaism: Restoring the First-Century Context to the Apostle.* Minneapolis: Fortress, 2015.

Sanders, E. P. *Paul and Palestinian Judaism: A Comparison of Patterns of Religion.* Minneapolis: Fortress, 1977.

Thiessen, Matthew. *Paul and the Gentile Problem.* Oxford: Oxford University Press, 2016.

Westerholm, S. *Perspectives Old and New on Paul: The "Lutheran" Paul and His Critics.* Grand Rapids: Eerdmans, 2004.

Zetterholm, M. *Approaches to Paul: A Student's Guide to Recent Scholarship.* Minneapolis: Fortress, 2009.

Paths to the Past: On Sources and Methods

Same Sources, Different Conclusions

Consider the following scenario. The year is 4020. An international group of archaeologists, textual scholars, and historians from the wealthy southern hemisphere are working on a collaborative project, aiming to uncover Swedish religious behavior during the 1900s—the period during which the country experienced an enormous economic boom. The limited primary source material available to the team consists of an assortment of texts, including some statistical material, that were discovered by accident in an archive, as well as approximately forty excavated churches and a couple of synagogues and mosques. The synagogues and mosques were discovered in larger urban centers, whereas the churches were found in rural settings as well as in cities of all sizes.

The statistical information reveals that, by the end of the century, approximately 80 percent of all Swedish citizens were members of the Lutheran state church. Additionally, one of the texts reveals that a copy of a new Swedish translation of the Bible, found in a previous excavation, was financed by the state. Another document, dated to the first half of the twentieth century, suggests that churches were in wide use at this time, filled with people on Sundays and other holidays. This was true of both urban and rural areas. In addition, new, larger churches were built around this time. Finally, the archaeological team also has access to a newspaper article from the second half of the twentieth century, which strongly advises individuals to leave the state church, pointing to economic benefits for them if they do so, as they would avoid the church tax. How should one approach and interpret this diverse source material?

The members of the team disagree. The majority of the team subscribes to the theory that Christianity in the form of the state church was popular throughout the entirety of the twentieth century. As evidence, they point to the high membership rates and the overwhelming prevalence of churches in the archaeological material. They therefore see no reason to doubt that the information concerning widespread church attendance in the first half of the nineteenth century should also be applied to the second half of the twentieth century. Two factors validate this assumption. First, many of the churches that have thus far been found and excavated, and have been dated to the late twentieth century, showcase innovative architectural forms that had not been seen in any religious buildings prior to that time. The scholars interpret this as evidence for the existence of active and lively congregations that renovated their churches in accordance with the evolving needs of the masses. Second, a connection between the church and the state could be secured through the text mentioning that the translation of the Bible was funded by the Swedish state in the year 2000. According to the majority of the scholars, this supports the hypothesis that Christianity was a popular force in society on all levels: in urban and rural settings, in local congregations, and in national politics. The newspaper article advising people to leave the church is explained as a deviance from the norm, the product of an angry anti-Christian minority that for various reasons had come into conflict with the state.

A minority of scholars working within the team takes a different point of departure, however, placing special emphasis on the newspaper article and how it was worded, suggesting a widespread dissatisfaction with the church. These scholars argue that because economic arguments against church membership were used by the author, it is likely that the majority of its members were not active in their congregations. Had they been active members, the author would have been more likely to use religious reasoning to advocate against membership. From this perspective, foregrounding this article in the interpretative process, the construction of new church buildings was understood as attempts made by shrinking congregations to architecturally adapt to the zeitgeist for the purpose of attracting more members. The new translation of the Bible from the year 2000 is interpreted as the state wanting to preserve and make available a cultural and historical artifact that had played a large role in the formation of the country but whose religious importance was no longer widely appreciated. The information concerning widespread church attendance is interpreted as being applicable only to the early twentieth century, after which there occurred major sociocultural shifts, resulting in changed popular opinions about religion. These shifts may be traced, these scholars argue, to the two world wars and their devastating aftermath as well as to an increasing belief that the natural sciences had the potential of answering existential questions. These researchers thus attempt to understand the Swedish situation as part of a larger European context.

Simultaneously, the research team has studied the growth of Christianity in the so-called Two-Thirds World, or Global South, and found that very few buildings had survived from the twentieth century. The team concludes that Christianity did not experience much widespread growth in the southern hemisphere until the time of the great cathedrals, which came with the rapid economic growth a couple hundred years later, around the 2100s. Only a few cathedrals in this part of the world could be dated to the twentieth century.

The intention of this somewhat detailed (semi-)fictional example is to draw attention to the many challenges and difficulties historians may face. The problems range from scarcity of sources to the much-debated questions about how to actually go about reading and interpreting the sources that are in fact available. In other words, historical inquiry revolves around source material and methodology. The problems faced by our future fictional colleagues in the example above highlight many of the same issues faced by scholars today; the example illustrates how challenging it can be to acquire knowledge about the past.[1] Different historians have different opinions as to whether it is possible to reconstruct the past with any precision at all. The

1. For those unfamiliar with Swedish society and history, it may be noted that the scenario closest to the historical situation is the one suggested by the minority in this fictional example. Further, the final conclusion reached by the team, based on the existence or not of monumental church buildings in the Global South during this time period, is flawed, since, as statistics show, the majority of Christians live in this part of the world and have done so since around the 1970s. The total number of Christians in the world today is about the same as it was a hundred years ago, but there has been a shift in population patterns, from the north and west to the south and east.

axioms embedded in traditional historical-critical analytical discourses have come under increased fire from postmodern and postcolonial scholars in recent decades. Such critique, which we unfortunately do not have the space to expand on here but which at its core deals with the impossibility of objectivity, has compelled historical scholarship to find new ways to improve its methodology.

Intersubjectivity

Few historians today would maintain that objective knowledge about the past is possible. Instead, historical inquiry should be approached as an *intersubjective* conversation, in which the degrees of likelihood of various theories are discussed and debated. This has led to an emphasis on the word "construction" when dealing with historical *re*construction. The same source material may be interpreted in a variety of ways, opening up a certain degree of legitimate diversity with regard to conclusions drawn. Depending on the nature of the individual sources, the range of interpretations may vary from source to source.

Instead of viewing historical inquiry as engaged in finding ways of fitting together a certain number of pieces in a jigsaw puzzle to create a larger picture, we should rather understand the process of historical reconstruction as first of all consisting of attempts at restoring diverse and incomplete fragments of information. The pieces themselves are not a given but need to be reconstructed before they can be combined with other sources in order for us to understand historical processes.

To this should be added that the majority of the pieces of the puzzle are in fact missing. Scholars need to fill in the gaps themselves, making assumptions about what happened on the basis of factors and insights gained from previous studies. We shall return to this part of the research process later on. Let us stop here for a moment and contemplate some of the problems of interpretation presented to us by the sources we actually have access to.

For example, if a Roman legal text from the sixth century contains an imperial ban on the building of synagogues, should this be interpreted as a sign that no synagogues were built at this time? Or could one hypothesize that the ban was issued precisely because synagogues were being built? Should we assume, if synagogues were indeed being built, that Jewish communities halted their construction when the ban was issued? How do we measure the effectiveness of imperial bans in various parts of the empire? As to the building of synagogues, we do have archaeological evidence from both Palestine and the diaspora that their construction continued despite the emperor's wishes. How does this affect our understanding of historical legal material?

Another example will further problematize the nature of the sources. A 1,500-year-old literary text accuses and condemns a specific group of people as marginalized and lacking any kind of position of power or influence in society. Can such a text give us direct information about social realities at the time? Or is the text more concerned with rhetoric than actual social reality? It could very well be that the situation described in the text reflects a scenario that the author *wishes* to see, rather than what actually happened. It could also be the case that the author wishes to *promote* the scenario he or she describes. To answer our question, we must carry out numerous investigations, including a rhetorical analysis of how ancient writers used diction and different forms of expression in order to communicate with their audience.

There are several cases in which scholars have found that the church fathers' description of the Jews and their place in society in fifth-century Palestine (which is what the previous example was about) can *not* be considered a historically accurate description of the social reality at the time. The texts concern themselves with Christian (theological) triumphalism and Jewish subordination. There is archaeological evidence, as discussed earlier, that points to the fact that Jews were, at this time, building impressive monuments across the land. Such remains point to Jewish self-confidence and economic independence in relation to their Christian neighbors both near and far. Thus, it must be kept in mind that literary sources may be worded (intentionally or unintentionally) in a way so as to create a view of reality that serves the purposes of the author. Studying the church fathers' theological worldview, on the one hand, and attempting to understand the historical context in which they lived, on the other, can thus constitute quite different endeavors, although such research questions are intertwined on a number of levels.

Game Rules

The fact that the same sources may be interpreted in a number of ways means that academic humility becomes an epistemological necessity rather than merely a likeable personal character trait, which some scholars happen to develop. Despite this, it must be emphasized that not every historical reconstruction should be viewed as equally legitimate. It is not possible to argue that, if no one can reach absolute objectivity in their interpretations, this must mean that any interpretation made by anyone is legitimate. The efforts put in to understand historical phenomena have led to the formation of a certain "discursive game," governed by certain "game rules," whose purpose is to keep discussions on track. These "rules" of historical research (composed of certain attitudes, approaches, and methodologies) are constantly tested and developed. They may be applied to any historical discipline, not only the study of ancient religion, and they aim to make possible a better understanding of the past.

From a historical perspective, there is thus no difference, in principle, between reconstructions of Alexander the Great, Jesus, or Mother Teresa, even though the types of sources available imply different kinds of challenges for each of the quests. The opinion has sometimes been voiced that the aim of religious texts is not to provide accurate historical information, and that historical investigations of the New

Testament therefore are misguided. From an academic point of view, such claims are hardly tenable. All historical artifacts, including texts, are open to historical interpretation regardless of the intentions of their authors. A work of art from the eighteenth century can, for example, be analyzed from a variety of perspectives, some of which the artist could never have dreamed of, such as detailed analysis of the chemical combination of the colors used to create the painting. The important thing for scholars is to make it clear to themselves, as well as to their readers, what kind of questions they bring to the table, how they intend to go about answering them, and in which ways the conclusions they will eventually draw are a product not only of the source material but also of the methodology employed and their own perspective. We shall return to this in just a moment.

At this point it should be noted that historical investigations of the New Testament do not rule supreme within the academic field of biblical studies. At the center are the texts themselves, and these may be read and interpreted in various ways, even ways that do not further historical understanding. For this reason, we have divided the section on methodology into two parts: one concerned with a more general historical approach and the other focusing on a more text-oriented approach, which also includes historical understanding of the texts (see ch. 6). In the following, we shall focus on aspects of historical reconstruction and take a closer look at how the questions that we pose are related to the source material and the methodology that we employ.

"The Answer Lies in the Question": Choosing Source Material and Methodology

It is important to keep in mind that the point of departure for all research is the questions that we ask. The historical artifacts, buildings, art, and texts remain silent until we approach them with our questions in an attempt to understand them. We are the ones giving them a voice. In other words, that which we call history is "created" in the tension between source and interpreter.

When we encounter historical phenomena (or any phenomena at all), the spontaneous interpretations we make are completely dependent on our previous experiences and our contemporary context. We interpret what we see using reference points and knowledge we already possess. Were we to travel to a foreign culture, we would have to learn to interpret the language, symbols, art, and architecture of that culture if our aim was to understand the people of that culture and their worldview. In the same way, we must train ourselves to think outside our own immediate frames of reference and our own culture when we seek a historical understanding of Jesus, his earliest followers, and the texts of the New Testament. Such a process requires practice and takes time. But it is not impossible.

There are two foundational preconditions for a historical understanding of our subject. The first may seem somewhat obvious but should be mentioned nonetheless: it is essential that we are aware of the historical context surrounding Jesus and his earliest followers. Context may be viewed as a three-dimensional figure in which the synchronous section moves in concentric circles from the religion and culture Jesus shared with the Jewish people to the Roman Empire, which ultimately controlled the land of Israel in the first century. Diachronically, the context is also defined by history, since the history of the Jewish people influenced the social, political, and religious situation in which Jesus and his disciples found themselves (see fig. 1.1). Our first step on the path toward a historical understanding is thus to try to modify our (modern) reference points. This is done through the study of Jesus's and the earliest Christ followers' surroundings, variously defined (see below), as well as the history of their context. This mode of procedure is mirrored in the structure of the historical section of this book.

The second precondition of historical analysis is related to the above-mentioned procedure and focuses on the questions that tend to arise after a first reading of the source material. We must reflect on *what* we know in relation to *how* we know what we think we know. Which tools, or methods, do we use in order to attain knowledge? How can they help us to interpret the source material? It is through questions such as these that historical research can progress beyond common-sense arguments. ("Common sense" itself represents culturally determined ideas of how "reality" works and may be a hindrance rather than a help in research focused on a culture not our own.)

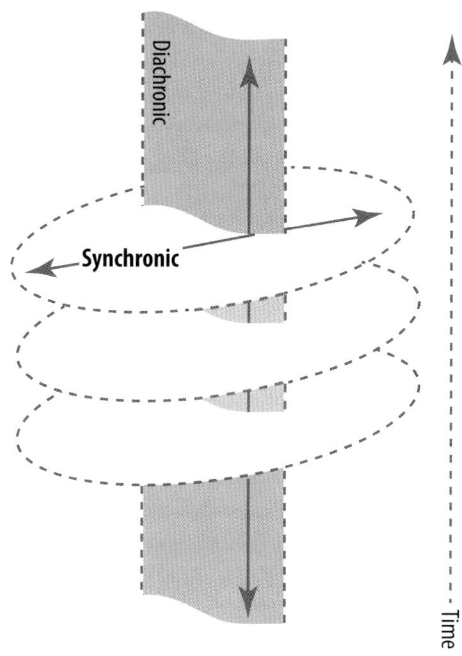

Figure 1.1 Contextual analysis: diachronic and synchronic perspectives on historical interactions and relationships.

With the above in mind, we may describe the basic parts of the research process in five steps. First, we need to understand that all historical investigations have their origins in our *questions*. Second, after choosing a research question, it is our job to select relevant *source material* that will help us answer our question. In a third step we move on to determine the *methodology* that will best enable us to interpret the source material. Fourth, we need to choose *conversations partners*; that is, we must decide which scholars we should read and interact with as we aim to answer our questions. Scholarship is not done in a vacuum; we need to learn from others. Lastly, we draw our *conclusions*.

It is crucial to understand that these six basic steps are interconnected. The conclusion must match the question asked; it should not attempt to say more than the source material and the methodology allow for. Further, the methodology we choose must be compatible with the selected source material and the questions asked, and the source material must be relevant to the original question. We cannot, for example, draw sociohistorical conclusions from a literary analysis of a text. Neither can we use a narrative methodology to answer a question that would require analysis of both textual and archaeological material. If our question is concerned with a group's social location in a specific geographic location, we must not work solely with archaeological analyses of buildings; we should also consider textual material and inscriptions, if such are available, to reach solid conclusions. The basic steps of the research process may be summarized as in figure 1.2.

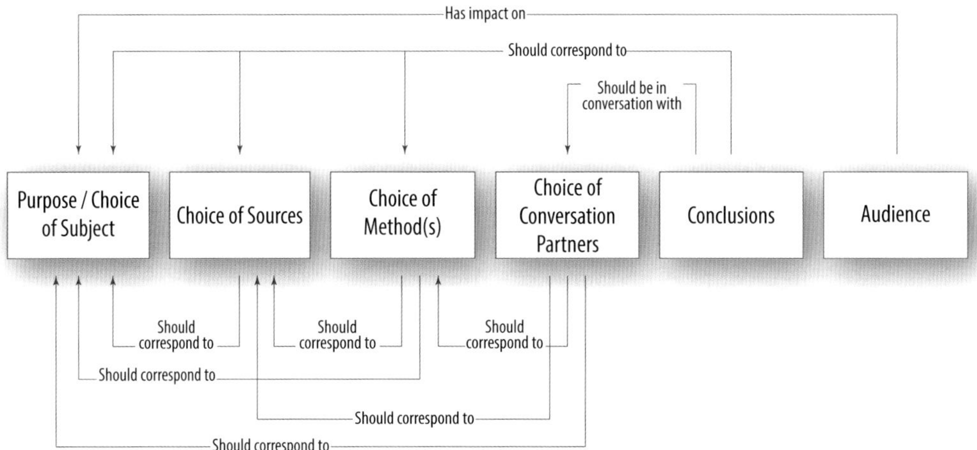

Regarding the interpreter: In the ideal case the interpreter's personal views and preferences should affect only the choice of subject. The scholarly debate itself is made possible and meaningful by not legitimizing the unavoidable bias of the individual researcher. The interpretative frame is set by the interpreter's choice of audience; the choice of audience will therefore determine the "game rules" for the interpretative activity.

Figure 1.2 The six basic steps of the research process.

With regard to source material, we have already noted that there are multiple types of sources. We have mentioned a few of the more important ones: *legal texts*, *literary texts*, *letters*, *inscriptions*, and *archaeological remains*. In addition, there is an important source type that has often been ignored in the past but that should be mentioned, since it has received increased attention in recent scholarship: *geography/topography*. These source types yield different kinds of information, which can later be woven together to create a fuller and more complete understanding of historical phenomena.

With regard to the *perspective* that the sources bring with them, it should be noted that legal and literary texts represent the upper strata of society, letters and inscriptions represent a somewhat wider sample of the population, and archaeological remains give us information concerning both the upper and lower strata of society (even though more expensive buildings usually last longer and are thus found in a better-preserved state than less expensive ones). The ruins of a fisherman's simple house may be analyzed just as much as the palace of an emperor, without the emperor's (biased) perspective on the social stratum to which the fisherman belonged. A literary text concerning fishing and fishermen, however, provides us with only indirect information (fishermen usually could not read or write; thus the author of the text was most likely not a fisherman), and should therefore be used with care and in combination with other sources. Perhaps geography/topography represents the most "democratic" source, since it frames all the different strata of a society within their physical boundaries. Pilgrim and trade routes, the time it takes to travel from one place to another, and thus the amount of contact that may have existed between people from different villages and cities are issues determined in large part by what the geography of a region allows. The career choices of individuals are also to a certain extent determined by what geography permits, even though we should put a larger emphasis on social and political factors when considering this aspect of ancient societies.

To clarify the arguments above and simultaneously invite the reader to develop an independent working relationship with the questions this book addresses, the following section will provide short and general examples of historical questions related to our field. The examples illustrate the challenges faced by scholars and provide a framework for the chapters to follow by indicating important steps in the research process, which preceded the authoring of this textbook.

We shall ask the following questions: Who was Jesus? What does the Gospel of Matthew say about judgment and salvation? How are the three earliest gospels connected? Was it Paul who created the form of Christianity we see today—that is, a Christianity separate from Judaism? The presentation and discussion of these questions will be general in nature; the reader is referred to the respective sections in chapters 2–5 for a more detailed discussion of the topics and technical terms used in historical inquiry. The concluding bibliography provides the reader with additional material for further study of methodology.

Jesus

If we begin with the question "Who was the Jesus of history?" and follow the previously outlined basic steps in the research process, the first question must be as follows: Which source material is relevant to answer this question? If one views the different types of sources as layered frames, where the inner frames give more direct information and the outer frames give more indirect, albeit necessary, information, the image in figure 1.3 emerges.

If we begin with the innermost frame, we see that all the sources consist of textual material: we have no inscriptions and no archaeological remains that provide us with *direct* information on Jesus. The texts listed inside the inner circle warrant further discussion. A majority of scholars hold that the gospels of the New Testament, in particular the Synoptic Gospels (Matthew, Mark, and Luke), provide us with the best information. *Agrapha* (meaning "not written" in Greek) refers to sayings attributed to Jesus that are not included in the Gospels but are quoted in other places, both within and outside the canon. There exist around 225 such Jesus sayings. Examples include John 7:53–8:11, since this text does not exist in the oldest versions of John's Gospel and did not appear in any of the other gospels until fairly late (although it had previously been linked to Luke at one point). Other examples within the New Testament are Acts 20:35 and 1 Cor 7:10–11. Papias (d. ca. 130), Justin Martyr (d. 165), and Tertullian (ca. 160–230) quote several noncanonical Jesus sayings, which they considered to be authentic, but most scholars have concluded that very few of the agrapha are useful for historical research. We can, further, obtain some information about Jesus from Paul, our oldest direct source. The value of the Gospel of Thomas is emphasized by some scholars as important for our task, but this remains disputed. Josephus (ca. 37–100), a Jewish historian who did not belong to the Jesus movement, contributes a brief note on the matter, and Tacitus (ca. 56–118) is considered to be among the few Greco-Roman authors whose (very limited) information about Jesus can be regarded as useful.

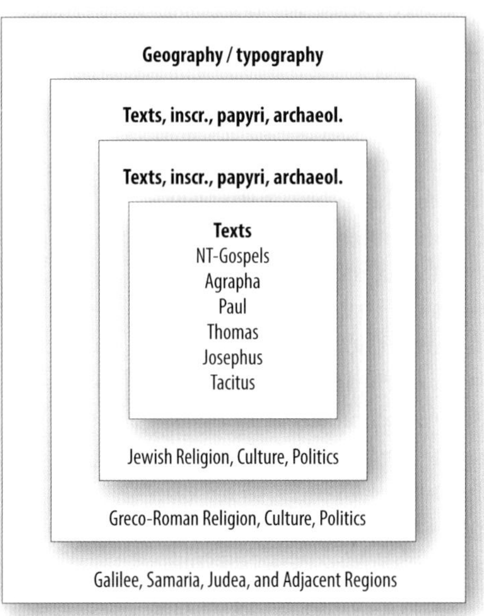

Figure 1.3 A schematic representation of source material relevant to the study of the historical Jesus.

These sources are discussed in more detail in chapter 3. The more indirect sources provide us with information concerning Judaism in the first century, and here we have at our disposal texts, inscriptions (e.g., the Theodotus inscription, which gives us information about a synagogue in Jerusalem), and archaeological remains (synagogues and private houses, as well as roads, towns, boats, tools, etc.). Through a study of the places where Jesus is said to have proclaimed his message, healed sick people, and exorcised demons, we can gain insight into how these people lived and the social strata to which they belonged. In this way, we may learn more about the people to whom Jesus primarily brought his message. Remains of simple houses in Capernaum, the village that Jesus, according to the texts, chose as the base for his mission, give us an idea of how his message about social change and the kingdom of God (or the "dominion of God," as the original texts may also be translated) may have been intended by him to be understood, and also how it was likely actually understood by his audience. Jesus chose primarily to speak publicly and gather followers in the rural districts and villages of Galilee, as opposed to the bigger and wealthier cities in the area.

The way Jesus died—crucified by the Roman authorities in the province of Judea—should lead us to include, among our sources, information about Roman imperial rule in the Middle East. This evidence should go beyond details such as the inscription found in Caesarea Maritima, which mentions Pontius Pilate, the man who sentenced Jesus to death, and include more general knowledge about how the Roman imperial presence—and the rule of their puppet tetrarch in Galilee, Herod Antipas—affected Jewish society and the general population culturally and politically. What laws were in place in Judea, a region that was under direct Roman rule, and what did the legal situation look like in Galilee, which was ruled indirectly by Rome via Antipas? What was the significance for Jesus of these two political regions not being united under one (Jewish) king? And *why* was Jesus executed by Pilate? The latter question is rather simple and straightforward, yet it is one that is absolutely central to the reconstruction of the historical Jesus.

Lastly, the geography/topography of Galilee and Judea gives us information about where and how Jesus traveled, which roads he took, which ones he could have taken but avoided instead, how far a day's journey could take a person, and what Jesus's pilgrimages to Jerusalem may have looked like.

Where the choice of methodology is concerned, it is perhaps easiest to state that archaeological excavation—and the reading and evaluation of excavation reports—requires knowledge of archaeological methodology. Further, an analysis of inscriptions must involve a good grasp of paleography (the study of the development of writing and the dating of different letter shapes), as well as an understanding of how inscriptions (dedications, injunctions, prohibitions, etc.) may be related to historical phenomena.[2] The geography/topography mode of analysis requires a combination of archaeology (ancient road systems, for example) and detailed knowledge of the landscape.[3] Finally, one must note that the texts that directly present or discuss Jesus are problematic from a methodological perspective since these texts represent interpretations of Jesus; they do not provide us with a direct window into his life. As opposed to Paul, Jesus never wrote anything himself—and Paul is difficult enough to understand!

We also have the problem of language and translation. The Gospels were written in Greek, but Jesus spoke Aramaic. Further, the texts were authored approximately

2. Kant, "Jewish Inscriptions in Greek and Latin."

3. Freyne, *Jesus, a Jewish Galilean.*

thirty-seven to seventy years after Jesus's death. Prior to being written down, the traditions about him were transmitted orally. Here we encounter an important problem: Can we decide which parts of the written gospels are "authentic"? Methodologies for such analysis have been developed, but they continue to be challenged and modified; a more detailed discussion of this is found in chapters 3 and 4. Generally, one may note that scholars today are moving away from methods involving the dissecting of the text in order to isolate authentic traditions. Instead, many are attempting to view the text in a more holistic manner, often taking a more sociological approach to the problem. Such approaches include the study of relevant geographical, cultural, and political realities.[4] Memory studies have also emerged as an important field relevant to our question. In other words, recently scholars have increasingly been integrating direct and indirect source material, which in turn has resulted in a more elaborate and diversified use of methodology.

It is important in the current situation to insist that the conclusions drawn about Jesus are considered in relation to the methodology that has been employed. It is difficult to compare and evaluate the results of investigations that have employed different methods.

Finally, on a more general note, it should be observed that the historical Jesus, whichever way he is reconstructed, does not correspond with any of the portraits painted of him by the individual gospel authors. The historical Jesus is a reconstruction based on the fragments of these and other texts, understood within a larger social, political, and religious context, a context that is itself a reconstruction of first-century Galilee and Judea.

The Gospels: Who Wrote First and Who Copied Whom?

Those interested in the historical Jesus are usually interested not only in the oral traditions about him and their transmission but also in the question of which of the texts written about him is the oldest. Attempts have been made by a minority of scholars (e.g., Helmut Koester and John D. Crossan) to show that several sections of the Gospel of Peter (ca. 200 CE) go back to around 50 CE. If correct, these sections would represent the oldest remaining text about Jesus. Others, also a minority, suggest that certain parts of the Gospel of Thomas (second century CE) are independent of the New Testament gospels and thus may go back farther in time than they do. Despite suggestions such as these, the consensus remains, after hundreds of years of research, that the oldest texts available to us are in fact the Gospels of Mark, Matthew, and Luke, also called the Synoptic Gospels. In addition, these gospels are at times so similar that it is highly likely that some sort of a literary dependency exists between them.

4. Freyne, *Jesus, a Jewish Galilean.*

For example, how does one explain the similarities and differences between Matthew's Sermon on the Mount (Matt 5–7) and Luke's Sermon on the Plain (Luke 6:17–49)? How are we to understand the different interpretations of the same Jesus tradition in Mark 7:1–23 and Matt 15:1–20? Who wrote first, and who copied whom? Who had the "original" version, and who revised or changed the text when he copied it? Even though such questions are related to the quest for the historical Jesus, they represent a separate area of investigation. For this reason, the source materials and methodologies applied must be different from what we saw above in the case of historical Jesus studies.

The source material here consists primarily of the first three gospels. Methodologically, we are dealing with what is called *source criticism*, the attempt to ascertain which sources the different authors have used. The texts are analyzed in much detail and certain (general) theories are applied in order to conclude who wrote first. Analyses such as these and the theories that have been employed are further explored in chapter 4.

In terms of results, it is important to remember, as we have mentioned, that conclusions cannot be drawn that extend beyond what the source material and the methodology allow. Source criticism provides us with information about which text is the oldest but says nothing about which of the texts most accurately portray the historical Jesus. The latter question requires wider use of sources and other methodologies, some of the most important of which we have already discussed above.

Analyzing Ancient Theology

If the first question about Jesus relates to a historical phenomenon beyond the texts, and the second question concerns itself with the technical task of ascertaining the relationship between the three Synoptic Gospels, then the third question, which deals with theological aspects of ancient texts, provides us with yet another example of a historical challenge.

When posing questions about key theological issues, such as, for example, how the Gospel of Matthew understands divine judgment and salvation, we may take either a historical-theological approach or a more general theological approach in which we are not dependent on first-century worldviews. The main difference between these tasks is the choice of source material. Certain scholars argue that the latter approach (i.e., a purely theological approach) is independent of historical context and thus ahistorical in nature. Such a statement can, however, hardly be sustained. It is fairly easy to show that ahistorical readings are impossible. When reading a text, we understand it on the basis of our previous experiences and knowledge, which we use in order to attribute meaning to the text in question. Meaning is thus dependent on our own background and identity. In other words, the real issue here is *which* historical and social reference points an individual wishes to understand a text within. A reading that is not based on first-century theological worldviews relocates the interpretation of the text to a different, more modern context. There is simply no way in which we can read a text outside or beyond a context. If we wish to understand our question from a nineteenth-century perspective, we must study what people wrote about the text at that time, as well as the worldviews that were prevalent when the nineteenth-century authors wrote. It is thus possible to study different interpretations of a text made throughout history through adjusting and shifting the historical reference points within which the text needs to be understood, but a text cannot be understood ahistorically.

This means that the source material we choose for the study of the theme of judgment in the Gospel of Matthew cannot be limited to Matthew only. If we made such an attempt at exclusive use of the text only, our modern experiences and worldviews would inevitably influence our analysis. Even though Matthew is the focus of our study, we need to understand the theological symbols and metaphors in the text through investigations into how other (Jewish) texts from the same time period use the same (or divergent) metaphors. Once we have reconstructed the appropriate historical reference points, we can proceed to focus on how the Matthean text deals with the theological concepts we have chosen for this methodological exercise.

An example of how important this methodological process really is surfaces when we consider the prejudices against various Jewish groups mentioned in New Testament texts, especially in the Gospel of Matthew. If we interpret the ancient rhetoric with our modern context as the reference point, we gain a very different understanding of these texts than we would have achieved had we viewed them from a first-century perspective. If we do not learn about how people expressed themselves in the first century and what they meant with their (in our ears) harsh, even violent rhetoric, our historical reading of the texts will be compromised.[5]

Since we are, in this example, interested in how the Gospel of Matthew presents the theme of divine judgment and salvation, and not how the historical Jesus viewed it, we must focus our analysis on the final version of the text, as we have it reconstructed today. This can be done in a variety of ways. *Redaction criticism* takes a closer look at how the author changed the traditions he adopted from his sources (most likely, in this case, Mark and Q, if the theory of Q is accepted). By studying the differences, one can glean the author's own perspective. A more developed version of redaction criticism, often called *composition criticism*, goes further and takes into consideration also those traditions that have been preserved unchanged in the gospel. The reason for this is the legitimate claim that even those Jesus sayings and stories that have been preserved unchanged acquire different meaning when placed in new literary contexts. Composition criticism is well suited for thematic investigations, such as the one we are dealing with here. Then, with the help of *narrative*

5. Johnson, "New Testament's Anti-Jewish Slander."

criticism, we can study how the story develops and how, if at all, the meaning of the theological concept under investigation shifts when the story moves forward. Are the criteria of God's judgment and salvation the same in the beginning of the story as they are at the end? Or do they change as the story unfolds? The most effective method for answering this type of question would be a combination of composition and narrative criticism. With regard to results, these must not move beyond conclusions relative to the first century, based on the research question and the methods used. We cannot, for example, draw many conclusions regarding the group that produced the Gospel of Matthew if our investigation focuses exclusively on the text; such questions would also require other, sociohistorical methods.

Did Paul Invent Christianity?

Lastly, if we take a closer look at our final question, which explores the important issue of whether it was Paul, rather than Jesus, who shaped what later became Christianity, we find that this is a very complex problem that requires a series of different investigations. The source material for such an inquiry will necessarily be diverse, and the methods many. Nevertheless, it is quite common in popular publications and discourses to ascribe to Paul a most crucial role in the development of Christianity without much thought dedicated to the complexity of the matter.

If we divide the inquiry into several consecutive sections, the first section needs to answer the question of whether Paul had any relationship whatsoever to what was to become the religion of the Roman Empire. If we can prove such a connection, we have secured a link between Paul and later mainstream Christianity. This would necessitate a historical analysis of both Paul and later Christian authors. If the results of such an investigation reveal a lack of continuity, the question about whether the historical Paul had a greater influence in the shaping of Christianity than Jesus had must be answered in the negative already at this point.

An equally important question concerns the continuity between Jesus and Paul. If Paul is considered to have direct connections to the future (i.e., to later forms of Christianity) but not to the past (i.e., to Jesus), then we naturally must assume that he had a crucial role in the development of Christendom. However, that would not be the case if one could establish continuity between Jesus and Paul; then Paul would simply become one of many disciples who carried on what Jesus had already begun. An investigation of this type would require not only a study of Paul but also a study of the historical Jesus (see above).

In both the first and second sections, the investigations would have to include theological themes as well as possible sociopolitical motives of Jesus, Paul, and later figures within mainstream Christianity. In terms of method, such a task necessitates historical-literary analyses and sociohistorical analyses, as well as the labor-intensive task of categorizing textual material from a comparative perspective. With the enormous scope of such a task in mind, it is surprising how easily certain authors make decided claims about the issue at hand. Of the research problems explored so far, this one is perhaps the most multifaceted, since it consists of several complex investigations, which must be linked together before any conclusions can be drawn. Chapters 3 and 5 below provide a starting point to understand the problems involved.

Can Modern Societies Shed Light on the Ancient World?

The four historical inquiries discussed above—the historical Jesus, the Synoptic Gospels, the Gospel of Matthew, and Paul—will suffice as examples of how source material and methodology can be selected in the research process. Beyond the specific methods we have already talked about, we shall, finally, look at some general methods borrowed from the social sciences—methods that are not directly shaped to suit investigations of specific sources but that may be applied to all source types. The emphasis here is more generally on our mode of procedure, which affects how we approach the source material and produce historical reconstructions. More specifically, we shall consider here the role of modern empirical studies and in which ways their results may or may not be relevant for historical investigations. Such studies may include social-psychological analyses, dealing with the ways in which individuals in certain situations, such as in a colonized society, tend to react and change their religious behavior. Can results of such studies help us understand the ancient world?

Scholars disagree about whether such methods and their results are compatible with historical investigations. Is it at all possible—and legitimate—to apply results gained from modern studies to first-century societies? Does such an approach run the risk of resulting in anachronistic interpretations of Jesus's time? Scholars who support the use of modern empirical studies in historical research argue that only those results that are based on analyses of several different cultural contexts may provide legitimate generalizations about people's behavioral patterns. These same scholars also argue that if such results are not used to interpret human behavior in antiquity, other tacit assumptions about what people think, do, or say given certain circumstances will illegitimately influence the interpretation. Such unspoken assumptions, unsupported by comparative material, are in reality more open to critique than approaches making explicit use of results generated by modern social-scientific methodologies, since the former have not been the object of a scientific investigation at all.

Among those who accept the use of modern empirical studies as a path to the past, people have different opinions about *how* such studies should relate to the source material. Some scholars believe that only when the sources—often textual—already indicate agreement with the results found using empirical studies can these studies be used in order to strengthen the argument made. Others argue that empirical results can also be used "against" the text, as a tool for a hermeneutic of suspicion. The latter position implies that the content of a text may be challenged as historically unreliable, if modern studies suggest that the behavior described is unlikely given the specific circumstances. In such cases, the text should be understood to reflect the author's bias, what he or she would like to see rather than what really happened. Such use of the social sciences is connected to the more generally accepted fact that ancient texts reflect primarily the perspective of the social elite, and thus must be used with care in historical reconstructions.

Lastly, there is some dispute between scholars who argue that modern empirical studies can only be used together with specific relevant source material and those who believe that results from modern social-scientific investigations may be used to "fill in the gaps." In the latter case, the idea behind the theory is that when textual sources lack the information searched for, it is possible to fill in these gaps using empirically tested theories, and thus create a reconstruction that is tailored to how individuals, according to these theories, act and react in certain situations. Examples where we have very limited access to direct source material include the situation and religious identity of the Jews in Syrian Antioch. We know that Jews lived in the city, since we have information about Jewish immigration in Antioch long before the first century CE. Just as all other people finding themselves in the position of a minority in a given population, it is reasonable to assume that Jews related to the majority within the population in one way or another. Instead of offering conjectures that are impossible to verify, it is possible, as Rodney Stark and Magnus Zetterholm have done,[6] to make use of modern empirical studies exploring how immigrants tend to develop their religious identity in foreign countries in different ways, in order to shed light on the situation in this ancient city.

Conclusion

When one focuses on the complexities that surface with the challenges faced by scholars today, one might ask oneself whether it is at all possible for an individual scholar to master all the source material and all the methodologies that are needed to arrive at historically plausible conclusions. The truth is that most scholars develop an expertise within a few areas only and rely on the results of other scholars who work in adjacent fields for the additional information they need. Few, if any, can master fully all the areas related to New Testament exegesis, although a more general competence is of course required. This state of affairs reflects well the reality of the academic discussion, which builds on both a scholar's individual expertise and his or her confidence and trust in the reliability of the work of colleagues. When the

6. Rodney Stark, *The Rise of Christianity*; Magnus Zetterholm, *The Formation of Christianity*.

university student, who initially is at the mercy of what the textbook claims, begins to gradually acquire the knowledge and skills necessary to discern what is historically reasonable, he or she has taken the first step to participating in this discussion of Jesus and his earliest followers.

Further Reading

Baird, William. "Biblical Criticism: New Testament Criticism." Pages 730–36 in *Anchor Bible Dictionary*. Vol. 1. Edited by David Noel Freedman. New York: Doubleday, 1992.

Black, David A. *New Testament Textual Criticism: A Concise Guide*. Grand Rapids: Baker, 1994.

Collins, John J. *Historical Criticism in a Postmodern Age*. Grand Rapids: Eerdmans, 2005.

Coogan, Michael D., ed. *The Oxford Encyclopedia of the Books of the Bible*. 2 vols. Oxford: Oxford University Press, 2011.

Elliott, John H. *What Is Social-Scientific Criticism?* Guides to Biblical Scholarship, New Testament Series. Minneapolis: Fortress, 1993.

Freyne, Sean. *Jesus, a Jewish Galilean: A New Reading of the Jesus Story*. London: T&T Clark, 2004.

Goodacre, Mark S. *The Synoptic Problem: A Way through the Maze*. Biblical Seminar 80. Sheffield: Sheffield Academic Press, 2001.

Holmberg, Bengt. *Sociology and the New Testament: An Appraisal*. Minneapolis: Fortress, 1990.

Johnson, Luke Timothy. "The New Testament's Anti-Jewish Slander and the Conventions of Ancient Polemic." *JBL* 108 (1989): 419–41.

Kant, Larry H. "Jewish Inscriptions in Greek and Latin." *ANRW* 20.2:671–713. Part 2, *Principat*, 20.2. Edited by H. Temporini and W. Haase. Berlin: de Gruyter, 1987.

McKenzie, Steven L., and Stephen R. Haynes. *To Each Its Own Meaning: An Introduction to Biblical Criticisms and Their Application*. Louisville: Westminster John Knox, 1999.

Moreland, Milton C. *Between Text and Artifact: Integrating Archaeology in Biblical Studies Teaching*. Atlanta: Society of Biblical Literature, 2003.

Novenson, Matthew V. *The Grammar of Messianism: An Ancient Political Idiom and Its Users*. New York: Oxford University Press, 2017.

Powell, Mark Allan. *Methods for Matthew*. Cambridge: Cambridge University Press, 2009.

Reed, Jonathan. *Archaeology and the Galilean Jesus: A Re-Examination of the Evidence*. Harrisburg: Trinity Press International, 2000.

Runesson, Anders. "The Historical Jesus, the Gospels, and First-Century Jewish Society: The Importance of the Synagogue for Understanding the New Testament." Pages

265–97 in *A City Set on a Hill: Essays in Honor of James F. Strange*. Edited by Daniel Warner and Donald D. Binder. Mountain Home, AR: BorderStone, 2014.

Ryan, Jordan J. *The Role of the Synagogue in the Aims of Jesus*. Minneapolis: Fortress, 2017. (Note especially Appendix A and B on historiographical method and hermeneutics.)

Soulen, Richard N., and R. Kendall Soulen. *Handbook of Biblical Criticism*. Louisville: Westminster John Knox, 2001.

Stark, Rodney. *The Rise of Christianity: How the Obscure, Marginal Jesus Movement Became the Dominant Religious Force in the Western World in a Few Centuries*. San Francisco: HarperSanFrancisco, 1996.

Udoh, Fabian E. *To Caesar What Is Caesar's: Tribute, Taxes, and Imperial Administration in Early Roman Palestine*. Providence: Brown Judaic Studies, 2005.

Zetterholm, Magnus. *The Formation of Christianity in Antioch: A Social-Scientific Approach to the Separation between Judaism and Christianity*. London: Routledge, 2003.

IVDAEA
CAPTA

2 Historical Background and Setting

In this chapter we shall attempt to specify the frame of reference within which the search for historical knowledge about Jesus and his first followers can take place. We begin by taking a closer look at Jewish history, in a diachronic deep dive, with the aim of increasing our understanding of the aspects that contributed to relevant historical developments in the first century CE. Many texts that were considered authoritative by Jews, including Jesus and his followers, were composed during the time period covered in the section "Jewish History from the Persian to the Roman Period," p. 52. We will learn more about how and when these texts came into being, which can help to inform us about the ways in which they were later interpreted.

From this diachronic study, we switch gears to a synchronic study of the ancient Mediterranean world during the time of Jesus and his first followers, providing what one may call concentric circles of context around the early Jesus Movement. The section "Greco-Roman Religions and Philosophies," p. 84, focuses on explaining and discussing the world in which the first Christ followers and their earliest recruits lived and worked. Understanding this world gives us the opportunity to better comprehend the historical context for some of Paul's statements and those of his coworkers: What were they writing against? Which aspects of their surrounding culture(s) did they view positively? How did surrounding cultures affect the way in which they chose to express their message?

Jesus, Paul, and the majority of other central figures in the Jesus Movement's early years were Jews and saw their belief in Jesus as an expression of how Judaism should be interpreted and lived. If we want to understand Jesus and his early followers, we must therefore also become well acquainted with contemporary interpretations of Jewish life and beliefs. This pertains both to specific Jewish groups that did not understand Jesus to be the messiah, and to Jewish life in the first century in general. Armed with this kind of knowledge, we can better account for the similarities and differences between the Jesus Movement and other Jewish groups. Such knowledge can help us to better answer the following questions: what were the most important questions for Jesus and his followers? Which issues tended to create conflicts? What issues did Jesus and his followers agree with other Jews on? The section "Beliefs and Practices in Second Temple Judaism," p. 114, deals with this narrower "context circle."

The final section of this chapter, "Men, Women, and Power in Ancient Society and the Early Jesus Movement," deals with a specific issue that affects both the synchronic timelines explored earlier and the Jesus Movement itself. This is a thematic-synchronic description of Greco-Roman and Jewish societies as they pertain to the role of women. This book as a whole aims to discuss all topics with an acute awareness of the different roles men and women had in antiquity. However, due to the importance of this question, we dedicate an entire section to exploring, in more detail, the different roles that men and women could have in the first century CE and how this relates to issues of gender and gender roles in the New Testament.

From Persians to Romans

Jewish History from the Persian to the Roman Period

This section gives an introduction to the history of the Jewish people and the land of Israel subsequent to the Babylonian exile in the sixth century BCE and up to Roman rule in the early second century CE. Situated at the intersection of Europe, Africa, and Asia, Israel was always a desirable geographical area of many empires. Therefore, as we shall see, the history of the people and the land is marked by domination by several empires, Jewish migration, and the people's interrelationship with dominant cultures. We will encounter some of the key figures from this period and also be introduced to some of the Jewish literature written at this time. Through these ancient authors we are fortunate to get insights into some of the varied theological ideas and worldviews current at the time.

The Persian Period

Following an unsuccessful revolt by the Kingdom of Judah against their Babylonian colonizers, Jerusalem and its temple were destroyed by Babylonian troops in 586/587 BCE. As punishment for the revolt, a portion of Judah's population were forced into exile in Babylon, while others fled to Egypt. Just a decade earlier, a similar wave of emigration had occurred. The context created by the exile left many of those now living in Babylon with a new need to define, clarify, and reinterpret their religio-cultural identity. This process had a significant influence on the biblical tradition and its development. Biblical texts give the impression that the land was in principle deserted during the Babylonian exile, but archaeological evidence, which suggests that the area was populated throughout the exile, indicates that this is an exaggeration. Life in the rural areas of Judah continued undisturbed, despite the fact that Jerusalem now lacked a temple. Those who lived in Babylonia as exiles were treated well, considering the circumstances, and they formed colonies that were granted a certain measure of autonomy. Many of the exiles took advantage of the wealth and agricultural fertility of their new home. The Babylonian Empire soon gave way to the Persians, who, led by King Cyrus II, conquered Babylon in 539 BCE, initiating what historians call the Persian period.

Unlike their Assyrian and Babylonian predecessors, the Persians did not use exile as a colonial and political strategy. Instead, Cyrus allowed the various groups in Babylonian exile, including the Jews, to return to their homelands. Cyrus's political strategy revolved around winning the loyalty of his diverse subjects via sympathetic acts, such as recognizing their religion and supporting their cultic centers. The expansion of his empire was accompanied by massive propaganda proclaiming him to be a humanitarian leader for all peoples. In the same vein, Second Isaiah (chs. 40–55 of the book of Isaiah) calls Cyrus "his [God's] anointed" (Isa 45:1), that is, his messiah—God's agent chosen to save the Jewish people. Second Isaiah is the label of the anonymous prophet who preached to the exiled Jews of Babylonia, and the book describes the return to Israel as a second exodus, led by God himself, in the guise of a victorious king (Isa 40:3–11). A large number of the exiled Jews had settled down in Babylonia, and many remained there even after Cyrus's edict. The Jews who chose to stay in Babylonia even after Cyrus's edict formed the basis for the significant Jewish population that prospered there during the following centuries, maintaining close ties with the Jews in Palestine.

Judah/Yehud: Biblical Sources

Judah, or Yehud, as the region was also known, was under Persian rule for about two hundred years. The region, now significantly smaller in size than before the exile (see map in the appendix), was part of the Persian province (*satrapy*) that encompassed the entire western section of the Persian Empire. Samaria was a separate province, but whether Galilee was as well is not known. Yehud was ruled by a Persian governor, while a council of priests spearheaded by a high priest had a significant amount of power in local administration. In addition, there was a non-priestly council consisting of clan leaders.[1] The sources we have access to from this period are first and foremost the historical descriptions found in Ezra and Nehemiah. These once comprised a single work, but in modern bibles they have been separated to form two books. The

1. Albertz, *From the Exile to the Maccabees.*

historical figures Ezra and Nehemiah originated from the eastern diaspora (Ezra was a priest, Nehemiah a governor) and were active in Jerusalem in the middle of the fifth century BCE, although not at the same time (the exact dating is still debated). Other sources from this period include the books of the prophets Haggai, Zechariah, Third Isaiah (chs. 55–66 of the book of Isaiah), and a number of lesser prophets (Malachi, Obadiah, Joel). Many scholars also believe that the second book of Chronicles was written around this time, but others argue that these historical works were composed early in the Hellenistic era. Additionally, much of the wisdom literature (Proverbs, Job) was composed during the Persian period. The priestly sections of the Torah (P), which include regulations concerning the tabernacle (temple), were also authored, to a certain extent, under the Persian period.

Return and Conflict

When the previously exiled Jews returned to the land, conflicts emerged between those who had left and those who had stayed. These conflicts, which continued for several generations, centered on the rights to land ownership but also represented a struggle for political power. The new leaders in Yehud were largely composed of returning Jews who were loyal to the Persians, and there seems to have been a great socioeconomic gap between them and the population who had remained in the land. The struggle for influence and control should be understood against the ideological

The so-called Cyrus cylinder, on which the successes and benefactions of Cyrus are recorded. The cylinder was found in 1878 during excavations in Babylon. The British Museum.

backdrop of the exile population. They argued that the land had been abandoned and uninhabited during the exile, which is reflected in many of the biblical texts from this period. This narrative was used as an important polemical tool against the indigenous population's demands to politically represent the province (see, e.g., Zech 7:7–14; 2 Kgs 25:8–11; Jer 52:15–16). In many passages, Ezra-Nehemiah appears to be ignoring the indigenous population in favor of the returned exiles, emphasizing that the latter should be seen as the "true Israel" (see, e.g., Ezra 2:1–70; 6:16, 21; 10:7–8; and Jer 24:2–10).

The conflict between the indigenous population and the returned exiles reached its pinnacle during the rebuilding of the temple. After the fall of the Jewish kingdom, the position of high priest grew in political significance—since Yehud had no Jewish king—and this also meant that the temple grew in political significance. Those who controlled the temple gained both political power and the economic wealth it generated. Certain indigenous groups consisting of both Samaritans and Jews (Ezra 4:4), who had nothing to gain and everything to lose from the project, opposed the rebuilding of the temple, since it increased the religio-political power of both the Persian rulers who supported it and the returning elite.

With the support of the Persian king Darius (522–486 BCE), the temple was at last rebuilt in 515 BCE. The prophets Haggai and Zechariah, who were part of the driving force behind the rebuilding of the temple, interpreted the occurrence in messianic terms, tying their hopes to the governor and a man called Zerubbabel, a descendant of David (Hag 2:21–23; Zech 3:8; 4:1–14).

Ezra's Reforms

Ezra arrived in Yehud (453 BCE according to Ezra 7:7–8) as a Persian representative, charged with the duty of teaching God's law to the Jews living within the province (Ezra 7:21). This was done in accordance with Persian policy, which stipulated that the nations under its rule codified their traditions and regulations and made them accessible to their rulers. Scholars have debated for a long time which law Ezra came to teach. The most common scholarly view is that it was the five books of Moses (Torah), in accordance with Ezra 7:6. If this is the case, it would represent the final stage in the long and arduous editing process of the Torah, which was intensified during the Persian period, in all likelihood because of the financial support of Darius.[2] In addition, the other sections of the Hebrew Bible (the Prophets and the Writings) were part of an intensified editing process at this time, and although scholars argue about how long this editing process continued, some of these texts attained a lasting and authoritative position during this period. The complete Jewish canon was, however, not finalized until after the first century CE, and thus many texts

2. Berquist, *Judaism in Persia's Shadow*.

that the Jewish community would come to consider authoritative had not yet been written during the Persian period. Still, it may be said that it was during this time that Judaism developed into a "textual religion"—that is, a religion that paid much attention to certain texts considered authoritative. This was to play an important role in later debates between different Jewish groups, including the Jesus movement. In the centuries following the amalgamation of the Jewish authoritative texts, groups would argue and debate about how to interpret these texts and what they actually said about what it means to live according the will of Israel's God.

Because Yehud was only a part of a large and powerful empire, the question of identity and belonging moved to the forefront of Jewish thinking. Malachi accused the male population living in Yehud of entering mixed marriages (Mal 2:10–16). Ezra argued that all men who had married "foreign women from the peoples of the land" (Ezra 10:2) had to send them away. Only the indigenous Jews who had distanced themselves from other peoples and their gods were accepted (Ezra 6:21). Scholars have interpreted these drastic measures differently. Some argue that they should be seen as a direct result of a minority group that felt their identity, and thus their survival, threatened by foreign cultures (cf. Neh 13:1–3, 23–31). Others would rather see it as a result of a Persian strategy to maintain distinctions between ethnic groups so that they could be more easily moved in times of political unrest.[3]

The perception of non-Jews that is to be found in Ezra, however, does not express a view shared by all Jews. This is revealed by other biblical texts from the same period, such as Ruth, Job, and Jonah, all of whom elevate non-Jews compared to their low status in Ezra. These books remained popular with the people, and thus it can be assumed that opinions on non-Jews were diverse rather than solely negative.

In the context of reforms undertaken, it should also be noted that Nehemiah himself attempted to curb the poverty of farmers, who were thrust into hardships by the urban elite, to which Nehemiah otherwise belonged (Neh 5:1–12). He also oversaw the rebuilding of the walls of Jerusalem.

The Hellenistic Period

In the short span of a decade (333–323 BCE), Alexander the Great managed to overthrow the Persians and build up his own empire, which stretched from Macedonia all the way to the river Indus (Pakistan/India). This marked the beginning of the Hellenistic period in Israel's history, a period that was to last until the Roman occupation in 66 BCE. After Alexander's death in 323 BCE, his empire was split into three sections, and Israel had the misfortune of ending up in the chaotic middle of two of these countries: Egypt, ruled by the Ptolemies, and the Seleucid kingdom in the

3. Hoglund, *Achaemenid Imperial Administration*.

north. After several war-torn years, Israel came under the jurisdiction of the Ptolemies (ca. 305 BCE), only to end up a century later under Seleucid rule (198 BCE).

Hellenism

Alexander's military success brought with it significant cultural changes to the territories he occupied, including Israel. Earlier oriental influences were replaced with influences from Greek culture—or Hellenism, as it is also known. Hellenism as a concept includes aspects such as philosophy, language (Greek), economy, politics, religion, communal buildings, architecture, fashion, lifestyle, and much more. The Romans embraced Hellenism and thus continued to spread it in their own empire later.

Generally, Hellenism affected the urban population of Israel more than the rural, which remained relatively undisturbed by the new ideas and lifestyles circulating in the cities. Alexander encouraged Greek immigration to the territories under his rule, and both he and his successors established Greek cities in the lands they conquered in which these immigrants would settle. These cities, both new and old, became centers for Hellenistic culture. They were organized according to the traditional Greek model—the *polis*—where every city was also a state (a city-state). This meant that Greek cities enjoyed a high degree of autonomy. Israel saw several such cities established on its land (see box 2.1).

As immigration of non-Jews to the land increased, so did the emigration of Jews from the land into the diaspora. Many settled down around the Mediterranean, where they were socioeconomically well integrated. This period thus saw many Jewish communities established in the area, and soon the Jewish population in the diaspora outnumbered the one remaining in the land.

Box 2.1
Polis

A *polis* (pl. *poleis*) in the classical sense was a Greek city that constituted an independent unit within a larger kingdom or empire, a kind of mini-state that encompassed the city with its surrounding land area. A polis was ruled by a democratically elected council. All free adult men had the right to vote at general meetings. Alexander the Great and his successors founded cities in the Greek style, but with limited self-rule (the degree of self-government could change over time and vary between cities). During the Seleucids, the Greek cities were given increased power.

A polis contained typical Hellenistic buildings and institutions: *gymnasion* (study center where young men from the upper class also received physical training), *agora* (market square), theaters, temples for the gods, stadium for competitions, and aqueducts. A polis also had the right to mint its own coins.

There was a strict distinction between official citizens of a polis and those who were residents but did not possess citizenship. Citizens had special responsibilities, a vote in the council, and also significant privileges, which varied from city to city.

Victor Tcherikover (*Hellenistic Civilization and the Jews*, 296) estimates that there were up to thirty Greek cities in Israel during the Hellenistic period, none of which were in Judea (except for the coastal area). There was a high concentration of poleis along the coast of Israel and in the region of the Decapolis (Gk. "ten cities") southeast of Galilee. Herod founded several Greek cities, including Caesarea Maritima and Sebaste, and subsequent rulers continued in his footsteps; for example, his son Herod Antipas founded Tiberias and Sepphoris as poleis. Sepphoris had a large Jewish population and was located only about seven kilometers (ca. four and a half miles) from Nazareth. The town was in the process of being built during Jesus's lifetime.

The indigenous people of the land of Israel could generally obtain citizenship in the poleis, although in some places this could lead to conflicts (Josephus, *Jewish Antiquities* 20.173–78; *Jewish War* 2.166). The Greek population (and Hellenized groups from other areas) in Israel consisted not so much of orators and philosophers as of Greek soldiers who immigrated to the eastern Mediterranean because they were given land to use. Other immigrants were craftsmen, peasants, and merchants who sought their fortune in new places. The Greeks brought their culture with them but were also influenced by the cultures they encountered. The inhabitants of the Hellenistic cities in Israel were of both Jewish and non-Jewish background, which during periods of unrest could lead to fighting between Jews and non-Jews.

Under Ptolemaic Rule

Under Ptolemaic rule, Israel and the area east of the river Jordan became part of a larger province that also encompassed Phoenicia (Lebanon) and southwestern Syria. The province was under the authority of a *stratēgos* and was split into several smaller administrative entities, called hyparchies, of which Judea was one. The Jewish population of the land continued to have a certain degree of autonomy, which made the century relatively stable and peaceful. The Ptolemies did not appoint a governor of Judea, and so the political power of the high priest increased drastically. The high priest was chairman of a council of elders (*gerousia*) and was in practice the leader of the Jewish people.[4] The sources we have access to from this period are very limited. Some of the more important include the Jewish historian Josephus, writing in the

4. Berquist, *Judaism in Persia's Shadow*.

first century CE, and the Letter of Aristeas, written in Egypt. These sources shed some light on the Jewish world during the Ptolemaic period and beyond. Jewish wisdom literature continued to develop during this period; Ecclesiastes (third century BCE), for example, offers a critical philosophical outlook on traditional theology, as well as bearing witness to the elite's abuse of the poor during this period.

Following in the footsteps of other colonial powers, the Ptolemies exploited the resources of the lands they colonized. This resulted in a policy where the right to collect taxes was given to the individual or group offering the highest sum to the Egyptians. At the same time, there was no set taxation sum, and this resulted in a suffering and over-taxed population. The majority of this population already had to work hard just to survive, so the Egyptian taxation system became for many what tipped the scale leading to poverty. Those who could not make ends meet under the Ptolemaic taxation system often had no choice but to sell themselves as slaves because of unpaid debts. Slave export stretching into the diaspora thus developed during this period.

The Jewish population in Egypt experienced a drastic increase during the Hellenistic period, largely because of exile and immigration. This was accompanied by a wave of Greco-Egyptian migrants, mainly soldiers, settling down in Israel. There had long been a substantial Jewish population living in Egypt (see Jer 44:1). Already during the fifth century BCE, there was a Jewish military colony on the island Elephantine in southern Egypt. This colony built, among other things, their own temple dedicated to the God of Israel (see box 2.3, p. 67). The relationship between the Jews and the Ptolemies was good: many Jews became soldiers in the Ptolemaic army, while others devoted themselves to agriculture. Additionally, the Jewish population in Alexandria would later come to dominate certain quarters of the new capital. One of the most important sources informing us of Egyptian Jewry is Philo, a Jewish author from Alexandria who was active at the same time as Jesus (we will discuss Philo in further detail later).

The Septuagint and Other Jewish Literature from Egypt

The Letter of Aristeas (third century BCE), mentioned above, contains a description of the first translation of the Torah into Greek, which took place in Alexandria (Let. Aris. 301–11). According to the legend, seventy-two scribes from Jerusalem carried out the translation, which explains the name the text was given; Septuagint means "seventy" in Greek. That a translation was deemed necessary suggests that the majority of Jews at this time had Greek as their mother tongue, and that Hebrew or Aramaic was not widely read. In addition to the Letter of Aristeas, the third book of the Sibylline Oracles, which, like the Letter of Aristeas, did not make it into the canon, was composed around this time. These documents share a favorable disposition toward non-Jews and express a desire for mutual understanding and peaceful coexistence between different peoples—a positive approach that, for various reasons, would be challenged during the Roman period (see below).

Revolt, which, like David's victory over Goliath, illustrated an unlikely Jewish success over foreign oppression and injustice.

Driven by nationalistic fervor combined with religious zeal, the Hasmoneans conquered new regions (the inhabitants of which they also proselytized) and established a tenuous control of the land. The borders of the nation were expanded to such a degree that it now included an area almost as large as David's kingdom eight hundred years earlier. All of Israel, except the very south and the areas east of the Jordan, was now under Hasmonean rule. Simon and his sons and grandsons all occupied the post of high priest, and starting with Aristobulus I (104–108 BCE), the Hasmonean leader was also given the title of king, which was very symbolic in the context of a people who had been continuously colonized for the last few centuries.

The Jewish population generally appreciated the Hasmoneans—dissatisfaction would emerge only later—but there were other ethnic groups living in the land of Israel that grew opposed to their rule. For example, the Samaritans became embittered enemies of the Jews after Hasmonean troops destroyed the two most important Samaritan cities, Samaria (which had a large Greek population) and Shechem. The Hasmoneans also demolished the Samaritan temple on Mount Gerizim. The enmity that grew out of this disaster forms the background for the conflicts between Jews and Samaritans that we come across in the New Testament (John 4:9) and gives Jesus's parable about the good Samaritan (Luke 10:29–37) an especially sharp edge.

The Hasmoneans, who had fought against the hellenization of the land, now initiated a Judaization of their kingdom. They did this by forcing inhabitants in occupied territories such as the Idumeans to convert to Judaism. Simultaneously, the Hasmoneans were influenced by Hellenistic culture: they took Greek names, had diplomatic ties with Greek regents, used Greek mercenary armies, and surrounded themselves with the same luxury and style as other royal courts in the region. Their military rule and colonization praxis created a general dissatisfaction among the Jewish population. This dissatisfaction eventually boiled over into a revolt under the rule of Alexander Janneus (103–76 BCE), which was brutally crushed.

It was during the Hasmonean period that the Sadducees and Pharisees emerged as political parties, each supporting different regents and fighting for influence. After the rule of Queen Salome Alexandra (76–67 BCE), her two sons fought for the throne. This caused a civil war, where both sides sought Roman support for their cause. Both brothers approached General Pompeii, who finally intervened with full military strength and conquered Jerusalem. He appointed Hyrcanus II as high priest and incorporated the land into the Roman Empire. With Jerusalem's fall in 63 BCE, almost eighty years of Jewish autonomy came to an end and the Roman period in Israel's history, the period that was to serve as the background for both the Jesus movement and the eventual development of rabbinic Judaism, descended on the land.

The Roman Period

Despite the fact that Hyrcanus II served as high priest, the real governing power lay in the hands of a wealthy Idumean named Antipater, who had a long history of supporting Rome. Antipater appointed two of his sons as governors. One of these sons was called Herod, the same man who would later be known as Herod the Great. When the Parthians invaded Israel and Syria in 40 BCE, the Roman senate appointed Herod "king" of the region, on the basis of his unswerving loyalty to them. In 37 BCE Roman troops, under the leadership of Herod, defeated the Parthians, and Herod could now properly begin his regency as client king. Herod's kingdom initially included Judea, Galilee, and several regions east of the Jordan, but during his reign he would expand his borders to include Samaria and parts of southern Syria (see map in the appendix).

It was a challenge for Herod to unite and rule a country whose population consisted of diverse ethnic groups that were more often than not hostile toward one another. In addition, the Jewish population was skeptical of his Idumean heritage. To this day, Herod remains a man shrouded in mystery. On the one hand, he is remembered for his authoritarianism and brutality. He executed many of his enemies, including his wife Mariamne, a Hasmonean princess, and two of her sons by him. (The story in Matt 2:1–18 about the killing of all infants in Bethlehem is in all historical probability false and should instead be viewed as the author's attempt to equate Jesus's birth with that of Moses: Moses was born, according to Exod 1:22–2:4, amid the murder of Jewish sons ordered by the Pharaoh.)

On the other hand, Herod helped his subjects a number of times when they were faced with famine, and his massive building projects created thousands of job opportunities. His many palaces and forts were magnificent. He built entire cities, of which the most famous is perhaps the port city Caesarea Maritima. He also rebuilt the city of Samaria, renaming it Sebaste after Emperor Augustus (whose name in Greek is Sebaste). Both cities were built in the Hellenistic fashion, with aqueducts, hippodromes, theaters, market squares, and Roman temples dedicated to the emperor cult. Moreover, Herod also initiated the restoration of the second temple in Jerusalem, which was completed in 64 CE, just six years before its destruction. The result of the restoration was one of the most impressive sanctuaries of the ancient world (see a reconstruction on p. 123; see also fig. 2.2 on p. 121). Herod died in 4 BCE.

Kingdom Divided

After the death of Herod, his kingdom was split between three of his surviving sons. Archelaus was given the largest section (Judea, Samaria, Idumea), Philip was allotted the regions east of Galilee, and Herod Antipas became tetrarch of Galilee and Perea, located east of the river Jordan (for more information, see the map). The regency of

Antipas, as well as that of his brother Philip, overlapped with the ministry of both John the Baptist and Jesus. According to the Gospels, John criticized Antipas to the extent that he had him executed.

The situation in Judea and Samaria saw a very different development than the relatively stable north. When Archelaus succeeded his father, revolts broke out. He crushed them so brutally that he was stripped of his post by Rome already in 6 CE. After his disposal, Rome ruled the area directly via a Roman governor. The most famous of these governors is, arguably, Pontius Pilate (26–36 CE), who has become known for his role in Jesus of Nazareth's execution.

Judea and Samaria became a Roman province with a single governor in the early years of the Roman period. The governor of Judea was subordinate in authority to the governor of Syria. In spite of this, Jewish representatives had quite a bit of influence on internal issues through a council called the Sanhedrin (a Hebrew word borrowed from the Greek *synedrion*, meaning "meeting"). The Sanhedrin was the highest Jewish legal authority in Judea and was presided over by the high priest. The council's sphere of influence varied according to fluctuations of politics, but generally included jurisprudence, the creation of laws, economic decisions, and care of the temple. The residence of the Roman governor was located in Caesarea Maritima, which also served as the capital of Judea. On the occasion of important pilgrim holidays, when Jerusalem experienced a great influx of visitors, the governor would relocate to his Jerusalem residence so that he could be available in case of problems. The governor's presence in Jerusalem was especially crucial during the Passover celebrations, with its emphasis on liberation from Egypt, a previous colonial oppressor in Israelite history.

Unlike Herod I ("the Great"), the Roman governors were not well acquainted with Jewish religious thinking and were not as sensitive to Jewish religious traditions. Their actions sometimes provoked the population and resulted in protests, which could escalate into brutal and bloody encounters between Jews and Romans. Josephus narrates how people protested when Pilate used the temple funds to build an aqueduct, which was illegal according to the Jewish population's way of thinking. The protest was brutally squashed (*Jewish War* 2.175–77). When a prophet leader in Samaria persuaded a large group of people to follow him to Mount Gerizim to see vessels from Moses, they were killed by Roman soldiers. This incident actually led to Pilate being deposed by Rome (*Jewish Antiquities* 18.85–89).

The relationship between the Jewish population and their Roman colonizers further deteriorated when the mentally unstable Emperor Caligula (37–41 CE) ordered a statue of himself to be erected on the Temple Mount in Jerusalem. (Caligula was murdered before the project could be realized.) The Jewish people rejoiced, however, at the appointment of Herod's grandson Agrippa I as client king of the entire land in 41 CE. The joy was short-lived, and Agrippa I died after only three years on the throne, in 44 CE. Agrippa I would be the last Jewish king to ever rule the entire land.

He was succeeded by Roman officers, known as procurators. These officers did not rule the entire region. Agrippa II controlled Ituraea and Trachonitis; because of his loyalty to Rome, he was allowed to retain his regency until his death in 100 CE.

The taxes owed to Rome and the temple tax caused widespread poverty in Israel and increased the gap between the higher and lower classes. We can see traces of this social inequality in many of Jesus's parables. Jesus was one of many charismatic leaders in the first century CE whose message focused on liberation from different types of oppression (see box 2.2).

The First Jewish War (66–70 CE)

A steady progression of religio-politically insensitive actions carried out by corrupted and incompetent Roman procurators resulted in an increasing dissatisfaction with Roman rule. This dissatisfaction led to the emergence of various resistance movements throughout the land, movements that had their roots among the poor. These movements were often motivated by religious ideals. The Zealots were an example of this. In the ancient world, religion was not seen as something separate from other aspects of life; political, military, and religious actions were synonymous. Therefore, the military and political goals of the Zealots are difficult, if not impossible, to distinguish from their religious motivations. Revolutionaries trusted that God would help them in their struggle, and they were often encouraged by the success of the Maccabees, who had defeated their enemies against all odds only a century earlier. Although there was widespread dissatisfaction with and dislike of Roman rule, it should be pointed out that not everybody was in favor of the revolt. Many Jews, even if they did not see the Roman occupation as positive, nonetheless believed that a struggle against the most powerful military in the world could only be hopeless. Still others were happy to be part of the larger, Roman world. Generally, the rural population supported the revolt more than the urban population did.[5]

The dissatisfaction of the population reached its boiling point when the procurator Gaius Florus (64–66 CE) decided to take a large amount of money from the temple fund. Protests followed, and when soldiers clashed with the protesters, resistance groups joined the struggle, thus marking the beginning of the First Jewish War. The rebels took control of Jerusalem early on in the struggle and put an end to the very symbolic daily sacrifices made there in the emperor's honor. The revolt spread throughout the land, and in many ethnically diverse cities, Jews and non-Jews rose against each other. The First Jewish War lasted four years (66–70 CE) and ended in the total annihilation of the Jewish troops and a horrible suffering for the people.

Through Josephus, who was a general of Jewish troops in the Galilee, we have

5. A. Levine, "Visions of Kingdoms."

access to primary source material about the First Jewish War. His texts describe how there was dissidence and disunity even within the Jewish troops. Under the leadership of Vespasian, Roman troops were able to quickly take control of large parts of the land and begin a siege of Jerusalem. After Vespasian was declared emperor in 69 CE, his son Titus inherited the task of defeating the Jews. The different Jewish groups operating within Jerusalem itself did not unite until the siege of their city was a fact. According to Josephus, this inability to unite would prove their downfall. In 70 CE, Titus's troops entered Jerusalem and burned the temple to the ground. Many revolutionaries fled with their families and took refuge in a fort called Masada by the Dead Sea, but they too were defeated three to four years later. According to Josephus's account (the historicity of which is debated by scholars), the revolutionaries of Masada chose to commit mass suicide rather than end up as prisoners of war.

Masada, looking east. Note the ramp on the right that was built by the Romans in order to gain access to the fortress. The wagon in the foreground is from a later time. Photo by Anders Runesson.

Box 2.2
Charismatic Preachers

In Josephus's writings we find several examples of charismatic leaders, preachers, prophets, and miracle men who became popular among the people and who were sometimes seen as a potential political threat to the status quo by the Roman authorities. If these charismatic individuals also had followers, the Romans viewed them as a bigger threat. These charismatics were driven by an apocalyptic agenda and foresaw the fall of their enemies, in most cases represented by the Romans—although other Jewish groups who did not accept their message were also sometimes portrayed as the enemy. Some had a revolutionary message, like Theudas (Acts 5:36; *Jewish Antiquities* 20.97–98), who during the 40s CE led a large group of people to the river Jordan, where he was meant to part the river and enter the land. The symbolic references to Moses, the exodus, and Joshua (who crossed the river before entering Israel) were seen as a political provocation. Another prophet worth mentioning is "the Egyptian" (Acts 21:38; *Jewish Antiquities* 20.169–72), who claimed to be the messiah and led a large group of people to the Mount of Olives in order to witness the destruction of Jerusalem's walls. In both of these cases, Theudas and "the Egyptian," Roman forces intervened with force against the gatherings. Another group, led by Samaritans, was massacred on Mount Gerizim, where they had gathered to witness holy artifacts that Moses allegedly buried there. One prophet, Jesus son of Ananias (60s CE), was tortured by soldiers after he had preached about the immanent destruction of the temple. He was, unlike most, released fairly quickly, having been declared mentally challenged and thus not dangerous (*Jewish War* 6.300–309). In light of these sources, the executions of the two main charismatic figures in the New Testament, John the Baptist and Jesus, were not unique events for their time and should be viewed within their larger religio-political context.

Box 2.3
The Temple in Jerusalem—More Than a Religious Institution

When the first temple, built during the reign of King Solomon (ca. 961–922 BCE), was destroyed in 587/586 BCE, the people lost the foremost cultic center dedicated to the God of Israel. With this in mind, it may seem strange that the entire population did not support the Persian-funded rebuilding of the temple, which was completed in 515 BCE. The explanation for this is that the temple was not only a religious center; it was also a political and economic center. This meant that the struggle for power in the land inevitably centered on who controlled the temple. The majority of Jewish society *did* support the rebuilding of the temple; for the prophets Haggai and Zechariah, the consecration of the second temple was a sign that God's presence was once again dwelling among the people. They foresaw a magnificent future for Judah, in which nations would send tribute to Jerusalem (Hag 2:6–9). The groups that were opposed to the rebuilding of the temple were more often than not groups that were marginalized by the new power center. These groups consisted mainly of Jews who had remained in the land during the exile, as well as Samaritans (Ezra 4:4; Isa 66:1–6; cf. Neh 4:1–3). The Jews who had remained during the exile did not need a new temple, as they had survived without one for a long time, carrying out sacrifices in its ruins. In addition, a reinstitution of temple practices would mean the introduction of new temple taxes. We should also keep in mind that the Persians gained from financially supporting the building of the second temple. Their generosity turned the local elite into loyal subjects, and the massive temple institution provided them with bureaucratic structures and native leaders, tools that they could use to more effectively rule the land (Berquist, *Judaism in Persia's Shadow*). The high priests occupied a role that was simultaneously religious and political, and the governor had connections to the temple.

The temple remained a wealthy institution throughout the Second Temple period, generating income via taxes and donations, and acting as a bank for the aristocracy. The temple funds were also used to donate to charities. By having both religious authority and economic control, the priestly families became increasingly wealthy and powerful, and the majority of conflicts arising during Seleucid rule revolved around who would occupy the desirable role of high priest. Later, the Hasmonean rulers would validate their authority by claiming the position of high priest and making it hereditary within their family. (According to many scholars, this was one factor behind the creation of the Qumran movement, a protest leading to voluntary social isolation in contrast to society at large.) Furthermore, during the Roman period, the high priest was the influential leader of the Jewish Council. Herod ("the Great") did not come from a priestly family and thus made sure to control the appointment of the high priests. He appointed those loyal to him and replaced them when he so desired. After Herod's death, the Romans continued appointing the high priest, either through the procurator or the governor of Syria.

Jews in Rome and Alexandria

There were many Jewish communities in the Hellenistic cities surrounding the Mediterranean. Two of the most important Jewish centers were located in Rome and Alexandria. The exile of Jewish rebels following Pompey's conquest of the land, and voluntary immigration to Italy in later times, caused the Jewish population of Rome to increase significantly during the middle of the first century CE. The Jews enjoyed a good standing in Rome under Julius Caesar (49–44 BCE) and Augustus (27 BCE–14 CE). This is evidenced by the fact that Jews were allowed to congregate to practice their religion, unlike many other religious minorities whose meetings Caesar prohibited. Romans, who generally appreciated old traditions from other cultures, viewed the Jewish religion favorably owing to its ancient roots. It was not until Jews became more prominent in Roman society that a noticeable backlash occurred. This backlash was expressed in anti-Jewish rhetoric and the exile of some Jewish groups from Rome. In Acts 18:2 the author mentions that Emperor Claudius (41–54 CE) exiled the Jews from Rome. Among those forced to leave the city were Priscilla and Aquila, a Jewish Christ-believing couple whom Paul later met in Corinth.

Despite such incidents, the Jewish traditions were still well respected in many circles.[6] The most common Roman accusations against Jews were that they had a hate-filled inclination toward others, "misanthropia" (perhaps a distorted interpretation of the Jewish purity and dietary laws), that they were lazy (because they did not work on the Sabbath), and that they were atheists (since they did not worship the Roman gods). The Jewish community in Rome remained strong despite the backlash, but the strain between Jews and Romans would never completely disappear.

The relationship between Jews and non-Jews in Egypt deteriorated during the Roman period (ca. 30 BCE and forward). Although the Jewish population of Alexandria enjoyed certain privileges, such as a degree of autonomy and the right to practice their religion, the average Jew was not given Alexandrian citizenship, which brought with it decreased taxes and social prestige. Conflicts between Jews and non-Jews increased for various reasons, including the fact that other minority groups were unhappy about the privileges enjoyed by the Jewish population and did not understand their refusal to partake in the Roman emperor cult. Toward the end of the 30s CE, during the reign of Emperor Caligula, these conflicts escalated into riots when murderous attacks were carried out against the Jews of Alexandria. This is the first known pogrom against Jews, which also involved attacks against their homes and desecration of the synagogues. These riots were followed by a Jewish counterattack after the death of Caligula in 41 CE. Clashes between non-Jews and Jews in Alexandria would occur sporadically during the following decades, to culminate during the First Jewish War in Israel. According to Josephus, the Romans mercilessly killed fifty thousand members of Alexandria's Jewish population (*Jewish War* 2.494–98) in retaliation for the Jewish revolt in the land of Israel.

The Wisdom of Solomon and 3 Maccabees, both written in Egypt, describe difficult conflicts between Jews and non-Jews. The Wisdom of Solomon deals with controversial theological concepts such as the suffering of the righteous, the arrogance of the ungodly, and the eventual justice that will be brought against the ungodly. Third Maccabees is a fictional rendition of persecution and miraculous salvation that encourages people to trust God in a world that is dangerous for Jews.

The Effects of the First Jewish War

The war of 66–70 CE left behind it a decimated Israel and tens of thousands of dead. The Romans confiscated large regions of the land and took thousands of Jews as slaves.

6. Barclay, *Jews in the Mediterranean Diaspora.*

The country was now ruled by a legate with a senate rank who answered directly to the emperor. The revolt had problematic consequences for Jews throughout the Roman diaspora; they were now seen even more as outsiders and came under suspicion of having treasonous inclinations. The yearly half-shekel that was paid as temple tax by every Jewish male was now replaced by a humiliating tax to Jupiter Capitoline's temple in Rome, something that was forced not only on Jews in the land but also on Jews throughout the diaspora, even if they had not participated in the revolt.

The destruction of Jerusalem's temple was a huge shock for the Jewish people as a whole. The temple had united Jews in the land and Jews in the diaspora in a shared cultic and symbolic focal point, where the meeting between God and God's people could take place. Many of the Jewish texts we encounter during the post-temple period deal with the complicated theological questions that arose from the ashes of the temple, especially the echoing question "Why?" (e.g., 2 Baruch and 4 Ezra). The council in Jerusalem disintegrated, the priesthood lost its income, and the people were forced to get used to worshiping without the Jerusalem temple, its cult, and the annual pilgrimages. Synagogues, the religious function of which had previously revolved around Torah readings, began to function more and more as the focal points of Jewish communities. The temple lived on in the collective memory of the people: the rabbis, for example, continued to discuss correct temple procedures for

The Arch of Titus in Rome. The relief tells of the victory of the Romans over the Jews and shows some of the spoils from the temple in Jerusalem, such as the menorah. Photo by Dieter Mitternacht.

centuries. Certain elements of the temple liturgy would come to play an important role in the later development of synagogue liturgy.

The temple's destruction and the failure of the revolt resulted in the disappearance of Jewish revolutionary groups as well as other Second Temple groups such as the Sadducees, who were popular among priests and hence tied to the temple. The Essenes also fade into history at this point. According to Josephus, they were massacred by Roman soldiers (*Jewish War* 2.152–53). They left behind them a large library in the caves around Qumran. The two groups that survived the fall of the temple and flourished during the post-temple period were the Pharisees and the Jesus movement. However, neither group remained unchanged by the event, and they both developed in different ways at the turn of the century. The Jesus movement gained a large number of non-Jewish members, contributing to a development that would eventually result in a Christianity separate from Judaism. The party of the Pharisees played an important role in the "coalition" of the different Jewish groups that would come to constitute early rabbinic Judaism. This form of Judaism took root and grew stronger in the post-temple period. It became the dominant form of Judaism perhaps as early as the fourth century CE, although many scholars would argue that the process was much longer and more complicated than such an early date would indicate. The Pharisaic rabbi Yohanan ben Zakkai founded a new religious center in Yahvne, located west of Jerusalem, which would become pivotal for the development of rabbinism. The Judaism we see today can trace its roots back to the rabbinic interpretation of the Jewish religion that emerged from the center at Yahvne.

The Diaspora Revolt (115–117 CE)

The revolt of 66–70 CE, also referred to as the First Jewish War, was more or less limited to within the borders of the land. However, it triggered a large-scale revolt among the Jews of Egypt, Cyprus, and Cyrenaica around 115–117 CE. The revolt, which had its basis in messianic theology, was first and foremost aimed at local Hellenistic groups, but developed into a war against Rome. The Roman army crushed the rebellion, and the Jewish diaspora population was drastically decreased. This war put obvious further strains on Jewish-Roman relations but did not lead to further diaspora revolts. However, unbeknownst to all, a new revolution was already brewing in Israel.

The Bar Kokhba Revolt (132–135 CE)

After the war of 66–70 CE, Israel became a Roman province called Judea. Despite the great losses incurred by the war, the Jewish people in the land had not yet given up their hope for autonomy. This hope eventually led to a new revolt during the reign of Hadrian (117–138 CE), triggered in part also by Hadrian's own anti-Jewish political policies. As part of a general law against dismemberment, the emperor outlawed circumcision, which obviously hit the Jews hard. Outlawing circumcision was in essence seen as outlawing Judaism, and it brought back bitter memories of Seleucid oppression. In addition to this new law, Hadrian also made plans to rebuild Jerusalem as a Roman city, with a Roman temple. The Jewish reaction was swift. A revolt began in 132 CE under the leadership of a man called Simon, also known as Bar Kokhba ("son of the star," a messianic title) by those who believed that he was the messiah sent by God to defeat the Roman colonizers and rebuild the Jewish kingdom. The prominent leader Rabbi Akiva was among those who believed that Simon was the messiah. Archaeologists have found letters written by members of the guerilla forces in the Judean desert, even letters written by Bar Kokhba himself. These letters are known as the Bar Kokhba Letters. The letters were written during the last stages of the revolt, when the hope for a free land was beginning to disappear.

The revolt was crushed in 135 CE by the Roman army. Cities and villages were destroyed once more. Hadrian rebuilt Jerusalem as a typical Roman city and called it Aelia Capitolina (after his family name Aelius). He built several Roman temples in the new city, including a temple to Jupiter that was built on the old Temple Mount. In addition to this humiliation, Jews were forbidden even to visit Jerusalem, the country's name was changed to Palestine (meaning "the land of the Philistines"), and Jews were forbidden to follow their traditional laws. After Hadrian's death in 138 CE, the situation was somewhat improved for the Jews in Palestine, but the Jerusalem temple would never be rebuilt.

Bar Kokhba tetradrachm; *obverse*: the Jewish temple facade with the rising star; *reverse*: a lulav, with the text: "to the freedom of Jerusalem." Courtesy of Classical Numismatic Group (https://www.cngcoins.com/Coin.aspx?CoinID=106925).

In this context, it is important to be aware that the cult centralization (the idea that the Jews can have only one temple, the one in Jerusalem) mentioned in biblical texts was a relatively late, postexilic development that took a long time to spread to the diaspora. The synagogue's development in the diaspora is thus best described as an effect of a liturgical revival, which saw the spread of cult-centralization ideology outside the borders of the land of Israel. (See box 2.4 on the synagogue.) Previous to these changes in cult patterns, Jews in the diaspora had used the same type of organizational structures for their ancestral worship as people around them did. In the Greco-Roman world, non-Jewish associations incorporated sacrificial cults in their activities. When cult-centralization ideology, already prevalent in the land, eventually spread into the diaspora, Jews began to adopt the practice from the land of regular communal readings of Torah, abandoning their previous cultic practices.

Box 2.4
The Synagogue

There were two types of institutions in the land that went under the name "synagogue" in the first century CE (the word "synagogue" comes from the Greek *synagōgē*, which in this context means "assembly" or "meeting house"). The first type were civic or *public institutions*, and the second type were Jewish associations; for convenience, we may call the first type public synagogues and the second type association synagogues (Runesson, *Origins of the Synagogue*, 232–35). For society as a whole and its basic administrative instruments, the more important of these two institutions was the public synagogue, which is best described as a local municipal institution with social, political, and religious functions. Here, religio-legal decisions were made and religio-political issues debated by the inhabitants of local towns and villages. In addition, public Torah readings were carried out once a week, every Sabbath (see, e.g., Luke 4:16–30; Mark 1:21–28). Men, women, and children participated in the meetings and, as far as we know, sat together (at this time we do not find the separation of sexes that is characteristic of the later period). These institutions were part of the administrative structure of Jewish society, but they were also a space where individuals and groups could express their opinions on religious issues. One did not have to be a member of the priesthood to read and discuss the Torah. Public synagogues represented a space where Torah was accessible, at least in theory and as far as our sources indicate, to everyone. The Jesus movement, like the Pharisees, used the public synagogues to spread their respective messages.

The association synagogues, on the other hand, were not public in the same sense as the municipal institutions, but catered to groups that organized themselves around certain interests or networks. For example, a Jewish association could be dedicated to nourishing similar ideas about the interpretation of the Torah, or simply bringing together people from different geographical locations or social strata. "The synagogue of the freedmen" in Jerusalem (Acts 6:9) belongs to this category, and so does the synagogue of the Essenes, which is mentioned by Philo (*That Every Good Person Is Free* 81). The Theodotos inscription in Jerusalem (dated to the first century CE) speaks of a synagogue dedicated to the teaching of the law and the commandments, and, as it seems, constructed especially for diaspora Jews who had come to visit the Jerusalem temple. Membership in these association synagogues was optional, and the associations themselves decided on the rules that would govern their group. Association synagogues resembled non-Jewish (Greek, Roman, Egyptian, etc.) associations in every way except for the centrality of the reading of Torah as a form of worship. Most Jewish associations existed in urban areas, as far as we know, but there is also general evidence for associations in rural areas. There are a number of examples in the New Testament where both Pharisees and members of the Jesus movement visited public synagogues in rural regions with the aim of winning supporters for their respective agendas.

The situation was different in the diaspora. The administrative and political functions of the public synagogues in the land of Israel did not apply outside its borders. While Jews had the right of free assembly, the societies in which they lived were still controlled, of course, by non-Jewish civic administrative institutions. Therefore, synagogues in the diaspora were understood by non-Jews and Jews alike as a form of association. As such, they had the right to take care of their internal affairs, and the emphasis on weekly Torah readings/studies remained an integral aspect of the synagogue's function, just as in the land (see, e.g., Acts 13:13–43). According to several New Testament and other sources, non-Jews were welcome in Jewish association synagogues. In many (most?) cases, these non-Jews remained non-Jews, while others converted fully to the Jewish tradition (proselytes). This process required circumcision for men. In all likelihood, Paul and other missionaries with similar aims targeted such non-Jews who were interested in Jewish life and tradition and had become convinced that the God of Israel was a powerful deity.

As is illustrated by the historical reconstruction above, the question of what exactly constituted a "synagogue" at the time of Jesus is quite complex. Because of this, the problem of the origins of these institutions becomes complex as well, which is evidenced by the multitude of differing scholarly opinions. What all agree on, however, is that anyone dealing with the issue of the origins of the synagogue has to use source material from both the land of Israel and the diaspora. One should also differentiate between the origins of the public and the association synagogues, since the beginnings of these were not the same. Anders Runesson, in *The Origins of the Synagogue*, has presented the following solution to the problem.

The public synagogue in the land of Israel in the first century CE was a sociopolitical and administrative civic institution whose functions resembled similar institutions within non-Jewish societies. All societies need to be organized, and public institutions are needed to achieve this organization. According to some scholars, this implies that the question of origins becomes rather meaningless, since such institutions have always, by necessity, existed. However, Jewish civic institutions were unique in one significant aspect: in the first century, they included weekly public Torah reading and interpretation. How do we explain this activity, which did not exist among other ethnic groups? If one can ascertain how and why public Torah reading began, and how it was integrated into an already existing sociopolitical and administrative institution, one has successfully identified the origins of the (public) synagogue.

This approach to the origins problem leads us back to the Persian period. More specifically, it takes us back to around the year 450 BCE, when the Persian king Artaxerxes II and the Jerusalemite elite decided to use the previously codified Israelite laws in order to introduce socio-structural changes in the land (Yehud), aiming to establish a common social, religious, and ethnic identity that could be shared by everyone living in the land. In this way, the reforms were legitimized by (interpretations of) Israel's own law. In order to disseminate knowledge of the law, interpreted in this way, to the people, it was read out loud on special occasions in public places where the local administration was based. In fortified cities, this place was the city gate (see, e.g., Neh 8). The public reading of the law was, at that time, thus controlled by the Jerusalemite elite, who could send out representatives to teach the law to the people (see 2 Chr 17:7–9, a passage most likely mirroring the time when the text was authored—that is, the late Persian/early Hellenistic period). Eventually, the Jerusalemite elite lost control of public Torah reading, as local elites interpreted the text according to local customs. A seven-day interval between readings was eventually introduced and became the accepted standard throughout the land. The evidence for this is late, but there are some indications that this practice could have begun under the Hasmoneans, who, as they expanded their kingdom, had a need to consolidate their reign and introduce a common law for all. In this way, the Sabbath became synonymous with Torah reading and interpretation in public synagogues, and this is the situation later reflected in the New Testament (the Gospels and Acts).

The origins of Jewish associations, or association synagogues, is a very different story. As mentioned previously, this institution may be understood as a Jewish form of the Greco-Roman social phenomenon that we usually refer to as associations, and which existed between the public and the private spheres of society; they were, we could say, semipublic, or semiprivate institutions. This form of organization most likely reached the land from the diaspora with the hellenization process that was described earlier in this chapter, the earliest evidence coming from the third century BCE (Sir 51:23). The developing parties of the Sadducees and the Pharisees were likely the result of such institutional-cultural changes, and thus the organization is best described as a form of association. This development happened as the Jerusalem authorities loosened their control of Torah interpretation as it related to the civic institutions. In any case, Jewish associations in the land related to Jewish civic institutions in ways similar to the way in which Greco-Roman associations related to Greco-Roman civic institutions outside the land. In the diaspora, of course, Jewish associations related to civic institutions in the same way as other Greco-Roman associations did, although there were some rights that the Jewish communities enjoyed since the time of Caesar that many other people-groups did not. The origins of the church and of the modern (rabbinic) synagogue can be found in such Jewish associations, which catered to different interest groups and often had a mixed membership. Somewhat simplified, one could say that both of these institutions were the result of the combination of (different) Jewish communal messages and Greco-Roman organizational patterns. On the other hand, the civic Jewish institutions in which Jesus proclaimed his message of the kingdom ceased to exist as the land was colonized in late antiquity first by Christians and then by Muslims, with the result that Jews lost their self-rule and thus the administrative institutions through which they had organized and run their cities and towns as well.

In the diaspora, the development of the synagogue occurred partly along different trajectories. The majority of our evidence indicates that during the Persian and Hellenistic periods, Jews organized themselves mainly around (Jewish) temples and temple cults. This is especially clear in Egypt, from where the majority of our sources originate. In addition to the nonbiblical sources mentioning Jewish temples in Elephantine and Leontopolis (papyri and Josephus, but the latter also mentioned in rabbinic literature), there are indications in the Hebrew Bible of such Jewish temples in Egypt (Isa 19:19; cf. Josephus, *Jewish Antiquities* 13.65–66). There are also several inscriptions from the second century BCE that mention Jewish *proseuchai* (Gk.; sing. *proseuchē*, meaning "house of prayer"), a term originally used to describe the temple in Jerusalem (cf. Isa 56:7 LXX; 1 Macc 7:37; Mark 11:17). Later, however, we know from Philo and Josephus that this term, *proseuchē*, was used to describe synagogues. It is likely that, with the arrival of Jewish immigrants, Jewish diaspora temples were reorganized through the incorporation of Torah-reading services, which were already a key component of the civic synagogues in the land. It is, in light of this, important to recognize that the cult-centralization mentioned in biblical, preexilic texts, that is, the ideology that Jews were allowed to worship only at the one temple in Jerusalem, was not successfully implemented until the postexilic period, and it did not spread immediately to the diaspora. The origin of the synagogue in the diaspora, as it included the gradual introduction of Torah-reading rituals, was thus connected to a liturgical renewal movement as cult-centralization ideology spread from the land throughout the diaspora. The organizational forms were otherwise the same as for other Greco-Roman and Egyptian associations, as we have noted, the Jews over a longer period of time exchanging the sacrificial cultic element (which all associations had) with Torah-reading rituals imported from the land of Israel. For sources on ancient synagogues, as well as of Jewish temples, from their origins to ca. 200 CE, see Runesson, Binder, and Olsson, *The Ancient Synagogue*. See also the illustrations on p. 79.

Literature from the Hellenistic and Roman Periods

Terminology and Scope

A great number of Jewish texts authored during the second half of the Second Temple period were not included in the Jewish or Christian canon. These texts were written both in Israel and in the diaspora. These texts are known as *pseudographs* or pseudepigrapha (from the Greek *pseudepigraphon*, meaning "false title"), because most of them were authored under pseudonyms. The authors often—but not always—present themselves to be historical persons who played an important role in Israel's history. This was a common way to legitimize one's text during this time period. Pseudographs are not the same as apocrypha (from the Greek *apokryphos*, meaning "hidden"). The latter were included in the Septuagint (see the section "The Septuagint and Other Jewish Literature from Egypt" on p. 59) but not in the traditional Hebrew Bible according to Jewish tradition. Many of these texts have a special

The Madaba map. The map is part of a mosaic on a church floor in the city of Madaba, located in present-day Jordan. The map is dated to circa 500 CE and illustrates the extent to which Byzantine Christianity had come to value the "holy land." Jerusalem is pictured as it was rebuilt by Hadrian—a typical Roman city with a main street (*cardo*) cutting the city in half. That the mosaic is Byzantine can be ascertained by the fact that the Holy Sepulcher, not the destroyed Temple Mount, is placed in the center of the city. Above (east of) Jerusalem, one can see the Dead Sea and the river Jordan. Photo by Anders Runesson.

place in the Roman Catholic tradition and are classed as deuterocanonical (i.e., they have been included in the Bible at a later date than the other Old Testament texts). In Protestant tradition, however, the apocrypha are not included in the canon, but may be included in a special section.

Because of the extensive amount of literature from this time and the scope, which spans several hundred years, the introduction below is very selective.[7] In addition to the pseudepigraphic and apocryphal texts, we will be looking at documents from Qumran, composed by members of a Jewish sect (in all likelihood the Essenes; see "The Essenes," p. 137). These texts are usually treated as a separate entity of texts from this period. The great literary works of Josephus and the philosopher Philo are usually categorized separately as well.

The large quantity of literature produced during the Greco-Roman period can likely be traced back to the now-established tradition of Torah reading and interpretation in public synagogues every Sabbath. Furthermore, the development of association synagogues gave different groups the opportunity to develop different interpretative traditions. The literature bears witness to a new generation of Jewish philosophers, theologians, and visionaries who sought to answer questions about God and society in a new age. Sometimes they found inspiration in Torah, and sometimes through divine messages thought to be delivered by angels or dreams. Many of the texts show an openness for contemporary ideas popular in the surrounding societies the authors found themselves in, and many of the texts express a freedom of experimentation with new methods of interpreting and reworking traditions found in the Torah. The majority of the texts were written in Hebrew or Greek but have been preserved—often by Christian groups—in other languages (e.g., Ethiopic or Latin). The rich diversity of the texts reflects the multifaceted nature of Judaism in the Greco-Roman period.

Literary Types

Literature from the Second Temple period can be divided into different literary types (genres), although more than one genre can often be detected in the same document. One group of texts from this period consisted of rather free rewritings of biblical texts, often called rewritten Scripture, through which authors could "solve" theological problems occurring in the original text as well as make the text more relevant to their own time by rewriting the words and actions of the biblical characters into their own context. To this category of texts belongs the book of Jubilees (second century BCE), which is a rewriting of Genesis and the first part of Exodus. In Jubilees' retelling, the story is dated according to a 364-day sun-based calendar, and the patriarch lives in accordance with the Mosaic law, unlike in the original biblical narrative. Another example is a text called Pseudo-Philo (written in the first

7. See Charlesworth, *Old Testament Pseudepigrapha*.

The synagogue in Gamla on the Golan Heights, looking southwest. Photo by Anders Runesson.

The Theodotus inscription. The inscription describes how a man named Theodotus, together with others, constructed a synagogue in Jerusalem with the aim that Torah should be taught there. Visitors to the synagogue also had the opportunity to sleep there and to use the synagogue's water installations. The inscription is dated to the first half of the first century CE. The Israel Museum, Jerusalem.

century CE), in which biblical stories are interwoven with legends. In this text, the resurrection of the dead (a nonbiblical motif) is emphasized, and women are given a prominent role. The Temple Scroll, in which God speaks to Moses in the first person (instead of in third person, as in the biblical narrative), the Genesis Apocryphon (both from Qumran), and Josephus's *Jewish Antiquities* 1–10 are further examples of this literary type.

Standing in stark contrast to such free interpretation of biblical narratives, *Bible commentaries*, which make a very clear distinction between the original text and the interpretation, represent another genre from this period. Some of Philo's writings that deal with the deeper philosophical meaning behind laws and stories in the Torah are examples of Bible commentaries. In these texts, Philo comments on the biblical texts verse by verse, an approach that clearly distinguishes these texts from the genre of Bible retellings, or rewritten Scripture. The *Pesher* literature from Qumran also offers a symbolic interpretation of prophetic texts and psalms. These interpretations aim to illustrate that the texts are actually concerned with the history of the sect. The early Jesus movement also used this interpretative method to find signs of Jesus in the prophetic books.

Other books can be classified as *novels* or *short stories*—that is, stories that do not claim historical authenticity. In this category we find apocryphal Tobit (ca. 200 BCE) and Judith (end of the second century BCE). These fictional stories were not merely written as entertainment. They aimed to indoctrinate their readers with the importance of living a righteous life and placing one's trust in God. Another genre is *historical depictions*. Although they are not meant to be works of fiction, they, like every other historical account from this time, must be read with a critical eye and an awareness of the author's bias. The monumental historical work of Josephus contains the most comprehensive historical descriptions from this time (*Jewish Antiquities* 11–20 and *Jewish War*, both from the second half of the first century CE), but there are other examples of this category as well, such as 1–2 Maccabees (end of the second century BCE).

The *testament* is another genre from this period. Testaments were written as speeches held by historically important men (never women) on their deathbed. In this category belong speeches attributed to Moses (the Testament of Moses, ca. first to second century CE), Job (the Testament of Job, 100 BCE–100 CE), and the twelve sons of Jacob (the Testaments of the Twelve Patriarchs, second century BCE with later additions). In the Testaments of the Twelve Patriarchs the sons give advice to future generations and tell stories from their lives. A stylistic feature of this category is the tendency of the ancestors to beg forgiveness for their sins, which is noteworthy since the testaments were written to improve the image of the patriarchs' characters. Throughout the texts of this genre, the patriarchs give general ethical instructions, encouraging readers to increase their self-control and in particular to refrain from sexual immorality.

Wisdom literature is another literary form; examples are the apocryphal books

Sirach and the Wisdom of Solomon. Contained in this literature is a universal message of morality and wisdom that is not necessarily tied to Torah. Jewish authors also wrote *prayers and hymns* that they often attributed to David and Solomon.

Much of the *apocalyptic literature* (from the Greek *apokalypsis*, meaning "revelation"; see box 2.5) from this time reflects a belief that the world would soon be replaced by a paradise-like world. This view is evident in Book of Watchers (= 1 Enoch 1:36, third to second century BCE) and the animal apocalypse (= 1 Enoch 83–90, second century BCE), and 2 Baruch and 4 Ezra (first century CE). These texts often describe the end of the world with strong and violent imagery (like Dan 7–12; see also the book of Revelation). Even if these texts share a strong apocalyptic hope, they present very different ideas as to how exactly the end times will be. A messianic figure may or may not be present in these texts.

Philo

The Jewish philosopher and theologian Philo of Alexandria (b. ca. 15–10 BCE, d. 45–50 CE), who lived at the same time as both Jesus and Paul, was a prolific writer. He came from the upper classes; one of his nephews, Tiberius Alexander, was the procurator in Judea (46–48 CE) and later governor in Egypt. In his texts, Philo interpreted the Jewish writings from a philosophical perspective, basing his commentaries on Greek traditions. According to Philo, biblical texts that can appear simple on the surface actually contain a deeper meaning. He presents this deeper meaning to his readers by interpreting the biblical texts allegorically. For example, Philo interprets the commandment against eating animals who chew the cud and have split hooves (Deut 14:6) as symbolizing that a student has to memorize (chew the cud) his newfound knowledge in order to really take it to heart.

Through his hermeneutics, Philo found elevated philosophical concepts in biblical texts. The division of reality into the world of the senses and the world that can only be reached via knowledge—a Platonic tradition—is central to his worldview. Also central is the intellectual power behind creation, which he called *Logos* (God's Word). Even though Philo found a symbolic meaning behind the Jewish laws, he himself observed them strictly and despised those who interpreted the law as so symbolic that they stopped following it. Philo used his advanced symbolic exegesis to create a synthesis between Greek philosophy and the Jewish tradition.

Philo's expositions give us insight into Jewish life in Alexandria, where Jews made up a large portion of the population. At the end of his life, he authored two historical books (*Against Flaccus* and *On the Embassy to Gaius*), which dealt with the tragic anti-Jewish pogroms in Alexandria in 38–41 CE. Philo himself was even part of a delegation to Rome that demanded justice following the Roman pogroms. The delegation was not successful, since Caligula was generally hostile toward the Jews. After Caligula's death the situation for Alexandrian Jews improved for a time.

Box 2.5
Apocalyptic Literature

Many of the texts from the Second Temple period exhibit an interest in eschatology (the doctrine concerning the end of the world) and have a strong apocalyptic perspective. An "apocalyptic perspective" refers to an expressed hope of a total reversal of the present world and the introduction of an ideal reality. In the same strain, many New Testament books bear witness to widespread apocalyptic expectations among the first Jesus followers, based on Jesus's teachings (Cohn, *Cosmos, Chaos and the World to Come*, 194–211).

The apocalyptic worldview exhibits several recognizable themes. Angels and demons play a prominent role, revelations are transmitted through supernatural creatures, there is a struggle between good and evil (dualism), history is divided into epochs, and the future is already decided (determinism). Heaven and hell are often described, and humanity will be punished or rewarded at the final judgment. John Collins's definition of the apocalyptic genre, which emphasizes the character of revelation, has been accepted by a number of scholars: An apocalypse is "a genre of revelatory literature with a narrative framework, in which a revelation is mediated by an otherworldly being to a human recipient, disclosing a transcendent reality which is both temporal, insofar as it envisages eschatological salvation, and spatial insofar as it involves another, supernatural world" (*Apocalyptic Imagination*, 5). According to this definition, only Dan 7–12 in the Hebrew Bible and the book of Revelation in the New Testament can be classed as true apocalypses. However, parts of other books have an apocalyptic character (e.g., Joel; Ezek 38–39; Zechariah; Isa 24–27 and sections of 40–66; Mark 13; 1 Thess 4:13–5:11).

Further Reading

Albertz, Rainer. *From the Exile to the Maccabees.* Vol. 2 of *A History of Israelite Religion in the Old Testament Period.* London: SCM, 1994.

Barclay, John M. G. *Jews in the Mediterranean Diaspora: From Alexander to Trajan (323 BCE–117 CE).* Berkeley: University of California Press, 1996.

Bauckham, Richard, Alexander Panayotov, and James R. Davila, eds. *Old Testament Pseudepigrapha: More Noncanonical Scriptures.* Vol. 1. Grand Rapids: Eerdmans, 2013.

Berquist, Jon L. *Judaism in Persia's Shadow: A Social and Historical Approach.* Minneapolis: Fortress, 1995.

Bilde, Per. *En religion bliver til: En undersøgelse af kristendommens forudsætninger og tilblivelse indtil år 110.* Copenhagen: Anis, 2001.

Charlesworth, James H., ed. *The Old Testament Pseudepigrapha*. 2 vols. New York: Doubleday, 1983–1985.

Clark, Gillian. *Christianity and Roman Society*. Cambridge: Cambridge University Press, 2004.

Cohen, Shaye J. D. *From the Maccabees to the Mishnah*. Philadelphia: Westminster, 1987.

Cohn, Norman. *Cosmos, Chaos and the World to Come: The Ancient Roots of Apocalyptic Faith*. New Haven: Yale University Press, 1993.

Collins, John J. *The Apocalyptic Imagination: An Introduction to the Jewish Matrix of Christianity*. 3rd ed. Grand Rapids: Eerdmans, 2016.

———. *The Invention of Judaism: Torah and Jewish Identity from Deuteronomy to Paul*. Oakland: University of California Press, 2017.

Collins, John J., and Daniel C. Harlow, eds. *The Eerdmans Dictionary of Early Judaism*. Grand Rapids: Eerdmans, 2010.

Dillon, Matthew, and Lynda Garland. *Ancient Greece: Social and Historical Documents from Archaic Times to the Death of Alexander the Great*. 3rd ed. London: Routledge, 2010.

Fiensy, David A., and James Riley Strange, eds. *Galilee in the Late Second Temple and Mishnaic Periods*. 2 vols. Minneapolis: Fortress, 2014–2015.

Grabbe, Lester, L. *A History of the Jews and Judaism in the Second Temple Period*. 2 vols. Edinburgh: T&T Clark, 2004.

———. *An Introduction to Second Temple Judaism: History and Religion of the Jews in the Time of Nehemiah, the Maccabees, Hillel, and Jesus*. London: T&T Clark, 2010.

Hoglund, Kenneth G. *Achaemenid Imperial Administration in Syria-Palestine and the Missions of Ezra and Nehemiah*. SBLDS 125. Atlanta: Scholars Press, 1992.

Levine, Amy-Jill. "Visions of Kingdoms: From Pompey to the First Jewish Revolt." Pages 352–87 in *The Oxford History of the Biblical World*. Edited by Michael D. Coogan. Oxford: Oxford University Press, 1998.

Levine, Lee I. *The Ancient Synagogue: The First Thousand Years*. 2nd ed. New Haven: Yale University Press, 2005.

Meyers, Eric M., and Mark A. Chancey. *Alexander to Constantine: Archaeology of the Land of the Bible*. New Haven: Yale University Press, 2012.

Nickelsburg, George W. E. *Jewish Literature between the Bible and the Mishnah: A Historical and Literary Introduction*. Philadelphia: Fortress, 1981.

Olsson, Birger, and Magnus Zetterholm, eds. *The Ancient Synagogue: From Its Origins until 200 CE. Papers Presented at an International Conference at Lund University, October 14–17, 2001*. Stockholm: Almqvist & Wiksell International, 2003.

Runesson, Anders, Donald D. Binder, and Birger Olsson. *The Ancient Synagogue from Its Origins to 200 C.E.: A Source Book*. Ancient Judaism and Early Christianity 72. Leiden: Brill, 2008.

Greco-Roman Religions and Philosophies

The Hellenistic-Roman Culture

After the decisive Roman victories over Macedonia, Greece, and Carthage in 146 BCE, the Hellenistic states that had won political independence after the death of Alexander the Great were gradually incorporated into the Roman Empire. Under the rule of Rome, these states saw both political and social changes that manifested as a well-developed administration, a better judicial system, new roads, better communication networks, and increased trade.

At the beginning of what we call the Common Era (CE), Greek could be used as a language of communication around the entire Mediterranean Sea, as well as quite far into the Near East. This did not mean that the different regional languages had died out, but rather that large groups of people became bi- or multilingual, resulting in the spreading of a version of ancient Greek called Koine Greek (*koinē* being Greek for "common," "normal"). In these regions, one could come across many common cultural features, such as architecture, educational ideals, and popular philosophies. Such common features indicate a Hellenistic-Roman cultural hybridity where traditional Greek and Roman aspects had come to mold together more and more with oriental culture. This new hybrid culture expanded quickly over political and national borders.

Hellenistic-Roman hybrid culture was characterized by cultural and religious syncretism and a more prominent individualism. Local cultures were torn loose from their geo-ethnic places of origin and spread throughout other regions, all the while mixing with different cultures and cults. Greeks and Romans were in general quite open to incorporating new gods and cults into their own native beliefs and practices. Such incorporation was facilitated by the Greek and Roman interpretation of foreign gods and cults as mirror images of their own traditions and myths (the so-called *interpretatio Graeca* and *interpretatio Romana*, respectively). By this thinking, traditional Egyptian gods, for example, came to be seen as identical to or analogous with the native Greek and Roman gods. In the context of this religio-cultural hybridity, it should come as no surprise that Hellenistic-Roman religio-culture also saw the ancestral traditions of the Jews as having supernatural powers. Because of this, there are several archaeological finds where magical blessings or curse inscriptions include slightly altered Hebrew names of gods, angels, and demons.

An expression of the aforementioned individualism in the Hellenistic-Roman culture was that philosophy came to supplement the role of religion, and in some circles even came to replace it. This was especially true of the educated classes. At the same time, the belief in fate continuously grew stronger; fate or chance was seen as the power that ruled the universe. Astrology, which in earlier times had primarily only interested kings and rulers, now came to attract the attention of the commoners as well. The idea of individual belief and salvation became increasingly prominent during this period and led to the flourishing of various forms of mystery religions (for definition, see below).

Within the Hellenistic-Roman culture, religion and religious duties existed on multiple levels. The official religion, or national cult, tied religion to the contemporary political situation. The goodwill of the gods was deemed necessary for society to prosper and live in peace. This idea also bound the citizens' loyalty to a specific city or nation and its civic or national cult, which the political rulers could exploit for their own benefit. Religion and politics were, simply put, inseparable. The minor deities of domestic religion, or house-cult, connected familial units to the same religious praxis, and the home came to play an important role in private religiosity. There was also, however, a type of "optional" religiosity, which was practiced first and foremost by various mystery religions or within different types of societies, such as an association or guild (Gk. *kollēgion*). These became particularly popular during the Roman period (see below).

Greek Religion

Greek religion has its roots in both Indo-European culture and the religions of the Near East. Many of the Greek religious ideas have their origins in the Minoan culture and religions of Crete during the Greek Bronze Age (3500–1050 BCE). Archaeological finds aside, the sources we have that describe Greek religious beliefs are above all *The Iliad* and *The Odyssey* by Homer, as well as Hesiod's *The Birth of the Gods* (*Theogony*) and *Work and Days*, which were all written during the eight century BCE.

In the seventh century BCE, the Greek city-states (*poleis*; see box 2.1, p. 57) began to emerge, and the Greek world came to consist of hundreds of these. The Greek city-states were located on the Greek peninsula, in western Asia Minor, Sicily, and Italy. Every city-state had a great degree of political and religious independence. Local cultures were mixed with national religious institutions, sanctuaries, and cults. There were also common cult centers that united hundreds of city-states. These contributed to the formation of a Greek national self-consciousness.

Greek religion was not built on coherent and systematic teachings with common holy scriptures but was rather centered on traditional and local rituals, processions, prayers, sacrifices, and feasts. That is to say, Greek religion consisted of cult, not creed. Individual religious expression and praxis could vary greatly. Common to all, however, was an open worldview, in which gods and the divine were a natural part of daily life. Piety (*eusebeia* in Greek) was demonstrated through respect, not love, for the gods. Religious ideas and practices permeated every aspect of life, both public and private; religion and social life were intimately woven together. The gods were normally addressed for purely practical reasons, such as for council in a difficult situation, deliverance from the Persians (or any other adversary), or perhaps for personal health and welfare.

Box 2.6
The Olympic Gods and Goddesses

Greek god	*Characteristics and function*
Aphrodite	Goddess of love and fertility
Apollo	God of healing, light, music, and poetry
Ares	God of war
Artemis	Goddess of hunting and protector of childbirth
Athena	Goddess of strategic warfare and craftsmanship
Demeter	Goddess of the field and agriculture
Dionysus	God of vegetation and wine
Hades	God of the underworld
Hephaestus	God of the blacksmiths, the limping god
Hera	Goddess; Zeus's wife, queen of the heavens
Hermes	God of interpretation, protector of merchants and thieves
Hestia	Goddess of the hearth and women
Poseidon	God of the sea and earth, creator of the horse
Zeus	God of the sky and thunder, ruler of heaven, father of the gods and god of kings

Greek Gods and Goddesses

In Greek religion, both humans and gods were seen as created beings. In other words, it was not the gods who had created the cosmos (which was seen as eternal and uncreated). The sun, moon, and stars were thus seen as "eternal" gods (as constituents of the cosmos), whereas gods like Zeus, Hera, and Poseidon were seen as "immortal." The gods were often described with anthropomorphic characteristics. Even if they were seen as more powerful than humans, they were, like humans, subject to *moira* (fate). The gods were seen as very powerful and wise, but it is important to note that they were *not* almighty and all-knowing. In Greek mythology, the gap between gods and humankind was often emphasized. The gods were seen as generally above earthly suffering and misery, detached from the world of humans.

The Greeks differentiated between three types of gods: Olympian gods, chthonic gods (from the Greek *chthōn*, "earth"), and heroes (or demigods). Homer's *Iliad* and *Odyssey* describe the Greek gods as a pantheon on Mount Olympus. It was not until the fourth century BCE, however, that we begin to see specific mentions of the twelve Olympic gods who together constituted a family: Zeus, Hera, Poseidon,

Hades, Apollo, Artemis, Hephaestus, Athena, Ares, Aphrodite, Hermes, and Hestia (see box 2.6).

The myths surrounding this family of gods were passed down by way of oral tradition and illustrations on various crafts and temple art. Children were told the tales of the gods at an early age, and the aristocracy appreciated hearing the myths at their *symposia*. Zeus, "the father of gods and humans," ruled over the gods of Olympus. At his side was his faithful wife, Hera, as well as various brothers, sisters, and children. Mount Olympus was also home to the limping smith Hephaestus, who was married to the goddess of love, the beautiful Aphrodite. In addition to these, Olympus housed Ares, the god of war; Hermes, the messenger and spokesman of the gods; Apollo and Artemis, the archer twins; Athena, the protector of cities and civilization; and Hestia, the goddess of the hearth. The depths of the oceans were ruled by Poseidon, and the underworld was governed by Hades. The deities of agriculture, Demeter and Dionysus, were neglected in Homer's account of the gods, but they came to be included once Athens had become a democracy (normally replacing Hades and Hestia).

According to the myths, the gods could take the shape of humans if they so pleased. When Paul and Barnabas cured a crippled man in Lystra, Acts describes how the people thought them to be two gods: "When the crowds saw what Paul had done, they shouted in the Lycaonian language, 'The gods have come down to us in human form!' Barnabas they called Zeus, and Paul they called Hermes, because he was the chief speaker" (Acts 14:11–12). In a piece of Greek mythology recounted by the Roman author Ovid, Zeus and Hermes visited the neighboring land of Phrygia and were welcomed there only by two old people, Philemon and Baucis. In gratitude for their welcome, Philemon and Baucis's hut was transformed into a temple for the two gods, and both elders were made priests.

The gods were often locally anchored to certain geographic places through different civic cults. These civic cults honored their gods through festivals and processions. Large amounts of money would be dedicated to the civic cult. As an example, the city of Ephesus claimed to be the birthplace of the hunter goddess Artemis. The Ephesians prided themselves not only on the fact that their goddess was worshiped throughout the entire Greek world but also on the fact that their city had been given the honor of housing the cult of Artemis (the Temple of Artemis in Ephesus was one of the seven wonders of the ancient world). Thereby Artemis kept especial vigil over the city of Ephesus.

Acts recounts how Paul comes into conflict with some of the local craftsmen of the Artemis temple. The conflict quickly becomes public and results in a riot inspired by the cry "Great is Artemis of the Ephesians!" (Acts 19:28, 34). The city's clerk manages to calm the people: "Citizens of Ephesus, who is there that does not know that the city of the Ephesians is the temple keeper of the great Artemis and of the statue that fell from heaven?" (19:35). What this "statue that fell from heaven" means is unclear, but it could refer to an old legend of the origins of the statue of Artemis. It was not uncommon in antiquity to worship meteorites.

The second group of Greek gods were the chthonic gods, which were more locally worshiped and associated with the earth, harvest, and the underworld. The most important of the chthonic gods was Hades. Hades ruled the underworld with his queen, Persephone.

The third group of gods consisted of heroes or demigods. They were thought to originally have been mortal creatures or humans, who had been deified either during or after their life on earth. There were incredibly many heroes; in Attica alone, 170 heroes were worshiped. Some of these demigods seem to originally have been gods, but then to have subsequently "lost rank" and become heroes (e.g., Asclepius and Helena). Others were mythical beings (e.g., Achilles, Oedipus, Theseus), while yet others were historical figures (e.g., war heroes, athletes, or founders of colonies). Hero cults were usually local, and heroes were often seen as protectors of the city-state where they were buried.

Prayers and Rituals

The Greeks normally used a variety of prayer formulations so that the gods they worshiped would not be offended by an improper invocation. Prayers were said out loud during larger public sacrifices. Prayers introduced public gathering and were sometimes also said before people went to war.

Sacrifice played the essential role in cult. The most common form of sacrifice in ancient Greek religious rituals was that of an animal (normally domesticated), but offerings of grain, bread, fruit, and wine also took place. While certain parts of the sacrifice were burned on an altar, other parts were eaten by those who performed the ritual. On particularly important occasions, a lamb or young goat was sacrificed. The meal, held in fellowship among the people, was the climax of the ceremony. Some gods demanded specific types of sacrifices; for example, Athena demanded cows and Demeter pigs. It was also very important to distinguish between sacrifices to Olympian and chthonic gods.

Processions were seen as pleasing to the gods; song, dance, competitions, and games were also included in this category. In a city like Athens, more than 120 days a year could be dedicated to various religious holidays and feasts. Most of these festivities had their origin in agricultural traditions. Among the most common celebrations in the ancient Greek world was the so-called Thesmophoria. The festivity was an esoteric female festival in honor of Demeter, the goddess of the fields. It was held during the month of the autumn sowing. Functionally, the ceremony served as an initiation rite for girls of marriageable age. All the activities took place outside the city boundaries and included drinking, various sexual jokes, and other things that would normally have been regarded as obscene. The celebrations in honor of

Dionysus, the god of wine and vegetation, began at the end of December. Among jest and expressions of happiness, a massive phallus was carried in a procession through the city while masked dancers called out to the god.

The earliest Greek temples had their origin in the eighth century BCE, most likely in connection with the founding of the early city-states. Most temples were rectangular with an inner room (*cella*) that contained a statue of the deity to which the temple was dedicated. Primarily, the temple served as a house for the god. Sometimes the likenesses in the temples could be gigantic, as was, for example, the statue of Athena Polias, the city-protecting goddess in the Parthenon on the acropolis of Athens. The statue was sculpted by Phidias, the most renowned sculptor of the fifth century BCE, and was twelve meters tall with inlaid gold and ivory ornamentation at a cost of 750 talents (corresponding to the yearly salary of 12,750 skilled workers!). Normally, there would be burning incense in the temple to honor the god, and the storage rooms would contain various forms of sacrifices and gifts. The sacrificial altar for animal offerings was always placed outside, usually in front of the temple where those participating in the festivities would gather and watch.

Oracles, Divination, and Magic

The gods let their will be known to humans in different ways, using different signs. To interpret the gods' symbolic messages, one might, for example, cast lots, observe the flight of birds, interpret the behavior of sacrificial animals, divine innards, or interpret dreams. Several cult places became known as oracle sites because they readily facilitated the reception of a god's answer to temple-goers' questions. The oldest oracle site in Hellas was a holy oak tree in Zeus's holy grove in Dodona, Epirus. Here, priestesses interpreted the sound of the leaves in the wind as containing the will of the god on particular issues. The most well-known oracle site was the oracle in Delphi, located northwest of Athens. Every month on the seventh day, visitors could pose their questions to an oracle called the Pythia (cf. Acts 16:16). She is described as a simple woman from a local area who had been chosen as a priestess and mouthpiece of Apollo, the god of the sun, light, and song. A male priest assisted the Pythia as she sat on a lofty tripod behind a curtain, transmitting her often incoherent and obscure answers to the questioner. The oracles were usually delivered in verse, either in writing or speech. Apollo was thought able

A calf is brought for sacrifice. The statue is dated to 570 BCE. Photo by Dieter Mitternacht.

to provide answers to questions ranging from state business and war strategies to inquiries regarding travel, marriage, or lost items. The oracle's answers were usually formulated with enigmatic language, but for a fee these words could be interpreted and explained. In Delphi, a common person would have to pay approximately two days' salary for such an interpretation/explanation, whereas a stately delegation had to pay ten times as much.

The line between religion and magic is diffuse, and the very distinction has been critiqued. Traditionally, magic refers to manipulative actions that aim to influence supernatural and occult powers. Popular religiosity in Greece included a great deal of such "magic." Fear of the powers of nature; reverence of old trees, stones, and life-giving springs; belief in oracles and diviners—all of these were components of Greek religious life. Although the Olympic gods in general were thought to be outside the influence of magical rites and actions, Hermes was an exception. There were other gods—and primarily goddesses—that one sought to influence with incantations, amulets, and magical rites. The Greek word for superstition (*deisidaimonia*) means "fear of *daimones*" (*daimones* was a collective term for supernatural creatures or lesser deities; the word is the origin of our "demons"). This is a reflection of the common understanding that these *daimones* were present in the world and were seen as the source of various afflictions.

Acts tell us how Christ-following missionaries met exorcists, magicians, and soothsayers during their travels, on multiple occasions (see, e.g., Acts 8:9–24; 13:8–12; 16:16–19; 19:13–20). The following quote from Didache (3.4) illuminates how Christ followers around year 90 could interact with the popular beliefs of the time: "My child, be no dealer in omens, since it leads to idolatry, nor an enchanter nor an astrologer nor a magician, neither be willing to look at them; for from all these things idolatry is engendered."

Family and the Home

Religion was also a familial concern. Roman law dictated that the (male) head of the family, the *pater familias*, should lead the religious rituals of the house. Everyday chores and the passage of the year were encapsulated in religious ceremonies. Cult bound families together. Common festivities united the society's citizens in a feeling of cohesion and belonging. Meals were prepared on the hearth, and the fire was kept alive for an entire year. During various rituals it was put out and relit the same day. The hearth functioned as the altar of the house; prayers were said around it in the morning and evening, and libations were poured beside it.

At the beginning of the Common Era, the Olympic gods were honored in public sacrifices and rituals. However, most scholars agree that for the general populace these gods became more and more distant from their everyday existence. Instead, classical Greek religion came to be supplemented and increasingly replaced by popular philosophies, mystery religions, and various forms of belief in fate.

Acropolis in Athens, with the agora in the foreground. Photo by Dieter Mitternacht.

Parthenon, the Temple of Athena, on the acropolis of Athens. Photo by Dieter Mitternacht.

Roman Religion

Roman religion has its most important roots in Etruscan civilization, which emerged north of Rome in the eighth century BCE. In the fourth century BCE, Rome expanded and quickly became ruler of all of Etruria. As a result of this expansion, Rome appropriated various Etruscan designations for deities, and they inherited the Etruscan enthusiasm for divination.

There are many accounts that provide us with accounts of Roman religiosity. Besides the archaeological finds, there are also a great many texts. Among the more significant ones are Pliny the Elder's (23–79 CE) thirty-seven-volume encyclopedia, *Natural History*; Titus Livius's (59 BCE–17 CE) history of Rome's growth in 142 volumes, *Ab urbe condita* (From the City's Founding); and literary works by the statesman Marcus Porcius Cato the elder (234–149 BCE) and the scientist Varro (116–27 BCE), as well as the two Roman poets Virgil (70 BCE–19 CE) and Ovid (43 BCE–18 CE).

Roman religiosity was built on the foundational concept of *pax deorum*, "peace with the gods." *Pax deorum* meant that a good relationship with the divine was essential for all political, economic, social, and personal welfare. Accidents, pests, natural catastrophes, defeats in warfare, and so on were all interpreted as signs of the gods' anger and that the peace with the gods had been broken. A successful *pax deorum* was therefore the basic premise to a successful *pax Romana*, "the Roman peace." There were several essential steps in attaining and maintaining "peace with the gods": (1) the gods must be appeased through sacrifice and prayer; (2) the will of the gods that have been interpreted must be followed carefully, and every oath or promise made to the gods must be held; (3) a city's protection from enemy armies depended on carefully performed cleansing rituals and processions to avert evil.

There are many similarities between Roman and Greek religion. This is clearly demonstrated in the following shared aspects: belief in a world of gods and in fate, and the practice of magic. Perhaps the greatest distinguishing factor would be that Romans were less inclined to rationalize, poeticize, and mythologize their gods and the world they lived in.

Roman Gods and Goddesses

It is possible to distinguish between several types of deities in Roman belief. The most important group was undoubtedly the independent gods, who are often described in triads (e.g., Jupiter, Mars, and Quirinus or Jupiter, Juno, and Minerva). Although epithets such as "father" or "mother" could be applied to these gods, they did not, unlike Greek gods, have any actual familial relations to each other. Nor did Romans have any kind of indigenous mythology that described the gods' genealogy, life, or adventures. The most important Roman god, Jupiter Optimus Maximus (Jupiter,

Box 2.7
The Most Important Roman Gods and Goddesses

Roman god	*Characteristics and function*	*Greek counterpart*
Asclepius	God of healing	Asklepios
Ceres	Goddess of earth and fertility, protector of married women	Demeter
Diana	Goddess of the moon, protector of the hunt and chastity	Artemis
Janus	"The god of all beginnings," watcher over thresholds and bridges	
Juno	Goddess of the female life force, youth, and fertile women	Hera
Juno Sospita	Goddess of war and fertility	
Jupiter	The highest god, god of weather and the oracles	Zeus
Neptune	God of the sea and sea-faring, creator of the horse	Poseidon
Mars	God of war and vegetation	Ares
Mercury	God of trade and merchants, protector of thieves	Hermes
Minerva	Goddess of war and knowledge, protector of cities	Athena
Quirinus	God of peace and the people, in the late republic identified with Romulus	
Venus	Goddess of fertility and women	Aphrodite
Vesta	Goddess of the hearth	Hestia
Vulcan	God of fire and fertility	Hephaestus

the best and foremost), had two "coworkers" or "associates" (*not* wives): Juno and Minerva. In the third century BCE, the twelve Olympian gods of the Greeks were introduced in Rome under the designation *di consentes*, "the united gods." It was at this time that the Roman gods received their Greek counterparts (see box 2.7).

There were also a group of lesser Roman gods. These were known under the umbrella term *indigitimenta*, and often exist in the source material only as long lists of names. These gods aided the greater gods in their tasks and supervised various parts of human life, sometimes in meticulous detail. A god called Redarator watched over the second ploughing of the field, Icitor over sowing, Messor over the harvest, Fornax over the leavening of bread, and so on. The lesser gods that watched over and protected agricultural processes, the home, and the family were called *lares* (and may be compared to the Scandinavian house gnome). People believed that these deities lived around the hearth of the house and were therefore associated with the goddess Vesta. The *lares* could also be present in other places, such as crossroads, certain parts of a city, or the battlefield. The house gods that specifically watched over the welfare of the house and made sure that the pantry was always full were called *penates* (from the Latin *penus*, meaning "pantry"). There were also *manes* that were "the spirits of the dead," which were in turn divided into good and evil factions. In addition to these, a seemingly infinite number of anonymous and secret beings were believed to continuously be helping or hindering the Romans in their daily tasks. These unknown spirits or beings put humans at a disadvantage, because their names were not known. Rituals in their honor could not be carried out, and so it was impossible to know whether they were appeased.

Priests, Temples, and Sacrifices

In Roman religion there were two groups of priests. The more noble of these, the *pontifices*, had the highest authority over religious life in Rome. The *pontifices* were led by a high priest, called *pontifex maximus*, who during the imperial period was none other than the emperor himself. The other group of priests were called the *flamines*, and they were normally in charge of the sacrificial cults of gods. During the imperial period, the term *flamen* was often a descriptor of one who was in charge of the emperor's personal cult. The higher the rank of a priest, the more rules he needed to abide by and the more precautionary measures he had to take. Since most priests worked only part-time and had other tasks aside from their priesthood, there was never any development in Rome of a specific coherent priestly social class.

Just as in Greek religion, public divination played a major role in the religion of Roman cities. Divination was seen as the most important way of ascertaining the will of the gods. Unusual events such as deformations, natural catastrophes, and lightning strikes were seen as signs of a disturbance in the "peace with the gods." These events were signs that the will of the gods had not been followed. There were different kinds of official diviners: those who interpreted the flight of birds, lightning strikes, and thunder (*augures*); those who interpreted the intestines of sacrificial animals or the shape of deformed children (*haruspices*); and those who guarded and interpreted the sibylline books (*quindecimviri*). These books were kept in the Temple of Jupiter in Rome and were consulted in times of crisis, with great solemnity. Among other things, the books contained texts about atonement rituals, omens, and Rome's coming fate. Divination was important for the success of Rome. During the Roman campaigns, for example, the feeding of chickens was very carefully observed as a form of divination. At one point when several holy chickens refused to eat, Admiral Publius Claudius Pulcher threw them into the sea, exclaiming, "Drink, then, if you refuse to eat!" This sacrilegious act was said to have caused the destruction of the majority of the fleet at the sea battle of Drepana, one of the greatest catastrophes in the Roman Republic's history.

Roman temple structures are very reminiscent of Greek temples. Normally they were rectangular in shape. In the inner room there was an incense altar as well as a statue of the god to which the temple was dedicated. Behind this room were storage chambers meant for treasure and gifts to the god. A stone altar usually stood outside, in front of the temple, where sacrificial rituals took place. Sacrifice was one of the most important aspects of Roman religion, both public and private. An important rule was that meat of male animals was sacrificed to male gods and that meat of female animals was sacrificed to the goddesses. The sacrifice needed to be entirely free of blemishes in order to be suitable for the gods. An animal walking voluntarily to the place of sacrifice was deemed a good omen. If a smaller animal was sacrificed, such as a goat or sheep, the meat left over was divided between the priests and those who had brought the animal to be sacrificed. In the case of a larger animal, such as an ox, one could hold a feast for a larger gathering of people or sell the leftover meat on the market. The result of this focus on sacrifice meant that almost all meat consumed in antiquity was sacrificial meat. Other types of sacrifices also took place. These included smoke offerings, libations with various liquids (normally wine), and, very seldom, human sacrifices (attempts were later made to curb this practice through various laws).

Reconstruction of the Temple of Jupiter on the Capitoline Hill of Rome. The Museum of the Roman Civilization, Rome, Italy. Photo by Jean-Pierre Dalbéra.

Prayers and Festivals

According to a rhetorically loaded statement by the Roman official and public speaker Cicero (106–43 BCE), the Romans saw themselves as the "most religious people in the world." The Romans treated their gods with the utmost respect. As an expression of this, prayer and sacrifice were normally performed while covering one's head. It was important to remember the names of the gods one wanted invoke and influence. In prayer rituals, Janus, the god of all beginnings, was normally the first to be called upon, followed by Jupiter, Mars, and Quirinus. Vesta, the goddess of the hearth, was called last. However, if by any chance some unknown god was present as well, a precaution was taken to call also upon this god, with formulations such as *si deus, si dea*, "if (you are) a god or goddess," or *sive quo alio nomine te appellari volueris*, "or whichever name you prefer to be called by." The Romans had an almost judicial understanding of the gods: *do ut des*, "I give such that you shall give in return." Typically, a promise (*votum*) was given during prayer. This had a binding nature, and the gods would punish the one who did not give what she had promised. In exchange, the gods were expected to give some form of gift. The Roman poet Horace (65–8 BCE) expresses this relationship with the words "It is because you submit to the gods that you control the world."

Roman religion had a well-developed calendar of festivals that followed the seasonal changes and mirrored older traditions. Under the reign of Augustus, there were approximately sixty festival days per year, amounting to about one festival day a week. Under the reign of Emperor Tiberius, however, this number increased to ninety per year, and under Trajan to 120! According to the old Roman calendar, the new year began on the first of March, when Vesta's hearth was both physically renewed (relit) and ritually renewed. Many festivals are worthy of mention. One such festival is the lady festival Caprotinia, when Rome's housewives and their slave girls would go out to the Field of Mars and sit beneath the olive trees. The festival is characterized by the reversal of social order that then occurred: the female slaves were dressed in their mistresses' clothes, and the mistresses had to obey their commands. In the middle of October the "October Horse" was celebrated, a festival that began with a two-competitor horse and chariot race on the Field of Mars. The horse that came in second place was butchered under specific ritual forms and sacrificed to Mars. The horse's tail was sent to the old royal palace, the Regia on the Forum Romanum, and the head of the horse became a prize that young men fought for. On the fifteenth of February, Rome celebrated the spring festival Lupercalia, a festival that involved the cattle being driven out to spring pasture. The climax of the festival was when two naked boys would run out on the streets, hitting people with straps of goatskin (called *februa* in Latin, likely the origin of "February"). This hitting targeted women of childbearing age, since it was considered to increase their fertility. Today, this "first day of spring" is celebrated by Valentine's Day, a day whose roots extend back to ancient Roman rituals of fertility.

Roman Imperial Cult

The Roman imperial cult can first and foremost be traced back to the Hellenistic worship of kings and rulers, which began with Alexander the Great and his successors in the fourth century BCE. Together with the Greek hero cults, the ruler cults blurred the line between mortality and immortality, between human and divine. In Hellenistic-Roman culture, each city had a specific deity that served as that city's protector and benefactor. These deities acted through the city's leader(s), meaning that a single person (the leader of the city) could represent an entire city and its god. In this manner, Emperor Augustus was seen as the personified deity of Rome (*thea Roma*) and could therefore be worshiped as a god.

The Roman imperial cult made use of contemporary trends: religion and politics were now bound together tighter than ever, something that can also be seen in the fact that the emperor had taken the role of *pontifex maximus* (see above), the high priest and bridge between gods and humans. With the deification of the emperors, the connection between "peace (with humankind) of the gods," *pax deorum*, and Roman welfare, *pax Romana*, became very explicit.

The Roman Forum. In the background one can see the Colosseum to the left and Titus's Arch of Triumph to the right. The smaller white structure in the center is what remains of the round Temple of Vesta, home to the constantly burning eternal fire, symbolic of Rome's eternal power. Photo by Dieter Mitternacht.

In a public ritual, the senate deified Julius Caesar after his death, and as *divus Julius* he entered the ranks of the Roman gods. (The Greek word *apotheōsis* is often used for this deification.) Caesar's successor, Augustus (31 BCE–14 CE), "the exalted," saw promotion of the cult of *divus Julius* as one of his tasks, but also drew personal gain from the situation. As the adopted son of Julius Caesar, Augustus could entitle himself *Divi filius*, "son of God." Augustus also claimed to have a special familial relationship with Apollo, Jupiter, and Mercury. Roman political ideology was now driven by a much clearer eschatological finesse. In the poems of Virgil (70–19 BCE), the emperor is described as a messianic savior figure that brings about a new golden age of welfare in the world. Inscriptions from Asia Minor (9 BCE) praise Augustus as "the god whose birthday marked the beginning of the good news [*euangelion*] for the world." After his death, Augustus was deified under the name *Divus Augustus*, and his cult was watched over by a special priest, called the *flamen augustalis*. To consolidate the cult, the emperors introduced special temples, altars, priests, priestesses, and sacrifices. Special months (e.g., July, after Julius, and August, after Augustus) and days were celebrated in honor of the emperors. Titles with divine connotations became more common; the names of emperors were combined with epithets such as "lord," "savior," "benefactor," and "ruler of all." Emperor Domitian (81–96 CE) ordered in a decree that he should be addressed as "our lord and god" (*dominus et deus noster*) in public contexts.

Emperor Augustus (31 BCE–14 CE), here depicted as the bridge between gods and humans, *pontifex maximus*. He took this title in 12 BCE. Palazzo Massimo, The National Roman Museum, Rome, Italy. Photo by Ryan Freisling.

In the first century CE, the cult was most diligently used (or abused) by Gaius Caligula (37–41 CE), Nero (54–68 CE), and Domitian. Driven by what in today's world can only be described more or less as maniacal megalomania, these emperors consciously played the roles of different gods and used the cult to serve their personal interests. Nero, for example, took the role of the poet god Apollo and the sun god Helios, and placed a colossal statue (thirty-five meters tall) of himself in his golden house (Domus Aurea). None of these emperors were deified after their deaths; instead the senate denounced them. Deification did, however, befall Augustus, Tiberius (14–37 CE), Claudius (41–54 CE), Vespasian (69–79 CE), and Titus (79–81 CE). With the exception of Augustus, these emperors all had a restricted relationship to the cult, even though they did make use of it as a cohesive structure, seeing it as a tool to unite the inhabitants of their empire.

The imperial cult came to play a greater role in the provinces than in Rome itself. It was used to strengthen the emperor's position and to ensure the loyalty of foreign subjects to Rome. In Asia Minor, a region that was to become significant for early Christ-following movement and mission, the imperial cult soon became the most important way to express and consolidate political relations with Rome. Most aspects of social life were permeated by reverence for Rome and the emperors. By means of everything from gladiator games to poetry competitions, inhabitants of cities competed among themselves to see who could best express their loyalty to Rome and thereby win the emperor's favor. As a reward, the city could receive the honor of being responsible for the provincial temple to the emperor.

The imperial cult became a direct cause of conflict between the early Christ followers and the Roman authorities. Like the Jews (see Philo and Josephus), Christ followers were in general willing to submit to the authorities and pray for the political leaders (Rom 13:1–7; 1 Tim 2:1–3; Titus 3:1; 1 Pet 2:13–17). This would only be acceptable, however, as long as it did not conflict with their confession of Jesus as Christ. Therefore, Christ followers could not participate in the imperial cult (because they believed that Jesus occupied that role). Although there was no specific law in the first century that compelled inhabitants of the empire to actively participate in cult practices, there was a strong local social pressure to demonstrate loyalty to Rome. To refrain from public worship of the emperor could be interpreted as a threat to the "peace with the gods" and be misinterpreted as an expression of hostility toward the state and disloyalty to the emperor. Against this background, it was problematic to consciously distance oneself from various practices of the imperial cult, or to present Jesus in terms of an emperor figure (e.g., Phil 2:9–11; Acts 17:6–7). The clearest sign of this conflict between the beliefs and practices of Christ groups and the emperor's claim to power is seen in Revelation. In this case, it is not the emperor but the Jewish God that is worshiped with the title that Domitian had made special claims to, "our Lord and God" (*dominus et deus noster*, Rev 4:11). Christ belief obtains clear political attributes when Jesus is described as "ruler of the kings of the earth" (Rev 1:5) and "the Lord of lords and King of kings" (Rev 17:14; 19:16).

Rome and Foreign Religions

The early imperial period is characterized by a positive Roman attitude toward foreign gods, as opposed to Rome when it was a republic. This was especially true in that many of the emperors supported various cults from Asia Minor and the Orient. Like the Greeks, the Romans called the gods of other peoples by the name of the god from their own pantheon that was most similar to the foreign god. The Greek gods more or less came to merge with the native Roman ones. It is, however, a misunderstanding to say that Romans would have taken the Greek gods as their own. That Romans did not "take over" foreign gods and make them Roman is illustrated by a solemn ritual called *evocatio* (calling in). Here, a military commander would call to the chief deity of a besieged city and promise this deity a temple in Rome. This ceremony had a religious-political background: by creating room for the foreign god in the pantheon of Rome, the conquered region was bound closer to the central power of the empire. The Romans were, however, very careful to always point out that their own gods were separate and superior to the gods of foreign peoples.

Which religions could be allowed in the Roman Empire was ultimately a question for the Roman senate. Intolerance could be shown toward certain cultures with ecstatic religious expressions, or those who employed magic and astrology, especially if these were seen as potential political threats. Accordingly, Egyptian Isis cults were forbidden in Rome by the emperors Augustus and Tiberius. Tolerance was shown to cultures with old traditions, which was beneficial for Jews, since Romans admired the antiquity of the Jewish traditions. Thanks to skillful diplomacy and strategic contact with the early emperors, the Jewish vassal kings and other leaders were able to negotiate their way to a kind of "religious freedom." As the only known monotheistic religion in antiquity, the Jewish religion's survival depended on Jews not being forced to actively participate in Greek or Roman cults. Despite protests from neighboring peoples, not least the Greek cities, Jews were granted their freedom, which, among other things, allowed them to regularly gather for Sabbath and to uphold Jewish laws of purity. They were also allowed to celebrate festivals, collect their own taxes (e.g., the temple tax), and avoid being drafted into the Roman army. Last but not least, they were exempt from active participation in the traditional Greco-Roman cults and the imperial cult. The Jews voluntarily agreed to pray and sacrifice *for* the Roman emperors but not *to* them. These privileges were generally of an ad hoc nature; they were not recorded in any general document that was applicable to Jews everywhere, and instead the Jews had to struggle locally for their religious independence to be upheld and respected.

Although the Jews enjoyed a great deal of privileges under Roman rule, it was not a relationship without its tension. Jews were met with differing attitudes by the Romans. Some sources give an impression of respect for Jewish morals and beliefs, whereas others demonstrate a classical Roman disgust at the foreign and the non-Roman (e.g., Juvenal, *Satires* 14.96–106, or Tacitus, *Histories* 5.2–13). The large Jewish community in Rome, totaling around thirty to forty thousand Jews, was on several occasions subject to the emperor's capriciousness: Tiberius, Gaius Caligula, and Claudius all banished the Jews from the city at different times. In general, it can be said that as long as the Jews refrained from disturbing the political and social order, Romans allowed them to tend to their own affairs.

For Christ followers, especially in the diaspora, it was more or less a matter of life or death to make use of the Jewish privileges within Hellenistic-Roman society. The Roman authorities originally saw the early assemblies of Christ followers as an intra-Jewish phenomenon, allowing Christ followers to avoid direct conflict (e.g., Acts 18:12–17; 23:29; 25:18–21). How long the Christ followers lived under the protection of the synagogue is under discussion, and there were surely regional differences. The first sign that the Romans began to view the Christ groups as something other than a strictly Jewish phenomenon is the Roman historian Tacitus, who in the early first century CE wrote about Roman political history. In his description of the origin of the fire of Rome in the year 64 CE, he places blame on the members of the Jesus movement (in Lat. *Christiani*, "those belonging to Christ"). The Jewish sources have nothing to say about any potential persecution of Jews at this time, which speaks for the idea that it was primarily Christ-following non-Jews who were persecuted. Similar attitudes to those that Romans could display toward Jews can be seen in Tacitus's text about early Christ followers. His contempt is especially apparent in his description of how their leader (Jesus) was crucified as a criminal by Roman authorities and in his accusation of Christ belief as a superstitious movement with poor morals. He also saw Christ belief as harboring hatred or dislike of humanity.

> But neither human help, nor imperial munificence, nor all the modes of placating Heaven, could stifle scandal or dispel the belief that the fire had taken place by order. Therefore, to scotch the rumour, Nero substituted as culprits, and punished with the utmost refinements of cruelty, a class of men, loathed for their vices, whom the crowd styled Christians. Christus, the founder of the name, had undergone the death penalty in the reign of Tiberius, by sentence of the procurator Pontius Pilatus, and the pernicious superstition was checked for a moment, only to break out once more, not merely in Judaea, the home of the disease, but in the capital itself, where all things horrible or shameful in the world collect and find a vogue. First, then, the confessed members of the sect were arrested; next, on their disclosures, vast numbers were convicted, not so much on the count of arson as for hatred of the human race. And derision accompanied their end: they were covered with wild beasts' skins and torn to death by dogs; or they were fastened on crosses, and when daylight failed were burned to serve as lamps by night. Nero had offered his Gardens for the spectacle, and gave an exhibition in his Circus, mixing with the crowd in the habit of a charioteer, or mounted on his car. Hence, in spite of a guilt which had earned the most exemplary punishment, there arose a sentiment of pity, due to the impression that they were being sacrificed not for the welfare of the state but to the ferocity of a single man. (Tacitus, *Annals* 15.44 [Jackson, LCL])

Mystery Religions

Aside from the more traditional and official religions practiced during the Hellenistic-Roman period, there were also a great deal of esoteric mystery cults (*mystēria* = secrets). These should not be seen as new or separate religions, but rather as a development of an already existing, more traditional cult. There were many mystery cults, and their contents and practices could vary locally. Common to all were well-known mythical fertility motifs and secret ceremonies that emphasized and dramatized death and rebirth. As opposed to traditional Roman religion, mystery cults placed the *individual* in the center of their praxis and offered salvation for those who participated in the rituals and sought proximity to the gods in the context of these secret associations. The purpose of the mysteries was to free the individual from the inevitable string of fate and give a blissful existence in the hereafter. Religious experiences were emphasized, but none of these experiences—or anything else that regarded the cult's inner workings—was allowed to be passed on to outsiders if the divinity of the message was to be retained. For this reason, we know very few details about the inner workings of the mystery cults today. Despite this, we know that they came to play an important role in many societies of antiquity, and that they could become quite popular locally.

The initiation rites of mystery religions were often structured in three stages and were led by someone called a *mystagōgos*. The first stage was one of separation, which sought to detach the human from the mystery. This could, for example, occur in the form of different types of cleansing and ritual bathing. The second phase consisted of the actual mystery itself and the symbolic rites associated with it, where the one being initiated was often made to take on degrading roles, designed to dissolve the contemporary norms. In the third phase, more rites were performed in order to bring the one being initiated back to his or her proper place in society. Common to all mystery cults was that the participants were thrown between anguish and hope, tragedy and happiness, death and rebirth. The participants were united in a communal meal that was eaten, surrounded by music, song, and dance. Cases of ecstasy and various forms of holy "madness" were frequent occurrences. In the mystery cults of Dionysus, the women—who were called "maenads" (from *mania*, "rage, frenzy, madness")—would go out at night toward the mountains in song and dance, holding burning torches, with snakes winding around their arms. The climax of the ritual was the sacrifice of an animal that had been hunted, torn into pieces, and eaten raw. Through this sacrificial meal, the participants thought themselves to come into union with the god himself (cf. 1 Cor 10:16–22).

Another well-known example of the Greek mystery cults is the Eleusinian Mysteries, which originated in the larger cult of the harvest goddess, Demeter, in the seventh century BCE. In the middle of September, a large cultic event was held in Eleusis, twenty kilometers northwest of Athens, to celebrate Demeter's mysteries. Both the aristocracy and slaves, men and women, could be initiated into the secret mysteries of Demeter, consisting of processions, cleansing baths, and cultic meals. The cult became very popular and was eventually included in the Attic festival calendar of the sixth century BCE. It was popular not only among the Greeks but also among Romans. The Roman counterpart to Demeter, Ceres, was given her own temple and priesthood in Rome.

The Mithras mystery cult was developed mainly to cater to Roman soldiers. According to the myth, Mithras was the son of the sun god Helios. Hence, the initiations and mysteries of the Mithras cult emphasized light and sound. The initiation rituals consisted of seven degrees of inauguration, each of which was designed to test the courage of the initiate in some way. In contrast to many of the other mystery cults, the cult of Mithras emphasized high morals and discipline. The ritual praxis of the cult mainly consisted of the participants partaking in a sacramental meal of bloody meat, bread, and wine. One of the festivals took place on "the birthday of the undefeated sun," December 25. When Rome was Christianized in the fourth century CE, this day was deemed an appropriate symbolic birthday of the Christian Savior.

There were a great many more mystery cults than the ones we have briefly touched on here. Among the more popular of these were the mysteries surrounding the goddess Cybele (or Magna Mater, "the Great Mother") and her young lover Attis, the priesthood of which was self-castrated. There were also Isis and Osiris mysteries that, with their oriental origins and exotic rites, attracted many Greeks and Romans. One of the best-known texts describing the ritual praxis of mystery cults comes from the Roman rhetorician Apuleius's account of the Isis mysteries from around 150 CE (*Metamorphoses*, or *The Golden Ass*, as it is also known):

> I kept these rules with the restraint of true veneration and ritual precision, and now the day was at hand in which I must answer my divine summons; the Sun swerved downward, pulling Night behind it. Then crowds came pouring in from all directions, each person with a different gift in my honor, according to the ancient custom. Then when all the uninitiated had been removed, I was covered with a brand-new linen garment, and the priest seized my hand and led me into the shrine's inmost sanctuary.
>
> Perhaps, eager reader, you have a certain pressing curiosity about what was said and done at this point. I would tell you if telling were permitted; you could learn of it if you were allowed to hear. But your ears and my tongue would incur equal blame, the latter for its impious loquacity, the former for its foolhardy prying. Yet I do not intend to torment you, to draw out your anguish—perhaps a religious longing makes you anxious to know. Hear, then, and believe, since what I relate is true. I approached the boundary of death and placed my foot on Proserpina's threshold. I made my way through every level of the universe and back. In the middle of the night I saw the sun flashing in the purest brightness. I came face to face with the gods below and the gods above. In unmediated nearness, I worshiped them. So there it is: I have related what you must truly know, though now you have heard about it. Likewise, I shall continue to report only what can without sin be revealed to the minds of the uninitiated.

> The next morning was brought into being, the rites were completed, and I stepped forth in the twelve stoles of an initiate. It is certainly a holy vestment, but I am by no means forbidden to speak of it, as at the time a great many people were there to see. In the very heart of the holy habitation, before the goddess's statue, I stood as ordered on a dais built of wood. My robe was only linen, but it was all a-blossom with embroidery and made a striking sight out of me. From my shoulders, a costly cloak draped down my back clear to my ankles. And all around, wherever you looked on me, I was emblazoned with multicolored animals: Indian serpents on one side and griffins from the Far North on the other—these looked like winged birds, offspring of another world. This is the robe the members of the cult call Olympian. In my right hand I held a torch in full-blown flame, and my head's handsome encirclement was a diadem with gleaming white palm leaves projecting like rays. Once I was decked out in this way as the Sun god and set up to serve as a statue, the curtains were suddenly pulled back, and people were let in to look at me. After this, I celebrated the first birthday of my initiation very merrily indeed with a refined banquet and a witty drinking party. On the third day, parallel observances took place, with the addition of a ritual breakfast and the initiation's last formal stage. (*The Golden Ass* 11.23–24 [Ruden, 266–67])

Within the study of the history of religion, scholars often draw many parallels between various mystery cults and Christ belief. Just like the mystery religions, Christ followers emphasized personal salvation for all people, independent of social class or gender. Furthermore, comparing the Christ groups' baptism and communion rituals with the mystery cults' initiation rites, we can see several similarities as well. Most evident, perhaps, is the common theme of death, resurrection, and rebirth. Both Christ belief and the mystery cults speak of a god who suffers, but the decisive difference is that within mystery cults the gods alternate between death and life, therefore resurrecting in a very different way from how the Jesus movement describes Jesus of Nazareth's single, historical journey from death to life. Church fathers such as Tertullian and Justin Martyr argued that the mystery cults were "devilish mimicry" of Christianity. Clement of Alexandria saw Christianity as the only true mystery, in contrast to the "shameful" and "corrupt" Greco-Roman mysteries. The fact that mystery cults and Christ belief make use of several common terms and concepts is evident. What exactly this means in terms of overlap, dependence, and interrelationship is unclear.

Popular Philosophies

With its center in Athens, Greek philosophy occupied a significant role in Greek culture from the sixth century BCE onward. Many philosophical schools developed during this period. Each respective school tried to define human existence and give practical counsel about how life should be lived. The most well-known philosopher from antiquity is without a doubt Socrates (ca. 469–399 BCE), a brilliant "lover of wisdom" with a great sense of humor. Instead of attempting to give answers about the meaning of life, as was the practice of contemporary schools, Socrates came to be known for his rational questioning of the accepted "truths" about religion, morals, and human existence. He eventually accumulated a great many influential enemies, who managed to bring him to trial and have him sentenced to death. Socrates did not author any texts of his own, but his disciple Plato (ca. 427–347 BCE) recorded some of his dialogues with intellectual opponents. The only other source of knowledge about Socrates was written by the Greek author Xenophon (ca. 430–355 BCE), whose accounts of the philosopher differ markedly from those of Plato.

Plato dedicated his life to proving the existence of eternal values. His philosophy builds on an array of divisions of reality into two separate worlds. One of these is the physical and bodily world that is perishable, and the other is the invisible and spiritual world of ideas that is complete and eternal. The true nature of the human—the soul—has its origin in the invisible world and returns to the abode of the gods after being cleansed by a range of human lives. The wise person is the one who seeks the eternal truths of this invisible realm. These truths can free the human from the undue unison of spirit and matter, thereby releasing the soul from its bodily prison.

Plato's dualistic worldview came to be the foundation for much of the philosophical thinking that developed during the Hellenistic-Roman period. Aristotle (384–322 BCE) was an exception to this rule. He tried to divorce his thinking from the Platonic worldview that the body was the prison of the soul. Instead, he argued that body and soul are one, and that everything consists of matter on a rising scale, starting with the first and most simple matter. Aristotle created a system of taxonomy that could define, classify, and distinguish the things we see around us. Plato and Aristotle's significance for Western philosophy, psychology, and theory of knowledge cannot be emphasized enough.

Greek philosophy during the Hellenistic-Roman period went from the previous, classical focus on political, public, and scientific issues to embracing a focus on individual, practical, and ethical concepts. The philosophies of the Hellenistic-Roman period answered questions about the meaning of life and how a human could acquire and enjoy the best things in life. The philosopher became a kind of therapist and counselor that comforted and gave practical advice on how to make good decisions. While the mystery cults supplemented or replaced many of the traditional cults of the common people, different philosophies came to serve the same supplementing/replacing function for intellectuals. With time, the philosophies were popularized by wandering philosophers, which eventually turned philosophy into common knowledge. When Paul, according to Acts (17:16–21), came to Athens in the beginning of the 50s, he quickly became involved in a discussion with representatives of two of the most influential contemporary popular philosophies—that is, Epicureanism and Stoicism. Both of these philosophies were directed at the individual with counsel as to how she or he could find a meaningful and happy life (a "happy life" was designated by the technical term *eudaimonia*).

Epicureanism

Drawing on the teachings of Democritus, Epicurus (ca. 341–270 BCE) developed his material thinking as a form of the "gospel of the atom": all existence is physical and is therefore dissolved into nothingness upon death. Epicurus wanted to free humankind from the power that the gods and religion held over them. He did not deny the existence of the gods but argued that the gods had no greater interest in human life. Because of this, humans in turn did not need to care much about the gods; prayers and sacrifices would not reach them anyway. Further, as no human could survive death, no human needed to worry about judgment, punishment, or the afterlife. The only benefit of religion was that it could grant a feeling of mental and social well-being to the individual.

According to Epicurus, there is no divine providence, nor any form of predestined goals for the world. For an Epicurean, the meaning of life is attained in the here and now. (The well-known saying *Carpe diem*, "Seize the day" or "Enjoy the day," is taken from the poet Horace [65–8 BCE], an eager advocate of the Epicurean lifestyle.) Epicurean individuals must create their own meaning in life through constant contemplation. Epicurus's motto became "Live withdrawn," and his advice was thus to withdraw from public life in favor of the private, individual life. A balanced psyche can be attained in careful reflection on which actions would promote a positive state of mind.

The best that a human can do is to enjoy this life by using wisdom to find the best course of action in each unique situation. This being said, insatiable desires and a life of excess must be avoided. Epicurus distinguished between active pleasure, where desire receives full satisfaction, and passive pleasure, which consisted of the absence of pain. The more coveted of the two was the latter. On the basic principle that pain should be avoided and pleasure sought, Epicurus developed a fairly pragmatic view on life. For example, he concluded that drinking oneself into a stupor was not worth the unpleasant hangover that arose the next day; physical training of the body can be unpleasant, but in a long-term perspective such training induces well-being and a good quality of life. The hunt for political positions can grant certain pleasures in the form of power, but should all the same be avoided, seeing as conflicts and disappointments are sure to follow. As a result of this philosophical worldview, Epicurus urged his followers to remove themselves from public life and create an alternative community among friends who shared the same philosophical convictions.

The teachings of Epicurus were appreciated primarily because of their simplicity and clarity. Epicureanism also encountered some disagreement, seeing as its focus was on the well-being and happiness of the individual and had nothing to say about the public and political life. The Epicureans were criticized for only seeking pleasure in this life without caring about life after death. Within Judaism, an "Epicurean" became equivalent to one who denied the belief in a future resurrection and lived only for this life. In the eyes of the Greco-Roman public, the Epicureans were generally seen as "atheists."

Stoicism

The teachings of the Stoics stand in clear contrast to Epicureanism. Stoicism was founded by the philosopher Zeno (ca. 336–263 BCE), who in the year 304 BCE began teaching at one of public porches in Athens, called the Painted Porch (*stoa poikilē*) because of its many wall paintings. Zeno's teachings were in large part developed by his followers, so much so that modern scholars think of Stoicism as divided into early, middle, and late Stoicism. Characteristic of late Stoicism, which emerged during the first and second centuries CE, was an emphasis on ethics and practical action.

Stoic teachings are best summarized in the terms "monism," "materialism," "immanence," and "pantheism." Monism means that the divine is seen as a unit; the world too was seen as a single unit. The divine is not divorced from the created, but rather permeates it and completes it. Nothing exists beyond the world and its matter; there is no world of ideas or transcendent creator-god. The universe is filled with the divine *logos* (the Greek term for "word" or "cosmic wisdom") and its power, the rational principle of creation through which the entire cosmos is ordered. By recognizing and respecting nature's order and laws, humans can access this divine power that flows through all creation. The human, who is naturally permeated by the divine, and whose soul is a spark of the divine *logos*, ought to see herself as a part of this all-encompassing nature and adjust her life in accordance with this. This is done by seeking to live in harmony with the natural order. This worldview can be summarized as a form of pantheism.

For a Stoic, the goal of life is not reached through pleasures and desires. The ideal life is brought about through an inner independence of all that binds the human being to this world. For this reason, Stoics do not strive for possessions or material gain, nor do they allow themselves to be influenced by suffering and disease. There is an unchanging and restraining regularity that creates order in the world, but Stoics, unlike others, do not interpret this as a blind and meaningless fate. This fate steers the world and does what it wants; whatever happens is accepted as an expression of divine providence and will, as an order that grants meaning and protection. In everything, the Stoic strives to reach a position of self-control and inner self-sufficiency, that which later came to be known as "the stoic calm." With their respect for the guiding fate behind everything, the Stoics were criticized for their deterministic worldview. Who is actually free? Stoicism's answer is classic: the wise person owns riches, beauty, and freedom. Freedom has to do with an inner stability, grounded in the knowledge that objects of fear can be avoided and that hopes can be achieved. As long as one fears or covets things that lie within the power of others and not oneself, true inner freedom cannot be obtained. There is, however, one area where we ourselves are the unquestioned masters—namely, in the ability to decide for ourselves what value we ascribe to that which we encounter.

Epictetus (ca. 55–135 CE) was a former slave who lectured as a popular Stoic philosopher in Rome and Nicopolis. The following excerpt is from *The Art of Living*, a manual (*Enchiridion*, as the work is also known) that presents some of the basic tenets of the Stoic teachings:

> Some things are within our power, while others are not. Within our power are opinion, motivation, desire, aversion, and, in a word, whatever is of our own doing; not within our power are our body, our property, reputation, office, and, in a word, whatever is not of our own doing. . . .
>
> With regard to everything that happens to you, remember to look inside yourself and see what capacity you have to enable you to deal with it. If you catch sight of a beautiful boy or woman, you'll find that you have self-control to enable you to deal with that; if hard work lies in store for you, you'll find endurance; if vilification, you'll find forbearance. And if you get into the habit of following this course, you won't get swept away by your impressions. . . .
>
> Remember that you're an actor in a play, which will be as the author chooses, short if he wants it to be short, and long if he wants it to be long. If he wants you to play the part of a beggar, act even that part with all your skill; and likewise if you're playing a cripple, an official, or a private citizen. For that is your business, to act the role that is assigned to you as well as you can; but it is another's part to select that role. . . .
>
> As regards piety towards the gods, you should know that the most important point is to hold correct opinions about them, regarding them as beings who exist and govern the universe well and justly, and to have made up your mind to obey them and submit to everything that comes about, and to fall in with it of your own free will, as something that has been brought to pass by the highest intelligence. For if you follow that course, you'll never find fault with the gods or accuse them of having neglected you. (*Enchiridion* 1, 10, 17, 31 [Hard, 287, 290, 291, 295])

Epictetus saw the entirety of life as a grand feast that should be received with appreciation and praise; to die was nothing but taking leave of this life, in thankfulness and obedience to the gods. A true Stoic did not fear death; indeed, most Stoics believed that the soul lived on after death, albeit with certain limitations. Stoics believed that the world perished periodically in a massive fire (*ekpyrōsis*), after which it once again was filled with life. Everything and everyone fall victim of these flames—gods, humans, animals, and nature; only Zeus, the highest god (whom some Stoics equated with the fire itself), survives. The Stoics dismissed the idea that the soul existed in a subterranean underworld after death. Rather, they believed that the soul would go to a kind of heavenly place, above the earth. Therefore, death served more as a liberator than anything else, exemplified by the Stoic view of suicide as something positive. Epictetus and Seneca saw suicide as the ultimate sign of human freedom.

Human ability to think rationally was connected to the divinity that Stoics believed dwelled within the human being. Following from this, rational thinking *was* the divine, and it served as a type of guardian, or guide, that ensured that the individual acted in harmony with the laws of nature. The concept is comparable to our idea of a conscience (a term that was also employed by the Stoics). Humans have within themselves the unique ability to live in harmony with nature and to be able to distinguish between right and wrong. For a Stoic, the differences between humans do not matter, since all—rich and poor, Greeks and barbarians, men and women—are a part of the cosmic order (cf. Gal 3:28). Although the Stoics distinguished themselves by seeing all people as equal, they seldom demonstrated this view by fighting social injustices (at least openly).

Stoic philosophy and ethics were especially appreciated by the Romans. Roman pragmatism used Stoic teachings to shape Roman ideological thinking. The Roman Empire was seen as a cosmopolitan community where every human was expected to understand and fulfill the function granted him or her by the gods. Thus, many Stoic philosophers gained popularity and influence in Rome. In the works of Cicero, Stoic teachings were reformulated into politically applicable rules. The great Stoic philosopher Seneca (4 BCE–65 CE) served for several years as mentor to the emperor Nero and had significant influence on imperial ideology. Another emperor, Marcus Aurelius (r. 161–180 CE), was himself a dedicated Stoic, and his writings represent some of the finest works of later Stoic philosophy.

In the book of Acts, Paul enters into discussion with some Stoics before the Council of the Areopagus in Athens. He quotes the Stoic poet Aratus's (ca. 310–240 BCE) statement about Zeus: "We have our origins in him" (cf. Acts 17:28), with the important distinction that Paul is referring to the Jewish God. Additionally, he latches on to the Stoic view of humankind having been given the divine gift to seek God and find out his will. Like the Stoics, Paul bases his views on the common revelation that God may be found in the laws and order of nature, but he adds that God has now revealed himself and "judge[s] in righteousness by a man whom he has appointed" (Acts 17:31). After Paul declares his belief in Christ's resurrection, he is interrupted by those gathered: some mock his speech (likely the Epicureans), while others become curious and wish to hear more (likely the Stoics; see Acts 17:32–34).

In the New Testament letters, several texts appear to have been written as dialogues with contemporary Stoic views. Just like the Stoics, Paul in Rom 1:19–23 bases his arguments on the aforementioned common revelation, but also points out that this revelation has several flaws: even though human beings have knowledge of God, they do not honor God as they should. In Phil 4:8–9 we find a list of virtues that is basically in agreement with that of the Stoics (here we find one of the Stoic's favorite terms, the Greek *aretē*, "virtue"). The difference, of course, is that Paul connects said virtues to typically Christ-related ideals. In Phil 4:11, Paul alludes to the Stoics' self-sufficiency ideal, *autarkeia*: "I have learned to be content [*autarkēs*] with whatever I have." For Paul, it is the belief in Jesus Christ that gives him the ability to have such contentment: "I can do all things through him who strengthens me" (Phil 4:13).

Cynicism

Cynicism was the forerunner to Stoicism. A Cynic rejected all forms of pleasure and advertised a life of simplicity, asceticism, and self-denial. One of the movement's founders, Diogenes (ca. 404–323 BCE), became known for living with very meager resources in a barrel in Corinth. His slogan was "Fear nothing, wish for nothing, own nothing." The ascetic way of life that the movement's followers favored came to be known among common people as a "dog's life" (Gk. *kynikos* = like a dog). Cynicism was hardly a coherent movement during the first and second centuries CE. The Cynics' teachings never became as popular as those of the Stoics or Epicureans, primarily because of the harsher way of life and extreme views the Cynics advertised.

During the first century CE, Cynicism was characterized by wandering teachers who, armed with a cloak of wool and some basic necessities in a small pack, walked from city to city and taught their philosophy. This draws some clear parallels to the missionary work of Jesus and his disciples (cf. Jesus's instructions to the disciples in the commission in Matt 10:9–10). Paul, however, seems anxious to avoid being confused with a wandering Cynic teacher. They did not always have a good reputation (cf. 1 Cor 9:3–18; 2 Cor 11:7–9).

"Gnosticism"

Late antiquity saw the development of a dualistic worldview incorporated into many religions and philosophies. This growing concept emphasized the spiritual insight or knowledge (Gk. *gnōsis*) as the savior from a material, evil world. These ideas are normally clustered together under the debated umbrella category "Gnosticism." The question of Gnosticism's origins is complicated, as its roots can be traced to everything from Persian philosophy (Zoroastrianism) and Platonic dualism to Jewish apocalyptic beliefs and wisdom literature. Although there is no consensus among scholars today as to the origins of Gnosticism, most agree on the idea that it existed before the Jesus movement. Certain scholars feel that the words *gnōsis* and *Gnos-*

ticism are distinct from one another: *gnōsis* is a wider term that includes all forms of gnostic ideas and expressions of both pre-Christian and Christian origin, while *Gnosticism* is used more specifically for the gnostic ways of thinking that flourished during the second and third centuries CE. Others choose not to make any clear distinction between the two terms and instead use the word *Gnosticism* as designating more or less all forms of *gnōsis* teachings.

For a long time, gnostic thinking was only known through the early church fathers' polemical writings from the second and third centuries (the two most significant authors on this subject are Irenaeus of Lyon and Hippolytus of Rome). The problem with these texts is that they are evidently drenched in criticism and a clear renunciation of the Gnostics. Logically, they thus lack a more neutral and in-depth presentation of the *gnōsis* teachings that they attack. A breakthrough in this subject was the finding of multiple Coptic texts at the end of 1945. When some Egyptian brothers were searching for saltpeter with which to fertilize their fields, they accidentally found an approximately one-meter-tall urn containing thirteen books of papyrus, bound in leather. After having been moved to multiple locations, these books finally found their way into the hands of experts, who noted with excitement that around 80 percent of the material was entirely new information to researchers. They came to be known as the Nag Hammadi texts, named after the village ten kilometers from the place of discovery. Eventually, even more finds were made. Today the collection of literature consists of some fifty treatises that are normally dated to around 100–300 CE. Among these are some texts especially worthy of mention: the Gospel of Thomas, the Gospel of Truth, the Trimorphic Protennoia, the Apocryphon of James, the Gospel of Philip, and the Dialogue of the Savior. Most Nag Hammadi texts (notably not *all*) have clear gnostic tendencies. Some forty contain *gnōsis*—thought that was either originally based on Christ belief or later Christianized.

Another source that is important in the task of understanding *gnōsis* thinking is the *Corpus Hermeticum* (after the god Hermes, who was thought to give secret revelations). This is a collection of eighteen, mostly Greek, treatises from Egypt that are dated to approximately 50–250 CE. The most well-known of these is *Poimandres*, a treatise characterized by a clear dualistic thinking and usually assumed to be of non-Christian origin. Beyond these sources, there are several other writings available today that exhibit gnostic tendencies with Coptic, Syrian, and Aramaic origins, among others.

Gnosticism did not constitute a coherent system of belief, even though most *gnōsis*-related views share certain basic characteristics. One of these characteristics is a cosmic dualism. According to this dualism, the highest god is transcendent, exalted, unknown, and unreachable. With regard to humans and the world in relation to this "highest god," there are primarily two dualistic explanatory models, both of which have their origins in the problem of theodicy (the question of a good god's relationship to evil). Manichaeism (a religion founded by Mani [ca. 216–276 CE] with hints of Zoroastrianism, Buddhism, and Christianity) is characterized by a metaphysical dualism that assumes an evil higher power that originally existed together with the highest god. The physical world has its origins in this evil power but is also permeated by particles from the good world of light. A more common way of describing the beginning of the world within Gnosticism would be the idea of "falling." To understand this concept, we must first understand the nature of the highest god himself. The highest god emanates various eons (creatures, powers), which fill the upper world (Gk. *plērōma*, "fullness"). Wisdom (*sophia*) is one of these eons. One of the lowest eons, however, does not remain in this upper world but sinks to the lower, material world because of its desires, and is there shattered and trapped. This material world is not created by the highest god, but rather by a lower, evil deity, the Demiurge (in Greek *demiourgos* means "craftsman"), who was equated by some gnostic Christ followers with the biblical creator-god. Explanations as to how the "fall" occurred vary within different gnostic myths, but a recurring characteristic is that one of the first humans (or the very first) is the object of the fall. Hermeticism, for example, means that the first human, who was born of the upper world, stepped down through the seven planetary realms to nature and was loved by it, thereby giving rise to the human race. Humans, therefore, do not bear any personal guilt in the matter of their fall but are instead seen as trapped by the material—the perishable, evil powers.

A basic thought in most *gnōsis* teachings is that all humans have within themselves a divine, sleeping spark of light that longs for freedom. Such a freedom of the spirit or soul from the prison of the body can only be attained through the right form of spiritual insight: *gnōsis*. Through the soul's "illumination," the human being is freed from the physical evil and is reunited with divine completeness. By means of *gnōsis*, it is also possible to master the forces that exist in the physical world and make use of them for one's own benefit. In different gnostic persuasions, there are different figures of salvation that bring with them the essential teachings of *gnōsis*. Christ-following Gnosticism sees Christ himself as this figure leading the way to freedom (see the section "Gnosticism and 'the Gnostics'" on p. 455).

Eschatology plays a minor role in Gnosticism. For a gnostic, it is far more important to understand the past than to understand the future. Because the physical was something evil that one needed to be freed from, bodily resurrection was not an accepted belief. For the person who had attained enlightenment, resurrection had already occurred on the spiritual plane. Life after death is usually described as the soul and spirit's ascent to the highest (seventh) heaven (a thought central to Mandaeanism, for example). During this ascent, the soul/spirit meets evil powers and eventually the Demiurge himself, who attempts to hinder ultimate unification with the divine. Once more, it is insight that serves as salvation at this stage. Finally, the soul and spirit are separated from one another; only the spirit returns to the upper world (*plērōma*), and the soul dissipates. *Poimandres* contains an explicit description of this entire process.

The human was originally seen as androgynous (both sexes); separate male and female sexes were a result of the fall. Gnostic anthropology is usually markedly divided in two (dichotomy), sometimes even in three (trichotomy): humankind was seen as the undue unison between a divine and intelligent spark of light (the spirit/soul) and a material and demonic dust (the body/psyche).

Many women were attracted to the gnostic movements, where it was not unusual to find female leaders, teachers, prophets, or missionaries. The gnostic, androgynous view of humankind also became a way of seeking emancipation from contemporary patriarchal gender roles within the public spheres of society. There is a remarkably large number of statements about women in gnostic texts, both positive and negative.

The scholarly literature often claims that gnostic dualist thinking resulted in just two apparently opposing ethical core principles, which both demonstrated contempt for the evil creator-god and the material world: one principle led its followers into a more ascetic way of life, and the other led toward a more libertine existence. Such a view of "gnostic ethics" is no longer possible. Although there are texts that advertise an ascetic way of life, and some that seem to indicate libertine ideas, it is misguided to present these two versions of reality as the only, or even the primary, ethical alternatives among the gnostics. In general, having a specific ethical approach and moral lifestyle could be seen as a method by which one could become more like the divine.

Further Reading

Beard, Mary, John North, and Simon Price. *Religions of Rome*. 2 vols. Cambridge: Cambridge University Press, 1998.

Brodd, Jeffrey, and Jonathan L. Reed. *Rome and Religion: A Cross-Disciplinary Dialogue on the Imperial Cult.* Atlanta: Society of Biblical Literature, 2011.

Dowden, Ken. *Religions and the Romans*. London: Duckworth, 1998.

Eidinow, Esther, and Julia Kindt, eds. *The Oxford Handbook of Greek Religion.* Reprint edition. Oxford: Oxford University Press, 2017.

Fishwick, Duncan. *The Imperial Cult in the Latin West.* Vol. 3, parts 1–4, *Provincial Cult*. Leiden: Brill, 2002–2005.

Friesen, Steven J. *Imperial Cult and the Apocalypse of John: Reading Revelation in the Ruins.* Oxford: Oxford University Press, 2001.

Garland, Robert. *Religions and the Greek.* London: Duckworth, 1995.

Johnson, Luke Timothy. *Among the Gentiles: Greco-Roman Religion and Christianity*. New Haven: Yale University Press, 2009.

Johnston, Sarah Iles, ed. *Religions of the Ancient World: A Guide*. Cambridge, MA: Harvard University Press, 2004.

King, Karen L. *What Is Gnosticism?* Cambridge, MA: Harvard University Press, 2003.
Klauck, Hans-Josef. *The Religious Context of Early Christianity: A Guide to Graeco-Roman Religions.* Minneapolis: Fortress, 2003.
Pearson, Birger A. *Ancient Gnosticism: Traditions and Literature.* Minneapolis: Fortress, 2007.
Perkins, Pheme. *Gnosticism and the New Testament.* Minneapolis: Fortress, 1993.
Price, Simon. *Religions of the Ancient Greeks.* Cambridge: Cambridge University Press, 1999.
———. *Rituals and Power: The Roman Imperial Cult in Asia Minor.* Cambridge: Cambridge University Press, 1984.
Rüpke, Jörg. *Pantheon: A New History on Roman Religion.* Princeton: Princeton University Press, 2018.
———. *Religion: Antiquity and Its Legacy*. Oxford: Oxford University Press, 2013.
Sellars, John. *Hellenistic Philosophy.* Oxford: Oxford University Press, 2018.

Beliefs and Practices in Second Temple Judaism

This section will take a closer look at Jewish beliefs and practices in and around the first century. Jesus and his disciples were all Jews who lived in a Jewish society. When the Jesus movement spread into the diaspora, it did so via Jewish institutions. Synagogues provided the context in which non-Jews first came into contact with the Christ followers. Therefore, in order to fully understand Jesus and his first followers, it is essential that we first acquaint ourselves with the different expressions of the Jewish faith that were prevalent during the Second Temple period.

The New Testament (which should in large part be viewed as a collection of Jewish texts) provides us with some information in this regard. The Jewish lifestyle and context form the given background of many narratives and discussions (e.g., see Jesus's circumcision in Luke 2:21, his activities during Jewish holidays in John 2:13 and 7:2, and the fact that his disciples kept the Sabbath). We must, however, be cautious in this respect when relying on New Testament texts. They are written from a specific perspective, and the authors often present other Jewish groups in a polemical light. The New Testament texts often reflect conflicts between the Jesus movement and other Jewish groups. We can see a number of examples of this in the Gospels, Pauline letters, and other letters.

To gain a balanced perspective of Second Temple Judaism, it is necessary to study other Jewish texts as well. Several such texts have been presented throughout chapter 2 (see also the appendix). In older research, we often encounter quite negative presentations of Judaism. There Judaism was frequently depicted as the monolithic and gloomy background to Christianity, which was presented in brighter terms.

New Testament texts were sometimes used to fuel this misconception, not the least the Gospel of Matthew, with its polemical attacks on the Pharisees. During the last decades, such views of Judaism have been criticized by scholars.[8] Contemporary scholars point out that religious polemics in the New Testament should not be regarded as historical facts, and biased descriptions of the other should always be seen as problematic. In addition to this, the diversity of Second Temple Judaism was lost when older scholarship presented "Judaism" as an antithesis to "Christianity." The fact that the Jesus movement was one of many Jewish groups further reveals the problems with such a monolithic reconstruction of the Jewish tradition during the Second Temple period (cf. chapter 5 below).

In what follows, we will explore Jewish beliefs and practices across three main topics. We will start by analyzing rituals and holy days as the everyday pattern of Jewish life. We will continue with a summary of the Jewish belief system, focusing on both theology and praxis. Lastly, we will turn our attention to authority and interpretation in Jewish society; this section will include a discussion of the different Jewish groups active at the time, each of which, like the Jesus movement, had its distinctive ways of understanding how Jewish life and culture should be lived out.

Rituals as the Rhythm of the Week, the Year, and the Lifespan

In the previous section outlining Greco-Roman religiosity, we saw that there were a multitude of festivals and holidays celebrated each year, in honor of different deities. These festivals created a feeling of community and strengthened both the identity of the individual and the group. One fact that is easily neglected is that the weekly rhythm we are used to today was absent in antiquity. Only the Jews organized the week around a day of rest, the Sabbath. The Sabbath was a Jewish innovation. The Sabbath, together with other Jewish holidays such as Pesach and Shavuot, defined and strengthened Jewish identity. The latter holidays are related to central occurrences in the Hebrew Bible, and thus emphasized the common historical heritage of the Jews and their status as the chosen people of God. It could be argued that the holiday that has shaped Jewish identity most significantly is the Sabbath, which is also the most frequently recurring one.

The Sabbath

According to Jewish tradition, the seventh day of the week is holy. Genesis 2:1–3 describes how God completed the creation of the world on the seventh day and

8. Sanders, *Judaism*; Sanders, *Paul and Palestinian Judaism*, 7–12.

spends it resting. God also sanctifies or blesses the seventh day. The Decalogue (Exod 20:8–11) encourages the people to follow God's example and rest on this day as well. Deuteronomy 5:12–15 connects the sanctification of the Sabbath with the liberation from Egypt. The Sabbath is thus both a day of rest and a holy day.

The Sabbath began at sundown on Friday and lasted until sundown on Saturday. The sounding of shofars, rams' horns, indicated these times. The communal meal held on Friday was characterized by joy and celebration. The remainder of the Sabbath was to be spent in worship, resting, and recreation. Thus, the Sabbath was not a burdensome day; rather, it brought joy and rest. In order that the people would not neglect the holiness of the Sabbath, they were not allowed to carry out any labor, or work, on that day. In the first century CE, different Jewish groups had different opinions on what constituted "work" (this debate continues to this day in Jewish communities). Examples of activities that were generally agreed as constituting work include starting fires, carrying heavy objects, and making long journeys. The food that was eaten on the Sabbath had to be prepared beforehand. The Essenes had among the strictest interpretation of the Sabbath laws: they did not allow speaking about work or helping animals in need during the day of rest (CD X, 15–XI, 22).

Despite the sanctity of the Sabbath, there were certain things that superseded the commandment against work, things that should be done despite being classified as work. The temple cult with its sacrifices and liturgies did not pause for the Sabbath, and the circumcision of newborn sons could also take place on the Sabbath, since the importance of these things was placed above that of the Sabbath commandment (cf. Matt 12:5–6). Even more important than these exceptions was the saving of lives. If a life was threatened, one was obliged to defend it. Helping people in need by giving out food was also permitted and recommended. During war, defending oneself was generally believed to be permitted, but according to most, attacking was not. The lawfulness of defending oneself on the Sabbath became painfully evident during the reign of the Hasmoneans, where those who refused to defend themselves during the Sabbath were mercilessly mowed down (1 Macc 2:32–38). The Hasmoneans then decided that self-defense (1 Macc 2:39–41) should be allowed when an enemy attacked, and this ruling has remained the consensus.

The Calendar and the Jewish Feasts

The Sabbath was not the only religious holiday to punctuate Jewish life during the Second Temple period. The entire year, especially during spring and autumn, was filled with different religious holidays and feast days. The Jewish calendar, which regulated the Jewish holidays and festivals, was based on the phases of the moon. Those in control of the temple generally controlled the calendar as well. A new month was signaled by a new moon, and the full moon indicated the middle of a month. Some of the most important holidays were celebrated during the full moon, such as Pesach (Passover) and Sukkot (Feast of Booths). The year was divided into twelve months, each consisting of either thirty or twenty-nine days. The lunar year consisted of 354 days (see fig. 2.1), and in order for the most important holidays to continually occur during the right seasons (e.g., Sukkot has to occur early in autumn, and Pesach in the first phases of spring), an extra month is added approximately every third year. Thus, the religious calendar can be described as both a lunar and a solar calendar,

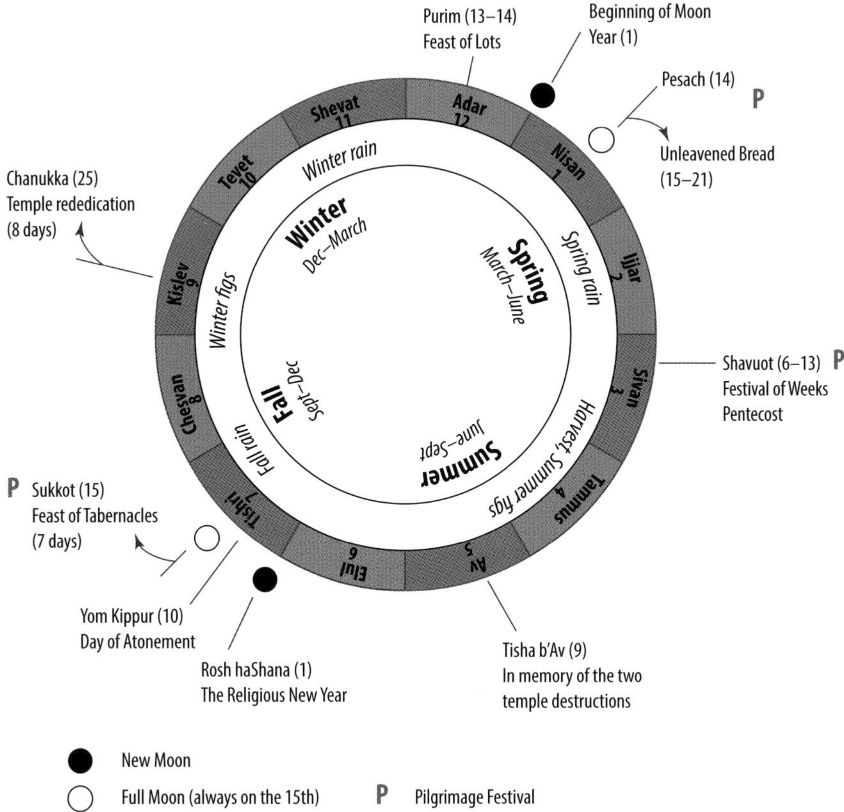

Figure 2.1 The Jewish year. Unlike the solar year, which has 365 days, the Jewish calendar has 354 days, divided into twelve months, each consisting of twenty-nine or thirty days. The lunar year was adapted to the solar year by adding an extra Adar between Shevat and Adar every time the difference between the solar and lunar year became greater than thirty days.

since the basis of the calendar is the phases of the moon and an extra month is added to make sure that the holidays occur during their correct season.

Box 2.8
Calendars and Conflicts

The calendar described in the section "The Calendar and the Jewish Feasts," p. 116, was most likely an innovation introduced sometime during the third century BCE. The older calendar was based on a quarterly system where a cycle of seven weeks constituted the base. The year was made up of fifty-two weeks and 364 days. The first day of the week was the fourth (our Wednesday), since the sun and the moon were created on that day (Gen 1:14–19). The positive aspects of such a system included that the high holy days occurred on the same days every year, and that they rarely fell on a Sabbath. Such a solar calendar was the preference for those who produced and associated with the Enoch literature. The text that most clearly indicates the usage of the solar calendar is the book of Jubilees, and the sectarians at Qumran also followed this calendar. In the alternative solar calendar, the month of Nisan was also counted as the first month of the year.

Because of the limited space available here, we shall focus only on the most important Jewish holidays, in particular those connected to the temple. According to the dominating solar-lunar calendar, the Jewish year was ushered in during autumn, with *Rosh Hashanah,* the Jewish New Year day. The start of a new year was signaled by the shofars. Contracts and pardons could be reviewed and regulated at this time, as could the validity of oaths.

The two main holidays celebrated during the fall were *Yom Kippur*, or the Day of Atonement, and *Sukkot*, Feast of the Booths. *Yom Kippur* was celebrated ten days after *Rosh Hashanah* and was a day set aside for serious contemplation and atonement. Fasting, not washing, and refraining from using perfumes and oils marked the seriousness of the day, compared with ordinary daily routines. People were also expected to refrain from sexual activities and wearing leather sandals. The day was also known as the day of fasting. The central aspect of *Yom Kippur* was the high priest's liturgy in the temple, which is described in Lev 16. Prior to the Day of Atonement, the high priest was separated from the other priests and prepared for his duties. Two male goats had already been selected, one of which would be sacrificed in the temple while the other was sent out into the desert (the so-called scapegoat). After the sacrifice of the first goat, the high priest went into the holy of holies and spattered the blood, after which he brought forth a smoke offering. When the day of contemplation and atonement was over, it was customary for various celebrations to be held.

Five days after *Yom Kippur*, on the fifteenth of *Tishri*, the Feast of Booths, or *Sukkot*, was celebrated. *Sukkot* was one of three holidays that were considered to be especially important, since pilgrimage to Jerusalem was encouraged; this was also the case with Passover and the Feast of Weeks. Scholars estimate that the population of Jerusalem increased significantly during the pilgrimage holidays. Pilgrims normally stayed in the city for a week. The pilgrim holidays were a source of economic income for Jerusalem, since pilgrims brought with them both money and gifts for the temple as well as money to pay for living accommodations. When the city, and especially the temple, was filled with so many people, the risk of riots increased significantly. Thus, the Roman occupiers were on their guard during these holidays (see John 11:54–57). The Roman prefect even traveled from his residence in Caesarea Maritima to Jerusalem every *Passover*, to make sure order was maintained. His mere presence was meant to intimidate the population.

Even though *Sukkot* had certain characteristics of a harvest celebration, it was officially celebrated as a reminder of the time the Israelites wandered the desert and lived in booths (*sukkot* in Hebrew). Booths meant to mimic these were built in gardens or on the roofs of houses. Specific liturgies were carried out in the temple, including processions and water sprinkling ceremonies. The water was collected from the Gihon spring, located near the temple. Those celebrating the festival in the temple wore the so-called *lulavim*, comprised of palm leaves, myrrh leaves, and willow leaves. A citrus fruit called an *etrog* was also carried by participants. In John 7:2–53, Jesus is described as making a pilgrimage to Jerusalem for *Sukkot*, and the evangelist describes how Jesus benefited from the large masses of people in order to preach his message. His metaphorical allusions to water should be viewed against the background of the water sprinkling ceremony (John 7:37).

The most prominent pilgrimage festival was *Pesach*, or Passover. The biggest theme of the *Pesach* celebrations was remembrance of the exodus from Egypt. The food, liturgy, and Torah readings were all meant to serve as reminders of how God led his people out of slavery, to freedom. The festivities began on the fourteenth of *Nisan* with the eating of the Passover meal. This was done together with one's family or, if one was a pilgrim in Jerusalem, with the company one traveled with. On the same day as the meal, the Passover lambs had been sacrificed in the temple, and they were later consumed during the dinner. During the meal, a special order (*Seder*) was followed, which included readings and prayers. During Passover, no yeast was allowed in the household, so no leavened bread or beer could be consumed. Thus, unleavened bread (*matzo*) was consumed during the holiday. According to the Synoptic Gospels, Jesus and his disciples ate such a *seder* dinner just prior to Jesus's arrest (Mark 14:12–52 and parallels).

Seven weeks after Passover was celebrated, *Shavuot* began, which is also another pilgrimage holiday. The word *Shavuot* is translated "the feast of the week." Within

which housed sacrificial altars and buildings for sacrificial animals. As the name suggests, only priests were allowed access to this courtyard. From the courtyard of the priests, there was a staircase leading up to the temple. After passing a forecourt, one would come to the first chamber, known as "the holy." The first chamber was adorned with incense altars and the menorah, a candlestick with seven branches. A beautiful curtain separated the first, outer chamber from the inner chamber, which was known as the "holy of holies." Only the high priest was allowed to enter the holy of holies, which he did on only one day of the year, on Yom Kippur (the Day of Atonement). During the time of the second temple, the holy of holes was empty. The ark of the covenant, which had previously been housed there, had in all likelihood been destroyed during the fall of the first temple in 586 BCE.

The Jerusalem temple was the center of Jewish cult. The most important function of the temple was its daily sacrifices. The liturgy and worship were led by priests. Priests were also responsible for teaching and education, which was offered at the temple in addition to cult praxis. Education can thereby be described as the second most important function of the temple. The temple housed a large library that was used for the collection and compilation of theological and ritual literature. Priests were assisted in their more practical duties by Levites. Both priests and Levites were divided into twenty-four groups that took turns running the temple one week at a time. When it was their turn to carry out the temple duties, priests and Levites who did not live in Jerusalem traveled to the city. After their week of service, they returned to their ordinary lives and livelihoods.

The temple's structure and activities were organized and carried out in minute detail. They were very comprehensive. In order for the sacrificial cult to run smoothly, the temple needed a steady supply of wood, water, and sacrificial animals. These animals came from different parts of the land. A popular sacrificial animal used by the common folk was the dove. The animals were carefully scrutinized before being allowed into the temple to make sure they would not pollute it with uncleanness (i.e., through blemishes). There was even a separate bakery for the bread used in the temple area.

People came to the temple to pray, participate in worship services, offer sacrifices, partake in discussions or lessons, and donate to the temple funds. There were several obligatory donations, including the temple tax that was paid once a year (cf. Matt 17:24–27). The temple tax consisted of half a shekel, which was about two day's pay. Another obligatory donation was to pay tithe, which meant that one had to pay 10 percent of the profit made from agriculture or commerce. Tithe was usually paid in the form of seeds, oil, or wine. Some of this was given to the priests, and the rest was used in the temple activities. In antiquity, the temple was not only the center of the religious cult but also the place where the wealth of the land was kept safe—a sort of bank. There were several adjacent buildings that housed enormous riches in the form of votive gifts and money.

A reconstruction of the Jerusalem temple during the time of Jesus. Photo by Anders Runesson.

The Soreg inscription, discovered in 1871, an inscription forbidding non-Jews from continuing past the so-called Courtyard of the Gentiles in the temple. Istanbul Archaeological Museum, Istanbul, Turkey.

The daily sacrifices of the temple cult provided a certain rhythm for the passing of time. In addition to the pilgrimage holidays, when the Jerusalem temple was the central attraction, there was a daily religious rhythm inside the temple that maintained and nurtured the relationship between the Jewish people and the God of Israel. The sacrificial cult was maintained for the well-being of the Jewish people as a whole, but also for non-Jews (e.g., special sacrifices were carried out in honor of the Roman emperors). The individual for whom the sacrifice was being carried out did not have to be physically present in the temple for the sacrifice to have the desired effect. Thus, the worship praxis was very different from worship praxis in modern Judaism (and Christianity and Islam for that matter), in which the place of worship is connected to the actual worship and its effect. The ancient counterpart for our modern view of worship praxis and space would be the ancient synagogue. The synagogue, and all the different institutions hiding beneath this term, has already been discussed (see box 2.4, p. 73).

The pattern of the seven-day week was, through the Sabbath, connected not only to individual homes and the temple but also to the synagogue. The public synagogue institution in Israel had both a sociopolitical function and a religious function on the local level. Every Sabbath, people would come to the synagogues to hear the Holy Scripture being read, explained, and discussed. Beyond the reading and explaining of Scripture, we do not know much about the praxis of these synagogues. We have some evidence for the existence of prayer associated with the public reading of Scripture. In the diaspora, specifically in Egypt, there may even have been incense and vegetable offerings. We do not have any evidence for the existence of such offerings in Israel, and it is doubtful that it was common practice anywhere other than Egypt.[9]

The priesthood did not run the synagogue. Rather, laymen were responsible for the buildings and services. Earlier research has often attempted to assert that the Pharisees acted as leaders of the synagogues, but this theory is no longer relevant and has been abandoned by scholars. We have no evidence that would suggest that a particular group had control of the public synagogues, even though there were both individuals and groups who tried to exert their influence on society via this institution (see the section "Jewish Christ Followers and the Emergence of Christianity and Judaism," p. 365).

The synagogue was also the place where education could be received. During the time of the New Testament, the synagogue was a well-established institution and as such would have been a natural part of Jesus's religious life (see Luke 4:16–37) and the mission of Paul (see Acts 13:5) and others.

9. Runesson, *Origins of the Synagogue*, 436–59.

From Birth to Death

As we have seen, Jewish life had three natural cornerstones that punctuated and defined the religious rhythm of the Jewish traditions: the temple, the synagogue, and the home. The family/home has always been the core of the Jewish tradition; it is the space in which you are born, grow up, age, and die.

To marry and start a family was the foundational responsibility for both the Jewish man and the Jewish woman. It is legitimized as the religio-cultural norm already in the first chapter of Genesis. The ethnic dimensions of Judaism meant that the Jewish people was first and foremost increased when each new generation grew up, even though conversions did happen occasionally. According to some groups, the only legitimate and justifiable reason to abstain from having a family was to devote one's entire life to Torah study and piety. The majority of marriages were arranged by parents. The parents were also responsible for helping the young couple establish their household. The first stage of marriage was betrothal, in which a man and a woman were promised to each other. In all likelihood, this involved the signing of a binding contract according to which the father of the bride was given a certain sum of money. Normally, the woman continued to live with her parents during the betrothal period. Women could be betrothed as early as thirteen years of age. It was important that a woman be a virgin prior to her marriage (see Matt 1:18–19).

The marriage itself was a grand and festive occasion both for the families and for their entire neighborhoods. The ceremony consisted of the bride being brought to the house of the groom. A ceremony blessing the couple was carried out under a canopy. After the ceremony, a party spanning several days began. Even though polygamy was not forbidden during this time, it was a rare occurrence outside the royal courts. Herod I, for example, had multiple wives, but the average Jewish man would only have had one wife.

As in the cultures around them, the Jewish family structure was patriarchal. The husband was expected to provide for his wife, and the wife was expected to take care of the household. According to the Mishnah, which reflects a certain strain of later rabbinic Judaism, the role of the woman was to grind flour, bake, wash clothing, cook food, look after children, make the beds, and spin yarn (Ketubbot 5:5). The man, on the other hand, was not allowed to move or leave the house for a lengthy period of time without the approval of his wife. Divorce was permitted if either party could prove that the other had not lived up to their marital obligations. Acceptable reasons for divorce included barrenness, adultery, or idolatry. There were mixed opinions about this among, for example, the Pharisees and other Jewish denominations from this period. Around the turn of the century, there were two major theological schools of thought (there were, of course, many smaller schools as well), named after the rabbis who inspired them: Hillel and Shammai (see b. Shabbat 15a, but keep in mind that it was written several hundred years after the events it describes). Shammai often had the stricter interpretation of the law. For example, Hillel permitted divorce if there were good reasons, but Shammai did not.

Once married, women were expected to give birth to children. Miscarriages were relatively common, and the birth of a healthy baby was celebrated with much joy. During the birth, the laboring mother was assisted by other women. After the delivery, the woman was considered unclean for fourteen days if she had given birth to a girl, and seven if she had given birth to a boy. This was based on Lev 12:1–8. A newborn son was to be circumcised on the eighth day after his birth. A doctor carried out the circumcision, and in all likelihood the baby was also named during this ceremony. The circumcision was especially important because it was a concrete sign that the boy was Jewish, a sign of the covenant between God and his people. The transition from childhood to adulthood corresponded with the coming of puberty. The tradition of becoming a *bar-mitzvah* (a "son of the law") is probably a later tradition. Girls could be betrothed already as preteens, but boys most likely waited until they were around eighteen.

Just like the birth of a person was marked by certain rituals, the death of a person was marked by even more rituals and laws. Taking care of the body of a deceased person and making sure he or she was properly buried was the family's natural responsibility (see Matt 8:21 and Jesus's remarkable answer in 8:22). It was important that the body be buried prior to the evening on the same day that the death had occurred. This practice seems to have been especially popular in the region in and around Jerusalem. The body of the deceased was first anointed with oil and then washed (Acts 9:37). The body was wrapped in a burial cloth, which could be very expensive and beautiful if the economic means were there. At the actual burial, there were official female mourners and at least two flute players. Those who grieved for the dead showed their grief by tearing their clothes: sorrow and pain were physically manifested. Well-to-do families often had their own graves consisting of a large, shallow cave with small niches in the walls for the individual graves of the family members. The body was kept in the cave until the corpse had decayed, at which point the bones were collected and put into smaller bone boxes, known as ossuaries. The practice of secondary burial in ossuaries was a relatively short-lived burial ritual in Israel, starting around the turn of the century and ending before the Bar Kokhba revolt. Prior to ossuaries, the decomposed bones of the dead were simply collected and put into communal pits or other storage areas in order to make room for new bodies in the expensive cave graves. Scholars are still debating the significance of the ossuary. Some see it as an indication that the concept of bodily resurrection was popular during this period, whereas others see it as an adoption of foreign burial practices. It is crucial to note that burial in cave graves was a luxury. Only the wealthy could afford this kind of burial (note that Jesus had to be buried in another man's grave—a rich man's grave; see Matt 27:57–60). Likewise, only the wealthy could afford ossuaries. Archaeological remains of the burial practices of the majority population have not survived.

Tombs hewn in rock. These tombs are found inside the Holy Sepulcher in Jerusalem, just east of the tomb where Jesus was buried, according to tradition. Photo by Anders Runesson.

Because a corpse was ritually unclean, those who had been in contact with it were also made unclean. This impurity extended to their household, their vessels, and, of course, the grave itself (see Num 19:16 and Matt 23:27, which uses the imagery of ritually unclean graves to criticize the Pharisees). The period of immediate mourning after the death lasted for seven days and carried with it certain restrictions for those in mourning. If it was someone close to you who had died, the mourning period could be longer, up to a year.[10]

Belief, Theology, and Praxis

Scholars have tried to establish exactly what connected Jewish groups in antiquity. What was the factor that united them despite such great denominational and geographic differences? The aspects of Jewish life that we have already discussed—the holidays, sacred Scriptures, the temple, synagogues, and the land—were in many ways crucial ingredients for the creation of this precarious unity. All Jews, no matter their denomination, had some sort of relationship with these institutions and texts. If we look a little closer, however, we soon find that there are extreme variations in how different denominations of Second Temple Jews viewed and related to these in-

10. Safrai, "Religion in Everyday Life," 782.

stitutions. Samaritans (who, although technically not a Jewish denomination, traced their origin back to preexilic Israel; see box 2.10, p. 145) and Sadducees only accepted the five books of Moses, or the Pentateuch, as normative and authoritative, while the Pharisaic movement also accepted the prophetic literature, the Psalms, and a rich and growing oral tradition. The Essenes generally distanced themselves from the Jerusalem temple, its calendar and cult. Even though not all Jews lived in the land of Israel, even those in the diaspora had some sort of relationship to the homeland. The great differences between the Jewish groups in the Second Temple period have sometimes led scholars to speak in terms of "Judaisms" rather than just one Judaism in the singular. The pluralism of Second Temple Judaism should be emphasized, but not at the cost of forgetting the aspects of Jewish life that actually united them. E. P. Sanders has argued for the existence of what he terms "Common Judaism." The term is meant to reflect all the common practices and beliefs that united the Jews of this period, and many scholars are in agreement with him.[11]

Worship of One God Only

One such central, uniting belief for all Jewish groups was the belief in one God—the God of Israel—as expressed both in prayer and liturgy: "Hear, O Israel: The LORD is our God, the LORD alone. You shall love the LORD your God with all your heart, and with all your soul, and with all your might" (Deut 6:4–5).

The belief in the God of Israel implies a belief in God as the creator and upholder of the entire world. It also implies a belief in the close relationship between the people of Israel and the God of Israel. God's special concern for Israel was seen in the fact that he chose them to be his people and he made a covenant with them on Mount Sinai (Exod 34). According to the covenant that God made with Israel, the Jewish people were expected to prioritize their relationship with God, expressed in love, respect, and participation (see Deut 6:4–5 above). This relationship is supposed to act as an example of relationships between human beings: "You shall love your neighbor as yourself. I am the LORD" (Lev 19:18). This love was meant not only for members of the Jewish people but also for the immigrant: "The alien who resides with you shall be to you as the citizen among you; you shall love the alien as yourself" (Lev 19:34).

Respecting God meant worshiping only the God of Israel and no other gods. This is evident in the Decalogue: "You shall have no other gods before me. You shall not make for yourself an idol, whether in the form of anything that is in heaven above, or that is on the earth beneath, or that is in the water under the earth" (Exod 20:3–4). Thus, in stark contrast to many other peoples and cultures around the Mediterranean in this period, Jews abstained from the creation of idols and other decorative images. This was probably not interpreted as a rule against *all* kinds of images, since we have

11. Sanders, *Judaism*, 47.

recent archaeological evidence of images in synagogues, often in the form of zodiacs and sun images. There are many examples of these "zodiac synagogues," but they are all dated to later than the first century CE. They generally did not begin appearing until the third century CE and onward. Coins with images on them seem to have been allowed. The Tyrian shekel, used to pay the temple tax, contained an image of the Phoenician god Melqart. Controversies did appear, however, regarding coins with images of the Roman emperor. This was related not only to the rule against the making of graven images but also to the Roman occupation of Judea (see Mark 12:13–17).

Perhaps the greatest social implication of Jewish worship exclusivity was its rejection of the polytheistic Greco-Roman cult. As mentioned in previous chapters, this rejection sometimes led to persecution against Jews in the diaspora, since local gods were believed to protect the city from disease and war. If misfortune befell the city, this could easily be blamed on those who had not participated in the cult of the local gods and thereby displeased them. Thus, Jews could be perceived as atheists and traitors.

Jewish respect and worship of their God was concretized and ritualized already during the Second Temple period. In continuation of the quotation from Deut 6:4–5 above, the following is said: "Keep these words that I am commanding you today in your heart. . . . Bind them as a sign on your hand, fix them as an emblem on your forehead" (6:6, 8). Today, the use of prayer capsules, or teffilin, is common practice during weekly prayers and services. This practice came into use already during the beginning of the Common Era (see Matt 23:5; note that the critique directed toward the Pharisees is that their phylacteries and fringes are too long, not against the actual use of them). Both capsules of the teffilin contain the words of Deut 6:8 and other

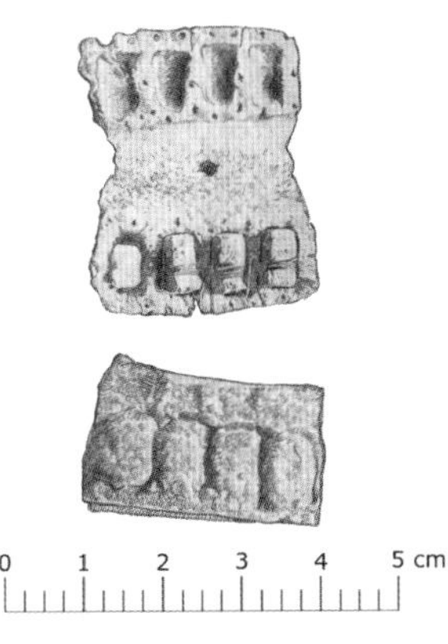

On the left, tefillin (prayer boxes), also called phylacteries (from the Greek *phylaktērion*, "guard, defense"); photo by Håkan Bengtsson. On the right, open and closed ancient tefillin cases found at Qumran; sketch by Per Gyllenör.

central words of the Hebrew Bible and are fastened onto the forehead and the arm. Such teffilin have been found in excavations of the Qumran settlement.

The Concept of the Covenant

The belief that God instituted a covenant with the Jewish people on Mount Sinai is the cornerstone of the Jewish faith. At Sinai, God gave instructions to the Israelites outlining how their relationship with God would look. These instructions are known as the Torah, manifested in the two stone tablets received by Moses with the Decalogue inscribed on them. The Jewish people are the only ones obliged to keep the law expounded in Torah. This does not mean that non-Jews (Heb. *goyim*) were excluded from salvation or did not have the opportunity to cultivate a relationship with God. In and around the first century CE, we find a plethora of different Jewish theologies concerning non-Jews, and most of them argue that there are both righteous people and sinners among the gentiles, just as there are both righteous people and sinners among Jews. Righteous non-Jews would, just like righteous Jews, have a place in the life of the world to come. Different Jewish groups had different ideas about what was required of non-Jews to enter the world to come. Some suggested that non-Jews had to keep a smaller number of laws (see Acts 15:20 and the discussion in chapter 5). Later, the rabbis would develop a theology around this based on what they called the seven Noachian laws, which consisted of seven ethical and ritual laws ensuring righteousness for non-Jews. This idea is still dominant in modern rabbinic Judaism.

A common misconception about the covenant concept in Judaism is the idea that it was based on the belief that the Jewish people were superior to all other ethnic groups, and that their election as God's people was based on some special merit. According to the Jewish self-understanding, the covenant is an expression of God's compassion and grace (see Deut 7:7–8). The covenant means that God takes it upon himself to protect and bless his people, and in return for such compassion, the people are obliged to show their faithfulness. If the people deviate from God's commandments by worshiping other gods, God has the right to punish them. Some of the misfortunes that have befallen the Jewish people over time have been explained as such punishment. The possibility of regret and repentance is always available, and as long as the temple was standing, it was a concrete sign that God had forgiven the people their sins. The mechanisms of atonement and forgiveness are built into the very framework and structure of the law, since the law prescribes the temple cult.

The weakness and shortcomings of the people form a recurring theme in the Hebrew Bible and in later rabbinic literature. Already in Jer 31:31–33 we see the introduction of a renewed covenant, which would be instituted by God: "I will put my law within them, and I will write it on their hearts; and I will be their God, and they shall be my people." There is evidence that the group living in Qumran saw themselves as such a new covenant (CD VI, 19), especially since they believed the rest of the Jewish people to be lost. When discussing the Jewish covenant concept, it is important to remember that there was more than one covenant in Jewish thinking. These covenants are mentioned in different places in the Hebrew Bible, and they are instituted between God himself and, for example, Noah (Gen 9:12); Abraham (Gen 15:18–21; 17:4, 7–8; note that Sarah is included in 17:16); the people at Sinai, when the Torah is given; and David (2 Sam 7:12–16; 23:5). There is even a covenant that reaches beyond the Jewish people and includes the nations (gentiles) (Isa 42:6). Scholarly literature has often focused solely on the covenant at Sinai, and New Testament research often emphasizes the covenant Jesus instituted during the Last Supper (Mark 14:22–25 and synoptic parallels; 1 Cor 11:23–25). Many modern ideas about the covenant are based on the belief that a newer covenant by definition supersedes an older one, but this is hardly an accurate representation of how people thought about covenants in antiquity. For example, in Gal 3:15–17 Paul, a Jewish Christ-following Pharisee, explains that a new covenant does not render the old one obsolete. Thus, a better and more accurate way of viewing covenants is to think about them as layered.

The description of Jewish life as defined by the covenant and laws given at Sinai has long been dominated by a polarizing Christian perspective. This perspective presents works of the law as constituting the sole means of salvation in ancient Judaism. Such terminology is Christian, not Jewish, and it leads to a thoroughly problematic and misconstrued reconstruction of ancient Jewish life. Instead, living according to the covenant of Sinai should be described as living in obedience and reverence to God, partly expressed by following the law of the Torah. E. P. Sanders has described this relationship as having two stages: first, "entering the covenant," and second, "remaining in the covenant." Membership in the covenant is already a given. Staying faithful to the covenant by living in accordance with the laws meant to show respect for God. The law was understood not as a collection of merits or a way to prove one's piety but rather as a way to show loyalty to the covenant and the God who instituted it.[12] The loyalty to the covenant could be manifested and lived out both in a minimalist and in a maximalist manner.

A recurring theological problem in Jewish literature from the Second Temple period is why non-Jews were allowed to triumph over God's chosen people (e.g., Pss. Sol. 2). Should these defeats and humiliations be interpreted as punishment or trial (see Jdt 8:25–27)? Different groups answered this question differently. One way to answer the question was by asserting that when the end of the ages comes, non-Jews will come up to Zion and see the glory of God (Pss. Sol. 17:31). The Qumranites represent the most extreme answer in their assertion and hopeful expectation that all non-Jews would be completely defeated and erased from history (1QM I, 6–15).

Another way of dealing with this issue of the people's suffering was to place one's hope in the restitution and reestablishment of the entire people as a whole, but also for the individual. This idea of restitution could take several forms: the reestablishment of the twelve tribes and the reclaimed glory of Jerusalem was one (Pss. Sol. 11:2–9);

12. Sanders, *Paul and Palestinian Judaism*, 422–23.

another was the idea of a future king, a messiah. The Hebrew word *mashiakh* means "anointed one," someone elected into the office of prophet, priest, or king. The idea that such an anointed person would save and reestablish the nation was prevalent during this time, as illustrated by texts such as Psalms of Solomon (17:32; 18:5). The messianic expectation differed according to which strand of Second Temple Judaism you belonged to. For example, the Qumranites expected two messianic figures: one priest and one king, "the anointed ones from Aaron and Israel" (CD XII, 23; IX, 11; XIV, 19).

Ritual Purity

We have already noted that purity was an important part of Jewish life, and we will presently delve a little deeper into the concept. The idea of purity originated in the precepts laid out in Leviticus (chs. 11–15). Purity could be related to the moral life, since sins with a moral dimension, like illicit sexuality or idolatry, could render an individual unclean. In this section, however, we will focus on ritual purity.

In order for the divine and the human to meet in ancient Judaism, it was very important for the human aspect of that meeting to be both physically and ritually pure. Therefore, ritual purity rules were an integral part of temple praxis in this period. Impurity was primarily transmitted by touch, and many situations and phenomena were believed to render a person unclean—for example, different kinds of bodily fluids exiting the body, contact with leprosy, or the touching of human or animal

A *miqveh* (bath, either natural or constructed, used for ritual immersion and purification of persons and objects) from the first century, found next to a building in Jericho that may have been a synagogue. Photo by Anders Runesson.

corpses. Degrees or levels of impurity were determined according to how long it took the person to become clean again. For example, sexual intercourse between a man and a woman resulted in both becoming unclean, and the state of impurity lasted until the evening and could be cleansed by a ritual bath. Ritual bathing was done in a pool known as a *miqveh* (plural *miqvaot*). A large number of such *miqvaot* have been discovered all over Israel, indicating that ritual purity was an important part of everyday life during this period, not only in direct relation to the Jerusalem temple.

Regarding the degrees of impurity, touching the corpse of an animal, a fairly normal occurrence in an agricultural society, was considered a lighter form of uncleanness. The uncleanness caused by menstruation or contact with leprosy was much worse. Contact with human corpses was even worse. The process of purifying oneself before being able to visit the temple after contact with a human corpse was extensive and included a water-sprinkling ceremony using water containing special ingredients. The most famous of these ingredients was the ashes of an unblemished red cow that had been brought up and slaughtered for this very purpose (see Num 19:2–10).

From a modern Western perspective, one can ask oneself how people managed to live their lives under such circumstances. Was everyone as careful about following every little ritual purity law? We can safely assume that those involved in temple service, such as priests and Levites and their families, had good reason to be very careful about properly observing the ritual purity laws. Other groups were also more observant in this regard, like the Essenes and some of the Pharisaic denominations. A plausible solution to this question is that the majority of the people found practical ways of both observing and compromising on these laws so that the issue of purity did not problematically hinder their daily lives. One way of doing this was to use stone vessels instead of ceramic ones, since stone did not transmit impurity. Such vessels have been found in large quantity throughout Israel, and together with the *miqvaot*, they suggest that ritual purity was an important aspect of first-century Jewish belief and praxis, and that issues of ritual purity permeated the everyday lives of Jews in a way that did not hinder their other activities.

Who Had the Power? The Jewish Parties and Common People

During the greater part of the period this book deals with, the Romans held political power of the land (by direct rule in Judea and by indirect rule in Galilee and the northeastern regions). There was, nevertheless, a Jewish institution that had managed to retain a certain degree of autonomy. This institution was known as the Council or the Great Council. In Greek, the council was known as *synedrion* (meaning "gathering"), which is the foundation for the Hebrew word for the council—namely, the Sanhedrin.

The Council, which was active in different constellations from around the 130s

BCE to the fall of the temple in 70 CE, consisted of seventy or seventy-one members recruited from the priestly aristocracy, the influential families of Jerusalem, and the scribes. The high priest was the chair of the council. The exact jurisdiction and power of the council is debated, especially concerning whether they had the authority to carry out the death sentence (see Mark 14:55; John 11:47–53). In all likelihood, the power of the council changed depending on the political changes and fluctuations of the land. Another factor that may have affected the council was the power struggle between different Jewish parties; for example, the struggle between the Sadducees and the Pharisees for control over the council is well documented.

In his documentation of Jewish life in Israel, the Jewish historian Josephus describes the different Jewish parties from this period. The largest and most important of these groups are the Pharisees, Sadducees, and Essenes. Josephus explains the phenomenon of such parties/denominations using the Greek phrase *eidē philosopheitai* (*Jewish War* 2.119; *Jewish Antiquities* 18.11) or *haireseis tōn Ioudaiōn* (*Jewish Antiquities* 13.171), the approximate meaning of which is philosophical schools or Jewish parties. By examining Josephus's descriptions of these groups, we know that they had existed in Israel since 130–100 BCE.

One can ask exactly how these groups were organized and what their function was. In all likelihood, the reason for the existence of different groups was different interpretations of religious practices and central beliefs. The members of these parties could join around a common idea or ideal but could choose how much and to what degree they wished to participate and be active in the group. The Pharisees and Essenes, in particular, could be described as popular, grassroots movements, of which the Essene party was the more elitist and hierarchical choice. Several scholars have described the Essenes as a *collegium*—that is, a voluntary association in the Greco-Roman style—and some even argue that the Pharisees and Sadducees were organized in a similar way (see box 2.4, p. 73, about associations in antiquity).

The Pharisees

The most well known, but also the most critiqued, of the Jewish parties in the New Testament is that of the Pharisees. The Gospel of Matthew, in particular, is marked by a polemical attitude toward this group (cf. Matt 23). This attitude has lived on in (non-Jewish) Christian tradition, which has often endorsed a stereotyped image of Pharisees as hypocrites and religious traitors. In addition, many scholars have attempted to portray the Pharisees as the party with the most authority—practically ruling all religious life in Israel. If this is combined with an uncritical approach to the critique of the Pharisees in the New Testament, the result is a very negative portrayal of the Pharisees as a powerful party imposing their own religious practices and beliefs on the population and exercising control over them. Today, this reconstruction has been abandoned in favor of a more pluralistic and positive reconstruction of

Jewish life during in this period. As in any group, there were, of course, good and bad Pharisees, something that is also discussed in the Talmud (b. Sota 22b).

The Pharisees shared the idea of the covenant between God and Israel with the rest of the Jewish people. The commandments of the Torah were central for the Pharisees, and it was therefore crucial that they should discuss and interpret the Holy Scripture in order to decide just how the commandments should be followed. They had what we call a written and an oral Torah. The latter consisted of the oral tradition of the Pharisees. The movement was characterized by applying the Torah to their daily lives. Because of this, education played an important role. Acts 22:3 is an example of this, as it describes how Paul studied with the famous Pharisaic teacher, Gamaliel the Elder, indicating the importance of education in the Pharisaic tradition.

The term "Pharisee" is originally not a word that the movement used to describe itself (like the term "Christian," which was used to describe the Jesus movement by those outside it). The Greek word *pharisaioi* is assumed to come from the Hebrew word *perushim*, which means "the separate ones." This does not mean that the Pharisees were separated from other Jews, nor that they had an elitist attitude toward them. In fact, Pharisees were represented in every social class, and, in contrast to the more elitist Sadducees, they can be classified as a movement of the people. "Separation" here is in all likelihood a reference to their careful observance of the purity laws regarding the preparation and communal consumption of food. Eating and table fellowship could be a source of conflict, as we can see in Gal 2:12. The scholar Jacob Neusner has suggested that the laws and practices around food and eating, as well as their way of observing the religious holidays, made up the core of the Pharisaic belief system. According to Neusner, the Pharisees originated in an influential political party under the Hasmoneans—they were especially influential under the reign of Salome Alexandra—and then developed into a more religiously oriented community under the reign of Herod I.[13]

The Pharisaic movement was not a homogeneous movement. The rabbinic discussions preserved in the Mishnah indicate that there were at least two competing schools within the party. The more liberal school was called *bet Hillel*, and the stricter school was known as *bet Shammai* (in Hebrew, *bet* means the "school" or "movement" of Hillel and Shammai). Hillel (ca. 50 BCE–10 CE) had the epitaph "the mild" and often emphasized the intention and importance of following the minimum amount of halakic practices. This interpretative tradition, which attempts to summarize the law into overarching commandments, can also be found in the Gospels (see Mark 12:28–34; Matt 7:12) and in the writings of Paul (Gal 5:14; Rom 13:10). Hillel's colleague Shammai was stricter in his interpretation and emphasized the importance of following the maximum amount of halakic practices. Because of this, he can sometimes be interpreted as being harsher and less willing to compro-

13. Neusner, *From Politics to Piety*, 153–54.

mise. A question up for debate between these two schools could, for example, be how a meal should be prepared in order to meet the requirements of religious purity. According to the school of Hillel, one could tolerate a certain degree of impurity concerning the hands, vessels, and preparation of the meal, as long as the result was blessed and proclaimed to be clean. According to the school of Shammai, however, the entire process had to be clean in order for the end product to be considered clean. Today, we often interpret Hillel to be the more sympathetic of the two, but, as previously mentioned, in the issue of divorce the ruling of Shammai against divorce actually protected the position of the woman. The school of Hillel was generally favored in later rabbinic literature.

The heart of the Pharisaic tradition could therefore be said to consist of the study of Torah, the ongoing discussion of the Scriptures, and an emphasis on ritual purity. Initially, many of the discussions within the movement were preserved in the form of oral traditions that later became the so-called pillars that carried the movement forward. Pharisaism could thereby be characterized by an ongoing discussion. Because of this, the Pharisaic tradition was in principle flexible and open to new idea, both in terms of commandments and theology. Examples of the innovative and new thinking of the Pharisees include the belief in resurrection and angels, something they shared with the Jesus movement. This openness and theological innovation stood in stark contrast to their traditional opponents, the Sadducees.

The Sadducees

The Sadducees are the most clearly characterized group, yet also the most difficult of the Jewish parties to clearly define. In general, they are assumed to have been members of the aristocracy and priesthood of Jerusalem. However, not all members of the aristocracy and priesthood were Sadducees. The recruiting base that the group had was important, since it gave them representation in and around the Jerusalem temple and thus provided them with a great deal of influence over the political power and cult associated with the temple. Despite this, we do not have access to much source material concerning the Sadducees, especially since the Mishnah is so clearly biased against them in favor of the Pharisees. Even the New Testament reflects the antagonism between the Sadducees and the Pharisees (see Acts 23:6–9) but does not provide us with a great deal of further information about the Sadducees. In rabbinic literature, a group known as the Boethusians is also mentioned, named after the high priest Boethus. Boethusians are mentioned as opponents of the Pharisees and are grouped together with the Sadducees. Such information indicates that our perspective of the Jewish parties has been heavily influenced by Josephus's three categories: Pharisees, Sadducees, Essenes. In all likelihood, there were other groups besides these, including subgroups and groups that existed in the spaces between the three mentioned.

The connection between the Sadducees and the temple aristocracy of Jerusalem is a general scholarly consensus. This is supported by the etymology of the word "Sadducee," which comes from the name Zadok, a man who became high priest during the time of Solomon (1 Kgs 2:35). The New Testament also associated Sadducees with leaders among the temple priests (Acts 4:1; 5:17).

The conflict between the Sadducees and the Pharisees is usually believed to have revolved around the following points of contention: halakic purity, the oral interpretative tradition, the belief in angels, and the resurrection of the dead. In questions of purity, the interpretation of the Sadducees was often stricter and more rigorous than that of the Pharisees. Because of the Sadducees' connection to the temple, their purity praxis was adapted to the level of rigor demanded for those associated with the temple. Seen from this perspective, there is more similarity between the Sadducees and the Qumranites than between the Sadducees and the Pharisees. Where the other points of contention are concerned, the position of the Sadducees is best understood in light of the fact that they accepted only the Pentateuch as authoritative and normative Scripture. They rejected the oral tradition as an important part of the revelation, even though they had their own interpretative praxis. Having these facts as a point of departure makes it easier to understand why the Sadducees, according to many scholars, rejected the belief in the existence of any sort of hierarchy of angelic beings—which, however, was an important belief for the Qumranites—and the belief in the resurrection of the dead. The Sadducee position concerning the resurrection of the dead is also found in the New Testament, where Jesus is questioned by them about this belief (Mark 12:18–27). Even Paul is confronted by and confronts the Sadducees in this question (Acts 23:6–10).

The study of the Sadducees is often plagued by negative presuppositions about them, in this case not only stemming from Christian tradition but also stemming from Jewish tradition. Sometimes the Sadducees are portrayed as priests and aristocrats who were completely corrupted by power and money. However, we have no evidence for the "tradition" that the temple priests, and more specifically the Sadducees as a group, were corrupted by power and money. It was likely important for them to retain good relations to whichever ruler was in power, whether it be the Hasmoneans, puppet kings, or the Romans, since this would ensure that the temple cult could continue to run smoothly. This was important for the well-being of all of Israel. This meant that they often had to balance the will of the rulers and the pressure of the people, resulting in their negative portrayal in contemporary literature.

The Essenes

For a long time, the Essenes were seen as the most mysterious and nebulous of the Jewish parties. They are mentioned by Philo, Josephus, and Pliny the Elder, but the New Testament makes no mention of them. After the discovery of the Dead Sea Scrolls at Qumran in 1947, the scholarly consensus has been that the Qumranites were Essenes. Although this theory has been criticized, there is nevertheless considerable evidence supporting it. This means that the Essenes are no longer quite such a mystery. Because we now have access to the writings of an Essene group, writings that include prayers, liturgies, Bible commentaries, and so forth, we actually know a great deal more about them than we do about the Sadducees.

Cave 4 in Qumran, where thousands of text fragments were discovered in the 1950s.

Box 2.9
The Qumran Literature

The texts found in the caves by the northwestern shore of the Dead Sea between 1947 and 1956 are often referred to as the Dead Sea Scrolls. A more accurate term is "Qumran texts," which refers more directly to the particular documents with religious content discovered in the area around the ruins of the settlement Khirbet Qumran. The texts were found dispersed in eleven caves. The material consists of Bible texts, so-called apocryphal and pseudepigraphic literature (e.g., Book of Enoch and Jubilees), as well as previously unknown prayers, liturgies, Bible commentaries, and community rules. The texts from the latter category were in all probability composed by the group living at Qumran. The majority of scholars assume that the group was part of the Essene movement.

In total, more than nine hundred documents have thus far been discovered, most of them fragmentary. The first documents were discovered by Bedouin boys in what would later be named Cave 1. The Community Rule, War Scroll, Thanksgiving Hymns, Habakkuk Commentary, and two copies of the book of Isaiah are examples of some of the more well-preserved scrolls found. These texts were published relatively quickly during the 1950s. In Cave 4, however, all the texts discovered were in fragments, and it took many years to painstakingly piece them together into scrolls. These were not published for a couple of decades because the international team of scholars working on them had no clear structure or publishing plan. Internal conflicts and illnesses further delayed the process. Today, all the material found at Qumran is published and translated.

To keep track of the hundreds of documents found at Qumran, scholars have developed a system of abbreviations. The shorthand for the well-known Community Rule, 1QS, is as follows:

1 means the document was found in Cave 1
Q means the document was found at Qumran
S stands for the Hebrew word *serech*, meaning "rule," and indicates the genre

Another example is 4QpNah:

4 means the document comes from Cave 4
Q means the document was found at Qumran
p stands for the genre: *pesher*, meaning Bible commentary
Nah stands for Nahum, indicating which book the commentary is about

The most well-known documents found at Qumran are the following:

1QS: The Community Rule. This document contains rules and instructions for the members of the congregation living at Qumran. In the beginning of the document, a liturgy for the renewal of the covenant at Sinai, probably Shavuot, is described. In this document we also find teachings concerning the "spirit of lies" and the "spirit of truth."

CD: The so-called Damascus Document. It was known to us already from the beginning of the twentieth century when it was, together with a wealth of other texts, discovered in a genizah in a synagogue in Cairo. Fragments of the document were found in Cave 4 at Qumran and can therefore be assumed to belong to the literature of the Qumranites. The document describes the early history of the movement, as well as outlining halakic rules and principles.

1QH: The Thanksgiving Hymns. *H* stands for Hodayot, which means "thanksgiving hymns" in Hebrew. These psalms were inspired by the Psalter and were in all likelihood composed by a community leader with prophetic insight.

1QpHab: The Commentary to Habakkuk. This commentary deals with Habakkuk's first chapters and was discovered in relatively good condition. The texts include allusions to the history of the Qumranites and their self-understanding.

1QM: The War Scroll. The *M* stands for the Hebrew word *milkhamah*, meaning "war." The document is a description of what can be assumed to be the expected apocalyptic war between the sons of light (Qumranites themselves) and the sons of darkness (nonbelievers, non-Qumranites).

***4QMMT* (4Q394–399):** *MMT* stands for the Hebrew *Miksat Ma'aseh ha-Torah*, meaning "some principles for how to live the Torah." The document begins with an account of calendar data and continues in the form of a letter to the priesthood in Jerusalem. It was written by someone with a leadership position at Qumran who was attempting to convince the priests in Jerusalem to adopt stricter halakic interpretations.

***11QTemple* (11Q19):** The Temple Scroll. This is the longest document discovered, as long as nine meters. It contains a new halakic interpretation of Torah. Many of the passages deal with the temple cult, and some scholars identify this text as one of the earliest and most important documents for the Qumranites.

Khirbet Qumran ("Khirbet" designates "ruin" in Arabic), which consists of a complex of buildings and a graveyard with over 1,200 graves, seems to have been a center for the Essene movement. A traditional theory asserts that the sect was founded by a figure known as the "teacher of righteousness," who led a group of followers out into the desert to Qumran in order to wait for the day of the Lord by studying Scripture. This is described in 1QS VIII, 12b–16b: "When such men as these [come to be] in Israel, [conforming to these doctrines], they shall separate from the session of perverse men to go to the wilderness, there to prepare the way of truth/the LORD, as it is written, 'in the wilderness prepare the way of the LORD, make straight in the desert a highway for our God' (Isa 40:3). This means the expounding of the law, decreed by God through Moses for obedience, that being defined by what has been revealed for each age, and by what the prophets have revealed by His holy spirit."[14] One problem with this theory is that the ruins at Qumran have been redated to the second century BCE at the earliest.[15] Since 1QS is considerably older than that, it is difficult to believe that it could be speaking about the particular settlement at Qumran. Like

14. Parry and Tov, *Dead Sea Scrolls Reader*, 1:33.
15. Magness, *Archaeology of Qumran and the Dead Sea Scrolls*, 63–69.

the Pharisees, the Essenes were not a homogeneous movement. The texts found at Qumran indicate a diversity of interpretations of laws and rules. Some scholars have suggested that the community at Qumran broke away from other Essenes to start their own movement (this theory is known as the Groningen hypothesis).

The etymology of the word "Essene" (Gk. *essaioi* or *essēnoi*) is debated. The word either comes from the Greek word *hosios*, meaning "holy" (Philo, *That Every Good Person Is Free* 75), or, as the Qumranites themselves suggest in one of their Bible commentaries, stems from the Hebrew *oseh ha-Torah*, which roughly translates to "the one who keeps Torah." Another etymological alternative is the Aramaic word *khase*, meaning "pious." Either way, all the alternatives point to the fact that the group saw itself more exclusive than other groups.

In both Josephus (*Jewish War* 2.119–61; *Jewish Antiquities* 18.18–22) and Philo (*That Every Good Person Is Free* 75–91; *Hypothetica* 11.1–18) the Essene movement is described as interpreting and prioritizing purity and food laws in such a way that it made it difficult for them to associate closely with other Jews or non-Jews. Josephus writes that there were about four thousand Essenes in Israel during the reign of Herod. In all likelihood, they lived in separate enclaves among the villages and towns of the land so as to be able to preserve their traditions. By all accounts, the Essenes were greatly appreciated for their hospitality, especially toward travelers.

When attempting to reconstruct the Qumran congregation, we can use their own texts, especially the so-called Community Rule, since it corresponds in large part to what Josephus writes about the Essenes. A strict hierarchy defined the congregation, where the leadership consisted of a group of elders. To enter the congregation, one had to go through a trial period of several years, after which the candidate was evaluated as appropriate or not. The group had a communal worship life and also engaged in intensive studying and interpreting of the Holy Scriptures. They also had communal meals with ritual characteristics. Simplicity and humbleness defined the lifestyle of the members, in both dress and food. Members were most likely engaged in light agriculture

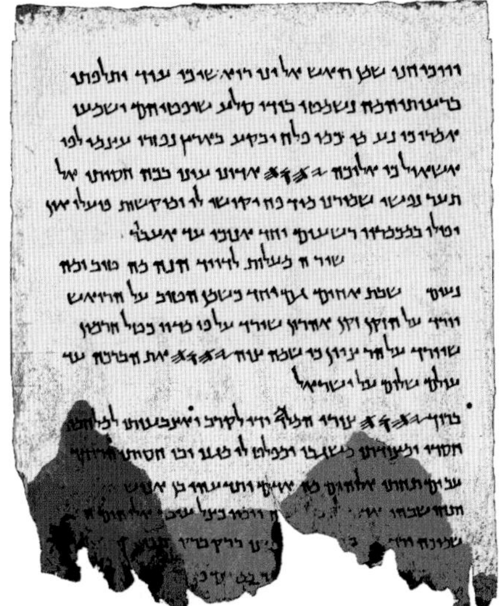

Column X from the Habakkuk commentary (1QpHab). Note the fourth word from the right on the fourth line, where the name of God is written in paleo-Hebraic letters. Find the other two instances of paleo-Hebraic writing on the same page. Photo by Dieter Mitternacht.

and animal rearing. Individual members were allowed only certain private belongings, such as their clothing. All other belongings were communal. A large sum of money was found at Qumran, which is usually explained by the theory that the congregation traded with nearby cities, such as Jericho and Ein-Gedi.

Everyday life consisted of agricultural work, Scripture study, communal meals, and worship services. According to Josephus, Essenes rose before the sun in order to pray facing in its direction. Another interesting and defining aspect of the group was that it used another calendar than the one used by the temple cult. The Qumranites followed an older, sun-based calendar (see above). It is possible that they also counted the days as beginning when the sun rose instead of when it set, as other Jewish groups did. The separate calendar meant that the Qumranites celebrated the holidays on different days than other Jews. It was not only the matter of calendars that separated the Qumranites from other Jews; the group had a much stricter and less compromising purity halakhah. From this perspective, the halakhah of the Pharisees appears mild and opportunistic. In the commentary to the prophet Nahum's book (4QpNah), the Pharisees are given the humiliating nickname "those who seek easy interpretations."

Typical characteristics of Qumranite theology include their dualistic view of the world and a strong eschatological expectation. In the Community Rule's introduction, the "sons of light" and the "prince of light" are contrasted with the "sons of

Remains of buildings at Khirbet Qumran. In room 4 (to the right) were found benches, indicating that the room was used for meetings. To the left is the larger room 30, which was probably a scriptorium. Photo by Anders Runesson.

destruction" and the "angel of darkness." The entire world was seen as being divided into two sections—the spirit of darkness and the spirit of truth—and it is up to everyone to pick sides (1QS III–IV). Such a black-and-white theology was common in Jewish apocalypticism, according to which God would soon destroy all the forces of evil. The expectation of a restitution in the near future via the concrete interaction of God with the world can be found in the War Scroll (1QM), which describes an apocalyptic war between the sons of darkness and the sons of light. We can even sense this expectation in the commentary to Habakkuk, in which the author writes about the restitution of the "men of truth who keep the Torah . . . in the end times" (1QpHab VII, 10–12). Such a dualistic perspective brought with it social isolation from Jewish society at large.

In ancient descriptions of the Essenes in Greco-Roman literature, they are described as celibate, with the exception of a certain strand, which, according to Josephus, married. This does not correspond with the information we have from the Qumran literature. With the exception of the Community Rule, all the other texts of rules and laws—such as the Damascus Document, the Community Order (1QSa), and the Community Texts (4Q265)—address members who are clearly married. In fact, it seems as though marriage was common in Qumran. There is evidence of the fact that women could take part in decision-making[16] and occupy leadership positions.[17] It is, however, likely that men and women did not normally occupy the same roles. There is much research left to be done on this topic.

There are many similarities between the Essenes and the early Jesus movement. The simple lifestyle, communal meals, communal property and belongings, and eschatological expectations are a few examples. Because of this, many people have wanted to see connections between the Essenes and Christ followers. It is important to note that there is no evidence for such direct connections. In fact, there are great differences between the groups—from how they viewed the world and communicated with non-Jews and marginalized members of society to how they interpreted halakic questions.

Zealots and Sicarii

The anger at Rome's occupation of the land was accentuated when Herod Archelaus was deposed by Rome, and Judea and Samaria became provinces under direct rule of Rome in 6 CE. The Jewish resistance became increasingly organized over the years, and eventually the small-time robbers and crooks that normally roamed the countryside found their way into the movement.

16. Wassén, *Women in the Damascus Document*, 188.
17. Schuller, *Dead Sea Scrolls*, 96–97.

A special group, known as Sicarii (from the Latin word *sica*, meaning "dagger"), was active during the 40s CE. One common strategy was to attack their victims in crowded places. They would come near their victims with their daggers hidden under their cloaks and disappear into the crowd after the assault. The usual victims of the Sicarii were Jews whom they believed to have betrayed the Jewish freedom cause. Paul was accused of being such a "dagger man" when he was arrested in the tumult on the Temple Mount in Acts 21:38.

Josephus mentions another resistance group active during the Jewish revolt, which he calls Zealots (from the Greek *zēlōtēs*, meaning "zealous"). The term should probably be understood as more of a name than an epithet. The foundation for the Zealots' struggle was religious. Most likely they shared many of their ideals with the Pharisees. They viewed the Roman occupation as a religious affront. Josephus, from whom we have the most extensive description, was negative in his assessment of the Zealots, blaming them for the fall of Jerusalem and the destruction of the temple. He names several individual representatives for this "fourth party," as he calls it (*Jewish Antiquities* 18.23), indicating that many different groups were involved in the opposition against Rome.

Ordinary People

Our point of departure should be that the lives of ordinary people in antiquity were not so different from the lives of regular people today. Their days were defined by the need to attain the basic needs of life, such as food, work, and security. Urban life was different from rural life. Those who lived in the city enjoyed advanced education, and a small minority could afford to live in luxury, while the majority of the inhabitants had to work hard for their daily living under feudal-like circumstances. Common professions included merchants, construction workers, and day laborers (usually agricultural work). Slaves carried out the heavy labor. In New Testament times, people lived their lives in the presence of the Roman military. The Roman military presence was especially felt along the Mediterranean coast, in Judea and in Jerusalem. Caesarea Maritima was the center of the Roman administration. Because Galilee was ruled by a Jewish puppet king (Herod Antipas, 4 BCE–37 CE), the Roman presence was not as palpable there. Poverty, military oppression, and an increased taxation was still a constant reminder of the deplorable state of the land. The discontent of the people occasionally bubbled up in sporadic riots, which eventually led to the Jewish revolt in 66 CE. The hope of Jewish sovereignty did not disappear when the Romans crushed the revolt and destroyed the Jerusalem temple in 70 CE. The Bar Kokhba revolt from 132–135 CE proves that the Jews did not give up the struggle for their homeland even after the fall of the temple.

Box 2.10
The Samaritans

The groups we have discussed so far have been geographically limited to Judea first and foremost, but also to the Galilee. We know, however, that there were Pharisees in the diaspora, and we find mention of yet another group, the Therapeutae, in the writings of Philo. The Therapeutae were sectarian and had their base in Egypt, outside Alexandria, but according to Philo, they had members all over the Mediterranean world. They lived a quiet life, viewed men and women as equal, and were against slavery, which they saw as contradicting the order of nature. All of these groups were Jewish.

A group that did not (and still today does not) define itself as Jewish was (and is) the Samaritans. This ethnic/religious group survived the fall of the Northern Kingdom in 721 BCE and traces its origins to the preexilic era. Samaritans saw themselves as heirs of the old traditions of Israel, just like the returning Jews who rebuilt the temple in Jerusalem did after the exile. The Samaritans rejected the Jerusalem temple; Mount Gerizim, near modern-day Nablus, was the site of the Samaritans' temple. The Samaritans share the Pentateuch with the Jews, although they have their own version of it, and they also adhere to monotheism and the conviction that they have a covenant relationship with God. The big difference lay in the fact that they believed the rightful place for the cultic worship of Israel's God was on Mount Gerizim rather than on Mount Moriah (the mountain on which the Jerusalem temple was built). Conflicts between Judeans and Samaritans were intensified in the 170s BCE when the Hasmonean rulers expanded their territory to include Samaria. Samaritans were described by the Hasmoneans as "unclean" and idolaters, and were given the derogatory nickname Cuteans (after the Mesopotamian city Kut, where the Hasmoneans claimed the Samaritans came from; this designation lived on in rabbinic literature). This name implied an accusation that the Samaritans did not have a legitimate claim on the traditions of Israel but should rather be seen as aliens who had occupied the land. The Hasmonean ruler John Hyrcanus eventually destroyed the Samaritan temple in 128 BCE. The tensions between Jews and Samaritans constitute an important context for understanding some of Jesus's parables and actions (Matt 10:5; Luke 9:51–56; 10:25–37; 17:11–19; John 4:1–42; 8:48; Acts 8:25). In relation to Luke 10:25–37 it might be mentioned that the exemplary concern shown by the Samaritan enemy in Jesus's parable is the origin of the modern concept of "Samaritans" as organizations or persons committed to humanitarian support.

The Samaritans still sacrifice pascal lambs at the site of their temple on Mount Gerizim, even though their temple was never rebuilt after its destruction at the hands of the Hasmoneans. Reinhard Pummer, in *The Samaritans: A Profile*, provides a good introduction to Samaritan history and culture for those interested in further reading on this interesting and often under-studied group.

Further Reading

Barclay, John M. G. *Jews in the Mediterranean Diaspora: From Alexander to Trajan (323 BCE–117 CE)*. Berkeley: University of California Press, 1996.

Brooke, George J. *Reading the Dead Sea Scrolls: Essays in Method*. EJL 39. Atlanta: Society of Biblical Literature, 2013.

Crossley, James G. *The New Testament and Jewish Law: A Guide for the Perplexed*. London: T&T Clark, 2010.

Eshel, Hanan. *The Dead Sea Scrolls and the Hasmonean State*. Jerusalem: Yad Ben-Zvi Press, 2008.

Grabbe, Lester L. *An Introduction to First Century Judaism: Jewish Religion and History in the Second Temple Period*. Edinburgh: T&T Clark, 1996.

Knoppers, Gary N. *Jews and Samaritans: The Origins and History of Their Early Relations*. Oxford: Oxford University Press, 2013.

Lau, Binyamin. *From Yavneh to the Bar-Kokhba Revolt*. Vol. 2 of *The Sages: Character, Context and Creativity*. Jerusalem: Maggid Books, 2011.

Magness, Jodi. *The Archaeology of Qumran and the Dead Sea Scrolls*. Grand Rapids: Eerdmans, 2002.

———. *Stone and Dung, Oil and Spit: Jewish Daily Life in the Time of Jesus*. Grand Rapids: Eerdmans, 2011.

Meyers, Carol. "Temple, Jerusalem." Pages 350–69 in *The Anchor Bible Dictionary*. Vol. 6. New York: Doubleday, 1992.

Neusner, Jacob. *From Politics to Piety: The Emergence of Pharisaic Judaism*. 2nd ed. Eugene, OR: Wipf and Stock, 2003.

Neusner, Jacob, and Bruce D. Chilton, eds. *In Quest of the Historical Pharisees*. Waco: Baylor University Press, 2007.

Parry, Donald W., and Emanuel Tov, in association with Geraldine I. Clements. *The Dead Sea Scrolls Reader*. 2 vols. 2nd ed., revised and expanded. Leiden: Brill, 2014.

Pummer, Reinhardt. *The Samaritans: A Profile*. Grand Rapids: Eerdmans, 2016.

Runesson, Anders. *The Origins of the Synagogue: A Socio-Historical Study*. ConBNT 37. Stockholm: Almqvist & Wiksell International, 2001.

Safrai, Shmuel. "Religion in Everyday Life." Pages 793–833 in *The Jewish People in the First Century: Historical Geography, Political History, Social, Cultural and Religious Life and Institutions*. CRINT, Section One. Assen: Van Gorum, 1987.

Saldarini, A. J. *Pharisees, Scribes and Sadducees in Palestinian Society*. Edinburgh: T&T Clark, 1989.

Sanders, E. P. *Judaism: Practice and Belief 63 BCE–66 CE*. London: SCM, 1992.

———. *Paul and Palestinian Judaism: A Comparison of Patterns of Religion*. Philadelphia: Fortress, 1977.

Schäfer, Peter. *Judeophobia: Attitudes towards the Jew in the Ancient World*. Cambridge, MA: Harvard University Press, 1997.
Schuller, Eileen. *The Dead Sea Scrolls: What Have We Learned 50 Years On?* London: SCM, 2006.
Stemberger, Gunter. *Jewish Contemporaries of Jesus: Pharisees, Sadducees, Essenes*. Minneapolis: Fortress, 1995.
VanderKam, James C. *An Introduction to Early Judaism*. Grand Rapids: Eerdmans, 2001.
Vermes, Geza. *Who's Who in the Age of Jesus?* London: Penguin Books, 2005.
Wassén, Cecilia. *Women in the Damascus Document*. Leiden: Brill, 2005.

Men, Women, and Power in Ancient Society and the Early Jesus Movement

Ancient society was patriarchal, the Greco-Roman no less than the Jewish. This claim is often repeated in research literature and textbooks. Still, a number of primary sources point in directions that undermine any simplistic understandings of such labeling. In addition to inscriptions and papyri, in various New Testament texts, including the Gospels and the Pauline letters, there are indications that the presence and active involvement of women in the early Jesus movement was the norm. This is noteworthy since the texts in question were written by men and in general present an androcentric worldview. Given such initial observations, the problem of whether women occupied leadership roles in the early Jesus movement emerges as a valid and interesting question. Were there female apostles in the first century CE? If so, how should such a phenomenon be understood in relation to the surrounding Greco-Roman and Jewish societies?

In Rom 16:7, according to many Bible translations, Paul sends greetings to a Jewish man called Junias, who, together with a certain Andronicus, is described by Paul as a highly respected apostle. In the oldest Greek manuscripts, the name is written with capital letters: IUONIAN. The grammatical form of this name leaves us with two options: either it is the accusative case of a woman's name, Junia, or it is a man's name, Junius. The choice between these two options depends on where the accent is placed in the Greek. Because the oldest preserved texts lack accents, it is difficult to establish whether the name refers to a man or a woman. Despite this ambiguity, the evidence points to the conclusion that this name belongs to a woman, as Eldon Epp, Wayne Meeks, Bernadette Brooten, and several other scholars have argued.[18] The male version of the name has no predecessor in Greco-Roman literature or inscriptions, and the church fathers, with the possible exception of Epiphanius, seem to believe the name referred to a woman.

18. Epp, *Junia*; Meeks, *First Urban Christians*; Brooten, "Junia." See also Stegemann and Stegemann, *Jesus Movement*.

John Chrysostom (ca. 347–407) wrote the following in his commentary on Rom 16:7: "To be an apostle is something great! But to be outstanding among the apostles—just think what a wonderful song of praise that is! They were outstanding on the basis of their works and virtuous actions. Indeed, how great the wisdom of this woman must have been that she was even deemed worthy of the title of apostle."[19]

Interestingly, of the thirty-nine Greek versions of the New Testament published from the time of Erasmus (1516) into the nineteenth century, only one (Alford, 1844–1857, 1888) chose to place the accent on the last letter and in this way create a male name.[20] The others placed the accent on the penultimate letter and thus interpreted the name to be female. Around the middle of the nineteenth century, however, something changed, and Junia became a man in many critical editions. As late as in the Nestle-Alands's twenty-seventh edition of the Greek text (1993), the apostle is referred to as Junias—a man—but in the footnotes (or, as they are called in the academic world, the text-critical apparatus) the strong evidence in favor of a female name is listed. In the twenty-eighth edition (2013) this is corrected, so that the text now refers to a female name. Looking at translations, the influential King James Version (1611, with later revisions) uses Junia, as does the New Revised Standard Version. A sample of translations less common in the Western academic world shows that Yunia is used in the Swahili Bible (United Bible Societies, 1952) and in the Norwegian translation of 2011 (Bibelselskapet). The Swedish translation of 1981 (republished in the new Bible edition of 2000 without change), however, chooses to write Junias, a minority position today.[21]

If we can be almost certain that the person in question was in fact a woman named Junia—based on current research, the ancient manuscripts, the absolute majority of critical editions of the New Testament since the sixteenth century, as well as interpretations by the church fathers and the fact that the male version of the name is otherwise unknown in ancient texts—can we also be sure that she was an apostle? The Greek (*episēmoi en tois apostolois*) could, grammatically speaking, be interpreted in two ways. One option is that Andronicus and Junia (who were probably a married couple, as suggested by Meeks and Cranfield) were respected or well known *as* apostles, and the other option is that they were respected or well known *by* the apostles. This ambiguity may be used as evidence by those who are convinced that we are dealing with a woman but who simultaneously believe that Paul would never address a woman as an apostle. All patristic commentators nonetheless interpret the

19. John Chrysostom, *Homilies on Romans* 31.2, cited in Brooten, "Junia."

20. Epp, *Junia*.

21. Compare, however, Luther's translation, revised by the council of the Evangelical Church in Germany in 1964 (Württembergische Bibelanstalt, 1970), which also uses "Junias."

two individuals mentioned in the text as *being* apostles.[22] This is also Chrysostom's interpretation, as we saw above.

Icon of Junia and Andronicus, with Saint Athanasius, Bishop of Christianoupolis, in the center.

In addition, scholars still debate exactly what Paul meant by the word "apostle." (When investigating this question, it can be helpful to analyze texts where Paul describes himself as an apostle: Rom 1:1–5; 1 Cor 1:1; 9:1–2; Gal 1:1, 15–17). On the basis of both linguistic and patristic evidence, it is difficult to deny that Rom 16:7 refers to a man and a woman, Andronicus and Junia, whom Paul describes as highly respected apostles. Regardless of what meaning we attribute to the word "apostle," all can agree that for Paul the word represented the most important office in the early Christ groups. This is evident in 1 Cor 12:28 (in the Greek text there is a clear hierarchy among the duties, though in some modern translations this is lost). In sum, then, according to the oldest sources on the early Jesus movement we have access to—Paul's own letters—apostleship was regarded as the most important office, and it could be held by both men and women.

Now, having said this, several follow-up questions surface. Was this view of men and women, according to which they could have, in these communal settings, the same titles and carry out the same duties, the norm in ancient society? Could women generally carry titles that men were honored with, and occupy leadership roles? Have we not been taught that men dominated ancient society on all levels? Why would the early Jesus movement be any different? Junia opens up for us new discussions, and she forces us to reconsider what we have learned, reread the sources, and ask new questions. The answers to these new questions may provide us with information about the place of the earliest Christ groups in societies in which they lived. Were they more "radical" about issues of female status and leadership than other groups at the time? And why

22. Cranfield, *Romans*; Epp, *Junia*. Cranfield argues that this interpretation of Paul's text is "virtually certain" (2:789).

did the emerging majority church become such a male-dominated institution, if it had its genesis in a more gender-inclusive milieu, with regard to titles and leadership? In the following section, we will take a closer look at women in the ancient world, basing our analysis on Greco-Roman and Jewish sources, as well as sources related to Christ followers, whether Jewish or non-Jewish.

Women in Ancient Society: How Do We Ask the Question?

When we discuss men, women, power, and social roles, we are not speaking about the "natural" roles of men and women in society, despite the fact that this is how our sources often present the situation. In this section we shall discuss ancient constructions of gender without delving into the discussion of whether these constructs reflect some biologically or divinely motivated differences in terms of what is expected of respective sexes. This means that ideologically or theologically motivated beliefs about the place of women in society should be understood as just that: constructions.

When investigating the question of whether women in antiquity had access to social power, we first have to realize that the scope of that question is far too wide and needs to be specified in order for us to accurately interpret our sources and draw balanced conclusions. When we do this, certain patterns emerge that suggest that the situation of women could vary greatly depending on the circumstances in which they lived. A multitude of parameters need to be taken into account, and these can be divided into two main groups. The first group deals with factors influencing general differences in gender expectations:

(A) 1. Social strata
2. Type of society (rural or urban)
3. Marital status (married, unmarried, widow)
4. Culture (broadly divided into eastern or western parts of the Roman Empire)

In our analysis, we must also include the possible differences that come with changing role expectations, laws, and rules at different levels of society. Just as religion was expressed differently depending on *where* in society an individual was located in the Roman Empire, so also gender expectations varied. Consequently, we need to distinguish between the following:

(B) 1. Public/civic level (politics, state and city administration)
2. Private/domestic level (individual and family level)
3. Semipublic/association level (groups based on a variety of network connections)

The parameters listed under category A may be considered in comparative perspective. For example, a married woman (A3) from the upper strata of society (A1) in the western part of the empire (A4) can be compared to an unmarried woman (A3) from the lower strata of society (A1) in the eastern part of the empire (A4). However, the parameters under A should also be considered in conjunction with the relevant levels labeled B. The opportunities for a married woman (A3) from the upper strata of society (A1) to occupy a position of power/leadership varied depending on whether she was active in the public, political sphere (B1), within an association (B3), or in the private, domestic sphere (B2). The same is true for an analysis of men and the various role expectations attached to them.

It is important that we keep these social spheres and other parameters separated in our analysis, since it is not uncommon for scholars to study sources originating in and/or concerned with the public sphere of society and then apply their conclusions to the association level as well, despite the fact that these respective contexts offered very different options for both men and women. Such generalizations are especially problematic because it is at the association level that we find Christ groups and other Jewish groups in first-century Mediterranean societies.

The Public Sphere: Politics, the Right to Vote, and Municipal Administration

In order to get a better appreciation of the situation, it is necessary first to take a closer look at the public, administrative, and political spheres of Greco-Roman society. Looking at this part of many ancient societies, we should state from the start that free adult men with citizenship were those who enjoyed direct political influence through the right to vote and the ability to hold administrative offices. The population of Greco-Roman societies may be divided into three general sections: free men and women, freed slaves (men and women), and slaves (men and women). The majority of the population was not given the opportunity to influence society directly. Slaves, both men and women, could be freed and granted citizenship. In the case of freed slaves, only the freed*men* could aspire to play an influential role in the public sphere, as women were in general excluded from the polis-administration. The conclusion to draw from this is that women, whatever their status, had the lowest chance of influencing their society via voting or political activities. This conclusion is valid across the social spectrum; it affected those both high and low on the social scale, free individuals and slaves. A free woman had as little right to vote in ancient Greece as a male slave did.

This did not mean that women had no influence on their societies at all. As we see in some sources, women could influence political decisions in indirect ways. Here we must draw a line between women of different social and marital statuses. Ancient (male/elite) authors were horrified at what they sometimes called "manly women," who, according to them, had an "improper" influence over political decisions; they were part of conspiracies, influenced decisions related to war, or both. In cases such as these, we are dealing with women from the upper strata of society, who were married to, or mothers of, influential and important men. These men could be emperors or governors of Roman provinces (in both the east and the west), and their positions indirectly opened up the path for the women related to them to have an impact on political decisions. For example, we may note how Berenice appears in official settings with King Agrippa in Acts 25:23, and how, according to Matt 27:19, Pilate's wife attempted to sway the decisions Pilate was making in a court setting.

The political and administrative systems of Greco-Roman society were completely male-dominated,[23] and democracy as we know it today did not exist. Ancient literature does, however, provide us with valuable information about high-ranking women and how they navigated the roles attached to them. These texts show that, despite what we would understand as a repressive political structure, women still possessed the will to power and influence in areas that society was structured to keep beyond their reach. Indeed, many of these women seem to have been successful in their aspirations, despite their lack of access to official political channels.

Another example of how women may have influenced society can be found as we analyze sources relating to different social strata. Wealthy women, without being members of the elite, could still act as philanthropists or patrons and in this manner forge a platform for active participation in society, achieving positions of honor outside the domestic sphere. In this context, marital status plays a minor role. There are examples of married and unmarried female patrons, as well as widows. Legally, women had a valid claim to parts of their husbands' fortunes, but they could also have achieved wealth themselves, sometimes even supporting their husbands financially.[24] Women could, thus, use their own financial assets—not only their influential husbands or sons—to exercise a degree of power and achieve a standing in society.

By donating money to various undertakings, such as building projects, these women managed to make a name for themselves and were honored in inscriptions and sometimes even with statues by those who benefited from their donations. Such honors were displayed in public space and therefore made these women visible in society. They could be honored with titles normally conferred on men, but there is some debate regarding how we should interpret these sources. These debates concern the next level of society that we will soon discuss: the association level. Were these titles merely honorary titles lacking real meaning, or did the conferring of a title mean that women could in essence occupy the same position as a man? Where political administration in a polis is concerned, the latter is highly unlikely when one considers the overwhelming evidence pointing in the opposite direction. However,

23. Of course, we have examples from Greco-Roman, Egyptian, and Jewish societies of high-ranking women in political roles, such as queens, but these are exceptions to the rule.

24. Stegemann and Stegemann, *Jesus Movement*.

in an association the situation may not have been the same, and therefore we will delve deeper into this issue below. But before we do this, we will take a brief look at the role of women in what we would call religious settings at the public level.

Women were active in Greco-Roman cultic life at various levels and fulfilled different roles. They could be priestesses and in some cases carry out sacrifices. Women could also have prophetic functions. A variant of this is found in the famous oracle of Delphi, where a woman, Pythia, answered the questions of visitors, who were often prominent men (the answers were often cryptic and had to be interpreted by priests). This institution lost its political power already during the Hellenistic era, even though it was in use until the fourth century CE. In Greek cities, the role of prophet was often considered to be a female function. To remain in the favor of the gods was important in the political sphere as well as in the private sphere, which points to these women contributing to key aspects of society. One should be careful, though, not to overemphasize the role of women in such cultic settings. In the public sphere, men still dominated the scene, since the cultic sphere was intimately connected to the same structure as the polis, in which only men had important roles. Taking a step back, then, it becomes clear that although women played an important part in the cultic lives of cities, men still ultimately held the reins. The practice of religion in the domestic sphere followed a similar pattern; to this sphere we now turn.

Remains of the Temple of Vesta (virgin goddess of hearth, home, and family) in the Roman Forum, in which the eternal fire, the foremost symbol of Roman power, burned. Beside the round temple we find the house of the vestals (Atrium Vestae). The six vestals constituted the female priesthood who were in charge of the temple and the fire. They were chosen when they were young and served the temple for thirty years, after which they were retired. The vestals lived in celibacy during their time as priestesses but could marry upon their retirement. If a vestal broke her vow of celibacy, she was condemned to death. Since the blood of a vestal could not be spilled, those condemned to death were buried alive. Our sources tell us that this punishment was rare, but it was carried out during the reign of Domitian. Photo by Dieter Mitternacht.

The Private Sphere: Women inside and outside the Home

Texts written by (male) authors in antiquity reveal that they considered the home to be the proper place for women. In these texts we even find descriptions of the different ways households could be constructed spatially. In such descriptions, women had their own section of the home, where men were commonly not allowed. This was the case only in the upper strata, however, not the lower; neither can we generalize this to be true for all parts of the Mediterranean world. This detail does reveal, though, the extent of the separation between men and women in the Greco-Roman world, at least in some contexts. The separation was not only political but, in some cases, also private, expressed spatially. Overall, Greco-Roman society was relatively segregated, with men and women assigned different roles and different spheres, resulting in a situation where their paths crossed more rarely than they do today. This does not mean, however, that there was *absolute* gender segregation, something that is supported by our third set of sources, those that speak to the sphere between the private and the public: the associations (see the next section below).

In Greco-Roman society, a woman was more often than not regarded as the man's "property," which also meant that her behavior as a wife or a daughter reflected back on the man. The public honor of the man was therefore linked to the manners and actions of the wife or daughter. If she crossed the boundaries of social role expectations, this would reflect poorly on her husband or father and could tarnish his reputation. It is difficult to ascertain how prevalent such an honor/shame system was in the different strata of society, and we also have to take cultural differences between geographic regions into consideration. Role expectations varied according to a person's social location, but there would also have been differences between geographical/cultural locations. In addition, the texts we have access to today were written by a small minority of which the vast majority were men belonging to the literary elite, and as such they inevitably reflect their biases about how men and women should behave. Overall, this makes it difficult to make generalized statements about the roles of women in antiquity.

The literary constructions of female roles that we find in our sources must be balanced against what we know about the working lives of women. Among both the rich and the poor, we find examples of women who work. Women could own estates, workshops, stores, shipyards, wine industries, and so on. From Ostia we have an inscription about a certain Julia Fortunata, who was involved in the lead pipeline industry, and there are also examples of women leading brick and stone-cutting industries. Lower down on the social scale, we find examples of women who own or work in the weaving and textile industry (cf. Acts 16:14). Poorer women in the lower strata of society could be fisherwomen, nail sellers, makers of wreaths, or leather workers—like Paul's friend and companion Priscilla (Acts 18:2–3; she is also mentioned in Rom 16:3 and 1 Cor 16:19). We also find examples of women working in hotels and as nurses, doctors, midwives, bakers, perfume sellers, writers, and even miners and gladiators. In the countryside, women often worked in the fields. The majority of working women on the lower rungs of society were either slaves or freed slaves; very few were free women.

With this information in mind, we may draw several conclusions. Despite the fact that a few occupations were reserved for men (e.g., carpentry and metal work), and some for women (e.g., textile production), the number of occupations open to both genders is striking. We have already mentioned that Priscilla was a leather worker, but we should add that she shared this occupation with her husband, Aquila. Paul had a related occupation. This must have meant that men and women often worked together, even cooperated, which problematizes the assumption of a complete gender separation in ancient societies, from which would follow only marginal interaction. In everyday life, men and women met not only in the home but also in their professional lives.

It seems that the amount of interaction between the genders increases steadily as one moves lower and lower on the rungs of society, since slaves and freedwomen dominate the sources we have that speak of women who work. However, if we view society as a whole, this means that the majority of the female population worked, since women who were born free constituted a minority of the population. As we noted previously, the literary sources reflect only the upper strata of society and therefore provide us with a skewed view of women. Individuals in the workforce practically never produced literary works, but a minority consisting of elite, literate men did, and it is from them that we have inherited our view of what the "woman's role" in the home and in society consisted of.

The second conclusion we can draw from this is related to the fact that the majority of individuals in the workforce were likely members of guilds. This means that women in the workforce were also part of these institutions, which had certain structural functions in society. This then effects the way we understand the role of women in society—wedged between the public political sphere and the private apolitical sphere. As we will see below, in this observation lies a key to understanding the role of women in Christ groups, whether these groups were Jewish or non-Jewish or mixed.

Associations: Men and Women as Leaders and Members

Greco-Roman society was host to an extensive network of associations. These were not organizations in today's sense but consisted rather of associations of different types that shared a similar organizational structure and, at least in certain periods and cases, had to have the approval of the Roman authorities. There are examples where emperors dismantled associations (except for the oldest ones), which could be perceived by the rulers as facades for underground or political activity disturbing the status quo. For example, in a correspondence between Pliny the Younger and Emperor Trajan, the emperor prevents the establishment of a *collegium* for local firemen in Nicomedia, a city in Asia Minor. The reason for this was the emperor's fear that these associations could potentially begin involving themselves in political activity, something the Roman authorities wished to prevent.

Such imperial measures reveal something about what an association was and how people organized themselves outside the official political and administrative spheres of society. Roman rule exercised limited power over such groups, in which individuals who usually did not have a voice in society could organize themselves in ways that gave them influence, sometimes even beyond the framework of what the association originally intended.

There were many types of associations, and they may be categorized according to the networks from which they drew their membership. Philip Harland has suggested five such basic categories:

1. Household networks
2. Ethnic and geographic networks
3. Neighborhood networks
4. Occupational networks
5. Cult or temple networks[25]

Slaves, freed slaves, and free citizens could all be members of the same association (even though there were associations designated for each specific group, such as only for slaves or free citizens). An association thus provided a somewhat different context for interaction between men and women belonging to different social strata than the political structure did. Many of the associations were more egalitarian in this regard, one could say, although not in the full modern sense of the word.

Among the varied career groups that made up different guilds, we inevitably find working women. The guilds therefore created a platform for interaction between men and women from a more equal point of departure than existed outside their institutional frames. Associations could meet in large private houses of wealthy individuals, in rented space (such as temple dining rooms), in workshops and public baths, and in cemeteries. Some associations had special meeting houses constructed, if they could afford it. There are several examples of such buildings in Ostia. Meetings were held privately, parties were often hosted, and each association included some sort of cult (not only those listed in the fifth category above, which were *exclusively* meant for the worship of a specific deity). The associations also offered social security by taking communal responsibility for the burial of deceased members. Social involvement like this was very common in antiquity.

25. Harland, *Associations, Synagogues, and Congregations*, 28–53.

People were sometimes members of more than one association, which was natural since one's profession alone more or less required participation in networks connected to it. This could place Jews and Christ followers (both Jewish and non-Jewish) in a difficult position, since they worshiped the God of Israel exclusively and therefore could not participate in the non-Jewish rituals that came with membership. In all likelihood, this created tensions and probably led to compromises in individual cases.

For the purposes of this chapter, we may note that Jewish diaspora groups were organized in a pattern very similar to that of the associations (see box 2.4, p. 73). Indeed, Roman authorities considered diaspora synagogues as similar to all the other associations, but regarded them as trusted because of their age. For example, when the emperor dismantled all associations, with the exception of those going back far enough in history, Jewish synagogues were exempted. Presumably, they had proven over time that they did not engage in dangerous activities leading to unrest.

Now, if we look closer at the role of women in these synagogues, we find that not only could non-Jewish men and women be honored as benefactors supporting the construction and/or renovation of Jewish community buildings; Jewish women could also be given leadership titles otherwise assigned only to men. Previously, scholars assumed that these titles were simply honorary titles, void of any real leadership implications. However, this theory is problematic, and an increasing number of scholars are today considering the possibility of women

The association, or guild, of the builders in Ostia met in this building. The smaller rooms to the side of the large hall are called *triclinia*, a type of dining room in which the diners reclined on wide benches. The building is dated to the first half of the second century CE. Photos by Anders Runesson.

occupying leadership positions in synagogue communities.[26] Indeed, as noted in the section "Beliefs and Practices in Second Temple Judaism," p. 114, the sectarian group at Qumran has often been described as an association by scholars. Even in such an association, it has been argued, women could be part of decision-making processes[27] and could occupy leadership positions.[28]

In the same way, older theories claiming that men and women were separated in ancient synagogues have now been discarded. There are no examples of such partitions in any of the excavated synagogues, neither in Israel nor in the diaspora.[29] The division of the cultic room into separate spaces for men and women appeared during the Middle Ages, and the influence of the Christian church on the synagogue in this regard seems likely. In antiquity, as far as the early sources can tell us, men, women, and children gathered in the same room for worship and meetings. There is only one text that describes a low partition between men and women during meetings. This is Philo's description of the sectarian synagogue of the Therapeutae in his work *On the Contemplative Life*. This is, however, a single case without parallels, and no archaeological evidence of the synagogues of the Therapeutae has been found. (In this regard, it may be of interest to note that this particular group, according to Philo, was against slavery and viewed men and women as equals.)

If one understands the synagogues of the diaspora within the framework of Greco-Roman associations, such circumstances are not surprising. Associations offered a different type of setting for men and women to interact than was possible in the public political sphere. Female leadership was not common but nonetheless did exist in some regions around the Mediterranean, as can be seen in the inscriptional evidence that explicitly mentions women as leaders.[30]

Junia: Exception or Rule?

If we return now to the apostle Junia and the question of women in the early Jesus movement, we may draw several general conclusions. First, it should be noted that the earliest Christ followers, like Junia, were Jews and therefore belonged within what we would call a synagogue context. The evidence available points to Christ followers often constituting subgroups within Jewish associations, or synagogues, before they eventually formed their own associations independent of other Jewish groups. This means that the earliest Christ followers were socialized within an institution where women had the possibility of interacting with other (male and female) members on

26. So, e.g., Levine, *Ancient Synagogue*, 509–11.
27. Wassén, *Women in the Damascus Document*.
28. Schuller, *Dead Sea Scrolls*, 95–97.
29. Levine, *Ancient Synagogue*, 500–505.
30. See Brooten, *Women Leaders in the Ancient Synagogue*, for more extensive discussion.

somewhat equal terms and could, potentially, occupy leadership positions. The same would be the case with non-Jewish Christ groups, as they would form in a similar institutional framework of Greco-Roman associations. We should therefore be wary of portraying the position of the first Christ-believing women against the background of Greco-Roman marginalization of women in the public or civic sphere of society. A more productive approach would be to seek an understanding of their position against the backdrop of the organizations in which they existed in their everyday lives—that is, the associations, the social space between the private and the civic. From this perspective, the idea of women as leaders in Christ groups emerges not as unique, but as growing from a broader institutional pattern.

The claim that Christ groups were more radical in this regard than their surroundings is relatively common, and there could very well be a grain of truth in this. The reasoning behind such an argument is usually that Christ groups were more charismatic than other associations, and as such were open to both male and female leadership. Gender was subordinate to charisma in the construction of leadership roles. We have examples from other centuries of charismatic women occupying important leadership roles in Christ groups (e.g., Prisca's and Maximilla's roles within the Montanist movement, which emphasized the end of the ages and the imminent final judgment). However, this has to be balanced against what we know about the Jewish associations, the synagogues, of the first century—and associations in general—and the role of women within them. A charismatic leadership definition cannot be the only factor behind the influence and prominence of women in the early Jesus movement.

But what happened within the majority church that developed during the following centuries? Where did all the women go? This is a complex and difficult question to answer, but, in broad brush strokes, we may think along the following lines. First, the emerging church redefined itself as non-Jewish (see the section "Jewish Christ Followers and the Emergence of Christianity and Judaism," p. 365, for a description of the so-called parting of the ways). In this complicated process, Christ-following non-Jews had to assert their right to form independent associations. To leave the Jewish institutional setting and identity behind effectively meant that they were now identified as independent from the Jewish community, and thus could not claim the rights the Jews already had in Roman society. Various examples indicate that non-Jewish Christ followers were sometimes persecuted and even executed. Had they stayed within the folds of the Jewish community, or synagogue, the risks could have been reduced, since the Jewish way of life, including the refusal to worship local divinities and the emperor, was accepted within the Roman Empire. Outside Jewish communities, Christ followers appeared to constitute a new cult, or "superstition," whose members wanted to organize themselves, and this was politically sensitive.

Because of this, it became more important for (non-Jewish) Christians to present themselves to authorities and others in the societies in which they lived as law-abiding and orderly members of society with a stable organizational structure (cf. 1 Pet 2:13–3:1). In all likelihood, it was during this process that Christ followers increasingly started imitating gender roles in public society and attempting to tone down charismatic aspects of their worship. In such processes, which took place at different times in different places, women were given fewer and fewer opportunities to function as leaders. The Pastoral Letters may be a product of this development (see the section "Successors of Paul," p. 430).

To this may be added the above observation regarding the number of women in the workforce. The higher status a woman had, the less likely she was to be part of the workforce. Thus, interaction between men and women was more common in the lower strata of society, and most—but not all—of our evidence points to the majority of the early Christ followers being members of the lower strata of society. From this follows a greater openness for the active participation of women in these groups. When the (non-Jewish) Christ groups then spread to the upper social strata—even as far as to the political elite—this openness was diminished because of the culture of gender separation prevalent in that part of society. Changes in how Christ followers defined leadership also had an effect, as the leadership shifted from charismatic to institutional. The desire to identify the movement as "normal" and legitimate in an attempt to avoid harassment or worse, and the spread of the Christian faith to the upper echelons of society, all contributed to the marginalization of women in terms of leadership in the emerging majority church. This was the state the church found itself in when, before the end of the fourth century CE, it became the only accepted religion in the Roman Empire. And this was the version of the church that would subsequently spread throughout the world.

In sum, while these processes were extended over time and varied from place to place, there is good reason to suggest that Christian women lost their right to the same titles and leadership roles as men in a process of social adaptation. The daughters of the Jewish Junia and Paul's gentile followers would soon forget what had been a matter of course to their ancestors.

Closing Remarks

As we have seen, it is essential that the primary sources we use in our analysis be organized and categorized, since this helps us acquire a clearer view of ancient society and the role of women in its various spheres and on different social levels. It is clear that the Mediterranean region was dominated by a patriarchal culture, which becomes especially obvious when one studies its politics and cultic cultures. However, this does not mean that women were invisible in society, or that they had no opportunities whatsoever to occupy leadership roles in various contexts. The sources we have access to on women in the workforce and in associations provide important information attesting to this. Nonetheless, researchers are still debating the extent of women's influence in these different social settings. Many scholars, arguing from a minimalistic perspective, have a tendency to emphasize the public and political sphere, where the role of women was indeed limited. As we have attempted to illustrate in this chapter, though, such a one-sided perspective provides us with a skewed and misleading understanding of the historical reality of most women in antiquity.

Owing to limitations of space, the presentation of the Mediterranean world has, of course, been only an overview, with little opportunity to delve into the details. We have not been able to discuss Jewish society in Judea and Galilee, for example, apart from some brief comments on the lack of spatial partitions in synagogues based on gender. To this we may add that there is evidence suggesting that women participated in public meetings of both political and religious nature (the ancients did not distinguish, as many societies and cultures do today, between religion and politics). We know less about the attitudes of the various association synagogues, even though later rabbinic sources provide us with some information about the rabbinic view of the matter. We have also not discussed Jesus's attitude to women, which is a topic meriting its own chapter. We may, however, note here that there were women among his followers, and they accompanied him on his journey all the way to the cross. All four gospels identify the first witnesses of the resurrection of Jesus as women—which is significant since the resurrection is the defining doctrine of what became the church. Several scholars link Jesus's open attitude to women with the roles they would occupy in the first Christ groups after his death.

It is important to be aware that the attitude toward women as active members of Christ groups could vary from place to place. Such differences existed early on in the history of the Jesus movement. We find evidence of this already in 1 Cor 11, where Paul attempts to balance an ideology of equality with the argument that women should be veiled when they prophesy or pray at gatherings, something the women of Corinth clearly did not feel obligated to do. The main takeaway from this passage, however, should be that women did prophesy at these gatherings.

We have also not had the opportunity to discuss the oft-cited text about women in 1 Cor 14:33–36, which seems to stand in opposition to Paul's perspective as it appears in the rest of his letters (in addition to Romans, see also Phil 4:2–3, where two women, Euodia and Syntyche, are said to be Paul's coworkers, struggling together with him to spread the gospel together with Clement and others). What are we to make of the words of 1 Cor 14 that state that women should be quiet during assemblies and ask their husbands any questions they might have only once they returned home? Such a rule seems strange when one considers that earlier in the same letter (ch. 11) women are described as legitimate prophets and are portrayed as publicly praying during gatherings. This contradiction, and the fact that a (western) text fragment shows an uncertainty about where the section should be placed in the letter, has resulted in several scholars suggesting that the passage is a later, post-Pauline addition.[31] This suggestion fits well with what we already know about the later marginalization of women in the Jesus movement as it began developing into what became the mainstream church. A similar development is evident in the Pastoral Letters (1 Tim 2:11–12), which the majority of scholars believe are post-Pauline. It would appear that Paul's followers indeed felt a need to adapt their group's behavior to the social norms of the upper strata of society (see 1 Tim 3:7; 6:1), whereas Paul did not. No matter how one solves this particular problem, the passage remains historically challenging and presents the scholar with contradictions that have to be addressed. For more detailed discussion of Paul and his followers, see the section "Paul, His Assemblies, and His Successors," p. 399.

Much more could be said about the presentation of women in the Gospels—how John lets Martha identify Jesus as the Messiah (John 11:27), whereas Matthew gives this very important job to Peter (Matt 16:16), for example. The aim of this chapter about women, men, and power in antiquity has, however, only been to offer an interpretative tool and a wider framework within which the reader can continue to study local variations and more or less pronounced differences between ancient gender constructions.

Further Reading

Brooten, Bernadette J. *Women Leaders in the Ancient Synagogue: Inscriptional Evidence and Background Issues.* Chico, CA: Scholars Press, 1982.

Cranfield, C. E. B. *A Critical and Exegetical Commentary on the Epistle to the Romans.* 2 vols. Edinburgh: T&T Clark, 1979.

Epp, Eldon J. *Junia: The First Woman Apostle.* Minneapolis: Fortress, 2005.

Harland, Philip A. *Associations, Synagogues, and Congregations: Claiming a Place in Ancient Mediterranean Society.* Minneapolis: Fortress, 2003.

Kloppenborg, John S. *Christ's Associations: Connecting and Belonging in the Ancient City.* New Haven: Yale University Press, 2019.

Kraemer, Ross Shepherd, ed. *Women's Religion in the Greco-Roman World: A Source Book.* New York: Oxford University Press, 2004.

Lefkowitz, Mary R., and Maureen B. Fant. *Women's Life in Greece and Rome: A Source Book in Translation.* 3rd ed. Baltimore: Johns Hopkins University Press, 2005.

31. Wire, *Corinthian Women Prophets*; Witherington, *Conflict and Community in Corinth.*

Levine, Lee I. *The Ancient Synagogue: The First Thousand Years*. 2nd ed. New Haven: Yale University Press, 2005.

MacDonald, Margaret Y. *The Power of Children: The Construction of Christian Families in the Greco-Roman World*. Waco: Baylor University Press, 2014.

Meyers, Carol L. "Was Ancient Israel a Patriarchal Society?" *JBL* 133 (2014): 8–27.

Miller, Patricia Cox. *Women in Early Christianity: Translations from Greek Texts*. Washington, DC: Catholic University of America Press, 2005.

Osiek, Carolyn, and Margaret Y. MacDonald, with Janet H. Tulloch. *A Woman's Place: House Churches in Earliest Christianity*. Minneapolis: Fortress, 2006.

Rowlandson, Jane. *Women and Society in Greek and Roman Egypt: A Sourcebook*. Cambridge: Cambridge University Press, 1998.

Schuller, Eileen. *The Dead Sea Scrolls: What Have We Learned 50 Years On?* London: SCM, 2006.

Stegemann, Ekkehard, and Wolfgang Stegemann. *The Jesus Movement: A Social History of Its First Century*. Edinburgh: T&T Clark, 1999.

Wire, Antoinette C. *The Corinthian Women Prophets: A Reconstruction through Paul's Rhetoric*. Minneapolis: Fortress, 1990.

Witherington, Ben, III. *Conflict and Community in Corinth*. Grand Rapids: Eerdmans, 1995.

3 The Historical Jesus

The term "the historical Jesus" is used to describe a Jew who lived in Galilee at the beginning of the first century, and who was crucified by Roman soldiers outside the walls of Jerusalem around the year 30 CE. He is one of the historical figures from the first century that we know most about (about the same as Julius Caesar and Herod the Great), since we have access to a considerable number of sources about him that were written not too long after his death.

Sources about Jesus

Several ancient sources outside the New Testament mention Jesus. The most important of these is the Jewish historian Flavius Josephus's (ca. 37–100 CE) work *Jewish Antiquities* (see the section "Jewish History from the Persian to the Roman Period," p. 52), which was published in the 90s CE in Rome. Together with his earlier book, *Jewish War*, this is the most important source on Jewish history in the first century both BCE and CE. In the eighteenth volume of *Antiquities*, Josephus writes,

> About this time there lived Jesus, a wise man, *if indeed one ought to call him a man*. For he was one who wrought surprising feats and was a teacher of such people as accept the truth gladly. He won over many Jews and many of the Greeks. He was *the Christ* [Greek for Messiah]. When Pilate, upon hearing him accused by men of the highest standing amongst us, had condemned him to be crucified, those who had in the first place come to love him did not give up their affection for him. *On the third day he appeared to them restored to life, for the prophets of God had prophesied these and countless other marvellous things about him*. And the tribe of

the Christians, so called after him, has still to this day not disappeared. (*Jewish Antiquities* 18.63–64 [Feldman])

Josephus was not Christian, and thus could not have written the italicized text. These words are easily identified as interpolations, added by later Christian copyists or editors. Apart from the interpolations, however, the text appears as a detached, mildly benevolent note by Josephus himself. One need not conclude, however, that the whole passage is a Christian interpolation. The role of the Jewish leaders in the execution of Jesus is mentioned without the critique that often surfaces in the New Testament and other texts by Christ followers. And an author acquainted with the Gospels would hardly have made the mistake of stating that some of the disciples were Greek. Here Josephus probably confuses Jesus's disciples with the Christ followers of his own time, the "Christians" who are "called after him." When Josephus later writes (*Jewish Antiquities* 20.9.1) about how the high priest Ananus (ca. 62 CE) had a certain Jacob killed in Jerusalem, he specifies who this person was by describing him as the "brother of Jesus, the so-called Christ" [Greek: *ho legomenos Christos*]. This specification is so short and without explanation that it is natural to assume that Josephus has recently mentioned this "so-called Christ" in the previous text. Naturally, a Christian interpolator would want to delete Josephus's ironic *ho legomenos*, just as he wanted to "improve" the impression that Jesus was just a "man" or that his execution was his end.

In all likelihood, then, the so-called Testimonium Flavianum quoted above was indeed written originally by Josephus (without the interpolations). His information seems independent of the gospels and was more likely based on his own and not perfectly accurate knowledge of the matter, acquired when he grew up in a priestly family in Jerusalem in the middle of the first century. This makes this text from the late first century a source of prime historical importance: a non-partisan first-century piece of information about Jesus, predating, yet in some aspects corroborating, the Christian gospels.

There is no mention of Jesus in rabbinic literature prior to the year 200 CE, and the references that do occur in the Talmud are not independent sources but rather polemical texts based on and directed against Christian theology concerning Jesus. These texts describe how Jesus was condemned as a sorcerer and someone who misled the people. They also question his lineage, stating that his father was a legionary named Panthera.

Early in the second century, several Roman authors mention Jesus, calling him "Christ." Tacitus writes about how the emperor Nero blamed the fire in Rome (64 CE) on the Christians, and how he punished them with excessive cruelty. He adds that the group was named after a certain "Christ" who had been condemned to death by Pontius Pilate during the reign of Tiberius (he may have based this information on Josephus). This, together with mentions of Christ in the works of Pliny the Younger and Suetonius, represents indirect literary evidence of the historical existence of Jesus of Nazareth.

Christian Sources

The oldest source describing Jesus is a fixed oral tradition that Paul quotes in 1 Cor 15:3–7 (written ca. 55 CE). The tradition is thought to have been formulated in Jerusalem in the early 30s CE. It describes how Jesus was crucified and buried, only to rise again, as testified by a number of witnesses, of which Paul counts himself as the last. From other Pauline letters, we learn that Jesus was a Jew (Gal 4:4), that he was a descendant of David (Rom 1:3), had brothers (1 Cor 9:5), of which Paul met James around 33 CE (Gal 1:19). On the same occasion, he also met one of Jesus's disciples, Cephas (Peter), and interviewed him for two weeks (Gal 1:18). This information, however, only confirms what all serious historians already agree on: that Jesus of Nazareth was a historical individual who lived and died in the land of Israel during the first third of the first century.

An inscription mentioning "Pontius Pilate, prefect (*praefectus*) of Judea" dated to circa 26–37 CE. The inscription was unearthed during the excavations of Caesarea Maritima in 1961. Caesarea Maritima was the residence city of the Roman prefects. The inscription describes how Pilate built a temple dedicated to the emperor Tiberius (r. 14–37 CE). The photograph shows a copy of the original, housed in the Vatican Museum, Rome. The original can be found in the Israel Museum in Jerusalem. Photo by Dieter Mitternacht.

A variety of apocryphal gospels were written by Christian writers in the second century, which attempt to fill in the gaps left by the canonical gospels (such as Jesus's childhood and the period between the resurrection and the ascension), often in rather imaginative or fantastic ways. Among these texts, only one may contain elements of historical value: the Gospel of Thomas. This text is a collection of 114 "Jesus sayings," written in the second century CE (see the section "Secret Gospels: Thomas, Mary, and Judas," p. 463). Several of these Jesus sayings are clearly dependent of the canonical gospels or present a rather un-Jewish Jesus. However, other sayings have a more concise character than their parallels in the New Testament, leading some scholars to assert that the Gospel of Thomas has preserved them in their original form (cf. Mark 12:1–12 with Gos. Thom. 65). Despite these exceptions, it has to be concluded that the Gospel of Thomas contributes only minimally, if at all, to historical knowledge about the person of Jesus.

The conclusion is clear: the four canonical gospels constitute the most important primary sources about the life of the historical Jesus that are available to us. They are much more comprehensive than most other texts, and as a rule they were written closer in time to the events they describe.

The Canonical Gospels as Historical Sources

Despite the fact that the Gospels are the most important sources we have in the quest for the historical Jesus, they have some very obvious deficiencies as resources for historical reconstruction. For example, they are not complete biographies, since—with the exception of the nativity stories in Matthew and Luke (and the story of Jesus in the temple at the age of twelve in Luke 2)—they begin their narratives with the baptism of Jesus, which occurred when he was an adult. In addition, the narratives are not ordered chronologically in a way we can be sure of historically, apart from the fact that the narratives move from baptism to death and resurrection. It is not possible to use the chronological order described in the Gospels as the basis for a historical reconstruction of a sequence of events or of the developing self-awareness of Jesus.

Even such central texts as the Beatitudes, the prayer known as Our Father, and the words of institution of the Eucharist are conveyed differently in the Gospels. In the first three gospels, there is a general similarity in content, while specific details vary quite a bit. Thus, the Gospels do not aim to convey the exact words of Jesus. When one further considers the fact that all the gospels can be dated to around 65–100 CE, according to a majority of scholars, and that they have made use of preexisting oral and possibly textual sources, it is evident that one cannot simply reconstruct an image of the historical Jesus from the plain text of the Gospels. The Gospels as historical sources need to be studied and analyzed thoroughly if one wishes to extract historical information from them, not only because of the problems we have pointed out above, but also because of their bias and their nature as documents representing religious convictions.

The Bias of the Gospels

The gospel that is likely the oldest one, Mark, begins with the following words: "The beginning of the good news of Jesus Christ, the Son of God." So, from the very start, the author is stating the following:

- Jesus was the Christ (the Greek word for "Messiah," the anointed one, a term applied to the kings of Israel).
- This Jesus is in fact God's son, way more than just a normal human or king.
- The story of Jesus is in itself a singularly joyful and meaningful message for the reader, despite the fact that the main character is executed at the end of the story.

This example serves to illustrate the fact that the basic historical information about Jesus is saturated with a deep religious belief that he was sent and equipped by God, and that his entire life was marked by his unique relationship to the divine. The question is whether one can use such deeply biased texts as valid historical sources.

Which Jesus Are We Speaking About?

Is it possible to extract unbiased historical knowledge concerning a person one knows only via accounts written by his most devoted worshipers and disciples? Who is the "real Jesus," the man behind the Christ of faith in which Christians believe? The same question can, of course, be asked in relation to founders of other world religions, such as Buddhism and Islam. The oldest sources about Siddhartha Gautama and Muhammad also come from devoted disciples. Nobody can historically doubt that these individuals existed, but who exactly were they, beneath and beyond the religious traditions within which they have been embedded for centuries?

Can a Historical Human Being Be Fully Understood and Reconstructed?

When answering the question of whether a historical person can be fully understood and reconstructed, we need to take a step back and first note that this is an unrealistic goal for any historical study. Who exactly was Alexander the Great, or Winston Churchill, really? The words "exactly" and "really" indicate a desire to find a deeper and more complete truth, hidden behind the surface "persona" visible to any observer. In Churchill's case, we have access to thousands more pages of historical documentation (along with voice recordings, photographs, and eyewitnesses) than we have about Alexander, but the difficulty of the task does not lie only in the (too small or too large) amount of historical data we have access to. It lies rather in the difficulty of reconstructing in a convincing, testable way who the individual really and truly was behind his or her observable surface. (Do we understand even ourselves that well?) Human beings are much too complex, contradictory, and unfathomable to be well grasped and understood by historical methods.

As historians, we must be reconciled to the fact that we will never be able to reconstruct much more than the visible actions of any historical actor. One should keep in mind that "the historical Jesus" is simply a convenient name for a portrait of him that is based on the comparatively small portion of Jesus's life that historians can study and draw the contours of.

The Divine Cannot Be Investigated

If, on top of the general difficulty of historical reconstruction just mentioned, one also claims that a historical person is in some way divine (both Alexander and Jesus were claimed to be sons of God), the task moves even further away from the domain of historical research. The question whether Jesus really was a commissioned representative ("Son") of the God of Israel, or rather possessed by Beelzebul, is not a historical one, as historical research can answer questions only within human reality. What it ascertains as historical facts must be observable and verifiable by other historians, regardless of their religious convictions. A healing like the one reported in John 9 could rather easily be investigated and found to be a historical fact ("yes, X was blind from birth but now can see"), while the question whether this was a real miracle, that is, effected by an act of God through Jesus, cannot be answered by historical methods.

That is so because a statement on the action of God himself in human reality cannot be corroborated through observation by independent others; historians have to resort to agnosticism on such matters ("we don't know and can't know"). Supernatural occurrences and divine information have to be considered to lie outside the domain that can be investigated by historical research—simply because even if what such sources say *may* be true, they cannot be intersubjectively *known* (by others) to be true. (So, for example, Swedish Saint Bridget's detailed fourteenth-century mystical vision of the birth of Christ is not intersubjective knowledge, and therefore not admissible evidence for historical research on Jesus.)

This is not to say, however, that historians are bound to assume or claim that God does not exist, only that God himself or his decisive action within historical events cannot be investigated or included in historical explanations. Historical research on Jesus does not have an ontology of its own (a fundamental conviction or axiomatic understanding of what really exists or does not exist); it is neither inherently theistic nor atheistic, but simply *agnostic*, that is, aware that God is not knowable as a historical object among others and cannot be fitted into historical reconstructions.

The question of who Jesus actually was can be answered in different ways. The majority of Christians would say that Jesus was actually God's Son, who became human (was incarnated), while those who are not Christian would most likely say that he was a mere human, around whom people have spun religious legends and tales. Since the breakthrough of critically investigative historical research unfettered by church doctrine that occurred in the mid-1700s (conveniently labeled the Enlightenment), the scholarly consensus of Jesus research has been to choose the latter alternative. Most historical investigations of Jesus have taken as a point of departure that he was a normal, ordinary human being who did not much resemble the "divine" image of him painted by the evangelists, with miracles, genuine prophecies, and a grandiose self-understanding.

It should not be denied, however, that this presupposition (Jesus was an ordinary man) is more than the basic methodological decision of the academic discipline of history, made for practical purposes ("practical agnosticism"): historians can investigate only that which is within the realm of normal human reality, and they should leave ontological questions to philosophers. That decision or custom has also been influenced by the rationalistic and naturalistic Enlightenment philosophy with its often anti-Christian and anti-metaphysical bias.

Naturalism is an ontological axiom stating that everything that exists ("nature") can be studied and explained with scientific methods. If any thing or being cannot be so studied, it is a mere figment of the imagination and does not exist. So, for some Jesus historians, the boundaries and limitations of historical method as practiced were seen to constitute the boundaries of reality as well, so that anything that must be placed outside historical treatment (such as miracles, prophecies, the incarnation, God, etc.) is *a priori* nonexistent.

This faulty epistemological assumption of naturalistic historiography has rightly been considered problematic by later historians and scholars in the philosophy of history. It should not be equated with the historical method in Jesus research as such, which operates within the self-selected limitations of practical agnosticism, but refrains from claiming that any *historical* (reconstruction of) *Jesus* is synonymous with the *real* person of *Jesus*.

To sum up the preceding discussion, the following differentiations are useful when attempting to keep the "historical Jesus" separate from the actual or real Jesus:

- *the Jesus of history*: the man Jesus who lived in first-century Galilee and Judea and whose life is just as open for historical study as that of any other historical figure;
- *the historical Jesus*: a scholar's portrait of the Jesus of history, based on data acquired by historical methods;
- *the real Jesus*: the actual person of Jesus—who, like any other historical figure, cannot be fully reconstructed using historical research.

The chapter about the Jesus of history that you are now reading aims only at treating those aspects of him that are accessible to historians. It is thus one variant of the "historical Jesus"—one research-based portrait of a human Jesus rather than an attempt to say who he really was or was not.

How to Find the Historical Jesus

How, then, should one approach the task of achieving a well-grounded, research-based portrait of Jesus? We cannot simply use the four gospels as they stand in order to write history, even if they are the most proximate sources, geographically, chronologically, and personally. Between the ministry of Jesus in Galilee and Judea circa 28–30 CE and the final redaction of the Gospels lie two generations of oral and written tradition in a movement led by his devout disciples, a process that was anything but a collecting of impartial observer reports about Jesus.

Since the beginning of the quest for the historical Jesus in the eighteenth century, a guiding assumption has therefore been that the Gospels in general must be seen as reflecting the life and faith of the early church rather than that of Jesus and his ministry. The conviction that the historical Jesus must have been different from the all-too-Christian portrait of him given in the Gospels led to the application of various sifting processes to the gospel material. Dominant through the whole of the nineteenth century was the idea that source criticism and the search for the oldest strata in the material would lead the researcher to the most reliable historical information about Jesus, information untouched by later Christian accretions such as the miracle stories and claims of divine sonship.

The form-critical school (started by the German scholars Martin Dibelius, Karl Ludwig Schmidt, and Rudolf Bultmann in 1919–1921 and influential throughout a large part of the twentieth century) wanted to go one step further. They and their followers attempted to investigate the thirty-year period of oral Jesus tradition preceding the earliest written sources. They did this through analyzing especially the sayings of Jesus and by applying what they believed to be the laws governing the development of oral tradition into specific literary "forms" (genres). By separating redaction from tradition, and later tradition from earlier tradition, they believed that one could penetrate the thick barrier of Christian oral transmission and interpretation otherwise separating the gospel readers from the "authentic" Jesus. From the form-critical perspective, the task of a Jesus historian was to identify and put aside those parts of the Gospels that might have originated in the oral transmission process between 30 and 60 CE, and that were therefore not authentic.

The basic idea in both source analysis and form criticism was that the tradition was chronologically layered. Since later material was considered always to build on earlier material, the chronologically later was considered "inauthentic" and not reliable enough to be used as a source for historical reconstruction. Thus, the reconstruction of Jesus carried out by source critics and form critics was based only on what they deemed to be the earliest sources within the Gospels.

The Criterion of (Double) Dissimilarity

The main instrument for this separation between authentic and inauthentic sayings of Jesus was the criterion of double dissimilarity, formulated most sharply by Bultmann's pupil Ernst Käsemann in a famous 1953 essay on the problem of historical Jesus research: only those traditions that are dissimilar from Jesus's contemporary Judaism *and* from the early Christian community are to be deemed authentic—that is, delivering reliable information concerning what Jesus said or did. The small core of genuine words of Jesus and a few key acts and events in his life that are thus sifted out from the gospel tradition form the "secure" ground, on which the complete transmission process, from the root—the Jesus of history—up to the four gospels, can be reconstructed.

Criteria and Historical Probability

The weakness of the criterion of dissimilarity is that, when strictly applied, it conflicts with simple historical probability. A thousand fine threads connect everything historical to its surrounding context, both to what preceded it and to what followed it. But the criterion of dissimilarity operates with the opposite basic presupposition, namely that Jesus must have been absolutely unique and disconnected from everything in his own first-century world. Or, put more bluntly, the historical Jesus emerging from this type of approach is (and must be) both thoroughly un-Jewish and un-Christian.

Instead of being a tool for historical reconstruction, the presupposition behind the criterion of double dissimilarity reveals a hidden theological proposition about the uniqueness of Jesus, grounded in a combination of a firm belief in Jesus as a "sane" and "noble" genius (i.e., according to modern requirements) and the Enlightenment-related dislike of both the Jewish and the Christian faith, camouflaged as a principle of historical investigation. To start an investigation of a historical figure from a dogma-like conviction that he was so unique that no one in his time could possibly understand him, or even remember the gist of what he said and did, is an odd way of doing history, marked by a deep distrust of the sources.

In fact, this principle of dissimilarity is not known or used in other fields of historical research, and several scholars have recently urged that it should no longer be used as an instrument of historiography at all. Others think that this criterion could still be useful if modified in various ways, such as altering it into a criterion of single dissimilarity (with early Christianity) and, in doing so, not applying the criterion negatively (to disqualify material as inauthentic). To broaden the core of reliable material further, the criterion should be used together with other criteria of multiple attestation, embarrassment, and coherence—today widely seen as also basically flawed, and with increased awareness of the fact that the discontinuity presupposed is situated within a more pervasive and dominant continuity. Especially the last modification is an important step toward admitting the importance of historical probability in the quest for the Jesus of history.

Form criticism's understanding of oral tradition was based too much on analogies taken from the literary history of folklore through the centuries, which nowadays has been superseded by advances in research concerning memory, memorization, and techniques of transmission; the role of eyewitnesses in the shaping of social memory; and the oral history of a community. Since the criteria approach is organically connected to the basic ideas of form criticism, it must be put under more radical scrutiny and more thorough revision, if not abandonment.

The Criterion of Plausibility

In later years it has been claimed, with good reason, that it is actually better historiography to work from an assumption opposite to that of discontinuity, namely *both* that Jesus was influenced by and interacted with his own Jewish context *and* that he influenced the movement of his disciples and Christ followers that grew from his ministry. This does not rule out that there may have been conflicts between Jesus and his contemporary opponents or that his teaching was hard to follow for his adherents.

A "criterion of plausibility" could be formulated as follows: gospel traditions that both (a) plausibly fit into an early first-century Jewish context and (b) plausibly explain the impact of Jesus on the early Christian movement (e.g., Jesus's teaching on divorce) have a better claim to provide us with reliable historical information about Jesus.

How Should We Reconstruct the Jesus of History?

The initial question of this section still needs an answer: How should historical research on Jesus be carried out? Book-length answers can be given, but for our purposes a shorter summary shall have to suffice. To summarize the previous remarks and their logical extensions into a few guidelines, one could say that historical research on Jesus should be carried out in the following ways.

First, it should be carried out *with less distrust of the historical sources.* Three decades ago, E. P. Sanders wrote against the prevailing pessimism in this regard: "The dominant view today seems to be that we can know pretty well what Jesus set out to accomplish, that we can know a lot about what he said, and that those two things made sense within the world of first-century Judaism."[1] Responsible historiography analyzes and evaluates available sources with a balanced combination of trust and distrust, neither accepting nor discarding the information without reserve. It takes care to include and make sense of all available material.

1. Sanders, *Jesus and Judaism*, 2.

Second, historical research on Jesus should be carried out *with ordinary historical methods*—that is, proceeding from question and hypothesis to verification. The criteria approach is not historical enough, as it entails a problematic shortcut to historical results by starting with a rather unsophisticated process of selection and discarding of source material, in accordance with the historian's preconceived image of the object to be investigated, after which it uses the few remaining details to paint a "historical" portrait of Jesus. Historical results can be had only by following the normal procedure of interrogating the sources and formulating hypotheses of how to interpret and explain all the data. To explain "all data" means finding well-evidenced, larger, overarching patterns of ideas and actions in the gospel traditions with a good general level of probability, not attempting or claiming to reach final confidence concerning the authenticity of any individual saying or story. One's hypotheses should be verified by severe testing, to separate the probable ones from the merely plausible or possible.

Finally, historical research on Jesus should be carried out *with recognition of what historiography can and should achieve.* It should not be viewed as capable of completely "reconstructing the past," and even less reconstructing the "real Jesus." Past reality is represented by narrativized memories in the sources and made sense of, interpreted, by the modern historian. In this kind of work, the historical sources do not and cannot lead to one specific image of the past Jesus and exclude all others. The historian can aim only at presenting a reasoned, historically grounded image of Jesus.

The Origins of Jesus

When, Where, and How Was Jesus Born?

That Jesus was born in Bethlehem is something we are reminded of every Christmas, and as the calendar year count begins at the time of his birth, he should logically have been born in the year 1 (sometimes incorrectly called "year 0"). Historians, however, question both of these statements, mostly the "when."

The two evangelists that recount Jesus's birth say that it occurred in Bethlehem (Matt 2:1; Luke 2:4–6). This, however, agrees almost too well with the prophet Micah (5:2): "But you, O Bethlehem of Ephrathah, who are one of the little clans of Judah, from you shall come forth for me one who is to rule in Israel, whose origin is from of old, from ancient days" (in other words, a new David, the Lord's anointed). Such astonishing agreement between a prophecy and statements about Jesus's place of birth raises the suspicion that Bethlehem is mentioned by the two evangelists simply to create harmony and confirmation between a biblical prophecy and an event in Jesus's life, not because Jesus actually was born there.

Suspicions, however, prove nothing. The question of historical probability is influenced, not determined, by the fact that the two historical sources that speak of Jesus's birth "want" him to have been born in Bethlehem. It is important to remember that the presence of a theological agenda in a statement does not in itself undermine the historicity of its information. Does a certain *Tendenz* (bias) create history, or does history create the *Tendenz*? Both are possible hypotheses, and further arguments are necessary in order to determine which is the most likely.

What position, then, does a historian take on Matthew's and Luke's claims of a *virgin birth*, that Jesus was conceived without a man's participation? Academic historians do not use categories such as "impossible" or "must have happened," but rather speak in terms of degrees of probability. Since both sources, despite their common tendency of glorifying Jesus, say that Mary became pregnant without her husband Joseph—which in this culture was shameful for both Jesus and his mother—this information should be deemed "probable." The evangelists' information as to how the conception occurred—that God's spirit somehow created an embryo in Mary's womb that became Jesus—does not agree, however, with what is known of human biology, and must therefore be deemed as highly unlikely from a historical perspective.

The fact that none of the other New Testament writings mention the virgin birth is sometimes interpreted as evidence that the authors of these texts did not believe in it. This is, however, only an argument based on silence—that is, no argument at all, as silence in historical sources cannot be interpreted as either confirming or denying anything that they do not mention. Matthew, Luke, and the early Christ followers would probably have agreed that the virgin birth is highly unlikely and lies outside of the boundaries of what may be considered possible in normal human history. For them, however, this unlikeliness would probably rather have confirmed that the virgin birth belonged to the category of miracles: direct divine intervention in the bodies and lives of human beings.

Box 3.1
When Was Jesus Born?

According to the narrative of Matthew's and Luke's Gospels, Jesus was born during the reign of Herod the Great. Matthew also tells us that the king sent his soldiers to Bethlehem to kill all boys who were two years or younger (Matt 2:16). The gospel narratives seem to contradict the historical fact that Herod's death occurred in 4 BCE. Taking these two bits of information together, we may infer that Jesus was born at least six or seven years before the beginning of the Common Era (CE). Consequently, "the birth of Christ" is a chronological term—an imagined point in time—that occurs, as a result of a miscalculation, six or seven years after the actual time of Jesus's birth. In the beginning of the sixth century, Dionysius Exiguus introduced Rome to the idea of numbering years by the incarnation of Christ, rather than by Roman emperors. He determined Jesus's birth, incorrectly, to 754 years after the founding of the city of Rome.

Jesus's Family and Social Setting

The most detailed description of Jesus's family is found in Mark 6:1–6, which recounts a visit that Jesus makes to his hometown, Nazareth in Galilee. Surprised at what Jesus says in their synagogue, the audience cries out, "Where did this man get all this? What is this wisdom that has been given to him? What deeds of power are being done by his hands! Is not this the carpenter, the son of Mary and brother of James and Joses and Judas and Simon, and are not his sisters here with us?" From this we may conclude that the family of Jesus consisted of the parents, five identified sons, and two or more daughters. Because really poor families had no chance of feeding this many mouths, the number of surviving children in Jesus's family indicates that his family did not belong among the destitute.

There are several indications that Jesus grew up in a traditional and religiously observant family. He and his brothers all received biblical names, and he and his family made pilgrimage to Jerusalem every Passover (Luke 2:41; cf. John 7:2–10, where pilgrimage on Sukkoth is also mentioned). This was a physically and economically strenuous journey that far from every Galilean Jew undertook. The adult Jesus is described in the Gospels as never setting foot in any large cities in Galilee, such as Sepphoris or Tiberias, and visits only on exception non-Jewish settlements. It may therefore be assumed that Jesus and his family belonged to "the faithful in the land," a conservative, rural population that was careful to observe the law and prevent their Jewishness from being influenced by non-Jewish surroundings.

This may partly explain why Jesus appears so well versed in his tradition's Holy Scriptures, as well as the contemporary methods of discussing the contents and applications of these. Indeed, according to Luke 4:16–19, he could read from the Hebrew Bible (Aramaic was the spoken common tongue), which is worth noting in a society in which, scholars estimate, only around 10 percent of the population was literate. It is also plausible that Jesus, like many other Jews in the Galilean mixed population, could speak at least a few words of Greek for basic purposes.

Jesus's childhood, teenage years, and professional life as a "carpenter," or artisan (Gk. *tektōn*, referring to someone who works in hard materials such as wood or stone), go practically unmentioned in the Gospels—probably because these years of his life were not all that remarkable. It is likely that Jesus was unmarried and had been working the same job as his father for around fifteen to twenty years when he left home for good and emerged from the obscurity of Nazareth.

John the Baptist as the Mentor of Jesus

The first thing mentioned about the adult life of Jesus, by all four gospels, is that he was baptized by John the Baptist in the river Jordan. This says a great deal about Jesus.

The Church of the Nativity in Bethlehem marks the location where Jesus, according to tradition, was born. The church, which has been remodeled and extended incessantly over the centuries, was first built in the fourth century. Photo by Anders Runesson.

John was a stern prophet who emphasized judgment and repentance in the classic biblical style, attracting droves of people to him. His preaching, briefly summarized, aimed at communicating that God's judgment would soon be passed on all God's people and that there was no protection against this devastating encounter with God's righteousness except repentance, expressed and confirmed by the cleansing action of allowing oneself to be baptized in water by John himself. Repentance was necessary specifically for the people of the covenant, the Jewish people—even those considered the most pious among them.

John made no exception for the powerful, and openly opposed his ruler, Herod Antipas, for breaking God's holy law by marrying his still living brother's wife (Matt 14:3–4; Luke 3:19; the prohibition mentioned in Lev 18:16). Of course, he knew that such a reprimand would question the political legitimacy of the leader in the eyes of his Jewish subjects, and that direct provocation of the political power put one's life in danger. All the same, John entered his role as Elijah (Sir 48:10), the prophet that God would send to cleanse and prepare his people, especially by confronting unrighteous rulers who led the population to ruin through their disobedience to God. John's death as a martyr for God's truth emphatically confirmed his prophetic authenticity and courage—just as it did Herod's guilt—for Josephus (see *Jewish Antiquities* 18.116–19), Jesus, the evangelists, and many other Jews.

John may indeed be called the mentor (educator, supervisor) of Jesus, since Jesus learned from and aligned himself with John on multiple important matters:

1. Jesus allows himself to be baptized by John, which indicates that he agrees with John on the matter of Israel's need of repentance and wishes to be a part of the necessary preparation for the impending judgment. Both John and Jesus saw the covenant not as protection against God's judgment but rather as a reason for repenting.
2. The origins of Jesus's calling and his work lie in the work of the Baptist, and when John died, Jesus wished to continue this work—perhaps even with John's baptisms as well (John 3:22; 4:1–2). Jesus saw himself and John as messengers of God, sent as a pair to accomplish radical repentance in his people Israel. God's attempt to reach his people through John and Jesus is, however, refused by many, especially by the Jewish leaders.
3. When Jesus is asked the serious (and dangerous) question as to what authority he has to disturb the peace in the temple in Jerusalem the way he did, he answers with a reference to John's authority to baptize for the forgiveness of sins (Mark 11:27–33). The answer is not an evasion but an argument: just as God has authorized John to provide forgiveness outside of the temple's prescribed methods, so too has God authorized Jesus when he acts against the temple. This implies a severe criticism of the contemporary priesthood's way of managing the temple, a criticism that Jesus took over from John.
4. Both John and Jesus reckon with a prophet's fate for themselves: martyrdom (Matt 17:12–13; Luke 13:33). Jesus seems to have seen important aspects of his own life as formed after the Baptist's. Additionally, John's violent, unjust death for admonishing a ruler may have been interpreted by Jesus as an indication of what his own end would look like.

Jesus did, however, carry out his task in a manner that in many aspects differed from that of his mentor. Ultimately, he even placed his own mission above that of John. Sure, repentance is important in the face of impending judgment, but Jesus puts far greater emphasis on the kingdom of God—*already present*—healing, freeing, and pardoning people who wish to receive it. This is for Jesus a joyous reality: already *now*, one can be freed, cured from disease, both in body and spirit, and salvation begins *now* for the most unlikely of groups (Matt 5:3–12). He emphatically highlights God's mercy, which is demonstrated not least by the fact that he did not choose an ascetic role out in the desert but rather visits "tax collectors and sinners." Jesus eats and drinks with those lacking in religious "merits," who do not care about God or his laws. In doing so, he brings them into communion with himself, and thereby the kingdom of God (Luke 7:33–34).

What John did and said is for Jesus something true and admirable: "Among those born of women there is no one greater than John," yet the kingdom is unfathomably greater (Luke 7:28). Therefore, Jesus identifies John with Elijah, who, according to the prophet Malachi's book, is the great preparer of the arrival of the Lord (Mark 9:12–13). Unstated, yet quite clear, is that Jesus ascribes to himself a more central role in the kingdom than John—the role of the one who performs and completes rather than the one who prepares. This interpretation, of course, also became that of the Christian church.

The Kingdom of God: The Center of Jesus's Proclamation

After his baptism by John the Baptist, Jesus chose the public sphere as his way of living and teaching, since he wanted to be heard by and make an impression on many. He stays in the populated regions around the Sea of Galilee, where he wanders from place to place, speaks in synagogues and in open-air settings, heals the sick, and acts publicly. It is clear that Jesus sees himself as having a task that involves all of Galilee's Jews—indeed, all of the Jewish people, since he also visits and preaches at the center of the Jewish religion, the holy city of Jerusalem.

Jesus's contact with non-Jews, however, is minor and of a temporary nature. It is almost unwillingly that he sometimes heals people who are not Jewish. Matthew the evangelist allows him to summarize his mission accordingly: "I was sent only to the lost sheep of the house of Israel" (Matt 15:24). This attitude is seen in both his social network and the passion that drives his whole mission. It is his own people, Israel, that he wishes to return to the Shepherd (God). He wants them to open themselves to God, so that God's kingdom can be opened in turn to them.

In the Hebrew Bible, "the kingdom of God/heaven" refers to God's dominion over creation (Ps 95) and his chosen people, Israel. The biblical hope is, then, that this dominion will spread and be established worldwide, with Israel at the center. In the time of Jesus, the expectation of the coming kingdom most commonly took a political form, focused on the nation of Israel. God will, through a new anointed king in Jerusalem, a new "David" or Messiah, liberate the Jews from Rome and all tyrants. This was also the conviction among certain groups within the Jesus movement, as we see in Acts 1:6–7. Some Jewish groups also looked further than the boundaries of the nation and hoped for a future in which Israel would rule over all other nations (cf. Matt 18:18–20).

There was, however, no uniform idea among the Jews of what such a process would look like. The eschatological future could be imagined either with or without a messiah. In the texts preserved we can observe large-scale, cosmically inclusive variants as well as more politically oriented visions. In the former, the divine is expected to break through into our time and world, which is then destroyed in a final judgment, after which God creates a completely new world (e.g., Isa 65). There are also more introverted interpretations, where the kingdom of God means that the hearts of first all Jews and then all others will be transformed, bending to God's will.

Area around Lake Tiberias (Sea of Galilee), where Jesus began his ministry and gathered his first disciples. Photo by Anders Runesson.

That the kingdom of God was central to Jesus's teachings is demonstrated by the fact that the term is used around one hundred times in the Gospels (but very seldom in any other Christian text). God's dominion on earth was, for Jesus, not the same as what we would call political success (including over other peoples) but rather—as for the Baptist—a total transformation and an ultimate act of God, mixed with strong elements of final judgment and a new creation. "The kingdom," then, is the state of things emerging after God has intervened, ultimately, in order to judge and bring salvation to humankind. Nobody can expect to be saved automatically, not even the people of the covenant.

The Kingdom Is Here Now, but Not Yet

What was unusual in Jesus's proclamation of the kingdom of God was his belief in its proximity and immediacy. The kingdom is so close that it can be noticed by those who "have ears and eyes," and every person must make a decision to become part of it, here and now. How persons, or a collectivity like a city, respond to Jesus, in faith or lack thereof, will determine whether they will ever enter the kingdom of God. Jesus says in Matthew's Gospel, "Woe to you, Chorazin! Woe to you, Bethsaida! For if the deeds of power done in you had been done in Tyre and Sidon, they would have repented long ago in sackcloth and ashes. But I tell you, on the day of judgement it will be more tolerable for Tyre and Sidon than for you" (Matt 11:20–22).

According to the evangelists' Jesus, one can enter the future dominion of God already in the present by entering into communion with him—believe in his word, obey his (interpretation of God's) commandments, break bread with him, change one's life according to his teachings. It seems, therefore, that Jesus claims that his person somehow unites the future with the present, and that because of this the coming dominion of God is here *now*, in and through him. "But if it is by the finger of God that I cast out the demons, then the kingdom of God has come to you" (Luke 11:20). In Matt 11:2–6, John the Baptist, through his disciples, asks Jesus, "Are you the one who is to come, or are we to wait for another?" Jesus answers, "Go and tell John what you hear and see: the blind receive their sight, the lame walk, the lepers are cleansed, the deaf hear, the dead are raised, and the poor have good news brought to them. And blessed is anyone who takes no offense at me." The answer is formulated with words from the book of Isaiah about the time of salvation/redemption. Jesus's reply thus implies that his intention was to challenge John to use this quotation from Isaiah as an interpretative key to Jesus's actions and understand that the answer is "Yes, I am the one."

Model of Jerusalem at the time of Jesus, looking toward the north with the Antonia Fortress and the temple on the far right. The model can be seen at the Israel Museum, Jerusalem. Photo by Anders Runesson.

The Kingdom Requires Repentance

To be able to accept the change of reality that is "the kingdom of God," the individual must also change. Mark 1:15 summarizes Jesus's preaching as "the time is fulfilled, and the kingdom of God has come near; repent, and believe in the good news." The biblical term "repentance" designates an inner change (from the heart) and its manifestation in the person's outward actions. To turn away entirely from evil and selfishness, and in every aspect of one's life strive to realize God's dominion, is to truly believe in the news of the kingdom.

What, then, does God's idea of a righteous human life look like, according to Jesus? In terms of content, he presents no new ethics: one shall act with good intentions toward all humans, even the enemy, and not judge, curse, or reject but forgive, bless, share, speak truth to, and love all others as oneself. Faithfulness, including sexual faithfulness, is a matter of course (so much so that marriages are indissoluble; see Mark 10:9–11; Luke 16:18), as is generosity and absence of greed, as well as compassion and mercy in interaction with others. One should not be fixated on or worried about food and clothes, nor live to attain material security, but rather trust that God is a merciful Father. One should strive to copy that mercy: the marginal and weak are of particular interest to God, and they are his representatives on earth; how one treats them is a measure of true goodness and love.

Jesus is clearly suspicious of money and ownership, which he views as God's primary rival (next to family; see Matt 10:37; Luke 14:26). Money self-evidently corrupts humans and prevents them from entering the kingdom of God. The same goes for those precious things called status and honor, which originate in others' appreciation ("Woe to you when all speak well of you" [Luke 6:26; cf. Matt 5:11–12]). Both money and status are idols, strong driving forces that compete with God for the principal place in a human's life. It is necessary, in this regard, to prioritize: "But strive first for the kingdom of God and his righteousness, and all these things will be given to you as well" (Matt 6:33).

Of decisive importance is allowing God's demands to penetrate so deep into one's own consciousness and actions that good deeds do not become superficial and merely constitute an external pattern of (pretended) piety. A person's deeds and thoughts need to be solid, honest, and, quite simply, undivided in terms of purpose. Jesus is an enemy of hypocrisy, pretense, and half-heartedness. For this reason, good deeds must be carried out with love for God and one's neighbor, and not in a way that is meant only to attract attention and gain status in the eyes of others (Matt 6:1–18).

Symbolic Actions

Prophets in the Hebrew Bible performed symbolic actions as a (pedagogical) means of enhancing and clarifying their preaching, such as when Jeremiah crushed a pot as a prophecy of the catastrophe that would befall Jerusalem (Jer 19), or when Isaiah walked around naked for three years to make a point about the precarious situation of Egypt and Ethiopia in relation to the then powerful Assyria, in order to warn his own people, or when Hosea enters into a deliberately failed marriage that served to demonstrate the relationship between God and Israel. Jesus, too, was not only a speaker; he also carried out many telling actions. He ate with "sinners," he touched unclean people, he chose twelve men to be near him, he played the role of the righteous king riding into Jerusalem on a donkey (Zech 9:9), and on one occasion he violently prevented commerce in the temple involving sacrificial animals and currency exchange.

Within this category of telling actions, we also find Jesus's healings, exorcisms of demons, and other miracles, which many scholars today are inclined to see as historical occurrences, even though they cannot explain them historically. These healings were performed, of course, to help people in need, but were also meant to communicate a message: this is what the kingdom of God looks like. Or perhaps: this *is* the kingdom of God. God wishes to grant you a healthy life like this—no more disease, no more hunger, and no more death. His healing encompasses the entirety of the human being, not just the body. In the kingdom there are no lies or pretense, no injustice, no sin, and no guilt.

The Jesus of the Gospels does not focus on socio-ethical issues or the need for political freedom, and does not initiate a program for social reform, as we would define these terms. However, his caring for the sick and hungry, together with his sharp criticism of the demonic power associated with money and of the violent rampages of rulers, embody the promise of change for the better with God's dominion—a change also affecting the political reality. Religion and politics cannot be easily separated from each other, especially not in a deeply religious culture. If society and its basic institutions are built around a divine revelation, such as Torah in ancient Judaism (or *sharia* in Muslim states), then a prophet or theologian who is heard and believed by many is a very real political factor in that society. One who preaches a new "kingdom of God" questions the contemporary political dominion. Therefore, criticizing rulers or authoritative teachers as not obeying God, or not being able to see what God truly wants, is a revolutionary and, in the long term, dangerous thing to do. The political dimension of Jesus's proclamation of God's kingdom is undeniable.

Jesus—a Charismatic in Word and Action

Jesus attracted droves of listeners, help seekers, and the curious. The primary reason for this was probably his reputation as a powerful healer and exorcist, a reputation that was confirmed on multiple occasions at multiple locations. However, Jesus also seems to have attracted attention by the way he preached: "They were astounded at his teaching, for he taught them as one having authority, and not as the scribes. . . . They were all amazed, and they kept on asking one another, 'What is this? A new teaching—with authority!'" (Mark 1:22, 27). Jesus's persona is typical of the kind of authority that is called "charismatic." The speech of a charismatic draws its authority from the person's personal power, which is manifested both in the content and form of delivery of the message and in powerful actions that confirm it.

The content of Jesus's public preaching was similar to that of John the Baptist and the biblical prophets, in their demand for repentance and "righteousness"—that is, an obedience to God that surpassed even that of the most pious (Matt 5:20). At the same time, he emphasized the promise of the kingdom, or dominion, of God, which was so close that its power could change reality itself for those willing to accept it. Jesus thus takes up his own religious tradition's promises and demands but claims that these promises are already being fulfilled by God in the here and now, which is why there is currently nothing more important than to listen to and trust in Jesus's proclamation and act accordingly.

The way Jesus said this was distinct. He never referred to the interpretative traditions of earlier teachers or used the biblical prophetic formula "Thus says the Lord." He spoke with his own authority and laid claim to being one who (or even *the* one who) completely knows, understands, and mediates the will of God. Furthermore, it is apparent, even in the Greek translation of Jesus's Aramaic, that he was rhetorically skilled. Jesus used clearly formulated, powerful sentences, often structured as rhythmical and easily memorized parallelisms, and was a master of using imagery both in short comparisons and in longer parables.

Finally, Jesus could demonstrate, his followers were convinced, his word's power by turning it against disease, forcing it to leave a human's body. Word and action become two sides of the same coin, where the coin is the preaching of God's kingdom. In an ancient religious context, such palpable physical confirmation of the words spoken would be interpreted as the speaker truly having a mission from God, *or* that the speech and power came from the other supernatural power, the devil (Mark 3:22).

Jesus's Followers and Disciples

It is typical for a charismatic to be surrounded by a group of people who strongly believe in the charismatic's divine inspiration/power and authority, and who therefore willingly place themselves under this person's leadership. Jesus, being a charismatic, also became such a leader. He was followed from place to place by people (men and women, Luke 8:1–3) who left their own families and work to be his "full-time disciples," sharing his life and being shaped by his way of thinking, speaking, and acting. From this group of people, Jesus selected an inner circle of twelve disciples.

The relationship between Jesus and the inner circle of disciples lacks parallels in the contemporary culture, where known master-disciple relations had more of a school character. For Jesus's inner circle, the emphasis lies on the twelve disciples simply being with their master. Their primary task was still in the future. Jesus promises, according to Matt 19:28, "Truly I tell you, at the renewal of all things, when the Son of Man is seated on the throne of his glory, you who have followed me will also sit on twelve thrones, judging the twelve tribes of Israel." His vision of the future is that all twelve tribes, several of which no longer existed in his own time, would be reconstituted and united as a single Israel, and that the twelve near him would be rulers of one tribe each, under the king. This tradition very likely originated with Jesus himself, since neither in the early church nor in the Jewish people such a ruling group of twelve was ever put in place, which would have caused a need to invent such a tradition in order to seek legitimacy. This enormous, but not yet fulfilled, promise may be the reason behind the disciples' discussion on several occasions—against Jesus wishes (Mark 9:33–37; 10:35–45; Luke 22:24–30)—as to which of them would be the foremost (when Jesus becomes king, who among us will be prime minister?).

Jesus the Teacher

Although the disciples had not been chosen for their academic merits, one of their tasks was to receive education from Jesus and learn his way of thinking. In this teaching, Jesus made use of the pedagogy of his time: *rote learning* (memorization). The teacher summarized, in densely formulated sentences or stories, several points that he wanted the students to memorize. This summary was drenched with repetition, rhythm, and rhymes, such that it would be easy to memorize, and was then repeated word for word by the disciples until they could recite it from memory (four times given and four times repeated being enough for well-trained disciples). Thereafter, the memorized lessons could be brought up and used in later teachings.

Jesus in all likelihood told his parables more than once and would likely have returned many times to the core sayings of his preaching, both publicly and among his full-time disciples. His teaching spanned over a period between one and three years, and what he said was obviously much more than the Gospels record—an entire gospel may be read aloud in a few hours. That which *is* recorded in the Gospels probably represents a selection, processed by memory and the Christian faith, of the core information, that which was repeated most often and with most emphasis during the disciples' lessons. It is therefore likely that the disciples had, already while Jesus was alive, a good amount of memorized teachings from their master that they could use themselves—for example, when he sent them out to proclaim the kingdom of God with words and healings (Matt 10; Luke 10). As is usual in oral tradition, the central elements of certain teachings and memorable events would have been formulated quite firmly, whereas the details would have varied every time the speech/event was retold.

It is not impossible that parts of Jesus's teachings were *esoteric*—that is, reserved for the disciples that followed him. For most of Jesus's parables there is no explanation, but where there is one, it is given specifically to the disciples, not to everybody. For the occasional listener, according to Mark, the parables concealed the secrets of God's kingdom, but for the disciple, Jesus wished to reveal the hidden meaning (Mark 4:10–12). To understand what the kingdom actually is all about, one needs to have a follower relationship with Jesus. This is applicable perhaps even more to the intimate relationship between the kingdom and Jesus's own person, which eventually becomes so clear to the disciples in their own experience, but which is never actually formulated publicly. The same secrecy characterizes the accounts regarding the necessity of his passion, his suffering and death, which was only relayed to an inner circle that neither could nor wished to comprehend it—until afterward.

Jesus's Rivals and Opponents

To know God's law and be able to apply it to the daily needs of the people was a task given to the priestly tribe of Levi. In the time of Jesus, there had emerged groups of other literate text-interpreters, who in the New Testament are called "teachers of the law." It is hardly surprising that all these keepers of a large, authoritative teaching tradition were provoked by the Galilean artisan, who did not have formal education but still claimed he knew more about God's will than they did. Worse yet was that Jesus, despite his claim to represent and mediate God's will and kingdom, chose to socialize with Jews who were evidently worldly and often nonchalant toward the law—so-called sinners. Through his actions, Jesus claimed, he opened the way for their forgiveness, as they put their trust (Gk. *pistis*) in him and repented.

He was also reported to have said things that seemed to contradict the Mosaic law, such as when he claimed that God in fact does not agree with divorce, even though Moses's law allows it as a concession to the hardness of human hearts (Mark 10:1–12; but cf. Matt 19:3–9). In the kingdom, which Jesus claimed was already being established as he carried out his mission, such hardness of human hearts must be no more, and thus, finally, God's original intention, also found in the Torah (in Genesis), would be fulfilled. So, astoundingly, God's will and the law of Moses are not identical. Most Jewish teachers of the law would naturally reject such an idea as totally unacceptable. Jesus himself, on the other hand, accused his opponents of breaking the law (e.g., Mark 7:8, 13; Matt 5:20; 15:3, 6).

Contrary to later Christian perception, Jesus can hardly be understood as neglecting the law of Moses and putting himself above it when it suited him. On two points, however, he seems to have been particularly unconcerned about what the contemporary interpretative elite understood the law to mean, behavior that is typical for a charismatic leader. One of these concerns the laws of ritual purity, which really state only that, in order to come before the face of God and sacrifice in the temple, Israelites must be purified of contact with things unclean. For some contemporary authorities, however, these requirements were understood to reach deep into everyday life, so that ritual purity was required not only in relation to the Jerusalem temple. Yet Jesus comes into contact with all sorts of impurities, as he encounters people with leprosy and a hemorrhaging woman, as well as dead people. He also enters the homes of people labeled "sinners" by the texts. We are not told explicitly about any details as he visits these people, but such remarks may have implied a general understanding of Jesus contracting impurity in such settings. Further, in a discussion regarding purity and impurity that unfolds after an encounter between Jesus and a group of Pharisees from Jerusalem, Jesus is presented as giving a decisive answer on the matter to his audience. Jesus is asked why his followers do not respect the Pharisees' purity rule regarding the washing of hands before a meal, a rule with no basis in the written law (cf. Matt 15:3). In his reply, Jesus places ritual impurity in the larger context of moral impurity. In this way, it becomes clear that, while Jesus does not explicitly reject ritual purity as stated in the written law, he understands moral impurity to be the real concern; without attending to moral purity, ritual purity is of no consequence before God (Mark 7; Matt 15; cf. Matt 23:23–24).

The second point is his position on the Sabbath commandment. Jesus purposely chose to heal sick people also on Saturdays, even though this was considered by many authorities as "work" and should therefore be forbidden on the Sabbath (Luke 13:14). For Jesus, though, what happens around him is to be understood as the coming of the kingdom, and therefore nothing could be more important than the healing of the sick and the feeding of the hungry, since that is what the kingdom is about, to restore the world to God's intentions. If, as both Matthew and Mark claim, Jesus pointed out King David once broke the law in the temple (in Nob) when his men were hungry, would it not be much more right for the Son of David to feed the hungry when the kingdom is being established? And if the priests in the Jerusalem temple break the law as they work on the Sabbath, without being guilty of wrongdoing, why would Jesus and his followers be guilty of breaking the law as they work for the kingdom, which is more important even than the temple (Matt 12:1–8; Mark 2:23–3:6)? Jesus's argument regarding the Sabbath is not only based on a technical debate about how "work" should be defined, although those aspects are involved too, but rests on a more fundamental conviction about what is happening around Jesus—namely, the beginning of the fulfillment of God's eschatological promises. If Jesus and his opponents cannot agree on this, then there is little chance that the latter would accept the former's interpretation of the law, since for Jesus the kingdom constitutes an indispensable frame of reference when the law is to be interpreted. For Jesus, then, it is crucial to know what time it is in order to be able to grasp his teaching on the law.

It is not difficult to understand why this mix of authoritative claims by an unlearned artisan and an attitude toward the law dependent on the conviction that the kingdom is arriving, is already here, would provoke the teachers of the law and the priests, resulting in increased tensions and distrust of Jesus. The truly dangerous enemy, however, was the priestly aristocracy in Jerusalem, which had the real political and judicial power to remove people they saw as a threat to the existing order (cf. John 11:48–50).

Why Did Jesus's Life End on the Cross?

Of the events in Jesus's life, one of the things associated with the least amount of historical doubt is that he was crucified by Roman soldiers in Jerusalem during a Jewish Passover in the beginning of the 30s. However, historical inquiry not only involves stating that something took place; it also attempts to interpret and explain a particular event in relation to a network of other events as well as the aims of the historical agents involved. Jesus's execution has, therefore, often served as a checkpoint, or a criterion of authenticity (in addition to the ones mentioned earlier), in the reconstruction of the historical Jesus. A historical portrait of Jesus must be able to make sense of his death as an understandable consequence of what he did and said. A portrait of Jesus as a meek philosophical conversationalist and helper of people, who was in no real conflict with anybody, has rightly been criticized for not responding to the concerns this criterion aims to give voice to. Why would anybody wish to kill such a nice person? "A Jesus whose words and actions do not disturb or provoke people, especially the powerful, is *not* the historical Jesus."[2]

The Church of the Holy Sepulcher in Jerusalem, located at the site where Jesus was executed and buried, according to early tradition and later scholars. The site has different names, in Western tradition referring to the grave (Lat. *sepulcrum*) of Jesus, in Eastern tradition referring to his resurrection (Gk. *anastasis*). Other graves are also found inside the church walls. Photo by Anders Runesson.

The Key Events of the Passion

Already at the beginning of this chapter it was stated that the Jewish historian Josephus reports, independently of the gospel writers, that Jesus, "due to an accusation from our leading men," was sentenced to death on the cross by the Roman prefect Pontius Pilate. The gospel accounts are far more detailed in their descrip-

2. Meier, *A Marginal Jew*, 1:177.

tions of Jesus's death and the events leading up to it. The story of Jesus's suffering and death is made up of around twenty sections with largely the same sequence of events in all four gospels: the decision of the Jewish authorities in Jerusalem to eliminate Jesus, the last supper with the disciples, the betrayal of Jesus by one of his own, the arrest in Gethsemane, the hearing before Jewish authorities, the Roman trial and sentencing, the crucifixion, Jesus's death, and finally his burial.

All the evangelists agree that, in this sequence, the active group on the Jewish side is the Jerusalemite priestly aristocracy, with scribes and elders in the background. The Pharisees are not involved at all in this process. Those who arrest Jesus in Gethsemane are sent by the high priest and probably represent a group from the temple police (only John includes Roman soldiers).

After the nightly arrest, Jesus is brought to the high priest Caiaphas, where, Mark and Matthew report, a kind of hearing takes place. Luke and John have no nightly "trial," but all four write about a council session early on the Friday morning, which decides to deliver Jesus to the Roman judicial system.

In the scene where Jesus stands before Pilate on the Friday morning, Mark and Matthew emphasize Jesus's complete silence, and all four gospels reports the unwillingness of the governor to judge him; Luke alone says that Jesus was brought before the Galilean (vassal) ruler Herod Antipas, to whom he does not say a word. John includes an entire dialogue between Pilate and Jesus.

The end is the same: Pilate sentences Jesus to the cross; he is flogged (Mark and Matthew), receives help in carrying the cross from Simon of Cyrene (not in John), and finally is crucified. In Mark and Matthew, Jesus remains completely silent, save for a final cry of "*Elōi elōi lema sabachtani*," which Luke and John do not include; as if compensating for this, they have Jesus speak several times. Jesus dies in the afternoon of the same day that he was crucified and is buried before sundown.

The extensive overall agreement about the most significant events of the passion—despite several differences in the details—between the Synoptic Gospels and the Gospel of John speaks in favor of the hypothesis that the first generation of Christ followers had access to a basic story of the passion. In other words, it is probable that the passion narrative is older than all the gospels.

Box 3.2
The Day and Year of Jesus's Death

The four canonical gospels agree that Jesus was crucified and died on a Friday, then laid in a tomb shortly before the beginning of the Sabbath; further, that the women who saw this and wished to anoint his body did not go to the tomb on the Sabbath (Saturday) but waited until early Sunday morning, when they (or she: according to John, only Mary Magdalene) discovered that the tomb was empty.

Relating this to the first-century Jewish calendar, one should keep in mind that a new day begins with the setting of the sun. Therefore, the Sabbath begins at sunset on Friday evening and lasts until sundown on Saturday. According to Matthew, Mark, and Luke, Jesus's last supper with his disciples was a Passover meal, prepared on Thursday, the fourteenth of Nisan, and eaten as soon as the setting sun had initiated the fifteenth of Nisan. From John 18:28 we learn that the council members who delivered Jesus to Pilate did not want to enter his residence, as this would have made them ritually unclean and therefore unable to partake in the consumption of the Passover lamb on the evening of the same day. Also, according to John 19:31, Jesus's death occurred toward the end of the day of preparation, when thousands of paschal lambs were slaughtered at the temple of Jerusalem. This would entail that the dead Jesus was already in his tomb when the Passover meal began for all other Jews in Jerusalem.

While a majority of scholars sees a discrepancy here between the Synoptics and John (Brown, 1994), some have recently argued that all four gospels agree that both the last meal and the crucifixion of Jesus occurred on the fifteenth of Nisan (Pitre, 2015).

As for the year of the death of Jesus, we need to take into account that the Jewish calendar was (and is, like the Muslim and Chinese calendars) a lunar calendar. The beginning of a new month—and thus also a new year—was decided according to the cycle of the moon. Nowadays, we can determine the astronomically precise time for a new moon (and month) in any year and place on our planet, and so we can find out which years around 30 CE had the fifteenth of Nisan on a Friday. But in the first century the determining of a new month was dependent on the actual sighting of the new moon by two reliable witnesses. If clouds prevented the sighting—which we cannot know from a distance of two thousand years—the new moon/month had to be postponed at least one day. This and other uncertainties affecting the calendar (the need for inserting an extra month in order to fit agricultural realities and the increasing discrepancies between the lunar and the solar year) make it necessary to conclude that, based on astronomy, we cannot know exactly which year and day Jesus was crucified. The nearest approximation would be that it was on a date in March or April, in a year not earlier than 30 CE or later than 33 CE.

The Trials of Jesus

Josephus and the evangelists agree that both Jewish and Roman authorities were involved in Jesus's death—the former in their accusation against Jesus and the latter (Pilate) in the actual judgment and execution. Both must have deemed him sufficiently dangerous to necessitate elimination, therefore cooperating to this end.

What is questioned most intensely in terms of historicity is the information about the Jewish council's (Sanhedrin) arrest and hearing of Jesus. This part of the passion narrative has often been attributed to later Christian anti-Judaism.[3] However, even if the Jewish leaders' part in the process eventually leading to Jesus's execution has been used in the horrible history of Christian anti-Semitism as ammunition against Jews, this is not sufficient to undo the historicity of that tradition. The procedure was probably not a formal trial but rather a guilt-confirming hearing with a predetermined outcome, which needed to be completed in a short period of time. There were good religio-political reasons for stopping Jesus, and doing so quickly. Jesus was political dynamite, an unpredictable person with well-known messianic tendencies (e.g., the entry into Jerusalem and his actions in the temple) and a rebellious attitude against authorities (cf. the harsh criticism of the Jerusalemite leadership in the parable of the wicked tenants in the vineyard in Mark 12:1–12). And, importantly, he was popular among the pilgrim masses. The situation was explosive, and making things even worse, Jesus's actions seemed to be founded on a self-perception that to the council members most likely appeared insolent and false, perhaps even blasphemous.

The Jewish leaders' political sensitivity resonated with that of the Roman prefect, whose most important function was to maintain law and order, suppressing everything that could unsettle the pilgrim masses. It was not necessary at all to produce a detailed or even believable formulation of the accusation against Jesus; Pilate would quickly have realized that it was in both his and the Jewish leaders' best interests to eliminate the accused.

Was Jesus Sentenced for Blasphemy?

If blasphemy means to clearly utter and curse the holy name of God, then Jesus did not blaspheme. The definition of blasphemy is in practice, however, much wider than this. The term may also refer to actions or words that are understood to offend God's power and majesty and lay claim to an authority that belongs only to God himself. The accusation against Jesus for blasphemy had at least three components: (a) Jesus's claim to be the chosen agent for God's actions in Israel, as the Son of Man; (b) his perceived threat against the temple; and (c) false prophecy in the sense that he was seen as leading others astray (Matt 27:63; John 7:12, 47). The scene itself, Jesus standing beaten, bound, powerless, and abandoned before the Jewish council, would have spoken against any claims that he was the divine Son of Man. Thus, the conclusion that he must be a liar seems logical. So, yes, in this sense Jesus did blaspheme when he placed himself at the right hand of God—him, a captured rebel and false prophet

3. See, e.g., P. Winter, *On the Trial of Jesus*; Crossan, *Who Killed Jesus?*

who had, at least according to what the texts call false witnesses (Mark 14:56–59), threatened to destroy the temple and in various ways undermined what the authorities were convinced was the correct understanding of the law. Therefore, handing Jesus over to the Roman authorities and seeking the death penalty may have been more for the Jerusalemite leaders than just a measure to secure political stability. The action of the Council could also have been, for some of them (not Nicodemus and Joseph of Arimathea), a necessary and just measure to defend God's honor, and so, at the deepest level, the will of God.

Did Jesus Want to Die as a Sacrifice for the Sins of Others?

That Jesus died voluntarily is evident. He had ample opportunities to flee if he so wished, even at the end—ten minutes from Gethsemane up the Mount of Olives and nobody would have been able to find him. The question is why he chose to be captured and killed. A possible, perhaps even probable, answer could be that he saw it as God's will and part of his calling. He could not have stayed in Galilee, and spared his own life by hiding, if his mission was to prepare all of Israel for "God's visit" (Luke 13:33; 19:44). On the contrary, such a mission necessitated that he met his people, as publicly and centrally as possible, which meant that he had to go to Jerusalem at the time of a great pilgrim festival.

Did Jesus believe that the masses, headed by their leaders, would finally repent and believe his good news of God's kingdom, the promises of which reached them in the present through his person? Or did he anticipate that his life would end in a way similar to John the Baptist's? If the latter were the case, what meaning did he ascribe to the rejection of his message by the authorities?

Jesus's final act in freedom, his last supper with the Twelve, answers this question. During the Passover meal, Jews remember God's liberation of the people from slavery, as well as the covenant God made with them on Mount Sinai (Exod 12–19). Jesus gives the bread and wine of the meal new meaning: they are an image of his own death. The broken bread represents his broken body "given for you"; the wine his drained blood, the blood of the new covenant (Luke 22:19–20; 1 Cor 11:24–25; Mark 14:24; Matt 26:28). Jesus's death, as he came to anticipate it, was very likely understood by him not as a failure but as deeply imbued with meaning—a sacrifice that would atone for sins and renew the covenant. Such an interpretation of an execution of an innocent person had roots in contemporary Jewish thought about the redemptive power of a righteous person's martyrdom, which is probably what Jesus based his ideas on. This interpretation was also taken over by his followers as the key to understanding the master's actions. The kingdom of God was thus not made impossible by Jesus's death, but rather made possible by it.

The Crucifixion and Burial

The punishment corresponded to the crime: insurgents were executed with all forms of public cruelty possible. Crucifixion was a punishment meant to deeply humiliate the executed, while killing him slowly. If the entire weight of a body hangs by the arms, suffocation occurs after a short time. In order to get air, the crucified would support himself on the nails in his feet, bear the pain for a few minutes, and then sink down into the hanging position again. And then up again, and down, hour after hour, giving the appearance of attempting to pry oneself loose from the cross (cf. the mocking cries in Mark 15:30–32). This process is repeated a couple of hundred times, causing restricted breathing, blood loss, and exhaustion, until suffocation occurs after one or two days. If the legs of the crucified are crushed, suffocation will occur much quicker, as the body weight will be supported only by the arms (John 19:31–34).

Jesus died after a few hours on the cross, which a soldier present confirmed by thrusting a lance in his side. The lance must have pierced the heart or one of the larger blood vessels, as blood and other liquid flowed from the wound. As the execution is described in the texts, Jesus was certainly dead.

Family or friends could obtain permission to take down the body and bury it, and in Jesus's case, all the gospels recount that this was done by a member of the Jewish council in Jerusalem called Joseph of Arimathea. After the body was removed from the cross, it was wrapped in linen cloth and placed in a carved cave tomb outside the city walls (the dead could not be buried within the confines of the city). Such graves were meant for continuous usage, which is why a large, round boulder was rolled up in front of the opening.

Both the place of execution and the grave were located close to Jerusalem, and it was not difficult for the women who had remained at Jesus's execution (including his death, removal from the cross, and burial) to note the place of his grave. They decided, according to Luke 23:56, to go to the tomb after the Sabbath and express their love and reverence for the dead by anointing his body with spiced ointment. It is at this point that they notice, early on Sunday morning, that the large boulder has been removed and that the tomb is empty.

Box 3.3
The Place of Jesus's Death and His Tomb

According to John 19:41 the place of Jesus's death and his tomb were located near each other. Archaeological studies have shown that the Church of the Holy Sepulcher contains what at the time of Jesus was an old quarry outside Jerusalem's northwest wall, with vegetation and some minor cultivation. At its western border, tombs were hewn in the rock, and on the eastern side, fifty meters closer to the city wall, was a mound of poor-quality and unusable rock, the so-called Place of the Skull (Golgotha); the difference in height is approximately five meters.

The church, built between 326 and 335 CE by Emperor Constantine, encompasses what, according to local Christians, was the tomb of Jesus. The building project necessitated the dismantling of a large temple built by Hadrian when he, in 135 CE, exiled the Jews and rebuilt Jerusalem into the Roman Aelia Capitolina. To rediscover the location of Golgotha and the tomb, Constantine's builders had to carry out an extensive excavation of the partially deep quarry that had been filled two hundred years earlier in order to serve as the foundation for the Capitoline Temple.

The choice of such a difficult location to build on was probably due to Hadrian's intention to build Roman temples on locations that were holy to Palestinian Jews, in order to quell them after the second serious rebellion in less than a hundred years. He also built a temple to Jupiter where the great Jewish temple had been, and the cave in Bethlehem where Jesus was said to have been born was changed into a place of worship for Adonis, the god of fertility. Two hundred years later, when public Christian cult was allowed and churches could be built, there was thus little doubt as to which locations had served as places of worship for early Christ followers. Because of this, there is a fairly large probability that the modern-day Church of the Holy Sepulcher really is the place where Jesus died and was buried.

Resurrection?

What happened in the tomb between Friday and Sunday? That Jesus's body was, after a short period, no longer in the tomb is indisputable, and that the disciples would have stolen the body and invented the resurrection (Matt 28:13–15) is very unlikely. The historically accessible aspects of the "resurrection" as an event are that the tomb was noted quite early as being empty and that there were people who claimed—all factors considered, in good faith—that they met Jesus alive, after his execution. However, since historical research lacks the explanatory category "miracle," the incident can only be labeled inexplicable; it is beyond the reach of the historian. The event is also described in the Gospels as completely unexpected and incredible, but with enormous aftereffects for those who were convinced that they had met Jesus again, alive. True or false, this conviction is the root of the history of Christianity.

Further Reading

Allison, Dale C. *The Historical Christ and the Theological Jesus*. Grand Rapids: Eerdmans, 2009.

Bernier, Jonathan. *The Quest for the Historical Jesus after the Demise of Authenticity:*

Toward a Critical-Realist Philosophy of History in Jesus Studies. London: Bloomsbury, 2016.

Bock, Darrell L., and J. Ed Komoszewski, eds. *Jesus, Skepticism, and the Problem of History: Criteria and Content in the Study of Christian Origins*. Grand Rapids: Zondervan, 2019.

Bond, Helen K. *The Historical Jesus: A Guide for the Perplexed*. London: T&T Clark, 2012.

Brown, Raymond E. *The Birth of the Messiah: A Commentary on the Infancy Narratives in the Gospels of Matthew and Luke*. AYBRL. New York: Doubleday, 1993.

———. *The Death of the Messiah: From Gethsemane to the Grave; A Commentary on the Passion Narratives in the Four Gospels*. AYBRL. 2 vols. New York: Doubleday, 1994.

Byrskog, Samuel. *Story as History—History as Story: The Gospel Tradition in the Context of Ancient Oral History*. Leiden: Brill, 2002.

Dawes, Gregory W. *The Historical Jesus Quest: Landmarks in the Search for the Jesus of History*. Louisville: Westminster John Knox, 2000.

Dunn, James D. G. *Jesus Remembered*. Vol. 1 of *Christianity in the Making*. Grand Rapids: Eerdmans, 2003.

———. *A New Perspective on Jesus: What the Quest for the Historical Jesus Missed*. Grand Rapids: Baker Academic, 2005.

Freyne, Sean. *Jesus, a Jewish Galilean: A New Reading of the Jesus Story*. London: T&T Clark, 2004.

Gaventa, Beverly Roberts, and Richard B. Hays, eds. *Seeking the Identity of Jesus: A Pilgrimage*. Grand Rapids: Eerdmans, 2008.

Holmén, Tom, and Stanley E. Porter. *Handbook for the Study of the Historical Jesus*. 4 vols. Leiden: Brill, 2011.

Johnson, Luke Timothy. *The Real Jesus: The Misguided Quest for the Historical Jesus and the Truth of the Traditional Gospels*. San Francisco: HarperSanFrancisco, 1996.

Kazen, Thomas. *Jesus and Purity* Halakhah*: Was Jesus Indifferent to Impurity?* Rev. ed. ConBNT 38. Winona Lake, IN: Eisenbrauns, 2010 (originally published 2002).

Keith, Chris. *Jesus against the Scribal Elite: The Origins of the Conflict*. Grand Rapids: Baker Academic, 2014.

Keith, Chris, and Anthony Le Donne, eds. *Jesus, Criteria, and the Demise of Authenticity*. London: T&T Clark, 2012.

Kloppenborg, John, and John W. Marshall. *Apocalypticism, Anti-Semitism and the Historical Jesus: Subtexts in Criticism*. JSNTSup 275. London: T&T Clark, 2005.

Le Donne, Anthony. *The Historical Jesus: What Can We Know and How Can We Know It?* Grand Rapids: Eerdmans, 2011.

Meier, John P. *A Marginal Jew: Rethinking the Historical Jesus*. AYBRL. 5 vols. New York: Doubleday, 1991–2016.

Meyer, Ben F. *The Aims of Jesus*. London: SCM, 1979.

Pitre, Brant. *Jesus and the Last Supper*. Grand Rapids: Eerdmans, 2015.

Ryan, Jordan. *The Role of the Synagogue in the Aims of Jesus*. Minneapolis: Fortress, 2017.

Sanders, E. P. *Jesus and Judaism*. London: SCM, 1985.

———. *The Historical Figure of Jesus*. London: Penguin Press, 1993.

Schröter, Jens. *Jesus of Nazareth: Jew from Galilee, Savior of the World*. Waco: Baylor University Press, 2014.

Stewart, Robert B. *The Resurrection of Jesus: John Dominic Crossan and N. T. Wright in Dialogue*. Minneapolis: Fortress, 2006.

Theissen, Gerd. *The Quest for the Plausible Jesus: The Question of Criteria*. Louisville: Westminster John Knox, 2002.

Uro, Risto, ed. *Thomas at the Crossroads: Essays on the Gospel of Thomas*. Edinburgh: T&T Clark, 1998.

Van Voorst, Robert E. *Jesus Outside the New Testament: An Introduction to the Ancient Evidence*. Grand Rapids: Eerdmans, 2000.

4 The Texts

Chapter 2 presented the different religious, political, and social settings that contributed in various ways to form the contexts within which Jesus and his earliest followers lived. Many of the texts and sources that were used to re-create these contexts will not be examined in this book. The student who is interested in learning more about this evidence independently will find useful the chart about ancient sources for Jesus and his first followers in appendix 1. In addition, the recommended readings found at the end of the chapter will provide the interested student with material with which to delve deeper into the subject. A brief list of noncanonical texts written by Christ followers is discussed in the section "Which Texts Belong to the New Testament? The Canonization Process," p. 211. A list of explanations of difficult terms, names, and geographical places can be found in the glossary.

The present chapter deals with the twenty-seven texts of the New Testament. We begin with a short history of the texts, discussing their origins and transmission. How can we determine which version of a text is the most original? Which texts actually "belong" in the New Testament? What are the criteria for distinguishing between forgeries and new interpretations? What do we know about the traditions about Jesus that went on to form the basis for the gospel narratives? What role do geographical and political parameters play in the creation of the canon? These are the types of questions that will be asked in this section.

Turning to the texts themselves, we will first focus on the four gospels and the Acts of the Apostles. Key issues that we will deal with include the relationship between the first three gospels (the Synoptic Gospels). Which gospel is the oldest? What other sources were used as they were composed? Why did one of the authors choose to write a second book, the so-called Acts of the Apostles? How should one explain the unique and special characteristics of the Fourth Gospel? What are the main thoughts, individual characteristics, and general structure of each book?

We will then look at the Pauline letters. An introductory section discusses the general characteristics of ancient letters. A chronological chart of Paul's life and ministry is also provided before we delve into the specifics of each letter. The letters will be presented in three categories. The first category includes the seven letters that scholars agree were written by Paul himself. The second category deals with the three letters whose authorship is debated. The third category includes the three letters that a majority of scholars are convinced could not have been written by Paul but were in all likelihood formulated by Paul's disciples and heirs.

In the final section of the chapter, we will discuss the remaining nine texts of the New Testament. Many of these texts are called letters or contain letters. In this category, we have texts attributed to Peter, the foremost of the apostles, and letters that were, according to tradition, written by relatives of Jesus. Another text that we will examine was written "to the Hebrews," which reminds us of Christianity's roots in Jewish texts and traditions. Without the "old covenant," a "new" one—described in various ways in the New Testament—would not have been possible. In this section, we will also deal with the mysterious book of Revelation, which has made such a special impact on readers throughout history with its dramatic imagery.

The different sections in this chapter employ different criteria in terms of the order in which the texts are presented. For the Gospels and Acts, a chronological order is used (which is very useful when discussing the Synoptic problem), whereas the section on the Pauline literature applies an order based on assumed authorship, which only partly follows a chronological order. The last section categorizes the texts according to a traditional division between the seven short texts known as the Catholic Letters, since they are addressed to a wider, universal (catholic) audience; thereafter follow Hebrews and Revelation, two larger texts.

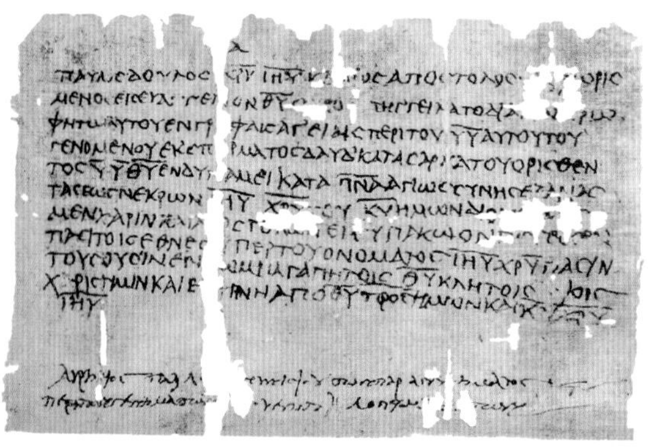

The so-called Peasant papyrus (P.Oxy. 209), dated to the beginning of the fourth century CE, was found in Oxyrhynchus in Egypt. It contains a copy of the first lines of Paul's letter to the Romans. The uneven and casual writing style corresponds to how letters were usually written and resembles the original probably more than most of the copies produced by professional scribes. The papyrus may have been used as an amulet.

The following table provides an overview of the chronological situation in terms of the production of the texts, based on recent scholarship. When the date is followed by a question mark, the time of composition is uncertain. The second column of the table is a reminder that the texts are all based on older, oral traditions and that written and oral traditions were often mixed and mingled. The last columns deal with debated texts, which were recognized by some church officials during the canonization process as authentic, but which ultimately did not make the cut.

Box 4.1
Text Chronology

Time line	Oral ( ) and written transmission	Pauline letters	Other texts	Apostolic Fathers
	Eyewitnesses and tradents			
40				
50	Oral and written tradition in interaction	1 Thess (~50), Gal (54), 1, 2 Cor (55–57), Rom (56–58), Phil (~60), Phlm (58–62), Col (58–62?)		
60				
70	Mark (~71)			
80				
	Matt 80–95		Heb (~65,~85,~95?)	
			1 Peter (70–95?)	
90	Luke (~90) Acts (~92)			
		2 Thess (98?)	Jas (~98?) Jude (~98?) Rev (~98)	1 Clem. (96)
	John (90–110)			
100		Eph (98?)	1, 2, 3 John (~100)	Did. (~100)
110		1 Tim (100–140) 2 Tim (100–140?) Tit (100–140)	2 Pet (100–140)	Ign. *Rom.* (~110) Pol. *Phil.*
				Apoc. Pet. (second century)
120				
				Barn. (130s) Herm. (130–140)

The Origins and Transmission of the Texts

None of the New Testament texts have been preserved in their original form. The earliest surviving manuscripts from the middle of the second century are written on papyrus in the codex (book) format, although the early Christians would have been familiar with the roll format, which was used for the Hebrew Scriptures and the Greek Septuagint. In the Gospel of Luke, Jesus unrolls a book of the prophet Isaiah and reads in the synagogue at Capernaum before he rolls it up again (Luke 4:17–20). From the third century, Christians started to copy their books on parchment (animal hide), which later outrivaled papyrus as the preferred writing material.

All the early manuscripts are written in majuscule script without spaces between words and with meagre, if any, reading aids (punctuation, breathing, and accent marks). An interesting and universal feature, however, is that they include abbreviations of the so-called *nomina sacra*, the holy names. For example, the word for God, *theos*, is written using only the first and last letter, adding a horizontal line above the two letters. Other names and titles, like "Jesus," "Christ," "Son," and "Lord," are abbreviated in similar ways.

The use of cursive writing in Greek gradually developed into the minuscule script used in New Testament manuscripts from the ninth century, and by the eleventh century the majuscule manuscripts had disappeared almost entirely. The editions of the Greek text of the New Testament used today, the editions on which modern translations are based, are reconstructed from more or less carefully copied manuscripts, as well as from quotations appearing in the patristic literature and ancient translations into a variety of languages. It is the task of the text critic to use these sources in the quest to reconstruct an original, or initial, text (we will say more about "original" and "initial" below). Another crucial aspect of textual criticism is to understand how the various ancient textual traditions developed in their variety.

Reconstructing the New Testament Texts

Before the invention of printing in the fifteenth century, the text of the New Testament was transmitted by scribes who copied texts letter by letter and word by word from previous copies, first on papyrus and later on parchment and paper. Attempting to fulfill their task to make faithful copies of the text, scribes nevertheless made textual changes, that is, additions, omissions, substitutions, or transpositions. Some of these changes were errors of spelling or obvious slips that did not change the meaning and were most often corrected, but at times the changes resulted in new meaningful readings, more likely to be perpetuated.

As an example of this, some manuscripts (MSS) of 1 Cor 2:1 speak of the "mystery [*mystērion*] of God," whereas others refer to the "testimony [*martyrion*] of God," with the root word in Greek being quite similar. It seems that a scribe at some point substituted one word for another that looked very similar to it. Which one is original?

If two similar words, or a similar beginning or ending of a word (*homoioarcton/homoioteleuton*), stood near each other on the same line, the scribe's eye could easily jump from the first to the second word or letter(s), which would result in an omission (called *haplography*), or, conversely, the eye could jump back in the text so that the same sequence of text was copied twice (called *dittography*).

In a case like 1 Thess 2:7, a letter was either accidentally omitted or repeated:

> "We were gentle [*egenēthēmen ēpioi*] among you." (NRSV)
>
> "We were like young children [*egenēthēmen nēpioi*] among you." (NIV)

At times scribes attempted to improve a text because it had an error or was lacking in some way. They could substitute or add what seemed to be a more appropriate word or form. In the Gospels in particular, scribes frequently harmonized one account with its parallel(s). After a copy had been made, a different manuscript (MS) could be used to compare with and correct readings with varied success. In the margin of the famous Codex Vaticanus, next to Heb 1:3 we find an interesting note: "Fool and knave, leave the old reading and do not change it!"

Thus, in the transmission process, words and phrases were sometimes omitted, inserted, substituted, or transposed, and sentences could be rewritten. In a few instances, whole sections were added—the long ending of Mark (Mark 16:9–20) and the pericope of the adulteress (John 7:53–8:11), which are both missing from the best MSS.

Textual Criticism

The original writings are now lost, but because of the intense use of the Christian Scriptures over the centuries, more than five thousand Greek New Testament MSS of varying age, material, handwriting, and textual character have been preserved. The earliest papyrus fragment from a gospel codex (John 18:31–33, 37–38) is dated to the middle of the second century (P^{52}), only decades removed from the composition of the gospel.

New Testament textual criticism is the study of these ancient MSS and other textual witnesses, such as early translations (versions) into Syriac, Latin, Coptic, and other languages, and quotations of the New Testament by early Christian writers (church fathers), in order to determine the original text of the New Testament. Having said this, one should note that, because of the problem of how exactly to define the term "original text" (intended text, autographic text, authorial text, initial form of the text, published text, etc.), most scholars now prefer to talk about the earliest recoverable text, or the "initial text."

Apart from this classic task, textual criticism is also concerned with other aspects of the textual transmission. As early Christian artifacts, the MSS can reveal much about the sociocultural and intellectual character of the communities who produced and used them. In fact, the textual variants themselves, although secondary, may serve as windows into the history, culture, and theology of the Jesus movement in its different stages of development.

Hence, the text-critical task has three major aspects: (1) to collect and organize the evidence (MSS, early versions, and patristic citations); (2) to develop a methodology that is able to evaluate this mass of material, in order to determine the initial text wherever there is textual variation; and (3) to reconstruct the whole history of transmission in correlation with church history, as far as the evidence allows.

The Textual Evidence

The vast amount of available source material for the text of the New Testament is a cause for optimism: this textual tradition is far richer than that of any other ancient literature. Therefore, New Testament text critics have generally been reluctant to emend the text, assuming that the original reading is present somewhere in the surviving material.

Greek Manuscripts

The most important materials are the Greek MSS, now numbering more than 5,700. They are characterized in three ways: (1) by the material (papyrus, parchment, or paper); (2) by the kind of script (majuscule/uncial or minuscule/cursive); and (3) by the function of the document (continuous-text MS or lectionary with church lessons). These categories overlap in the traditional manner of listing MSS.

Papyri The New Testament was first written on papyrus. Today there are 140 known papyrus MSS of the New Testament, each of which is identified by the letter P (or 𝔓) and a number. Nearly all of them have been found in Egypt, where they have survived in the dry desert climate. About one-half are dated prior to or around the turn of the third/fourth centuries and are particularly significant for our knowledge of the early text of the New Testament. Virtually all the New Testament papyri are in codex (book) form, reflecting the fact that Christ followers almost immediately adopted this format, whereas the roll continued to dominate secular literature for centuries.

The vast majority of papyri are highly fragmentary, with some notable examples. In 1930–1931 the collector Chester Beatty purchased three early and important papyri, which preserved extensive portions of the New Testament (see table 4.1).

Table 4.1. The Chester Beatty papyri

Manuscript	Date	Content
P^{45}	200–250	Portions of the four gospels and Acts (30 leaves)
P^{46}	200–225	Portions of Romans, Hebrews, 1–2 Corinthians, Ephesians, Galatians, Philippians, Colossians, and 1 Thessalonians (86 leaves)
P^{47}	200–300	Portion of Revelation (10 leaves)

The discovery of the Chester Beatty papyri was followed in the mid-1950s by the competing collector Martin Bodmer acquiring four other important papyrus codices (see table 4.2).

Table 4.2. The Bodmer papyri

Manuscript	Date	Content
P^{66}	200–250	Portion of John (75 leaves)
P^{72}	300–350	1–2 Peter and Jude (95 leaves), part of a miscellaneous codex with five other noncanonical texts
P^{74}	Seventh century	Portions of Acts and the Catholic Letters (124 fragments)
P^{75}	200–250	Portions of Luke and John (50 leaves)

New papyri come to light in a steady stream, not least from the Oxyrhynchus find in Egypt, which so far has yielded about 60 percent of the extant New Testament papyri.

Majuscules There are currently 323 known majuscules written on parchment, which are identified by a number starting from 01 (some also have a letter siglum stemming from an older system). Only three fragmentary majuscules are securely dated to the pre-Constantinian period (before 313) and belong with the papyri to the era before the production of the monumental majuscule codices. Six of the extensive majuscules arguably stand out because of their age (fourth or fifth century CE) and crucial importance for the history of the text.

Table 4.3. Six important majuscules

Manuscript	Date	Content and Textual Character (see text types below)
Codex Sinaiticus (א 01)	Fourth century	OT (LXX), NT, the Letter of Barnabas, the Shepherd of Hermas; "Alexandrian" text ("Western" in John 1–8)

Codex Alexandrinus (A 02)	Fifth century	OT (LXX), most of the NT, 1–2 Clement; akin to the Byzantine text in the Gospels; akin to "Alexandrian" in the rest of NT (particularly valuable in Revelation)
Codex Vaticanus (B 03)	Fourth century	OT (LXX), most of the NT; prime representative of the "Alexandrian" text, considered by many to be the most valuable MS of the NT
Codex Ephraemi Syri Rescriptus (C 04)	Fifth century	A palimpsest (biblical text overwritten) preserving parts of the OT (LXX) and NT; the text is of mixed quality (particularly valuable in Revelation)
Codex Bezae Cantabrigensis (D 05)	Fifth century	A Greek-Latin codex with the four gospels, Acts (ca. 8 percent longer than the general text), and a fragment of 3 John; chief Greek representative of the "Western" text type
Codex Washingtonianus (W 032), also known as the Freer Gospels	Fifth century	Four gospels; a mixed text copied from several exemplars; similar to P^{45} in Mark, representing a very early type of text

Most of the later majuscules conform to the mainstream text of the Byzantine church (see below). With the gradual transition to minuscule script, the majuscules soon passed out of use. The last twenty or so were written in the tenth century, perhaps one or two in the eleventh.

Minuscules The oldest dated minuscule of the New Testament is the Uspenski Gospels of the year 835 written in Byzantine minuscule script, which developed from earlier informal, cursive scripts that had been in use for a long time for documents rather than literature. During this period, the Byzantine text type had come to dominate the Greek MS tradition, so that the great majority of the approximately 2,850 extant minuscules represent the Byzantine Majority Text. (The official numbers of minuscules and lectionaries are higher than the numbers indicated here because of double registrations.) Minuscules are identified with a number starting from 1.

For practical reasons, the majority of MSS (mostly minuscules) with a similar Byzantine text are subsumed under a common siglum in critical editions ($\mathfrak{M}$ or Byz). However, some 10 percent of the minuscules are known to represent other textual streams and are therefore more valuable in the reconstruction of the initial text. It will take many years to examine these MSS and their place in the genealogy of the text for all parts of the New Testament.

Lectionaries In contrast to the continuous-text MSS, lectionary MSS, identified by the letter *l* (or L) followed by a number, have their New Testament text arranged in separate pericopes, or lessons, to be read in church on particular days during the ecclesiastical year. Although more research is necessary, by and large the lectionaries—currently numbering about 2,400—reproduce the Byzantine Majority Text, and therefore few are cited in the standard critical editions.

Versions

The earliest translations, or versions, of the New Testament are the Syriac, Latin, and Coptic versions. Each of them has a distinct textual tradition with several successive revisions and new translations. Because of this, the earliest and most important translations in these languages are actually the Old Syriac, the Old Latin, and, in Coptic, the Sahidic and Bohairic versions. These earliest translations, prepared by missionaries from ancient Greek exemplars in the second and third centuries, are of great value for textual criticism.

At the same time, there are serious limitations, primarily because certain features of the Greek language cannot be conveyed in a translation; there is no one-to-one relationship between a reading in Greek and its counterpart in a version. Hence, it is difficult to reconstruct the Greek reading behind a particular rendering, whether in Syriac, Latin, or Coptic. A sound use of versional evidence therefore requires detailed knowledge of the possibilities and limitations of each version to express the Greek source language.

Patristic Citations

In addition to Greek MSS and early versions, the vast number of scriptural citations in the works of early Christian writers (primarily the church fathers) constitute an important body of data for textual study. Examples of such early Christian authors include Clement of Alexandria (d. 212), Origen (185–254 CE), and Eusebius of Caesarea (263–339 CE). One particularly useful feature of patristic citations is that they serve to date and localize readings geographically.

On the other hand, patristic evidence involves several challenges. First, the text of the church fathers may have been modified in the course of transmission; scriptural quotations in particular were subject to changes by scribes. Second, it may be difficult to ascertain whether a church father cites from an existing MS or from memory, or whether he chooses to paraphrase rather than quote a passage verbatim. For non-Greek church fathers, matters are even more complicated because of translation.

Sorting Out the Evidence: The Theory of Text Types

Since the relationship between these varied textual witnesses is so complex, scholars since the eighteenth century have attempted to classify and divide them into textual groupings, or text types. Until the major papyrus discoveries of the previous century, classifications of texts were made mainly on the basis of the earliest majuscules. The New Testament text was divided into the following major text types: Alexandrian (א and B), Caesarean (W and Θ), Western (D and other bilinguals), and Byzantine (A and the majority of MSS).

The two Cambridge professors B. F. Westcott (1825–1901) and F. J. A. Hort (1828–1892) labeled the earliest stage of the Alexandrian text type as a "Neutral text," meaning it was virtually uncorrupted. The Neutral text, chiefly represented by the fourth-century codices Sinaiticus (א 01) and Vaticanus (B 03), formed the basis of their edition *The New Testament in the Original Greek* (1881). Their endeavor, and the theory and methods on which it was based, led to the final overthrow of the traditional New Testament text, the *Textus Receptus* (the "received text"), which had dominated Greek editions and, indirectly, Bible translations (most famously the King James Version) ever since Erasmus of Rotterdam published the first edition of the Greek New Testament in 1516.

However, new papyrus discoveries from the 1930s onward caused many scholars to question whether the Neutral text really represented a pure line of transmission from the earliest time, as Westcott and Hort had proposed. These early papyri did not clearly align with any of the established text types but reflected a more diverse and fluid state of transmission than expected. This led some scholars to assume that the earliest era was characterized entirely by a wild and uncontrolled textual transmission, and that the Neutral (or Alexandrian) text was instead the result of an ecclesiastical recension that probably took place in Alexandria in the fourth century. The aim of this hypothesized recension was to produce a standardized text and bring order to the chaotic textual state of the New Testament.

The recension theory, however, received a serious blow when the text of P^{75} became known and turned out to be nearly identical to Codex Vaticanus. This papyrus more than any other demonstrated the stability of this type of text during at least a century and a half in an era of textual transmission that was presumed "uncontrolled." Today, most scholars still think of the P^{75}–Vaticanus type of text as the best representative of a "strict" line of transmission, reaching back at least into the second century, if not ultimately derived from the initial text. On the other hand, a current scholarly debate concerning the dating of the early papyri (including P^{75}) may raise the issue again, although there are other "strict" papyri more securely dated to around 200 CE.

The text-type theory still prevails in current practice, most notably as reflected in Bruce Metzger's widely used *Textual Commentary* (a companion volume to the

United Bible Societies' *Greek New Testament*). More recently, however, leading scholars, who are now editing the standard text-critical editions, have advocated for the abandonment of the concept of text types in light of new computer-assisted methods for determining manuscript relationships in a more exact way. There is already a consensus that the various geographic locations traditionally assigned to the text types are incorrect and misleading. Some prefer to speak of "textual clusters" rather than text types. Further, the existence of a distinct Caesarean text type has been called into serious question.

The Practice of Textual Criticism

Since no single MS or text type can be followed automatically, decisions must be made on a passage-by-passage basis. The evaluation of variant readings in individual passages is generally based on certain guiding principles or criteria. The most profound principle is to prefer that reading which best explains the rise of all the others. All other criteria are subordinate to this one and utilized, where possible, in the reconstruction of a genealogical tree (*stemma*) of variant readings.

Westcott and Hort made a useful distinction between (1) external evidence pertaining to the MSS themselves and (2) internal evidence involving two kinds of considerations: (a) transcriptional probabilities relating to what scribes were more likely to have copied and (b) intrinsic probabilities relating to what an author was more likely to have written. In practically all current methodologies in New Testament textual criticism, criteria related to external and internal evidence are taken into account in varying combinations. The approach known as "thoroughgoing eclecticism," for example, relies primarily on internal evidence, whereas "reasoned eclecticism"—the dominant force in contemporary textual criticism—applies a combination of external and internal evidence.

The problem that has remained, however, is how to combine the entire set of criteria in order to determine the originality of readings. That is, *which* criteria should be applied *when*, and what weight should each be given? Very often the criteria will compete with one another in different ways such that decisions are based on a balance of probabilities. Moreover, no criterion can be applied in mechanical fashion; there are many exceptions.

External Evidence

External evidence relates to the date and textual character of witnesses. The support of early witnesses increases the likelihood that a reading has priority. The early witnesses, however, are often divided between several readings.

More important than the age of the physical MS is the age and character of the text it carries. Westcott and Hort attempted to demonstrate the superiority of the

Neutral text (Alexandrian), as represented chiefly by the codices Vaticanus and Sinaiticus, by examining a large number of textual variants. They showed how the Byzantine text more often than not displayed a smoother text, where difficulties had presumably been eliminated by scribes. The Western text, although very early, displayed periphrastic and harmonizing tendencies.

Today, most text critics generally favor the Alexandrian text type, but occasionally the associated MSS are divided between two or more readings. The support of several text types, or a variety of patristic and versional attestation, indicates that a reading is widespread and therefore early.

Internal Evidence

Internal evidence depends on transcriptional and intrinsic probabilities. The criteria related to transcriptional probabilities are based on the study of scribal habits in general, although it is crucial to study the individual documents to acquire knowledge of particular scribal tendencies.

A well-established transcriptional criterion is to prefer the more difficult reading. This criterion, known as *lectio difficilior potior* (the more difficult reading is stronger), suggests that it is more likely that a scribe makes the text smoother than more complicated. In practice, it may often be hard to judge the difference between a difficult reading and a reading that results from an error in copying. Hence, the criterion does not apply in cases where another, more specific transcriptional factor better explains the origin of the difficulty.

Another common criterion is to prefer the shorter reading. This criterion, known as *lectio brevior potior* (the shorter reading is stronger), is based on the assumption that scribes tended to add rather than omit words from the text. It is one of the most debated criteria and has proven to be in such need of qualification that some regard it as relatively useless, in particular for the early papyri.

Since scribes would frequently bring divergent parallel passages into harmony with one another—for example, with synoptic parallels or citations from the Septuagint in the New Testament—one should prefer the least harmonistic reading.

Intrinsic evidence depends on considerations of what the author was more likely to have written. This means that we have to take into account his theology, style, and vocabulary, as well as the immediate historical context. It is sometimes difficult, however, to determine which part of a text really originates from the author and not from other sources, redactors, or scribes.

Transcriptional probabilities often stand in direct opposition to intrinsic probabilities, since the scribes could potentially bring a passage in conformity with what they perceived as the author's style. They especially tended to harmonize to the immediate context. The intrinsic criterion seems to be particularly useful in relation to an author's theology or ideology, which involve matters of content and substance rather than language or style, which is more susceptible to scribal change.

The Monastery of Saint Catherine at the foot of Mount Sinai, Egypt, where Moses, according to tradition, received the law from the God of Israel. It was in this monastery that C. von Tischendorf (1815–1874) found the biblical uncial manuscript that is now called Codex Sinaiticus. Photo by Berthold Werner.

Which Texts Belong to the New Testament? The Canonization Process

When the painstaking text-critical work is completed, we have traveled as far back in time as is possible, for the time being. Still, we have not reached the "original" text. The truth is that we have no original texts, either of Paul's letters or of any of the gospels. And even if we found ourselves one day with an original letter in our hand, new questions would emerge. Did Paul write it, or was it someone else? Who is the audience? Where the Gospels are concerned, there are yet further steps to take before we arrive at the scenes they depict: What sources can be traced behind the narratives? How has the Jesus tradition grown and developed from the first transmitters to the composing of the gospel texts? And is it possible to access the historical course of events behind the narrative? We shall soon delve deeper into these fascinating questions, but before we can do so, we need to identify the texts we shall discuss and ask ourselves why they became part of what we today call the New Testament.

At first, the emerging Jesus movement used a large number of Jewish texts, some of which became part of the Hebrew Bible and others that were popular. Because the emerging Jesus movement soon spread throughout the Greco-Roman diaspora, it more often than not used Greek translations of the Hebrew Scriptures, known to us as the Septuagint (LXX). The LXX contains more books than the Hebrew Bible, some of which were authored in Greek. This emphasizes the fact that there was no fixed canon at this time. The texts were first and foremost read during the liturgy, a model that the early Jesus movement adopted from synagogue praxis. The service was also the natural platform for delivering messages from prominent leaders. Paul's letters to the congregations he founded were circulated and read in this manner. Already during the 50s CE, when they were first composed, they may have been copied and shared with other congregations. Galatians is an obvious example of a letter meant to be circulated among several congregations, and Colossians bears witness to the fact that letters were exchanged between congregations, even though the time period here is a little later. Eventually, the Pauline letters were made into a collection, and they were circulated in this format at the least by the year 100 CE. The youngest text of the New Testament, 2 Peter, which may be dated to the middle of the second century CE, takes it for granted that the content of the Pauline letters was accessible to the Christ groups it addresses. During the time between Paul and 2 Peter, many letters were composed that were attributed to Paul or other apostles. Most of these are easily identified as letters meant to circulate widely, to a larger audience (e.g., 1 Peter, Hebrews, and Ephesians—the words "in Ephesus" are missing in the oldest and best-preserved manuscripts we have).

The teaching in the early Jesus movement included Jesus traditions of various kinds. To begin with, these were transmitted first and foremost orally. Toward the end of the first century, these traditions were collected and integrated into cohesive written narratives of the life of Jesus. These narratives, the Gospels, are based on both oral and written traditions and came to be read in liturgical settings. We shall return to the question of the origins and usage of the Gospels later on in this chapter.

An Emerging Canon

As the canon began to take form, it was not self-evident which texts to include in the New Testament. The formation of the canon was a long and protracted process, which spanned the first four hundred years of the Christ movement. The old and rather common perception that the canonization process began with Marcion (c. 85–c. 160) and ended with Athanasius (ca. 295–373)—specifically, with the patriarch of Alexandria's Easter Letter in 367—is a deceptively simple and academically unsustainable hypothesis. Admittedly, Marcion's attempt to limit the texts used by Christ followers in the mid-second century to a cleaned-up version of Luke and ten Pauline letters preceded the first lists and the first delimitations found in various church fathers. Marcion's aim was to distance the Jesus movement from the image of God presented in the Hebrew Bible. But even if this affected the formation of the canon, many scholars today would argue that it is unlikely that it represents its origin. The point of departure for canon formation was rather the issue of which texts were used in the congregations and a desire for unity. The texts that were accepted and used by a majority of the Jesus movement early on make up the bulk of what was to become the Christian canon. These texts include the four gospels and the undisputed Pauline letters. The latter were probably collected into a textual entity already toward the end of the first century.

The Pastoral Letters are missing from Marcion's list of acceptable books but are present in later canonization lists from the third century onward (for further details, see box 4.2, p. 230). In addition to the Pastoral Letters, 2 Thessalonians and Philemon are also missing from the earliest collection of Pauline texts, the crucial papyrus manuscript P^{46}, which contains the other letters as well as Hebrews. First and Second Timothy are not included in any papyrus manuscripts at all.

Other texts that were disputed during the first centuries of the Jesus movement include Hebrews, 1 and especially 2 Peter, 2 and 3 John, James, Jude, and Revelation. In the oldest list of approved New Testament texts, the so-called Canon Muratori, probably from the end of the second century, 1 and 2 Peter, James, Hebrews, and one of the Johannine letters are missing.

If we turn the spotlight toward the church fathers, Irenaeus (bishop of Lyon, d. ca. 202) leaves out Philemon, 2 Peter, 3 John, James, Jude, and possibly also Hebrews. Origen (Alexandria, ca. 185–254) viewed 2 Peter and 2–3 John as disputed. The position he allots to James and Jude is unclear. During the fourth century, Eusebius of Caesarea (ca. 263–340) counted 1 Peter and 1 John as undisputed. He includes Hebrews, since he counts it among the Pauline letters, but points out that some reject it, because it is disputed by the church of Rome. The remainder of the "Catholic Letters" were, according to Eusebius, among the disputed texts, "even though well known to many." Revelation has a unique position since it is counted as both a disputed and undisputed text, depending on which is preferred. Eusebius's ambivalence toward the canonical status of Revelation mirrors that of the early church.

The first instance of Hebrews and Revelation being recognized with no further motivation is found in a widely circulated letter from Athanasius in 367. The Church Council of Hippo in 393 confirmed this view. However, in the Syrian churches, the Catholic Letters either were missing or were questioned for a long time, and Revelation was viewed with suspicion in the East for almost a thousand years.

Important Extracanonical Texts

A number of texts read by many early Christ groups were not included in the Christian canon. Some of these texts are today categorized as belonging to the writings of the *apostolic fathers*, such as the Didache (Teaching of the Twelve Apostles), the Shepherd of Hermas, 1 Clement, and the Letter of Barnabas. Some of these texts are dated to about the same time as the youngest texts in the canon. In both Rome and Alexandria, an apocalypse attributed to Peter was used toward the late second and early third century and was actually included in the Canon Muratori and the Codex

Claromontanus. Clement of Alexandria accepted all five of the aforementioned texts. The Syrian churches made use of a third letter to the Corinthians. Jesus followers in Syria used gospels that seem to have been variants of the Gospel of Matthew and that went under the names Gospel of the Hebrews, Gospel of the Nazarene, and Gospel of the Ebionites. The relationship between these gospels is uncertain, especially since only a small number of citations have survived via the church fathers.

Toward the end of the second century onward, we see the flourishing of a number of apostle legends, written in the genre of the so-called *acta* literature. These acts of various apostles represent a development of the genre of Acts, and they became very popular. They describe the journeys of a specific apostle and his heroic actions, miracles, and success. The narratives often contain erotic aspects, and the apostles are described as aesthetically appealing, to the degree that many prominent women are drawn to the apostle, adopting the teachings of abstinence and asceticism. This brings down the wrath of the prominent men of the city, leading to persecution and martyrdom. This kind of literature was never used as authorized reading in religious services, except for, perhaps, during the memorial days of the martyrs they dealt with.

The plethora of Christian texts with gnostic characteristics (see the section "Gnosticism and 'the Gnostics,'" p. 455, for more information about Gnosticism), which began flourishing around the same time as *acta* literature, does not appear in the early lists and discussions that we have access to. However, we may assume that such texts are represented in some of the lists of apocryphal texts that are available to us, for example, the Gelasian Decree (sixth century). Of course, gnostic texts were held in high esteem and actively used by the parts of the church that adopted such theology. Like the *acta* literature, texts with gnostic traits were mostly composed at a time when the major contours of the New Testament canon were already drawn. If one takes into consideration the polemic of the majority church against gnostic forms of Christianity, it is not surprising that texts with gnostic traits were rejected or regarded as spurious.

More Than Four Gospels?

A number of gospels or gospel fragments with roots in the same time period as the later texts of the New Testament were often viewed as heterodox (gnosticizing, docetic, Jewish, etc.) but actually might have made it into the New Testament canon if the circumstances had been different. The Gospel of Thomas, the entirety of which is today found only in a Coptic document from Nag Hammadi, is based on an older Greek version. Prior to the discovery of the Coptic document at Nag Hammadi, scholars had already discovered fragments of Greek papyri, which were later proved to be parts of the Gospel of Thomas. Even though it is unclear whether these particular papyrus fragments represent an older Greek version, a Gospel of Thomas is also mentioned by several church fathers. And even though the Coptic version of the gospel was used by "gnostic" Christians, the text itself contains no explicit gnostic characteristics or any clear traces of gnostic mythology. Thus, Thomas could be said to represent, like the Gospel of John, a special kind of "spiritualizing Christianity" rather than a "gnostic Christianity." In addition, several scholars have argued that the material behind the Gospel of Thomas shows similarity to the (hypothetical) Q document (see the section "The Gospels and the Acts of the Apostles," p. 238), in that both consist of a collection of Jesus sayings unconnected by any sort of narrative progression or context.

We may also consider the Gospel of Peter along similar lines, as it is also mentioned by the church fathers. Toward the end of the second century, Bishop Serapion of Antioch approved the use of the gospel by the congregation at Rhossus, although he later changed his mind after it was brought to his attention that the gospel might contain traces of docetism. The fragments of the gospel that have been found indicate that the document has undergone a great deal of change over time; nevertheless, the relatively late fragment found at Akhmim does not exhibit any explicit traces of docetism. Certain formulations may be interpreted as leaning toward the docetic, but all in all the document does not deviate from Serapion's first ruling that it was sound in its teaching. The mention of the gospel by the church fathers, as well as the discovery of fragments in Akhmim, indicates that it had a wide readership, since it existed not only in Syria but also in Egypt. It is possible that an early form of the Gospel of Peter could be dated to around the same time as the Gospels of Luke and John, or slightly later.

There is also a possibility that Papyrus Egerton 2 and Papyrus Oxyrhynchus 840 represent fragments of older gospels. This is especially likely in the case of Papyrus Egerton 2, since it contains several Jesus traditions in a continuous narrative, some of which overlap with Jesus traditions in the canonical gospels, albeit with distinct characteristics. All attempts to anchor these fragments in a specific sectarian context have failed. The material does not seem to reflect anything but mainline traditions in the early church, and it is thus within the realm of possibility that the fragments could be what is left of an independent gospel, one based on earlier sources and oral traditions, without necessarily being directly dependent on any of the canonical gospels. We have no evidence that would indicate the name of this gospel. If we move on to Papyrus Oxyrhynchus 840, the situation becomes more uncertain. This is in part because we have access only to one fragment, and in part because the fragment is so small that at least this particular copy could not possibly have been intended for public readings. However, the fragment contains the transition between two narrative structures, indicating that it is a part of a gospel. The text has been criticized for reflecting an anti-Jewish cult critique and containing unhistorical information, but the critique that Jesus directs against a temple priest is not so different from the critique the prophets of the Hebrew Bible directed toward the same institution, and several of the "unhistorical" details have, over time, been verified. Thus, it is possible that this papyrus fragment represents the remnants of yet another gospel with roots in early Jesus tradition. There are, of course, a plethora of other fragments that contain the remnants of Jesus traditions, but most of these are limited in scope, and it is impossible to verify whether they were once part of an unknown gospel.

Criteria of Selection

Why were such texts not universally accepted? What led to them being put outside the canon? As we have previously implied, the canon formation process was first and foremost a confirmation of the texts that were already frequently used and universally accepted by congregations of Christ followers. But, when there was doubt as to the legitimacy of a text, the primary question was, did it represent correct doctrine or not? The answer to this question relied in part on the individual examining the text and in part on whether the text was used by "heretical" groups to legitimize "unacceptable" teaching.

The latter criterion, however, could not have been decisive. Marcion used Luke, the Carpocrates (gnosticizing Christ followers active during the second century) used a version of Mark, Christ-believing Jewish groups appear to have based their gospels on Matthew, and John was popular among gnosticizing Christians. But, in the case of gospels that did not already enjoy wide acceptance, usage by groups deemed by the majority to be heretical could be compromising. The odds in favor of the Gospel of Peter were significantly decreased by Serapion's condemnation of it. The Gospel of Thomas's problems may in part have been due to its form: the lack of a narrative structure separated it from other gospels. Similarly, the sayings source (Q), also lacking a narrative structure, did not survive as an independent text. We have no information about the spread or readership of the gospels behind the fragments.

These observations lead us to pose some critical questions about the role of power in the process of canon formation. Although the process itself was far from centralized or systematic, the power center of Christendom began moving westward. The majority of New Testament texts were written in the East, but many of the texts recognized at a late stage were penned in the West, indicating that it was difficult for newer Eastern texts to gain a wide readership. For example, Syrian texts that were not already universally accepted would have had a much harder time making it into the canon than, for example, a text written in Rome. In all likelihood, some of the fragments found in Egypt come from North African gospels that never reached other parts of Christendom.

Practical considerations must also be taken into account. The more texts began appearing, the more important it became to limit what was read in worship services. This is where the *apostolic* criterion comes into play. Historically, it has often been considered the most important criterion but today has become less certain. In addition, the issue of apostolic origin is complicated. The adjective "apostolic" could mean "dogmatically correct" rather than implying that it originated with an actual apostle. Tertullian (North African theologian, d. ca. 220) indicates that it was not the apostolic *authorship* that was considered important; rather, the most important criterion was that the text was in agreement with apostolic *belief*.

In time, apostolic texts were identified with apostolic authors. When new texts appeared, texts that could hardly have been written by an apostle, the church had to question their authenticity. Maybe this can serve as an explanation as to why certain texts, which were recognized early on, did not make it into the canon, whereas others, which were under suspicion earlier, were later accepted. Eventually, texts like 2 Peter, 2–3 John, and Jude were accepted. Even Hebrews and Revelation, which were under a great deal of theological suspicion (Hebrews: no opportunity for a second penance; Revelation: exaggerated apocalypticism), came to be accepted through being associated with Paul and John, respectively. In such a context, it becomes impossible to accept texts such as the Letter of Barnabas or the Shepherd of Hermas, both of which were obviously not composed by a disciple of Jesus. The authority of Mark and Luke was already attested because Mark was viewed as Peter's interpreter and Luke was believed to have been a companion of Paul. This means that many of the texts of the New Testament were not composed by the apostolic authors mentioned in either the text itself or the tradition surrounding them. Today, most of these texts are categorized as *pseudepigrapha*. This could constitute a problem for those who have been taught that these texts are reliable and view them as the only cornerstones of Christian faith. We must therefore reflect on the ancient phenomenon of writing under pseudonyms.

Pious Forgeries or Necessary Reinterpretations?

The majority of New Testament texts came to be attributed to apostolic authors. This is true for the gospels as well as the letters. Where the gospels are concerned, none of the texts make any explicit claims to be written by a specific person. The author of Luke is assumed to be known. The author of John is linked to the disciple whom "Jesus loved," which church tradition has identified as the disciple John. The Gospel of Matthew has traditionally been linked to the disciple Matthew. Where Mark and Luke are concerned, the tradition has not even attempted to claim that they were written by a disciple, although during the process of canon formation they were linked to individuals supposed to have been associated with an apostle (Peter and Paul, respectively). Thus, none of the gospels can be classified as pseudepigrapha. Instead, they should be categorized as anonymous texts.

The same cannot be said for the letters. While Hebrews—like, for example, John's Gospel—implies in its conclusion whom the writer would like the audience to believe the author is, and 1–3 John remain cryptic about the authorship of the texts, the rest of the letters state one or more authors. Many of these texts are today classified as pseudepigrapha; that is, they were written after the death of the stated author by individuals using his name and authority. Even though there is no consensus about the authorship of the letters, the vast majority of scholars today believe the Pastoral Letters and the Catholic Letters to be pseudepigraphic. There are diverging opinions regarding 2 Thessalonians and Colossians, and the most common view of Ephesians is that it depends on Colossians and was written by a disciple of Paul (see the section "The Pauline Letters," p. 282). The reason for the complex authorship of these texts can be traced back to the leadership vacuum created by the death of the first generation of leadership and the more developed hierarchical and authoritarian structures that began to take form during the second century. During this period, it became increasingly important to adapt the Christian tradition to the changing circumstances and to adapt the legacy of the apostles' teaching to the partly changing contexts.

Motivation and Aims

Why would such methods be used? Scholars often point to Jewish pseudepigraphic literature. It is true that we have many examples of pseudepigrapha in the Jewish literary world in the centuries close to the turn of the era. Possibly, some of the roots of Jewish pseudepigraphy could be traced to the way in which several books of the Hebrew Bible were attributed to specific historical figures—for example, the five books of Moses and parts of the wisdom literature. However, the majority of explicit pseudepigraphic writings that we have access to today are apocalyptic books with visions, revelations, heavenly journeys, and expressive imagery. These books are attributed to biblical characters, such as Enoch, Adam, and Abraham. The writings often include specific predictions leading up to the time of their real composition. The book of Daniel can be classified as such a work. In the New Testament, only one book fits this description: the book of Revelation. In contrast to its Jewish counterparts, Revelation is not pseudepigraphic. The author clearly identifies himself as "God's servant" John and makes no apostolic claims. The New Testament texts that we usually classify as pseudepigraphic are of a completely different nature. They claim to be written by one of the apostles to a certain Christian congregation. The identified authors were well known to the audience and were alive a few decades prior to the composition of the letters.

Letters and collections of letters that claimed to originate with well-known individuals were a common occurrence in the Hellenistic world. For example, there is a collection of letters from Plato of which it is certain that not all were written by him. We can also see examples of how the collection of letters Ignatius of Antioch left behind was expanded and edited after his death, possibly by his followers. It was not uncommon for the disciples of a teacher to attribute to their master the expanded teaching they themselves developed. The Pythagoreans were said to attribute their teaching to Pythagoras. These observations suggest a slightly different background to the pseudepigraphic New Testament letters than pseudepigraphic Jewish apocalyptic writings.

Passing on the Legacy

Paul's own letters contain some important clues about the pseudepigraphic letters. Many of his letters mention not only him but also his companions as coauthors, although it is clear that Paul was the one dictating, since he often mentions a coauthor in the third person later in the text. One could, however, imagine that someone like Timothy, a recurring companion of Paul, could have been allotted the task of composing a letter independently, even during the lifetime of Paul. This is a *possible* hypothesis about the authorship of 2 Thessalonians, Colossians, and maybe Ephesians. A more *likely* hypothesis is that these three letters were composed after the death of Paul, by his disciples, in order to make what was deemed as necessary adjustments and expansions of his ideas. Just as the Gospels are based on traditions from and about Jesus, there must have been a large number of traditions from and about Paul that flourished during this period. These traditions may have been used by some of his coworkers in order to formulate the letters whose authenticity is debated. In any case, it is evident that these letters are intimately connected to the undisputed Pauline letters in that they further develop the ideas outlined there. Second Thessalonians adjusts an eschatology that already turned out to be a little too hasty. Colossians and Ephesians develop Paul's theology in a speculative manner, especially with regard to his views on Christ and the church. Both letters, especially Ephesians, seem to reflect a time later than Paul's.

The situation is somewhat different where the Pastoral Letters are concerned. Even though it is possible that there are oral traditions that can be traced back to Paul and might have informed certain details of the letters, these letters are obviously fictitious. All three are addressed to famous companions of Paul: two to Timothy and one to Titus. There are a number of intimate details that give the letters a feeling of familiarity. At the same time, they all contain the same signals and repeat "reminders" about various issues in ways that would hardly have been necessary for the stated recipients to hear. On the other hand, such instructions would have been very fitting for regulating Christian life and doctrine among the *real* recipients, which were congregations living in the Pauline tradition, a generation or so after Paul. When the Pastoral Letters were recognized and read together with the other undisputed Pauline letters, they would soon have the effect of modifying the image of the "apostle to the gentiles"; thus they provide us with a different portrait of Paul, the effect of which can still be felt today.

Calling these letters forgeries, however, is not an entirely obvious choice. The real authors of the post-Pauline letters were well acquainted with the Pauline tradition, and they probably saw themselves as tradents of Paul's message. The Pastoral Letters also have their likely background in a continuous development of the Pauline tradition. They reflect a wish to hear Paul speak to the various situations faced by the Christianity of a later period. In the case of the Pastoral Letters, we may speak about a more evident exploitation of Paul's authority than in the other post-Pauline letters.

A similar situation arises when we study the Catholic Letters more closely. These letters use the names James, Peter, and Jude (Hebrews and 1–3 John differ since they name no explicit author) to authorize their message. In these instances, however, there is little evidence that the real authors stood in continuity with, and developed a tradition stemming from, the aforementioned apostles. All of these letters must have been written after the Pauline letters, since they use them either as a model or as something to argue against. While James and Jude could be said to represent a more Jewish adjustment of (what was at that point interpreted to be) Pauline theology, the First Epistle of Peter embodies more of a middle path, ascribing a modified Pauline theology to Peter and prescribing this as a general norm. Even though neither oral tradition nor certain theological schools seem to have much to do with these letters, they reflect the theological significance attributed by later generations to a Jewish interpretation of Christianity according to James and to a Petrine middle road for the development of Christianity. In view of this, it might not be completely fair to call these letters forgeries. Moreover, they are not all of the same ilk. The letter that comes closest to being an outright forgery is 2 Peter, although its fictitious authorship is so obvious that one can almost wonder whether its audience was really meant to believe that the disciple had penned it himself.

Regardless of how we choose to view these texts, we should note that they significantly modify our overall understanding of the New Testament. Without these letters, the imminent eschatology of the New Testament would be given more space and prominence, and the early Jesus movement would appear less hierarchical and patriarchal.

From Jesus Traditions to Gospels

Even though the Pauline letters were the first texts of the New Testament to be collected and disseminated, the four gospels soon developed a special standing within the main stream of the Jesus movement and became its most important documents. There are examples of Christ groups with particular tendencies that based themselves on only one of the gospels. For Irenaeus, this was a strong argument for the validity and importance of having four gospels. The gospel harmony (Diatessaron, which means "through four") of Tatian (second-century Syrian apologetic and theologian) gained popularity only within the Syrian church, and lost even this support during the fifth century when the Syrian translation of the Bible, the Peshitta, came to include all four gospels separately.

The question about how the four gospels relate to each other has been discussed and debated by modern scholars since the eighteenth century. The different hypotheses mainly concern the relationship between the first three gospels, Matthew, Mark, and Luke (known as the Synoptic Gospels), since John differs significantly from them in both character and content. Although theories about oral traditions behind the Gospels appeared early on, the focus came to rest on the *literary* relationship between the Synoptics.

The Two-Source Hypothesis

The most widely accepted solution to the Synoptic problem is still the so-called *two-source hypothesis*, which will be described in more detail below in the section "The Gospels and the Acts of the Apostles," p. 236. According to this theory, Mark and a now lost Greek document, Q (which mainly contained Jesus sayings), provide the foundation for both Matthew and Luke. In addition, Matthew and Luke build on material specific to them. The hypothesis is based on the assumption that Matthew and Luke were written independently of each other. The arguments for the two-source hypothesis are based on easily observable features of the texts in question. Matthew includes almost all of Mark's material, and Luke includes between two-thirds and three-fourths of it, depending on how one counts. Mark's material has often been edited according to the aims of the authors of Matthew and Luke. Material shared by Matthew and Luke that is not present in Mark (attributed to the Q source) often appears in the same internal order, albeit not inserted in the same places within the frame provided by the material taken from Mark. In addition to this, the linguistic agreements between Matthew and Luke are often significantly greater in the material taken from Q than in the material taken from Mark. All of this makes it difficult for a majority of scholars to avoid the hypothesis of a literary sayings source (Q).

However, the two-source hypothesis is accompanied by a number of complications that require us to ask some critical questions. Examples are the so-called *minor agreements* between Matthew and Luke, against Mark, and the unique Markan *duality*, the repeated (unnecessary) expressions used by the author, of which Matthew often reflects one and Luke the other. Such observations might suggest the existence of more than one version of the Gospel of Mark, or Lukan access to Matthew, as in the Farrer hypothesis (for more details, see the section "The Gospels and the Acts of the Apostles," p. 237). In any case, the two-source hypothesis requires a degree of modification. The Cribbs-Shellard hypothesis from the late 1990s also includes John in Luke's sources. Such alternative theories do not solve all the complications, however, and they create many new problems. Without Q, Luke is required to have chopped up Matthew's thematic speeches and redistributed much of Matthew's non-Markan material in different locations within the Markan framework. Perhaps the basic tenets of the two-source theory could be combined with Luke having access to other sources, too, including Matthew, but prioritizing the older ones. In view of the growing tendency to assign a late date to Luke, this is at least becoming a possibility.

Oral and Written Transmission

One of the weaknesses of many theories is that the focus is entirely on the *written* sources behind the documents. Speculations about the different versions of Mark and Q risk portraying the origins of the gospels as pure deskwork. In opposition to this trend, a number of scholars have attempted to shift the focus to the role of *oral tradition* in the formation of the gospels. The fact that Matthew and Luke used Mark for their frames and copied large parts of his text is a given, but much of the material unique to them may have come from oral traditions that existed within the networks of the early communities. It is difficult to ascertain to what degree the author of Mark made use of written sources before him, but it is plausible that, prior to the composition of Mark, a number of gospel stories circulated in written form. There is some support for Mark making use in a few cases of earlier written sources in Greek. Some scholars have even suggested that he made use of Aramaic sources, but so far no certain evidence can be adduced to back this up. We should thus assume a number of oral traditions underlying Mark.

Recently some scholars have also suggested that some of the shared material between Matthew and Luke, usually explained as stemming from modifications of Q, might actually originate in shared oral traditions, especially in those cases where there is little verbatim agreement between the authors but where the core of the story is nevertheless the same. It has even been suggested that certain cases where Matthew or Luke deviates considerably from Mark, despite a common core, could be explained by the former's choice to follow oral alternatives of the same story rather than the version preserved in Mark. Prior to the composition of the gospels, oral tradition was the only way of preserving the common, identity-forming stories about Jesus, his life, and his teaching. The oral retelling did not die out just because the written gospels came into existence. At the same time, speculative suggestions about oral versions are not necessarily required, since there was great freedom in how authors could use written sources, something to which we shall return shortly.

The discussion about the oral phase of the formation of gospel traditions is, for many, associated with the question of whether the gospels are to be seen as historically reliable or not. To what degree do the gospel narratives correspond to the sayings and teachings of Jesus, which were first heard a couple of generations earlier? The question of the preconditions of historical research and the historical reconstruction of Jesus shall not be dealt with here. Instead, we will focus on the relationship between oral tradition and the written gospels. Did the disciples' focus on and belief in the resurrection shape the material to the degree that the gospels reflect more of Christian post-Easter preaching than the activity of the historical Jesus? Did the prophetic characteristics of the early Christ followers provide new and different impulses to the effect that the Jesus tradition was blended with the spiritual experiences of the believers?

Form and Function

For the form critics of the 1920s onward (Rudolf Bultmann, Martin Dibelius, and others), the *form* of the gospel traditions was of the utmost importance. The Gospels were viewed as collections of independent entities, anonymous oral traditions that had been molded into stereotypical forms such as "laws," "parables," "miracle stories," and so on. These forms were each associated with a different context and a different function, and could therefore provide scholars with information about the place of the traditions in the early church. The idea that a Jesus tradition has a *Sitz im Leben*—that is, that it has functioned and been meaningful in a real-life situation or context of the early church—is quite legitimate. It is also reasonable to suggest that the context influences the form of a tradition. The weakness of classical form criticism, however, lay in its assumptions about clear-cut forms, in romanticized analogies with the origins and formation of Germanic folktales, as well as an unrealistic belief in the scholar's ability to differentiate between Hellenistic "layers" and Palestinian "layers" in individual traditions. This led to the *Sitz im Leben* basically becoming a generalized explanation for the *origins* of the traditions. The result was a far-reaching skepticism, in which many of the Jesus sayings, and in particular the narrative traditions, were seen as inventions by prophets of the early church and based on their belief in the resurrection of Jesus.

Transmission and Memory

One of the strongest protests against this kind of form criticism came from Birger Gerhardsson in his book *Memory and Manuscript* (1961), a protest that was continued in subsequent publications. Gerhardsson suggests that in antiquity, the process of transmitting and memorizing traditions was different from our own, especially in rabbinic circles. He emphasizes memorization via repetition as the basic teaching technique of the time, basing his assertion mainly on rabbinic texts. He assumes that Jesus taught his disciples in a way similar to the teaching of the rabbis, and that, because of his venerated position as the Messiah and Son of God, his words, along with the narrative material we find in the Gospels, must have been memorized and transmitted even more carefully than rabbinic material. The traditions had, of course, undergone changes and been adapted to new environments and situations before being written down, but they had not appeared anonymously out of nowhere. They had been *shaped by* but not *created by* the needs of the early church.

Gerhardsson was criticized by other scholars for simplifying the problem and for uncritically accepting the traditions of the gospel as plain history. This is an exaggeration, since Gerhardsson in other contexts discusses the tradition's flexibility. However, the emphasis on comparison with rabbinic material and on memorization requires a number of conditions that cannot be evidenced. Gerhardsson does separate between halakic (law) and haggadic (story) traditions, and admits that the comparison does not work as well for all parts of the gospel tradition. But his basic presupposition is that even narrative parables were taught and memorized. While it is true that memorization and repetition played a larger role in antiquity than in our time, anyone comparing Jesus sayings to rabbinic sayings has to acknowledge that the transmission processes of each resulted in very different end products in different genres. The rabbinic Mishnah and Talmud represent quite a different genre than the Gospels. The highly stylized rabbinic material is adapted for oral transmission but hardly claims to be an exact repetition of the sayings of the rabbis. Rather, it represents the *content* of the teaching or the different *standpoints* in an ongoing discussion. The venerated position of Jesus that came with emerging Christology can help us understand the prominence of the Jesus tradition within the early church, but it can hardly be used to explain its *origins* and its *formation* in the period before the first "Christian" Easter, as Gerhardsson would have it.

Early eyewitnesses could have hindered the gospel traditions from developing or being innovated beyond all control, but it is hard to ascertain how many of the first disciples played an important role in the explosive development and growth that followed the resurrection experience. It does not take long before Peter and John are the only disciples mentioned, with the exception of Jesus's brother James, who does not seem to have followed Jesus during his lifetime. Greater prominence is allotted to apostles such as Paul and other less known figures. A large part of the early mission of the Jesus movement seems to have been carried out by individuals unknown to us, who adapted the traditions about Jesus to suit new settings. Here we see the relevance of form criticism when it makes the connection between form and function, although it is not necessary to deny a tradition any historical background, just because it was shaped or functioned in a certain environment.

Oral Tradition and Eyewitnesses

The issue of the origins and development of the oral Jesus tradition has continued to occupy scholars over the years. How flexible was the transmission process? What role did the *individual* play in relation to the *group*—that is, individual tradents in relation to congregations? And how does oral tradition relate to written text? What role did eyewitnesses have when traditions were written down? We shall mention here only a few of the scholars active in the debate.

Werner Kelber took an important initiative in the research on oral tradition with his book *The Oral and the Written Gospel* (1983), in which he argues that written gospels emerged as a kind of countermove and that the low proportion of sayings in Mark was due to suspicion of the oral genre. Kelber has emphasized the difference between oral performance and literary transmission of traditions. Oral performances are defined as constant variations of a base story with fixed and flexible formulations. Thus, even speaking about an original form of a tradition is problematized by this theory. Such oral retellings of Jesus traditions must have commenced already during the lifetime of Jesus, but it is problematic to categorize such retellings as "sources" the same way we do with the written sources for a new text. Kelber's view of transmission thus gives more room for creativity and variation than Gerhardsson's, but it has been criticized for being speculative and difficult to ascertain.

Another influential participant in this discussion is Samuel Byrskog, who in *Story as History—History as Story* (2000) has developed the idea of oral history further and has discussed the issue of eyewitnesses and the role of oral tradition in ancient history writing and in the formation of the gospels. In subsequent publications, Byrskog has continued to emphasize the role of the individual in relation to the group, collective memory, and social identity. In contrast to Kelber, Byrskog suggests that the Jesus tradition was put into writing in order to *preserve* oral history rather than outcompete it. At the same time he is more interested in how ancient writers viewed the relationship between their narratives and historical memories than in proving the historicity of singular traditions. It is rarely possible to tie eyewitnesses to specific stories.

In *Jesus and the Eyewitnesses* (2006), Richard Bauckham makes much more extensive claims. Referring to Byrskog, Bauckham argues that up to the point when the gospels were written, the Jesus tradition was transmitted mainly by eyewitnesses, who are also mentioned in the texts. Eyewitnesses are said to stand behind the primary sources for Mark as well as John. Bauckham's theories have received much attention in conservative circles, since he explicitly uses them to argue for the *historical* reliability of the texts. However, he rarely demonstrates his model on the texts in detail, and scholars at large remain highly skeptical.

Another model worth mentioning due to its influence during this period is James Dunn's modification of Kenneth Bailey's three categories for oral transmission, in *Jesus Remembered* (2003). The model builds on Bailey's experiences in rural villages in the Middle East, and differentiates between *informal uncontrolled* tradition (gossip, rumors; cf. Bultmann), *formal controlled* traditions (poetry, adages; cf. Gerhardsson), and *informal controlled* tradition (parables, narratives). The latter category is constantly reworked into different variations, while the core of the narrative stays the same, and the community functions as a control instance, correcting deviations. This last category (informal controlled tradition) encompasses stories that are important for the identity formation of the village/group. Traditions that are deemed irrelevant to the specific group are transmitted both informally and uncontrolled. Bailey suggests that the category of informal controlled transmission best represents the transmission of Jesus traditions from the death of Jesus to the First Jewish Revolt. Dunn proposes that certain synoptic and Q material might be better explained by oral tradition than as textual redaction, especially when deviations are large while the core and the key words remain the same.

The hypothesis has been criticized by scholars from different camps, and today it has fewer adherents than when it was first launched. An important question is whether Bailey's three categories accurately reflect the observations made in his study. Even if this were the case, it is not clear to what degree anecdotal evidence from rural villages in the twentieth century can be applied with any validity to ancient transmission of tradition. Another issue that has been raised is the freedom with which ancient authors made use of their sources. John Kloppenborg has shown how the same author has, in the same text, sometimes copied his source almost verbatim, and sometimes taken the freedom of considerably deviating from the source. Kloppenborg proved this using ancient texts that we can say with all certainty were reliant on written sources. In ancient handbooks of writing, we also find instructions for how to create a longer, freer version of a shorter text (e.g., a minimal *chreia*), and many scholars point to traces of these techniques in the Gospels. Thus, the existence of oral sources is neither necessary nor urgent as an explanatory model for the literary relationship between the Synoptic Gospels, even where large deviations are concerned. The question of what exactly ancient writing techniques can tell us about the relationship between literary gospel traditions and possible underlying oral traditions can thus be answered in a number of ways.

In more recent times, discussions about oral tradition and eyewitnesses have led to an increased interest in the role of memory, especially with regard to what is known as social or collective memory. The work of French sociologist Maurice Halbwachs (1877–1945) has been an important source of inspiration for this renewed interest, especially with regard to his theories on how our present state and its contextual frameworks influence our reconstructions of the past. However, the "memory" that is constantly "refracted" through new contextual frameworks and social settings is more of a collective tradition than individual recollections. Collective "memory" may therefore be understood as a negotiation between the past and the present, through which a contemporary relevant history is created and social identity maintained. The model can thus explain the emergence and function of a tradition, but it cannot guarantee that this tradition is based on historical events, even when this may be the case.

Hence it is questionable whether terms such as "collective or social memory" can bridge the gap between traditions and the history behind them. In order to really speak about the role of the individual's memory (e.g., the memories of eyewitnesses), something more is required. Some New Testament scholars have recently begun to enter into dialogue with memory research in modern psychology, which includes empirical investigations, but the results hardly give reason for any high expectations, since they rather point to the unreliability of memory in general and the difficulties in recalling details from memory. The more successful experiments usually build on intentional memorization. In the end, psychological memory research also fails to provide us with easy access to the history behind the traditions.

While some have high expectations of various types of orality and memory research, others are more skeptical, in particular of claims to thereby retrieve the history behind tradition. One of the sharpest critics recently is Paul Foster, who suggests that both research on memory and oral tradition and a renewed interest in the Gospel of John are dead ends with regard to the attempts to reconstruct Jesus behind the traditions. At the same time, critics and advocates alike usually agree that we cannot analyze the past, only its traces—and this cannot be satisfactorily done without acknowledging the role of oral tradition. Whether memory research will play any major role in the future remains to be seen.

While there is reason to point out the role of orality, it is important not to lose focus on the fact that the problem at hand revolves around the *texts* of the Gospels, especially the internal relationship between the Synoptic Gospels. This relationship is primarily literary and in Greek. No underlying Aramaic sources are preserved, and all ideas about Aramaic originals for Q or Mark remain unproven speculations. Singular Aramaic words provide little guidance. No attempts to reach beyond the tradition to Jesus's Aramaic teaching have proved to be sufficiently convincing.

As we have seen, the transmission process included a number of complicating factors. If our views about the reliability or value of these texts depend on their historical accuracy and require access to Jesus's own words, or the eyewitness accounts of his disciples, we will inevitably run into problems that no scholar of memory or transmission can solve. The only thing we have is tradition—but this tradition is, on the other hand, the prerequisite, the *sine qua non*, without which no story about Jesus would have been transmitted. The Gospels carry traces of the impression Jesus made on his followers and the Jesus tradition continued to make on the first Christ followers as they reflected further upon it. What scholars can do is suggest various hypotheses concerning the sort of events, sayings, and attitudes that provide us with the best and most plausible explanations for the diverging and occasionally contradicting effects we encounter in the subsequent Jesus tradition. What are the possible scenarios that best serve to explain the origins, shaping, and further developments of the traditions about Jesus?

For Whom Were the Texts Meant?

In our attempt to trace the path of the Jesus traditions into the Gospels, we have noted that the audience and users of the traditions and texts play an important role in what is transmitted and how the material is shaped. Individual stories may have had various meanings in their own diverse contexts, but as a part of a whole, integrated into a larger narrative, separate traditions also acquired a common overarching aim. Scholars have for a long time analyzed the different themes and theological aims of the different gospels, and even though there is no consensus on these issues, there is a large measure of agreement. But why were the gospels written, and for whom? The majority of scholars agree that Mark and Luke seem to be written for a more non-Jewish audience, whereas Matthew's character seems more Jewish. There is more dissent regarding the location of the gospels and their intended audience, but the question of why the gospels were written is about more than just this.

The Context of Author and Community

A common approach to this question is to assert that the gospels were shaped for use in specific communities, or for groups of communities in a specific region. We have evidence early on for communities initially using one or two gospels only in their services and readings. This does not necessarily mean that the other gospels were unknown to them; it simply means that they preferred one over the other since it was, in all likelihood, a better fit with their own Jesus traditions. We should not be misled into thinking that communities had no access to Jesus traditions before written gospels were made available. The interesting and intriguing question is why the oral tradition, which was so highly esteemed in the early congregations, even after the composition of the written gospels (see, e.g., Papias), was written down in the systematic way and in the specific form of the gospels from about 70 CE onward.

Maybe this was a natural development when, after the first generation, the need increased to bring some order among the ever-growing variant stories and provide the Jesus traditions with an overall structure. Maybe it was a result of the First Jewish Revolt, after which many of the Palestinian communities that formerly provided the base for continuous transmission no longer could continue that role. Maybe the need first arose in the rapidly growing communities of the Hellenistic cities, where the conditions for the transmission of oral traditions would have been slightly different, and where it may have been natural to complement the biblical texts already available in Greek form (the Septuagint) with both some Pauline letters and written Jesus traditions.

To All Christ Followers?

The intended audience of the Gospels has been the subject of intense debate. In a much-discussed article from 1998, Richard Bauckham claims that the Gospels were not at all written for a specific community of a certain region. Similar views were also argued by Martin Hengel around the same time. Their arguments are based on our understanding of ancient communication, road networks, the travel patterns of the apostles, and the extensive letter writing of Christ followers. With this in mind, the Gospels could be viewed as conscious attempts to spread different versions of the Jesus tradition into the whole world (though they could still be interpreted contextually).

This discussion is connected to a growing critique against reading the Gospels allegorically—that is, as allegories of the communities where, or for which, they were supposedly written. This criticism is not entirely unfounded. Extreme mirror-reading often becomes fanciful. The transmission of tradition invariably includes material that is not *directly* relevant to the individual or the group, and, as we have seen, the idea that the traditions were *created* by the needs of the contexts in which they were written down is rarely plausible. At the same time, as we have touched on, the perspective of those using the traditions has *shaped* the material, and the relevance of the traditions to the identity of the group has been crucial for its transmission. We can hardly hope to reconstruct in detail the details of a local community's history on the basis of a gospel. But we can determine certain important and characteristic contours and traits of that community, and occasionally of the region, in which the gospel in question originated.

One of Bauckham's arguments is that the authors of the Gospels, like the authors of the letters, would hardly have put such effort into producing the texts if they were meant only for their immediate community. But letters and gospels are not the same genre. The only New Testament texts that we can reasonably suppose were written for "all Christians" are the pseudepigraphic letters. Paul's authentic letters are, however, usually written to a *specific* community in which he is not present. Considering their biographical character, the Gospels would admittedly be of interest to a broader group. But if one of the main purposes of the Gospels was public reading in worship assemblies, why would an author bother writing with *another* community, or region, in mind, and why would that author not make use of the frames of reference provided by his own community context?

It is interesting to note that, for many of the noncanonical gospels that we have mentioned, one could easily make claims, equal to the four gospels, of being "universal," but they have often been said to have originated in sectarian environments. The conception that the four gospels specifically were written for "all Christians," without having to be interpreted through the framework of a particular local context, makes it easier to view them as universally authoritative, not only for the early church, but for later generations, too. This is the way they have traditionally been understood in the church. But does this understanding of them accurately reflect the aims of the authors? Could such understandings of the Gospels lead to a tendency to decontextualize their interpretation?

A text cannot restrict its audience to an intended audience or to those people who first encountered it. The New Testament is worth studying not least because, through two millennia, so many people have continued to find its texts fascinating and relevant to their lives. Because of this, one could say that the texts are meant for us as well. But this is only possible *because* they are firmly established in concrete contexts and directed to specific audiences. The contextuality of the texts does not constitute a hindrance for further interpretation of them but, on the contrary, is a precondition for it.

The Historical Development of the Canon and Other Early Circulation of Texts

The list in box 4.2 illustrates variations in the usage of texts within early Christianity. All examples, with the exception of Marcion, belong more or less to "mainstream Christendom" during the respective periods. Gnostic groups are not represented. The information on which this chart is built is of diverse character and neither conclusive nor certain. Although Canon Muratori and Codex Claromontanus present us with lists, the information gathered from many of the church fathers is based on which texts they cite and which texts they describe as being "apostolic," or as "Scripture," rather than on any conclusive list. There are many uncertainties.

Box 4.2
Canon Lists

Source	Status	Texts
Marcion, Rome, mid-second century	Accepted	Luke*, Rom, 1–2 Cor, Gal, 1–2 Thess, Laodicea Letter* (= Eph, Col, Phlm, Phil) **Marcion's accepted texts were rid of "Jewish" aspects*
	"Missing"	Matt, Mark, John, Acts, 1–2 Tim, Titus, Jas, 1–2 Pet, 1–3 John, Jude, Rev
Irenaeus, Lyon, 185	Accepted	Matt, Mark, Luke, John, Acts (albeit citing unknown Jesus sayings and referring to older traditions from Papias the Elder), Rom, 1–2 Cor, Gal, Eph, Phil, Col, 1–2 Thess, 1–2 Tim, Titus, 1 Pet, 1–2 John, Rev, Herm., 1 Clem., Pol. *Phil.*
	Rejected	Gospel of Truth, possibly all Valentinian texts
	"Missing"	Phlm, Heb*, Jas, 2 Pet, 3 John, Jude **According to Eusebius, Irenaeus cites Heb*
Canon Muratori, Rome, ca. 200	Accepted	[Matt, Mark]*, Luke, John, Acts, Rom, 1–2 Cor, Gal, Eph, Phil, Col, 1–2 Thess, 1–2 Tim, Titus, Phlm, 1–2 John, Jude, Wis, Rev, Apoc. Pet. **Fragments of the first lines are missing, but Luke is referred to as the Third Gospel*

	Debated	Herm. (good but too late, thus should not be read in worship services), Apoc. Pet. (not accepted by everyone to be read in services)
	Rejected	Paul's letter to Laodicea and Alexandria; gnostic texts
	"Missing"	Heb, 1–2 Pet, Jas, 3 John
Clement of Alexandria, ca. 200	Accepted	Matt, Mark, Luke, John, Acts, Rom, 1–2 Cor, Gal, Eph, Phil, Col, 1–2 Thess, 1–2 Tim, Titus, Heb, 1 Pet, 1–2 John, Jude, Rev, Apoc. Pet., Did., Herm., Barn., 1 Clem., a Jesus tradition from the Acts of John; also quotes a number of other Jesus traditions
	Debated	Greek Gospel of the Egyptians (cited with reservation), Secret Gospel of Mark (maybe a forgery)
	"Missing"	Phlm, Jas
Origen, Alexandria, mid-third century (partly reconstructed using Eusebius)	Accepted	Matt, Mark, Luke, John, Acts, Rom, 1–2 Cor, Gal, Eph, Phil, Col, 1–2 Thess, 1–2 Tim, Titus, Phlm, Jas*, 1 Pet, 1 John, Jude*, Rev **Missing in Eusebius's list, but cited by Origen*
	Debated	Heb (thoughts come from the apostle [Paul], but only God knows who wrote it), 2 Pet, 2–3 John
	Rejected	Greek Gospel of the Egyptians, Did., Gospel of Basilides, Gospel of Matthias, and "some others" (commentary added in Eusebius)
	"Missing"	Jas, Jude (missing in Eusebius's list, but cited by Origen)
Eusebius, Caesarea, ca. 300 CE	Accepted	Matt, Mark, Luke, Acts, Rom, 1–2 Cor, Gal, Eph, Phil, Col, 1–2 Thess, 1–2 Tim, Titus, Phlm, Heb, 1 Pet, 1 John, Rev ("if it is correct")
	Debated	"Appreciated by most": Jas, 2 Pet, 2–3 John, Jude "Doubtful": Rev*, Heb**, Apoc. Pet., Did., Herm., Barn., Acts of Paul **"if it is correct"* ***According to many, but appreciated by Jewish Christ followers*

	Rejected	Gos. Pet., Gos. Thom., Gospel of Matthias, and all other gospels; Acts of Andrew, Acts of John, and all other Acts
Codex Claromontanus, ca. fourth century	Accepted	Matt, Mark, Luke, John, Acts, Rom, 1–2 Cor, Gal, Eph, [Phil, 1–2 Thess]*, Col, 1–2 Tim, Titus, Phlm, Barn. = Heb(?), Jas, 1–2 Pet, 1–3 John, Jude, Rev, Apoc. Pet., Herm., Acts of Paul _* three lines missing in the manuscript, with space enough for these titles_
	"Missing"	Heb (?)
Athanasius, Alexandria, Easter Letter of 367	Accepted	Matt, Mark, Luke, John, Acts, Rom, 1–2 Cor, Gal, Eph, Phil, Col, 1–2 Thess, 1–2 Tim, Titus, Phlm, Heb, Jas, 1–2 Pet, 1–3 John, Jude, Rev
	Debated	"Recommended by the fathers": Did., Herm.
	Rejected	Apocryphal writings
Didymus, Alexandria, end of the fourth century	Accepted	Matt, Mark, Luke, John, Acts, Rom, 1–2 Cor, Gal, Eph, Phil, Col, 1–2 Thess, 1–2 Tim, Titus, Heb, Jas, 1–2 Pet, 1 John, Jude, Rev, Did., Herm., 1 Clem., Barn., Ign. *Rom.*
	Missing	Phlm, 2–3 John
Syrian churches, 300–400 CE	Accepted	Diatessaron (Tatian's gospel harmony), Acts, Rom, 1–2 Cor, 3 Cor*, Gal, Eph, Phil, Col, 1–2 Thess, 1–2 Tim, Titus, Heb _*Used by many churches during the fourth century, but not included in the Peshitta of the fifth century_
	Debated	Phlm, Jas, 1 Pet, 1 John; they were included in the Peshitta
	"Missing"	The four individual gospels, 2 Pet, 2–3 John, Jude, Rev

Further Reading

Burkett, Delbert. *Rethinking the Gospel Sources: From Proto-Mark to Mark*. London: T&T Clark, 2004.

Dunn, James D. G. *Jesus Remembered*. Vol. 1 of *Christianity in the Making*. Grand Rapids: Eerdmans, 2003.

Ehrman, Bart D., and Michael W. Holmes. *The Text of the New Testament in Contemporary Research: Essays on the Status Quaestionis.* 2nd ed. Leiden: Brill, 2013.
Foster, Paul. "Memory, Orality, and the Fourth Gospel: Three Dead-Ends in Historical Jesus Research." *JSHJ* 10 (2012): 191–227.
Haines-Eitzen, Kim. *Guardians of Letters: Literacy, Power, and the Transmitters of Early Christian Literature.* Oxford: Oxford University Press, 2000.
Hilhorst, Anton, ed. *The Apostolic Age in Patristic Thought.* Leiden: Brill, 2004.
Hill, Charles E., and Michael J. Kruger, eds. *The Early Text of the New Testament.* New York: Oxford University Press, 2012.
Kazen, Thomas. "Sectarian Gospels for Some Christians? Intention and Mirror Reading in the Light of Extra-Canonical Texts." *NTS* 51 (2005): 561–78.
Kelber, Werner H., and Samuel Byrskog, eds. *Jesus in Memory: Traditions in Oral and Scribal Perspective.* Waco: Baylor University Press, 2009.
Kloppenborg, John S. "Memory, Performance, and the Sayings of Jesus." *JSHJ* 10 (2012): 97–132.
Luomanen, Petri. *Recovering Jewish-Christian Sects and Gospels.* Leiden: Brill, 2012.
Metzger, Bruce M. *The Canon of the New Testament: Its Origin, Development, and Significance.* Oxford: Clarendon, 1987.
Roukema, Riemer. "La tradition apostolique et le canon du noveau testament." Pages 86–103 in *The Apostolic Age in Patristic Thought.* Edited by Anton Hilhorst. Leiden: Brill, 2004.
Wachtel, Klaus, and Michael W. Holmes, eds. *The Textual History of the Greek New Testament: Changing Views in Contemporary Research.* Atlanta: Society of Biblical Literature, 2011.
Wasserman, Tommy, and Peter Gurry. *A New Approach to Textual Criticism: An Introduction to the Coherence-Based Genealogical Method.* Resources for Biblical Study 80. Atlanta: SBL Press, 2017.

The Gospels and the Acts of the Apostles

Gospel as Genre

When the word "gospel" is used today, it is usually associated with the books of the New Testament. However, when these books were written, the word was not thought about in the same way. The word "gospel" means "good news" and probably has its roots in the Hellenistic ruler cult, where, for example, the life and actions of the emperors were described as good news for humanity. In early Christ groups, "good news" was used to refer to the message of God to humanity in the gospel about Jesus Christ. In the Greek translation of the Hebrew Bible, the Septuagint (LXX), the word *euangelizomai* is used to translate the Hebrew word *bsr*, which means "to convey the message of salvation." Thus the word "gospel" also has Semitic roots.

In Mark, Jesus is presented as the one proclaiming the gospel of God (Mark 1:14); at the same time, he is the subject of the author's own proclamation of salvation—ergo, the gospel *about* Jesus (Mark 1:1). Mark represents a literary expression of the theological belief that Jesus from Nazareth is the divine Savior. In the telling of his story, history, narrative, and sermons go hand in hand.

The Jesus narrative has been compared to the prophet and royal biographies of the Hebrew Bible, especially with regard to the stories of Moses, Elijah, and David. Scholars have also suggested that Mark has based his narrative on the suffering servant in Isa 53. In Hellenistic culture, Mark has been compared to the genre of Greco-Roman biography. None of the comparisons are completely satisfactory. While most scholars agree that the Gospels represent a form of ancient biography, some scholars have concluded that we have here a new literary genre that weaves together history, narrative, and sermon/mission and refers to the events with salvation-historical relevance for both the past and the present. When Matthew and Luke eventually follow in the footsteps of Mark, this new genre has become an established form.

The Synoptic Problem

As noted earlier, Matthew, Mark, and Luke are often referred to as the Synoptic Gospels, a term meant to reflect the fact that they are very similar. The problem constituted by this similarity is that we do not know in which order they were written or how exactly to explain the literary dependence between them. This problem is known as the Synoptic problem. Four basic observations about the tradition material have led to different theories about the literary dependence between the gospels. The observations are as follows:

1. *Triple tradition*: material shared by Mark, Matthew, and Luke
2. *Double tradition*: material found only in Matthew and Luke
3. *Special Matthew*: material found only in Matthew
4. *Special Luke*: material found only in Luke

An early Christian explanation of the problem can be found in the writings of the church father Augustine, who suggested that the order was the same as that of the New Testament: Matthew, Mark, Luke. Luke was thus seen as being based on Matthew, and maybe also on Mark (see fig. 4.1). Toward the end of the eighteenth century, solving the problem became a popular quest among scholars of the Bible again. The above observations led to a series of explanatory models. One was the *Ur-Gospel hypothesis*, according to which the Synoptics were independently influenced by a Hebrew or Aramaic original (*Ur*) source. The difficulty with this hypothesis is that it cannot be verified.

Another hypothesis was the *fragment hypothesis*, according to which the gospel authors had independently pieced together their unique narratives using documents and notes containing fragments of the Jesus narrative. The main criticism of this theory is that it cannot explain how the order of these fragments could to such a high degree be shared by the gospels. A third hypothesis, known as the *tradition or oral gospel hypothesis*, suggested the existence of an original, oral gospel that was translated into Greek by the gospel authors and interpreted by them in different ways. The problem with this theory is that the literary similarities between them are very close, sometimes verbatim, and, it has been argued, it is near impossible for an oral source to be transmitted with such accuracy.

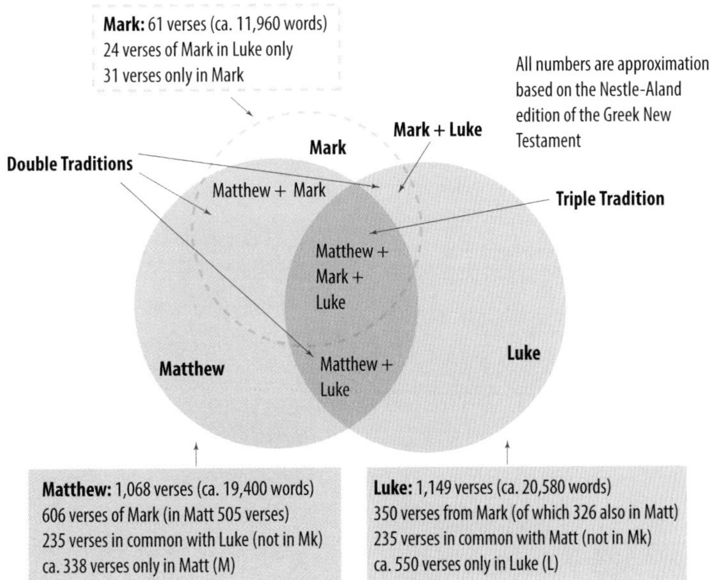

Figure 4.1 The relationships among the Synoptic Gospels: triple tradition, double tradition, and traditions unique to the individual gospels.

Soon scholars came to favor solutions building on the assumption of some sort of literary dependence of the three gospels. With this as the point of departure, Johann Jakob Griesbach suggested in 1789 that the order of composition was Matthew, Luke, Mark. Mark was seen as a summarized version of Matthew, using Luke as an additional source (see fig. 4.2).

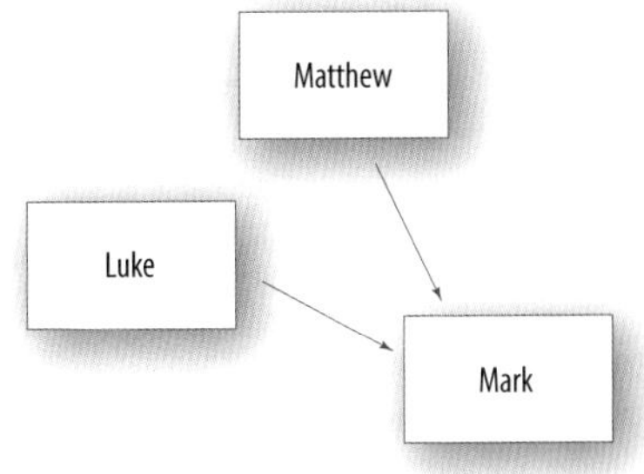

Figure 4.2 The Griesbach hypothesis.

The Griesbach theory left many questions unanswered, and it was not until Karl Lachmann radically reversed the order and questioned Matthean priority in 1835 that the first steps toward what many (but not all) see as the solution to the Synoptic problem could be taken. Lachmann's most important observation was that Matthew and Luke have the same wording only in pericopes they also share with Mark. In addition, Matthew and Luke rarely deviate from the Markan wording in the same way, and because of this Lachmann assumed that they cannot have had access to each other. Three years after

Lachmann's breakthrough, Christian Hermann Weisse introduced the theory that Matthew and Luke, written independently of each other, had both used a second, now lost, source containing only Jesus sayings. This hypothetical source was referred to as "Q," from the German word *Quelle*, meaning "source." The two-source hypothesis was born (see fig. 4.3).

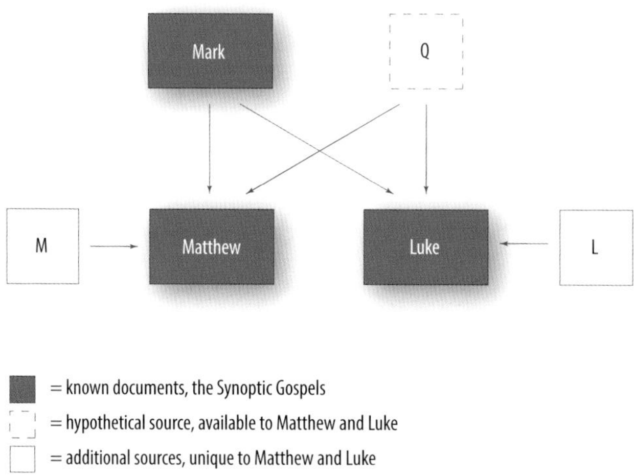

Figure 4.3 The two-source hypothesis.

According to this hypothesis, Matthew and Luke used material not only from Mark but also from an otherwise unknown source, Q, as well as some traditions known only to these authors, respectively (M and L). For this reason, this hypothesis is sometimes called the four-source hypothesis. However, since it is difficult to determine whether the special material unique to each of the two gospels comes from one or more sources, it is preferable to stay with the former designation (two-source hypothesis). The hypothesis is based on the assumption that Matthew and Luke were written independently of each other.

The differences between Matthew and Luke are explained by the fact that Matthew is more prone to systematizing his material thematically, most clearly exemplified by Matt 4:23–11:1, while Luke prefers to insert other materials into the Markan text, best exemplified by Luke 9:51–18:14 (the "great insertion"). Pericopes taken from Mark are shortened, and the wording/formulations have often been changed. In total, there are only three Markan pericopes (Mark 4:26–29; 7:31–37; 8:22–26) and a number of shorter sayings (Mark 2:27; 3:20–21; 9:48–49; 14:52–53; 15:44) that cannot be found in Matthew or Luke. Two of the missing pericopes tell the story of Jesus healing a deaf man and a blind man, respectively. Perhaps the authors of Matthew and Luke did not desire to portray Jesus as the typical miracle worker. It is more difficult to explain the absence of the parable of the growing seed (Mark 4:26–27).

According to many scholars, the linguistic and stylistic deviations from Mark in Matthew and Luke should be seen for the most part as corrections and improvements of the latter's weak Greek. Similarly, the changes to Mark's narrative content are explained as corrections of what the authors of Matthew and Luke see as factual errors, or simply as purposeful changes of the theological content.

One of the major problems with the two-source hypothesis is that it fails to explain the almost seven hundred cases where Matthew and Luke agree *against* Mark, in material coming from Mark. These so-called *minor agreements* consist of shared changes in wording, details, additions, and retractions. An example of a minor agreement is when Jesus is on trial before the council and is beaten and taunted while blindfolded. Matthew and Luke both have the addition "Who was it that hit you?," a phrase missing in the Markan material. In an attempt to explain such instances, some scholars have suggested that the Markan text we have access to today has actually been edited (deutero-Mark), and that the original version, which corresponded to Matthew and Luke's minor agreements and has now been lost, was the one actually used by Matthew and Luke when they composed their gospels.

As mentioned above, the hypothetical source Q is the key for the two-source hypothesis to work. The strongest arguments in favor of the existence of such a document are as follows: (1) the similarities in wording in Matthew and Luke are too great to not indicate some sort of literary connection; (2) the wording in Matthew and Luke of the material proposed to come from Q generally matches; and (3) Matthew and Luke share a number of doublets in relation to the Markan material. One of the strongest arguments for Matthew and Luke being composed independently of each other is that the Q material they use is almost never used in the same order in relation to the Markan material they both use.

The two-source hypothesis has, of course, not remained above criticism. The *Farrer hypothesis* is a well-known theory that has recently been attracting more adherents. This theory, first introduced by Austin Farrer in 1955, also assumes Markan priority but suggests that Matthew used and adjusted Mark, and that Luke had access to both Matthew and Mark as well as his own material in the composition of his gospel. Thus, the order here is Mark–Matthew–Luke, with Matthew having access to Mark, and Luke having access to both Mark and Matthew (see fig. 4.4).

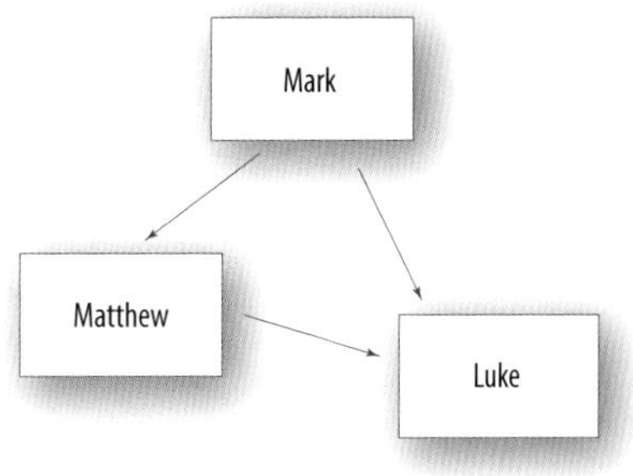

Figure 4.4 The Farrer hypothesis.

The Farrer hypothesis has had many supporters over the years and is today championed especially by M. D. Goulder and Mark Goodacre. One of the main criticisms of this theory is that it does not explain why Luke does not contain any typical Matthean characteristics.

Critics find it unlikely that texts such as the Sermon on the Mount and other carefully composed entities should be reorganized or excluded by Luke. Another criticism is that the theory fails to account for the great similarity in wording in the material supposedly stemming from Q (according to the two-source hypothesis) when the same is not true for other shared material. On the other hand, the Farrer hypothesis has no need for Q, and it is possible that the Jesus sayings could have been treated differently by Luke, who had access, according to this theory, to Matthew's Gospel.

Q as a Source and Historical Background

Q has been reconstructed backward from the non-Markan parallels in Matthew and Luke. The material almost exclusively consists of sayings, many of them dealing with warnings about the coming judgment. There are only a few stories, such as the story of Jesus's temptation and the healing of the officer's servant in Capernaum, included in Q. The Q material (= double tradition) begins with John the Baptist and ends with sayings about the end of the ages. The original wording is thought to be better preserved in Luke than in Matthew, since the Q material is almost exclusively found in the small and large Lukan insertions. The Q source, as reconstructed from Luke and Matthew, is believed to contain around four thousand words.

Because of the similarity between Matthew and Luke, Q is assumed to be a written Greek source. Scholars debate whether there is an underlying Aramaic tradition. Because of the content and geographical allusions in the Q material, it is assumed to have originated in a Jewish area, perhaps in Galilee, during the 40s CE. The existence of the temple is taken for granted, the ministry seems defined by wandering preachers, mission to non-Jews had begun, and so had persecution from other Jewish groups. The story of the officer in Capernaum could have been a story intended to open the door for non-Jews. Ideals of poverty and breaking away from normal social life are weaved together with practical teachings on stewardship and divorce. Because of this, the group behind the composition of Q is assumed to have consisted of both wandering missionaries and Christ followers living more normal, settled lives.

Jesus and his message are the core of the theology in Q. The way one relates to Jesus is soteriologically decisive (see, e.g., Luke 12:8–9Q). The death of Jesus is taken as fact (e.g., Luke 14:27Q), but the implications of the Easter events are not expanded on or dealt with. Instead, the earthly Jesus and the resurrected Jesus seem to be one and the same person.

Reconstructing a group and its theology on the basis of a hypothetical source is not without its problems. The entirety of the Q source may not even be included in the Gospels; there is no way of knowing this since Q is reconstructed only on the basis of double tradition. Nevertheless, from the material included in Matthew and Luke, we can piece together what we know about Q in the following fashion:

A The beginning
B Jesus's Sermon on the Plain
C The story of the God-fearing non-Jew
D John the Baptist
E Discipleship and mission
F Prayer
G Disputes and accusations
H Correct confession
I Correct focus and vigilance
J Parables and other Jesus sayings
K The end of the ages

The Gospel of Mark

Author

The title *The Gospel according to Mark* is not original to the manuscript. Papias of Hierapolis said circa 130 CE, "Mark was Peter's interpreter, and he carefully wrote down everything he remembered about what had been said and done by the Lord, however not in chronological order" (Eusebius, *Ecclesiastical History* 3.39.15 [author's trans.]). Papias emphasized the reliability of Mark by associating him with Peter, an eyewitness. According to Papias, this tradition can be traced back to the presbyter John. The question is whether this connection between Mark and Peter is historical. The assertion that the gospel had been authored by someone called Mark is likely reliable, since it would have been advantageous to attribute the gospel to a known apostle. Some have suggested that the author is the John Mark who is listed as a companion of Paul (Acts 12:25; Phlm 24). It is possible that there was indeed a connection to Peter via the letter bearing his name (1 Pet 5:13; cf. Acts 12:12). On the other hand, it is plausible that the tradition Papias is speaking of is not historical at all, especially with regard to the fact that the Gospel of Mark has no traces of Pauline or Petrine theology.

It is perhaps more plausible that the author of Mark was an author who is otherwise unknown to us. His mother tongue seems to have been Greek, but the usage of Aramaic and Hebrew expressions in his text implies at least cursory knowledge of these as well. The usage of many Latin words, such as *legio* and *centurio*, indicates that the gospel was written in a context where Latin was spoken. Many have therefore assumed the gospel to have been written in Rome, especially since Peter ended his days there. However, other large cities, such as Antioch in Syria, could also have been the place of composition; Syria certainly seems to be the preferred location for a majority of scholars today. The fact that Jewish customs are explained

(Mark 7:3–4) indicates that the gospel was written for a non-Jewish audience and/or for hellenized Jews in the diaspora with little or no connection with traditions practiced in the homeland.

Dating the Gospel

The gospel is usually dated to shortly prior to or following the destruction of the temple in 70 CE. In Mark 13:2 and 13:14, the fall of the temple is taken for granted, yet the allusions are vague and belong to the source material of the evangelist. If Mark wrote after 70 CE, some scholars argue, he surely would have placed more of an emphasis on the fulfillment of the prophecies about the temple (cf. Luke 21:21, 24). The apocalyptic material behind Mark 13 is without doubt relevant if one would date the gospel to 68–70 CE. Emperor Nero, the man who had ordered the brutal persecution of Christ followers in Rome, had been murdered in Rome. The First Jewish Revolt consumed Galilee and Judea. The threat to Jerusalem, including the Christ followers living there, was imminent. Maybe this atmosphere of fear and destruction is what led Mark to end his gospel with the words "So they went out and fled from the tomb, for terror and amazement had seized them; and they said nothing to anyone, for they were afraid" (16:8).

Mark 16:9–20 is a later addition made by a later author, since it is missing in all the best-preserved early manuscripts. The addition is an amalgamation of the endings of the other three gospels and Acts. Many scholars believe that the actual ending has been lost, assuming that Mark could not have meant to end the gospel with the words of 16:8. Perhaps a reference to Q is helpful here. Q, as reconstructed, does not include a passion narrative or any mention of the resurrection, but still makes reference to a risen Lord. In Mark, the realization that Jesus is the Messiah is supposed to be kept secret—a secret known to the readers of the gospel. In fact, the text is full of references to and repetitions of information that was common knowledge in the early Christ groups: "But after I am raised up, I will go before you to Galilee" (14:28). This verse foreshadows the words the angel utters at the end of the gospel: "But go, tell his disciples and Peter that he is going ahead of you to Galilee; there you will see him, just as he told you" (16:7).

Audience and Context

There are a number of indications that Mark was written with a larger non-Jewish audience in mind. Issues of morality and the double love commandments are central, but cultic rules are evidently missing. This does not exclude a Jewish audience, but it may make the message more relevant for non-Jews, especially, perhaps, after the destruction of the Jerusalem temple in 70 CE. It is reasonable to assume that an active mission to non-Jews was ongoing at that time (Mark 7:1–37). Other scholars point out that this pericope can hardly be described as a mission to non-Jews given Jesus's reluctant reply to the non-Jewish woman who asks him to exorcise a demon that possesses her daughter (7:26–27). Regardless of the views and actions of the historical Jesus, which we cannot determine with certainty, it appears to be taken for granted that Mark's audience presupposes a mission to the gentiles. Such a scenario is supported also by the two feeding miracles (6:30–44; 8:1–10). The first, where five thousand men plus women and children eat their fill, takes place among Jews, in a Jewish area. The second, where four thousand people are mentioned, takes place in a non-Jewish area, where we may assume the author implies non-Jews were also present. Moreover, the eucharistic overtones point to a time when the Lord's Supper is a integral part of community life.

A worldwide mission is implied in a number of passages: Mark 12:9; 13:10; and 14:9. One may also note that it is a Roman officer who, as Jesus dies on the cross, utters the words "Truly, this man was God's son!" (15:39).

The Colosseum, exterior and interior views. The Colosseum was planned and begun by Emperor Vespasian. His son Titus completed the structure in 80 CE. The underground structures were completed by Domitian. The term *Colosseum* comes from the ninth century and referred to the colossal bronze statue of Emperor Nero that stood just outside the amphitheater. In antiquity the Colosseum was known as *Amphitheatrum Caesareum*. Photos by Dieter Mitternacht.

Content and Redaction

The proclamation of Jesus as the Son of God is the theological core of Mark's Gospel. The book as a whole is about the "good news of Jesus Christ, the Son of God" (1:1). At the baptism of Jesus, a voice from heaven is heard (1:9–11), and demons realize the power of Jesus and tremble with fear (3:11; 5:7). On the Mount of Transfiguration, three of Jesus's disciples have this power revealed to them (9:7); the high priest later confronts Jesus, and the latter's response leads to his death (14:61–64). Finally, a Roman officer declares that he must have been the Son of God (15:39).

The gospel in its entirety represents a drama revolving around the purpose of Jesus's life and ministry. In an unhistorical yet dramatically effective way, the gospel traces the narrative from Jesus's baptism to his only, final, and theologically decisive journey to Jerusalem. The first half of the gospel tells the story of Jesus's ministry and its aim, all within a Galilean context (1:1–8:26). Already at this stage of the narrative, we can see a foreshadowing of resistance, suffering, and death (2:6–7; 3:6). In Mark 8:27 we see a geographical and theological turning point. Jesus begins his journey to Jerusalem, and his coming suffering is predicted three times (8:27–10:52). The third part of the gospel takes place in Jerusalem (11:1–16:8). Jesus is greeted like a king by the people (11:9–10) and is later executed as a messiah claimant (15:2–4, 26).

It is difficult to say anything about the sources behind the gospel with any degree of certainty. However, most scholars agree on the fact that the passion narrative (14:1–16:8) is based on an older source, and that both oral and written material was added into the eschatological speech (Mark 13). Even the parables of Mark 4 have their origins in pre-Markan material.

The Structure of the Gospel of Mark

1:1–13	Introduction: John the Baptist's ministry, Jesus's baptism
1:14–8:26	*I. Jesus's ministry in the Galilee and the surrounding region*
1:14–45	Jesus calls his disciples, preaches, and performs miracles
2:1–3:6	Conflicts with the scribes and Pharisees
3:7–35	The Twelve are selected; Jesus and his family
4:1–34	Parables
4:35–5:43	Miracle stories
6:1–56	Continued ministry in the Galilee; the feeding of the five thousand
7:1–23	Questions of purity and defilement
7:24–8:10	Miracles performed among non-Jews; the feeding of the four thousand
8:11–26	To be able to interpret the signs and see

8:27–10:52	*II. The journey to Jerusalem*
8:27–9:1	Peter's confession; the first prediction of suffering
9:2–50	The transfiguration; the second prediction of suffering
10:1–52	Nearing Jerusalem; the third prediction of suffering
11:1–16:8	*III. The dramatic conclusion in Jerusalem*
11:1–25	The entry into Jerusalem and the cleansing of the temple
11:27–12:44	Conflicts and adversarial dialogues
13:1–37	Eschatological speech about the end of the ages
14:1–15:47	The passion narrative
16:1–8	The empty tomb
16:9–20	Later addition—the risen Christ reveals himself

Box 4.3
On the Structure of Mark

The structure suggested here is one of many different interpretations of Mark's structure. It is based on the observation that every section begins with a key to the entirety of the section. Part one begins with the core of Jesus's preaching (1:14–15), part two begins with the climax and turning point of the story (8:27–30), and part three begins with a manifestation of the realization that Jesus is the Messiah (11:1–11). "Hosanna! Blessed is he who comes in the name of the Lord. Blessed is the coming kingdom of our ancestor David! Hosanna in the highest!" (11:9–10). Even the endings of the sections seem to match. Parts one and two both end with a story of how blind men regain their sight, and part three ends with the angel telling the disciples (through the women at the tomb) to go to Galilee, where they will see the risen Jesus (16:1–8). Thus, the core of the gospel is to see and to realize the (secret) messiahship of Jesus.

Many scholars divide the gospel into two roughly equivalent sections. The first section consists of Jesus's ministry (1:1–8:26), and the second section consists of Jesus's path to suffering and death (8:27–16:8). Such a division does not differ much from the above three-partite suggestion in terms of the significant aspects of the text. Perhaps the thematic observations speak in favor of a division of the text into three parts rather than two. If one reads Mark as a story, the dramatic characteristics of the text emerge more clearly and 8:31–14:42 could be viewed as the major turning point in the narrative. The (narrative) situation worsens for Jesus, and confrontations between him and his opponents become successively more aggressive and serious in nature. The narratives of the preparations for the Passover, the maneuvers of the traitor, and the Last Supper build on each other and culminate in Judas's betrayal of Jesus and Jesus's subsequent arrest, torture, and death (14:43–15:47).

Key Theological Thoughts

A foundational theological thought in Mark is that Jesus's true identity is a secret. The demons know who he is, but they are sternly ordered to keep silent. Exorcisms and miracles are, according to Mark, not enough of an indication of Jesus's true identity. When Jesus performs a miracle, he forbids those he heals to speak of the event, but rumors about him spread nonetheless (e.g., 7:36). Not even the disciples are able to fully grasp who Jesus is. They do not understand his actions or his parables. Eventually, Peter realizes that Jesus is the Messiah (8:29), but he is immediately reproached by Jesus for his lack of understanding of the necessity of Jesus's suffering (8:33). Mark offers his audience the chance to have a better understanding of Jesus's identity than do the characters in his narrative. An important aspect of the messianic secret is that the disciples are forbidden to reveal Jesus's true identity (8:30 and 9:9). The truth is not allowed to become public knowledge until *after* the Son of Man has suffered and been resurrected from the dead. Any true discipleship has to be characterized by this realization: "If any want to become my followers, let them deny themselves and take up their cross and follow me" (8:34).

Behind Mark's theology lie hidden a number of important problems and questions that the author has obviously wrestled with. For example, if Jesus was the Messiah, why did he not evict the Romans from the Holy Land? If Jesus was the Son of Man, why did he not arrive on the clouds in order to judge the world? An important answer to these questions was the necessity of Jesus's suffering and death. The problem with this perspective, however, is that we have no evidence of this messianic model in contemporary Jewish thought. The belief in a suffering messiah had to be developed by the early Christ followers, who based it in large part on texts such as Ps 22, Ps 69, and Isa 53. An important theological thought in Mark is that the Son of Man gave his life as "a ransom for many" (10:45). That the curtain in the temple was torn in two when Jesus died is symbolic, signifying that Jesus was the final and perfect offering (15:38).

The kingdom of God is as yet only close (1:15), but it has been made visible through the words and deeds of Jesus. The disciples followed him without hesitation (1:16–20). Jesus taught and performed miracles with the same power behind his words (1:22, 27). He did not come to call the righteous; rather, he came to call sinners (2:17). Jesus was lord over the Sabbath (2:28). When Jesus healed the sick and forgave sins, evil had to give way, and the kingdom of God could break forth. The author of Mark was convinced that Jesus would be revealed as an apocalyptic judge at the end of the ages (13:24–37). That the kingdom and reign of God was fast-approaching and would soon be established is one of the most important and central messages of the gospel (9:1).

The Gospel of Matthew

Author

Papias of Hierapolis (ca. 130 CE) said the following of Matthew: "Matthew collected and organized words/sayings (*logia*) in Hebrew dialect and each one translated/interpreted them according to his ability" (Eusebius, *Ecclesiastical History* 3.39.16 [author's trans.]). Papias is probably referring to Aramaic when he speaks of a "Hebrew dialect." The words of Papias are notoriously difficult to interpret, and the main question is whether they are reliable. In all likelihood, by "Matthew" Papias was referring to the disciple Matthew. As a historian, however, one can ask oneself how logical it would be for an eyewitness to use material from someone who was not an eyewitness (Mark). In the Gospel of Matthew itself, the disciple is identified as a tax collector, called Levi in Mark (Matt 9:9; Mark 2:14). This could be an indication that Matthew was an important figure in the community from which the gospel sprung. The reference to the disciple by Papias may be seen as an attempt to lend legitimacy to the gospel by linking it to an apostle. In any case, the author seems to have been a well-educated scribe and teacher of Scripture.

The most disputed question concerning the author of the gospel is whether he was a Jew or a non-Jew. In favor of a Jewish author, scholars refer to the emphasis in the gospel on the continued validity of the Mosaic law (5:17–20), the references to the fulfillment of Scripture (1:22–23), the sending of the disciples to the "lost sheep of the house of Israel" only (10:5–6), the validity of the Sabbath commandment (24:20), and the continued authority of the scribes and Pharisees in settings frequented by Jesus followers (23:2–3). In addition, Jesus is portrayed as the new Moses (4:1–2; 5:1). In favor of a non-Jewish argument, scholars refer to the theory that the entire gospel culminates in 28:18–20, where Jesus sends his disciples out to the nations. In the Sermon on the Mount, Jesus is portrayed as a lawgiver superior to Moses (esp. 5:21–48), and the Pharisaic authority and interpretation of the law is continually questioned and challenged. Matthew replaces Aramaic expressions with Greek ones (e.g., 7:11 and 15:5). In addition, the ritual laws seem to be relativized, at least to some degree (15:20, but cf. 23:23), and perhaps some of the more detailed Sabbath rules have undergone a similar process (12:8). However, this "relativization" does not necessarily have to situate the gospel outside a Jewish setting. Rather, it could instead reflect an inner-Jewish debate about the specifics of the Sabbath commandment. Some scholars argue that the expression "your synagogues" indicates a social distancing from Jewish life (e.g., 23:34), whereas others argue that this is yet another reflection of an inner-Jewish conflict, where one Jewish group is criticizing the association synagogue of the other (see box 2.4, p. 73). Matthew 21:33–46 has sometimes been used as evidence for the non-Jewish authorship of the gospel. However, the concluding comment indicates that the group under criticism is not the Jewish people as a whole but rather the Jewish leadership. In verse 46 the people are portrayed as being on Jesus's side, against the leaders.

Further, there is tension in the gospel with regard to the concept of mission. From forbidding mission to non-Jews (10:5–6), the gospel ends with the Great Commission (28:18–20), in which Jesus orders the disciples to carry out mission to all nations. Some scholars explain this seemingly strange turn of events by suggesting that the gospel consists of two layers of traditions from different time periods; others would rather note the narrative progression of the gospel, where the ending becomes the interpretative key to the previous parts of the story. It is not until Jesus has acquired all power in heaven and on earth (28:18) that a worldwide mission can begin. One could also imagine that the two positions—mission to Jews only and mission to both Jews and non-Jews—represent the scope of convictions about mission present in the context from which the Gospel of Matthew originated. For obvious reasons, these observations complicate the issue of the religio-ethnic identity of the author.

Dating the Gospel

If we assume that Matthew used Mark as a source for his own gospel, we must of course assume that Matthew was written after Mark. Several features in Matthew would seem to justify this hypothesis. One such detail is that the destruction of the temple in Jerusalem seems to be taken for granted (22:7; 23:38; 24:1–2). Related to this, the temple is described in Mark as a "house of prayer *for all nations*" (Mark 11:17), whereas in Matthew this saying excludes "for all nations," thus signaling a focus on the Jewish people (Matt 21:13). Matthew seems, further, to distance the main character of his gospel from some contemporary Jewish terminology with regard to hierarchies: "But you are not to be called rabbi, for you have one teacher, and you are all students" (23:8). It is possible such a ruling indicates that the gospel was written sometime after the fall of the temple. Stronger arguments suggesting a late date of the text are those that highlight time-related comments that the suffering, death, and resurrection of Jesus occurred quite a long time ago, such as "still today" and "even to this day" (27:8; 28:15). In terms of Christology, Jesus is described as being one person of a larger triad consisting of himself, God, and the Holy Spirit (28:19). Even though it is difficult to say anything positive about the development of Trinitarianism—Matthew is certainly not an example of the doctrine of the Trinity decided on in Nicaea in the fourth century—most scholars would suggest that, even if not a conclusive argument, the mention of the three as cosmic powers (cf. 28:18) would likely date Matthew later than Mark. While it is difficult to say anything certain about how early Matthew was written, the reception of the gospel could provide a *terminus ante quem*. If one agrees that Ignatius of Antioch quoted from Matthew's Gospel, then we would have a rather certain indication that the gospel must have been written sometime before 110 CE, the approximate time when Ignatius was executed. Because of these arguments, most scholars date the gospel to around 80–90 CE.

The location where Matthew was written is the object of debate among scholars. A majority of scholars argue that the text was composed in Syria, and more specifically in Antioch. There is a comment in Matthew, which is absent from the other gospels, in which the author writes that "his fame spread throughout all Syria" (4:24). The gospel seems to have been known and used by the authors of the Didache and, as noted, Bishop Ignatius of Antioch. The problem is that while it is clear that the Didache is closely related to Matthew, the location of the Didache itself is far from certain. Antioch had a large Jewish population, which could speak in favor of this gospel being written there. Other locations in Syria have also been suggested, but an increasing number of scholars now argue that the gospel was composed in one of the Galilean cities, such as Sepphoris or Tiberias, or even in a smaller town like Capernaum.

Audience and Context

Matthew's earliest audience or audiences seem to have experience with persecution, which would have meant, among other things, punishment within the framework of different synagogues (10:17–18; 23:34). This indicates a situation *within* Judaism, while also pointing to growing tensions between the Matthean group(s) and other Jews. Some scholars suggest that much of the criticism directed by the Matthean Jesus at the scribes and Pharisees was actually meant by the author to target his own contemporaries in the late first century. The problem with this is that a Pharisee during the time of Jesus and a Pharisee in Antioch during the 80–90s CE are far from identical. These scholars argue, then, that in Matthew's narrative the descriptions of the two are woven together, which, if nothing else, raises some interesting questions in terms of the interpretation of the Bible. The author of the gospel asserts, in what often appears to modern Christians as a contradiction, that followers of Jesus have to exceed the Pharisees in their righteousness.

An important aim of the author seems to have been to provide his readers with guidance based on the Jewish law (5:17), and to encourage a faith expressed in good deeds—requiring, even, that followers be "perfect" (5:48). Perhaps Matthew's demanding attitude in this regard should be attributed to the fact that there may have been Christ groups in the same area who believed that the Torah no longer had a salvific function. The warnings against false prophets may have been directed against Christ followers of this persuasion (7:15–23; cf. 5:19). According to Matthew, one should not throw the baby out with the bathwater.

A majority of scholars today agree that Matthew's Gospel was very likely written by a Jew or Jews in a Jewish setting, as it mirrors Jewish concerns that were common among other Jewish groups. Some would also point to the gospel's anti-gentile bias as excluding the possibility of a non-Jewish author. The so-called Great Commission (28:18–20) has been taken by many, but not all, as indicating an openness of this Jewish group to including non-Jewish members in their *ekklēsia* (cf. 16:17–19; 18:15–17), with or without requiring male converts to be circumcised.

Content and Redaction

One of the most important observations about the structure of Matthew is that the gospel contains five larger discourses by Jesus, all concluded with the words "when Jesus had finished saying these things." The discourses, or speeches, include the Sermon on the Mount (5:1–7:29), the commissioning of the disciples (10:1–11:1), the parable discourse (13:1–53), rules for the *ekklēsia* (18:1–19:1), and the eschatological discourse (24:1–26:1). Matthew is also littered with smaller structural divisions, indicated by formulations such as "From that time Jesus began to proclaim, 'Repent, for the kingdom of heaven has come near'" (4:17) and "From that time on, Jesus began to show his disciples that he must go to Jerusalem and undergo great suffering at the hands of the elders and the chief priests and the scribes, and be killed, and on the third day be raised" (16:21). These formulations show how Mark's structure has been handled and, at least partly, preserved in Matthew. At the same time, Matthew has included some new units, which becomes most clear when one observes summaries of major undertakings, such as "Jesus went throughout Galilee, teaching in their synagogues and proclaiming the good news of the kingdom and curing every disease and every sickness among the people" (almost identical formulations in 4:23 and 9:35). These words frame the Sermon on the Mount and the following stories about healings and exorcisms. A redaction-historical observation one might make is how the author of Matthew has inserted the Sermon on the Mount neatly between Mark 1:21 and 1:22.

The most obvious differences between Mark and Matthew are that Matthew spends time describing Jesus's genealogy, birth, and early childhood, and that Matt 28 describes how the risen Jesus reveals himself to the women at the tomb and later to the male disciples in Galilee. Matthew also introduces some of his own terminology. For example, Mark speaks of a "kingdom of God," whereas Matthew uses the term "kingdom of heaven" instead.

Another redaction-historical question that arises is how Q material, if we accept the Q hypothesis, has been incorporated into Matthew. Q (or double tradition) more or less appears in chunks within the framework provided by Mark. In addition, relevant Q material also makes an appearance in several of the Matthean speeches. In fact, Matthew's portrayal of Jesus as a teacher builds in large part on Q/double tradition. Matthew also contains a number of citations from the Hebrew Bible—for example, "Then was fulfilled what had been spoken through the prophet Jeremiah: 'A voice was heard in Ramah . . .'" (2:17–18). It may be that the author of Matthew made use of an already existing compilation of quotes from the Bible, which had the aim of emphasizing Jesus's role in the history of salvation.

The Structure of the Gospel of Matthew

1:1–2:23	*I. Jesus's genealogy, birth, and childhood in exile*
1:1–25	Jesus's genealogy and birth
2:1–23	The wise men from the East; the flight to Egypt
3:1–4:25	*II. Proclamation that the kingdom of heaven is near*
3:1–4:11	John the Baptist preaches and performs; Jesus is baptized in the Jordan
4:12–22	Jesus begins preaching and gathering disciples
4:23–25	Summary and transition
5:1–7:29	*III. The Sermon on the Mount (Discourse 1)*
5:1–2	Jesus ascends the mountain
5:3–7:27	The speech
7:28–29	Transition formula
8:1–9:38	*IV. Ten miracle stories*
8:1–9:8	Jesus heals the sick, calms the storm, drives out demons
9:9–17	Jesus calls the tax collector known as Matthew
9:18–34	More sick are healed
9:35–38	Summary and transition
10:1–11:1	*V. The disciples are sent out (Discourse 2)*
10:1–4	The Twelve are sent out
10:5–42	The speech
11:1	Transition formula
11:2–12:50	*VI. Jesus preaches, heals, and enters into conflicts*
11:2–19	John the Baptist's questions and Jesus's answers
11:20–30	Some Jesus sayings
12:1–50	Conflicts with the Pharisees; Jesus and his family
13:1–53	*VII. Collection of parables (Discourse 3)*
13:1–2	Jesus sits in a boat preaching while people flock to the shore
13:3–52	The speech
13:53	Transition formula
13:54–17:27	*VIII. Jesus's ministry and questions about his identity*
13:54–14:36	Continued ministry in Galilee; the feeding of the five thousand
15:1–20	Miracles among non-Jews; the feeding of the four thousand
16:1–12	On the interpretation of signs
16:13–28	Peter's confession; first prediction of suffering
17:1–27	The transfiguration; second prediction of suffering

18:1–19:1	*IX. A rule for* ekklēsia *(Discourse 4)*
18:1–2	Disciples wonder who is the greatest in the kingdom of heaven
18:3–20	First part of the speech
18:21–22	Peter's question about forgiveness
18:23–35	Second part of the speech
19:1	Transition formula
19:2–23:39	*X. Jesus's ministry in Judea and Jerusalem*
19:2–20:34	Close to Jerusalem; third prediction of suffering
21:1–22	Entry into Jerusalem and the cleansing of the temple
21:23–22:46	Conflicts and testing inquiries
23:1–39	Accusations against the scribes and Pharisees
24:1–26:1	*XI. Eschatological discourse (Discourse 5)*
24:1–3	Introductory conversation about the temple and its impeding fall
24:4–25:46	The speech
26:1	Transition formula
26:2–28:20	*XII. Jesus's suffering, death, and resurrection*
26:2–27:66	The passion narrative
28:1–20	Jesus's resurrection; the Great Commission

Box 4.4
On the Structure of Matthew

How one classifies chapters 3 and 4 is essential for any structuring of Matthew. If one views Mark's structure as guiding Matthew's narrative, then the introduction of Mark, consisting of John the Baptist, Jesus's baptism, and Jesus's temptation, is reflected in expanded form in Matthew (3:1–4:11). However, one can also view Matt 3:1–4:25 as a narrative entity, consisting of information on John the Baptist (3:2) and Jesus (4:17), who both proclaim the coming of the kingdom (identical wording for both; according to Mark, this proclamation is unique to Jesus). The latter interpretation emphasizes the independence and originality of the author of Matthew.

A similar key issue is to what degree Matthew has retained the climax and turning point of the Markan narrative (Mark 8:27–30). Some scholars assert that a new structural entity begins in the corresponding place in the Matthean narrative (Matt 16:13). The confession of Peter also plays an important role in Matthew (16:13–20), but it has another function, as an episode wedged inside the parable discourse and the discourse on the rule of the *ekklēsia*, rather than being its own entity. The power to bind and loose things on earth and in heaven is given to Peter in this context (new in relation to Mark) and should be seen as a foreshadowing of the discourse on the rule of the *ekklēsia* (18:18), which in its turn creates a large gap between the second and third predictions of suffering. Nevertheless, many scholars assert that the first prediction of suffering constitutes the beginning of the new main section of the Gospel (16:21–20:34 or 16:21–28:20). In the structural analysis suggested here, the five discourses play the central role in defining the frameworks of the narrative. Some scholars have interpreted these five discourses as an intentional structural choice by the author of Matthew, made to reflect the five books of Moses.

Key Theological Thoughts

In Matthew, Jesus's baptism is presented as a theophany (a revelation of God). The baptism is no longer a matter of Jesus's personal calling, as it is in Mark ("*You* are my Son, the Beloved," Mark 1:11), but rather becomes a manifestation of Jesus's identity, visible to all ("*This* is my Son, the Beloved," Matt 3:17). This is the start of a gospel-long trend: throughout all of Matthew, Jesus's identity, while not always understood, is clearly enunciated. The messianic secret of Mark has been downplayed and is visible only in some remaining passages taken over by Matthew. Joseph receives a revelation that Mary is pregnant through the Holy Spirit. The Magi from the East realize that Jesus's birth is the birth of the Messiah with universal authority. John the Baptist does not want to baptize Jesus, because he is fully aware of who the latter is. The disciples prostrate before Jesus when they see him walking on water, unlike in Mark's version, where the disciples do not even understand what they are witnessing (Mark 6:51–52). When the realization of Jesus's identity begins to dawn on Peter, he does not hesitate to formulate it with the following strong wording: "You are the Messiah, the Son of the living God" (Matt 16:16). Overall, there is a palpable christological development in the narrative. Jesus is a new Moses who saves his people and transmits correct teaching of the Jewish law. He saves his people from their sins (1:21), and he is the Savior of the entire world (12:21; 28:18–20). He is the Son who knows the Father (11:27), but he is also linked to the Holy Spirit when Christ followers are instructed to baptize in the name of the Father, the Son, and the Holy Spirit (28:19). Indeed, before the resurrection, as much as God is greater than Jesus in Matthew (19:17), the Holy Spirit is also more important than Jesus himself (12:31–32).

The climax of the Matthean narrative is the elevation of Jesus to Lord, with "all authority in heaven and on earth" (28:18). The immediate consequence of this elevation is that the disciples are to go out into the world to teach and baptize all nations/gentiles (28:19–20). The very ending of Matthew, "And remember, I am with you always, to the end of the age" (28:20), forms an *inclusio* with the beginning of the gospel, as Matt 1:23 ensures the reader that Jesus's name, Immanuel, means "God with us." The importance of this perspective on Jesus's presence among his own is further emphasized in the discourse devoted to the *ekklēsia* (18:20).

Another central theological theme is intimately connected with the former: the universality of Jesus's message. Non-Jews are referred to in several places in the narrative. Already in Jesus's genealogy we find mention of three non-Jewish women (possibly proselytes, according to some scholars). The Magi from the East, further, come to pay homage to the newborn Messiah. When the officer in Capernaum asks Jesus to heal his servant, Jesus says of him, "Truly I tell you, in no one in Israel have I found such faith. I tell you, many will come from east and west and will eat with Abraham and Isaac and Jacob in the kingdom of heaven" (8:10–11). While researchers have pointed out that those who lack faith here include Jesus's own disciples, since they are presented as part of Israel in Matthew, these passages show that while for Matthew, during Jesus's pre-resurrection lifetime, non-Jews were coming to him and not the other way around (cf. 10:5–6), this will all be reversed after the resurrection, when the teaching of the kingdom will be proclaimed universally.

The Church of the Beatitudes, located on the hills just north of the Sea of Galilee, Israel. According to tradition, this is where Jesus spoke the Sermon on the Mount. Photo by Anders Runesson.

The will of God and righteousness are also central concepts in the gospel. The law plays an important role here. In the Sermon on the Mount, Jesus sharpens the law; a simple glance of desire directed toward a married woman is enough to break the commandment against adultery. With the power of his authority, Jesus sets a high standard: "But I say to you, Love you enemies and pray for those who persecute you" (5:44). "For if you forgive others their trespasses, your heavenly Father will also forgive you; but if you do not forgive others, neither will your heavenly Father forgive your trespasses" (6:14–15). "Be perfect, therefore, as your heavenly Father is perfect" (5:48). An oft-debated issue concerns whether these interpretations of the commandments are realistic; can they actually be followed? Is it humanly possible for a person's thoughts, words, and deeds to be so completely saturated with love and righteousness? Either way, the radical message of the Sermon on the Mount has spoken to the hearts of millions of people for over two thousand years, challenging both Christians and non-Christians to engage in ethical reflection.

The Gospel of Luke

Author and Addressees

One and the same author is very likely responsible for the composition of both Luke and Acts, but exactly who this author is remains to us a mystery. The church father Irenaeus claimed (ca. 180 CE) that Luke was the companion of Paul. He based this claim on certain parts of Acts that are written in "we" form (e.g., Acts 16:10–17). In Col 4:14 the author makes mention of a certain "Luke, the beloved physician" as a valued companion of Paul (cf. Phlm 24). Second Timothy 4:11 also speaks of a Luke, who is said to have remained with Paul during his captivity in Rome.

There is no reason to doubt that Paul could indeed have traveled with a companion named Luke, but this does not necessarily mean that the gospel in question was written by that same Luke. Indeed, there is much that would suggest that the author of Luke-Acts did *not* have a close association with Paul. The theology of Luke-Acts differs from that of Paul in a number of significant ways. In addition, many historical events do not correspond in Paul and Luke-Acts. According to Acts, Paul traveled to Jerusalem five times, whereas Paul himself insists that he has been there only twice. The third visit would be his last. The depictions of the meeting of the apostles in Jerusalem are significantly different in Acts 15 and Gal 2. Regardless of who the author is, we have evidence that the Gospel of Luke was in use already in 140 CE, since Marcion based his heavily reduced canon on a version of it.

We can glean some information about the author from the introduction of the gospel (1:1–4). He is well read and initiated into the traditions of the Jesus movement, and aims to portray the life of Jesus according to the standards of Hellenistic history writing. At the same time, it is apparent that the author is a theologian who belongs to the Christ-believing tradition. It is very difficult to ascertain whether this Hellenistically educated author was Jewish. He is well acquainted with the Septuagint and the synagogue service, but he avoids Semitic expressions and discussions of issues of cult. Because of this, it is not unjustified to suggest that the gospel is directed to a mostly non-Jewish audience. At the same time, there is much in the gospel that anchors it in the context of Hellenistic diaspora Judaism. We have examples of diaspora synagogues attracting non-Jews. Some of these non-Jews converted to Judaism fully, but others continued to attend the synagogue and honor the God of Israel without a full conversion; such non-Jews were known as God-fearers. Perhaps the author of Luke was a proselyte, or a God-fearing non-Jew, who had accepted Jesus as the Messiah.

Theophilus, the name of the person to whom both Luke and Acts are dedicated, could have been a wealthy sponsor, but we do not have any specific information about him. Since the name means "friend of God," we cannot exclude the possibility that it could be a general address to a larger, otherwise undefined audience.

Dating the Gospel

Like Matthew, Luke also makes use of Mark as a source, which means that Luke too must be dated after Mark. Luke appears to have been written with the destruction of Jerusalem (70 CE) as the backdrop, although there seems to be a certain amount of distance between the catastrophic event and the composition of the gospel. In Acts, too, there is a distinct distance between the events it describes. Despite the fact that the narrative ends with Paul proclaiming the kingdom of God in Rome, it is clear that his martyrdom is in the past (Acts 20:25, 38). One could say that the author of Luke writes a kind of salvation history. The author depicts the crucial epochs of God's intervention in the world—Jesus's life and deeds as well as the birth of the *ekklēsia*—as a background and basis for the communities of the author's own time. It is almost impossible to determine an exact date for the gospel. In all probability, it was written somewhere around the time of Matthew, with 90 CE as the most common suggestion. A group of scholars argue that Luke-Acts should be dated much later. Some of them see this literary collection as an attempt at distancing the Jesus movement from Judaism, and as an adaptation of the message to a Greco-Roman context. Others who prefer a later dating do not agree that we find here a distancing from Judaism; on the contrary, they understand the collection as an attempt at overcoming diversity within the Jesus movement through a highly idealized portrayal of its early history. Many arguments speak against such a late dating of Luke-Acts. First, the gospel seems to have been known to the author of John's Gospel. Second, if the two-source hypothesis is accepted, Luke and Matthew were written independently of each other, which is harder to believe the farther apart they are dated. Third, 1 Clement, usually dated to the end of the 90s CE, appears to be even more distant from the first Christ-believing heroes than does Luke (1 Clem. 5 and 42).

There are many different suggestions concerning the geographical origins of the gospel. Different places in Greece, Macedonia, and Asia Minor have been suggested by scholars, not least because of the extensive travel descriptions in Acts. Caesarea Maritima and Syrian Antioch are also up for discussion. Because of the pivotal role of Rome in Acts, this city is also an option. Given that Jerusalem is the ideological center of the world in the Lukan literature, it is plausible that there were a significant number of Jewish Christ followers among Luke's readers, regardless of their location in the Roman Empire. Whether the author came from Rome, Beroea, or some other city is still an open question.

Audience and Context

It is interesting to reflect on the intended audience of Luke-Acts. In this regard, the ending of Acts is significant. When Paul arrives in Rome, he assembles the Jewish leaders in the city and speaks with them. "Some were convinced by what he had said, while others refused to believe" (Acts 28:24). According to Acts 28:28, Paul arrives at the following conclusion: "Let it be known to you then that this salvation of God has been sent to the Gentiles; they will listen."

The Lukan version of the Jesus story appears to have seen the belief in a fast-approaching parousia as a problem. Because of this, Luke states that the kingdom of God is not something one can see with one's eyes (Luke 17:20–21; 19:11; 21:8 and Acts 1:6–7). The coming of the Son of Man is not denied, but it is pushed into the future (Acts 1:11; 3:20–21). Until that day (which will not come with the same speed as is indicated in Pauline theology), Christ followers are to be patient and live as the master taught, carrying their cross "daily" and following Jesus (Luke 9:23), and proclaiming the gospel to "the ends of the earth" (Acts 1:8).

The relationship between the rich and the poor seems to have been a major concern of the Lukan Christ followers. Luke contains more information about this than any of the other gospels. Paul is described in Acts as uttering an otherwise unknown Jesus saying: "It is more blessed to give than to receive" (Acts 20:35). In several longer passages, Luke warns his audience of wealth and possessions (Luke 12:13–34; 16:1–31). The criteria given by Jesus for following him are quite strict in this regard: "So therefore, none of you can become my disciple if you do not give up all your possessions" (Luke 14:33). The first Christ followers in Jerusalem are portrayed as excellent examples of this. They share all property (Acts 2:44–45; 4:34). It is doubtful whether the idea of shared property should be practiced to its logical extreme, according to Luke, but there are several passages where there seems to be no compromise to the rule. "Blessed are you who are hungry now, for you will be filled" (Luke 6:21).

Luke-Acts has sometimes been interpreted as an apologetic text defending the Jesus movement in the Roman Empire. This is hardly the case, though, since the Lukan works are clearly directed toward Christ followers rather than Roman administrators. Nevertheless, because of the nature of Christ belief, the author of Luke moves on a political minefield simply by writing. The author appears to be aware of this, attempting to soften the blow. Pilate says three times that he cannot find Jesus guilty of the crimes he is accused of, thus placing the majority of the blame for Jesus's death on the Jewish high priests rather than the Romans (Luke 23:1–25). The Christ-following Jew Paul is portrayed as a model Roman citizen, saved by the Romans from the claws of his Jewish attackers (Acts 23:27; 25:7–12). Despite the fact that Paul was most likely martyred by the Romans, this unpleasant detail is not mentioned, and Paul's imprisonment in Rome appears almost idyllic (Acts 28:16, 30–31).

Content and Redaction

The parallel presentation of John the Baptist and Jesus is a uniquely Lukan characteristic (Luke 1:5–2:52). When Jesus's ministry in Galilee begins, it is introduced by a programmatic sermon by Jesus in the synagogue in Nazareth (Luke 4:16–30).

Referring to Isa 61, Jesus begins his sermon with the words: "Today this scripture has been fulfilled in your hearing." After the sermon, the townspeople tried to lynch him, and thus drove him from his hometown. Concerning Jesus's Galilean ministry, Luke more or less follows Mark's lead, apart from inserting double tradition (Q), such as the Sermon on the Plain (Luke 6:20–49), and some material unique to Luke, such as the story of the widow's son in Nain (Luke 7:11–17). There is also a significant amount of Markan material (Mark 6:45–8:26) missing here (known as the "great gap"). The most striking aspect unique to Luke is the long travel story (Luke 9:51–19:27), which consists of double tradition/Q material and special Lukan material. The Markan narrative does not return until Luke 18:15. Luke contains more resurrection stories than Matthew, and the gospel ends with Jesus ascending into heaven (Luke 24:1–53).

The Lukan literature has a clear aim to be both biographical and historical in the ancient, Hellenistic sense of those words. Many important events are verified by concretely connecting them to history (Luke 1:5; 2:1–2; 3:1–2; Acts 11:28; 18:12). Even the rhetoric in the literature indicates Hellenistic education, thus suggesting that the genre of Luke-Acts is history, in Greco-Roman style. Except for Mark and double tradition/Q, the author of Luke also based his works on material unique to him ("L"). Different theories have been suggested concerning this L material. For example, some scholars have argued that at least part of the material has its origins in a source coming from the oldest *ekklēsia* in Jerusalem.

The Structure of the Gospel of Luke

1:1–4	Introductory speech
1:5–2:52	*I. Birth and childhood stories*
1:5–80	Two annunciations; the birth of John the Baptist
2:1–52	Jesus's birth; the twelve-year-old Jesus in the temple
3:1–4:13	*II. Preparation for Jesus's ministry*
3:1–20	John the Baptist's ministry
3:21–4:13	Jesus's baptism and genealogy; the Son of God is tested
4:14–9:50	*III. Jesus's ministry in the Galilee*
4:14–30	Jesus's sermon in a synagogue in Nazareth
4:31–5:16	Jesus performs miracles; the first disciples are called
5:17–6:11	The Twelve are selected
6:12–49	The Sermon on the Plain
7:1–17	Two miracle stories
7:18–35	John the Baptist's questions and Jesus's answers
7:36–8:3	Women around Jesus
8:4–56	Parables and miracle stories
9:1–17	The Twelve are sent out
9:18–27	Peter's confession; first prediction of suffering

9:28–50	The transfiguration; second prediction of suffering
9:51–19:27	*IV. Jesus's journey to Jerusalem*
9:51–10:24	Persecution; the seventy-two are sent out
10:25–42	Parable of the good Samaritan; Mary and Martha
11:1–13	Jesus teaches about prayer
11:14–54	Conflict; accusations against the scribes and Pharisees
12:1–13:21	Parables and other Jesus sayings; a woman with a bad back is healed
13:22–35	The goal of the journey is Jerusalem
14:1–35	A man with water in his body is healed; parables and Jesus sayings
15:1–32	Parables about lost things being found
16:1–31	Parables about the choice between God and mammon
17:1–18:14	Parables and other Jesus sayings; ten lepers are cured
18:15–30	Criteria for entering the kingdom of God
18:31–19:27	Third prediction of suffering
19:28–21:38	*V. Jesus's ministry in Jerusalem*
19:28–48	Entry into Jerusalem and the cleansing of the temple
20:1–21:4	Conflicts and testing inquiries
21:5–38	Speech about the end of the age
22:1–23:56	*VI. Jesus's suffering and death (passion narrative)*
24:1–53	*VII. Resurrection stories*
24:1–12	The empty tomb
24:13–49	The risen Jesus reveals himself in the region around Jerusalem
24:50–53	The ascension

Box 4.5
On the Structure of Luke

Luke's geography differs significantly from Mark's. In Mark, Jesus travels north, toward Tyre in Phoenicia, and visits the Decapolis region of Galilee at least twice. According to Luke, Jesus carried out the majority of his ministry in Galilee, with the exception of the miracle of the swine, where he healed a man by expelling the demons possessing him and letting them enter a herd of pigs, which promptly rushed off a cliff and drown in the lake. This event takes place on the eastern shores of the Sea of Galilee (Luke 8:26–39). The fact that Luke keeps Jesus firmly anchored in Jewish areas of the land could explain why he does not locate Peter's confession in Caesarea Philippi, a city located in Ituraea (Luke 9:18; cf. Mark 8:27; note, however, that this area is ruled by one of the sons of Herod I). When Luke tells the story of Jesus's journey to Jerusalem (Luke 9:51–19:27), the narrative takes place mostly in the borderlands between Galilee and Samaria (9:51–56; 17:11). Samaritans play an important narrative role here (10:25–37; 17:12–19).

An important section of the text in terms of redaction is the lengthy unit describing Jesus's journey to Jerusalem, a journey that will culminate in him offering up his life in prophetic fashion. In the presence of some Pharisees who try to save his life by warning him that Herod wants to kill him (Luke 13:31), Jesus attacks the leaders in Jerusalem with the words "You will not see me until the time comes when you say, 'Blessed is the one who comes in the name of the Lord'" (13:35). In this context, the saying is probably a reference to the impending entry into Jerusalem, but it could very well also be a reference to the parousia (see Acts 1:6–7, 11); this means that this saying, which is double tradition/Q material, probably had eschatological meaning in its original context. It is somewhat strange and worthwhile to note that Jesus's lengthy journey along the border between Galilee and Samaria suddenly transitions to Jesus's arrival outside Jericho (Luke 18:55). This means that the significantly longer journey through the Jordan valley has been passed over in silence. From this we can gather that the symbolic and thematic significance of the geography is important to the author of the Gospel. This also becomes clear in Luke's resurrection stories (24:13–49). Luke connects both the visions of the resurrected one and the birth of the *ekklēsia* of the Christ followers to Jerusalem and the region around it, whereas Mark and Matthew contain references to Galilee only (compare, too, John's Gospel, which in its second ending claims that the disciples returned to Galilee after the resurrection).

The Lukan account of Jesus's journey gives the impression of being rather disparate. The connection between the different pericopes is not always clear. If one were to analyze the Gospel from a purely redaction-historical perspective, it appears that Luke has used the journey to insert the majority of the double tradition/Q and L material, which is especially interesting since the journey takes up almost all of the "great insertion." There are also a couple of miracle stories. In sum, one could say that Jesus's journey to Jerusalem offers a way for the author to collect and present important parts of Jesus's teaching, often in the form of parables.

Key Theological Thoughts

The history of salvation runs through the entirety of Luke. The story of Jesus is anchored not only in secular history but also in the history of God's relationship and interactions with his people. Jesus's entire ministry is characterized by the guidance and actions of God's spirit (Luke 4:18–19). When Jesus begins his journey toward Jerusalem, this comes to the fore in a theologically important sentence: "When the days drew near for him to be taken up, he set his face to go to Jerusalem" (9:51). Suffering, death, resurrection, and ascension are all viewed in light of one another—indeed, as one and the same thing (24:26). During the journey to Jerusalem, Jesus teaches his disciples, and by extension Luke's readers, about how to live in the right way after the ascension, before the parousia.

In his classic construction of Lukan theology, Hans Conzelmann argues that Luke's history of salvation is divided into three sections: the period of the law and the prophets, the period of Jesus, and the period of the church.[1] John the Baptist exists in the borderland between the first two periods. The ascension and, in particular, the giving of the Holy Spirit at Pentecost are the indicators of the shift from the second to the third period. Although this categorization is still very relevant, it is not without its problems. John the Baptist, for example, poses a problem, as he is part of the prophetic period, yet he also proclaims the good news to the people (3:18), which means that his character permeates the border between the first two periods. In addition, the function of the ascension becomes difficult to grasp. It should function as the bridge between the gospel and Acts (compare Luke 24:50–53 with Acts 1:9–11), and as such actually speaks more in favor of a division into two periods (Luke and Acts): Jesus was taken into heaven just like Elijah, and just like Elisha, his disciples pick up his mantle and continue his mission on earth (2 Kgs 2:1–18). Like Elisha, Jesus's disciples inherit a double share when they are given the Spirit at Pentecost.

Another important theological thought in Luke pertains to the twelve disciples. The apostles were important both as eyewitnesses (Luke 1:1–2; Acts 1:21–22) and as models of leadership in the early Jesus movement. The number twelve was symbolic and highly charged, representing the twelve tribes of Israel, and we see this importance in Acts 1:15–26, when the disciples have to select a replacement for Judas (this is unique to Luke). It was apparently of crucial importance for the author to show the continuity between the twelve tribes of Israel and the twelve disciples of Jesus.

While the Synoptic Gospels all emphasize the role of the Holy Spirit in Jesus's life, from conception (Matthew and Luke only) onward, Luke's repeated references to the Spirit create a certain emphasis that differs from the other gospels. Jesus's conception and birth is dependent on the Holy Spirit (Luke 1:35). When Jesus is baptized, the Holy Spirit descends on him (Luke 3:22), and he himself baptizes others with Spirit and fire (Luke 3:16; Acts 1:5). Jesus's life and ministry is wholly characterized by the Holy Spirit (Luke 4:18; 23:46). His disciples were filled with the Holy Spirit on Pentecost, and everyone they baptized was filled with it as well (Acts 2:38). The *ekklēsia* was guided by the Spirit of the Lord in its missionary work (Acts 8:29; 11:11–12) and in all its important decision-making (Acts 15:28).

Further, Luke's Gospel in large part portrays Jesus as a prophet (Luke 7:16; 24:19). His entire life is a model for his followers. He is a model of prayer both during his baptism and at Gethsemane (3:21; 22:46). He even dies with a prayer on his lips and gets

1. Conzelmann, *Theology of St Luke*.

evaluated in the following way by those watching: "Certainly this man was innocent [righteous, *dikaios*]" (23:47). This is the point of departure for Luke's Christology.

Acts of the Apostles

Author and Dating

The same author is responsible for the composition of both Luke and Acts, as previously mentioned. Even the individual addressed in the beginning is the same, Theophilus (Acts 1:1). The title "Acts of the Apostles" appears for the first time in the writings of the church father Irenaeus, and it is unlikely that it is the original title of the work. The question of authorship and geographical origins has already been dealt with in the section on Luke. Where dating the work is concerned, it was in all likelihood written not too long after the gospel, which puts it around 90 CE or slightly later.

Content

Acts 1:8 provides us with some insight as to the program of the work and can function as a key to understanding the character of Acts: "But you will receive power when the Holy Spirit has come upon you; and you will be my witnesses in Jerusalem, in all Judea and Samaria, and to the ends of the earth."

The Holy Spirit is the force that drives the story forward, and the narrative exhibits a general pattern of movement from Jerusalem to Rome. Ironically, Rome is called the "furthest end of the earth" in Jewish polemical literature (Pss. Sol. 8:15). Acts ends with Paul reaching Rome. Perhaps there is a hidden criticism of Rome behind the facade of the narrative, since it is the city/empire that ends up martyring Paul. Either way, Jerusalem is the center of the world in the history of salvation, as it is the point from which salvation flows.

In the beginning of the work, the author describes the apostles and everyday life for the *ekklēsia* in Jerusalem. Greek-speaking Christ-believing Jews play a central role in spreading the gospel (Acts 6:1–7). The good news is preached in Samaria and the coastal regions. An important step is taken when non-Jews begin converting and being baptized. Peter plays a key role in this development (10:1–11:18). In the next phase of the story, the northern Syrian city of Antioch, where Christ followers are for the first time called "Christians," plays an important role (11:26). From Antioch, Barnabas and Paul are sent out for missionary purposes. In a crucial meeting in Jerusalem, where Paul and Barnabas represent Antioch, the leadership of the Jesus movement discusses what to do about the increasing number of non-Jews being baptized, and to what degree they should be required to follow the Jewish law. As a result of this meeting, non-Jews are not required to get circumcised in order to join the Jesus movement (15:1–35). From this point onward, Paul becomes the main character of the story. He selects Silas and Timothy as companions and travels extensively throughout Asia Minor, Macedonia, and Greece, spreading the gospel. According to the author of Acts, Paul decides in Ephesus to travel to Jerusalem, and from there to continue onward to Rome (19:21).

The journey to Jerusalem ends with Paul's arrest and a series of trials, wherein Paul demands of the emperor a final trial in Rome, something he has a right to because of his Roman citizenship. After a shipwreck and a series of other events, he finally arrives in Rome as a prisoner. The story ends with Paul "proclaiming the kingdom of God and teaching about the Lord Jesus Christ with all boldness and without hindrance" (28:31). His martyrdom is not mentioned.

This marble statue representing the Ephesian Artemis, also called "Artemis the beautiful," is dated to the beginning of the second century CE. Artemis was worshiped as the goddess of nature and hunting; she was identified by the Romans with the goddess Diana (an example of *interpretatio Romana*). In this representation, the goddess is stretching forth her hands and is flanked by two deer, her most holy animals. The breast-like protrusions on her body have been interpreted in diverse ways: as breasts, as bees (Ephesus's emblem included bees), or as testicles from the bulls that were sacrificed to her. The Temple of Artemis in Ephesus is counted among the seven wonders of the ancient world. The statue is located in the museum in Selçuk, close to Ephesus. Photo by Dieter Mitternacht.

Style and Composition

Like Luke, Acts is written in good Hellenistic Greek and fits well into the genre of Greco-Roman history. The imagery of LXX is imitated here and there, and in the speech in the Areopagus in Athens, a classical style is used (Acts 17:22–32). The linguistic style is a narrative tool, but the main theological mode of communication are the stories themselves. The theology of the text is made clear in dramatic stories rather than abstract sayings. In some places we find examples of summarizing comments, as well as explicit comments on and interpretations of events (e.g., 2:42–47).

Acts contains over twenty speeches of varied length. Peter and Paul are the most avid speakers, but Stephen and James, the Lord's brother, also give speeches. The speeches are reminiscent of each other in that they contain similar theology, imagery, and diction in strategic places. Like many ancient history writers, the author appears to have chosen key words unique to each speaker

Theater in Ephesus. According to Acts 19:29 citizens gathered in the theater, furious about Paul and others, who they claimed had threatened the good reputation of Artemis and the silver smiths.

(e.g., "faith" and "righteousness" for Paul in Acts 13:38–39) and proceeds to give the speeches in an appropriate style (e.g., a biblical style). When all is said and done, however, the author is transmitting his own worldview and take on history through these speeches. The so-called missionary speeches likely contain traditions from early missionary speeches (e.g., 3:19–21), which have been heavily edited with the aim of highlighting specific aspects of the early history of the *ekklēsia*. It is noteworthy that Gamaliel, the member of the Jewish council, and Festus, the Roman governor, are allowed to speak.

A Text-Critical Problem

A particular problem for anyone studying Acts is how to approach it from a text-critical perspective. The so-called Western text is 8 percent longer than the so-called Alexandrian version, which is generally viewed as having a more reliable text (see the section "The Origins and Transmission of the Texts," p. 202). This noteworthy fact is perhaps best explained by the theory that the Western text represents an intended edited and changed version of the Alexandrian, perhaps in Syria sometime during the third century. With the exception of some presumably original readings (e.g., Acts 19:1), the Western version is in general more stylistically and linguistically ironed out, and it clarifies and/or corrects confusing aspects of the texts.

Sources

Acts is likely based on a number of sources. Perhaps some of these sources were traditions written down in Jerusalem. Many scholars are convinced that much of the source material used by the author has its origins in the community located in Antioch (parts of Acts 6–15), but it is far from easy to come to any definite conclusion.

Many scholars have suggested that one of the sources may have been a short description of the missionary journeys of Paul and his companion, written in "we" form, which the author has copied closely, albeit inserting several of his own sections into its framework (Acts 16:10–17; 20:5–15; 21:1–18; 27:1–28:16). Another explanation for this "we" form is that the author of the texts is the same Luke (the physician) mentioned in some of the Pauline letters, and that he uses this diction because he in fact traveled with Paul. Scholars who argue against this theory usually bring up the point that not all the travel accounts are told in the "we" form, and that the author never gives any evidence of having personally known Paul or his thinking, which would, presumably, have been a source of legitimacy for him. We could, perhaps, view the "we" form as a literary convention, used to really bring the stories alive, especially the sea journeys. Since the changes from "we" form to the normal phrasing of the author occur so suddenly and abruptly, it is perhaps most logical to assert that the author is closely copying a source relaying the journeys in the "we" form, perhaps written by one of Paul's companions. The author then adds some of his own details and comments to this narrative core.

In sum, the author of Acts can be assumed to have had access to a large and varied number of sources. Some of the sources were written, others oral. Some were rather trustworthy, others more legendary in nature. Some of the traditions could reflect the beliefs of a certain group of Christ followers, while others could be more general. Faced with this diversity of sources, it is the author himself who collects, edits, summarizes, speaks, writes speeches, and creates new traditions.

The Structure of Acts of the Apostles

1:1–1:26	*I. Introduction with transition from Luke's Gospel*
1:1–14	Forty days with the resurrected Jesus; ascension
1:15–26	Waiting and preparing
2:1–47	*II. Pentecost and the first Jewish Christ followers*
2:1–13	The Holy Spirit
2:14–40	Peter's speech
2:41–47	The fellowship of the believers
3:1–8:3	*III. The apostles evangelize in Jerusalem*
3:1–4:31	Peter and John heal the sick, preach, and are arrested
4:32–6:7	Communal property, crises, and successes
6:8–8:3	Stephen's arrest, speech, and stoning
8:4–12:25	*IV. The apostles evangelize in Judea, Samaria, and Syria*
8:4–40	Philip in Samaria and on the road to Gaza
9:1–30	Saul on the road to Damascus, in Damascus, and back to Jerusalem
9:31–10:33	Peter in Lydda, in Joppa, and with Cornelius in Caesarea
10:34–11:18	Peter speaks about the conversion of non-Jews

11:19–30	Barnabas and Saul in Antioch; journey to Jerusalem
12:1–25	Peter's arrest and freeing
13:1–28:31	*V. Paul's missionary work in Asia Minor, Greece, and Rome*
13:1–14:28	Barnabas and Paul travel to Asia Minor via Cyprus; return to Antioch
15:1–35	Meeting of the apostles in Jerusalem
15:36–17:15	Paul, Silas, and Timothy travel through Asia Minor and Macedonia
17:16–34	Paul speaks before the Areopagus in Athens
18:1–17	Paul stays in Corinth for one and a half years
18:18–23	Paul travels to Jerusalem and then to Antioch
18:24–28	Apollos in Ephesus and Achaia
19:1–41	Paul in Ephesus
20:1–12	Paul's travels in Macedonia, Greece, and Troas
20:13–21:16	Paul's farewell speech in Miletus; journey to Jerusalem
21:17–23:22	Paul meets James (the Lord's brother) in Jerusalem, is arrested, and is put on trial
23:23–24:27	Paul on trial before the governor Felix in Caesarea; arrested for two years
25:1–26:32	Paul on trial before the governor Festus and King Agrippa II
27:1–28:31	Boat journey, shipwreck, and two-year stay in Rome

---

Box 4.6
On the Structure of Acts

Many scholars have chosen to divide Acts into two sections, the first (Acts 1–12) dealing with Peter, and the second (Acts 13–28) focusing on Paul. Such a division is an oversimplification, since Paul is introduced already in the first part (7:54–8:3; 9:1–30; 11:19–30), and Peter continues to play a central role well into the second section (15:1–21). Perhaps a better and more useful division could be made according to the development of how non-Jews are dealt with.

The structure here is in large part based on a geographical and thematic analysis of Acts. In comparison to Luke, Acts exhibits a reversed movement, geographically speaking. Luke begins with a reference to the emperor ordering the entire world to register, followed by the story of Jesus's ministry described in three phases: his ministry in Galilee, his journey to Jerusalem via the border between Galilee and Samaria, and, finally, his triumphant entry into Jerusalem, violent death, and subsequent burial (Luke 19:28–23:46). Indeed, all of the resurrection stories as well as the ascension take place in and around Jerusalem (Luke 24:1–53). In contrast, Acts begins in Jerusalem with the ascension as the starting point, followed by Pentecost and mission in Jerusalem. After this, even if the leaders stay in Jerusalem, there is a general movement from Jerusalem out into the world—reaching as far as Rome itself. Here, the ministry of the Christ followers is also portrayed in three phases. First, the mission of the apostles in Jerusalem is described (Acts 3:1–8:3). This is followed by several stories about the apostles who went out into the other parts of Judea, Samaria, and Syria to spread the gospel. This section could possibly be split into two subsections, the first being in Judea and Samaria and Damascus and the second being in Phoenicia, Cyprus, and Antioch. Paul is in focus in the third section, which revolves around his missionary journeys in Asia Minor, Greece, and Rome (13:1–28:31).

Despite the large geographical span of the narrative, Jerusalem remains the center from which everything else flows. Paul returns to Jerusalem and describes the conversion of the gentiles (11:1–18). In fact, Paul returns to Jerusalem no less than five times (9:26; 11:29–30; 15:1–6; 18:22; 21:14–17). It is important to note that Jerusalem does not only have positive connotations; Jerusalem is also the place of persecution and conspiracy. Every important section mentioned in the structure suggested here ends with the arrest of an important character in this city: Stephen is arrested, stoned, and martyred (6:8–8:3); Peter is arrested but saved by the angel of the Lord (12:1–19); Paul is arrested in Jerusalem (21:33) and then held in arrest for several years, waiting for his trial in Rome (28:16). In all likelihood, the readers of Acts knew that both Peter and Paul had died as martyrs. The message of the text could thus be interpreted to be that neither persecution nor martyrdom can stand in the way of the expansion of God's kingdom.

Key Theological Thoughts

The main theological thoughts of Luke and Acts correspond with each other. We should, however, add that Acts expresses the idea that the good news is meant not only for Jews but also for non-Jews. The movement from Jerusalem to Rome emphasizes this. The ministry of the apostles is widened step by step, both geographically and theologically. That the Holy Spirit is granted not only to Jews but to non-Jews as well (Acts 10:44–48) indicates that the missionary work of the apostles is sanctioned by God, whose plan for salvation includes the entire world. Paul is the main instrument for this to happen in Acts. Proclaiming the word of God first to the Jew and then to the non-Jew is a theme that runs like a red thread throughout Paul's missionary journeys (e.g., Acts 13:45–49). According to Acts, many Jews did not accept Paul's message, and distanced themselves from him, whereas many non-Jews were attracted to his mission and began converting. This reality, matching the Jewish eschatological thought of gentiles coming to Zion as the end of the ages approaches, was viewed as divine legitimization of the mission to non-Jews.

If one views Luke and Acts as an entity, Jerusalem's centrality becomes obvious. The story of Jesus and the universal soteriological plan of God converge here: "it is impossible for a prophet to be killed outside of Jerusalem" (Luke 13:33). All the resurrection stories take place in Jerusalem and its immediate surroundings in Luke-Acts, unlike in the other gospels, which situate them in Galilee. The holy city becomes the starting point of the spread of Christ belief (Acts 2), and the assembly of the apostles, which paves the way for non-Jews to enter the *ekklēsia* (Acts 15), also takes place here. Moreover, Jerusalem is the place of the arrest of the Christ-believing Jew Paul, the apostle to the gentiles (Acts 21). Paradoxically, Acts ends with Paul being taken to Rome by Roman soldiers, as a Roman citizen, where he proclaims the kingdom of God to both Jews and non-Jews—entirely according to God's plan of salvation, as the author of Acts could have added.

The Gospel of John

The Johannine Tradition

The Johannine tradition consists of the Gospel of John, the three Johannine letters, and possibly also Revelation, although the character of the latter differs significantly from the other texts. Scholars sometimes even speak of a "Johannine school." The theological similarities are substantial, such as the unity between the Father and the Son, the incarnation, the dualistic contrast between God and the world, the knowledge of God, the Christ-believing individual's unity with God, and the commandment to love. Except for Revelation, the books are similar also on the linguistic level; there is a clear connection between the texts. A signature mark of Johannine literature is the term "and *we know* that his testimony is true" in relation to the testimony of the disciple that "Jesus loved" (John 21:24). The individual or the group who put together and produced the gospel has named the "disciple Jesus loved" as its author. The real author has also reworked the relationship between Jesus and Peter. In connection to this, the author also dwells on ecclesiological issues, traces of which can be seen in the references to disciples calling each other friends, God's children, and brother and sister. The ethical commandment to love is first and foremost directed toward these brothers and sisters.

The so-called Johannine school is often linked to Ephesus. History tells us that the Gospel of John was used avidly in Asia Minor by Christians with gnostic tendencies and Montanists, among others. Polycarp knew of 1 John (which we know from his letter to the Philippians: Pol. *Phil.* 7:1–2). Both 2 and 3 John can with some degree of certainty be placed in Ephesus and its surroundings. Even Revelation seems to be connected to this region (see Rev 2–3).

The issue of how the Gospel of John is related to the Johannine letters is a complex one. Scholars debate whether 1 John and the gospel were composed by the same author, as well as which one was written first. The first question (if both works are the product of the same author) loses some of its significance if one assumes the existence of a Johannine school of thought. Concerning the second question (of who wrote first), the traditional view is that the letter uses the theology of the gospel and applies it in new congregational and historical contexts. The letter has, for example, been interpreted as a follow-up to the gospel, meant to explain how the gospel should be correctly read and interpreted. The letter never makes any direct references to the gospel. Indeed, whether the author of the letter was aware of the theological overlap between his own text and the gospel remains to be proven. One thing that we can say with a greater degree of certainty pertains to the difference between the texts in their usage of the Greek word *archē* (meaning "beginning" or "origin"). In 1 John 1–4 the emphasis is placed on the origins or beginning of the *ekklēsia*—the way in which the first Jesus followers heard, experienced, and physically touched Jesus. In John 1:1–5 the term is used to describe Jesus's preexistence and participation in the creation of the world. Another example of the difference between the two texts is the theological issue of the "Helper," the *paraklētos*. In John 14:16 Jesus's promise of *another* Helper indicates that Jesus is the original *paraklētos*, the original Helper (1 John 2:1). In 1 John there is no mention at all of the Holy Spirit being the *paraklētos*. From these observations, it is possible to hypothesize that the gospel was written after the dramatic conflict within the movement described indirectly in 1 John. But this is far from a conclusive argument, and more research is needed before this can be established with any certainty.

Author and Dating

The church father Irenaeus asserted in 180 CE that the Gospel of John was written by John, son of Zebedee, whom he identified as the disciple whom Jesus loved (John 13:23). He, according to Irenaeus, wrote the gospel during the later years of his life, in Ephesus during the reign of Emperor Trajan (98–117 CE). Irenaeus supported this claim with reference to both Polycarp and Papias, whom he viewed as disciples of John. One problem with this is that Polycarp makes no mention in his writings of being John's disciple, which is strange since that would likely have been a source of legitimacy for him. Papias does make reference to an apostle and presbyter named John, but does not directly connect this individual with the gospel. Papias does, however, make a clear distinction between the apostles and their disciples, and places the presbyter John in the latter category. It is quite likely that Papias could have met this presbyter.

Most scholars reject Irenaeus's claims about the authorship of the gospel. It is historically very unlikely that an eyewitness wrote the gospel. The theological perspective of the text is better suited to a later time period. While the Synoptics emphasize Jesus's ministry to preach about the coming of the kingdom of God, the term is mentioned in only one pericope in John (3:3, 5; cf. the formulation in 18:36). Instead, Jesus himself becomes the core of his own message—he is the "bread of life" (6:35–48) and the "the way, the truth, and the life" (14:6). The eschatology of the Synoptics, focused on the future, has evolved into a realized eschatology in John: "Very truly, I tell you, anyone who hears my word and believes him who sent me has eternal life" (5:24). Indeed, it is not until chapter 21, added to chapters 1–20 during a later stage of editing, that the "disciple whom Jesus loved" is identified as the author of the gospel. Before this addition, he was perhaps seen as the source of the tradition on which the gospel is based. It is thus not a coincidence that the sons of Zebedee are mentioned only in John 21:2. We may conclude, then, that the disciple whom Jesus loved was, at some point in the evolution of the Johannine tradition/school, identified with John, the son of Zebedee.

John 11:48 likely indicates that the gospel was composed after the destruction of the temple. Based on the fact that Valentinus's disciple Heracleon used the gospel during the second half of the second century, and since the manuscript P^{52}, usually dated to around 125 CE, contains a fragment of it, the gospel is most often dated to somewhere between 90 and 110 CE.

Audience and Context

One can sense decisive conflicts lingering behind the text of John. In all likelihood, most of these conflicts were already historical by the time the gospel was written. It seems that conflict and rivalry between the Johannine community and followers of John the Baptist erupted early on in the history of the Jesus movement. Some of Jesus's disciples seem to have been disciples of John the Baptist before following Jesus (John 1:35–39). Therefore, the Baptist's importance may have been toned down by the author of the gospel. In reality, we know that the Baptist's movement was widespread and successful, not least in Asia Minor, and specifically around Ephesus, where the gospel is often assumed to have been written (cf. Acts 19:1–7).

One especially problematic aspect of the gospel is that it may appear to us as anti-Jewish. In a very stern statement, Jesus is quoted as saying that by not acknowledging him as the Messiah, the "Jews" have rejected God and are in reality children of the devil (John 8:37–45). In situations such as this, it is important to keep track of the terminology. While it is accurate to assert that the word "Jews" is used to describe the opponents of Jesus, it must be kept in mind that Jesus was himself a Jew, as were his disciples and important role models such as Nicodemus and Joseph of Arimathea. With this in mind, it becomes clear that the term "Jews" needs to be decoded and analyzed.

A way of explaining what appears to be the anti-Jewish nature of the Gospel is to take a closer look at the dualistic theology that forms its backdrop. An underlying assumption in the gospel is that Christ followers are met with misunderstanding and hatred by the world around them. This becomes especially clear in Jesus's Farewell Discourse, where it is emphasized that "the world" did not accept Jesus. In the same way, "the world" will hate and persecute the disciples. Within the framework of the Jesus narrative, "the Jews" often, but not always, come to represent "the world"—that is, the opponents of Jesus. When the gospel was written, however, "the world" was understood in a wider sense as the enemy. Thus, the usage of the terms ("Jews" and "world") may be attributed to the dualistic worldview of the gospel.

The question remains whether there actually was widespread conflict between the Christ followers and other Jews in the context in which the gospel was written, and whether this conflict is what fueled the negative statements about "Jews" in the text. It is not unthinkable that the Johannine Jesus movement, previously a movement defined by Christ-centered Judaism, had recently experienced a painful separation from the other, non-Christ-believing Jews of the region. First John 2:18–24 could be interpreted along such lines. Those who deny that Jesus is the Christ are called "anti-Christs." This critique has traditionally been interpreted as being directed toward docetic Christians, who deny the human nature of Jesus, but it may also have been directed toward Christ-believing Jews who began to hesitate to call Jesus "Messiah" (= Christ). To call Jesus "Messiah" was equivalent to calling him "king" (John 1:41, 49). There seem to have been good reasons for Christ-believing Jews in the context of the author of 1 John to stop calling Jesus "Messiah." In the beginning of the 90s CE, there were persecutions against Christ followers in parts of Asia Minor (including Ephesus). Emperor Domitian demanded to be worshiped as a king and a god. Jews were exempted by Roman law from such worship. Christ-believing non-Jews likely bore the brunt of this persecution since they were not exempted from the worship yet could not participate in it without going against their beliefs. Thus, it is not strange at all that Christ-believing Jews during this period may have begun emphasizing their Jewishness and downplaying the messianic claims about Jesus. This context could also explain some of the statements made in Revelation (2:8–11; 3:7–13).

Another reason for Jewish Christ followers to hesitate calling Jesus "Messiah" may have been the introduction in some Jewish circles of the Birkat Haminim into the so-called Eighteen Benedictions, a move that could be interpreted as a condemnation of Christ-believing Jews as heretics. However, while this has been a traditional interpretation of the three passages claiming that followers of Jesus were expelled from synagogues (John 9:22; 12:42; 16:2), such a reading can no longer be maintained.[2] As scholars have pointed out, not only is this prayer/curse dated later than John's Gospel, but rabbinic Judaism, which emerged in the decades following the fall of the temple in 70 CE, and which eventually authored the prayer, did not become mainstream Judaism until the third or fourth century CE at the earliest, and did not control

2. Bernier, Aposynagōgos *and the Historical Jesus in John.*

public synagogues before that time. In addition, it is historically very unlikely to assume that members of John's community would have been attending the meetings ("synagogues") of the rabbis as a subgroup, which is a necessary precondition for envisioning this prayer/curse to be related to the expulsion passages in John's Gospel, since these two groups have very little in common.

In any case, in some diaspora synagogues it may have become important to exclude Christ-believing Jews from the community so as not to be targeted by the imperial persecution of Christians. In this context, it no longer seems strange that John should be at once so Jewish in his theology while simultaneously distancing himself so overtly from "the Jews."

It is noteworthy that almost the entire trial of Jesus before Pilate, and the subsequent crucifixion, revolves around the question of whether Jesus is the king of the Jews (John 18:19–19:22). In this section "the Jews" shout, "Everyone who claims to be a king sets himself against the emperor" (19:12). And the most crucial quote before the crucifixion is when "the Jews" cry out, "We have no king but the emperor" (19:15). Jesus, on the other hand, had said, "My kingdom is not of this world" (18:36). Perhaps these statements represent the boundaries being erected between Christ followers and other Jews, and the christological difference created between them by the religious persecution of the 90s CE.

The context for the composition of the gospel is dependent not only on the existence of division, persecution, and conflict, but also on the idea that Christ followers are tied to or connected with Jesus in a special way. The "Helper" is a crucial link in this connecting chain (John 14:16–17, 26). A human link is the disciple whom Jesus loved, who bore witness to his ministry, suffering, death, and resurrection. It is possible that this disciple is a literary figure, representing the presbyter John, the founder of the Johannine school. The past, present, and future are merged in the gospel; the boundaries of time are blurred in order to connect things happening in the present to Jesus's past ministry, and in order to base expectations of the future on prophecies of the past and realities of the present. Jesus, the disciple he loved, and the "Helper" were part of the Johannine community's reality, a reality in which everyone was seen as God's disciple, filled with knowledge from God (John 6:45).

During the larger part of the twentieth century, scholars assumed that John was marked by a gnostic tendency (for more information about gnosticizing interpretations of Christianity, see the section "Gnosticism and 'the Gnostics,'" p. 455). Some scholars today would still assert this to be the case. The question is, however, whether it is possible to prove the existence of Gnosticism during the time of the gospel's composition. The oldest literature that we can, with certainty, categorize as gnosticizing is the Apocryphon of John, which was most likely written in the mid-second century CE. Because of this, it is fairly safe to assume that the categorization of John as a gnostic text is flawed. Instead, one should view the tensions in the gospel more as an expression of the increased distance between the Johannine Jesus movement and other Jewish groups. This distance, when combined with a Platonic worldview, could have opened up for the development of gnostic tendencies in nascent Christianity. To acquire a historical understanding of the gospel, it is sufficient to read it in the context of the Hebrew Bible, the Dead Sea Scrolls, different expressions of Hellenistic Judaism, and other New Testament texts.

Content and Redaction

The gospel begins with a prologue (1:1–18), which functions as a theological introduction of sorts to the rest of the narrative. The prologue is complemented by a short epilogue that highlights the purpose of the gospel, which includes encouraging and strengthening a deeper conviction that Jesus is the Messiah, the Son of God (20:30–31). The gospel itself consists of material that is in large part thematically constructed as a theological reflection on Jesus and his mission and ministry, revolving around the Jewish holidays.

The following observations on the redaction of the gospel should be noted:

- In the Synoptics, the cleansing of the temple takes place a couple of days before Jesus's death and seems to play an important role in the trial against him. In John, however, the cleansing functions as an introduction to Jesus's ministry (2:13–22). John's placement of the event may be a reflection of a historical reality that the synoptic authors were unaware of, or its placement may have the narrative function of emphasizing the conflict between Jesus and the temple priests from the very onset of his public ministry.
- In contrast to the Synoptics, the Johannine Jesus visits Jerusalem four times. While the synoptic authors spend little time describing the Last Supper, the author of John inserts the lengthy Farewell Discourse into this context. The discourse is about Jesus's love and stewardship, and also about the disciples and how they should live in the world after the Son has returned to the Father. In the middle of the Farewell Discourse, Jesus says, "Rise, let us be on our way" (14:31), but it takes three chapters until anyone actually moves or goes anywhere (18:1). It is possible that new material was added to a more original, shorter version of the discourse (ch. 14). It is also possible that Jesus's statement is simply a way to heighten the tension of the passage, an attempt to keep the aim of the story in mind amid a very long speech.
- At one point, Jesus is described as crossing to the other side of the Sea of Galilee (6:1), even though he has just held a speech in Jerusalem (ch. 5). Because this sudden geographical shift is not explained by the author, some scholars have attempted to shift the speech in chapter 5 to Galilee rather than Jerusalem, but since this creates more (new) questions than it answers, it is perhaps more logical to suggest that the author is more interested in

the thematic significance of the Jewish holidays for the role of Jesus than in chronological consistency.

- Chapter 21 is a later addition to the gospel. The gospel has two well-defined endings: 20:30–31 and 21:24–25. The "disciple whom Jesus loved" is identified as the author of the gospel in chapter 21. In addition, the added section emphasizes Peter as a leader of the movement, which can tell us a great deal about the development of the Johannine tradition in the early history of the *ekklēsia*.

The sources and traditions behind the Gospel of John have long been debated by scholars. Rudolf Bultmann believed that something that came to be called the "Sign Source" was used by the author. The source was believed to contain a series of miracles, or signs, as they are called in John. The assumption was that some of these miracles were picked up by the author, who incorporated them into his gospel (see 2:11; 4:54; cf. 20:30–31). The majority of scholars today, however, are more or less in agreement that the miracle stories of the gospel have different origins and that the existence of a single unified source is highly unlikely.

A more important question is whether the author of John had access to Mark. The two gospels share approximately fifteen stories and about ten Jesus sayings. The fact that many of these stories occur in the same order increases the likelihood of there being a literary connection between the gospels. Some scholars assert that John had access to Luke as well, and even Matthew, since these gospels also have a number of shared traditions.

The Structure of the Gospel of John

1:1–18	Prologue
1:19–2:12	*I. From Jordan to Cana in Galilee (Jesus's first "week")*
1:19–28	John the Baptist's identity (day 1)
1:29–34	John the Baptist witnesses about Jesus (day 2)
1:35–42	John the Baptist's disciples follow Jesus; Simon becomes Peter (day 3)
1:43–51	Jesus calls disciples in Galilee (day 4)
2:1–12	The first sign: water turned to wine ("on the third day")
2:13–3:21	*II. Passover in Jerusalem*
2:13–25	Cleansing of the temple
3:1–21	Jesus and Nicodemus
3:22–4:54	*III. From Jordan to Cana in Galilee*
3:22–36	John the Baptist bears witness one last time
4:1–42	Jesus in Samaria

4:43–54	The second sign: the son of a royal official is healed
5:1–47	*IV. Festival and Sabbath in Jerusalem*
5:1–9	A sick man is healed by the pool of Bethesda
5:10–18	Conflict
5:19–47	Jesus speaks about his mission
6:1–7:1	*V. Passover by the Sea of Galilee*
6:1–15	The feeding of the five thousand
6:16–21	Jesus walks on water
6:22–59	Jesus speaks about the bread of life
6:60–7:1	Division among the disciples: Peter's confession
7:2–10:21	*VI. Sukkot in Jerusalem*
7:2–52	Jesus speaks during some of the days of the holiday
7:53–8:11	Later addition to the gospel: the adulteress
8:12–59	Jesus continues speaking in the temple
9:1–41	A man born blind is healed
10:1–21	The parable of the sheep and the good shepherd
10:22–39	*VII. Temple Dedication in Jerusalem*
10:40–11:54	*VIII. From Jordan to Bethany*
10:40–42	John the Baptist's witnessing is confirmed
11:1–44	The greatest sign: Lazarus is raised from the dead
11:45–54	The decision to have Jesus killed is made
11:55–12:50	*IX. Passover in Jerusalem (Jesus's last week)*
11:55–12:11	The passion narrative begins (six days before Passover)
12:12–19	Entry into Jerusalem (the next day)
12:20–50	Jesus speaks about his death and mission
13:1–38	*X. Jesus's last night with his disciples*
13:1–17	Jesus washes the disciple's feet
13:18–38	Jesus identifies who will betray him and predicts Peter's denial of him
14:1–17:26	*XI. The Farewell Discourse*
14:1–31	Part 1
15:1–17:26	Part 2
18:1–19:42	*XII. Jesus's suffering and death (passion narrative)*
20:1–29	*XIII. Resurrection stories*
20:1–10	The empty tomb
20:11–29	The risen Jesus reveals himself in the areas surrounding Jerusalem
20:30–31	Epilogue
21:1–23	Redactional addition to the gospel: Jesus reveals himself by the Sea of Galilee
21:24–25	A second epilogue (redactional addition)

Box 4.7
On the Structure of John

Many analyses of John's structure have emphasized the role of "signs" in the narrative. Usually, seven such miracle stories are identified and interpreted as signs that say something about Jesus and who he is. The seven "sign stories" are as follows: water is turned into wine (2:1–11), the son of a royal official is healed (4:46–54), a sick man is healed by the pool of Bethesda (5:1–9), the five thousand are fed (6:1–15), Jesus walks on water (6:16–21), a man born blind is healed (9:1–41), and Lazarus is raised from the dead (11:1–44). Most scholars agree up to this point. The first two signs are, however, the only ones explicitly referred to as signs (2:11 and 4:54). The seventh and greatest sign (the raising of Lazarus) is clearly viewed as a sign (11:47 and 12:18), but it is not explicitly numbered as such. In addition to this, the word "sign" is often used in an imprecise way in the plural. It is especially noteworthy that the author emphasizes that many came to believe in him when "they saw the signs that he was doing" (2:23), and yet, at that point, only one of the signs, the first one, had been spoken of explicitly (2:11).

By far the most common way in which modern scholarship interprets the structure of John is in terms of two main sections: the "book of signs" (1:19–12:50) and the "book of glory" (13:1–20:31). The book of signs is preceded by the prologue (1:1–18), and the book of glory is followed by the added ending (21:1–25). This theory has its origins in the work of Raymond E. Brown. The book of signs includes the above-mentioned seven miracles, which are interpreted as signs that reveal and explain the deepest meaning of Jesus's identity and ministry. In the book of glory, which begins on the last night before the passion begins, when Jesus washes the feet of his disciples, and which ends with resurrection stories, the focus is on how the suffering and death of Jesus is actually a victorious triumph. One of the arguments in favor of this theory is that the term "sign" occurs only between 2:11 and 12:37, as well as in the epilogue (20:30). Another argument is that the word "glorified" is connected to Jesus's suffering and death. This argument is, however, rather weak, since the term is in fact used already in 7:39 and 17:10. See 12:28 in particular, where Jesus prays to the Father to "glorify" his name, after which a voice from heaven says, "I have glorified it, and I will glorify it again." Thus, the glorification of Jesus has at least already partially occurred prior to the passion narrative, during Jesus's ministry (e.g., 2:11). Not even the revelation that Jesus already knew when his moment was to come in the putatively important verse in 13:1 carries much significance. On the one hand, Jesus says that the moment for his glorification has come already in 12:23, and on the other hand, the glorification comes to some sort of climax in 17:1. The strongest argument in favor of 13:1 as a decisive start of a new section are the comments of the author (13:1–3). Authorial comments such as these are interspersed throughout the narrative (e.g., 2:23–25; 6:15; 12:1–2; and the entire section 12:12–19).

If John is to be divided into two main sections, as most scholars believe it should be, this division should occur in 11:55 rather than 13:1. Indeed, if there is to be any clear boundary on a higher hierarchical level, it should be 11:55. Geographically, it marks the beginning of the ascent to Jerusalem, and thus also shifts the geographical focus of the story from Galilee to Jerusalem as the center. In terms of chronology, it is now time for Passover. This is the third Passover in the narrative, which points toward the climax of the story. The passion narrative begins and Jesus's last week is introduced (11:55–20:29), which corresponds to the first week in the beginning of the Gospel. In addition, the decision to have Jesus killed has just been made (11:53–54). Caiaphas has, according to the Gospel, even spoken prophetically about it: "it is better for you to have one man die for the people than to have the whole nation destroyed" (11:49–52). The council of the high priests is described against the backdrop of the final and greatest of Jesus's signs: the raising of Lazarus from the dead. In addition, chapter 11 revolves around the theme of life. In chapter 12, however, the theme shifts to death. Jesus is anointed before his burial and struggles with anxiety over his own death (12:27). Thus, there are plenty of indicators in the text linked with or pointing to 11:55 as a turning point.

The chronological markers in the gospel are mostly relative. Comments like "after this" are common but stereotypical transition markers (e.g., 2:12; 3:22; 21:1). A more meaningful chronological marker is "the next day" (e.g., 6:22 and 12:12). Days function as a principle structuring the gospel during the first half of Jesus's ministry (1:19–2:12). Altogether, a week of Jesus's life is described (albeit not a week in real time but rather a week in the narrative). Jewish festivals make up the most important chronological markers. They also play a significant thematic role. It is interesting to note that the formulation "the Passover of the Jews was near" occurs in two places (2:13 and 11:55). A similar expression is used to transition the narrative to the Passover Jesus spends by the Sea of Galilee (6:4). In sum, it could be said that the narrative is in large part constructed around three Passovers (II, V, and IX) and three other Jewish festivals (IV, VI, and VII).

Since there is much that speaks in favor of the author of John having access to Mark while composing his gospel, it is important to say some words about the structural effect of the author's redactions. In Mark, the passion narrative begins partly with the news that the high priests were looking for a way to arrest Jesus during the Passover festivities (Mark 14:1–2), and partly with the story of the woman with the jar of costly ointment (Mark 14:3–9). In John, the passion narrative also begins with the high priests making plans to arrest Jesus during the Passover festivities (John 11:55–57). After this follows the story of how Mary anoints Jesus (12:1–8). This section provides the most convincing argument in favor of John having used Mark: the expression "costly perfume made of pure nard" and Judas's words about why the ointment had not been sold for three hundred denarii and given to the poor (12:3, 5). The formulations of this section are the same in the two gospels, thus supporting the theory that there is a relationship of literary dependence between them. It should be noted that the passion narrative in John begins before that of Mark, since the entry into Jerusalem occurs the day after Mary has anointed Jesus for his burial. In addition, Mark's telling of the entry into Jerusalem and the cleansing of the temple has been separated in John: the order has been rearranged and the occurrences have been connected to two different Passovers (II and IX).

A thematic pattern is visible in the structure in that there are three sections consisting of Jesus and his followers moving from the river Jordan (II, III, and VIII), and all three sections are preceded by the mention of John the Baptist bearing witness. It is likely of some significance that the only two signs explicitly called signs occur in these sections. The greatest sign, the raising of Lazarus, can also be found within its framework. In all probability, it is no coincidence that the final appraisal of John the Baptist's witnessing is as follows: "John performed no sign, but everything that John said about this man was true" (10:41). Jesus is the one who performs signs, which is confirmed later in the section when Lazarus is raised from the dead (11:1–44).

Another structural theme relates to the significance of the three Passovers. At the first Passover, Jesus cleanses the temple. This section concludes with a comment about the body of Jesus being the actual temple that would be destroyed and rebuilt in three days (2:18–22). At the second Passover, the feeding of the five thousand occurs, and Jesus speaks about himself as the bread of life. This section moves on to a sacramental level: "Those who eat my flesh and drink my blood have eternal life, and I will raise them up on the last day" (6:54). At the third Passover, Jesus is put to death. Thus, the first two Passovers foreshadow the third. Jesus's death and resurrection and the significance and meaning of the Eucharist are all themes present within the framework of the structure. Finally, it should be noted that Jesus's "first week" (1:19–2:12) thematically corresponds to his "last week" (11:55–20:29). The first week is both symbolic and schematic; it ends with Jesus's glory being revealed (2:11). The last week begins six days before Passover (12:1) and ends with Jesus being glorified both in death and via his resurrection on the morning after the Sabbath (20:1).

Key Theological Thoughts

Conceptions of the Spirit play a crucial role in John. The Spirit is sometimes referred to as the Helper and identified as the guide, teacher, and defender of the community. The Helper is Jesus's presence in the here and now. Behind these statements about the Spirit we can intercept a foundational ecclesiology. The *ekklēsia* is organically connected to Jesus, like the branches of a vine (15:5). The Eucharist is an important part of the life of the *ekklēsia*. The meal is the incarnation of the sacramental unity with God. The one who eats and drinks of it will have eternal life (6:53–58).

John emphasizes the unity between the Father and the Son (10:30). Because of this, many scholars assert that the gospel has a high Christology. Jesus is the *logos*, the Word. The Word was preexistent and actively present during the creation of the world (1:1–5). The Word became flesh; it was incarnated, which meant that God became a human in the person of Jesus Christ (1:14). This mystery is sometimes expressed by Jesus saying, "I am the light of the world" (8:12), a statement that is characteristic for John. (In Matthew, Jesus says this of the Jewish crowds and the disciples hearing the Sermon on the Mount [Matt 5:14].) Another such statement is "I am the resurrection and the life" (John 11:25). These "I am" statements are formulations based on the unnameable name of God, YHWH. Although it can be misperceived as a contrast to the high Christology in John, Jesus's entire ministry is centered on suffering and death (1:29). In fact, the very crucifixion itself is interpreted as a glorification of Jesus (12:27–33). The gospel thus revolves around the paradox of an incarnated God who dies and in his death triumphs. All of this is an expression of the Father's will and God's love for humanity.

There is a clear dualism present in Johannine thinking. The dualism relates, for the most part, to the struggle between light and darkness. The dualism is not absolute, since it has to do with the creator and the world he created. Either people are children of light, belonging to God and with access to truth, or they belong to the world, which does not know God. By receiving the incarnated Word, humans can become free. The belief in Jesus is also a belief in the one who sent him. "For God so loved the world that he gave his only Son, so that everyone who believes in him may not perish but may have eternal life" (3:16). While Mark and Luke speak about the kingdom of God, John focuses on eternal life—a whole other dimension than the Synoptic Gospels.

To a large degree, the teaching about the end of the ages, known as eschatology, is presented as realized, rather than future, in John. Those who do not believe in Jesus have already been condemned (3:18). Those who listen to Jesus and believe in the Father *have* eternal life and have *already* gone over from death to life (5:24–25). This realized eschatology does not, however, negate an eschatology oriented toward the future. It is obvious from the gospel that Johannine communities were indeed waiting for the return of the Christ (14:2–3) and the resurrection of the dead (5:28–29).

Further Reading

General

Barton, Stephen C., ed., *The Cambridge Companion to the Gospels*. Cambridge: Cambridge University Press, 2006.

Bauckham, Richard. *Jesus and the Eyewitnesses: The Gospels as Eyewitness Testimony*. 2nd ed. Grand Rapids: Eerdmans, 2017.

Bockmuehl, Markus, and Donald A. Hagner, eds. *The Written Gospel*. Cambridge: Cambridge University Press, 2005.

Burridge, Richard. *What Are the Gospels? A Comparison with Graeco-Roman Biography*. 2nd ed. Grand Rapids: Eerdmans, 2004.

Cotter, Wendy J. *The Christ of the Miracle Stories: Portraits through Encounter*. Grand Rapids: Baker Academic, 2010.

Goodacre, M. S. *The Synoptic Problem: A Way through the Maze*. London: T&T Clark, 2001.

Keith, Chris, and Larry W. Hurtado. *Jesus among Friends and Enemies: A Historical and Literary Introduction to Jesus in the Gospels*. Grand Rapids: Baker Academic, 2011.

Kloppenborg, John S. *Q, the Earliest Gospel: An Introduction to the Original Stories and Sayings of Jesus*. Louisville: Westminster John Knox, 2008.

———. *The Tenants in the Vineyard: Ideology, Economics, and Agrarian Conflict in Jewish Palestine*. WUNT 195. Tübingen: Mohr Siebeck, 2006.

Levine, Amy-Jill. *Short Stories by Jesus: The Enigmatic Parables of a Controversial Rabbi*. Nashville: Abingdon, 2018.

McIver, Robert K. *Memory, Jesus, and the Synoptic Gospels*. Atlanta: Society of Biblical Literature, 2011.

Robinson, James M., Paul Hoffmann, and John S. Kloppenborg. *The Critical Edition of Q*. Hermeneia. Minneapolis: Fortress, 2000.

Stuckenbruck, Loren T., and Gabriele Boccaccini, eds. *Enoch and the Synoptic Gospels: Reminiscences, Allusions, Intertextuality*. EJL 44. Atlanta: SBL Press, 2016.

Watson, Francis. *Gospel Writing: A Canonical Perspective*. Grand Rapids, Eerdmans, 2013.

Mark

Becker, Eve-Marie. *The Birth of Christian History: Memory and Time from Mark to Luke-Acts*. New Haven: Yale University Press, 2017.

Collins, Adela Yarbro. *Mark: A Commentary*. Hermeneia. Minneapolis: Fortress, 2007.

Levine, Amy-Jill, with Marianne Blickenstaff, eds. *A Feminist Companion to Mark*. Cleveland: Pilgrim Press, 2004.

Marcus, Joel. *Mark: A New Translation with Introduction and Commentary*. 2 vols. AYBC 27A–B. New Haven: Yale University Press, 2002–2009.

Telford, W. R. *The Theology of the Gospel of Mark*. Cambridge: Cambridge University Press, 1999.

Matthew

Davies, W. D., and Dale C. Allison. *Matthew*. 3 vols. ICC. London: T&T Clark, 2004.

Gurtner, Daniel M., and John Nolland, eds. *Built upon the Rock: Studies in the Gospel of Matthew*. Grand Rapids: Eerdmans, 2008.

Hamilton, Catherine Sider. *The Death of Jesus in Matthew: Innocent Blood and the End of Exile*. SNTSMS 167. Cambridge: Cambridge University Press, 2017.

Levine, Amy-Jill, with Marianne Blickenstaff, eds. *A Feminist Companion to Matthew*. Cleveland: Pilgrim Press, 2004.

Luz, Ulrich. *The Theology of the Gospel of Matthew*. Cambridge: Cambridge University Press, 1995.

Nolland, John. *The Gospel of Matthew*. NIGTC. Grand Rapids: Eerdmans, 2005.

Riches, John, and David C. Sim, eds. *The Gospel of Matthew in Its Roman Imperial Context*. London: T&T Clark, 2005.

Runesson, Anders. *Divine Wrath and Salvation in Matthew: The Narrative World of the First Gospel*. Minneapolis: Fortress, 2016.

Sim, David C. *The Gospel of Matthew and Christian Judaism: The History and Social Setting of the Matthean Community*. London: T&T Clark, 1998.

Luke

Bovon, François. *Luke*. 3 vols. Hermeneia. Minneapolis: Fortress, 2002–2013.

Conzelmann, Hans. *The Theology of St. Luke*. New York: Harper, 1961.

Fitzmyer, Joseph A. *The Gospel according to Luke: A New Translation with Introduction and Commentary*. 2 vols. AYBC 28–28A. New Haven: Yale University Press, 1985.

Green, Joel B. *The Theology of the Gospel of Luke*. Cambridge: Cambridge University Press, 1995.

Knight, Jonathan. *Luke's Gospel*. New Testament Readings. London: Routledge, 1998.

Levine, Amy-Jill, with Marianne Blickenstaff, eds. *A Feminist Companion to Luke*. Cleveland: Pilgrim Press, 2004.

Levine, Amy-Jill, and Ben Witherington III. *The Gospel of Luke*. Cambridge: Cambridge University Press, 2018.

Metzger, James A. *Consumption and Wealth in Luke's Gospel*. Leiden: Brill, 2007.

Nolland, John. *Luke*. 3 vols. WBC 35A–C. Grand Rapids: Zondervan, 1989–1993.

Acts

Fitzmyer, John F. *The Acts of the Apostles: A New Translation with Introduction and Commentary*. AYBC 31. New Haven: Yale University Press, 1998.

Jervell, Jacob. *The Theology of the Acts of the Apostles*. Cambridge: Cambridge University Press, 1996.

Levine, Amy-Jill, with Marianne Blickenstaff, eds. *A Feminist Companion to Acts*. Cleveland: Pilgrim Press, 2004.

Levinskaya, Irina. *Diaspora Setting*. Vol. 5 of *The Book of Acts in Its First-Century Setting*. Grand Rapids: Eerdmans, 1996.

Marguerat, Daniel. *The First Christian Historian: Writing the Acts of the Apostles*. Cambridge: Cambridge University Press, 2004.

Talbert, Charles. *Reading Acts: A Literary and Theological Commentary*. Rev. ed. Macon, GA: Smyth & Helwys, 2013.

John

Anderson, Paul N. *The Riddles of the Fourth Gospel: An Introduction to John*. Minneapolis: Fortress, 2011.

Bernier, Jonathan. Aposynagōgos *and the Historical Jesus in John: Rethinking the Historicity of the Johannine Expulsion Passages*. Leiden: Brill, 2013.

Bieringer, Reimund, Didier Pollefeyt, and Frederique Vandecasteele-Vanneuville. *Anti-Judaism and the Fourth Gospel*. Louisville: Westminster John Knox, 2001.

Brown, Raymond E. *The Gospel according to John: A New Introduction with Translation and Commentary*. AYBC 29–29A. New Haven: Yale University Press, 1966–1970.

Culpepper, R. Alan. *Anatomy of the Fourth Gospel: A Study in Literary Design*. Minneapolis: Fortress, 1983.

Levine, Amy-Jill, with Marianne Blickenstaff, eds. *A Feminist Companion to John*. 2 vols. Cleveland: Pilgrim Press, 2003.

Michaels, J. Ramsey. *The Gospel of John*. NICNT. Grand Rapids: Eerdmans, 2010.

Moloney, Francis J. *The Gospel of John*. SP 4. Collegeville, MN: Liturgical Press, 1998.

Thatcher, Tom, and Stephen D. Moore, eds. *Anatomies of Narrative Criticism: Gospel of John as Literature*. RBS 55. Atlanta: Society of Biblical Literature, 2008.

The Pauline Letters

In the New Testament, thirteen letters are attributed to Paul: Romans, First Corinthians, Second Corinthians, Galatians, Ephesians, Philippians, Colossians, First Thessalonians, Second Thessalonians, First Timothy, Second Timothy, Titus, and Philemon. In all likelihood, Paul wrote more letters than have been preserved in the New Testament. In 1 Cor 5:9 and 2 Cor 2:3–4 Paul mentions previous letters written to the Corinthians, and in Col 4:16 there is mention of a letter sent to the assembly at Laodicea. These letters have been lost. Some scholars, however, argue that the letters mentioned in 1 Cor 5:9 and 2 Cor 2:3–4 have actually been worked into 1 Corinthians by a later editor, and others have identified the letter mentioned in Col 4:16 as the Letter to the Ephesians.

The letters can be categorized in a variety of ways. The term "Prison Letters" is used for the letters written while Paul was imprisoned. The Prison Letters include Ephesians, Philippians, Colossians, and Philemon. The "Pastoral Letters" (from the Latin *pastor*, meaning "shepherd") is a collective description referring to the letters aimed at leaders of Christ groups. The Pastoral Letters include 1 and 2 Timothy as well as Titus. The categorization of these letters based on issues of authorship are discussed below.

The order of the Pauline letters in the modern translations of the New Testament is the same as the one presented in the Vulgate, the famous Latin translation of the Christian canon from the fifth century. The order is not chronological but rather based on other factors. The nine letters to specific assemblies come first, followed by the four addressed to specific individuals. Within these two categories, the order seems to be based on length. In addition, letters addressed to the same assemblies or individuals have been placed together.

The so-called New Testament Apocrypha, a collection of noncanonical writings from the early centuries of the Common Era, contains a number of texts claiming to be Pauline letters. Here one can find the letter to the assembly at Laodicea, a correspondence between Paul and the Roman philosopher Seneca, and a correspondence between Paul and the assembly at Corinth. Both the style and the content of these texts indicate that they were written much later than the Pauline letters in the New Testament.

The Question of Authorship

The Pastoral Letters (1 Timothy, 2 Timothy, Titus) exhibit great similarity between themselves in language but deviate from the other Pauline letters in the New Testament in that respect. Many of the central theological terms in the Pastoral Letters (e.g., *eusebeia*, "piety") are missing in the other letters and vice versa (e.g., *eleutheria*, "freedom"). Conjunctions and other particles are used differently in the Pastoral Letters than in the other Pauline letters. This is noteworthy because the usage of particles tends to be fairly constant from author to author; that is, they are usually a good indicator of authorship. One can also note the difference in presentation techniques and argumentation. In the Pastoral Letters, the lively and engaging style of the other letters has been replaced with a more restrained and formal diction. Opponents are rebutted with references to tradition rather than with theological arguments. These differences in language, diction, and style are so significant that the vast majority of biblical scholars today believe that it is unlikely that the Pastoral Letters and the other Pauline letters have been composed by the same author.

The Pastoral Letters are set apart also in other ways. For example, they are not present in the list of canonical books put together by Marcion around 140 CE; neither are they present in the oldest preserved collection of Paul's letters (P^{46} from around 200 CE). In addition, they seem to assume a more complex community structure than the other letters do.

As regards the other Pauline letters, there is a strong consensus that Romans, 1 and 2 Corinthians, Galatians, Philippians, 1 Thessalonians, and Philemon were composed by the same author. Concerning the three remaining letters—Ephesians, Colossians, and 2 Thessalonians—opinions differ among scholars. These texts deviate linguistically and stylistically from the first-mentioned seven letters, but not to the extent or in the same way as the Pastoral Letters. The deviations are most obvious in Ephesians. The linguistic constructions are longer, and there are more modifiers. There is also a comparatively large number of words not used in other Pauline letters. One can also note certain changes in theology—for example, that salvation is seen not only as a future occurrence but also as a present reality (Eph 2:4–5; cf. Rom 5:9–10 and 1 Cor 3:15). For these reasons, a majority of scholars hold the view that Ephesians was probably not written by the same person who wrote the seven letters.

Many scholars also assume that Colossians has a different author than the seven letters. Colossians deviates from them in much the same ways as Ephesians, with which it also shares certain structural and content-related similarities. As in Ephesians, there are certain theological changes, most notably that the author of Colossians assumes that the believer has already died and been raised together with Christ (Col 2:12; 3:1–2); in the seven undisputed letters (e.g., Rom 6:5; Phil 3:10–12), the resurrection with Christ is situated in the future. However, the linguistic deviations are not as significant as they are in Ephesians.

Second Thessalonians does not deviate linguistically from the seven undisputed letters as much as do Ephesians and Colossians. The reason why some scholars want to separate it from the seven letters is that it differs theologically from them in certain respects. Perhaps the most obvious example of this is that the statements about the "day of the Lord" in 1 and 2 Thessalonians are not consistent with each other. In 2 Thess 2:1–12 the audience is told that the day of the Lord has not yet come, since the lawless people first have to be revealed and carry out their evil deeds. In 1 Thess 5:1–11, however, the author asserts that the day of the Lord comes like a thief in the night and that the audience should stay alert and sober. But arguments of authorship based solely on content are somewhat risky. Emphases can shift even within the same context, and thoughts and perspectives can change and develop within a relatively short time span. Therefore, there are more scholars who are prepared to categorize 2 Thessalonians as having the same author as the seven letters than there are those who would add Ephesians and Colossians to this list.

How can one then explain that the Pauline letters seem to have been written by more than one individual? Usually, one of the following three explanations are given. First, in antiquity it was not considered problematic to write a text in someone else's name—someone from whom the actual author had drawn inspiration. In fact, this was common practice among disciples of a great teacher, who not only collected the works of their master but also wrote independently in their master's name. For example, this was done by the disciples of the Greek philosopher Pythagoras (sixth century BCE). Another example, this time from the Hebrew Bible, is the book of Isaiah, which in all likelihood consists of traditions from several centuries (from the eighth until the sixth or the fifth century BCE), but is, as a whole, attributed to the same prophet. According to this explanation, Paul's disciples have published letters in his name after his death, and this might explain the differences between the seven letters and the ones with a more dubious authorship.

Second, in antiquity it was common practice to employ a scribe to write one's letters. The role of the scribe could vary. It could consist of writing what the sender was saying word for word, or capturing only the main message, or freely composing a text on behalf of the sender. It is clear from the texts themselves that Paul sometimes made use of scribes (see Rom 16:22; 1 Cor 16:21; Gal 6:11; Col 4:18; 2 Thess 3:17). If the scribe was sometimes given the freedom to independently formulate the letter, this could explain the differences between the letters previously noted, both content-related and linguistic. One should also make note of the fact that some letters contain references to more than one sender in the introduction (1 Corinthians, 2 Corinthians, Galatians, Philippians, Colossians, 1 Thessalonians, 2 Thessalonians, and Philemon).

A third possibility is that some of the Pauline letters were written by persons wishing to have their audience believe that Paul was the real author. One reason for this would be to gain support for one's theology from a known religious authority.

There are reasons to believe that at least Romans, 1 and 2 Corinthians, Galatians, Philippians, 1 Thessalonians, and Philemon stem directly from Paul. They are more or less uniform in style, vocabulary, and theology, and they fit within the time frame of Paul's mission. In addition, several of them are so important and/or written with such a personal commitment that it seems strange for Paul to have let someone else formulate them.

How should we view the remaining letters? Here we must weigh the problems against the difficulties that each of the three models of explanation above brings with it, and every letter must be judged by itself. That Ephesians, Colossians, and 2 Thessalonians should be purposefully falsified letters is not likely. The letters were well known and were attributed to Paul already by Polycarp of Smyrna (all three) and Ignatius of Antioch (Ephesians and perhaps Colossians). Both of these community leaders lived and worked only a couple of decades after the death of Paul and had personal connections to assemblies in the regions to which Paul wrote. For the Pastoral Letters, the situation is different in this respect. We have no certain evidence of their existence until the Canon Muratori (from the second half of the second century). In addition, they display the format of private letters, which means that fewer people could witness either for or against their authenticity.

In the field of biblical studies, scholars often call the letters Paul himself wrote the "authentic" letters, and the letters whose authorship is debated are referred to as "pseudo-Pauline" or "deutero-Pauline." In this book, these terms are avoided, since they create the false impression of a simplified and one-sided position on the issue of authorship. In the presentation of the individual letters below, the letters will instead be divided into the following categories:

- A. Letters most likely formulated by Paul himself: Romans, 1 Corinthians, 2 Corinthians, Galatians, Philippians, 1 Thessalonians, and Philemon (the "undisputed" letters)
- B. Disputed letters: Ephesians, Colossians, and 2 Thessalonians
- C. Letters most likely not formulated by Paul himself: 1 Timothy, 2 Timothy, and Titus

Letters as a Literary Form

Despite the fact that it is a linguistic anachronism, it has long been customary to distinguish between letters and epistles. "Letter," using this vocabulary, refers to a text that functioned as a method of communication between the letter's author and the specific recipients. "Epistle" refers to a text that takes the form of a letter but is actually more of a tractate—that is to say, written for a wide audience. In later years, another category is often added: a middle form, which refers to a text written to a specific audience in a specific context but simultaneously meant to be normative outside that immediate context.

How should we evaluate the Pauline letters on the basis of these distinctions? On the one hand, the letters believed to have been authored by Paul himself were doubtlessly written to a specific audience in a specific context. On the other hand, the letters have been written with such care and thought that it seems that they were meant to carry relevance even outside the immediate situations they address. One may also note that at least Galatians is addressed to more than one assembly (Gal 1:2; cf. Col 4:16).

The Pauline letters have the same basic form as other ancient letters. Letters in antiquity were usually divided into three sections: (1) the introduction of the letter, (2) the body of the letter, and (3) the conclusion. The introduction of the letter usually had a formulaic character, consisting of (a) a reference to the sender in the nominative, (b) a reference to the audience (receiver) in the dative, and (c) a greeting. In Greco-Roman letters the greeting often consisted of the verb *chairein* (to be glad) in the infinitive, but in the Pauline letters the greeting is more similar to Jewish-oriented letter-writing conventions: "grace to you and peace from God our Father and the Lord Jesus Christ." In the Pauline letters the three parts, a, b, and c, are often construed such that they are extended in a way that prepares the reader for what is to come in the body of the letter. See the section "'Am I Now Seeking Human Approval?' A Rhetorical-Epistolary Reading of Gal 1:10," p. 547, for a discussion of a letter introduction.The subject matter of the letter is then dealt with in the body of the letter. The text can be organized in different ways, depending on the subject matter. In the Pauline letters, the body of the letter often opens with a favorable assessment of the situation of the audience, through a formulation like "I always thank God for you because . . ." In this way, a positive relationship is established between the sender and receivers of the letter, while the readers are simultaneously encouraged to behave in such a way that the situation is maintained. There are also other formulaic openings of the letter body, such as God being declared blessed for what he has done for "us" (2 Cor 1:3–7; Eph 1:3–14).

The body of the letter can contain formulaic expressions, sometimes collected in so-called clusters, which function as markers for the structure of the letter. For example, when Paul combines a personal address ("brothers") with an appeal to the audience (see Rom 12:1; Gal 4:12), contemporary readers may have interpreted this as an important marker. One should also note that the body of the letters have a general tendency to be concluded with some sort of an expression of what the writer wants and hopes for the audience—for example, a section with exhortations and/or wishes.

The endings of the letters consist of (a) greetings to the audience that the sender conveys on behalf of someone else, (b) greetings from the sender that he requests the audience to convey to someone else (sometimes b-a), and (c) a concluding greeting from the sender to the receiver. In Greco-Roman letters the imperative of *errōso* or *errōsthe*, meaning "be strong," is often used as an ending, but in the Pauline letters this literary formula has once again been replaced with another, special Christ-believing phrase: "grace from our Lord Jesus Christ to you all." If the letter had been dictated or written by a secretary, the concluding greeting could be written by the sender himself as a kind of signature (e.g., 1 Cor 16:21; 2 Thess 3:17). In Galatians the concluding part written by the author himself is rather long (6:11–18) and seems to have functioned both as an assurance of the identity of the author and as a summary of the letter.

Paul's Life and Ministry

The two most important sources we have access to regarding the life and ministry of Paul are the Pauline letters, especially the seven most likely formulated by himself, and the Acts of the Apostles. Other mentions of Paul in early texts written by Christ followers are often dependent on these two sources and rarely contribute new information. The Acts of Paul, which is part of the apocryphal literature, was composed much later (latter part of the second century CE) and has a distinct legendary character.

The Pauline letters are the oldest sources we have concerning Paul's life and ministry, and they contain valuable firsthand information. Because of this, the letters should have precedence over Acts in any attempt to reconstruct Paul's life. The letters, however, rarely provide us with any descriptions of wide-ranging events in Paul's life; most of the descriptions are highly fragmentary or determined by motives other than narrative retelling. The only time a larger context is described is Gal 1:11–2:21, and even here the description is in large part dependent on a limited perspective.

Thus, in order to gain an overview of the life and ministry of Paul, we are forced to base most of our reconstruction on Acts, even though it is a source that should be used with care since it was written using secondhand information and organized according to a set theological paradigm (see the section "The Gospels and the Acts of the Apostles," p. 260). There are several examples of discrepancies between the letters and Acts. According to Acts 17:10–15, Timothy and Silas stayed in Beroea while Paul traveled to Athens and Corinth, but in 1 Thess 3:1–3 Paul tells us how he sent out Timothy from Athens. In Gal 1:15–20 Paul is described as traveling to Jerusalem to speak with Cephas three years after his vision on the road to Damascus, whereas in Acts 9:10–30 the reader is left with the impression that only a small amount of time passed between Paul's vision and his meeting with the apostles in Jerusalem. That is consistent with the general tendency in Acts to illustrate the good relationship and doctrinal unity between Paul and the other apostles. Even the result of the so-called meeting of the apostles in Jerusalem is described differently in Acts and Gal (cf. Gal 2:6–10 and Acts 15:28–29). Thus, there are good reasons to exercise caution when making use of Acts as a source to reconstruct Paul's life and ministry, although it should not be discarded entirely (see also box 4.7).

Bema from the synagogue in Beroea. The three steps lead up to the bema that Paul allegedly stood on in Acts 17:10–15, successfully preaching his message. The steps can today be found in a memorial to Paul. Archaeologists have not found evidence to support the dating of the structure to the first century CE. Photo by Dieter Mitternacht.

There are no details about how Paul's life ended either in the Acts narrative or in the undisputed Pauline letters. In the Pastoral Letters, it appears that the author takes it for granted that Paul was eventually released from Rome, traveled to the east of the Mediterranean region, sent out Timothy and Titus, was imprisoned again, perhaps in Troas (2 Tim 4:13), and ended up in Rome once again (2 Tim 1:17). In 1 Clement (written sometime during the mid-90s CE) there are indications that Paul eventually did reach Spain (cf. Rom 15:24), before being martyred (1 Clem. 5:7). These pieces of information are difficult to assess.

According to an old tradition, reported also in Eusebius's *Ecclesiastical History* (ca. 300 CE), Paul was martyred during Emperor Nero's persecution of Christians in Rome (64–68).

Box 4.8 ***Chronology of Paul***

The following reconstruction of Paul's life and ministry is based on an amalgamation of information from both the Pauline letters and Acts. The events found only in Acts are set within square brackets. The approximate dates on the left hand of the column are based on certain known historical events mentioned in either Acts or the letters, as well as relative information about time indicated by these texts.

Mid-30s CE

- Is a Pharisee (Phil 3:5; Acts 22:3).
- Persecutes Christ followers (Gal 1:13, 23; 1 Cor 15:9; Phil 3:6; Acts 7:58; 8:1–3; 22:4).
- Has vision of Jesus on the road to Damascus (Gal 1:12, 16; 1 Cor 15:8; Acts 9:3–9; 22:6–11; 26:12–16).
- Travels to Arabia (Gal 1:17) and later returns to Damascus (Gal 1:17; Acts 9:10–25).
- Escapes from Damascus and King Aretas (2 Cor 11:32–33; Acts 9:23–25).

End of the 30s CE

- Travels to Jerusalem, where he meets with Peter and James "the Lord's brother" during fifteen days (Gal 1:18–19; Acts 9:26–30).
- Arrives in Syria and Cilicia (Gal 1:21–24); [travels to Antioch in Syria] (Acts 11:25–26).

End of 40s CE

- ["First missionary journey" with Barnabas and Mark: Antioch in Syria, Cyprus, Perga, Antioch in Galatia, Iconium, Lystra, Derbe, Lystra, Iconium, Antioch in Galatia, Perga, Attalia, Antioch in Syria). Conflicts with Jewish groups in Antioch in Galatia, Iconium, Lystra, and Derbe result in persecution, which culminates in Paul's stoning in Lystra] (Acts 13–14; cf. 2 Cor 11:24–25).

- The apostolic council in Jerusalem: Paul travels to Jerusalem with Barnabas and Titus in order to lay his gospel before the Christ-following leaders there. Of these leaders, we are made aware of the presence of James "the Lord's brother," Peter, and John. The reason for the meeting being called was the development of a conflict concerning the incorporation of gentiles into the Jesus movement. Should they (the males) be circumcised or not? The result of the meeting was that gentile members of the Jesus movement would not have to be circumcised (or follow the full extent of the Mosaic law) in order to join in the fellowship (Gal 2:1–10; Acts 15:1–29).
- Travels to Antioch in Syria, where he, among other things, chastises Peter for ceasing to eat together with gentile Christ followers (Gal 2:11–21; cf. Acts 15:30–35).

Beginning of 50s CE

- "Second missionary journey," carried out in the company of Silas and Timothy: [Antioch in Syria, Derbe, Lystra, Phrygia], Galatia, [Mysia, Troas, Samothrace, Neapolis], Philippi, [Amphipolis], Thessalonica, [Beroea], Athens, Corinth, [Ephesus, Caesarea, Jerusalem, Antioch in Syria].
- Arrives in Galatia because of some sort of illness or weakness, is humiliated in Philippi, forced to leave Thessalonica because of persecution, and stays for a longer period of time in Corinth [according to Acts, he stays for one and a half years] (Gal 4:13; 1 Thess 2:2; 2:17–3:10; Acts 15:36–18:22).

Mid-50s

- "Third missionary journey": [Antioch in Syria, Galatia, Phrygia], Ephesus, Macedonia, Greece, [Macedonia, Troas, Assos, Mitylene, Samos, Miletos, Cos, Rhodes, Patara, Tyre, Ptolemais, Caesarea, Jerusalem].
- Stays for a longer period of time in Ephesus [according to Acts, for about two years]. Plans to travel to Corinth via Macedonia and then onward to Jerusalem with the money he has collected for the congregation there. He also develops plans to travel to Rome and Spain (1 Cor 16:1–9; 2 Cor 1:8, 16, 23; 2:12–13; 7:5; Rom 1:10, 15; 15:22–32; Acts 18:23–21:16).

End of 50s CE

- [Jailed in Jerusalem] (Acts 21:27–23:22).
- [Jailed in Caesarea for two years] (Acts 23:23–26:32).

- [Travels to Rome as a prisoner: Caesarea, Sidon, Myra, Malta [?], Syracuse, Rhegium, Puteoli, Rome] (Acts 27:1–16).

Beginning of the 60s CE

- [Is in Rome for at least two years] (Acts 28:17–28:31).

Letters Likely Formulated by Paul Himself

The seven letters that will be discussed under this heading are arranged in the most likely order of composition: 1 Thessalonians, Galatians, 1 Corinthians, 2 Corinthians, Romans, Philippians, and Philemon.

First Thessalonians

Context and Dating

Thessalonica is located on the northwestern shores of the Aegean Sea. In New Testament times the city was the capital of Macedonia and home to the most important port in the region. It was also close to the Via Egnatia, the imperial Roman road to the east.

The letter describes how the senders, that is, Paul, Silvanus (Silas), and Timothy, had suffered and been "humiliated" in Philippi. They had then gone on to preach the gospel under severe difficulties in Thessalonica (2:2), before being forced to flee to Athens. Because they felt worried about the Christ followers they had left behind in Thessalonica (to whom the letter is addressed), they sent Timothy back to the city in order to strengthen them (3:1–5). After Timothy had returned to Paul and Silas with reassuring news (3:6–10), Paul wrote the letter to express his joy and gratitude as well as to comfort his readers with encouragement and guidance.

Many commentators assume that the letter also comments on specific problems in this Christ group. The section 2:1–12 is assumed to deal with back talk against the sender, 4:3–8 with a lacking sexual morality, and 4:13–5:11 with unclear or faulty assumptions about the return of the Lord. But such problems are never explicitly mentioned in the letter, and the above-cited passages can also be interpreted as statements meant to encourage and strengthen the readers as they experience persecution (see below).

The information provided by the letter corresponds in large part to the information provided in Acts 16–18 about how Paul, Silas, and Timothy established an assembly in Thessalonica during their "second missionary journey." This indicates that the letter may have been composed around the year 50 CE in Corinth, where, according to Acts 18:1–5, the three missionaries were reunited. The assembly seems to have been composed mainly of non-Jewish Christ followers (see 1 Thess 2:14 and Acts 17:4).

Communication Strategy

An important aspect of the letter's communication strategy is to compliment the readers for what they have already accomplished in this difficult time. No other Pauline letter has such a lengthy or encouraging thanksgiving section as this one. The thanksgiving is reformulated several times in the first half of the letter (1:2–10; 2:13–16; 3:7–10), sometimes with great emphasis (esp. 3:7–10). Great appreciation of addressees is also expressed in other ways in this part of the letter—for example, in 2:17–20: "for what is our hope or joy . . . is it not you?"

The reason for the compliments and the appreciation is described in terms of *imitatio.* The readers have made themselves worthy of this praise because of the fact that they have followed the example of the Lord, the senders of the letter, and the assembly in Judea (1:6; 2:14–16). Through this imitation, they have themselves become models of Christ-believing behavior for all the faithful in Macedonia and Achaia (1:7–10). Because the praise actualizes several models of faith/behavior (including the readers themselves), it functions as both comfort and guidance. Comfort and guidance are also given through the references to Jesus's ethical and eschatological teaching (4:2, 15).

Content and Structure

Apart from a short introduction (1:1) and a short conclusion (5:26–28), the letter consists of two main sections, one that is descriptive (1:2–3:13) and one that is exhortative (4:1–5:25). The two sections are similar in length and have similar conclusions.

The descriptive section is introduced with a reference to the senders' thankfulness to God for what the group has accomplished in an attitude of faith, love, and hope. They have followed the example of the Lord and the senders and have themselves become models of Christ-believing behavior for others (1:2–10). The character of the imitation is indicated through a reference to how the author and his companions behaved despite being persecuted. They were brave and self-denying; they preached the gospel openly and worked hard to not be a burden for the group (2:1–12). This reminder is followed by a new formulation about how the senders are thankful to God for the sake of the addressees. This time the author compares them to the Christ followers of Judea, with a short reference to all the hardships the Judean group has had to endure (2:13–16). The remainder of the first main section is composed of references to how worried the senders were about the assembly, but how their hope was renewed by the good news about the group's strong faith (2:17–3:10). The section ends with well-wishes for the addressees (3:11–13).

The second main section starts with an exhortation to the readers to continue doing that which they are already doing, after which the author reminds them of Jesus's teaching. Each one of them should strive for holiness and brotherly/sisterly love, which encompasses, among other things, minding one's own business (4:1–12; cf. 2:9–10). After this, the author spends some time teaching the group about the day of the Lord (4:13–5:11), a day that the members of the assembly should see as a great comfort. The teaching is based on the resurrection of Jesus and his eschatological teaching, and it describes how the dead will be brought back to life upon the return of the Lord (4:13–18). This return will occur when "those who are in the darkness" least expect it (5:1–11). The author proceeds with yet more exhortations meant to strengthen the unity of the group. These exhortations are mostly concerned with showing appreciation for leaders, keeping peace with one another, and encouraging/comforting those who have lost courage or hope (5:12–22). The second main section, like the first, is concluded with well-wishes for the assembly (5:23–25).

The content of the letter can be summarized as follows:

1:1	*Introduction*
1:2–3:13	*Descriptive section*
1:2–2:16	The senders' gratitude for the way the assembly has dealt with persecution
2:17–3:10	The senders' previous worry but current renewed hope following positive reports concerning the faith of the assembly
3:11–13	Well-wishes for the assembly
4:1–5:25	*Exhortative section*
4:1–12	Exhortation to continue on the path of imitation of Christ's ethical teaching
4:13–5:11	Exhortation to comfort one another with the teaching of the Lord's return
5:12–22	Exhortation meant to strengthen the assembly as a group (unity)
5:23–25	Well-wishes for the assembly
5:26–28	*Conclusion*

Key Theological Thoughts

One of the foundational characteristics of the letter is the idea of *imitatio*. Jesus is the ultimate paradigm. The sender, the readers, or others can also function as role models, inasmuch as they themselves conform to the paradigm exemplified by Jesus. In this way, their lives become a proclamation of the gospel (see 1:5–10; 2:14–16).

In 2:14–16 the letter states that "the Jews/Judeans" killed Jesus, defied God, and are the enemies of humanity. These sentences have, for obvious reasons, been the subject of much discussion. They are reminiscent of later Christian anti-Semitism, and because of this similarity, several scholars have argued that they are in fact a later addition to the original letter. But if one reads the entire section carefully, one will find that the purpose of the text is *not* to portray "the Jews" as more evil than other people. Indeed, the purpose of the text is the opposite: the Thessalonians have experienced *the exact same* persecution by their Greek society as the Jewish Christ followers in Judea experienced by their society. (Note that the Greek *Ioudaioi* does not distinguish between "Jews" and the geographical designation "Judeans"; the comparison made by Paul—Greek society/Judean society—strongly suggests that the translation here should be "Judeans.")

Another characteristic aspect of the letter that has received a great deal of attention is 4:13–5:11, which concerns itself with the day of the Lord. It would appear that the author of the letter expected the day of the Lord to occur very soon. But the wording of this section should perhaps not be overinterpreted, since the purpose of the text is to say that the day of the Lord will be unexpected, "like a thief in the night" (5:2), and that the readers should therefore be awake and sober at all times (5:6). Yet the author seems to take it for granted that the day of the Lord at least *could* occur in the very near future (see also the section "Paul, His Assemblies, and His Successors," p. 405).

Letter to the Galatians

Context and Dating

The region of Galatia was located in middle of Asia Minor, approximately in the areas surrounding modern-day Ankara. The Roman province with the same name extended further south, also including parts of Phrygia and Pisidia. If the name Galatia in Gal 1:2 refers to this province, the letter could be addressed to the Christ groups in Iconium and Lystra. If the name refers to the region, it has to be addressed to groups farther north. In Acts, Galatia is used to refer to the region, and we may assume that this reflects common usage, thus settling for the hypothesis that Paul here writes to Christ groups in the region rather than in the province.

In the letter it becomes clear that "certain" people have appeared in the Galatian assemblies, trying to induce them to be circumcised (5:2–10; 6:12–13). Paul does not seem to know exactly who they are (e.g., 1:7; 5:7, 10). He does, however, believe that they are advocating circumcision solely to escape persecution for the sake of the cross of Christ (6:12). According to traditional interpretation, the people advocating circumcision were believed to have been Jewish Christ followers, probably from Jerusalem, who had come to Galatia. However, the individuals in question could also have been non-Jews acting under pressure from Jewish or other groups in their proximity. The letter was written in order to persuade the addressees not to follow their advice. In addition to himself, Paul lists "all the brothers with him" as the senders.

Paul seems to have visited the group at least twice (4:13). If the letter is addressed to the assemblies in the region of Galatia, we can chronologically trace it, via Acts, to sometime after his visit there in the beginning of "the third missionary journey." At the same time, there is reason to believe that Romans and 2 Corinthians build on the material in Galatians. This would indicate that the letter originated sometime during the first part of Paul's stay in Ephesus, which in all likelihood occurred around 54–56 CE. The assemblies apparently consisted mostly of non-Jewish Christ followers (e.g., 4:8).

Communication Strategy

In order to keep the assemblies from listening to those advocating circumcision, Paul carries out a comprehensive argumentation in favor of himself and his interpretation of the gospel, an argumentation that eventually lands in exhortation directed to the assemblies to take his side (4:12) and to live their lives according to his interpretation of the gospel (5:1; 5:13–6:10).

The argumentation occurs in large part through references to both Paul's and the group's own experiences, respectively, interpreted in light of the career of Jesus and various citations of Scripture. The Abraham narrative is used extensively in the argumentation. The letter is written with personal commitment. The introductory tone is very rebuking (1:6–10) but is gradually softened, and later on in the letter it becomes appealing and hopeful (4:12; 5:10).

The engaging phraseology gives the impression of being both impulsive and hurried, but behind this facade is a highly structured and carefully formulated letter that clearly indicates that the author understood and made use of the rhetoric of his time. Not least, the author's use of narrative self-presentation (*ethos*), combined with theological arguments (*logos*) and emotional arguments (*pathos*), reveals a well-thought-out communication strategy.

Content and Structure

Already in the introduction to the letter (1:1–5) there is a foreshadowing of the two perspectives that Paul intends to argue in favor of in the letter. He claims to have been called directly by Jesus Christ and God the Father to be an apostle (1:1), and his gospel is about Jesus having sacrificed himself for "our" sins to save "us" from the present evil age (1:4). This is not followed by a section of thanksgiving, as is common in the Pauline letters. Instead, the body of the letter starts with Paul voicing his astonishment over how quickly the addressees are deserting God for another gospel, and then he puts a curse on anyone who preaches a gospel different from his own (1:6–10). This harsh introduction indicates how seriously Paul takes this issue.

The curse is followed by argumentation for Paul's gospel being no human message (1:11). It neither stems from humans nor aims to please humans. This argumentation begins with a reference to Paul's own experiences. The gospel came to him through a revelation of Jesus Christ himself (1:12). As a result, he who—true to his interpretation of Judaism—had persecuted "the church of God" became an apostle to the gentiles, and as such was persecuted himself (1:13–24). His gospel was confirmed and legitimized by James, Cephas, and John, the "acknowledged pillars" of the assembly in Jerusalem (2:1–10). Later, when Peter, in Antioch, did not dare admit to this for fear of the "circumcised," Paul publicly reminded him of its significance. A person is made righteous not through works of law but rather through faith. As a Christ follower, Paul has been crucified with Christ and been rendered dead to the law in order to be alive to God. His life is now characterized and lived by Christ, who is in him (2:11–21).

The argumentation then continues with a reference to the audience's own experiences. They did not receive the Spirit through works of law, but rather through faith (3:1–5). With an intricate exposition of Scripture, Paul "proves" that their experiences are in line with what is told about Abraham in Scripture. He was counted as righteous because of his faith and received the message that all nations would be blessed through him (3:6–14). This promise was given to Abraham and his descendant, which Paul identifies as Christ. Only later was the law given, after this promise had already been made, in order to function as a guardian until Christ came. Now that faith has arrived in the form of Christ, the law is no longer needed *as a guardian* (3:15–25). Those who have been baptized into Christ become themselves descendants and heirs in accordance with the promise, and God sends the spirit of his Son into their hearts (3:26–4:7). After this exposition, Paul expresses his astonishment that the audience now seems prepared to abandon their position in Christ and again be subject to weak and beggarly forces (4:8–11).

Instead, he encourages them to be like him (4:12). This encouragement is followed by a renewed reference to the experiences of the addressees. When he previously visited them, they welcomed him with great enthusiasm, despite the fact that he was physically very weak (4:12–20). The next exhortation is introduced with a complex allegory of the story of Abraham's two sons, where slavery under the law is contrasted with the freedom of the addressees. This time, it is also used to illustrate their marginalization (4:21–30). The exposition of Scripture leads to an encouragement to stand firm and not let themselves be enslaved again (5:1). Like the encouragement in 4:12, this is ultimately about taking Paul's side and directing their lives in accordance with his gospel. Both exhortations are followed by a formal assurance that each and every one who is circumcised is obliged to keep the law in its entirety, and that the addressees will be outside the grace in Christ if they seek their righteousness in the law (5:2–12). In 5:13–6:10 Paul encourages the addressees to live their life in faith and in the freedom of the Spirit, a freedom that consists of serving one another in love and not being conceited or jealous. The law and Spirit agree on this and fight in their own ways against the flesh.

The letter is concluded with Paul contrasting himself with those who aim to force the addressees to be circumcised. They seek status through outward means in order to avoid being persecuted for the sake of Christ. Paul, on the other hand, does not wish to boast of anything but the cross of Christ, through which he is crucified to the world and becomes a new creation (6:11–17). The conclusion of the letter (6:18) is short and concise, ending in the conciliatory phrase "brothers and sisters, amen."

The content of the letter can be summarized as follows:

1:1–5	Introduction
1:6–10	Criticism of the addressees' behavior and a curse on those creating confusion
1:11–2:21	Argument for Paul's gospel, as based on his experiences
3:1–4:11	Argument based on the addressees' experiences and Scripture
4:12–20	Exhortation to be like Paul against the background of previous experiences
4:21–5:1	Exhortation to stand free from the law, as based on an allegorical exegesis of Scripture
5:2–12	Consequences of being circumcised
5:13–6:10	Exhortation to live a life in faith and in the freedom of the Spirit
6:11–17	The real aims of Paul's opponents and Paul's wishes for himself
6:18	Conclusion

Key Theological Thoughts

As in 1 Thessalonians, in Galatians the idea of *imitatio* plays an important role in interpreting experiences (e.g., 6:17) and when searching for guidance (e.g., 5:25). But in Galatians this idea is much more elaborated theologically. Christ followers should view themselves as crucified with Christ. They have died away from the old age, characterized by, for example, the law and negative "fleshly" impulses (5:24), and have been resurrected with Christ to a life under other conditions, as a new creation (6:15) with the Spirit of Christ in their heart (2:20; 4:6). With the help of Scripture, these beliefs are put into the perspective of a larger salvation history, stretching from Abraham's time via the time of the law and the arrival of Jesus to the present-day situation of the Christ followers themselves (3:6–4:7). Such usage of Scripture is not present in 1 Thessalonians.

Scholars have different opinions about what exactly the issue being debated in Galatians consists of. In traditional Lutheran biblical scholarship, the conflict was usually interpreted as being between two types of religions, one seeing salvation as earned through works and the other claiming that salvation could only be received as a divine gift. The first type of religion was seen as Judaism, and the second as Christianity. The problem with this is that Paul never blames Christ-believing Jews for living a Jewish way of life. What he reacts so strongly against is not circumcision in and of itself but rather *who* was being circumcised and *why*. Compromises in terms of the law due to fear of reprisals is not reconcilable with Christ's cross. Paul himself is prepared to carry his cross. He carried the marks of Christ on his body (6:17), a burden that he would not need to carry, were he (still) preaching a gospel of circumcision (5:11).

Another question that has been thoroughly debated of late is how the Greek term *pistis Christou* is used in, for example, 2:16. The word *pistis* can mean both "faith" and "faithfulness/loyalty," and the construction could be interpreted as "faith in Christ" (as the NRSV translates it), "Christ's faith(fulness)," and/or "Christ-faith(fulness)." The question is thus whether Paul means to say that people are made righteous through their faith in Christ, through Christ's faith(fulness) toward God, and/or through a faith(fulness) that has its foundation and model in the faith(fulness) of Christ and is inspired by his Spirit. According to the last-mentioned interpretation, faith(fulness) means communion with Christ and participation in his faith(fulness); Christ became human so that humans would be able to become like him. The same interpretative crux can be found in 2:16, 2:20, and 3:22, as well as in Romans (3:22, 26), Philippians (3:9), and Ephesians (3:12).

First Letter to the Corinthians

Context and Dating

Ancient Corinth is located just west of the Isthmus, which connects Peloponnesus to the Greek mainland. The city had ports on both the Adriatic and Aegean Seas. In New Testament times, it had developed into a large, cosmopolitan trading city, housing around half a million inhabitants. It was the capital of the Roman province Achaia (the main area of classical Greek). Famous for its Aphrodite cult, it had also developed a reputation for widespread prostitution.

According to Acts 18, Paul founded an assembly in Corinth during his second missionary journey (cf. 1 Cor 4:15) and stayed there for one and a half years (probably around the year 51 CE). After his departure, another teacher named Apollos was active there (cf. 1 Cor 1:12; 16:12). The congregation seems to have consisted mainly of non-Jewish Christ followers from humble backgrounds (1 Cor 1:26; 12:2).

The letter reveals that Paul is writing from Ephesus, where he is working hard despite difficulties and persecution (15:32; 16:8–9). Rumors of the negative state of affairs in the Corinthian group have reached his ear (1:11; 5:1; 11:19, 20), and he has also received letters from them with specific questions (7:1). The negative state of affairs is due to many things, including that the assembly has become characterized by division based on different preachers (1:11–12); a case of sexual immorality (5:1); an inability to solve domestic disagreements (6:1–8); lack of order at gatherings where the assembly divides itself into different groups (11:18), some having to sit hungry while others drink themselves into a stupor during the Lord's Supper (11:21); and the gifts of grace not being used in a constructive manner (14:5, 27–28). In addition to all this, there are some members of the assembly who deny the resurrection of the dead (15:12). The questions in the letter the Corinthians sent to Paul seem to have revolved mainly around marriage (7:1–40), meat from Greco-Roman ("pagan") sacrifices (8:1–11:1), worship services (chs. 11–14), and the resurrection (ch. 15).

Corinth's main street, the Lechaion, which leads up to the agora via stairs and monumental gates (*propylaea*). On either side of the street we can see sidewalks and gutters. Photo by Dieter Mitternacht.

Paul writes 1 Corinthians in order to answer these questions, as well as in an attempt to lead the group back to what he understands to be the right path. In addition, he sends Timothy to Corinth (4:17; 16:10–11). A certain Sosthenes is listed as co-sender, but the identity of this individual is unclear (cf. Acts 18:17). Paul himself plans on staying in Ephesus until Pentecost (1 Cor 16:8–9). After Pentecost, his aim is to travel to Corinth via Macedonia in order to organize a collection of charity for the assembly in Jerusalem, among other things (16:1–7). If it is worth it, he will then join the group leaving for Jerusalem to hand over the gift.

The context indicated in the letter is a rather neat fit with the context of the latter half of Paul's stay in Ephesus during the "third missionary journey," as described in Acts 19. This would place the composition of the letter somewhere between the years 55 and 56 CE.

Communication Strategy

As in Galatians, Paul writes 1 Corinthians in order to correct serious wrongs done within a Christ group. However, the communication strategy in 1 Corinthians differs significantly from that of Galatians. In Galatians, Paul begins the letter with strong words of condemnation and then progressively softens his style, becoming more hopeful. In 1 Corinthians, he begins with positive words about the group, thanking God for making them so rich in spiritual gifts (1:4–9). With this positive perspective as his point of departure, he then addresses first the rumors about the problematic state of affairs in the assembly (1:10–6:20) and then the assembly's questions to him (7:1–15:18). The fact that the problems are brought up before he answers the questions indicates how seriously Paul views the challenges the group is facing. In addition, the assembly's difficulties reappear later in the letter, where appropriate (e.g., 11:18), and in this way the problematic state of affairs in the group comes to characterize the entire letter. This leads to a situation that is somewhat unclear with regard to what is written as a result of the rumors and what represents answers to the group's questions, respectively.

The argumentation in the letter is multifaceted. As in Galatians, we find references to Jesus and the passion (e.g., 1:23; 15:3–7), the experiences of the author and addressees (e.g., 2:1–5; 4:9–13), Jesus's teaching (e.g., 7:10; 11:23), and references to Scripture (e.g., 10:1–11). But the argumentation is sometimes based on other concepts, such as nature (e.g., 11:14), different kinds of traditions (e.g., 11:16; 15:29), and "common knowledge/logic" (e.g., 11:13).

Content and Structure

Already in the introduction of the letter (1:1–3) one of the main aims of the letter is indicated, namely to try to stop the divisions threatening to destroy the unity of the assembly. It is done by the description of the addressees as part of a larger community.

After the introduction follows a short section of thanksgiving for the group and all the knowledge and spiritual gifts God has bestowed on its members (1:4–9). Then Paul begins to address the problematic state of affairs, about which he has heard through rumors. He starts by addressing the lack of unity in the group, as a result of different factions claiming to follow different teachers (1:10–4:21), mainly Paul himself and Apollos (1:12; 3:4). Paul's reply to this is that he proclaims a crucified Christ, a foolishness to the world (1:18–25). This proclamation wins the most support with the marginalized and weak (1:26–31). He and the other apostles are weak, marginalized, and scorned too (2:1–5; 4:9–13), and they are all servants of the same Lord (3:5–17). In this way, God has obliterated the wisdom of the world. Here, there is no space for the pride and "wisdom" lying behind the divisions within the assembly (1:18–31; 3:18–23). Division is the principal expression of the group's immaturity (3:1–4). This argument leads to an exhortation to the assembly to take Paul, their spiritual father, as an example (4:14–16).

In contrast to the addressees' self-confidence stands their inability to solve disputes between members. An obvious case of adultery—a man living together with his father's wife—has been allowed to continue without any measures having been taken to stop it (ch. 5). In addition, Christ followers have been going to public courts to accuse one another (ch. 6). Trials between Christ followers should, Paul claims, not exist at all, but if needed, disputes should be solved internally and not with the help of nonbelievers (6:1–11).

After this, Paul begins to answer the specific questions he has been sent by the assembly. The questions are about marriage, celibacy, and divorce (ch. 7), as well as whether it would be permissible for members to eat meat sacrificed to "idols" (8:1–11:1). The answers lead to a description of how Paul adjusts himself according to different contexts in order to save as many people as possible (ch. 9), and this in its turn leads to an exhortation to the group to take Paul as an example, just as he has taken Christ as an example (11:1). The following chapters deal with issues related to worship services. Paul begins by dealing with the issue of whether women should cover their heads during the services (11:3–16), after which he turns to the rumors about how the addressees divide into groups at the meetings, and how some are left hungry while others are getting drunk at the Lord's Supper. Paul condemns this as a sin against the body and blood of Christ (11:20–34). After this, Paul turns to the usage of the spiritual gifts (chs. 12–14), and their relative significance in comparison to love, which is crucial (ch. 13).

Lastly, Paul discusses the belief in the resurrection of the dead (ch. 15), apparently because some members of the Corinthian assembly have denied it. Paul bases his argument on the statement that if the dead do not rise, Christ has not risen. If Christ has not risen, the entire faith is empty and pointless. If this were the case, it would be better to enjoy life rather than to continually risk it, as Paul does. There is also no point in being baptized for the sake of the dead. But Christ has indeed risen from the dead, and just as everyone dies through Adam, everyone shall receive new life through Christ upon his return. After his return, and after everything has been conquered by him, Christ will hand the kingdom over to God, the Father, so that he shall become everything, everywhere (15:28). But first the Son must reign, until he has defeated all his enemies; as the seed must die in order to give birth to a new form, so too the earthly body will be transformed into a heavenly, indestructible body. Thus, the addressees shall not shy away from or fear dedicating themselves completely to the work of the Lord, as Paul and Christ have done (15:3, 10, 30–31, 58).

The content of the letter can be summarized as follows:

1:1–3	*Introduction*
1:4–9	*Reinforcing a positive connection to the addressees*
1:10–6:20	*Interventions on the basis of rumors*
1:10–4:21	Against party formation in the assembly
5:1–6:20	Against fornication and lawsuits between believers
7:1–15:58	*Discussions of questions put by the group in a letter*
7:1–40	Questions about marriage (answering group's letter)
8:1–11:1	Questions concerning meat from idolatrous sacrifices

11:2–14:40	Questions concerning worship services
15:1–58	Questions concerning the resurrection
16:1–18	*Practical questions and concluding remarks*
16:19–24	*Conclusion*

Key Theological Thoughts

Since there are a number of practical questions being dealt with in 1 Corinthians, the theology of the letter goes off in a number of directions, as opposed to 1 Thessalonians and Galatians. As in 1 Thessalonians and Galatians, *imitatio* theology (4:16; cf. 11:1) constitutes the major backbone of 1 Corinthians, with a special emphasis on the cross of Christ (1:18–25) and Paul's weakness and suffering (2:1–5; 4:9–13). But here this theology has a completely different function. In the earlier letters, the theology of imitation was used to encourage the addressees to stand firm in their faith despite persecution, whereas 1 Corinthians uses the same theology to counter the misguided self-confidence and competitive mentality of the assembly, inspiring them instead to be humble and be of service to one another. With this ambition in mind, Paul goes on to develop the image of the assembly as the body of Christ, where the different limbs are dependent on each other (ch. 12), an image that is followed up with a more comprehensive reflection on the role, nature, and consequences of love in the life of the group (chs. 13–14). The principle of love is pinpointed by Paul as the central pillar of congregational life, functioning as a guide in the various practical matters brought up in the letter (e.g., 8:13; 9:19; 10:24, 33). Other guiding principles include "all things are lawful, but not beneficial" (6:12; 10:23) and "remain as you were called," the latter applied not only to the issue of marriage but also to Jewish and non-Jewish identity in the *ekklēsia*, as well as social status (7:8, 17–24).

In 1 Thessalonians, Paul's teaching about the resurrection on the day of the Lord gave comfort to the marginalized Thessalonians. In 1 Corinthians, Paul is given the opportunity to develop his thoughts on resurrection (ch. 15), since belief in the resurrection is being questioned in Corinth. He does this by, among other things, viewing the resurrection from the perspective of the larger history of salvation, through a typology where Christ is compared with Adam (gives life/brings death, a life-giving spirit/a living creature). He also expands on and develops the description of Christ's career as a course of events in several stages: Christ's resurrection; his return; the resurrection of the dead; handing over the kingdom to God after Christ has defeated all his enemies and each of them, including death, has been gradually removed. In contrast to Galatians, this perspective is cosmic and Paul makes no reference to the story of Abraham, but rather to the story of creation.

One passage that has found itself under the theological and exegetical magnifying glass a great deal of late is 1 Cor 14:34–35, a passage stating that women should be silent in the assembly, and that they should be subordinate, as the law states. The passage breaks the train of thought in chapter 14 in a strange way. In fact, it appears in different places in different manuscripts, and it stands in stark contrast to 1 Cor 11:5 and other passages that Paul has formulated himself (e.g., Rom 16:1–2). For these reasons, many scholars assert that verses 34–35 are a later addition made to the original text. Even if the passage would be accepted as original, the difficult task of somehow reconciling and relating it to 1 Cor 11:5 remains (see also the section "Men, Women, and Power in Ancient Society and the Early Jesus Movement," p. 161).

Second Letter to the Corinthians

Composition

Many scholars believe that 2 Corinthians is a compilation of different letters. Some also believe there are interpolations in the text. The reasons for this are first and foremost that the atmosphere is significantly different in chapters 1–7 (comfort and atonement) and chapters 10–13 (polemical), that 6:14–7:1 breaks off the context in a strange way, that chapter 8 changes abruptly to a completely new topic, and that chapter 9 seems to repeat chapter 8. In addition, 2:3–4 and 7:8–13 mention a letter that Paul had written to the Corinthians "with a heavy heart"; this description could fit very well as a description of chapters 10–13. Thus, these chapters may have been composed before chapters 1–7.

There are a number of counterarguments to these theories. Foremost among them are that there is no agreement regarding how the composition of the compilation should be mapped out, if indeed we are dealing with a compilation, and that it is rather unclear why someone would edit the letter this way. Indeed, understanding the letter in the order we have it today, one may in fact see several connections between its different parts in terms of the motifs discussed. The theory of compilation may create more problems than it solves. The following analysis of the letter assumes that it is a unified composition rather than an edited compilation.

Context and Dating

The letter provides us with the following information about its context. The senders, Paul and Timothy, had risked their lives in the province of Asia (western part of Asia Minor) but were saved (1:8). Paul had thereafter planned on traveling to Corinth and Macedonia, and later onward to Judea (1:15–16). But someone in Corinth had behaved in such a way that Paul had decided to postpone the visit and instead write an admonishing letter (1:23–2:11). It is not clear exactly what this individual had done, but presumably Paul's authority had been questioned in favor of the "great apostles" (e.g., 10:2; 11:5, 22; cf. 5:12). There were also conflicts in the assembly (12:20), and several people were engaged in illicit sexual relationships and other lifestyles considered deviant by Paul (12:21). Paul had sent Titus in order to deliver the admonishing letter, and had himself continued to Troas and Macedonia (2:12–13). Titus had eventually joined him there, delivering a joyful message about the Corinthian group (7:5–16). The hope of traveling to Corinth in order to complete the collection for the Jerusalem assembly was reignited (8:1–24; cf. 1 Cor 16:1–7). Paul would, however, travel to Corinth a little after the others. It would be his third visit to the assembly (e.g., 12:14). It is in this situation the letter was written with the aim of following up on the previous conflict and supporting Titus and the others with the collection.

The information provided us in the letter is more or less a fit with the scenario given us in Acts 19–20. There we are told that there was a riot against Paul and his companions at the end of their stay in Ephesus (the most important city in the province of Asia) during the "third missionary journey," and that Paul afterward traveled first to Macedonia and then to Greece. This indicates that 2 Corinthians cannot have been composed too long after 1 Corinthians. The admonishing letter mentioned in 2 Cor 2:3–4 and 7:8–13 can, however, hardly be a reference to 1 Corinthians. We thus have to assume that a sufficient amount of time passed between the composition of 1 and 2 Corinthians to allow a worsening of the situation in the assembly and the composition of another letter, as well as Titus's journey to Corinth and later to Macedonia. If 2 Corinthians was thus written around six months after 1 Corinthians, it would be dated somewhere between 56 or 57 CE.

Communication Strategy

Paul's strategy for following up on the conflict in the Corinthian group is partly to comment on and evaluate what has happened and partly to warn and exhort the assembly in preparation for his forthcoming visit. The first aim, the reflection on the past conflict, is carried out from a positive point of view (chs. 1–7). It focuses on the success of the senders (despite their hardships), as well as reinforcing their authority (the rescue in Asia, the openness in Troas), and on the addressees' positive response to the admonishing letter. Using an at times strongly emotional style, especially when describing the addressees, Paul strengthens his positive connection to them (e.g., 2:4; 7:4, 7, 11–16). Paul does not deny that there are still problems in the group, but this is put in the background (e.g., 5:20; 6:1; 7:2–3). Paul then attempts to engage the addressees in the collection for the Jerusalem assembly by telling them how generous the Macedonians were in their donations, what high expectations everyone now has for the Corinthian assembly, and that God loves a cheerful giver (chs. 8–9).

The second aim of the letter, following up on the conflict, is carried out by a stern warning to the group that he will not shy away from interfering powerfully if he is met with more conflict when he arrives in Corinth (chs. 10–13). The tone is more reproachful here than it was before (e.g., 10:7; 11:7, 19–20; 12:11), but this is balanced by a repeated reassurance that what has been said has only been said with the aim of strengthening the addressees (10:8; 12:19; 13:10). The tone is lightened significantly through the use of a stylistically brilliant self-irony. This letter is also marked by a strong sense of *imitatio Christi* theology (e.g., 1:5; 4:10–14; 5:14–15; 13:3–6). The only part of Scripture on which Paul reflects is the story of Moses at Sinai in chapter 3.

Content and Structure

After a short introduction (1:1–2), Paul expresses how grateful he and the other senders are for the comfort they have experienced in the midst of their sufferings, and their hope that the addressees will also be comforted through it (1:3–7). He then explains what this comfort consists of by recounting how they were under severe pressure in Asia but were saved (1:8–14), and how Paul was tormented by the problems in Corinth (1:15–2:11) but was met with openness in Troas (2:12–13.).

This serves as a prelude to a larger section about glory and weakness. Paul expresses his gratitude that God always includes them in his triumphal procession (2:14–17), but he confesses that it is like a treasure stored in clay jars (4:7). The glory of the new covenant surpasses that of the old covenant and is expressed in the Spirit working in the hearts of humans, which is a result of their evangelism (3:1–4:6). But this glory is experienced only in weakness and fragility. Constantly persecuted, they carry the death of Jesus in their bodies in order that Jesus's life should also become visible in their work promoting atonement (4:7–5:19). He exhorts the addressees to be reconciled with God, make space for the senders in their hearts, and contribute to the lessening of their suffering (5:20–7:16). The Christ groups in Judea are also suffering, and Paul urges the Corinthians to take the generous Macedonians as an example and be generous too in their donations, and to remember that God loves a cheerful giver and gives himself in abundance (8:1–9:15).

Paul then warns his audience that, on his forthcoming visit to Corinth, he is prepared to intervene powerfully against those who claim that he is guided by human motives (10:1–2). The warning is substantiated by a long, often self-ironic explanation and defense of his authority. His authority comes from God and is manifested in the fact that he has spread the gospel as far as to the addressees themselves (10:3–18). Although he is a weak speaker, he has much knowledge and wisdom, which he has shared with the addressees free of charge (11:1–15). He is not in any way inferior to the "greater apostles" (11:16–33), even though in reality he only wants to boast about his weakness, through which others become strong (12:1–13). This exposition concludes in a renewed warning (12:14–13:11 and 13:12–13).

The content of the letter can be summarized as follows:

1:1–2	*Introduction*
1:3–7:16	*The senders' comfort in times of trial and suffering*
1:3–7	The senders' gratitude for comfort in their suffering
1:8–2:13	Senders' experiences in Asia and Troas
2:14–5:19	Glory and fragility in the calling and work of the senders
5:20–7:3	Exhortation for the addressees to be atoned with God and the senders
7:4–16	How the senders are comforted by the addressees' repentance
8:1–9:15	*Titus and the others visit Corinth in order to complete the Jerusalem collection*
8:1–15	Encouragement for the addressees to be as generous as the Macedonians
8:16–9:5	The organization of the collection and the expectations of the assembly
9:6–15	God loves a cheerful giver and gives himself in abundance
10:1–13:11	*Preparing for Paul's third trip to Corinth*
10:1–2	Warning of powerful intervention against those who back-talk Paul
10:3–12:13	Paul's authority and weakness
12:14–13:11	Warning of powerful intervention against conflicts and debauchery
13:12–13	*Conclusion*

Key Theological Thoughts

In 1 Cor 1–4 there was *imitatio* thinking focusing on Christ's cross and Paul's suffering. In 2 Corinthians there is similar *imitatio* thinking, but here "the aspect of weakness" is complemented with an "aspect of strength," which instead focuses on the resurrection of Jesus (2 Cor 4:11–14; 13:3–4) and Paul's successes (1:8–14; 2:12–13; 3:1–4:6; 10:12–18). This aspect of strength is, however, balanced against the aspect of weakness throughout (4:7–5:19; 6:3–10; 11:23–12:13).

In 2 Corinthians there are a number of theological motifs, which are also found in Galatians: for example, the idea of the two covenants (2 Cor 3:3–18; Gal 4:24–26), the law that kills and the Spirit that gives life (2 Cor 3:6; Gal 3:10–14), and the idea that the one who lives in Christ is a new creation (2 Cor 5:17; Gal 6:15). In 2 Corinthians, the purpose is to enable the addressees to see the greatness and glory of the work of Paul and his companions. The motifs are combined with a revelation theological phraseology that is reminiscent of the Johannine tradition: Christ is the image of God and the carrier of God's glory (3:17–18; 4:4–6). The glory is present in God's Spirit and glorifies all those who see it (3:18).

Another theological motif that appears in 2 Corinthians is the idea of "Israel's present hardening," as applied to those among the Jews who do not accept Jesus's messianic status. This is expressed in conjunction with Paul's reflection on how Moses veiled his face with a cloth so that the Israelites would not see the waning glory and light emanating from his face (3:12–18). This thought is further explored in Romans.

Letter to the Romans

Composition

Many scholars suggest that the doxology in 16:25–27 is a later addition to the letter. The reasons for this are that it is missing from some manuscripts and appears elsewhere in other manuscripts (after ch. 14 or 15), and that this passage exhibits some unique features in terms of style and content.

In addition, some scholars suggest that 16:1–23 is a letter of recommendation originally sent to the assembly in Ephesus. The main reason for this assertion is that they find it unlikely that Paul would have known so many people in an assembly he had never visited, and that 1 Corinthians and Acts identify some of these people as living in Ephesus. Arguments against this claim include the fact that it is unlikely that a letter would consist mostly of greetings, that travel was not unusual among the first Christ followers, and that the many greetings match the aim of Romans. The below description and discussion of the letter assumes that it is a uniform composition, even though questions remain about 16:25–27.

Context and Dating

We do not know when or how the Christ-believing assembly in Rome came into being. A note in the work of the prominent Roman historian Suetonius could be interpreted as evidence for the fact that there were Christ followers in Rome as early as 49 CE. The group was in all likelihood started by Christ followers who moved to the city. By the time of the composition of Romans, the group seems to consist mostly of non-Jewish Christ followers (Rom 1:5–6, 13–15).

The letter provides us with the following clue concerning the context: as the apostle to the gentiles, Paul believes that he carries a responsibility for the Christ followers in Rome (1:10–15; cf. 15:15–16), even though this particular assembly was not started by him. He has often thought about visiting them but has hitherto been unable to fulfill this desire (1:5–6, 13–15). He views his work in the eastern regions of the Mediterranean as completed, and now wishes to turn his attention westward, to Spain (15:23–24). On the way he wants to visit the Christ followers in Rome. He would like to share with them some spiritual gift (1:11–15) and hopes that they will help him along the way (15:23–24, 28–29). The aim of the letter seems to be for Paul to establish himself as the apostle to the gentiles in Rome, in preparation for his planed mission to the western part of the Roman Empire.

The information about the Jerusalem collection (15:25–27) in Romans indicates that the letter was written in chronological proximity to 2 Corinthians. According to Acts 20:1–3, Paul traveled from Macedonia to Corinth, where he stayed for three months before beginning his journey to Syria and Jerusalem. If this information is correct, the Letter to the Romans was most likely written during the three-month stay in Corinth. Thus, the year of its composition is likely to be either 56, 57, or, possibly, 58 CE.

Communication Strategy

Paul's strategy for establishing himself as the apostle to the gentiles in Rome may be outlined as follows. He wishes (a) to create a bond between himself and the addressees by describing them positively (1:6–8; 15:14; 16:19) and speaking about how much he has longed to meet them (1:9–12, 13, 15; 15:23), as well as carrying forth a number of greetings to a large number of named individuals (16:3–16, 21–23); (b) to clarify his role and his claims (1:1–6, 13–15; 15:14–32); (c) to describe God's plan of salvation, in relation to which his claims must be seen (1:16–11:36); and (d) to begin acting in the role he has taken on by revealing, in the form of exhortations, the practical consequences of this salvation plan (12:1–15:13).

The argumentation of the letter is based in large part on Jesus's career (e.g., 6:4–11) and Scripture (e.g., 4:1–25) but also, to a lesser degree, on Paul's and the addressees' experiences (e.g., 6:20–22; 7:14–25). The references to Scripture tend to be both longer and more numerous in Romans (e.g., 3:10–18) than in the other letters.

Content and Structure

Already in the letter opening (1:1–7), Paul outlines the purpose of the letter through a rather comprehensive self-presentation. He is the servant of Christ, called as an apostle to lead all gentiles, including the addressees, to obedience in faith. The addressees, in turn, are described as God's beloved, called to belong to Christ and be God's holy ones. Paul then begins the main body of the letter by telling his audience how he thanks God for them because of their well-known faith, and that he hopes he will soon have the opportunity to meet them (1:8–12). Following this, he clarifies his ambitions and his claims concerning the addressees. As the apostle to the gentiles, he sees himself as being responsible for all gentiles and thus wants to visit the group in Rome and preach the gospel there as well (1:13–15).

The long section (1:16–11:36) that follows can be seen as a further clarification of these ambitions and claims. It begins with a general proclamation of the gospel as the power of God for salvation to everyone who believes, the Jew first but also the Greek. In the gospel, God's righteousness is revealed "from faith to faith" (1:16–17). As a background for this, Paul explains how everyone is subject to the judgment of God (1:18–3:20). All unrighteousness is subject to God's wrath. Nobody can say that he or she is without sin, since everyone has knowledge of God through God's works (1:18–2:16). In addition, the Jews have the law. But the law does not make a person righteous; it can only give insight into what constitutes sin (2:17–3:20).

But the righteousness of God has been revealed through Jesus Christ, so that everyone—both Jew and Greek—may be liberated and find atonement and righteousness through faith in Jesus (or through Jesus's faith[fullness] (3:21–31); compare the discussion on *pistis Christou* in the section "Letter to the Galatians," p. 292, and the section "Justification by Faith and Participation in Christ," p. 418). This corresponds with what Scripture says about Abraham. He believed in God and was thus reckoned as righteous. It was through the righteousness of faith that he and his descendants were given the promise to inherit the world. This promise is applicable to everyone who, like Abraham, believes, and in this sense is one of Abraham's children (4:1–25).

Following this, Paul turns his attention to describing what life in God's righteousness looks like (5:1–8:39). Those who are made righteous are also reconciled with God. Adam's sin led to the judgment and death of all people, but Jesus's righteous deed means that all have access to justification and life (5:1–21). Everyone who has been baptized into Christ has died with him to sin and to the law, in order to live to God (6:1–7:25). They now have God's and Christ's Spirit in themselves and should live in accordance with it. If they do so, they will become the sons and heirs of God—the coheirs of Christ. If they share his suffering, they will also share his glory. Ultimately, this means liberation for all of creation. Reconciled with God and led by the Spirit, the faithful can be sure of reaching the goal (8:1–39).

The long description of God's plan of salvation is concluded with a reflection on the significance of the fact that the majority of Israel, the people to which Paul himself belongs, has not accepted Jesus as the Messiah (9:1–11:36). Israel was given the promises of God, but the majority of them sought righteousness based on works of the law rather than on faith (9:1–33). But their stumbling became the salvation of the gentiles. When the gentiles have reached the goal in their full number, "all Israel" will also be saved (10:1–11:36). Romans 9–11 is analyzed in a more comprehensive manner in chapter 5.

After the description of God's plan of salvation follows a section of exhortations of a rather general nature (12:1–15:13). The addressees are exhorted not to adapt to this world but rather to present themselves as holy sacrifices to God (12:1–2); not to think too highly of themselves but instead to outdo one another in showing honor and brotherly love and to serve the Lord and bless those who persecute them (12:3–21); to be subordinate to their superiors and not to be in debt to anyone (ch. 13); not to judge one another but instead to help the weak (14:1–15:6); and, finally, to accept one other, just as Christ Jesus, servant of the circumcised, has accepted them and other gentiles (15:7–12). The section is completed by well-wishes for the addressees (15:13).

The body of the letter is concluded with Paul returning to his ambitions and claims in relation to the addressees (15:14–33). He is convinced that they can guide one other, but as the apostle to the gentiles, he has still taken it upon himself to remind them of "a few things" (15:14–21). He now plans to travel to Spain via Rome; he hopes that they will help him along his way and that he in return might bring the blessings of Christ with him (15:22–33).

The conclusion of the letter is unusually long (16:1–27), with greetings to about twenty-five named individuals as well as people related to them in some way.

The content of the letter can be summarized as follows:

1:1–7	*Introduction*
1:8–12	*Establishing a positive connection to the addressees*
1:13–15	*Paul's ambitions and claims in relation to the addressees*
1:16–11:36	*God's plan of salvation, as the context for Paul's claims*
1:16–17	The nature of the gospel
1:18–3:20	Everyone is subject to God's judgment
3:21–4:25	God's righteousness through faith
5:1–8:39	Life in God's righteousness
9:1–11:36	Israel's role in God's plan
12:1–15:13	*Exhortations, as an expression of Paul's claims*
15:14–33	*Paul's ambitions and claims in relation to the addressees*
16:1–27	*Conclusion*

Key Theological Thoughts

In Romans we meet the majority of the theological ideas that Paul, in response to various situations, developed in the previous letters. Here they are combined into one large, comprehensive, and unified vision. The Abraham typology from Galatians (Rom 4) is intertwined with the Adam typology from 1 Corinthians (Rom 5), and the terminology of righteousness from Galatians (e.g., Rom 8:1–17) is combined with the terminology of glory from 2 Corinthians (e.g., Rom 8:18–21, 30).

But the letter is more than just a collection of motifs and ideas developed in previous letters. As they are combined into a large vision with a specific focus, they are reshaped, developed, and supplemented with new motifs. The large vision revolves around God's act of salvation in relation to Jews and gentiles. It begins with the guilt of humanity as a whole, both Jews and gentiles, before God (1:18–3:20) and ends with the final union of Jews and gentiles in the salvation of God (11:25–36). In this universal perspective, Paul has expanded his thoughts about righteousness through adding comments on how God has been revealed in creation (1:18–32), and the role of the law as a guardian (cf. Gal 3:24) has been toned down in favor of a more universal role as a revealer of sin (Rom 3:19–20). The universal perspective is taken so far that the entirety of creation is included in the drama of salvation. Enslaved under the rule of corruption, all of creation is waiting impatiently for liberation (8:19–22).

In the paraenetic section, we also find a number of images and motifs from earlier letters. They have, however, been generalized in Romans. In Rom 14:1–23, for example, Paul brings up a principle from 1 Cor 8–10—namely, that those who feel comfortable to eat certain food should not judge those who do not dare to do the same. In 1 Corinthians this thought is developed in response to a concrete problem—whether or not the Christ follower could eat food from pagan sacrifices. In Romans the idea is rather used as a general example of the principle that you should never judge your fellow siblings in faith (14:1, 13) or put a stumbling block in their path (14:13, 19).

Letter to the Philippians

Composition

Some scholars believe that Philippians is a compilation of several letters. The most important reasons for this are that (1) chapters 1–2 contain almost all of the traditional parts of a complete New Testament letter, (2) the harsh words of 3:2 stand in stark contrast to the positive wording that has hitherto characterized the letter, and (3) in 4:18 the reader gets the impression that Epaphroditus has recently arrived, whereas in 2:25–30 he has already had time to arrive, serve Paul, become seriously ill, and recover, at the same time as the rumor of his illness had both reached Philippi and had time to come back.

One of the strongest arguments against the theory of a compilation of more than one letters is the fact that much of the diction and many of the motifs of the letter recur throughout. It is difficult to explain how there could be such thematic unity in the letter if it is in fact a compilation of two letters. The presentation and discussion below assume that the letter is a unified composition.

Context and Dating

Philippi was a Roman colony, located a short distance from the coastline of eastern Macedonia. It was situated on the Roman road Via Egnatia. According to Acts 16, Paul established the assembly there during his second mission journey (cf. 1 Thess 2:2).

The Roman agora in Philippi. In the foreground we can see Via Egnatia, the Roman military and trade road from around 150 BCE. Via Egnatia connected Asia Minor and Europe, the Bosporus and the Adriatic Sea (see the map at the back of the book). Photo by Dieter Mitternacht.

The assembly appears to be made up mainly of non-Jewish Christ followers (Phil 3:3), who seem to be especially dear to Paul (4:15; cf. 2 Cor 11:9).

The letter reveals that Paul is imprisoned "for the sake of Christ" somewhere where there existed a *praetorium* (1:12–18) and a presence of people who worked for the "emperor's court" (4:22; see below). The situation seems serious, but Paul still counts on being released (1:18–26; 2:17). The addressees are also persecuted (1:27–30). They have sent a gift to Paul with a certain Epaphroditus (4:18). During the visit, Epaphroditus became seriously ill but eventually recovered. Paul now plans on sending him back to the assembly (2:25–30). He also plans on sending Timothy to Philippi in order to find out more about how the persecuted addressees fare (2:19–24). He also hopes to be able to visit them in person soon (2:24).

This is the context in which Paul composed the letter. The aim is threefold: (1) to inform the addressees of his situation (imprisonment, etc.), (2) to strengthen and encourage them in a time of persecution, and (3) to thank them for the gift they sent. The overarching purpose seems, naturally, to be the second aim. Timothy is listed as a sender together with Paul, but the entire letter is written in the first person and seems to express Paul's perspective.

Paul sits imprisoned in a place with a *praetorium* and people who work in the emperor's court. The word *praetorium* was used to designate the residence of a Roman governor, but it could also refer to the headquarter of the imperial lifeguard in Rome. "The court of the emperor" refers to the imperial court administration, which could be found in many places throughout the Roman Empire. The information is an approximate fit with the two imprisonments described in Acts, more specifically the one in Caesarea (Acts 23–26) and the one in Rome (Acts 28:16–31). The first imprisonment is usually dated to around 58–60 CE and the second one to around 60–62 CE. These two alternatives have been questioned because both cities are far from Philippi. Paul seems to assume that Timothy will be able to travel to Philippi and return before his own release (Phil 2:19, 24). A third option is that the letter was written in Ephesus. Ephesus was significantly closer to Philippi, and Paul stayed there for a longer period of time (ca. 54–56 CE). The city had a *praetorium* as well as an imperial court administration. But an imprisonment in Ephesus is not mentioned in any of the letters or in Acts. The discussion here will assume that the letter was written during the latter part of the 50s CE or the early years of the 60s CE.

Communication Strategy

Paul attempts to strengthen and encourage the persecuted addressees by communicating a positive perspective with regard to their situation. No other Pauline letter uses the phrase "be joyful" as much as this one. The entire first section of the letter (chs. 1–2) is written from the perspective that Paul is and will be joyful, and that he will be able to experience this joyfulness with the addressees soon (1:4, 18; 2:2, 17–18, 28). Important parts of the second section (3:1–4:7) are also written from the perspective that the addressees should be joyful (3:1; 4:4).

This joy is motivated by an *imitatio* theology revolving around Christ's suffering, death, and resurrection (e.g., 2:5–12; 3:10–11). Those who share in the suffering of Christ have the hope that they will also share in his resurrection. Paul's difficult situation and the gift he has received from the assembly are contextualized in the same way. Both become expressions of participation in the suffering, but also in the grace (1:5, 7; 4:15).

The positive connection Paul establishes to the group is a very important part of the letter, and the style is often highly emotional (e.g., 1:3–4, 8; 4:1, 10). *Imitatio* theology dominates the letter. Scriptural citations are missing, and allusions to specific passages are comparatively few.

Content and Structure

In the introduction of the letter (1:1–2), Paul presents himself not as an apostle but as a servant of Christ. He does not have to underline his authority when speaking to the Philippians, but rather inspires them to carry the suffering they are experiencing because of the gospel as imitators of Christ. The body of the letter starts with Paul thanking God for the addressees' fellowship in the work for the gospel and praying that they will continue to grow in love and insight (1:3–11).

After this, he describes his incarceration and how it has meant progress for the gospel and how this gladdens him. He is sure that the situation will contribute to his salvation, whether he lives or dies. Even though he would gladly be united with Christ—that is, die—he is convinced that he will survive, for the sake of the addressees (1:12–26).

In conjunction with this description, he encourages the addressees to make his joy complete by living a life worthy of Christ's gospel, letting the same mind be in them as was in Jesus Christ, the one who was in the form of God, but he gave it all up and became as human beings are, and he was obedient to the point of death on a cross and was therefore exalted by God over all things (1:27–2:18). This description of Jesus's career (2:6–11) is assumed by many scholars to be an excerpt from an ancient Christian hymn. The assumption is a tempting one, but it is difficult to find enough evidence to properly support it. After the exhortations, Paul discloses that he plans on sending Timothy and Epaphroditus to them and says that he hopes to soon be able to travel himself (2:19–30).

In a new section of exhortations (3:1–4:9), the former focus on Paul and his joy is abandoned, and the perspective shifts more unequivocally to the situation and joy of the addressees. They are encouraged to be joyful and face their situation, imitating Christ together with Paul (3:17)—he who was blameless as to righteousness under the law but who gave it all up to share in the suffering and death of Christ, hoping also to share his resurrection (3:4–16). The addressees are also encouraged to stand firm and united and, once again, to be joyful (4:1–9).

The body of the letter is concluded with Paul mentioning the gift he received from the assembly (4:10–20). He is gladdened by their compassion, which will be a benefit for themselves too. As for himself, he has everything he needs now. After this follows a short conclusion with greetings (4:21–23).

The content of the letter can be summarized as follows:

1:1–2	Introduction
1:3–11	Encouragement to continue participation in the work for the gospel
1:12–26	Account of Paul's situation and his model reaction to persecution
1:27–2:18	Exhortations in conjunction to the above account
2:19–30	Account of future contacts with the group
3:1–4:9	Exhortations based on the group's present situation
4:10–20	Account of Paul's joy over the gift the group sent
4:21–23	Conclusion

Key Theological Thoughts

Like 1 Thessalonians and Galatians, the letter to the Philippians makes ample use of *imitatio* theology, focusing on the cross of Christ in order to help the group stand firm in the midst of persecution. An important difference, though, is that the resurrection and glorification to come are more emphasized in this letter (e.g., 2:9–11; 3:10–16, 20–21; cf. 2 Cor 4:11–14, 13:3–4). This gives Paul the opportunity to interpret persecution in a positive light, going so far as to describe it as grace (1:7, 29–30). However, this tendency also leads him to imply a greater distance between the Christ follower and the world; he writes that it would be best for him to depart and be with Christ (1:21, 23). All those who are perfect should forget what lies behind them and instead focus on the prize waiting for them in heaven, to which God has called them (3:13–15); their homeland is in heaven (3:20).

Another difference in relation to earlier Pauline letters is that the perspective on Jesus's career has been widened, such that Jesus's self-sacrifice refers not only to his obedience to the point of death (2:8) but also to a giving up of a "God likeness" to adopt a "human likeness" (2:6–7).

Letter to Philemon

Context and Dating

The letter reveals that Paul is imprisoned when he writes it (Phlm 1). In prison, he has been paid a visit by a certain Onesimus, a slave who has run away from his owner, Philemon (11–16). Philemon owns a house, in which a Christ group assembles. The house is probably located in Colossae (cf. Col 4:17), and Philemon seems to occupy a leadership role in the group (Phlm 2). Onesimus became a Christ follower through the work of Paul and has helped him in many ways (10–13). With the letter, Paul is sending Onesimus back to Philemon (12), and he expects Philemon to receive Onesimus as a beloved brother (16). He himself also hopes to soon be able to visit the group and therefore asks Philemon to prepare for his arrival in the near future (22).

Timothy is listed as a co-sender, but the entire letter is authored from the perspective of Paul. Apphia, Archippus, and the group meeting in Philemon's house are listed as co-addressees, but the letter is first and foremost directed toward Philemon.

The issue of dating the letter is plagued by the same problems as the dating of Philippians. Onesimus's escape and Paul's planned visit to the group indicate that the distance between Paul and the addressees is not too large. At the same time, certain details in the letter would support a later dating (9), in which case it was most likely composed from Paul's imprisonment in Caesarea (ca. 58–60 CE) or in Rome (ca. 60–62 CE).

Communication Strategy

In order to convince Philemon to receive Onesimus as a beloved brother, Paul strategically relates positively to Philemon and gives a very positive portrayal of Onesimus. He also clarifies what he expects from Philemon. The tone of the letter is friendly and humble. Allusions to Paul's imprisonment are made no less than five times. The request in the letter is described as an appeal rather than an order (8–9), but in reality the letter comes closer to a command than an appeal, since a rejection of Onesimus would be a rejection of Paul (17). At the end of the letter, Paul goes so far as to clearly state that he *expects* Philemon to obey (21).

The letter does not contain much theological argumentation, other than the fact that Paul's request is set against the backdrop of values cherished by Christ followers, such as love and faithfulness.

Content and Structure

Already in the introduction of the letter (1–3), the relationship between Paul and Philemon is clarified. Paul writes to Philemon as a prisoner of Christ, describing the addressee as his dearly beloved friend and coworker.

Then he positively relates to Philemon by telling him how he thanks God for his faithfulness and love toward all Christ followers (4–7). This forms the background for Paul's requests on behalf of the now believing Onesimus (8–21). His request should be understood not as a command but rather as an appeal from an aged prisoner of Christ (8–9). The appeal is made on behalf of Onesimus, Paul's spiritual child, who is like a part of himself (10, 12). Indeed, as Philemon is not currently with Paul, Onesimus is very useful to Paul, talking the place of Philemon (11, 13). If he had a choice, Paul would rather that Onesimus stayed with him (13–16). If Philemon sees Paul as his friend, he should receive Onesimus as if he were Paul himself (17). Paul promises to pay all of Onesimus's debt, if there is any (18–19), even though it is really Philemon who is indebted to Paul. He trusts that Philemon will make him happy by obeying (20–21).

The body of the letter is concluded by Paul asking Philemon to make ready a room for him, as he hopes to soon be able to visit the assembly (22). Thereafter follows some concluding words and a greeting (23–25).

The content of the letter can be summarized as follows:

1–3	Introduction
4–7	Positive connection with Philemon emphasized
8–21	Appeal to Philemon to receive Onesimus as a beloved brother
22	Request for Philemon to prepare a room for Paul
23–25	Conclusion

Disputed Letters

The letters included in this category are presented in the order they would appear to place themselves in Paul's life (2 Thessalonians, Colossians, Ephesians). The presentation will include only what the letters themselves tell us of their context and dating, communication strategy, and so on. These aspects may then be further analyzed by the reader depending on what stance is adopted on the question of authorship.

Second Letter to the Thessalonians

Context and Dating

The letter assumes the following context: The addressees are suffering persecution (1:4). Some of the members have caused unrest in the group by claiming that the day of the Lord has arrived (2:2). Apparently, some of them also live "without order" at the expense of others (3:6). Possibly these two statements refer to the same group of individuals. The main aim of the letter is to encourage the addressees and help them stand firm in the face of persecution. They should not be troubled by false teachings about the day of the Lord. In addition, the addressees are encouraged to take measures against those who refuse to work. Senders are listed as Paul, Silvanus, and Timothy.

If Paul's signature (3:17) is authentic, the letter should have been authored soon after 1 Thessalonians, whose statements about the resurrection contributed, possibly, to some confusion about the day of the Lord (e.g., 1 Thess 4:17; 5:1–2). Scholars who doubt Pauline authorship often understand the letter to have been written toward the end of the first century.

Communication Strategy

The strategy used to persuade the addressees to stand firm in the face of persecution and not to let themselves be troubled in their faith by false doctrine is to encourage them to firmness by thanksgiving for their faith and endurance. This is followed by a number of direct exhortations not to let themselves be led astray by false teachings. Both the thanksgiving and the exhortations are supported with references to prior knowledge about the teaching of the day of the Lord.

The strategy for getting the members of the assembly to stand up to those who live off their charity without working is to encourage the group to refer to how the senders lived among them as a standard by which to judge others.

Content and Structure

After a short introduction (1:1–2) follows a longer section (1:3–2:17), which is composed from the perspective that the senders give thanks to God for the faith and endurance of the addressees (1:3–4; 2:13–14). In direct connection with the introductory thanksgiving is a more comprehensive reminder of how the day of the Lord will bring destruction for those who pester the addressees and strive only for their own advancement (1:5–10). This reminder ends with the senders asking God to help the addressees complete their actions in faith (1:11–12).

The section of thanksgiving is followed by an exhortation to the addressees not to be confused or alarmed if someone, with reference to the Spirit or something the senders would have said or written, tells them that the day of the Lord is already here (2:1–3). Such teaching cannot be true, because the day of the Lord cannot happen before the rebellion occurs and the lawless one is revealed, he who is opposed to all that is holy and says he is God, but is, in reality, destined for destruction. His arrival is the work of Satan, and he will be very powerful and lead astray those who have not put their faith in the truth (2:3–12).

The section is rounded off with a renewed thanksgiving, new exhortations to stand firm in the teaching provided them by the senders, and an expressed desire for God to strengthen the addressees in word and deed (2:13–17).

Thereafter follows a section with several exhortations of a different nature (3:1–16). First, the addressees are encouraged to pray for the senders and for the success of their mission (3:1–5). Second, the addressees are encouraged to stay away from those living "without order" at their expense but not to view them as enemies (3:6–15). They should view the senders as an example, since they worked and were not a burden on the addressees; indeed, the one who does not want to work should not be allowed to eat. The section is rounded off with a wish of peace for the addressees (3:16). Thereafter follows a short conclusion to the letter, ended with a personally written greeting from Paul himself (3:17–18).

The content of the letter can be summarized as follows:

1:1–2	Introduction
1:3–2:17	Exhortation to stand firm in times of persecution and to not be fooled by false teachings
3:1–16	Exhortation to pray for the senders and to stand up to those who refuse to work
3:17–18	Conclusion

Key Theological Thoughts

The letter is in many ways reminiscent of 1 Thessalonians. The theological reflection is, however, expanded on one point. It concerns the understanding of the Lord's arrival. In 1 Thessalonians, the author writes that the day of the Lord will arrive unexpectedly for "those who are in the darkness," and that they who have died in Christ will then be resurrected (1 Thess 4:13–5:11). In this letter, the author adds information about the various signs indicating that this day is close at hand: first the rebellion must occur and the lawless one be revealed (2 Thess 2:3–12). Similar thoughts about a "lawless person" cannot be found in other Pauline literature but can be found in the Johannine literature (1 John 2:18; 4:3).

Letter to the Colossians

Context and Dating

Colossae was located in Asia Minor about 170 kilometers east of Ephesus on the main road from Ephesus to Syria. The city, renowned for its wool industry, was destroyed in an earthquake in the year 61 CE and was never rebuilt. The Christ group there seems to have been composed mainly of gentiles (1:21, 27; 3:5–7).

The letter reflects the following context. Paul is imprisoned (4:10, 18). He does not know the group personally but has been told about them by Epaphras, the founder of the assembly (1:4, 7–9). The addressees have begun adhering to a certain "philosophy," with rules about food, drink, and festivals (2:8, 16, 20–23). The rules are motivated by respect for different cosmic powers (2:8, 18). The main aim of the letter is to convince the addressees to distance themselves from this philosophy and praxis and to adhere only to the gospel (2:4–8). Timothy is listed as co-sender of the letter. In addition to sending the letter, Paul plans to send his companion Tychicus to the addressees, so that he may inform them of Paul's situation (4:7–8). He will be followed by Onesimus (4:9; cf. Phlm above). Paul has also written a letter to the assembly in the neighboring city of Laodicea and suggests that the addressees also read this letter and vice versa (4:16).

If Paul's signature is authentic (4:18), the letter may be dated to around the same time as the letter to Philemon (see above). Those who view Paul's signature as inauthentic usually date Colossians to the latter part of the first century CE.

Communication Strategy

The letter's overall aim is to convince the addressees to distance themselves from a certain teaching (as in Galatians). Despite this, the communication strategy for the letter is largely positive. The senders begin by positively connecting to the addressees and encouraging them to stand firm in the gospel. They express themselves favorably concerning the group, praising them for their faith, reminding them of the gospel that led them to this faith as well as reminding them of Paul's role in their spiritual growth (1:1–2:5). Only then, in connection with an exhortation to the addressees to stand firm in the faith they have been taught, do the senders address and criticize the "philosophy" (2:6–23). After this interlude, the senders return to the positive strategy, with exhortations related to life in Christ (3:1–4:6).

The argument is built by referring to previously accepted teaching. The issue does not seem to be that the addressees have the wrong teaching, rather that they are drawing the wrong conclusions as they apply it. Citations from Scripture are missing. Some scholars argue that the somewhat rhythmic description of Christ in 1:15–20 is a citation from an ancient Christ hymn, but, as with the supposed hymn in Phil 2:6–11, support for this theory is hard to find.

Content and Structure

Already in the introduction of the letter (1:1–2), the sender connects favorably to the addressees by describing them as "saints" and "faithful brothers and sisters in Christ."

The positive connections are followed up with a longer section that aims to encourage the addressees to stand firm in the gospel (1:3–2:5). This section begins with the senders thanking God for the addressees' faith, love, and hope. The thanksgiving is connected to a reminder of the gospel that has led them to these spiritual gifts (1:3–8). After this, the senders pray that the addressees be filled with the knowledge of God's will, so that they might live in a fashion worthy of him. The prayer is developed into a reminder of the content of the gospel: God has reconciled everything and everyone, even the addressees, with himself through the death of Christ—who is the image of the invisible God, standing before and above everything, and through and for whom everything in heaven and on earth has been created. Each one of the addressees shall one day stand before him, holy and without blemish, as long as they stand firm in the gospel, of which Paul has become the servant (1:9–23). This encouragement is concluded with some comments on how Paul is glad to suffer and fight, following Christ's example, in order to fulfill his mission to let God's word come to fruition among the addressees and others (1:24–2:5).

It is against this background of positive buttressing and thanksgiving that the addressees are eventually asked to stand firm in the faith they have been taught and distance themselves from the "philosophy" that has become popular among them (2:6–23). The section is introduced with a few positive exhortations for the addressees to take a stand for the gospel (2:6–7), after which follow three admonitions about the wisdom philosophy (2:8–23). The three admonitions are mixed with comments about how the fullness of the divine is found in Christ, and how God through Christ's death and resurrection has disarmed all worldly rulers and powers. The addressees have, through their baptism, died and been resurrected with Christ, and thus cosmic powers have no power over them. The "philosophy" is described as the vain thoughts of humans.

Thereafter follows a more positive set of exhortations to live in Christ (3:1–4:6).

If the addressees have died and been resurrected with Christ, they ought to strive toward being with Christ in the heavenly sphere and "kill" the worldly, or sinful, aspects of their lives. These worldly aspects include sexual immorality, selfishness, anger, and lies. They should strive toward compassion, kindness, humility, and so on (3:1–17). This is exemplified in a so-called household code, with exhortations for different members of the household: men/women, children/parents, masters/slaves (3:18–4:1). The section is concluded with some general exhortations regarding prayer and interaction with non-group members (4:2–6).

The body of the letter is concluded with some practical information. Paul is sending Tychicus and Onesimus to the group, and these shall provide them with more information and encouragement (4:7–9).

The conclusion of the letter (4:10–18) includes, among other aspects, greetings to the addressees from a number of named individuals. This could be another way of positively connecting to the addressees, since the senders apparently do not know the assembly personally.

The content of the letter can be summarized as follows:

1:1–2	Introduction
1:3–2:5	Encouragement to stand firm in the gospel
2:6–23	Exhortations to take a stand for the gospel as opposed to the "philosophy"
3:1–4:6	Exhortations for the life in Christ
4:7–9	Practical information
4:10–18	Conclusion

Key Theological Thoughts

The argumentation aims to portray Christ's reign and his central role in both creation and salvation. The one who lives in Christ has died away from the cosmic powers of the world and should focus wholly on orienting his or her life around Christ.

There are some points in the letter in which the explanation of Christ's reign exceeds the descriptions of the same concept in the letters discussed above. One of these points is his involvement in creation. Christ is said to have existed before all else, and everything in heaven and on earth was created in, through, and to him (1:15–17). In Phil 2:6–7 we become acquainted with a Christ who went from a "likeness with God" to taking on "human form." Here we are presented with a Christ who played a central role in creation itself.

Another point that is similarly expanded on is the degree to which the reign of Christ has already been established. In 1 Cor 15:24–25 the final triumph over all "powers" is located in the future, while these same powers in Colossians have already been dethroned and exposed to the ridicule of all (Col 2:15). A similar conceptual shift has occurred on the anthropological level. In the earlier letters, the Christ follower is said to have died with Christ *in the hope* of also being resurrected with him (e.g., Phil 3:10–16). In contrast to this, Colossians claims that the addressees have *already* been resurrected with Christ (2:12; 3:1).

A third point concerns the word *plērōma*, the Greek word for "fullness," which is used in Colossians in a theologically new way in reflections on the reign of Christ (1:19; 2:9). The term seems to stand for the entirety of the riches of good things existing in God. A similar fullness is also said to exist in Christ. A comparable usage of this word is found in Ephesians (Eph 1:23; 3:19; 4:13) and in the Johannine prologue (John 1:16).

There is yet another difference worth mentioning here. In the other Pauline letters, Christ followers are portrayed as limbs of the body of Christ (e.g., 1 Cor 12:12–17; Rom 12:4–5). In Colossians, this metaphor has been developed in such a way that Christ is portrayed as the head of the body (Col 1:18). In this way, the metaphor is used to portray the authority and reign of Christ (see also the section "One Body with Many Members," p. 411).

Letter to the Ephesians

Context and Dating

Ephesus is located on the west coast of Asia Minor; in the Roman province of Asia, it was the main city. According to Acts 18:18–19:40, Paul was active there during both the second and third missionary journeys. It is, however, unclear whether the letter was originally meant to be addressed to a specific assembly. Some older manuscripts lack the specification "in Ephesus." There are also other aspects of the letter that do not match the circumstances of the assembly in Ephesus, such as the fact that Paul and the addressees do not seem to be acquainted (1:15–16; 3:2; cf. Acts 19:10). In addition, the content of the letter is of a general character and does not seem to be directed to a certain group. Because of this, several scholars assert that the letter originally was a circulating text without specific addressees. Others argue that it should be viewed as a tractate rather than a letter in the more strict sense. Yet others wish to identify it as the letter to the Christ group in Laodicea, which is mentioned in Col 4:16. Paul may not have known that assembly personally.

The letter does not provide us with much information concerning its context. Paul is said to be in prison (3:1; 4:1; 6:20) and the addressees are described as non-Jewish Christ followers (2:11–19; 3:1; 4:17; 5:8). Paul writes that he will send his companion Tychicus to the addressees so that they would know more about his situation and be encouraged (6:21–22). The letter shows signs of being connected to Colossians. There are several demonstrable similarities in structure, formulations, and ideology. Ephesians is, however, richer in content and seems to be written with somewhat different aims in mind.

The purpose of the letter appears to be to encourage non-Jewish Christ followers to live according to their calling and not like "pagans." The letter does not reveal any specific problems among the addressees. The theme of unity can be found in the text, which could indicate that there were divisions among them, but the main focus of the letter could as well indicate that the addressees had a tendency to live like "pagans" and/or that they were under pressure from their pagan compatriots.

If the letter was authored by Paul, it should have been composed around the same time as Colossians and Philemon. Those who argue that the letter is not Pauline usually opt for dating it to the end of the first century.

Communication Strategy

The strategy by which to persuade the readers to adhere to their calling as Christ followers and scorn "pagan" traditions consists largely of emphasizing the positive aspects of the calling, in contrast to the addressees' negative "pagan" point of departure. The text appears quite evaluative; this is partly due to the author using a lot of modifiers with appraisive words (e.g., 1:18–23), and partly due to the presentation taking place mainly within a frame of praise (1:3–14), prayer (1:15–3:21), and exhortation (4:1–6:20).

Despite the emphatically evaluative nature of the letter, the text radiates a certain calm, almost meditative feeling. It flows with often quite long sentences with elements of multiple subordinate clauses and phrases. Engaging rhetorical devices, such as direct addresses and rhetorical questions, frequently used in Galatians and Romans, are largely missing.

In contrast to Colossians, Ephesians contains several citations of Scripture (e.g., 4:8, 25–26). We also find a citation of what appears to be an older hymn or liturgical text (5:14). Furthermore, the text includes several references to Jesus's career (e.g., 1:20–23; 5:2) and, to a certain degree, references to the sender's and addressees' own experiences, all for the sake of construing a solid argumentation (e.g., 1:13; 3:1, 3).

Content and Structure

After a short introduction (1:1–2)—which is strikingly similar to that of Colossians—the body of the letter starts with an account written from the point of view of "Paul's prayers to God" (1:3–3:21). The first thing we see is a praising of God for all the blessings that have been given the sender and addressees in and through Christ (1:3–14). In Christ they have, in accordance with God's "secret" plan from before the creation of the world, been liberated and given their inheritance (1:7–12). As a pledge of the inheritance, they have received the Spirit (1:13–14). In this section, a distinction is made between "we who were the first to set our hope on Christ" and "you" (1:12–13). It is likely that this distinction refers to Jewish and non-Jewish Christ followers, respectively. Both groups have been allowed a share in the blessings.

Thereafter follows a thanksgiving for the addressees' faith and love, as well as a prayer that they may receive knowledge such that they can see what a rich inheritance it truly is that God is bestowing on the faithful (1:15–2:10). The power by which God raised and exalted Christ is still at work here and now, for their sake (1:18–23). They were dead through their trespasses, but God has made them alive in Christ and given them a place in heaven (2:1–10).

It gives the sender reason to remind the readers of the importance of Christ's salvation for them, more specifically (2:11–22). They were, by birth, gentiles with no citizenship in Israel and therefore no share in its covenant and the promises made to it (2:11–12). However, thanks to Christ they are no longer strangers but hold the same citizenship as the holy. For he made the two groups into one. He has abolished the law in order to create in himself a single human from the two, and through the cross reconcile them both to God in one body (2:13–22).

The descriptive section (1:3–3:21) is concluded by a new appearance of Paul's prayer for the addressees (3:1–21). This time, it is emphasized that the prayer is that of *Paul*—Paul who was given the mission to proclaim the gospel to the gentiles, and who is now in prison for their sake (3:1–13). His prayer is that God shall give the addressees power through the Spirit such that Christ may live in them and that they may grasp everything until God's "fullness" fills them (3:16–21).

Next follows a longer exhortative section (4:1–6:20). The first part is structured around exhortations encouraging the audience to live in a worthy manner and adhere to their call in humility and love, as well as to strive for spiritual unity (*one* body, *one* spirit, *one* hope, *one* Lord, *one* faith, *one* baptism, *one* God). Using the power that stems from Christ, the head, they shall allow the body to grow and be strengthened in love (4:1–16). These positive exhortations are then balanced by negative ones warning against a life in ignorance, egoism, deception, and rage (4:17–32). Instead, they ought to take God and Christ as models of love, epitomized by Christ's sacrifice of himself for others (5:1–14). The rather general exhortations are then specified into more practical ones. This part builds significantly on so-called household codes, with specific rules for women and men, children and parents, as well as slaves and masters (5:15–6:9). The exhortative section (4:1–6:20) is concluded with encouragements to find strength in God (6:10–20).

The body of the letter finishes with a practical piece of information mentioning that Paul is sending Tychicus to the addressees in order that he may tell them how

Paul is faring and be encouraged (6:21–22; cf. Col 4:8–9). After this follows a short conclusion without personal greetings.

The content of the letter can be summarized as follows:

1:1–2	*Introduction*
1:3–3:21	*Paul's prayers to God*
1:3–14	Praise to God for salvation in and through Christ
1:15–2:10	Thanksgiving and prayer for the addressees
2:11–2:22	Reminder of the significance of Christ's salvation for the addressees
3:1–21	Prayer for the addressees
4:1–6:20	*Exhortations*
4:1–16	Exhortation to live worthy of one's calling in love and unity
4:17–32	Exhortation to no longer live in ignorance
5:1–14	Exhortation to take God and Christ as models
5:15–6:9	Specific exhortations
6:10–20	Exhortation to find strength in God
6:21–22	*Practical information*
6:23–24	*Conclusion*

Key Theological Thoughts

The theological thinking in Ephesians ties in very nicely with that in Colossians. In Ephesians, as in Colossians, we find mention of Christ's cosmic dominion (e.g., 1:10, 20–23). In Ephesians, however, we find a lesser focus on the dominion as such, with emphasis placed rather on its consequences for the faithful. The same great power, through which Christ was raised and exalted, is said to still be at work for them (1:18–23). In Christ they are united, both Jews and non-Jews, into a single body, one *ekklēsia*, through which even the rulers and powers of the heavens will obtain knowledge of God's wisdom in its multiple layers (e.g., 1:10–14; 2:14–22; 3:6, 10; 4:3–6). Here, too, Christ is identified as the head of the body (1:22; 4:15; 5:23).

As in Colossians, the word "fullness," *plērōma*, is applied as a special theological term (1:23; 3:19; 4:13). In Colossians the term was used to claim that all of God's richness exists in Christ. In Ephesians, however, the word is used to express that all this also exists or will exist in the *ekklēsia*.

Another theological term of key importance in Ephesians is "secret," *mystērion* (1:9; 3:3–4, 9; 5:32; 6:19; cf. 1 Cor 2:1, 7; Rom 11:25). The term conveys the idea of hidden knowledge that is revealed. In Ephesians it is used primarily in describing God's plan for the world's salvation that is realized through Christ and the *ekklēsia* (1:9–10; 3:10). This plan has been hidden from the creation of the world but is now revealed (1:9–10; 3:5–6, 9–12). Through the emphasis on God's plan, the idea of a predetermined path, predestination, is strengthened in the theological pattern (1:4–5, 11; 2:10).

As in Colossians, the resurrection is spoken of as something already realized. With Christ, Christ followers are said to have been resurrected already, received salvation, and obtained a place in heaven (2:5–6).

Letters Likely Not Formulated by Paul Himself

The three letters that are taken up here are treated in the order that they appear in the New Testament (1 Timothy, 2 Timothy, and Titus). Here, too, the presentation will include only what the letters themselves tell us of their context and dating, communication strategy, and so on. These aspects may then be further analyzed by the reader depending on what stance is adopted on the question of authorship.

First Letter to Timothy

Context and Dating

According to the information provided by the letter itself, Paul is traveling to Macedonia and has left Timothy in Ephesus so that he will be able to admonish certain individuals there who are spreading false teaching (1:3–4). A couple of these individuals are named (1:20). The problematic teachings include speculations concerning myths and genealogies (1:4), interest in the Mosaic law without proper understanding of it (1:7–11), and the rejection of marriage and abstinence from certain foods (4:1–5). Paul writes the letter in order to support the young Timothy in his mission (4:12). Paul hopes to be able to visit him soon (3:14).

Those who argue that the letter in one way or another originates with Paul himself usually assume that it was written during Paul's incarceration in Rome, which is mentioned in Acts 28:30 (cf. 2 Tim 1:17; 4:6). If this is the case, the letter must be dated to the middle of the 60s CE. However, most scholars argue that the letter does not originate with Paul at all but that it was composed in his name. They usually opt for dating it to the first decades of the second century CE.

Communication Strategy

The strategy used to strengthen Timothy in his mission is to clarify for him what his mission actually consists of (1:3–7, 11–19), what its background is (1:4, 6–7, 18–19; 4:1–5; 6:20–21), what its aims are (2:1–4:5), and how he should go about approaching it (4:6–6:20).

The strategy Paul advises Timothy to have in his mission is not to enter into pointless discussions about the deviating teachings, but to focus on building a pious and dignified community through good leadership (1:3–6; 4:6–7; 6:20). He should do this through encouragement but also through being a good example in everything (4:11–16; 6:11–16) and making sure that other leaders in the assembly also serve as good examples (3:1–13; 5:17–22; cf. 5:10).

In agreement with these strategies, the letter does not contain a great deal of argumentation against the deviant teachings. Mostly the author just rejects them and their advocates in favor of Paul and his gospel, and that is often done with appraising words (e.g., 1:6–11, 14–15, 17; 4:1–3). To a certain extent, the author defends and justifies Paul's teachings using scriptural quotations (2:13–15; 5:18), other known and accepted teaching (1:8, 11; 3:16), references to the Spirit (4:1), and prophecies (1:18; 4:14).

Content and Structure

Following a short introduction (1:1–2), where Paul is described as the apostle of Jesus Christ and Timothy as the true child of Paul, the letter body begins with a section reporting on Timothy's mission and its background (1:3–20). The mission, which he has received from Paul in accordance with certain prophecies, consists of admonishing those who, with evil intent, are spreading deviant teachings in Ephesus about the law and the ancestors, teachings that go against the gospel that Jesus Christ has entrusted to Paul.

After this section follow instructions on how one should behave in an assembly (2:1–3:16). Members of the group should pray for and be thankful for all people, especially those who have power in the society, so that they can live peaceful, pious, and dignified lives (2:1–7). Men should pray with clean hands, without rage or reservations. Women should behave in an appropriate, self-disciplined manner (2:8–15). The leader of the assembly (*episkopos*) should be above any reprehension, be able to govern his own house, be experienced, and have a good reputation in the community. Deacons should be as dignified and worthy as the leader himself (3:1–13). Such behavior reflects both the assembly's and Christ's nature (3:14–16).

Following the description of the desired behavior in the group come a set of instructions for Timothy as to how he should go about establishing such a behavior (4:1–6:21a). He should maintain that the Spirit has predicted that some individuals will fall away from the true gospel, preaching against marriage and certain foods. But he should never be associated with such teachings (4:1–10). He should be an example in everything, read aloud from the Scriptures, encourage, and teach (4:11–5:2). He should award the dignity of widowhood only to those who truly are widows, complaints against the elders should not be brought up without fair reason, and slaves should show appropriate respect for their masters (5:3–6:2). He should carry out all his duties beyond reproach, and should tell the rich not to be conceited but rather to do good with what they have been given (6:3–19). Following some concluding exhortations for Timothy to take good care of those who have been put into his care and to avoid the false teachings (6:20–21a) comes a very short letter conclusion (6:21b).

The content of the letter can be summarized as follows:

1:1–2	Introduction
1:3–20	Timothy's mission
2:1–3:16	Rules for group behavior
4:1–6:21a	What Timothy must do
6:21b	Conclusion

Key Theological Thoughts

Theologically, the letter is clearly connected to the previously discussed Pauline letters. The ideas exhibited in 1:8–11 about the law as meant not for the righteous but rather for the unrighteous are reminiscent of discussions in, for example, Galatians and Romans (cf. Gal 3:21–25; 5:22–23; Rom 7:7; 8:2–3). In addition, the mention in 3:16 of how Christ was revealed as an earthly creature, seen by angels, proclaimed among gentiles, and taken up into heaven is easily associated with similar perspectives in Philippians and Colossians (cf. Phil 2:6–11; Col 1:15–20).

One point where the theology deviates somewhat from the other letters is the description of Paul as an example in joining the Christ followers. In 1:12–17 the letter states that Paul, in his earlier life, was a blasphemer and a merciless persecutor of Christ followers; he is therefore an archetype for the sinner who receives grace and mercy from Christ. In Phil 3:4, 11, 17, however, the text states that Paul, before his turning to Christ, was irreproachable in his righteousness according to the law, and that he therefore is a role model because he gave up all his gains and offered himself for Christ in the hope that he could share in Christ's resurrection. In this context, his persecution of Christ followers becomes part of his faithful zealousness (Phil 3:6). Paul's persecution is described in a similar way in Gal 1:13–14. In 1 Cor 15:8–10, the persecution is explained by the fact that Paul was "not yet born," like an embryo, when Christ revealed himself to him. In this case, however, the event was not interpreted typologically.

Second Letter to Timothy

Context and Dating

The letter assumes that Paul has been or is in Rome (1:17). He is imprisoned (1:8; 2:9), and his life is nearing its end (4:6–8). Timothy appears to be located in Ephesus (1:18; 4:19). The letter states that everyone in the province of Asia has turned away from Paul (1:15). In Timothy's assembly there are false teachers (2:17; cf. 1 Tim 1:20) who preach that the resurrection has already occurred (2:18), and probably they also engage in speculations about myths (4:4; cf. 1 Tim 1:4). The aim of the letter is to encourage Timothy to stand firm in the gospel, despite all the suffering this has brought him (1:6–9; 4:1–5), as well as to ask him to come to him, bringing Mark, a coat that Paul had left behind, and certain books (1:4; 4:9, 11, 13, 21). The letter names a number of individuals, many of whom are otherwise unknown to us.

If the letter is in any way connected to Paul in terms of authorship, it must be dated to the middle of the 60s CE. If not, scholars usually date it to somewhere between 100 and 140 CE.

Communication Strategy

The strategy used to encourage Timothy to stand firm in the gospel despite all his suffering is to praise him for his faith (1:3–5; 3:10–11) and to put it in a greater context by declaring that he is included in a community (e.g., 1:3–5, 16–18; 4:19–21); that he is taking care of a great inheritance (1:3–6, 10–14; 2:1–2; 3:14–15); that sufferings are to be expected (3:1–9, 12–13; 4:3–4); that he shares them with Paul (1:8, 12; 2:9–10; 3:11; 4:6–7, 14–17); and that they will result in something good (1:9–10; 2:8, 11; 3:15, 17; 4:8, 18).

The strategy that the author suggests for Timothy to employ against the teachers of false doctrine is, as in 1 Timothy, to not be dragged into meaningless discussions about these teachings (2:14, 16, 22–26; 3:5) but instead to proclaim "the sound teaching" (2:14, 24–25; 4:2, 5) and to entrust it to trustworthy individuals (2:2).

The argumentation of the letter is to a certain degree supported by scriptural citations (e.g., 2:19, 3:8). As in 1 Timothy, the Pentateuch is the main source of such citations, which could be explained by the false teachers' interest in precisely these books. There is also a short section explaining how those who teach and preach benefit from the Scriptures (3:15–17). In addition to scriptural citations, the author also makes use of references to Jesus traditions (e.g., 1:9–10; 2:8, 11) and Paul's experiences (2:10–11; 3:10–11).

Content and Structure

In the introduction of the letter (1:1–2), Paul's status as an apostle is connected to the promise of life in Christ. In this way, the author hints already here at an important strategy—namely, to encourage the suffering addressee with the fact that the one who shares in Paul's suffering will have something positive to look forward to (the promise of life in Christ).

The body of the letter begins with a short section of thanksgiving for Timothy, who, like Paul, the ancestors, his mother, and his grandmother, is a servant of God with a sincere faith. He is also reminded that he should enliven the gift of grace he received when Paul laid his hands on him (1:3–7). In this way, he is encouraged to stand firm in his faith.

The letter continues with a longer section about what Timothy should do about the actual situation he finds himself in (1:8–4:8). He should be ashamed neither of the gospel nor of Paul, but rather he should suffer with Paul for the sake of the gospel and of Christ, their Savior, who has eliminated death and brought life and immortality to light. Everyone in Asia has turned away from Paul, but Timothy should take strength from grace, let himself be inspired by Paul's struggle and Christ's resurrection, and entrust the message to reliable people (1:8–2:13). He should stay away from unproductive conversations with godless people who, for example, argue that the resurrection has already happened. Such people are to be expected at the end of the ages (2:14–3:9). But Timothy has followed Paul faithfully in his teaching, life, faith, and suffering. He should remain firm in that which he has learned from Paul and from the Holy Scriptures, which are inspired by God, and he should fulfill the duties of a preacher, even if this means a great struggle for him. Paul's own life is already being poured out like a sacrifice, and now he is looking forward to receiving the wreath of victory (3:10–4:8).

The body of the letter is concluded with some personal instructions (4:9–18). Paul has been abandoned by most and asks Timothy to come to him soon. He asks him to bring Mark and some of his belongings. In addition, he warns Timothy about Alexander the smith, who has caused Paul much harm.

The letter is concluded with greetings to several named individuals, as well as a final, general greeting (4:19–22).

The content of the letter can be summarized as follows:

1:1–2	Introduction
1:3–7	Exhortation to Timothy to stand firm in his faith
1:8–4:8	Instructions for Timothy
4:9–18	Personal remarks
4:19–22	Conclusion

Key Theological Thoughts

Like the earlier Pauline letters, 2 Timothy has references to Jesus's career and the Jesus tradition as comfort in times of persecution. In this letter, however, the focus is not on the *cross* and the *crucified* as an object of identification during persecution. Rather, Christ is depicted as the Savior (1:9–10). Through his resurrection (2:8), he has eradicated death and has brought life and immortality into the light (1:10; 2:11).

In 2:17–18, a couple of individuals are admonished for suggesting that the resurrection has already occurred. This is "profane chatter" (2:16) and reveals that these people have departed from the truth (2:18). In accordance with this, the author speaks of the resurrection with Christ in the future tense (2:11). This view of resurrection reflects the perspective of the seven undisputed Pauline letters (e.g., Phil 3:10–16) but stands in contrast to certain statements in Ephesians and Colossians, where the Christ followers are described as already being "resurrected with Christ" (Col 2:12; 3:1; Eph 2:5–6).

A novelty in 2 Timothy is the theological reflection around the Holy Scriptures (3:15–17). They are said to be inspired by God, to provide the knowledge necessary for salvation through faith, and to be useful for those who teach and guide other members of Christ groups.

The Letter to Titus

Context and Dating

According to the information provided by the letter, Paul is in Nicopolis (probably referring to a city on the Adriatic coastline, south of Corfu), where he has planned to spend the winter (3:12). He has left Titus on the island of Crete in order for him to organize everything that time did not permit earlier, including appointing elders in every city (1:5). There are false teachers in the Christ groups, especially among some Jewish Christ followers who believe in Jewish legends and keep certain purity laws (1:10–16). The letter is written to support Titus in this mission, as well as to ask him to come to Nicopolis, when someone whom Paul will send has arrived.

If the letter in any way originates with Paul, it would be dated to the middle of the 60s CE. If not, scholars usually date it to sometime between 100 and 140 CE.

Communication Strategy

The strategy for encouraging and supporting Titus in his mission is to state clearly what is required of different members of the assembly (1:5–9; 2:2–10; 3:1–2, 8–9), as well as to connect his mission to the greater plan of salvation (1:1–3; 2:12–14; 3:3–7). In connection with the author stating what is required of a community leader, those whom the leader must "quiet" are also mentioned (1:10–16; see also 3:10–11).

There are no direct references to Scripture in the letter, but there are references to Jesus's career (2:13–14; 3:6). At one point, the author also refers to a local prophecy (1:12). The text is full of judgments and opinions, expressed using appraisive words, although rarely backed up with argumentation (see 1:10–12, 14, 16).

Content and Structure

In the introduction of the letter (1:1–4), the sender of the letter is described in such a way that the apostleship of Paul is placed within the larger context of God's plan of salvation. In this way, Titus's own mission is also related to this plan.

After this, Titus's mission is dealt with directly (1:5–16). Paul left him in Crete so that he could organize the assemblies and appoint blameless elders (*presbyteroi*) in every city. It is important that the leader of the assembly (*episkopos*) is above reproach, since he is God's steward, and he should be able to strengthen others and refute opponents. The opponents are described as troublemakers among the "circumcised" and "deceitful Cretans," who believe in Jewish legends and commandments, which are not from God but from humans.

Following this is an account of what "the sound doctrine" requires (2:1–3:11). Older men must be sober and dignified, and older women should not badmouth others or abuse wine. Young women should love their husbands and children and behave in an appropriate, subordinate way. Young men should also behave in an appropriate way, and slaves should subordinate themselves to their masters. For the grace of God, which has become visible as the salvation of all, has taught the Christ followers to live decently while they wait for their great God and Savior, Jesus Christ, who shall return in glory. He sacrificed himself in order to redeem them from sin and to make them pure (2:1–15). They should subordinate themselves to those who have power and be humble toward all. They were themselves fools at one point, before God's love for humanity was revealed and he saved them through baptism and the Spirit. In addition, they should stay away from mindless disputes (3:1–11).

The body of the letter is concluded with a few personal remarks (3:12–14). Paul is sending some people to Titus and then asks Titus to come to him in Nicopolis. He also asks Titus to equip a few other travelers. The conclusion of the letter includes a few general greetings and a final greeting (3:15).

The content of the letter can be summarized as follows:

1:1–4	Introduction
1:5–16	Titus's mission
2:1–3:11	Description of "the sound teaching"
3:12–14	Personal remarks
3:15	Conclusion

Key Theological Thoughts

Theologically, the letter is reminiscent of the Pauline tradition in general and 1–2 Timothy in particular. In one regard, however, this letter goes further than the other Pauline letters: in Titus, Christ Jesus is expressly associated with *theos*, God (2:13; cf. 3:4, 6). In the other letters, Jesus is described as having God-like qualities and functions, but he is not directly referred to as God. The Johannine tradition is similar to Titus in this regard (e.g., John 1:18; 20:28; 1 John 5:20).

An additional aspect is worth mentioning. The text makes several references to Jesus's career (2:13–14; 3:4–7), but this is not done primarily to provide material for *imitatio*; rather, it is something that reveals the conditions of the Christ-oriented life.

For more information on the Pauline heritage see the section "Successors of Paul," p. 430.

Further Reading

Barth, Markus. *Ephesians: A New Translation with Introduction and Commentary*. 2 vols. AYBC 34–34A. New Haven: Yale University Press, 1974.

Barth, Markus, and Helmut Blanke. *Colossians: A New Translation with Introduction and Commentary*. AYBC 34B. New Haven: Yale University Press, 2005.

Dunn, James D. G. *The Cambridge Companion to St. Paul*. Cambridge: Cambridge University Press, 2003.

———. *The Epistles to the Colossians and to Philemon*. NIGTC. Grand Rapids: Eerdmans, 2014.

Fitzmyer, Joseph A. *First Corinthians: A New Translation with Introduction and Commentary*. AYBC 32. New Haven: Yale University Press, 2008.

Hawthorne, Gerald F. *Philippians*. WBC 43. Grand Rapids: Zondervan, 1983.

Jewett, Robert. *Romans: A Commentary*. Hermeneia. Minneapolis: Fortress, 2006.

Last, Richard. *The Pauline Church and the Corinthian* Ekklēsia: *Greco-Roman Associations in Comparative Context*. SNTSMS 164. Cambridge: Cambridge University Press, 2016.

Lincoln, A. T. *Ephesians*. WBC 42. Grand Rapids: Zondervan, 1990.

Longenecker, Bruce W., and Todd D. Still. *Thinking Through Paul: A Survey of His Life, Letters, and Theology*. Grand Rapids: Zondervan, 2014.

Malherbe, Abraham J. *The Letters to the Thessalonians: A New Translation with Introduction and Commentary*. AYBC 32B. New Haven: Yale University Press, 2004.

Mitchell, Margaret M. *Paul, the Corinthians and the Birth of Christian Hermeneutics*. Cambridge: Cambridge University Press, 2010.

Moo, Douglas J. *Galatians*. BECNT. Grand Rapids: Baker Academic, 2013.

———. *The Letter to the Romans*. 2nd ed. NICNT. Grand Rapids: Eerdmans, 2018.

Nanos, Mark D. *The Irony of Galatians: Paul's Letter in First-Century Context*. Minneapolis: Fortress, 2002.

———. *Reading Corinthians and Philippians within Judaism*. Eugene, OR: Cascade Books, 2017.

Neutel, Karin B. *A Cosmopolitan Ideal: Paul's Declaration "Neither Jew nor Greek, Neither Slave nor Free, nor Male and Female" in the Context of First-Century Thought*. LNTS 513. London: Bloomsbury, 2015.

Riches, John K. *Galatians through the Centuries.* Oxford: Blackwell, 2013.
Stendahl, Krister. *Final Account: Paul's Letter to the Romans.* Minneapolis: Fortress, 1995.
Stowers, Stanley K. *A Rereading of Romans: Justice, Jews, and Gentiles.* New Haven: Yale University Press, 1997.
Towner, Philip H. *The Letters to Timothy and Titus.* NICNT. Grand Rapids: Eerdmans, 2006.

Catholic Letters, the Letter to the Hebrews, and the Book of Revelation

The Term "Catholic Letters"

The seven letters 1–2 Peter, 1–3 John, James, and Jude are found toward the end of the New Testament. They are designated "the Catholic Letters" (*katholikos* = "general") in the church's tradition because they all address a broader audience, thus indicating letters that were meant for the entire church. Strictly speaking, only 2 Peter and Jude fulfill this criterion; the addressees in 1 Peter are specified as Christ followers in five Roman provinces in Asia Minor; 2 John is addressed to an unnamed assembly; in 3 John there is only one addressee, a man named Gaius; and James is an exception, as it addresses "the twelve tribes in the Dispersion." Decisive, however, seems to have been that the personal relationship between sender and receiver—save for 2 and 3 John—is not very explicit in these texts, wherefore it is possible to view them as inclusive, with a message to the entire church. See the section "Which Texts Belong to the New Testament? The Canonization Process," p. 213, for a description of the history of these texts during the canonical process.

The First Letter of Peter

The Letter's Context: Setting, Receiver, Author

According to 1:1–2 the letter is addressed "To the exiles of the Dispersion [*diaspora*] in Pontus, Galatia, Cappadocia, Asia, and Bithynia, who have been chosen." The provinces mentioned are in the west and north of modern-day Turkey. At the end of the letter (5:13), the author sends greetings from the assembly in "Babylon," a name frequently used in contemporary Jewish and Christian literature as a code name for Rome (cf. Rev 14:8; 18:2). The author wished to convey to the addressees a sender context that is characterized by isolation and exclusiveness. Marginalization is expressed through the epithet "exiles," while the terms "elect," "scattered," and "Babylon" identify the addressees with, and as equals of, Israel: a people, privileged but responsible before God, scattered and in various ways persecuted around the world (cf. the similar address in James: "To the twelve tribes in the Dispersion"). On account of the characterization of the addressees as "Once you were not a people, but now you are God's people" (2:10; cf. 1:14, 18; 4:3), it is very unlikely that they were Christ-following Jews.

Most scholars doubt that the letter originated from Jesus's disciple Peter. The letter gives certain hints about its author. Disregarding the fact that the name Peter is used in 1:1, it is only in 5:1 that the sender reveals anything about him- or herself. Informing the readers of being "an elder myself" and "a witness of the sufferings of Christ" does not necessarily indicate a link to Peter. Furthermore, it must also be noted that nowhere in the New Testament is there a special connection between Peter and Christ-following assemblies in Asia Minor, not to mention Paul's note on the "division of labor" between him and Peter (Gal 2:8), which makes it even less likely that the actual author of a letter aimed primarily at non-Jews is the historical Peter. In addition, the kind of persecution that the letter presumes does not seem to have occurred in Asia Minor before Peter's death (presumably in the middle of the 60s in Rome).

Beyond Peter being mentioned in the introduction as the sender of the letter, there is also special mention of Silvanus and Mark. Considering the manner in which Silvanus is presented (5:12), it is likely that he is the coauthor. Whether this means that he functioned as a scribe or a more independent writer is unclear; the latter is fully possible given the contemporary custom of writing under a known name in order to place more weight on one's own words. If he is the same Silvanus/Silas who is mentioned as an important Pauline coworker several times in various letters and Acts (co-sender of 1–2 Thessalonians, co-founder of the assembly in Corinth, co-traveler to Antioch and on the second missionary journey), this could help explain the many similarities between the letter and Pauline theology.

The epithet "my son" for Mark indicates an especially intimate relationship. This may connect to what Bishop Papias of Hierapolis (beginning of the 100s) says about Mark acting as Peter's interpreter in Rome and recording what he heard the disciple say about Jesus. At the same time, Mark is mentioned as one of Paul's coworkers with a special relationship to Asia Minor (Col 4:10; cf. Phlm 24; 2 Tim 4:11), and many scholars have claimed that, in several regards, Mark's theology compares well with Paul's. On the whole, these hints place the sender in a context charged with Pauline theology.

Dating

There are no clear hints in 1 Peter for dating the letter. The persecution against Christ followers that is evident could be linked to Emperor Nero in the 60s (although only in Rome for a short period of time), Domitian in the 90s, or Trajan in the 110s; unfortunately the text is too vague for any one of these periods to be pinpointed. As the letter includes thoughts of the world's imminent end, it could be linked to a fairly early time—that is, still in the disciple's generation: up to and including the 50s and/or 60s. It is, however, fully possible that this eschatological expectation (in the near future) was also prominent among groups of believers in Asia Minor in the following decades, which is corroborated by a text such as Revelation.

Genre and Communication Strategy

First Peter begins and ends like a letter—that is, with normal greeting and closing phrases (1:1–2; 5:12–14). In terms of style and content, however, it appears more as an inclusive text with a message of comfort to a general audience of Christ followers in Asia Minor. This is a common feature with other New Testament texts, such as Ephesians, Hebrews, and 1 John. There has also been a suggestion that 1 Peter functions as a sermon related to baptism and Easter, as there are several associations to these topics in the letter. But the argumentation is too vague for any safe conclusions about the original background. It is, however, likely that the text would have functioned well as a sermon to Christ-following assemblies.

Structure

1:1–2	Greeting and indication of sender and addressees.
1:3–2:10	A reminder of God's merciful actions (keyword "mercy" in 1:3 and 2:10), situated in a comforting speech of the Christ followers' hope and conservation of faith, as well as their identity as a holy people of God.
2:11–4:11	The exemplary behavior of the Christ followers will prevent the "non-Jews" from holding any criticism against them; also included is a list of behaviors in the so-called *Haustafeln* with regulations for slaves (2:18–25), women (3:1–6), and men (3:7), and the explanation that their suffering during the short period of time that remains before the end is a suffering for the sake of Christ.
4:12–5:11	Eschatologically grounded admonishment, focused on the assemblies' internal relationships (special admonishing of the assembly leaders, 5:1–4).
5:12–14	Conclusion with greetings and wishes of peace.

Theological Main Ideas

The identity of the Christ followers as a small minority is emphasized, as is the outer threat from those who accuse and in various manners persecute them. Enduring suffering according to the example set by Christ is a major focus, but such endurance is to be met with joy and reliance on God. Indeed, the reason for the suffering is that one has been called and chosen by God to be included in his "holy people"—taking over Israel's self-perception (compare 2:9 with Exod 19:6)—and therefore suffering gives a hope of vindication in the coming times, just as Jesus was raised to the heavens.

As a stranger to this world, one should follow Jesus's example and obey the laws of society and act with goodwill toward all in one's surroundings. The difference in attitude between 1 Peter and Revelation (e.g., ch. 13) is striking (2:17: "honor the emperor"; cf. 2:13). There is an eagerness to present Christian faith and conduct as something that does not challenge the existing social order. By writing in the name of Jesus's foremost disciple and conveying greetings from the assembly in "Babylon" (Rome), the sender emphasizes the authority of his message to the Christ followers in Asia Minor.

The Second Letter of Peter

The Letter's Context: Receiver, Author, Dating, and Setting

The second letter written in the name of Peter does not provide much concrete information regarding the context of its origins. No specific addressees are mentioned, and even though the author presents himself as Jesus's disciple Simon Peter, it is highly unlikely that this was the case (for more on pseudepigraphy in the New Testament and its historical context, see the section "Pious Forgeries or Necessary Reinterpretations?," p. 217). Of course, the author does adhere to Petrine tradition (the reference to 1 Peter in 3:1 and to the scene on the Mount of Transfiguration in 2:16–18), but this does little to strengthen the historical likelihood of the proposed identity. Potentially the reference to 1 Peter could be interpreted as indicating an audience with geographical proximity to that which 1 Peter addresses—that is, Asia Minor.

The letter's canonical position was quite weak in the ancient church (see the section "Which Texts Belong to the New Testament? The Canonization Process," p. 213). It is absent from the Canon Muratori and first begins to appear in lists (disputed according to Origen) of authoritative New Testament texts in the middle of the 200s. A prominent argument among those who reject that the letter could have been written by the historical Peter—and against an early date in general—is found in the reference to Paul and his letters in 3:15–16. Such a reference seems to indicate that 2 Peter was written at a time when the Pauline letters were already gathered together and had begun to be an object of debate—but such a collection can hardly have existed before the year 100 or so. Likewise, 2 Peter seems to have been used or referred to only in the late ancient church (again evidenced by Origen).

There are many similarities between 2 Peter and Jude. Indeed, a great deal of the content in the significantly shorter Jude is found in 2 Peter, except for the reference in Jude to biblical Pseudepigrapha in relation to the criticism of certain false teachings. Scholars dispute whether these similarities might trace back to a single source for both letters, or whether Jude served as a model for 2 Peter rather than vice versa. Jude's list of warning examples—gathered not only from the (subsequently) canonized books of the Bible but also from so-called pseudepigraphical and parabiblical literature (texts from outside the Bible that relate to, retell, or expand the canonical writings to be)—is edited; the pseudepigraphical content is omitted and supplemented with positive examples from the Scriptures (Noah and Lot). This could be an additional indicator of 2 Peter's late origins: the omission of references to the Pseudepigrapha in the battle against false teachings may have been due to the text's originating in a later phase of the Hebrew Bible's canonization. The letter could thus potentially be dated to the first decades of the 100s, which is why many scholars consider 2 Peter to be the youngest text in the New Testament.

With regard to the letter's setting, it is quite clear that the author wishes to warn the addressees of false teachings and strengthen their faith in the true path. Especially, questions concerning the parousia and the day of the Lord seem to be in focus (ch. 3), which could also indicate a late origin. Christianity has now been established for such a long time that the original expectation of eschatological proximity has been criticized by some, and these critics appear to openly flaunt their beliefs (3:3–5). In answer to this, the author suggests that the delay is actually something positive: God is waiting in order that there will be more time for all the people to repent (3:9), and thus it is of utter importance not to fall back into a previous, sinful life (1:4–9; 2:17–22; 3:17).

Genre and Communication Strategy

The genre of 2 Peter has characteristics of the so-called Jewish "testament literature"—that is, Scripture that, like large parts of the apocalyptic literature, makes use of the name of a known and authoritative person from the past to invite, warn, and comfort (already in the biblical texts there is a "testament model" in the form of the Letter of James and Moses's farewell speeches to the twelve sons and the tribes of Israel in Gen 49 and Deut 33, respectively). Especially good for comparison is the Testaments of the Twelve Patriarchs, which can be dated to the centuries just before the Common Era and belongs to the biblical Pseudepigrapha. With an increased eschatological awareness and expected imminence, this text and 2 Peter both warn especially of apostates and false teachings, which are signs of the final days. The primary purpose of 2 Peter seems, however, to be to encourage the addressees to hold fast to the true teachings about God and Jesus.

Structure

1:1–2	Generally formulated greeting that especially underlines the unity in faith of sender and receiver, as well as the correct knowledge of God and Jesus
1:3–11	Appeals to grow in knowledge while aiming for Christ's eternal kingdom
1:12–21	Emphasis on the author's commitment to the benefit of the addressees, and his authority as an eyewitness to Jesus's divine glory, as well as a warning against attempting to interpret the Scriptures' prophecies independently
2:1–22	Biblically grounded description of false teachers and their judgment
3:1–13	Teaching on the parousia and the day of the Lord against the background of the false teachers' mocking questions and criticism
3:14–18	Concluding admonishments with reference to Paul's letters, and appeals to growth in knowledge of Jesus Christ; festive praising ("doxology") of Christ instead of a closing greeting

Theological Main Ideas

Appealing to Peter's authority as the foremost of Jesus's disciples and a clear leader in the oldest Christian movement, the author attacks interpretations of Scripture and the Christian faith that do not agree with the apostolic testimony. For his authority, the sender refers to being an eyewitness to Jesus's transfiguration and revelation in divine glory on the mountain (1:16–18; cf. Mark 9 and par.), as well as claiming that Jesus had foretold the author's death as a martyr (1:14; cf. John 21:18).

By using Peter's authority and letting "him" remind the readers of the biblical prophecies and their credibility, the author generates legitimacy for his message. Contrary to Jude (see below), it is questions of eschatology that are the main focus for the criticism of false teachers, and perhaps it is with the teachings on Jesus's parousia in mind that the author in chapter 1 refers to the scene on the Mount of Transfiguration (the transfiguration that anticipates Jesus's glory at the parousia). While Jude warns against contemporary false teachers, the author of 2 Peter polemicizes against pending apostasy from and objections to the true faith.

It is precisely because questions about the day of the Lord and the parousia are relevant that the note in 3:15–16 about those who make faulty interpretations of what Paul wrote and said is interesting to observe; we can compare this with how the author of 2 Thessalonians also appears compelled to correct misunderstandings of what Paul is supposed to have said about the day of the Lord (2 Thess 2:2). Questions regarding the future and Jesus's return apparently belonged to, at least in some groups of Christ followers, the most debated subjects as the apostolic era neared its end.

A more foundational theme in 2 Peter is the emphasis on correct knowledge about God and Jesus. Faith appears secondary as it is presented as a teaching to be embraced (in Latin, *fides quae creditur*, as opposed to being a subjectively dedicated and trusting relationship, *fides qua creditur*). From this faith/knowledge, love shall emerge (1:5–7). The primary goal of the Christ followers is to "become participants of the divine nature" (1:4), an expression that, together with the weight of growing in and preserving the right and true knowledge of God, indicates the letter's context as a Hellenistic-Jewish philosophical and religious environment.

The Letter of Jude

The Letter's Context: Receiver, Author, Dating, and Setting

Just like 2 Peter, this letter is a pseudepigraph: that Jude, the brother of James (and thus also of Jesus), should have written the letter seems impossible, especially considering the reference to what was foretold by "the apostles of our Lord Jesus Christ" in verse 17; the time of the disciples/apostles seems to be something of the past. Normally the letter is dated to around or just before the year 100, so it would have been available to the author of 2 Peter for citation. In dating the letter, it is important to note that eschatology and Jesus's parousia are not, as in 2 Peter, central subjects. That these questions are not dealt with may imply that the text was written quite a bit earlier than 2 Peter.

The short letter reveals almost no concrete hints about its original setting, but there is a strong polemic against false teachers that may have found their way among the addressees. What the false teachings were about is unclear. Those who adhere to them, however, are described as ungodly people who "defile the flesh" (v. 8), "worldly people, devoid of the Spirit" (v. 19). It is therefore possible that the author aims his polemic at individuals who he sees as adherents of some form of gnostic libertinism (cf. the later church fathers' polemic against gnostics; see also the section "Gnosticism and 'the Gnostics,'" p. 455). In line with this interpretation, many scholars deem that the author and audience of Jude are Christ-following Jews, and that the threat to the true faith and way of life would thus be from non-Jews. At the same time, it is important to underline that the letter is stylistically and linguistically anchored in a Hellenistic setting, which may indicate a setting in diaspora Judaism.

Genre and Communication Strategy

Jude has a general address "To those who are called, who are beloved in God the Father and kept safe for Jesus Christ" (v. 1), a truly "catholic" letter. It is well structured according to contemporary patterns of rhetoric (see below), with an argumentative main body full of allusions to figures and motifs from biblical and nonbiblical texts (vv. 5–16). In this regard, Jude may be compared with the Qumranite so-called pesher comments—that is, an interpretation (midrash) of the Scriptures into an actual situation (see the section "Beliefs and Practices in Second Temple Judaism," p. 114), primarily with the purpose of pointing out enemies to the readers and encouraging faithfulness and endurance.

Structure (with Rhetorical Terms Describing the Text's Different Parts)

1–2	Generally formulated greeting (*praescriptum*)
3–4	The setting is given; warning for false teachers (*narratio*)
5–16	The main body of the letter, where false teachers are described and criticized against a background of biblical examples (*probatio*)
17–23	Admonishments based on the previous arguments (*peroratio*)
24–25	Closing doxology (*conclusio*)

Main Theological Ideas

Jude's main purpose is to warn its addressees of false teachers and to remind them to hold fast to the true faith. With the aid of examples from biblical history—Israel in the desert, the fall of the angels, Sodom and Gomorrah (vv. 5–7), and later also Cain, Balaam, and Korah (v. 11)—and mythological traditions known from the biblical Pseudepigrapha, specifically 1 Enoch and the Testament of Moses (the imprisoning of the fallen angels in the underworld and Michael's argument with the devil over Moses's body, respectively), the author warns of God's punishment of the ungodly and the apostates. At this point, 2 Peter differs from Jude in that 2 Peter places the three biblical examples in the "right" chronological order and omits the allusions to noncanonical traditions, which by most exegetes is seen as a sign that Jude is the older of the two writings.

The Letter of James

The Letter's Context: Receiver, Author, Dating, and Setting

In both modern critical editions of the Greek New Testament (Nestle-Aland and *Greek New Testament*), the Letter of James ranks first among the Catholic Letters. Its addressees are "the twelve tribes in the Dispersion" (1:1). This expression recalls both the biblical notions of Israel as God's chosen people, consisting of twelve tribes, and the Jewish people's exile and dispersion (Gk. *diaspora*) throughout the Mediterranean world. Prophetic and postbiblical traditions (Isa 49:6; 1QM II, 2–3; Pss. Sol.

17:18, 44) speak of the ideal people of God, gathered from their exile in the coming time of salvation. This could of course indicate that the author is, in fact, addressing Christ-following Jews outside the land of Israel, but it is also possible that the expression is used more as a metaphor for the people of God restored in Christ in the end times, and their vulnerable condition as they wait for the completion of salvation. Therefore, although Christ-following Jews are specifically addressed, the message may also be applicable to non-Jewish Christ followers.

The question of which James has written this letter must be determined in light of the text's dating. The introductory phrase "James, a servant of God and of the Lord Jesus Christ" does not directly identify the author with any of the apostles or with the James who was known as "the brother of the Lord," who appeared as a leading figure among the early Christ followers in Jerusalem after Jesus's resurrection (see, e.g., Acts 1:14; 15:13–21; 1 Cor 15:7; Gal 1:19, and the reference to James as a brother of Jude, the author of Jude). Outside the New Testament, this James is referred to as one of the first ancient church leaders even by the Jewish historian Josephus, and later in Hegesippus's church history, retold by Eusebius of Caesarea in the fourth century. Indeed, the simple and unpretentious introduction and presentation of the author might speak for him actually being James "the brother of the Lord," as a pseudepigraph would probably have emphasized the fame of the author more. It has also been pointed out that the letter's consistent paraenetic style may well be anchored in a Jewish Jerusalemite context, which further strengthens this notion. On the other hand, linguistic and stylistic factors, not least the good fluency in Greek and the usage of the Septuagint (the Greek translation of the Hebrew Bible), speak for a more hellenized original setting.

The introductory greeting of the letter follows the traditional Greek form with only the word *chairein* (approx. "hail"), while the greeting phrases in other New Testament texts are grammatically more detailed (so-called oriental style) and often contain the words "grace" (*charis*) and "peace" (*eirēnē*). In addition, we must consider the content of the letter, which deals with the relationship between faith and actions. This could be interpreted as a polemic against a twisted Pauline kind of Christianity (see the section "Paul, His Assemblies, and His Successors," p. 399). If the letter were to be dated to the time of the disciples in Jerusalem, and written by the James who was widely regarded as a leader of the first Christ-following assembly, it seems odd that there are so few traces of the author's personal relation to Jesus (apart from the introductory greeting, Jesus is named only once in the letter [2:1]!) or of the special historical situation at this time and place. The question of authorship and dating must furthermore consider that the letter appears to have been disputed in the ancient church canon history; it is absent in the Canon Muratori from the end of the 100s and finds general acceptance into canonical lists only in the fourth century.

The determination of James's date of origin and author has been subject to much debate. If it really was a letter from Jesus's brother James, it must be dated to before the year 62, when said brother was killed during the prelude to the Great Jewish Revolt against Rome in 66–70. Since the problems in the relationship between Jewish and non-Jewish Christ followers are not mentioned in the letter, it has been suggested that this letter, in fact, could be the oldest preserved text in the entire New Testament, originating in the 40s, even before the so-called meeting of the apostles in Jerusalem. However, if the letter has instead been authored under the name of James in order to make use of his authority (especially among Christ-following Jews), which still is the majority opinion, a dating toward the end of the first century would appear appropriate. The sender of the letter could in this case be strongly anchored in both Jewish thought and Hellenistic education, and this does not preclude that traditions originating in the time of the historical James, "the brother of the Lord," were included in his message.

Genre and Communication Strategy

Formally, James can hardly be called a proper letter: it starts out as a letter but lacks a closing greeting. It seems to be a form of inclusive text, meant to be read before an assembly as a form of paraenesis—that is, a kind of admonishing sermon (in a total of 108 verses, there are over fifty imperatives). The ethical teaching is firmly grounded in the Jewish wisdom tradition, albeit hellenized and affected by contemporary philosophy (e.g., Proverbs, Sirach, Wisdom of Solomon). James's form can partially be compared with the so-called diatribe style in contemporary popular philosophical writings. Such a style incorporates teaching into the form of a fictitious dialogue with short questions (often rhetorical) and answers. The dialogues are often characterized by wordplay and allusions, dismissing proposed objections and faulty conclusions, employing ironies and sarcasms against real or fictive opponents, and so on.

Structure

1:1	Prescript
1:2–18	About endurance in temptation
1:19–27	About being both the hearer of the word and one who acts on it
2:1–13	About not noting the reputation of a person
2:14–26	About the right relationship between faith and action
3:1–12	About the use of the tongue
3:13–18	About the right wisdom
4:1–17	Warning about discord, pride, and slander
5:1–20	Admonishments against the backdrop of living in the final days

Main Theological Ideas

The connection between the letter's various subjects is unclear; a generally accepted explanation of a logical relationship between them has yet to be found. The consistent paraenetic style with its emphasis on practical-ethical exhortation has contributed to its theology often being disregarded, or seen as less valuable, especially because of the assumption that Paul was proclaiming the law-free gospel (Martin Luther, for example, called James an "epistle of straw," as he did not see Christ playing a central role in its message). In modern Pauline scholarship, the relationship between Paul and James has been radically reassessed (see the section "The Peculiar Case of Pauline Scholarship and Judaism," p. 23), and it seems out of place not to respect the theological validity of the many admonitions presented in this letter, as there is in fact a center point in the content—namely, the conviction that faith in Christ is true only if it comes to expression in action (2:14–26). The author focuses on questions of the testing of faith (ch. 1) and of correct behavior in certain situations (chs. 2–4) and concludes by clarifying the eschatological horizon of the exhortations (ch. 5). The "last days" are mentioned (5:3), and the audience is encouraged to "be patient . . . until the coming of the Lord" (5:7). The connection to statements and thoughts related to Jesus's ethical teachings (primarily 5:12 but also 4:12) is quite natural, without having to assume that the author held a special relationship with him.

Since the relationship between faith and action is central to Christian faith, the question of whether James polemicizes against Paul or Pauline theology has special relevance. It is most likely that the author was aware of Paul's arguments concerning faith and works in Rom 3–4. This becomes apparent when James reproaches an incorrect understanding of human righteousness with references to Abraham as a biblical model for how faith and action must work together (2:21–24). This need not, however, indicate an actual conflict between the historical figures James and Paul; rather, it may be seen as a criticism of an all-too-intellectualized view on faith among certain Christ followers who follow Pauline theological tradition. Paul's own understanding of what characterizes Christian faith is not necessarily opposed to James's criticism but may in fact support it (one also needs to take into account the special relationship between Christ-following Jews and non-Jews in Rome—whom his arguments are directed toward—and the risk of a one-sided Lutheran reading of Paul that may give birth to fake and anachronistically conceived contradictions).

The Letters of John

For linguistic, stylistic, and content-related reasons, these three short texts, of which only two are actual letters, are counted to the sphere of Johannine texts centered on the Gospel of John. Second and Third John and their addressees—"the elect lady and her children" and "the beloved Gaius," respectively—do not strictly fulfill the criteria for a so-called catholic letter. Some include Revelation in this group, but there is considerably less similarity (see below). In the canonization process of the ancient church, 1 John seems to have been accepted already in the second century, whereas the other two, although known among the church fathers, were not accepted as canonical until toward the end of the fourth century. Theologically, they are fairly insignificant, and their brevity—they are the shortest texts in the New Testament—and highly personal design have also contributed to their neglect in church services.

The First Letter of John

Context of Origin: Receiver, Author, Dating, and Setting

Neither author nor addressees are given in 1 John. Nor are there any clear hints for dating or setting to be found in the text. The many linguistic, stylistic, and content-related similarities with the Gospel of John do, however, indicate a similar context—that is, a circle of Johannine Christ followers (for more on the Johannine tradition, see the section "Johannine Christ Followers," p. 437). The witnessing of Jesus as a revelation of the divine Word and life (1:1: "what we have seen with our eyes"; cf. John 1:14) is emphasized in the solemn introductory prologues of both texts. In the gospel's closing editorial note (John 21:24), the reader is ensured that "we know that his [the disciple who testifies to these things] testimony is true," which may be compared with the repeated "we know" in 1 John, especially in the final verses. This does not mean, however, that the identity of the author, or the setting of origin, of 1 John can be safely assumed as being the same as that of the Gospel of John.

Besides the aforementioned argumentation, the only hint as to 1 John's context of origin is in the mention of false teachers, "antichrists" who have gone out, whose behavior is seen by the author as a sign of the final days (2:18–19). These apostates are accused of rejecting Jesus as the Messiah and true human (2:22–23; 4:2), which could signify that 1 John originated from a time when gnostic and docetic perceptions of Jesus had begun to spread among certain Christ followers. This could indicate a time of origin that is fairly late in the New Testament period—that is, approximately concurrent with the Pastoral Letters.

Normally, 1 John—just like the other two Johannine letters, in which the sender is identified as "the elder"—is considered to be written after the Gospel of John, which would indicate a time of origin around the year 100. The dating is due in part to the observation that the struggle against "false teachers" (primarily docetics) has hardened, and in part to the traditional hypothesis that Jesus's disciple John is behind the writing of the gospel and the letters. However, the ancient church authority Bishop Papias of Hierapolis mentions in the first half of the second century (referred to by Eusebius of Caesarea in his fourth century work on the history of the early church) that there are two people with the name John who, at approximately the same time (toward the end of the first century), were active as leaders of the Christ followers in Asia Minor and whose graves were located in Ephesus: one was the disciple John, and the other a presbyter by the same name. Thus, the possibility that different people could be behind the Johannine texts should not be dismissed, nor is it impossible that 1 John was written before the final version of the Gospel of John (as discussed earlier).

Genre and Communication Strategy

Generically speaking, 1 John is not a letter. It lacks both opening and closing greetings and resembles a kind of sermon or admonishing tractate. The repeated addressing of "my children," "beloved," "brothers" mediates an impression of a near and warm relationship between the author and his readers. Further, an ambition to create an intimate group identity is clearly demonstrated by appeals such as "Beloved, let us love one another" (4:7). The message of love, based on God's love of the world through his Son, is an expression of the author's ideals regarding the true relationship between God and humans, as well as mutually between humans. Ideas of love and community also function argumentatively as a positive enclosure, within which there is no room for false teachings. The writer hence wants to remind his readers that right faith and right actions are intrinsically linked.

Structure

1:1–4	Prologue with connections to John 1 and Gen 1
1:5–2:17	Admonishments against the backdrop of what communion with God means
2:18–3:24	Admonishments against the backdrop of living in the final days
4:1–5:12	Admonishments and criteria regarding what is the right faith
5:13	Summary of the text's main purpose
5:14–21	Comfort and admonishment regarding hearing of prayer and sin

Theological Main Ideas

Just as in the Gospel of John, the theological language and message are characterized by dualistic expressions such as "light/darkness," "truth/lies," "love/hate" (or "to love/to hate"), and "come from the world/come from God." This special terminology (which can be compared not only to gnostic ideas but also to thoughts and expressions in Qumranite literature) makes very clear the main point that the author wished to convey. It is the commandment of love and warnings about "false teachers," primarily regarding different views of Jesus. Together with many other early "orthodox" Christ-following writers, 1 John attacks not only the docetists' view of Jesus but also the consequences of this view for a way of life, which the author sees as the result of their sharp separation between divine and human, as well as a result of their different view of the salvation of humankind. Because a right faith is expressed through right actions, and the basic commandment is to love one another with God's and Jesus's self-giving love as an example, the one who does not follow this example and love others does not perform the right actions and thus does not hold the right faith. Such a person cannot be other than a sinner, while one who is born of God/remains in God does not sin (3:6, 9–10; 5:18—and there is no contradiction between these passages and 1:8–10 or the speech about different kinds of sin in 5:16–17).

The Second and Third Letters of John

As mentioned above, these texts differ from 1 John in that they are actual letters. The sender refers to himself as "the elder" and addresses "the elect lady and her children" (2 John) and his "beloved Gaius" (3 John), but none of this information is particularly illuminating. The expression "the elder" (*presbyteros*) refers to the sender's authority rather than his age (see the above discussion regarding the "presbyter John" that Papias speaks of). It is quite likely that the addressee of 2 John, "the elect lady," is not actually a single person but rather a personified Christ-following assembly (cf. v. 13). Gaius in 3 John, however, *is* an individual, whom the author thanks for his kind reception and sends some remarks concerning a certain Diotrephes. This Diotrephes is criticized for attempting to overtake the leadership of Gaius's assembly, and the letter thus gives interesting insight into the power struggles of the early church. Some scholars have seen in the letter a struggle between different types of early Christianity ("the presbyter" and Gaius representing a charismatic, wandering type, and Diotrephes an early ministerial church), or between "those of the true faith" and "heretics" (with the three main characters in exchangeable positions). These hypotheses are interesting but cannot be ascertained.

That the letters are generally viewed as Johannine—primarily related to 1 John, secondarily to the Gospel of John—is due to linguistic and content-related characteristics: especially 2 John is reminiscent of 1 John in its emphasis on the foundational commandment of love and its warning about "false teachers" who deny Jesus's true humanity; and 3 John appears to have the same sender as 2 John and makes use of several Johannine terms ("truth," "love," "the good/the evil," "come from God," "see God," "witness," "our testimony is true"). The letters' context therefore also seems to be Johannine in nature, and they may be dated to near the end of the New Testament period—that is, around the year 100.

The Letter to the Hebrews

The Letter's Context: Genre, Author, Receiver, Setting, and Dating

Hebrews is not an actual letter, although it does conclude in a letter-like fashion with greetings and wishes of grace (13:22–25). It lacks, however, the introductory greeting, and the main body of the text is far more similar to a sermon centered on christological and theological teaching (primarily the presentation of and comments on the Scriptures), intermingled with admonitions. A summarizing description is given in 13:22, where the entirety of the previous text is referred to as *logos paraklēseōs*—that is, an edifying speech of admonishment.

Who, then, could have authored Hebrews, and for whom was the text meant? Where and when could it have been written? The information about Timothy in 13:23 could potentially point toward the Pauline circles of missionary work (one of Paul's coworkers in Acts 16:1 and Phil 2:19; the addressee of the two letters to Timothy). However, the authenticity of the note on Timothy is uncertain, and the language, style, and content of Hebrews differ markedly from the Pauline letters, especially from the undisputed ones. To this must be added that the author presents himself as a second-generation Christ follower (2:3), and that some time must have passed since the addressees joined the faith (5:12). Where these could have been located is unclear, as also the greeting from "those from Italy" in 13:24 is ambiguous: the author could be located on the Italian peninsula, from where the greetings come, but he could also be present in an entirely different setting and simply be passing on greetings from those from Italy. Both alternatives are possible, but in support of the former must be mentioned that the First Letter of Clement—the origins of which likely lie in Rome at the end of the first century—has many connections to Hebrews. Whatever the case, the author seems to be well acquainted with the addressees (6:9–10; 10:32–34).

The title "to the Hebrews" (which is absent in the oldest manuscripts) indicates, as does the content in general, that the letter was written to Christ-following Jews. The author makes use of an arsenal of scriptural citations, as well as references to the old covenant's sacrificial cult. Its argumentation is based on a comparison between Israel's old covenant and the new, superior one—a comparison that, in its entirety, recognizably originates from a Jewish perspective. Against this backdrop, some scholars have claimed that the addressees may have had a connection with Qumranic/Essenic Judaism (see the section "Beliefs and Practices in Second Temple Judaism," p. 114). At the same time, there is no indication of problems between Jews and non-Jews in the Christ-following people of God, which we see clearly in Paul's letters, for example. Hebrews could therefore also have been written so late in the theological development that the tensions between Christ-following Jews and non-Jews were a thing of the past (note, however, that conflicts between these two types of Christ belief occurred as late as the fifth century; see the section "Jewish Christ Followers and the Emergence of Christianity and Judaism," p. 365).

While scholars agree that Hebrews was written before the First Letter of Clement, there are some who date it as early as the time just before the Great Jewish Revolt against Rome in 66–70. The letter speaks much about the services and priesthood of the old covenant, yet without mentioning the fall of Jerusalem and the destruction of the temple in the year 70. Considering how the old covenant is consistently contrasted with the new, the fact of the Jewish catastrophe ought to have been used somehow in the letter's reasoning (if the text really *was* written after the destruction of the temple), or so the argument goes. At the same time, the contrasting occurs at a theoretical level, rather than at the level of concrete outer circumstances, so that a later dating is not impossible: the superiority of Christ is not compared with the cult during the Herodian Second Temple but with the worship of God in the biblical desert tabernacle. Hebrews could in fact be directed toward a predominantly non-Jewish Christ-following assembly, or to Christ followers in general. After all, it is an ancient Christian belief that the church inherited the promises given by the old covenant to God's people. The biblical Scriptures form the Holy Scripture of the church, which represents the true Israel. If Paul in his letter to the Galatians could use the Scriptures to such a great degree in his argumentation against the weak spirits in the assembly, how much more, then, could not Hebrews do so (especially considering that the educational and linguistic levels of this letter are much higher)? When the author reproaches the audience for their need of drinking milk like infants instead of consuming solid food (5:12–14), it is the foundational teachings of the mission to non-Jews to which he is referring: repentance from acts that lead to death, belief in God, and the teachings of baptism, the laying on of hands, the resurrection of the dead, and eternal judgment (6:1–3). For an exclusive Jewish-Christian audience, a reminder of Jesus's person and work and of the presence of the Spirit would seem more appropriate.

The admonition in chapter 13 is not so much directed toward the addressees of the letter as about human behavior in general: brotherly love, hospitality, concern for the abused, money, foreign teachings, and food laws. The warning to the assembly is not to remain in the infant stage (5:11–6:10), "not neglecting to meet together" (10:25), "not grow[ing] weary or los[ing] heart" (12:3), so that nobody will fall behind on the path to the city that is to come (4:1, 11; 12:1; 13:14). Some exegetes take these statements as proof that the text originates relatively late in the early church, even though such general admonitions cannot be reason enough for a late dating. In any case, the assembly as well as the author seem not to belong to the first generation of Christ followers. They have already endured suffering and persecution for the sake of their faith (10:32–34) but must now be reminded not to stray from the original path (2:1; 6:1–2). These people who have not themselves lived with Jesus but instead heard the gospel from others (2:3; cf. 13:7) can, however, belong just as much to the 60s as to the 80s or 90s.

In the ancient church, there were primarily three positions on the authorship of Hebrews: that it was written by Paul, or someone close to him in Alexandria; that it was written by Barnabas from North Africa, and therefore of a secondary rank as an apostolic text; or that it entirely lacked any connection to Paul, thereby disqualifying it from obtaining canonical status, and was written from Rome. The place of the letter in the oldest manuscripts and lists of New Testament texts shifts, depending on which view on authorship was favored. In the papyrus P^{46} from around 200, it appears between Romans and 1–2 Corinthians, a placement that cannot be explained solely as an ordering of texts by size, but may suggest the assumption of Pauline authorship and that great theological significance is attributed to the letter. The eastern part of the church—where its Pauline origins seem to have been widely accepted—normally places it at the end of the Pauline collection of letters (sometimes after the congregational letters, but before the private letters). In the western part of the church, for a long time Hebrews was either not included among the New Testament texts or seen as non-Pauline. Despite the fact that the church's central leadership toward the end of the fourth century agreed on including Hebrews in the New Testament canon, some reservations lingered on (Luther, for example, thought that it may have been written by the learned Apollos, who was a contemporary missionary, independent of Paul). For more on Hebrews in the canonization process, see the section "An Emerging Canon" on p. 212.

Model of Herod's temple, the Israel Museum, Jerusalem. Photo by Anders Runesson.

Language, Style, and Rhetorical Structure

With regard to both language and style, Hebrews is one of a kind. Some in the ancient church who claimed Pauline authorship thought that Paul wrote the letter in Hebrew and that it was translated into Greek by Luke or Clement of Rome; nothing in the text, however, supports such a proposition. On the contrary, the text boasts perhaps the best Greek in all of the New Testament, with regard to both grammar and vocabulary (words that occur only in this text and nowhere else in Greek—so-called *hapax legomena*; words that are also found in classical Greek but in no other New Testament text; words that are also found in the Septuagint but in no other New Testament text). Furthermore—perhaps the decisive argument—the many citations are all taken from the Septuagint. The letter exhibits none of Paul's grammatical gambades, with half-completed clauses, rhetorical questions, outcries, and the like. Similarities have also been noted between Hebrews and the writings of Philo, especially regarding the usage of Scripture. As in Philo, Scripture in Hebrews is interpreted allegorically, in search for deeper meaning (e.g., the comparison in chs. 8–9 between the high priest's sacrificial ceremony in the old covenant and Jesus's death on the cross, as well as the comment on those who in the time of the old covenant believed in the promises of God; see also 8:5; 10:1). Distinctive to Hebrews is also the usage of typological exegesis (e.g., when Melchizedek in ch. 7 is seen as "resembling the Son of God" [v. 3], and the earthly tabernacle in chs. 8–9 is related to the divine sanctuary).

Seeing that the formulations in the text appear well thought out and polished in order to give the greatest possible reading effect, it is not without reason that similarities have been noted to Hellenistic antiquity's rhetorical techniques (the first four verses of the letter are excellent examples of this, composed in a solemn style and with alliterations, which many translations attempt to reflect). Several studies have shown that the text has been carefully structured in accordance with the principles of ancient rhetoric, known from Aristotle, Quintilian, and others. For instance, Walter Übelacker claims that the author composed a kind of "deliberative" speech, the purpose of which was to convince the listeners of the accuracy of one's reasoning such that they not only were given insight into a matter but were persuaded to apply this insight to their action (Hebrews is, after all, generally seen as a sermon).[3] This may explain the peculiar blend of theological/christological inquiry and admonishing (paraenetic) sections.

Structure

1:1–4:13	Appeal to listen to God's speech through Jesus, who is higher than the angels and the old covenant's foremost representatives, Moses and Joshua

3. Übelacker, *Der Hebräerbrief als Appell*, 21.

4:14–10:18	Appeal to stand before Jesus, the divine high priest, and hold fast to the creed
10:19–13:21	Appeal to hold fast to the faith in Jesus and to profess the Christian hope
13:22–25	Closing of the letter

Hebrews' theological center of gravity lies in the teachings concerning Christ. An advanced Christology is presented already in its early chapters: as Son, Jesus is above all the angels, but after his humiliation—being made lower than the angels—by dying as a human and through his resurrection from the dead he has become the Savior of humanity. He is also above Moses—and how much more must one then follow the commandments and the example of Jesus in order to obtain that which was promised to God's people? At the same time and paradoxically, there is an emphasis on Jesus's humanity, especially in 2:14–18.

As a secondary main point, Jesus is presented as the one who through obedience and suffering is a perfect high priest, like Melchizedek (4:14–5:10; but already in 2:17–18). The theme returns in chapters 7–10 after the paraenetic aside (5:11–6:20), which warns of spiritual stagnation and falling away after having previously come to believe. Jesus is the holy, sinless high priest, who once and for all atoned for the sins of humanity and thereby gave the world eternal and complete salvation. His death on the cross, where Jesus is both the one sacrificing and the sacrifice, is a cultic cleansing that is far superior to the sacrificial ceremonies of the old covenant. What the assembly needs to do now is enduringly hold fast to their Christian hope—which they have done previously despite suffering and persecution—so that they may not sin by falling away from the faith and bringing upon themselves the wrath of God (10:19–39).

In chapter 11 the author illustrates his argumentation by recalling models of faith in the old covenant, from Abel via the patriarchs to the prostitute Rahab in Jericho, as well as to people like Gideon, Barak, Samson, Jephthah, David, Samuel, and the prophets—a chapter that ends with a statement that none of these people saw the fulfilling of the promise, and yet they believed. Thus, the addressees of Hebrews, who *have* seen the fulfilling of the promise, ought to hold fast to their faith in Jesus all the more. They have not received a revelation from God like the one on Mount Sinai in the form of fire, darkness, and terror; instead, they have come to Mount Zion, to the festive assembly in the heavenly Jerusalem. God's eschatological speech through Christ is definitive and may not be rejected (ch. 12). The practical consequences for the assembly follow as an appeal to love, marital fidelity, endurance in faith, and obedience to leaders (13:1–21).

Theological Main Ideas

In the theology of Hebrews, Christology and ecclesiology are two prominent elements, each with a special stance: one element elaborates Jesus as the new high priest of the covenant; the other develops the idea of the church as the wandering people of God.

Hebrews' identification of Jesus with Melchizedek is unique to the New Testament. This figure was previously only known from two texts, Gen 14 and Ps 110. Previously, the question of why Hebrews' author would choose to compare Jesus's role as high priest with this specific individual seemed quite inexplicable. However, in light of one of the Qumran texts (11Q13), dated to the middle of the first century BCE, this connection becomes particularly interesting. Melchizedek is mentioned in that text as an eschatological atoner with priestly and royal characteristics. Together with other sections of Hebrews, this theological similarity could be taken as an indication that the author's conceptual theological sphere somehow relates to Qumranic Judaism.

A common prerequisite of Christology and ecclesiology is the fundamental ancient Christian understanding of Jesus's death and resurrection (yet in Hebrews the focus is on his heavenly exaltation) as God's act of salvation, interpreted against the background of the biblical exodus—that is, a typological understanding of Scripture. In Jesus Christ, who is the most superior mediator between God and humans, a communion with God in the form of a new covenant is offered through faith and baptism. Those who are Christ followers can thus be seen, in analogy to Israel in the Scriptures, as the people of God, saved from the land of slavery and on their way to a promised land where there is completion and perfection in God. The old covenant from Sinai opened a path for the people of Israel to God, but now a new—better—means of salvation is presented that is open to Jew and Greek alike. Of utter importance in this new salvation is faith, something that the Christ follower must not lose, lest he or she risk not being allowed to rest in the heavenly city—that is, with God.

In this exodus theology lies the key to the characteristic ancient Christian tension between future and present eschatology, between "already now" and "not yet": salvation is already now a possibility for the people of God, through Jesus's death on the cross, but as salvation has not yet been completed, there is a risk of losing one's way on the path to it. God protects and guides the believer on the way to the final heavenly goal, just as he did for Israel in the desert. In Hebrews, the tension between "already now" and "not yet" is particularly evident in a comparison of 4:9–11 and 12:18–24. The readers are informed that ever since the time of Joshua, when the people of Israel could enter Canaan, there has been a Sabbath rest to come. Completion is still pending. Yet the readers are also informed that they have already arrived at the heavenly Jerusalem, standing at Mount Zion by the joyous crowd of angels; they are already partaking in the blessings of salvation. It is against this background that the statement in 6:4–6 about the impossibility of repentance for those who have already received the heavenly gifts but then have fallen away (cf. 10:26) ought to be understood. This view conflicted with the ancient Christian practices of repentance that emerged in Rome (cf. the Shepherd of Hermas) and contributed to a longstanding skepticism in the western part of the church concerning the canonical status of Hebrews. Christ's perfect sacrifice as high priest provides a basis for the faith and hope of the new people of the covenant. The people of God need to be warned and strengthened in order to manage the journey toward the ultimate heavenly goal. That this "theology of wandering" would be a kind of gnostic-influenced Christ belief seems unlikely; rather, Hebrews expresses a traditional early Christian typological understanding of the Scriptures, at times also exhibiting allegorical elements.

The Book of Revelation

Context: Receiver, Author, Dating, and Setting

The last writing in the New Testament, Revelation, is mysterious and disputed. In some regards, however, it provides clear information. The author addresses seven assemblies of Christ followers in the western part of modern-day Turkey: Ephesus, Smyrna, Pergamum, Thyatira, Sardis, Philadelphia, and Laodicea. Some of these, especially Ephesus and Smyrna, were significant cities in antiquity that are also known from the early history of Christianity. Even the place where the text was written is mentioned: the small island of Patmos, just off the Turkish west coast and not far southwest from Ephesus. Since the context of Revelation presumes an emerging persecution of Christ followers, the note in 1:9 about the author being on the island "because of the word of God and the testimony of Jesus" has been interpreted as John having been deported there. However, the text need not mean that and may simply articulate the divine mission. That Patmos was a place used for exile is a later Christian tradition.

John, the author, is clearly acquainted with the addressees, as he introduces himself by his name only (1:4). Chapters 2–3 reveal that he is familiar with local situations. The question, however, is *which* John is being referred to, which also begs the question of the relationship to other Johannine literature. Isolated occurrences of expressions such as "the Word of God" in 19:13, and "the water of life" in 22:17 have their clearest New Testament parallels in the Gospel of John, but differences in language, style, and content speak against a common authorship. A common "Johannine setting," however, is indeed possible. Already in the ancient church, it was understood that beyond the disciple and "evangelist" John, there was also a presbyter John who had connections to Ephesus (see discussion of Papias on the authorship of 1–3 John above).

The question about the identity of the addressees of Revelation is difficult to answer, but much speaks for a Jewish setting. The terminology, theological ideas, and ethical ideals are fashioned by models from Scripture that are entirely different from most of the other New Testament texts. By a careful count, 278 of the book's 404 verses exhibit some kind of connection to Scripture, an influence that does not seem to have been transmitted via the Septuagint. It is well known that the Asia Minor region long since had a significant Jewish presence (cf. Acts 19:1–7). Judging by Revelation's special language and conceptual sphere, it is plausible to assume that the author is primarily speaking to Christ-following Jews with his special ethical, christological, and eschatological teachings. Not least, the mentality and theological ideas of Revelation display many interesting similarities to Qumranic Judaism. The very sharp condemnations in 2:9 and 3:9 of those who call themselves Jews but who are actually a "synagogue of Satan" could be interpreted as the author speaking of *real* Jews who, because they are mocking Christ followers, are now to be categorized as "fake" Jews (cf. John 8:44). This could thus be an intra-Jewish polemic from the first (Jewish) Christ followers toward fellow Jews. In later history it has led to severe and tragic consequences when used by non-Jewish Christians with an "outside" perspective to theologically and ideologically motivate anti-Semitism.

In the messages to individual assemblies in chapters 2–3, warnings are given against different kinds of libertinism and syncretism, while the rest of the book emphasizes that the Roman state, personified by the emperor, is the greatest threat against the people of God. Both observations seem to imply that Revelation originated fairly late during the first century CE. Any form of widespread martyrdom of Christ followers appears as yet nonexistent, even though it is expected to begin soon as part of the suffering in the last days. Not until the end of Emperor Domitian's reign (81–96) does any form of general and active persecution of Christ followers occur on the part of the Roman state, which could explain Revelation's diabolizing of it. Of course, Nero's final year in power, with his documented hunt for Christ followers in Rome during the middle of the 60s, could be the occasion for Revelation, but the persecution seems to have been limited in both time and space. It is also striking that the attitude toward Roman state power in Revelation differs starkly from Paul's views (e.g., Rom 13).

The island of Patmos. In Greek mythology, the island of Patmos (like Delos) was raised from the sea by Zeus. Christian tradition tells of Jesus's disciple John coming to the island as a prisoner and there receiving revelations from Christ in the so-called Cave of the Apocalypse. In the middle of the picture, we see the Monastery of the Revelation, which was built around the aforementioned cave; furthest up is the Monastery of Saint John (since 1999 both are on the list of world heritage sites). The monastic life on Patmos began when Hosios Christodoulos came to the island in 1088. Photo by Dieter Mitternacht.

Text: Language and Style, Genre, and Structure

The expressions and content of Revelation are quite unique compared to the rest of the New Testament. The Greek text is permeated by grammatical errors and oddities, which have often been attributed to the author's poor linguistic capabilities but may actually be an attempt to write a "holy," Hebraicizing text. Above all, phrases from the prophetic literature (esp. Isaiah, Ezekiel, Joel), as well as the book of Daniel, abound, but there are also allusions to the Psalms and the books of Moses.

In terms of genre, Revelation resembles the rich flora of biblical and postbiblical Jewish and Christian apocalyptic literature such as Daniel, the books of Enoch, 4 Ezra, and 2 Baruch. The word "apocalypse" or "revelation" originates from the first word of Revelation: *apokalypsis*, "revelation, uncovering." The book contains Christ's revelations, which God has given him to pass on to John and his readers. Many of the conventional characteristics of apocalyptic style are there:

- A story of how an especially blessed person receives a special revelation from God through visions and auditions; the visionary's "journey to heaven" and conversation with a representative of the heavenly world (a "clarifying angel," *angelus interpres*)
- A description of the heavenly world with its many actors, and especially of God's throne
- An shift of focus back and forth between the heavenly scene and earthly events, between accounts of the heavenly harmonious world and grotesque and bloody images, often clad in a mythical, symbolic language
- A multifaceted numerology in which, for example, the beast is numbered as 666 (13:18)
- Actors presented as contrasting pairs—for example, the slaughtered but triumphing Lamb (ch. 5), whose counterpart is the mortally wounded beast (ch. 13); the divine woman who gives birth to the messianic child (ch. 12) with its counterpart in the prostitute sitting on the beast (ch. 17); the heavenly Jerusalem of the new creation (chs. 21–22) contrasted with evil Babylon's judgment and fall (chs. 17–18)
- A foundational dualistic and pessimistic worldview based on the belief that the world is in its final days, and that the decisive battle between God and evil is being fought
- A belief that after the final cosmic and earthly catastrophes and sufferings of the final days, and after God's judgment of his enemies, there will be a new creation and an age of peace for God's chosen people
- An ethical message that seeks to compel the readers, through alternate warnings and consolations, to lead their lives in strict compliance with God's will

Added to this rich symbolic language with a background in biblical ideas are images and motifs from the author's own time and context, with allusions to local situations in the seven Asia Minor assemblies and the Roman state's exertion of power.

The book distinguishes itself from contemporary apocalyptic literature by *not* using a pseudonym. Instead of claiming to be the work of some biblical or apostolic authority, the author calls himself simply "John." Another factor that distinguishes Revelation from other apocalyptic literature is that it features a coherent dramatic plotline throughout the entire text, from the first chapter to the last: The first vision of Christ is developed into the seven messages in chapters 2–3, and then into the heavenly vision in chapters 4–5. At this point the audience is introduced to the Lamb and the scroll that form the backbone of the visionary main body of Revelation (the series of seven seals, which develop into a series of seven trumpets and thereafter the seven bowls of God's wrath). Finally, the text closes with the visions of judgment and salvation in chapters 17–22. Characteristic for Revelation is the alternation between what "happens" on the heavenly scene versus the earthly one. The artistic composition of Revelation has inspired artistic creations throughout history, in many different forms—modern examples being movies such as *The Terminator* and *The Matrix*.

The author himself calls the text a "prophecy" (1:3)—that is, admonitions, warnings, and consolations from God in a crucial situation. By giving the message an outer frame in the form of a letter—with seven separate messages included in chapters 2–3—the text has even greater relevance for the audience.

In a text where the number seven plays such an important role (seven assemblies, seven letters, seven seals, seven trumpets, seven bowls of wrath, etc.), it is hardly surprising that many commentators find an overall composition related to the number seven. The following layout is just one among many possible alternatives.

Structure

1:1–3	Prologue: the mediator of the visions is here introduced; the content is characterized as prophecy; an expectation of eschatological proximity is articulated.
1:4–8	Letter-like introduction: this makes the entirety of Revelation appear very relevant to primarily the seven named assemblies; the number seven, however, as a symbol for wholeness, indicates that basically the entire church is addressed.
1:9–20	The calling vision: John here emphasizes that he shares with the addressees the sufferings, kingship, and endurance of Jesus.
2:1–3:22	Message to the seven assemblies—seven letters that are similarly structured:

a.	Formula of authorization of the message from the author with the help of christological motifs taken from the calling vision in chapter 1 ("These are the words of him who . . .")
b.	Criticism or praise, which demonstrates the author's knowledge of local situations, followed by an appeal to act righteously, as well as a threat or promise against the background of Jesus's second coming
c.	Auditory formulation ("whoever has ears . . .")
d.	Promises to the "one who is victorious" with connections to Revelation's closing visions of salvation
4:1–22:5	Visionary main part: within the frame of Revelation's visionary stories, seven larger entities may be identified:
I.	4:1–5:14: Vision of God's throne and of the Lamb with the scroll
II.	6:1–8:6: The seven seals
III.	8:7–15:8: The seven trumpets
IV.	16:1–21: Seven bowls of God's wrath poured out over the world
V.	17:1–19:10: The fall of Babylon
VI.	19:11–21:8: The world's judgment and new creation
VII.	21:9–22:5: The new Jerusalem
22:6–21	Relevant applications of the vision's messages in the lives of the readers, and closing authorization of the book, prayer, and greeting; Jesus again has the role of the conveyor of revelations, a role he also had in the introductory calling and sending scene in chapter 1.

Main Theological Ideas

Church theologians as well as biblical scholars have often viewed Revelation with suspicion. The obscure, grotesque, and often paradoxical imagery divulged an early form of Christian faith and theology that was not particularly appealing. In the last decades of the twentieth century, however, Revelation generated more positive attention. Its message of liberation from the oppressive powers of evil came to be used within South African liberation theology in the struggle against the apartheid regime. At the same time, exegetes, invigorated by an interest in literary and socio-rhetorical studies, were able to appreciate the "mytho-poetic" power of the "symbolic universe" of Revelation. New analytical methods from literary studies inspired by sociological theories began to be applied to this multifaceted text.

First and foremost, Revelation focuses on eschatology. Using John's own contextual description in 1:9 as a key, it becomes clear that the book's main concern is not only the future but also the present. Similar to other New Testament texts, Revelation presents Jesus's death and resurrection as the sign that the old age has ended and the new age has begun. Thus also, the sufferings endured by Christ followers confirm the beginning of the final battle between God and the forces of evil (cf. Dan 12:1). Time is short before God's definitive intervention and Jesus's triumphant arrival as the divine Son of Man. Contrary to what many scholars have claimed, there are no allusions in the text to the effect that a general martyrdom for followers of Christ had begun or was pending. The belief that faithfulness to God and Christ can cost the believers' their lives, however, is included in the rhetoric arsenal of the text (6:11; 17:6; 20:4). To have "Jesus's testimony," to be a *martys*, is about to assume the later Christian meaning of "blood witness."

The Cave of the Apocalypse on Patmos—the cave in which, according to tradition, John sought refuge and received revelations from Christ. A monastery has been built around the cave. Photo by Dieter Mitternacht.

The thorough usage of allusions to exodus traditions (e.g., the sufferings of the trumpet-and-bowl series, "Moses and the song of the Lamb" by the sea of glass) fits incredibly well into the book's special eschatological perspective: the readers are described in 1:6 as "a kingdom" and "priests" of God (cf. 5:10 and 20:6)—that is, their identity as Christ followers is seen as analogous to the old covenant's people of God at Sinai (Exod 19:6). Liberated from the power of sin and evil through the death of the Lamb, Jesus, they now stand under divine protection on their way to the promised land's perfect communion with God (cf. Isa 61:6 about Israel's coming restoration).

A special problem in the interpretation of Revelation is and has been how the faithful's thousand-year reign with Jesus (20:4–6) is to be understood. The belief in a "thousand-year kingdom" relates to Jewish apocalyptic traditions about an in-between period, with or without a messianic figure, that constitutes a transition between the present and coming ages (cf., e.g., 4 Ezra, 2 Baruch [Syriac Apocalypse]). The number one thousand fits into a particular view of the world's history where the seven days of creation model a calculation of the length of history as seven times one thousand years. The seventh day, God's day of rest, is the thousand-year-long messianic time, which marks the return of creation to paradisiacal conditions (cf. the Letter of Barnabas and 2 Enoch). The kingdom of a thousand years (the millennium) is closely connected to the "first resurrection" and the promise that the faithful will assume an existence that won't be affected by the "second" death, which according to 20:6 and 20:14 implies the final and definitive obliteration from existence.

The question is how literal the kingdom of a thousand years was meant to be understood, and what weight it ought to be given in the interpretation of Revelation's total message, not to mention within the frame of the entirety of the New Testament (it is the only time in all the New Testament that the expression occurs). In early interpretations it was taken as a prediction of a coming phase in salvation, when the faithful's divine reward will be expressed in concrete fashion. Throughout church history, there have been those who have interpreted the millennial kingdom as a prediction of a concrete and delimited period in the history of the world, thinking of themselves as contributors to the realization of this prophecy—not only today among fundamentalist groups like the "Branch Davidians" in Waco, Texas, but also among, for example, medieval charismatic-ecstatic reform and protest movements inspired by Bible scholars such as the southern Italian abbot Joachim of Fiore (1135–1202).

Even on the topic of Christology Revelation is unique within the New Testament, primarily by introducing the image of Jesus as the slaughtered but triumphant Lamb, which as of chapter 5 plays a decisive role in the unfolding of the apocalyptic drama. For one, the image points to Jesus's self-giving death for the salvation of humankind (cf. 1:5: "[he who] freed us from our sins by his blood"; and 5:9: "for you were slaughtered and by your blood you ransomed for God saints from every tribe and language and people and nation"). For another, quite paradoxically, the slaughtered Lamb is in fact the Lion of Judah and takes on a military role as God's agent in the final battle against the forces of evil. Thus, in one sense the image is an interpretation of the salvation through Jesus's death in biblical cultic-juridical terms, and in another sense it ascribes to Jesus a role in the apocalyptic conceptual world and drama (cf. the "dream-visions" in 1 En. 83–90, where Israel's people and their leaders are described as lambs or rams). Through such paradoxical images, Revelation depicts the simultaneous impression of Jesus's lowliness and his heavenly ascent (the same double nature and role is implied by the usage of the title "Son of Man" in the Gospels).

The question of where and how Revelation corresponds with the early christological development is highly interesting. The heavenly, exalted Jesus figure has really nothing in common with the Synoptic Gospels' earthly Jesus, nor hardly anything with the exalted revealer of the Father's secrets and nature of the Gospel of John. There may be, however, some hints at a common Johannine setting, as noted above: in 19:13 a divine rider appears under the name "The Word of God" (cf. John 1), and in 22:17 the "water of life" is offered to the faithful (cf. John 4:10, 14; 7:37–39). Just as in other New Testament letters, Jesus's death is interpreted in cultic-judicial terms as a removal of or atonement for the sins of humankind (cf., e.g., Rom 3:25). This, together with his resurrection from the dead and ascension to heavenly glory, motivates the worship of Jesus as the Savior and Lord of the entire world. It is not surprising, therefore, that Jesus as the triumphing Lamb can be related to God's throne and be praised together with God by the entirety of the heavenly world and all creation (5:11–13; cf. 7:10) while also being a mediator to God and to John (albeit the greatest: the faithful witness, the King of kings and Lord of lords, who holds the keys to Death and Hades)—and as such is not an object of formal worship (cf. 22:9).

From the History of Interpretation

The drawn-out reluctance to ascribe canonical status to Revelation depended not so much on the question of apostolic background as on objections to content and its interpretation by different people in the early church. Hardly surprising, the time perspective has emerged as a central concern. Is this apocalyptic drama with its series of sevens meant to progress in a chronological order? Is it the intent of the author that contemporary and future readers would be able to recognize themselves in specific images, periods of time, or the scenario as a whole? Or is the same eschatological message of the final days being repeated in the various visions? Does the book provide a timetable for the end times, or is its purpose to comfort and admonish John's contemporaries, simply expressing the assurance of God's salvation and judgment by using biblically and apocalyptically inspired language?

The many questions concerning its message and the multiple ways to interpret and use it have followed Revelation through the entirety of its history. Recently, occasion for comparisons was given by the Chernobyl catastrophe in 1986 (the meaning of the city name, "wormwood," has been highlighted by some interpreters; cf. Rev 8:11); the recent millennial shift has stirred speculations (as did the previous one); the chronic Middle Eastern conflict and related conflicts around the Persian Gulf (such as the so-called Gulf War in 1990–1991) has led to pretentious publications of books about the imminent Armageddon (cf. Rev 16:16).

The oldest interpretations of Revelation have been labeled as *futuristic-eschatological interpretations*: the visions are prophecies of the world's imminent destruction, of the faithful's vindication in the form of a thousand-year reign with Christ, and of the world's re-creation. This is the view put forward, for example, in the Letter of Barnabas, one of the so-called apostolic fathers' texts from the middle of the 100s CE. As expectations of the imminence of Christ's return, and with it the interest in a literal meaning of the biblical and postbiblical apocalypse literature, became more relaxed, the *church historical interpretation* of Revelation became more and more prominent among interpreters in the church. One of the most influential expressions of this reading—and to a large degree still accepted today—is found in Augustine's (ca. 400) understanding of the millennial kingdom as the time of the church. The section regarding the faithful's part in "the first resurrection" and the thousand-year reign with Christ is thought to signify in part baptism as the gate to the new creation and life in the new age, and in part the exaltation of the faithful to the highest possible human dignity before God.

As a variant of this, commentaries from the Middle Ages and later favor a *world historical interpretation*—not least through inspiration from Joachim of Fiore's view of Revelation's three series of seven-part visions as images of three phases in the world's history. That such a reading of Revelation is and has been popular within certain spheres of Christianity is apparent, for example, from the many identifications of the beast in chapter 13 (the catholic papacy, Charles XII of Sweden, Napoleon, Hitler, Stalin, etc.). Another favorite, quite popular in certain American circles in the 1970s, is the affiliation of the ten horns of the beast with the number of member states in the predecessor of the European Union.

Modern scientific commentaries of Revelation are dominated by a history of religions approach or a general historical interest, often both in combination. Of great relevance to these are studying how the author utilizes biblical and extrabiblical traditions and motifs, or how the texts corroborate contemporary historical, cultural, social, and religious contexts. The latest development has been an increased interest in the book's mytho-poetic and rhetorical aspects and language, focusing less on the author's historical world and more on how the readers and listeners now and then have been and are challenged by the "symbolic universe" of the apocalyptic drama and the message of God's judgment and salvation.

Further Reading

Hebrews

Attridge, Harold W. *Hebrews: A Commentary on the Epistle to the Hebrews*. Hermeneia. Philadelphia: Fortress, 1989.

Cockerill, Gareth L. *The Epistle to the Hebrews*. NICNT. Grand Rapids: Eerdmans, 2012.

DeSilva, David A. *Perseverance in Gratitude: A Socio-Rhetorical Commentary on the Epistle to the Hebrews*. Grand Rapids: Eerdmans, 2000.

Koester, Craig R. *Hebrews: A New Translation with Introduction and Commentary*. AYBC 36. New Haven: Yale University Press, 2001.

Lindars, Barnabas. *The Theology of the Letter to the Hebrews*. Cambridge: Cambridge University Press, 1991.

James, 1–2 Peter, and Jude

Achtemeier, Paul D. *1 Peter*. Hermeneia. Minneapolis: Fortress, 1996.

Allison, Dale C. *A Critical and Exegetical Commentary on the Epistle of James*. ICC. London. Bloomsbury, 2013.

Batten, Alicia J., and John S. Kloppenborg, eds. *James, 1–2 Peter, and Early Jesus Traditions*. London: Bloomsbury, 2014.

Bauckham, Richard. *Jude-2 Peter*. WBC. Grand Rapids: Zondervan, 2014.

Chester, Andrew, and Ralph P. Martin. *The Theology of the Letters of James, Peter, and Jude*. Cambridge: Cambridge University Press, 1994.

Elliott, John H. *A Home for the Homeless: A Sociological Exegesis of 1 Peter, Its Situation, and Strategy*. Philadelphia: Fortress, 1981.

———. *1 Peter: A New Translation with Introduction and Commentary*. AYBC 37B. New Haven: Yale University Press, 2001.

Johnson, Luke Timothy. *The Letter of James: A New Translation with Introduction and Commentary*. AYBC 37A. New Haven: Yale University Press, 2005.

Starr, James M. *Sharers in Divine Nature: 2 Peter 1:4 in Its Hellenistic Context*. ConBNT 33. Stockholm: Almqvist & Wiksell, 2000.

1–3 John

Brown, Raymond E. *The Community of the Beloved Disciple*. New York: Paulist Press, 1979.

———. *The Epistles of John: A New Translation with Introduction and Commentary*. AYBC 30. New Haven: Yale University Press, 1982.

Lieu, Judith M. *The Theology of the Johannine Epistles*. Cambridge: Cambridge University Press, 1991.

Olsson, Birger. *A Commentary on the Letters of John: An Intra-Jewish Perspective*. Eugene, OR: Pickwick, 2013.

Smalley, Stephen S. *1, 2, and 3 John*. WBC 51. Grand Rapids: Zondervan, 2015.

Revelation

Bauckham, Richard. *The Climax of Prophecy: Studies on the Book of Revelation*. Edinburgh: T&T Clark, 1993.

———. *The Theology of the Book of Revelation*. Cambridge: Cambridge University Press, 1993.

Collins, Adela Yarbro. *Crisis and Catharsis: The Power of the Apocalypse*. Philadelphia: Westminster John Knox, 1984.

Gregg, Steve. *Revelation: Four Views; A Parallel Commentary*. Rev. ed. Nashville: Thomas Nelson, 2013.

Koester, Craig R. *Revelation: A New Translation with Introduction and Commentary*. AYBC 38A. New Haven: Yale University Press, 2014.

Marshall, John W. *Parables of War: Reading John's Jewish Apocalypse*. Studies in Christianity and Judaism / Études sur le christianisme et le judaïsm. Waterloo: Wilfrid Laurier University Press, 2001.

Pippin, Tina. *Death and Desire: The Rhetoric of Gender in the Apocalypse of John*. Louisville: Westminster John Knox, 1992.

Rowland, Christopher. *The Open Heaven: A Study of Apocalyptic in Judaism and Early Christianity*. New York: Crossroad, 1982.

5 The Emergence of Early Christianity

In this chapter we will take a look at some major factions and trajectories of Christ affiliation that developed during the first century and from which early Christianity eventually emerged. The chapter consists of six studies of phenomena, processes, convictions, groupings, and communities. The outcome of the presentations in this chapter indicates that the diversity among Christ groups was substantial, to say the least. The first study traces the developments out of which Christianity and Judaism emerge as two distinct religions, from the first century to the fifth. Then follow two studies that focus on texts and groups that are documented in the New Testament. The three studies that complete the chapter highlight perspectives and developments that are affiliated with groups not documented in the New Testament.

The first study addresses two main topics: (1) the phenomenon of Jewish Christ followers and Christ-centered Judaism, and (2) the historical processes that led to Christianity becoming a religion separate from Judaism. The reason why these phenomena are studied together is simply that it is difficult, maybe impossible, to talk about one without touching on the other. Jesus was a Jew, as were Peter and Paul and just about every other early Christ follower. Early on in the history of the Jesus movement, however, groups began springing up that consisted mainly of non-Jews, and when, in the late fourth century, Christianity became the religion of the Roman Empire, it had become a non-Jewish religion. How did this come about, and what happened to the Jews who believed that Jesus was the messiah? Moreover, how can we envision the coexistence and co-worship of Jewish Christ followers and other Jews in the first century? These are some of the issues addressed in the section "Jewish Christ Followers and the Emergence of Judaism and Christianity," p. 365.

The second study focuses on Paul as a missionary, leader, and thinker, particularly as this relates to his assemblies and his successors. Paul's significance for emerging

Christianity can hardly be overstated, and his letters, the earliest texts in the New Testament, have exerted a tremendous influence over the centuries. Questions as to how his identity as a Jew shaped his thinking about Jesus and affected his mission to the gentiles are and have always been matters of intense contention. His assertions and convictions, when compared systematically, often seem puzzling, even to the point of contradiction. Did his concern for his individual assemblies with their specific problems, or the variety of exigencies to which the different letters testify, affect his argumentation so much that inconsistency was inevitable? And if so, can we identify a coherent theological core among his deliberations about faith, the law, and salvation? Moreover, how did his successors manage and relate to Paul's heritage? How do *their* interpretations and instructions compare to those of the historical Paul? These are some of the issues addressed in the section "Paul, His Assemblies, and His Successors," p. 399.

In the third study we meet the Johannine Christ followers, whose community formation is corroborated by the Gospel of John and the three Johannine letters. It seems to be a predominantly Jewish community of Christ followers that speaks of God as love and of itself in strongly relational terms as children, loved ones, brothers, siblings, and friends. The Johannine Christ followers pride themselves on their intimacy with Christ, characterizing themselves as sheep who know the shepherd and hear his voice, as indwelled by the Spirit, "the other advocate," who is with them forever. Yet, the community is afflicted and torn apart by divisions and conflicts, explicitly evident in the letters, which has led some to label the Johannine texts as "crisis literature." These and other issues are addressed in the section "Johannine Christ Followers," p. 437.

The fourth study in this chapter zooms in on texts from the first to the early fourth centuries, which describe and promote traditions from Second Temple Judaism but have been preserved only by Christians. Some of these works were probably originally Jewish texts that were later reworked by Christ followers who understood adherence to Jesus within a Jewish matrix. Other texts were composed entirely by Christ followers, who understood adherence to Jesus as being in continuity with Judaism. Some of these texts have traditionally been labeled "Jewish Christian." These and other issues are addressed in the section "Non-Rabbinic Jews and Varieties of Judaism," p. 446.

In the fifth study we meet the so-called Christian Gnostics, namely the Sethians, the school of Valentinus, and the Gospels of Thomas, Mary, and Judas. We ask questions concerning common features among these groups, such as myth and spiritual knowledge. Discussions aim to answer the following questions: Who was Jesus for them and what characterized his disciples? What distinguished the Gnostics from other Christ followers? Can the Gospel of Thomas with most of its content paralleled in the New Testament be labeled a 'gnostic gospel'? These and other issues are elaborated in the section "Gnosticism and the 'Gnostics,'" p. 455.

The sixth study concludes the chapter with a broad outline of the evolution from the diversity of faith and practice in the first century CE to a more uniform mainstream Christianity toward the end of the third century, and its culmination in the formation of Christianity as the official religion of the Roman Empire in the fourth century. The unifying processes that can be traced concern worship practices, congregational structures, scripture, and tradition. How can this development be characterized? Why did these communities from all over the Roman Empire strive toward unity rather than assert their own truths over and against each other? These and other questions are addressed in the section "Diversity and the Struggle for Unity," p. 467.

Jewish Christ Followers and the Emergence of Christianity and Judaism

A Story

Plotius Fortunatus counted himself lucky. After years of lobbying, documented in letters to several prominent Roman citizens, he had finally managed to collect enough money to finance the construction of a monumental building for the Jewish community he was in charge of in the city of Akmonostia. The highly esteemed Julia Severa, who not only organized the games in the city but also occupied the role of high priestess in the local temple, had agreed to donate a large sum of money in order that a house befitting the Jewish residents of the city might be built. Plotius had been competing with a number of other associations for this donation and was now busy with the preparation of various inscriptions that would honor Julia for her donation. Julia had been honored in similar inscriptions by other associations in the city, to which she had also donated money. Plotius and Julia had become good friends during the process, and she had introduced him to various prominent members of her family. These kinds of contacts were of the utmost importance for a leader of a synagogue such as Plotius.

Plotius was a wealthy man, of liberal standing and well integrated in Roman society, as his (Roman) name indicates. His open-mindedness was an important asset for his group, since it meant he was able to balance the different understandings of what it meant to be Jewish present in the assembly. If we take a closer look at the members of this Jewish association, or synagogue, we find there a certain Mindius Faustus, an aging, wealthy man who, despite his Roman name, was quite conservative. After the completion of the synagogue, Mindius donated a beautifully constructed cabinet, or ark, where the Torah rolls were to be kept. Plotius's group, like most other associations, was made up of individuals with diverse backgrounds and understandings of Jewish law. The synagogue was home to a large number of opinions even where the fundamental pillars of Judaism were concerned. A visit to the synagogue on a typical Sabbath would reveal interesting relationships between the members of this group, both Jews and non-Jews.

Mindius's daughter Judith was married to Antony, a young man who had converted to Judaism after having become convinced that Jesus of Nazareth was the Messiah, the one who would bring redemption to Israel and, most importantly for him, peace to the world. Antony's conversion was not only a fundamental part of his idea of what it meant to be a Jesus follower (there were a number of other members of the group who shared his messianic beliefs); it was also necessary in order to keep the peace in the family. Mindius Faustus would never have permitted Antony, as a member of his extended family, to pay homage to the Roman gods, as Nathaniel, a non-Jewish member of the synagogue, did. To worship Roman gods was both natural and necessary for him; it was self-preservation, as he knew that any god, whatever their internal rank in the pantheon, was stronger than any human. In addition, neglecting his duty to pay homage to the gods of the city would anger not only the gods but also his Greco-Roman neighbors, who would fear divine retribution if the gods were not kept happy through appropriate sacrificial rituals. The gods were, after all, protecting the city and should be taken care of; happy gods make for happy people.[1] Indeed, Nathaniel could be suspected of undermining the status quo not only of the city but also of the empire itself. As a Jew, Antony enjoyed the right of the Jewish people to worship the God of Israel only, a right granted them by Rome.

Nathaniel's situation was different from Antony's in several respects. Despite his Jewish name, he was not Jewish. Like his mother and father, he had worshiped the God of Israel for as long as he could remember. They avoided food deemed unclean by Jewish law and listened just as carefully as everybody else to the reading and interpretation of the Holy Scriptures every Sabbath. However, as non-Jewish citizens, they were careful to fulfill their duties toward the city as well. As long as they did this, nobody bothered them or others like them in the city. Nathaniel believed that his situation was very similar to Naaman's in the story of 2 Kgs 5:18. Naaman, who was not an Israelite but a Syrian, also worshiped the God of Israel. But, as the story goes, he also had to bow down to the god Rimmon for political reasons, as he served his master, the king, when he visited the temple. Plotius and the other leaders of the group had no problem with Nathaniel worshiping other gods, and even encouraged him and those like him not to ignore their religio-political obligations to city and empire. If people like Nathaniel no longer found it acceptable to worship the gods of the city, or the emperor, but wanted to pay homage to the God of Israel alone, they were told to convert fully to Judaism, as Antony had done. Preserving the status quo prevented squabbles with the municipality and unwanted attention, even riots, among the other inhabitants of the city. Such riots could easily erupt if an accident or calamity had occurred in the city, as misfortune was often understood as a result of divine indignation.

1. Fredriksen, *Augustine and the Jews*, 4–15.

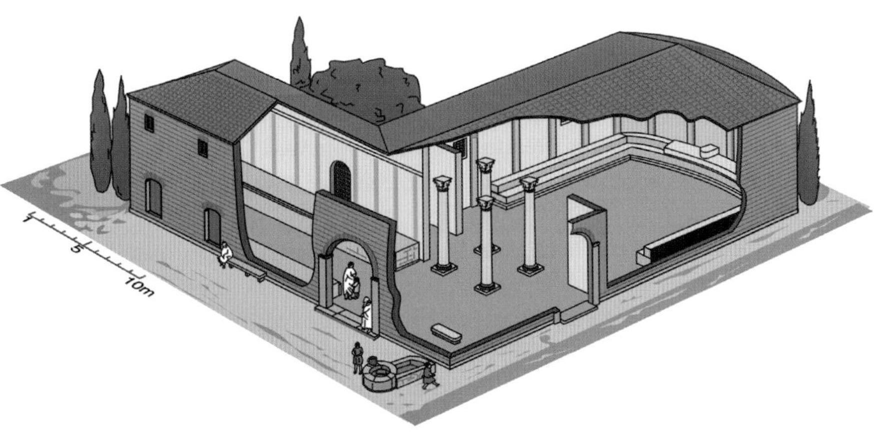

The synagogue in Ostia. Graphical reconstruction by Peter Lönegård, adapted by Dieter Mitternacht based on an archaeological plan by Anders Runesson.

Even a casual conversation with Nathaniel would reveal that he did not have much sympathy for the convictions of the Christ followers. His affinity with the synagogue was based firmly on what he would call the classical Jewish way of life. He could not understand how Jesus, a wandering agitator who had been executed by the empire, could be made to match the role of a messiah. He was also anxious to retain the balance between the Jewish people and the Roman authorities, both in his own city and in the empire as a whole. All this talk about Jesus, the end of the ages, and the coming of a new world order had, in his opinion, no support in the Holy Scriptures and could only mean trouble for anyone living in a world defined by the current empire, Rome.

Many of Nathaniel's acquaintances, among them his neighbors Avita and Mark, had a different opinion. Like Nathaniel, they were non-Jews who lived according to Jewish traditions, but unlike Nathaniel, they believed that Jesus was the Messiah. They longed for the day when he would return, but were anxious not to challenge social structures or disturb the peace until then. They placed a larger emphasis on Jewish ethical teaching than on apocalyptic expectations. They valued the synagogue community and being part of it but did not believe that their faith in Jesus as the Messiah required conversion to Judaism. However, because of the way they understood and interpreted the holy texts, they still kept many of the Jewish laws and customs, in the same way as most other members of this synagogue did. They had done this before they became Christ followers, and they saw no reason why that should change. After all, the Pentateuch is pretty clear that eating pork is forbidden! Because of Nathaniel's, Avita's, and Mark's Jewish lifestyle, it could be difficult for outsiders to determine whether they were Jewish or not, or even which of them was a Christ follower.

Gaius and Flavia, however, cousins of Avita, distinguished themselves clearly from the others. They were convinced that the kingdom of God was near; Jesus would soon return and all of creation would be renewed. They had chosen not to convert to Judaism, because they were convinced that it was God's will that they remain non-Jews. As non-Jewish Christ followers, they even understood themselves to be living proof that the end of the ages was at hand. What did they mean by this? At the end of the ages, they had been taught, non-Jews would flock to Zion, and in their world, Zion meant the Jewish people and the synagogue community. Yet this did not mean that they should convert. If everyone became Jewish, then, by definition, Israel's God could not be the God of the whole world, they reasoned. In other words, if all the nations converted to Judaism, the logical result would be the (theological) conclusion that God cared only for the Jewish people, that God's reach and dominion were limited to one ethnic group. And this is not what it says in the Torah.

Gaius and Flavia associated mostly with Jewish Christ followers, but did not keep the Jewish ritual commandments. Flavia's house, rather than the synagogue, became the place where they, together with other Jewish and non-Jewish followers of Jesus, performed rituals that other Jews would not accept, like the Eucharist. On such occasions, they would meet early on Sunday morning, before the working day began, and their rituals would be accompanied by hymns of praise to Jesus. In addition, they always met with other non-messianic Jews in the Jewish community house, the synagogue, on Sabbaths, where they participated in the discussions following the Scripture readings, often trying to point to evidence for their belief in Jesus as Messiah. In fact, they thought everything in the Hebrew Bible in one way or another should be interpreted in the light of the messianic event. While one of the reasons for them to stay with the synagogue was that their small messianic sub-group could not afford to buy their own copies of the Holy Scriptures, they also hoped to convince others of the truth they themselves saw as evident. Time was running out, and all opportunities to speak about Jesus had to be seized.

Problems started arising, however, when Gaius and Flavia refused to show respect for the deities of the city and the empire. This worried Plotius and the other leaders of the group. Such behavior could not only be interpreted as ungratefulness toward Julia Severa, who deserved respect on account of her donation. It could also be seen as though this Jewish association misled the inhabitants of the city and undermined the safety of the empire. Gods run in the blood; "religion" was an ethnic category.[2] Everyone knew that, and so did the gods. Non-Jews who refused to fulfill their religious duties toward their own people and the deities of their city were a threat to everyone's safety. To make things worse, the messianic movement used terms like

2. Fredriksen, *Augustine and the Jews.*

"savior," "son of god," and "lord" (Gk. *kyrios*) to describe and honor Jesus, titles that were normally reserved for the emperor. As if that wasn't bad enough, they also spread the message that the God of Israel would very soon reforge the world, making everyone and everything subservient to Jesus. Such a movement posed a significant political threat, despite the fact that its members often hastened to deny it.

Tension and division began to emerge in the association. Some argued that the Christ followers should give up their false convictions or else be forced to leave the synagogue. This had happened before in other places, although under different circumstances. The Therapeutae, a Jewish group that had left the Jewish community voluntarily and withdrawn from the world to a life of contemplation, were mentioned as an example of when a parting of the ways was made necessary. Why should not the Christ followers do the same?

Such suggestions frightened Antony, but they scared his wife, Judith, even more, since she did not share his messianic convictions. A division in the synagogue could lead to discord in the family. In addition, Jewish Christ followers could potentially become more vulnerable to critique from authorities, since they could be perceived, through the messianic affiliation, to be connected with non-Jewish Christ followers who refused to worship the gods of the city. In the long run, local rulers and the city's population would hardly care about the difference between Jewish and non-Jewish Jesus followers, if attachment to Jesus was foregrounded as the key identity marker rather than ethnicity; eventually they would all be seen as belonging to the same "superstition." The small-scale persecution against non-Jewish Christ followers that already happened from time to time on account of their refusal to worship the emperor could soon be affecting Jewish followers of Jesus as well. They all had the sense that hard times were coming their way, but many of them were still willing to take their chances. For them, loyalty to Jesus was worth more than life itself.

Mindius Faustus inscription: inscription honoring Mindius Faustus and his family for the torah shrine they donated to the synagogue in Ostia. Photo courtesy of the Photo Archive of the Excavations of Ostia, Ostia Antica Archaeological Park, Rome, Italy.

Because of their unwillingness to convert to Judaism, on the one hand, and their refusal to respect the Roman gods, on the other, Flavia and Gaius found themselves at the center of a storm of irritation and aggression. Some Jewish believers in Jesus joined Nathaniel and Plotius in their criticism of non-Jewish believers such as Flavia and Gaius, and Plotius realized that the line of what could be tolerated would soon be crossed. Unlikely coalitions between subgroups that seemed to have very little in common began to form, united by a "common enemy" more than anything else. The future looked very uncertain, at least in Akmonostia.

The History behind the Story

As the reader has surely pieced together by now, the narrative above is a fictional reconstruction of a situation and a series of developments that may very well have taken place somewhere in the Greco-Roman world around the second half of the first century CE or the early part of the second century. The name of the city, Akmonostia, is a combination of two actual cities: Ostia in Italy and Acmonia in Asia Minor. Plotius, Mindius, and Julia are all historical individuals. Plotius was the leader (*archisynagōgos*) of the synagogue in Ostia during the second half of the first century, and Mindius donated a Torah cabinet, or ark, to the group somewhat later. Julia served as high priestess of the imperial cult in Acmonia in the mid-first century. She was a prominent citizen and donated money for the construction of a synagogue for the Jewish community in her city. The building was later renovated with the help of other donations. These historical figures have been intertwined in the story with fictional characters (Judith, Antony, Nathaniel, Avita, Mark, Gaius, and Flavia), who all represent different factions and relationships that we know existed in diasporic Jewish associations. Indeed, the situation described is based on historical information that can be extracted from sources dating to this time.

So what was the purpose of telling this story? In fact, there were several purposes. First and foremost, the story aims to show the diversity that could exist within synagogue institutions. It is also important to note the sociopolitical implications that the religious convictions of different groups and individuals had. In addition, the relationship between synagogue institutions and Greco-Roman society more generally can help us understand the dynamics behind the scene. What actually happened when members of a synagogue that housed people of divergent convictions interacted with one another? The players in the drama that is the formation of the early Jesus movement did not live in an isolated social vacuum. Jews who did not believe that Jesus was the Messiah (Plotius, Mindius, Judith), the so-called "God-fearing" non-Jewish sympathizers (Nathaniel and his parents), the Jewish Christ followers (Antony, although he was a proselyte), non-Jewish Christ followers who adopted Jewish customs (Avita and Mark), and non-Jewish followers of Jesus who, for theological reasons, refrained from adopting Jewish customs (Gaius and Flavia)—they all related to each other not only as "religious" individuals but also on the basis of a large number of different social, cultural, ethnic, economic, and political factors. They cannot simply be defined according to their specific religious or ideological position;

they were not only Jews, God-fearers, or Christ-fearers;[3] they were also men and women, old and young, rich and poor, part of the workforce and unemployed, slaves and free, politically interested and not, and so on. With Greco-Roman society in all its complexities as the backdrop, we are in a better position to acquire a more comprehensive and nuanced understanding of the processes that led to the formation of Christianity and Judaism as two separate religions. It is not only about theology.

When we pay closer attention to the individual examples in the story above, the question soon arises: "Who exactly were these Jewish Christ followers?" Further, what exactly is Christ-centered Judaism? The impulse to pose two questions instead of just one is, as we shall soon see, justified. The classification "Jewish Christ followers" refers to individuals who identified themselves ethnically as Jews. This category includes proselytes like Antony, since a proselyte had shifted not only what we would call religious but also ethnic identity. "Christ-centered Judaism," on the other hand, refers to the various beliefs and practices that these Jewish Christ followers chose to uphold. Jewish Christ followers could, like all followers of Jesus, entertain divergent ideas about how their convictions should materialize; just because they were Jews did not mean they would all agree on how to embody their loyalty to Jesus. As for non-Jews, they could and often did choose to follow the same customs as non-Christ-following Jews, without converting to Judaism, as the characters Avita and Mark exemplified in our story.

An appropriate definition of Christ-centered Judaism pays special attention to the rites and customs practiced and adhered to by many Jewish Christ followers but also some non-Jewish followers of Jesus. Such practices would emanate from various understandings and interpretations of Jewish law, all of which characterized the Jewish way of life during this time. Such a criterion is sometimes called a praxis-oriented criterion, since it emphasizes embodied practices. Based on the discussion above we shall propose the following working definitions:

With a focus on ethnicity

- *Jewish Christ followers* refers to Christ-following individuals and groups who in different ways, in their own and in other people's eyes, belonged to the Jewish people. This includes proselytes.
- *Non-Jewish, or gentile, Christ followers* refers to Christ-following individuals and groups who were not seen as belonging to the Jewish people, neither in their own eyes nor in the eyes of others.

With a focus on different types of Christ belief (type of religion)

- *Christ-centered Judaism* refers to the kind of Christ affiliation/praxis that in

3. On this term, see Runesson, "Inventing Christian Identity," 73.

different ways emphasized the legitimacy of the Jewish law and its rites and customs, a Jewish way of life, whatever the specific interpretations of what such a life might look like.
- *Non-Jewish Christianity* is defined based on its principled dissociation from Jewish law and the rites, customs, and traditions prescribed by or associated with it. Such dissociation from Jewish tradition could and did take different forms.

If we apply these definitions to the sources to which we have access, we soon discover how important it is to distinguish between ethnic identity and various kinds of beliefs and practices (type of religion). As the fictional scenario above showed, there were many instances when the lines between groups were blurred or difficult to draw, even though most of our early sources indicate that ethnic identity should influence which kind of Christ affiliation a person identified with:

- Both Jews and non-Jews could and did embrace forms of Christ-centered Judaism, even though the majority of those who did were Jewish.
- Both Jews and non-Jews could and did embrace different forms of non-Jewish Christianity, even though the majority of those who did were non-Jews. It is quite likely, however, that the Jews who understood their affiliation with the Christ in this way were much fewer than the non-Jews who wanted to live "Jewishly."

If we imagine the members of Plotius's synagogue being seated separately, gathering according to factions (which is historically unlikely), the diagram in figure 5.1 could be a way of summarizing the above discussion.

It should be noted that our fictional story does not contain all types of Christ affiliation in the first century. For example, Jewish Christ followers who embraced a non-Jewish Christ affiliation are not accounted for in the diagram of figure 5.1. However, in this early period they formed only a marginal group, both in size and influence. Another type of Christ affiliation that has not been included in the diagram is the type of non-Jewish Christ affiliation that explicitly distanced itself from Judaism and Jewish associations. There are a number of reasons for excluding it here. First, there is no clear evidence of this type of Christ affiliation until the beginning of the second century. Second, for obvious reasons, this form of Christ affiliation would not be present in synagogue institutions. We shall explore this form of Christ belief in more detail later in this chapter, when we put the spotlight on Ignatius of Antioch and John Chrysosto.

The boundaries between ethnic identity and religious type were thus fluid rather than set in stone, and yet our sources indicate that the correlation between ethnicity and religion was crucial for many. This situation was not unique to Jews and

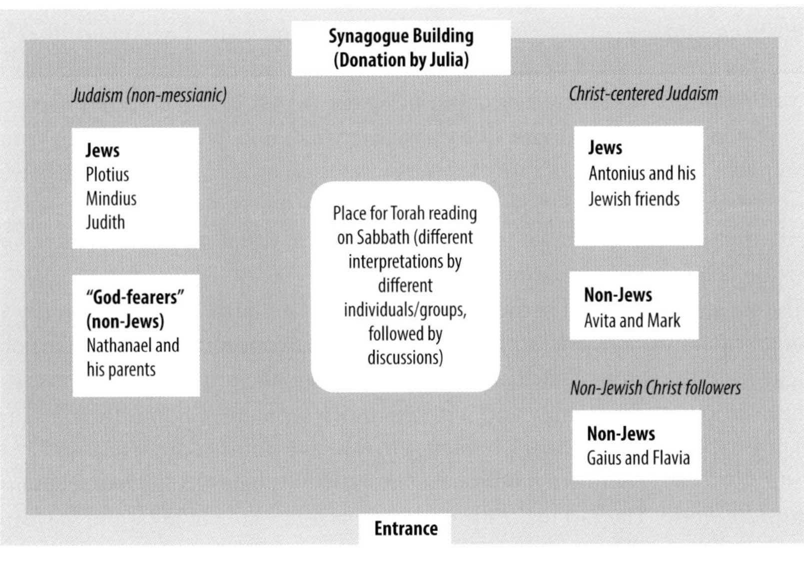

Figure 5.1 Possible groups and subgroups in first-century diaspora Jewish associations/synagogues.

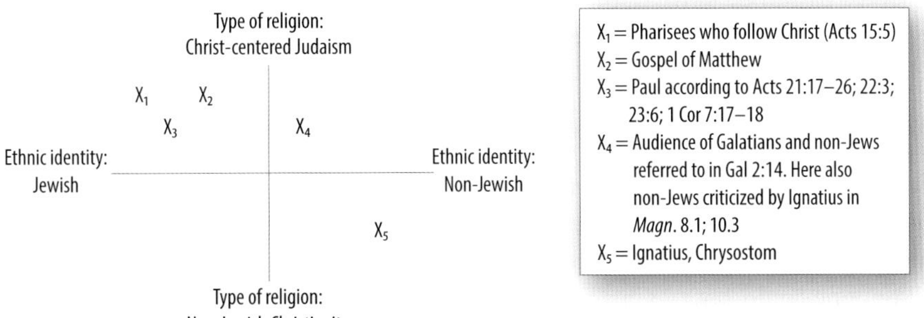

Figure 5.2 Relations between type of religion and ethnic identity: some examples.

non-Jews affiliated with synagogues, whether Christ followers or not. Similar "de-ethnosizing" processes took place in other Greco-Roman and Egyptian cults as well. The cult of Isis is a good example of this, as many non-Egyptians joined this cult around the same time. The key point, however, is that it was precisely the exotic element of a foreign ethnic cult that was attractive to non-Jews and non-Egyptians, respectively. They joined because they were interested in and believed in the power of these non-Roman and non-Greek deities. As for the Christ followers, one may summarize the situation as shown in figure 5.2. (We will discuss the examples brought up in the diagram as we continue our discussion.)

The situation described in the fictional story and in the diagram is obviously very different from how Christianity and Judaism relate to one another today. One of the difficulties in the study of Jewish Christ followers and the process that eventually led to the creation of Christianity and Judaism as two separate religions thus lies in our own presuppositions. We have a tendency to take as a point of departure and anachronistically impose our own modern-day relationships between the two religions on the ancient world. The vast majority of Christians today are not Jews, and the form of Christianity they adhere to is not defined as (a form of) Judaism, neither by Jews nor by Christians. It is therefore easy to fall into the terminological trap of using modern terminology in which Judaism and Christianity are two separate categories. But such discursive habits do not reflect the situation in antiquity. Indeed, the opposite was often true. Around the end of the first century, there were Jewish Christ followers who explicitly argued that Jesus, before his death and resurrection, had forbidden any mission to non-Jews (Matt 10:5–6). Gentile inclusion in the Jesus movement was not at all a given or an obvious wish or aim at this time—far from it. Indeed, even after Jesus's death, when gentile inclusion became desirable for most, there were a lot of debates and disagreements as to how this should be done, and which (Jewish) laws and regulations would apply to them. In Acts 15 we find some of these different suggestions about how to manage gentile inclusion, none of which went on to be accepted as authoritative in the emerging mainstream (non-Jewish) church.

In the beginning of the second century, the situation was, according to *some* Christian authors, reversed. Judaism and Jewish ways of life were seen as incompatible with what was now called, for the first time, "Christianity" (Gk. *Christianismos*). Or, perhaps better, Judaism was understood as the very antithesis of Christianity. Consequently, according to adherents of this type of Christ affiliation, Jewish believers in Jesus should be required to leave their Jewish heritage behind, and instead adopt the traditions and worship style of non-Jewish Christianity. The very definition, one could say, of Christianity was that it was *not* Judaism, in the same way as modern-day Canadians sometimes define themselves as *not* Americans, thereby revealing, unintentionally, how closely connected they are to the nation south of their border. Note the words "*some* Christian authors" above. The consistent anti-Jewishness exhibited by these authors was not representative of all types of Christ affiliation at this time. We have evidence of Christ followers, both Jewish and non-Jewish, who were part of or attracted to Judaism as late as the fifth century. At this time, however, the now Christian empire had begun producing anti-Jewish legislation, which, in the long run, would undermine and counteract such "in-between" positions as Christ-centered Judaism. The theology of the church fathers merged with the legislation of the state.

The non-Jewish definitions of Christianity that eventually became the official position of the mainstream churches took a long time to develop. It was never (and still is not) homogeneous. For a long time, non-Jewish definitions of Christianity stood side by side with other more or less Jewish interpretations and practices, until non-Jewish Christianity eventually gained complete dominance. Christ-centered forms of Judaism more or less disappeared from the historical scene until around the middle of the twentieth century, when various expressions of what is today referred to as messianic Judaism emerged. This early development, which we shall explore further in the next section, can be summarized in a simplified chart (see fig. 5.3).

Box 5.1
Who Was a Jew?

In the ancient world, drawing the line between who was Jewish and who was not was not always a straightforward task (Cohen, 1999). This holds true first and foremost for individuals and groups living at the margins of what the majority defined as Jewish. At the center, however, there have often been rather clear perceptions about who belongs where. This leads us to understand the question "From whose perspective?" as a central issue when discussing Jewish identity. In antiquity, in particular during the first century, we find several Jewish groups who identified themselves as Jews but who did not always accept the legitimacy of other Jewish groups claiming the same self-definition. We also have to take the Roman authorities into consideration, since it was important for them for several political reasons to distinguish between Jews and non-Jews. Jews had the right to be exempted from worshiping Greco-Roman gods, including deified emperors, whereas non-Jews were obligated to pay homage to both the gods of their city and to the emperor.

How did this process come about, and why did it take the direction it did? How can we explain the peculiar historical circumstance that a Jewish movement was "appropriated" by non-Jews, who then aggressively turned against Jews, both Christ followers and others? Who were the Christ-following Jews, really? And what role did the Christianization of the Roman Empire play in the emergence of rabbinic

Judaism and the disappearance of Christ-centered Judaism? The following sections are divided into two chronologically organized parts. The first, "From Jesus to the Acts of the Apostles," will deal with the first century, and the next, "Ignatius, Justin Martyr, and Chrysostom: From 'Synagogue' to 'Church,'" will focus on the period from the second to the fourth centuries and include some notes about the fifth to sixth centuries. We will conclude with a summary and some reflections.

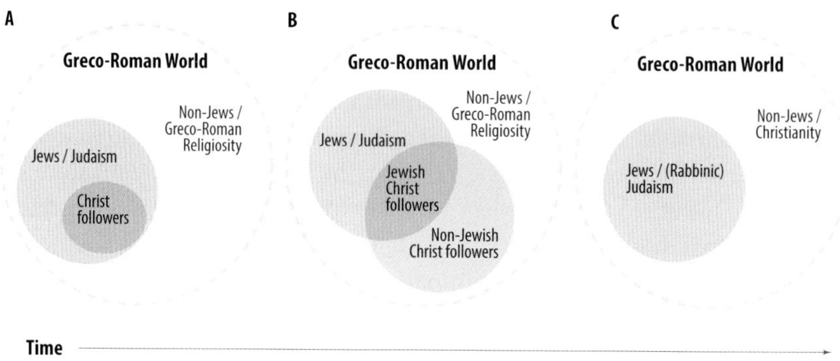

Figure 5.3 From Christ-centered Judaism to non-Jewish Christianity: three basic phases during the first five hundred to six hundred years.

From Jesus to the Acts of the Apostles

The Problem of Non-Jews in the Jesus Movement

It is not uncommon for secondary literature to describe the key issue in the Jesus movement of the first century as trying to solve "the place of the Jews in Christianity." Defining the problem in this way, however, means turning reality on its head, as the primary sources from this time are quite clear that the real question in the early Jesus movement was how to accommodate *gentiles* into the movement. The first definition of the problem illustrates what happens when we interpret the situation anachronistically, taking as the point of departure the third or fourth century (or even our own time) and then applying this to the first century. In the first century the real problem was that, a couple of decades after Jesus's death, different (Jewish Christ-following) groups were quite divided on what role gentiles should play within their movement. The sources reveal that the issue was a subject of debate at the highest levels.

Many scholars attribute the uncertainty regarding the place of non-Jews in the early Jesus movement to the fact that Jesus himself never saw his mission as extending beyond the Jewish people (see Matt 10:5–6). Had he done so, the early church would have had a pattern to follow, a tradition, and there would have been more unity and agreement on the question of how this issue should be handled. It seems clear, however, that Jesus interacted with a number of non-Jews during his lifetime, even though he never actively reached out to them. The texts of the New Testament agree that Jesus did not turn away such individuals, except in one case when he tried to resist dealing with a gentile help-seeking woman but was defeated by her in a verbal duel (Mark 7:24–30//Matt 15:21–28). It is equally clear that Jesus did not request that the non-Jews who approached him should become proselytes (that is, convert to Judaism, the religio-ethnic group he himself belonged to). It was enough for them to express their trust in him and his ability to help them. Jesus seems to have upheld a distinction that was, for him, important between Jew and non-Jew, but this did not mean that non-Jews could not receive a share of the blessings of the world to come. This view of Jews and non-Jews can be found also among other Jewish groups at that time: belonging to the Jewish people was not understood as a requirement for admittance into the kingdom of God, even though certain (ethical) behavior was understood as important for non-Jews just as much as for Jews. This gave rise to the theological notion of "righteous gentiles," which is common also in modern forms of Judaism.

Jesus, then, was securely anchored within the Judaism of his time, and the Jesus movement was one of many Jewish movements during the Second Temple period (see ch. 2 for more information on Judaism at this time). The followers of Jesus who were eagerly awaiting the coming of the kingdom were Jews, but they were joined by a small number of non-Jews who placed their hopes in the power of the resurrected Jesus.

It is important to remember that these non-Jews did not accompany Jesus during his lifetime (see Mark 5:18–20//Matt 8:33–34//Luke 8:37–39); they were thus not part of the movement as such at that time. It is not clear exactly what happened in this regard after the death of Jesus. What we can say with a large degree of certainty, however, is that the number of non-Jews who decided to follow Jesus increased significantly and at some speed. This was a direct result of the mission carried out by Jewish Christ followers (Paul being the best known of them), and later also by those non-Jews who had joined them. Thus, we can trace the development of mission from an initially centripetal one, where non-Jews sought out Jesus (albeit in limited numbers), to a centrifugal movement in which Jews actively reached out to non-Jews. This development can be observed in the Gospels; indeed, both movements are represented in the Gospel of Matthew (compare Matt 10:5–6/15:21–28 with 28:19–20).

Two questions arise. First, *why* was this Jewish mission to non-Jews initiated? It was not an obvious development for a Jewish group. Second, what were the consequences of the success this mission enjoyed, that is, how did the various factions of Jewish Christ followers view the incorporation of non-Jews into their movements? There were many different opinions about this controversial matter, despite the fact that a consensus was attempted already in the 50s CE. Let us begin by analyzing the first question.

Eschatology and Mission

The idea that a messiah would come and inaugurate a new age was a common belief among Jews in the Second Temple period. At that time Israel would be liberated from its colonial oppressors and reestablished as a sovereign kingdom (cf. Acts 1:6–7); sin would be eradicated, and righteousness would become a universal reality. Such a transformation would affect not only Israel but also the rest of the world. The coming of the Messiah would mean a fundamental change not only for Israel but also for the entire world (cf. Isa 42:1–13; 49:1–7). Different Jewish groups took different positions on this, appealing to support from a variety of traditions contained within Scripture. Sometimes there is even evidence of more than one type of tradition within one and the same text, or collection of texts. Some groups looked forward to the annihilation of their oppressors (see Isa 61:5; 63:1–6), while others believed that the righteous individuals among the nations would be saved along with Israel and share in the blessings of the world to come (e.g., Isa 56:1–8; contrasting the pattern of thought expressed in Deut 23:1–8). There were also people who believed that when the end of the ages had come, missionaries should be sent out to the nations, explaining what had transpired or was about to happen and proclaiming "the glory of God." The pattern of thought in such texts expressed hope that the result of this mission would be that the nations would abandon their old gods and flock to Zion in order to worship the God of Israel (cf. Isa 66:12–24).

Thus, a focus on the Jewish people did not exclude the idea of salvation for those outside this people group or *ethnos*. In fact, the reverse could be asserted: the salvation of Israel was a prerequisite for the salvation of the world. Certain Jewish groups of this era, such as the Pharisees, connected these eschatological ideas with the idea of the resurrection of the dead. As the end of the ages approached, the dead would be resurrected and then judged together with the living by God. Other groups, such as the Sadducees, denounced the idea of resurrection, but both Jesus and his followers joined the Pharisees in this matter (see Acts 23:6–8). A few days after his execution and burial, those who had believed Jesus to be the Messiah became convinced that Israel's God had resurrected him from the dead. Several individuals claimed to have met or spoken with the risen Jesus. In the Gospels, this development is portrayed as completely unexpected, even for those who belonged to Jesus's inner circle of disciples.

In all probability, Jesus's followers believed him to be the Messiah during his lifetime, the one who was to reestablish Israel and bring righteousness to the world. Jesus's entry into Jerusalem during Passover, the festival of liberation from slavery, was carefully planned, and most of his followers were in all likelihood convinced that the entry would trigger some sort of miraculous intervention from God; a disruption of the status quo that would do away with the religio-political elite and establish Jesus as king of Israel. The disappointment and disillusionment of the disciples when Jesus was arrested and executed indicate that the dreams of Peter, John, and James were also killed on the cross. Jesus's death seemed to confirm that the end of the ages had in fact not come, and that the promise of liberation remained unfulfilled.

The belief that Jesus had risen from the dead changed all of that. (Historical scholarship cannot solve the issue of whether Jesus was resurrected or not, but can study the social, political, and other effects of this belief. For discussion of this, see chapter 3 above.) In the theological world of the first Jesus followers, Jesus's resurrection marked the beginning of the end of the ages. The proclamation that Jesus had risen from the dead was, as far as we know, from early on seen as the first step toward Israel's God's ultimate victory: the establishment of God's kingdom with Jesus as its king. Within the span of a week, the disciples had gone from hope to despair, from the belief that God's Messiah would soon reestablish Israel to the dismayed realization that they had been wrong—after which they again became convinced that their initial hope was to be realized after all, albeit in a way no one could have predicted. Thus, the resurrection did not initially have much to do with immortality, as later Western tradition has so often understood it. Rather, the resurrection was seen as part of the eschatological expectation that anticipated the coming of the kingdom of God. That the soul continued to exist after death, albeit in Hades (or, as in the Hebrew Bible, Sheol), was already a common belief at this time among most people in the Mediterranean world, including the Jews. What the Jesus movement now claimed, however, was that a person could be released from Hades; indeed that one person, Jesus, had already left the realm of the dead, and that this process was part of a new world order. Jesus was the first to be resurrected, but others would follow. (For Paul's understanding of this anticipated sequence of events, see 1 Cor 15:17–28, 35–56.)

It is at this point that the tradition about non-Jews flocking to Zion to worship the God of Israel becomes relevant for the Jesus movement. During Jesus's lifetime, these types of references to such traditions for making sense of the Jesus event could hardly have been possible, since the basic belief was that the Messiah would first be crowned king of Israel *and then* be recognized by the world. Jesus's death on the cross put an end to such speculation, but the belief in his resurrection promptly brought it to life again, albeit in a way no one had predicted. The unfolding mission to both Jews and non-Jews produced results, but theologically the mission to non-Jews became more important to the early Jesus movement, precisely for this reason. When non-Jews began joining the movement, they confirmed to the original Jewish members that they were in fact right in their beliefs. The end of the ages had indeed come; everything they had hoped for would soon be fulfilled. The social-psychological effects of such very concrete "evidence," confirming a fundamental aspect of a theological worldview, should not be underestimated. What Isa 66:19–21 spoke about, they were doing, and the response was—to them—exactly what the prophet had predicted (see Rom 12:1; 15:16).

Non-Jewish Christ Followers: Three Ancient Solutions

The reaction from other Jewish groups, in particular the religio-political leadership, was rarely positive. The latter were attempting to balance between the demands and privileges of Rome on the one hand, and the needs of the people, burdened by taxes, on the other. All this talk of resurrection was almost as dangerous as a rebel leader claiming a throne in Jerusalem (see John 11:48–50). It is not surprising at all, in fact, that these leaders attempted to repress this sort of messianic fervor, which even attracted a following among non-Jews, not only in Israel, but also in the diaspora. The first Jewish Christ followers were thus in a tight spot, fearing the very real possibility of repression by the Jewish political leadership, which realized the political danger these messianics posed to occupied Judea.

Among the Jews who joined the Jesus movement, including Pharisees who saw Jesus's resurrection as confirmation of their belief in the resurrection (cf. Acts 23:6–9), we find different views on how non-Jews should be incorporated. Most were convinced *that* a mission to non-Jews was necessary, even essential, but there was less agreement about *how* exactly they should be included in the movement. This leads us to the second question we asked above: the "how" question. Jesus himself had not left any clear instructions on this matter. With some simplification, we could say that there were three main solutions to the gentile problem in the second half of the first century. All of them can be found in the New Testament, but none of them would be accepted by the type of Christianity that, much later, would become the religion of the Roman Empire.

The first solution was that non-Jews who wished to be incorporated into the Jesus movement should also be fully incorporated into the Jewish *ethnos*, which was interpreted as a full conversion to Judaism (which necessitated circumcision for men). The non-Jewish Christ followers would, in this scenario, become Jewish Christ followers. In Acts 15:5 this solution is linked to the members of the Jesus movement who belonged to the party of the Pharisees (cf. Gal 5:2–3). In modern terms, one could call this solution *unity in uniformity*. If we refer to the fictional story in the introduction to this chapter, Antony represents this approach.

The meeting of the apostles in Jerusalem came to a different conclusion, however. Instead of speaking in terms of homogeneity, they began to formulate a new way of being a Christ follower that was applicable only to non-Jews. Those who were not Jewish should remain (ethnically) non-Jewish, they decided, and would only be required to keep a minimum of four specific laws, of which three were ritual in nature and one was what we would call ethical (Acts 15:19–20). The point of departure for this alternative was that Jewish Christ followers would continue to keep the law in its entirety, as interpreted by Jesus, and in this way maintain their Jewish identity (see Acts 15:21; 21:17–27; cf. Matt 5:17–19). According to this solution, which we can call *unity in diversity*, non-Jews were dependent on the existence of Jewish Christ followers, who made up the theological and socioreligious core of the movement. The focus was on Jerusalem, rather than Rome, the latter eventually becoming the center for the type of Christianity adopted by the empire. This solution comes close to the example of Gaius and Flavia in our story, the only difference being that these two characters did not understand it to be necessary to keep the three ritual laws. Avita and Mark, however, kept more than the four laws prescribed in Acts and are therefore a less suitable example here; their lifestyle rather weakened the boundaries between Jewish and non-Jewish ways of life.

The third solution is represented by Paul. Here, as in the second solution, the focus is still on Jewish Christ followers, and the vision represents a further development of the *unity in diversity* theme. The solution differs from the one in Acts 15 in that it rejects the idea that non-Jews should strive to keep even a small section of the law. The core of this vision is Paul's belief that the God of Israel is the God of the entire world, not just of the Jews (Rom 3:28–31). If non-Jews were to become Jews, and thus keep the Jewish law when they joined the Jesus movement, that would undermine this fundamental principle; everyone would become Jews, and thus God would be God of the Jewish people only. This would contradict the Holy Scriptures (the Hebrew Bible), in which God is described as the God of the entire world (see, among others, the references to Isaiah made in the preceding section; we can also find similar statements frequently in the book of Psalms). In our story, Gaius and Flavia represent Paul's solution. Avita and Mark, however, represent the group that Paul forcefully argues against, especially in Galatians.

According to several passages by and about Paul, he believed, like the apostles at the Jerusalem meeting in Acts 15, that Jewish Christ followers should remain Jewish. The logic must go both ways in order to make sense. If Jewish Christ followers ceased to be Jews, then the God of Israel would not be the God of the whole world, but only the God of the non-Jewish world (see 1 Cor 7:17–24; Gal 5:3; Acts 21:17–26; 22:3; 23:6). In Rom 9–11 we find Paul's most clearly formulated theology of Jews and non-Jews in the movement, but also, with regard to the Jewish people, outside the movement. Paul describes the Jewish people as a cultivated olive tree. A wild olive branch, an image of gentile Christ followers, has been grafted onto this tree. In this way, the wild olive branch is nurtured by and dependent on the cultivated olive tree (Rom 11:17). The non-Jewish Christ followers, according to this theology, have no way of sustaining themselves but would be lost without the nutrition provided for them through the Jewish Christ followers, who are firmly anchored and sustained, in turn, by the roots of the tree, that is, the patriarchs (Abraham, Isaac, and Jacob): "it is not you that support the root, but the root that supports you" (Rom 11:18).

Romans 9–11 represents the first "defense" in literature written by followers of Jesus of Jews who did not join the Jesus movement. After much anxiety and sorrow (Rom 9:1–5) over the fact that the majority of Jews did not accept Jesus as the Messiah, and thus did not agree that the end of the ages had come, Paul then turns what actually is into a theological necessity. He argues that their declining of the offer to join the Jesus movement was planned by God; they cannot but act as they do (11:25). The Jewish Christ followers (Paul himself being among them) now play a vital eschatological role, but this does not mean that non-Christ-following Jews had lost their status as God's people. They remain Israel, and they are loved by God, just as they have been since their election; "the gifts and the calling of God are irrevocable" (11:28–29). When non-Jews have joined the worship of the God of Israel through Jesus Christ, in their "full number," "all Israel will be saved" (11:25–26). It seems that Paul's defense of the Jewish people—not only of Jewish Christ followers but of all Jews—was motivated by a growing resentment among non-Jewish Christ followers against Jewish ways of being, a sense of superiority over against the Jews (11:18, 20–22). Paul saw or had heard of these first signs of primitive anti-Jewish tendencies and wished, it seems, to quench any such developments before they became interwoven with the very fabric of the theology of the movement. Sadly, he failed, and it took until the mid-1900s and the Second Vatican Council until the church would begin to realize its mistake in this regard.[4]

Retaining Jewish Identity in Christ

The debate about the place of non-Jews in the Jesus movement reveals a number of important and interesting things about Jewish affiliation to Christ. The first thing to note is that there was no theological or praxis-oriented homogeneity among the Jewish followers of Jesus at this time. What bound the group together was their Jewish identity, which had its foundation in a sense of ethno-religious and cultural belonging. This sense of shared identity is what kept them together as a larger group and provided the context within which they discussed issues such as gentile followers of Jesus and the validity of the Jewish law. With regard to both gentiles and the law, these Jewish Christ followers could and did differ in opinion (see, for example, Acts 21:20–22; Gal 2:1–6, 11–14). The vast majority of Jewish believers in Jesus seem to have understood their faith in Jesus as fully compatible with and confirming the law of Moses. Indeed, the law was, together with trust in Jesus as the Messiah, the cornerstone of their religious identity (see Rom 3:31; Matt 5:17–19; 23:23; 24:20; Luke 23:56; Acts 21:20). Within this foundational conviction of the importance of Jewish law, we can then observe a diversity of opinion in terms of *how* the law should be interpreted. Among these interpretations, Paul's is one of the more complex.

Jewish Christ followers, like other Jews, attended the public or civic synagogues in the land of Israel, but were also present in many Jewish associations ("synagogues") in the diaspora. (For a definition of what a "synagogue" was in the first century, as

4. See Stendahl, *Final Account*. See also the next section of ch. 5 in this volume for a more detailed discussion of Paul's theology and developments of the Pauline tradition after Paul's death.

well as a description of different kinds of synagogues, see box 2.4, p. 73). At the same time, and as a result of such shared institutional contexts, we see many examples in the primary sources of debates and conflicts between Jewish Christ followers and other Jews. These conflicts sometimes resulted in Jewish Christ followers, who had belonged to a specific Jewish association ("synagogue," e.g., the synagogue of the Pharisees), breaking with or being expelled from these associations.[5] Being expelled or breaking away from association synagogues did not mean that the person or group in question ceased to be viewed as Jewish. Other Jews still understood them as Jewish, albeit with a flawed understanding of Judaism, and this also continued to be their self-understanding. Such examples are thus not indications of a parting of the ways between "Judaism" and "Christianity," but rather evidence of a parting process *within* Judaism.

Such partings were not uncommon in Judaism at that time, even as unrelated to Christ followers. For example, in some of the sectarian Dead Sea Scrolls, other Jews, who did not belong to the Scroll writers' group, are condemned in no uncertain terms. The process, and some of the rhetoric, is similar to that of the Christ groups, but no one would suggest that the sectarians at Qumran were not Jews, or that they had "parted from Judaism."

Scholars have often asserted that it was Christology—the Jewish Christ followers' faith in Christ—that set the Jesus movement apart from "Judaism" and made it "un-Jewish." This is, however, an unsustainable position, influenced rather by later, modern criteria deciding the difference between Christianity and Judaism. (Today, Christology is indeed the key issue separating between these religions.) In and around the time of Jesus, there are several examples of messianic claimants. Adherence to such a figure would have been an expression of a strong Jewish identity rather than a lack thereof. One of these messianic examples comes from the first half of the second century CE—that is, before rabbinic Judaism had come to define, normatively, what Judaism should be. A famous rabbi, Rabbi Akiva, at that time placed his hope in a certain Bar Kokhba, believing him to be the messiah who was to defeat the Romans and reestablish Israel as a nation. The reaction to his decision was not always positive within the rabbinic movement, despite the fact that both Akiva and Bar Kokhba had many followers. However, no one considered excluding him from the rabbinic fold based on his declared position on this matter, and no one understood his thinking to be un-Jewish. Other examples of messianic figures were more of the prophetic or even priestly kind. In the case of Jewish Christ followers, there is a lot of evidence of conflict with non-Christ-following Jews, but, just as was the case with Rabbi Akiva, this did not mean that those followers of Jesus were considered un-Jewish, not even

5. Runesson, "Inventing Christian Identity," argues that this was likely the case with the author of the Gospel of Matthew, breaking away from the larger Pharisaic community, but see also John 9:22; 12:42; 16:2.

by those outside the Jewish people (see Acts 18:15–16). Indeed, not even the claim that Jesus was resurrected, or that he was the son of God, can really be explained if it is not understood as an expression of Judaism.

During the first years following the death of Jesus, we have examples of Jewish Christ followers who were located *within* already-existent Jewish groups. The Pharisees are an interesting group to study in this regard, since some pharisees joined the Jesus movement without ceasing to identify as Pharisees (see, for example, Acts 15:5). Thus, we can speak of Pharisaic Christ followers, who presumably continued to affiliate themselves with Pharisaic association synagogues after they decided to accept Jesus as the Messiah, in a way similar to Rabbi Akiva continuing to identify as someone within the rabbinic movement some decades later, even after endorsing Bar Kochba as the messiah. Not only did acceptance of Jesus as the Messiah not mean parting with "Judaism"; it did not necessarily mean even parting with a special group identity within Judaism. This may explain some of the diversity within the Jesus movement, even early on in its history.

Jewish Christ followers who did not already belong to an association also began organizing themselves into smaller Christ groups, so that we see the rise of local Christ groups that formed exclusively on the basis of their messianic convictions. At the same time, a leadership structure was beginning to form in Jerusalem, which was independent from other Jewish associations, headed by Peter, James, and John. This messianic-Jewish leadership functioned as a unifying force among Christ followers from different backgrounds, even though its power was in all likelihood limited and also at times challenged. (See Gal 2:1–10, where Paul's rhetoric implies that the Jerusalem group had a very real position of authority, even while the way he phrases his sentences seems to relativize this very authority. In Acts the Jerusalem group is more obviously the unquestioned center of the Jesus movement.)

Over time, the division between Jewish Christ followers and other Jews grew deeper, so that Christ followers were eventually either expelled or voluntarily left these association synagogues. This led to the formation of association synagogues organized by and for Christ followers, institutions in which they themselves set the rules. We can follow this drawn-out and complicated development, which occurred during different times in different places, in several New Testament texts, especially Acts (e.g., 19:8–9) and Matthew, two texts written toward the end of the first century (Acts possibly written in the early second century). Two important factors triggering this development were the eschatological expectations of the Christ followers, which may have been seen as threatening the social and political status quo, and their emphasis on mission to non-Jews and the way in which non-Jews were incorporated into the Jesus movement. In their own association synagogues, Christ followers were free to formulate the rules of membership themselves, as all associations did, without having to take the opinions of non-Christ-following Jews into consideration.

During this early period—the first century—we can thus observe that Jewish

Christ followers from different backgrounds and interpretative traditions were involved in various conflicts with other, non-Christ-following Jews, but also with the Jewish religio-political, civic leadership. The causes of these conflicts were both what we would call religious and political, since religion and politics were two sides of the same coin in antiquity. Despite these conflicts, Jewish followers of Jesus were firmly embedded within Judaism; it is precisely the conflicts with other Jews that are evidence of this. It was the proximity of Christ-following Jews and other Jews that fed these conflicts and led to schisms. It is important to keep in mind that a Jewish Christ-following group that went through a split with another Jewish group did not for that reason cease to be identified as Jewish. As historians, we have to be careful about the assumptions we bring to the ancient evidence with regard to what it meant to be Jewish and live according to a Jewish lifestyle in the first century and onward. During the first century, we still find ourselves within category A in figure 5.3, even though the development toward category B does begin to take shape already at this time.

When the first century gives way to the second, there are a number of very interesting developments that merit our attention. These developments have to do with the fact that non-Jewish voices begin to dominate within some parts of the Jesus movement. In the first century, Christ-following Jews and non-Jews moved relatively freely between the more public synagogues and their own associations, but toward the beginning of the second century, we encounter several non-Jewish Christ followers who openly criticize this practice, claiming that their own way of being a Christ follower should be universalized and practiced by all, even Jewish followers of Jesus. Here we see, for the first time, a very real attempt at distancing a belief in Jesus as the Christ from Judaism and Jewish ways of life.

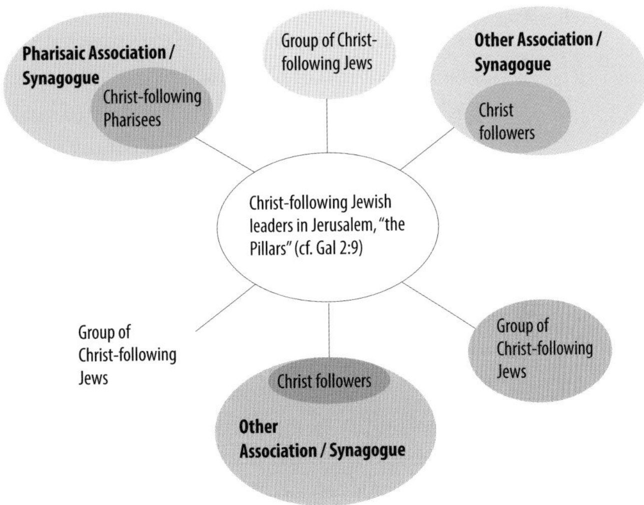

Figure 5.4. Groups of Jewish Christ followers. The different colors of the boxes signal the diversity of these Jewish groups, which is then reflected in the diversity among the followers of Jesus. The diversity of first-century Judaism is thus reflected in the diversity of first-century (and later) Christ groups, but all of this takes place within Judaism, which functions as an umbrella term for these different ways of being Jewish (cf. fig. 5.3 above, phase A). Note that, while challenged by some groups of Christ followers, the centrality, or authority, of the Jerusalem group extended beyond the land of Israel, as we see both in Paul's letters and in Acts.

Ignatius, Justin Martyr, and Chrysostom: From "Synagogue" to "Church"

From the beginning of the second century, non-Jews began to gain prominence within the Jesus movement, organizing themselves apart from Jewish Christ followers, sometimes explicitly excluding variants of Christ-centered Judaism. The reasons behind this development were likely linked to social-psychological and sociological factors, but in the texts the justifications for this development are presented as theological. The theological model—with institutional implications—that Paul and others had outlined formed a movement with Jewish Christ followers at the center and gentile Christ followers attached to them. As Paul wrote in Rom 11, it was not the gentiles in the movement who supported the root but the root, that is, the Jews, who supported them. Now strong non-Jewish leaders began to emerge, claiming non-Jewish ways of being a follower of Jesus as the only universally legitimate ways. These were ways that no longer orbited Jewish forms of Christ belief. In these settings, Christ-centered Judaism thus no longer functioned as a theological and socio-institutional centripetal force.

In what can be described as a hermeneutical adventure, driven by a vision of *unity through uniformity*, Paul's texts were reread and reinterpreted to support this non-Jewish form of Christ following. It is in such contexts that we see the beginnings of what became Christianity. Because of such readings, Paul became increasingly important and revered in groups run by gentiles, which led to many Jewish Christ followers distancing themselves from his teachings.[6] The Jewish law, ancestral customs, and rituals were now interpreted as being unnecessary or even invalid and superseded not only for gentiles but also for Jews. The "Christian" identity was proclaimed to be one and the same for all Christ followers: "law-free" and independent of Jewish ethno-religious identity.

In this process, which led to considerable conflict among Christ followers, we even find non-Jewish Christians discussing whether Jewish Christ followers are beyond salvation. Many decided not to associate with them at all. One of the last texts we have access to that displays more of a spirit of compromise was written by Justin Martyr, a non-Jewish apologist who lived around the middle of the second century. In his *Dialogue with Trypho*, he distances himself from non-Jewish Christians who refuse to associate with Jewish Christ followers. He further declares that he believes that Jewish followers of Jesus can, *despite* keeping the Mosaic law, attain salvation (ch. 47). It is, however, very clear that Justin views these Christ-following Jews as weak, as a kind of second-class Christians, because they understand the Jewish law as important and legitimate. In Justin's writings we encounter a clear anti-Jewish triumphalism, albeit at times tempered by a certain level of openness to the idea of unity in diversity. Here is an excerpt from the relevant passage:

6. Lüdemann, *Opposition to Paul in Jewish Christianity*.

> **Trypho**: "But," Trypho again objected, "if a man knows that what you say is true, and, professing Jesus to be the Christ, believes in and obeys Him, yet desires also to observe the commandments of the Mosaic Law, shall he be saved?"
>
> **Justin**: "In my opinion," I replied, "I say such a man will be saved, unless he exerts every effort to influence other men (I have in mind the Gentiles whom Christ circumcised from all error) to practice the same rites as himself, informing them that they cannot be saved unless they do so. You yourself did this at the opening of our discussion, when you said that I would not be saved unless I kept the Mosaic precepts."
>
> **Trypho**: "But why," pressed Trypho, "did you say, 'In my opinion such a man will be saved?' There must, therefore, be other Christians who hold a different opinion."
>
> **Justin**: "Yes, Trypho," I conceded, "there are some Christians who boldly refuse to have conversations or meals with such persons. I don't agree with such Christians. But if some [Jewish converts], due to their instability of will, desire to observe as many of the Mosaic precepts as possible—precepts which we think were instituted because of your hardness of heart—while at the same time they place their hope in Christ, and if they desire to perform the eternal and natural acts of justice and piety, yet wish to live with us Christians and believers, as I already stated, not persuading them to be circumcised like themselves or to keep the Sabbath, or to perform any other similar acts, then it is my opinion that we Christians should receive them and associate with them in every way as kinsmen and brethren." (*Dial.* 47 [Falls])

Even before Justin wrote his apologetic works, we have evidence of an even more radical anti-Jewish understanding of what a Christ follower should be or do. In the beginning of the second century,[7] Ignatius, bishop of Antioch in Syria, argued that "Christianity" (Gk. *Christianismos*; this is the first evidence we have of this term in the Greek language) was the antithesis of "Judaism" (Gk. *Ioudaismos*). In letters penned by him to different Christ groups as he was on his way to be martyred in Rome, it becomes clear that he views the two as separate traditions. The truth of the one, Christianity, required the delegitimizing of the other, Judaism. It is therefore, according to Ignatius, impossible to merge Judaism and Christianity into what we would call Christ-centered Judaism. Christianity comes in one form only, the non-Jewish form, and anyone who wants to be a part of it, regardless of ethnic background, has to accept this form. "It is outlandish to proclaim Jesus Christ and

7. The dating of Ignatius's letters is complicated; some scholars suggest a much later date for their production.

practice Judaism, for Christianity did not believe in Judaism but Judaism in Christianity—in which every tongue that believes in God has been gathered together" (Ign. *Magn.* 10.3).[8] This is the type of Christianity that became dominant in the later mainstream church. And it is this form of Christianity that became the state religion of the Roman Empire toward the end of the fourth century under Emperor Theodosius I. It is therefore noteworthy that it is precisely followers of Jesus such as Ignatius and Justin who were executed by the Roman authorities. How can we explain such a development?

The Persecution of Non-Jewish Christ Followers: Causes

The persecution of Christ followers was mostly local, but on some rare occasions it took place on a larger scale, ordered by the emperor. The details around this are quite complex, and a full description is not possible here. A larger pattern is discernible, however. Jews were often well integrated in Greco-Roman society, and Roman legislation allowed Jewish ancestral customs to be practiced within the empire. The first-century Jewish historian Josephus did report several occasions when local rioters attacked Jews. On such occasions, however, the Jews could write to Roman authorities to protest, and the authorities would respond by restating and reinforcing Jewish rights. The Jewish author Philo, a contemporary with Jesus, reported similar cases. One of the reasons for local outbreaks of anti-Jewish riots was surely that Jews refused to worship gods other than the God of Israel, and that such refusal was seen as "atheism." Atheism implied disrespecting the local Greco-Roman gods as well as the emperor, who protected both the city and the empire. Not honoring these gods could be interpreted as treason or, at the very least, as exposing the city to the significant danger that could follow when gods were displeased.

Following Jewish customs without being ethnically Jewish was considered by many to be deeply problematic, even, according to some belonging to the elite, treasonous. According to the Roman author Dio Cassius (67.14.1–3; 68.2), such behavior sometimes resulted in executions. There were examples of this under Emperor Domitian (r. 81–96 CE), who considered non-Jews following Jewish customs to be equivalent to the crime of *asebeia* (impiousness, ungodliness). Distinguished Roman citizens, like Flavius Clemens and his wife Domitilla, lost their lives (Flavius Clemens) or were exiled (Domitilla) as a consequence of their adherence to Jewish customs. It was thus not only the Jews who attached great significance to the connection between ethnic belonging and religious praxis, as we have also discussed above. This has to do with the fact that people in antiquity did not define "religion" the way we do today. Rather, in antiquity, religion, politics, ethnicity, and national loyalty were all intertwined.

8. Ehrman, *Apostolic Fathers*, vol. 1.

As long as Christ followers were associated with Jews within the context of Jewish associations ("synagogues"), they were safer than if they were exposed as non-Jews who refused to pay homage to the gods. Thus, Ignatius, Justin, and the growing number of non-Jews who distanced themselves from the Jewish people put themselves in a politically difficult and potentially dangerous situation. Not only did they worship a man who had been executed by the Roman imperial authorities in Judea; they now began to be visible as a special breed of cultic association, dedicated to the exclusive worship of a foreign Eastern god.

In the letters of Pliny the Younger to Emperor Trajan (r. 98–117 CE), we can see how (non-Jewish) Christians were on their way to becoming criminalized. To be a Christian became associated, through the spreading of rumors, with a number of horrific crimes, like cannibalism, crimes that then constituted the basis for the accusations against them as criminals. This led to a situation in which being a Christian in and of itself became a crime, regardless of other accusations. This Roman attitude toward Christianity was directed toward non-Jewish Christ followers, as long as a distinction could be made between them and Jewish followers of Jesus. Being Jewish, regardless of which version of Judaism was practiced, was not a crime (cf. Acts 18:12–16). An accusation against a Jew, Christ follower or not, required further evidence of a crime having actually been committed.

Anti-Jewish Replacement Theology as a Defense Mechanism

In a situation like the one described above, it became important for non-Jewish Christ followers to gain acceptance from the local and imperial authorities. There are two patterns discernible in the ancient sources in this regard. The first of these consisted of attempts to prove that (non-Jewish) Christianity was in fact *not* a new religion but could be traced all the way back to the prophets, and even to Abraham, the claim being that Christianity stood in continuity with ancient Israelite tradition. Christians had replaced Jews as the heirs of God's promises to Israel, and for this to be possible they had to argue that they, as opposed to the Jewish people, *were* Israel—the true or new Israel. The Jews, the church fathers claimed, had (contrary to Rom 9–11) forfeited their inheritance through rejecting the Christ. This constitutes the second rhetorical pattern found in this literature.

Such hermeneutical processes led to what is today called Christian replacement theology, or Christian supersessionist theology, terms used to describe the theological attempt to legitimize non-Jewish Christians as replacing the Jews as the people of God. The political situation in antiquity thus influenced to a significant degree the emergence of Christian anti-Judaism, a Christian theology of contempt that deeply affected Jewish-Christian relations until the second half of the twentieth century. The paradox in this lies in the fact that these non-Jewish Christians, while rejecting Judaism, appropriated the Jewish Scriptures and the history of Israel for themselves.

The "theological logic" of the reasoning behind this appropriation was based on the construal that the exclusion of the Jewish people was necessary for non-Jewish Christians to claim their heritage. (Today, most of the larger church traditions have rejected this type of reasoning and regard the Jewish people as siblings being true to their tradition.)

As a consequence of this early Christian reasoning among the church fathers, Jesus came to be understood within a non-Jewish cultural frame of reference. The Jewishness of Jesus became a problem, since seeing him in this way would mean admitting that Jesus, like the Jews of their own time, complied with the ritual parts of the laws, for example, the Sabbath and the food laws. This would have created an all-too-clear connection between Jesus and the Judaism of their time, including Christ-centered Judaism, something that was deemed unacceptable by these non-Jewish Christians. This in turn would have made difficult the claim that Judaism had been superseded by Christianity. Jesus was thus reinterpreted as critical of or even as abolishing the Jewish law, so that he would fit into the context of gentile Christianity, in which Jewish law and ethnicity had no legitimacy.

From the horizon of such a theological worldview, those non-Jewish Christ followers who identified with Jewish history and Holy Scriptures, and also kept the ritual laws of the Hebrew Bible (like Avita and Mark in our fictional story), became a very real threat for the emerging proto-orthodox Christian majority. It was theologically and politically important for these mainstream Christians to be able to clearly distinguish themselves from "the Jews." Those who ritually wandered freely and eclectically between the blurred lines separating Jews and Christians undermined the theological idea that the Christ event resulted in God's replacing the Jews as his people with the Christians. Thus (non-Jewish) Christians were very forceful in their rejection of such "heretics." One of the most famous examples of this type of rejection of Jews and Judaism, and of people who did not distinguish clearly enough between Judaism and Christianity, is John Chrysostom's sermons against the Jews in the fourth century. What especially provoked him was that members of his own assembly not only visited church on Sunday but also went to the synagogue on Sabbaths and during the Jewish holidays. (As our fictional story illustrates, especially with regard to Avita and Mark, such participation was the norm rather than a deviation during the first century.) With the aim of putting an end to such blurring of the (institutional and religious) lines, Chrysostom gave a number of sermons directed against Jews and Judaism in an attempt to make Judaism less attractive to those who wanted to call themselves Christians.

Marginalization and Otherness

It is self-evident at this point that Jewish Christ followers became more and more marginalized as non-Jewish Christ followers grew in number and influence. Jewish Christ followers identified themselves ethnically with other Jews and were thus understood, as one scholar puts it, as "the dangerous ones in-between." Their interpretation of Jesus was based on Jewish customs and law, and thus undermined the non-Jewish Christians' struggle for legitimacy, especially as this legitimacy depended on replacement theology, or supersessionism (cf. Rom 11:1), which in turn was a prerequisite, to their minds, for the non-Jewish appropriation of Jewish Scripture and history. The Jewish Christ followers, about whom we have the most information in the writings of the church fathers (see box 5.1, p. 375), were thus rejected as heretics together with the non-Jews who did not refrain from following the Jewish law and traditions. The inclusive attitude we find in the writings of Justin Martyr, where ethnic identity created the foundation for a (limited) legitimate difference between different kinds of Christ belief, was discarded by the emerging majority church, which declared ethnic identity invalid as an identity marker for believers in Jesus. The disappearance of ethnicity as an identity marker resulted in the establishment—contrary not only to Justin but also to Acts and Paul, as discussed above—of only one kind of Christ faith, the non-Jewish kind. Because Jewish ethnicity had no role to play when the church fathers construed the foundations of their version of a universal church, Jewish and non-Jewish Christ followers who believed that the Jewish law was still valid could be declared heretics. Christ-centered Judaism as a way of life was, for these authors, just as wrong as Judaism. Since the identity-forming rhetoric of the church fathers aimed at claiming the role of the people of God for the Christians, the anti-Judaism they developed in the process was very much intertwined with their struggle against Jewish believers in Jesus.

If we now turn our attention to the relationship between Jewish Christ followers and other Jews, which is essential to the question of the emergence of Judaism and Christianity as distinct traditions, we find that rabbinic Judaism, which gained more and more prominence in late antiquity, had a crucial role to play in this development. Jewish Christ followers, who had previously frequently been associated with other Jewish groups, none of which dominated Jewish life, became more and more marginalized as rabbinic Judaism gained a more central position in Jewish society. Previous scholarship has often dated this development as early as the second century, and sometimes even earlier, to the decades immediately after the fall of the Jerusalem temple in 70 CE. Today, however, a majority of scholars agree that rabbinic Judaism did not come to dominate Jewish life until the fourth or fifth century, some arguing for an even later date.[9] In any case, it seems clear that the dominance of rabbinic Judaism in Jewish society was linked to the triumph of (non-Jewish) Christianity in Roman society (see fig. 5.3, phases B and C). Rabbinic Judaism offered a dynamic interpretation of Jewish life, of what it meant to be Jewish and to worship the God of Israel, an interpretation that was clearly distinguishable from Christianity, which

9. Schwartz, *Imperialism and Jewish Society*.

claimed to be the new people of God. Rabbinic Judaism thus strengthened the identity of Jews who were increasingly marginalized in what was turning into a Christian society in the Mediterranean world. (One example of such marginalization was the anti-Jewish legislation of the fifth and sixth centuries, including prohibitions against the construction of synagogues, intermarriage, etc.) The strength of rabbinic Judaism is proven not least by the fact that it became the accepted and normative form of Judaism by the vast majority of Jews. Indeed, rabbinic Judaism constitutes the foundation for all mainstream forms of modern Judaism (Orthodox, Conservative, and Reform).

Therefore, the dating of the process that led to (non-Jewish) Christianity becoming the state religion of the Roman Empire, on the one hand, and rabbinic Judaism becoming the normative interpretation of Jewish life and tradition, on the other hand, is of great importance for understanding the development of the situation of the Jewish Christ followers. When rabbinic Judaism became the dominant form of Judaism, other Jewish groups, including Christ-centered forms of Judaism, were pushed to the margins of Jewish society, identified as heretics by the rabbis. Even if Christ-centered Judaism was marginalized in relation to non-Jewish Christianity rather early on in the diaspora, this did not mean that Christ-centered Judaism decreased in popularity or ceased to exist in Palestine and elsewhere in the East. In all probability, this had to do with the fact that rabbinic Judaism did not become the dominant interpretation of Judaism until the late fourth century at the earliest.

Examples of Jewish Christ Groups and Their Characteristics

Our knowledge of Christ-centered Judaism at this time is limited and cannot be reconstructed in detail. This has to do with certain problems with the sources. Most of the information we have access to comes from quotations and discussions in the works of the church fathers. Thus, this evidence consists of indirect information. We also need to keep in mind that the church fathers' portrayal of these groups is intentionally critical, written with the aim of proving them to be heretics. The texts are therefore biased against their subject. Thus, we need to approach the sources in a different manner than when we are dealing with earlier time periods, for which we have firsthand information, written by Jewish Christ followers themselves (e.g., Gospel of Matthew, the Didache, the Letter of James, etc.).

An additional complication is that the church fathers used the term "Ebionites" to describe a Jewish Christ group they judged to be heretical. The problem is that behind this term lie hidden several groups or individuals who practiced different forms of Christ-centered Judaism. The harmonizing label hides the diversity in beliefs and practices that existed, but which the church fathers lumped together in order to reject them. The diverse characteristics of these groups include (1) reading of the Gospel of Matthew only, (2) circumcision of sons, (3) following Jewish practices and traditions, and (4) seeing Jerusalem, rather than Rome, as the geographical center of their worldview. Some of these groups or individuals are said to have rejected the virgin birth (which does not seem consistent with their use of Matthew's Gospel), and they apparently rejected Paul's interpretation of Christianity completely (Irenaeus, *Against Heresies* 1.26.2; 3.11.7; 4.33.4; 5.1.3). Thus, these groups not only chose to emphasize the Jewish law; they also chose to reject some of the beliefs that were normative in non-Jewish Christianity. It is worth noting the fact that the Jewish Christ followers rejected Paul because he was understood to be a preacher of a law-free gospel, an interpretation that had by now come to define Paul for all of his readers, Jews and non-Jews alike.

This description of the "Ebionites" can be compared to the information we have about the Nazarenes, who, according to most scholars, were a homogeneous group. This group kept itself for the most part within the boundaries of what was then known as orthodoxy, but also kept a number of Jewish traditions. This led to them being labeled heretics by the authorities in the majority church. According to these authorities, Nazarenes read both the Hebrew Bible and the New Testament (although they used a Hebrew version of the Gospel of Matthew) and believed in the resurrection of the dead, in one God, and in his Son Jesus Christ (Epiphanius, *Refutation of All Heresies* 29.7.2–5); they even seem to have accepted what at this time was the mainstream understanding of the Pauline interpretation of Christianity and were critical of the "scribes and Pharisees" (Jerome, *Commentary on Isaiah* 8.14.19–22; 9.1–4; 29.17–21).

One of the most interesting examples of a variant of Christ-centered Judaism during this time is the Pseudo-Clementine literature, which places a large emphasis on the need for those who belong to Christ to keep the part of the Mosaic law that applies to non-Jews as outlined in Lev 17–18, while simultaneously rejecting the idea of ethnicity as a prerequisite for following it. Circumcision is not deemed a necessary prerequisite for following the law, but law observance is still viewed as a must for a true Christ follower. The self-identity of the author's group is *theosebeis*, defined as those who worship the one God and observe his law. The *theosebeis* included two distinct groups, Jews and baptized gentiles, who are united in their belief in the one God. An interesting component of this literature is that parts of it have an inclusive soteriology: Jews who do not accept Jesus as the Messiah are saved in the final judgment because they keep the Mosaic law. Jesus and Moses represent two parallel paths to salvation.

The Pseudo-Clementine literature consists of two main works, the *Homilies* and the *Recognitions*, both of which use a common source dated to the third century. The description of the Pseudo-Clementines above is largely based on the *Homilies*. Both of the texts were composed in the fourth century. They were, however, read and translated during the fifth century, indicating that the kind of Christ-centeredness within a Jewish sphere that they represent was relevant as late as that.

As long as Judaism lacked a dominating interpretative tradition, these versions of Christ-centered Judaism could coexist with other variants as expressions of Judaism, even though the lack of clarity regarding the question of ethnicity probably led to some tension. When rabbinic Judaism came to define Judaism, this was no longer possible. It is easy to imagine in this setting the social pressure related to being a Jewish Christ follower or a non-Jew who joined their movement without being ethnically Jewish. Because of such pressure, it is likely that many left their affiliation with the Christ group behind in order to remain integrated in Jewish society. Others, maybe an even larger number, probably decided to adapt their beliefs and practices to the type of Christianity that became the religion of the Roman Empire, especially once the anti-Jewish legislation was introduced. For example, the law against mixed marriages between Jews and non-Jews made it difficult to follow Jewish ancestral practices while simultaneously interacting with non-Jewish Christ followers. The ethnic identity of Jewish Christ followers, with its cultural and ritual markers, would have been toned down in such settings. Thus, such Jewish Christ followers joined with non-Jewish Christians, practicing their Christ tradition in the same way as these non-Jewish Christians did, soon forgetting their Jewish identity and the customs that came with it.

At this point, Christianity had become synonymous with non-Jewish Christianity, and Judaism was equated with rabbinic Judaism. This is the period to which we can trace the formation of the two traditions that eventually became modern Judaism and Christianity. The birth of these religions was thus interlinked with and dependent on the disappearance of Christ-centered Judaism as well as other marginalized Jewish and Christian groups from history.

Box 5.2
Christ-Centered Judaism: Texts and Groups

Information concerning Christ-centered Judaism after the first century can mostly be found in the works of the church fathers. The following authors should be noted:

- Ignatius (ca. 35–107)
- Justin Martyr (ca. 100–165)
- Irenaeus (ca. 130–200)
- Hippolytus (? – ca. 236)
- Origen (ca. 185–254)
- Eusebius (ca. 260–339)
- Epiphanius (ca. 310–403)
- Jerome (ca. 347–420)

Through studying references and citations from the writings of the church fathers, scholars have reconstructed three extracanonical gospels used by Christ-centered Jews: the Gospel of the Hebrews, the Gospel of the Ebionites, and the Gospel of the Nazarenes. These texts, often dated to the second century CE, are part of the New Testament Apocrypha. A short summary of these can be found in Hans-Josef Klauck, *Apocryphal Gospels: An Introduction* (London: T&T Clark, 2003).

The most important Christ-centered Jewish groups are the Ebionites, the Nazarenes, and the Elkesaites. The majority of scholars agree that the term "Ebionite" is an umbrella concept used by the church fathers to describe a number of groups that they deemed heretical.

The Pseudo-Clementine literature is an especially important source for the study of Christ-centered Judaism in late antiquity. The literature consists of two works: *Homilies* and *Recognitions*. An English translation of these texts is available in the seventh volume of *The Ante-Nicene Fathers*. Translations of other Christ-centered Jewish texts, together with other apocrypha, can be found in, for example, Bart Ehrman, *Lost Scriptures: Books That Did Not Make It into the New Testament* (Oxford: Oxford University Press, 2003). See also Appendix 1, "Nonbiblical Sources."

Summary and Outlook

Jewish Christ followers and Christ-centered Judaism should be studied in conjunction with the process that led to the establishment of non-Jewish Christianity as the normative version of Christ belief and of rabbinic Judaism as the normative version of Judaism. In this chapter, we have noted the importance of distinguishing between the basic aspects of *type of religion* and *ethnic identity* in order to see more clearly in the sources when these aspects overlap and when they do not. In the diversity of interpretations of what it meant to adopt an identity involving belief in Jesus as the Christ during the first centuries, we have found several examples that placed an emphasis on Jewish identity, in accordance with what we have called a *praxis-oriented criterion*. The validity and legitimacy of the Mosaic law stand at the center of these interpretations. These variants of Judaism have been referred to using the label Christ-centered Judaism, a label that should not be understood to indicate in any way a homogenous interpretation and practice of tradition.

We have also noted the importance of *ethno-cultural identity*, especially with regard to the early period, and its implications for the choice of type of religion. We saw examples of this in Greco-Roman society as well as in Jewish society, including in Christ-centered Judaism. This connection between ethnic identity and type of religion was important for the author of Acts and for Paul. Not all Christ groups were in agreement, however, and we saw several examples of this, both within and outside the New Testament: non-Jews who practiced Christ-centered Judaism and Jewish Christ followers who leaned toward non-Jewish interpretations of Christianity (see fig. 5.2; each of these examples can, and should, be the object of continuing discussion).

From our initial fictional story, we have learned that the terms "Christ-centered Judaism" and "non-Jewish Christianity" are rather general terms, and that within them there is room for considerable diversity. Non-Jewish Christ followers, like the kind represented by Gaius and Flavia, understood their faith quite differently from what Ignatius and Chrysostom preached, the distinguishing mark being the view of the relationship between Christ belief and the Jewish people: for Gaius and Flavia, as for Paul, Jewish Christ followers/Christ-centered Judaism was at the center of the messianic community; for Ignatius and Chrysostom, Christ-centered Judaism was heretical. Justin Martyr represents a middle ground between these two types of Christ followers, as he accepts the former's insistence on Jewish identity and the Mosaic law and wants community with them, as long as they do not evangelize non-Jews, but clearly prefers the latter as the superior form of Christ adherence.

It is noteworthy that the kind of non-Jewish belief in Jesus as the Christ represented by Gaius and Flavia in the fictional story, as well as the non-Jews to whom the decision of Acts 15 caters, was designed by Jewish Christ followers to be applied to non-Jewish Christ followers only. This was a decision made for both practical and theological reasons, in order to deal with the increased interest of non-Jews in eschatologically oriented Christ-centered Judaism. This form of Christ belief was never meant by its creators to be practiced by Jews. This unity-in-diversity type of solution disappeared rather soon, however. Ultimately, its departure from history paved the way for other kinds of Christ belief, especially non-Jewish kinds, of which we have early examples in, for example, the writings of Ignatius. The Christ-centered Judaism practiced by Jews (represented by Antony in the fictional story) as well as by some non-Jews (like Avita and Mark) survived for several centuries. This form of Judaism, however, eventually came to a similar end: adherents were marginalized, defeated by the "Ignatian" interpretation of Christianity, which had at this point become the religion of the empire.

We should not be fooled into thinking that the (non-Jewish) Christianity that triumphed had lost all contact with Jewish traditions and customs. From Christ-centered Judaism, Christianity inherited Easter (Passover), although it was eventually celebrated on a different day than the Jewish holiday, as well as the Jewish Scriptures, which remained holy for non-Jewish Christians, albeit under a different name (the Old Testament). Christianity also inherited most of the New Testament texts (e.g., the Gospel of Matthew, the Pauline letters, the Epistle of James) from Jewish Christ followers. Other texts added to the canon were authored by Christ followers who were more influenced by forms of Christ belief that are not immediately recognizable as Jewish (e.g., the Pastoral Letters). Within the canon of the New Testament, we thus find theological arguments for the validity of different forms of

Christ belief, even though this was probably not the intention of those who put it together (at least not where Christ-centered Judaism was concerned).

It is, of course, possible to argue that all kinds of belief in Jesus are in some way connected to or expressions of Jewish beliefs, and therefore describe even modern (non-Jewish) Christianity as "Judaism for non-Jews." However, the historian should be careful to observe and distinguish nuances beyond such generalizations. The main theme of continuity in Christian history moves between conflict and reconciliation in a process in which A would have some, but not all, parts in common with B, and B in turn have some parts in common with C, but C, ultimately, has very little to do with A.

In light of these early developments, it is interesting to note that Jewish believers in Jesus, now often referred to as messianic Jews, have once again surfaced more prominently on the stage of history. These developments are located mostly in North America and in Israel, but there are also several groups in other countries. As in antiquity, they make up a heterogeneous group with divergent views on what it means to be a Jewish Christ follower. Some place less emphasis on the Mosaic law and are rather charismatically oriented, similar to other modern charismatic forms of Christianity. Others express their Jewish identity by following the Mosaic law according to traditions very similar to those of rabbinic Judaism. At the same time, some (non-Jewish) churches have begun emphasizing Jewish traditions and customs, without considering converting to Judaism. The boundaries between Christianity and Judaism are thus once again shifting, often being blurred. This, of course, has generated considerable debate and often even conflict. This tells us something not only about these traditions but perhaps even more so about the socio-political context in which these developments transpire. When connections between state and religion are disentangled, as in most modern Western nations, and consequently religion has become a more private affair (although often with political reverberations), diversity and renegotiations of boundaries become more frequent. The older churches, with their roots in the second century, are no longer the only alternatives for those who in various ways identify Jesus as key to their search for the meaning of life, even though the vast majority of Christians still identify with traditional forms of Christianity. Only time will tell how the established church traditions (Catholic, Orthodox, Protestant) and the modern Jewish denominations (Orthodox, Conservative, Reform) will ultimately relate to these Jewish followers of Jesus.

Further Reading

Becker, Adam H., and Annette Yoshiko Reed, eds. *The Ways That Never Parted: Jews and Christians in Late Antiquity and the Early Middle Ages*. Minneapolis: Fortress, 2007.

Burns, Joshua Ezra. *The Christian Schism in Jewish History and Jewish Memory*. Cambridge: Cambridge University Press, 2016.

Campbell, William S. *The Nations in the Divine Economy: Paul's Covenantal Hermeneutics and Participation in Christ*. Lanham, MD: Lexington Books/Fortress Academic, 2018.

Carleton-Paget, James. "Jewish Christianity." Pages 731–75 in *The Early Roman Period*. Volume 3 of *The Cambridge History of Judaism*. Cambridge: Cambridge University Press, 1999.

Cohen, Shaye J. D. *The Beginnings of Jewishness: Boundaries, Varieties, Uncertainties*. Berkeley: University of California Press, 1999.

Cook, John Granger. *Roman Attitudes toward the Christians: From Claudius to Hadrian*. Wissenschaftliche Untersuchungen zum Neuen Testament 261. Tübingen: Mohr Siebeck, 2010.

Donaldson, Terence L. *Gentile Christian Identity from Cornelius to Constantine: The Nations, the Parting of the Ways, and Roman Imperial Ideology*. Grand Rapids: Eerdmans, 2020.

———. *Judaism and the Gentiles: Jewish Patterns of Universalism (to 135 CE)*. Waco: Baylor University Press, 2007.

Dunn, James D. G., ed. *Jews and Christians: The Partings of the Ways A.D. 70 to 135*. Grand Rapids: Eerdmans, 1999.

Fredriksen, Paula. *Augustine and the Jews: A Christian Defense of Jews and Judaism*. New Haven: Yale University Press, 2008.

———. *When Christians Were Jews: The First Generation*. New Haven: Yale University Press, 2018.

Gager, John G. *The Origins of Anti-Semitism: Attitudes toward Judaism in Pagan and Christian Antiquity*. Oxford: Oxford University Press, 1983.

Klijn, Albertus Frederik Johannes, and G. J. Reinink. *Patristic Evidence for Jewish-Christian Sects*. Leiden: Brill, 1973.

Kloppenborg, John. *Christ's Associations: Connecting and Belonging in the Ancient City*. New Haven: Yale University Press, 2019.

Lüdemann, Gerd. *Opposition to Paul in Jewish Christianity*. Minneapolis: Fortress, 1989.

Luomanen, Petri. *Recovering Jewish-Christian Sects and Gospels*. Vigiliae Christianae, Supplements, 110. Leiden: Brill, 2011.

Novenson, Matthew. *The Grammar of Messianism: An Ancient Jewish Political Idiom and Its Users*. Oxford: Oxford University Press, 2017.

Runesson, Anders. "Inventing Christian Identity: Paul, Ignatius, and Theodosius I." Pages 59–92 in *Exploring Early Christian Identity*. Edited by Bengt Holmberg. Tübingen: Mohr Siebeck, 2008.

———. "Jewish and Christian Interaction from the First to the Fifth Centuries." Pages 244–64 in *The Early Christian World*. Edited by Philip F. Esler. 2nd ed. London: Routledge, 2017.

Schwartz, Seth. *Imperialism and Jewish Society, 200 B.C.E. to 640 C.E.* Princeton: Princeton University Press, 2001.
Thiessen, Matthew. *Paul and the Gentile Problem.* New York: Oxford University Press, 2016.
Wilson, Stephen G. *Related Strangers: Jews and Christians 70–170 C.E.* Minneapolis: Fortress, 1995.
Zetterholm, Karin Hedner. "Jewish Teachings for Gentiles in the Pseudo-Clementine Homilies: A Reception of Ideas in Paul and Acts Shaped by a Jewish Milieu?" *Journal of the Jesus Movement in Its Jewish Setting* 6 (2019): 68–87.
Zetterholm, Magnus. *The Formation of Christianity in Antioch: A Social-Scientific Approach to the Separation between Judaism and Christianity.* London: Routledge, 2003.

Paul, His Assemblies, and His Successors

Paul is in Ephesus and receives visitors from Corinth. Some of Chloe's people have come to tell him that the assembly has been divided into different camps. Leaders are pitted against each other, some claiming to belong to Paul, others to Apollos or Peter, and some even to be exclusively related to Christ. In a letter that later comes to be known as the First Letter to the Corinthians, Paul lets his views on the matter be known. Judging by the sarcastic tone, he is upset by the report. "Was Paul crucified for you? Or were you baptized in the name of Paul?" he asks, and scathingly points out that thankfully he did not baptize many of them (1 Cor 1:10–15). What was happening in Corinth? Somewhat later in the same letter, we receive more clues. It turns out that the disagreements were so serious that members of the assembly were taking each other to court over worldly disputes. Even the Eucharist had become a cause for division (1 Cor 6:1–3; 11:17–34).

Still, the discord in Corinth seems to have been only the tip of the iceberg. What really troubled the water beneath the surface were doubts regarding Paul's right to call himself an apostle of Christ. "If I am not an apostle to others, at least I am to you," he writes and assures them that *they* are the seal of his apostleship, *they* are the work he has performed in the name of the Lord (1 Cor 9:1–2). With some irony, he admits later in the letter that he is the least of the apostles, yes, perhaps not even worthy of being called an apostle at all; what he has accomplished, however, nobody can repudiate. By the grace of God, he has worked more than any of the other apostles (1 Cor 15:9–11).

Almost two thousand years have passed, Paul's letters are part of the New Testament, and the apostle's reputation within Christianity around the globe is great and widely acknowledged. It is easy to forget that it was not always so. Paul's overwhelming experience of being called by God had given him absolute confidence that he was to "proclaim [the word] among the Gentiles" (Gal 1:16). His selflessness and effectiveness were beyond reproach, and his progress impressive by any standard. Yet a seed of doubt remained among the established leadership. Despite all his declarations to the contrary (1 Cor 9:1; 15:8), many felt that he did not fulfill the basic criteria. He had not met the risen Christ or been chosen and sent out by him in person.

Paul must soon have realized that it was his own life's work that would have to substantiate his legitimacy. Consequently, he refers to his assemblies as his letter of recommendation, "known and read by all . . . a letter of Christ, prepared by us, written not with ink but with the Spirit of the living God" (2 Cor 3:2–3). He notes with pride that "the people of those regions report . . . how you turned to God from idols, to serve a living and true God" (1 Thess 1:9). He does not hesitate to speak of his affection for those he loves, as a father, or even a mother in birth pangs (1 Cor 4:15; Gal 4:19; 1 Thess 1:8), and of his great longing for them (Phil 1:7–8). He reacts very strongly against that which he dislikes ("What would you prefer? Am I to come to you with a stick . . . ?") and seems convinced that they will take him seriously (1 Cor 4:21; see also 2 Cor 12:11–18; Gal 4:15–18; Phil 3:2–6).

After Paul's death, many claimed to be his heirs. His preaching of Christ and life in him was contextualized into new circumstances. At the end of this section, we will consider one of the trajectories of the Pauline tradition, the Pastoral Letters. First, however, our main focus is the communities that Paul himself laid the foundations for (1 Cor 3:10), the people on which he sought to imprint his ideals, the "brothers" who he wished would follow his example (1 Cor 4:16; Gal 4:12; Phil 3:17). What did he offer them? How did he manage to convince them of his views? What did life look like in the Christ groups in Galatia, Corinth, and Philippi? How did his preaching of Christ affect the lives and self-understanding of people around him? What did he want the church in Rome to learn from him? These are the kinds of questions that we wish to illuminate in the following section.

Calling and Strategy

Gospel to the Uncircumcised

Who were these people who accepted Paul's preaching in place after place, who came to believe in his gospel and gathered to "call on the name of our Lord Jesus Christ" (1 Cor 1:2)? What did the "testimony of Christ" (1 Cor 1:6) entail that made them accept this wandering preacher as an angel from God (Gal 4:14)? Despite his being a Jew and an educated Pharisee (Gal 1:14; Phil 3:4–6), it was not his own people whom he tried to persuade to follow the Christ (Messiah); instead, he saw himself as having been "entrusted with the gospel for the uncircumcised." And so he agreed with "the pillars" in Jerusalem that he and Barnabas would bring Greeks and other non-Jews into the fold, whereas they should go to the circumcised (Gal 2:6–10).

The book of Acts seems to tell a somewhat different story. There Paul's primary target group, from the start until his imprisonment in Rome, is his own kin (Acts 13:5, 14; 14:1; 16:13; 17:1–3, 10; 18:4, 19; 19:8; 28:17, 23). Notwithstanding the fact that Jewish rejection at the very start in Antioch of Pisidia prompted the "turn" to the gentiles (Acts 13:46: "It was necessary that the word of God should be spoken first to you. Since you reject it . . . , we are now turning to the Gentiles"), the continuation of synagogue visits indicates that the events in Antioch of Pisidia were not really a turning point but rather the pronouncement of an outreach pattern. Rejection by Jewish authorities and then mission to gentiles, in that chronological order, was an unremitting necessity since the pattern is validated by Scripture references (Acts 13:47 [Isa 49:6]; Acts 28:24–28 [Isa 9:9–10]). Nevertheless, the Lukan account may not be so much at odds with Paul's own affirmations. For one, as a pattern, the chronological order corroborates Paul's repeated formula in Romans that the gospel is "to the Jews first, and also to the Greeks" (Rom 1:16). Second, the Acts accounts fit Paul's own record of punishments by synagogue authorities (see below). Third, the Acts accounts also fit Paul's idea of a necessary give-and-take between Jewish rejection and gentile reception in God's overall plan for the salvation of all, as elaborated in Rom 9–11 (see below).

Even from a practical perspective, the most suitable place for the proclamation of a Jewish Messiah in a gentile city would seem to be the local synagogue. There, apart from Jews, Paul could find the so-called God-fearers (Gk. *theosebeis*, also *sebomenoi*, or *phoboumenoi ton theon*), non-Jews who were already familiar with the Jewish way of life through participation in the activities of the synagogue (see the section "Jewish Christ Followers and the Emergence of Christianity and Judaism," p. 365). They would know of God's promise to his people, share in Judaism's moral foundations, appreciate the social networks of the synagogue, and believe in Israel's invisible and righteous God. They would know that God's promises and election were for Israel, ratified through an eternal covenant with Abraham (Gen 17:10–13). And they would also expect that they themselves would *fully* share in those promises *only* by becoming Jews.

As Paul proclaimed to these God-fearers that the messianic age had begun, however, he added the astonishing novelty that from now on people *from all nations* could be in full communion with God and receive the blessings and promises that this entailed without becoming Jews. No circumcision required, indeed no circumcision of non-Jews allowed! All they were supposed to do was to call on the name of God's Son, Jesus Christ. In Paul's view, Israel's God had revealed his mysterious wisdom and power by letting a crucified Messiah (Christ) become the Savior of the world—to the great surprise and aggravation of the powers of this world (1 Cor 2:8). The new age had begun and the final phase in God's plan of salvation had been

The agora in ancient Corinth, with Acrocorinth in the background and the court (*bēma*) in the foreground. According to Acts 18:12–17, Paul was brought here to stand trial before the governor Gallio. Photo by Dieter Mitternacht.

ushered in. In Christ, the discrimination between Jews and Greeks, slaves and free, men and women, had ceased to exist. They were all "one in Christ," as he expresses it, part of a new covenant, a new creation, and a new communion. Israel and the other peoples could worship God together. In Christ, circumcision and uncircumcision were equal in value and honor (1 Cor 7:19, 23; 2 Cor 5:17; Gal 3:28; 5:6; 6:15).

Paul could refer to his agreement with the respected leaders in Jerusalem, implying that non-Jews could believe in Jesus and should not become Jews (Gal 2:1–10). That such an agreement was at all necessary may seem a little strange from later perspectives, but at the time the matter was important and controversial. According to Acts, it was also agreed that non-Jews should follow a certain minimum of regulations ("abstain only from things polluted by idols and from fornication and from whatever has been strangled and from blood," Acts 15:19–20) in order to ease the coexistence with Jewish Christ followers.

That following these regulations would mean full communion with the God of Israel was not recognized by Jews outside the circles of Christ followers. Thus, wherever Paul proclaimed his gospel, he came into conflict with the leaders of the local synagogues. The confrontations in Acts (13:45, 50; 14:2, 4, 19; 17:5, 13; 18:12–13) are corroborated by his own letters. Repeatedly he was imprisoned and flogged and risked his life (2 Cor 11:23–29). The hardships could become so intense that he "despaired of life itself" (2 Cor 1:8). Paul's report of how he "five times . . . received from the Jews the forty lashes minus one" (2 Cor 11:24) demonstrates that he conducted his activities under the jurisdiction and sovereignty of the synagogue and accepted its punishment. Following in the footsteps of his crucified Lord, he defied any objections to full fellowship with non-Jews in Christ and accepted the consequences of his "rebellious" actions.

The Pauline Network

In the beginning, Paul organized his activities from Antioch in Syria. From there he journeyed from province to province, synagogue to synagogue, and preached his gospel to the gentiles. Together with a growing team of coworkers, and in less than ten years, he organized a network of assemblies (*ekklēsiai*) consisting of people from different social classes, rich and poor, free and slaves, men and women, who worshiped the one God and Father of Jesus Christ.

The network stretched from Antioch in the province of Galatia over Ephesus in Asia Minor, Philippi and Thessalonica in Macedonia, all the way to Corinth on the Peloponnesus, which was at the time part of the Roman province of Achaia. Through his coworkers and messengers, Paul kept himself updated on how things were progressing in "his" various Christ groups; he sent letters, admonished, comforted, and taught. He saw them as a resource, as bridgeheads from which to expand the lordship of Christ, and as participants in a power struggle that could entail significant hardships. With great satisfaction, he confirms to the assembly in Thessalonica that in much affliction "the word of the Lord has sounded forth from you not only in Macedonia and Achaia, but in every place where your faith in God has become known, so that we have no need to speak about it" (1 Thess 1:8).

Among Paul's more renowned coworkers is Timothy, who worked with him for fifteen years. He coauthored several letters and acted as Paul's envoy to Thessalonica, Corinth, and Philippi. Titus was present at the meeting in Jerusalem (Gal 2:1) and seems to have conducted intricate mediations between Paul and the assembly in Corinth (see 2 Cor 7–8). Silvanus (who in Acts is called Silas) appears to have been Paul's first coworker (after Barnabas). According to Acts 15, he was sent by the assembly in Jerusalem with Paul to Antioch to deliver the news from the council, and then followed Paul on a missionary journey through Greece. He is mentioned as coauthor of both the first and second letters to the Thessalonians. Epaphras, Paul's messenger to Philippi, was imprisoned with him and may have been the founder of the assembly in Colossae. Priscilla and Aquila, to our knowledge, never actually traveled with Paul but are mentioned as people who risked their lives for him. Apollos, a gifted preacher who established himself first in Ephesus and later in Corinth, is described by Paul as an independent coworker: "I planted, Apollos watered, but God gave the growth" (1 Cor 3:6). Among female coworkers we find, besides Priscilla and Chloe, who led assemblies in their houses, Phoebe from Cenchreae (a port city near Corinth), who supported Paul in his activities (Rom 16:1–2); Junia, highly regarded as an apostle (Rom 16:7); and Euodia and Syntyche, who struggled together with Paul in the name of the gospel (Phil 4:2–3). (On women's roles in the ancient world and the early Christ groups, see the section "Men, Women, and Power in Ancient Society and the Early Jesus Movement," p. 147.)

Convictions and Contexts

The Message of the Crucified Christ

In two of his letters, Paul emphatically points out that his message is about the crucified Christ (= Messiah). He reminds the Christ groups in Galatia that "it was before your eyes that Jesus Christ was publicly exhibited as crucified" (Gal 3:1), and tells the assembly in Corinth that he had decided "to know nothing among you except Jesus Christ and him crucified" (1 Cor 2:2). In both cases, the audiences seem to have received the message with enthusiasm, yet the message did not take root in a manner hoped for by Paul. In fact, the Galatians are accused of being foolish (Gk. *anoētoi*), and the Corinthians are reminded and admonished to embrace Paul's preaching, even though it appears foolish to the world (1 Cor 1:18–30): "For the message about the cross is foolishness to those who are perishing, but to us who are being saved it is the power of God. For it is written, 'I will destroy the wisdom of the wise, and the discernment of the discerning I will thwart'" (vv. 18–19).

One of the obstacles of the message of a crucified Messiah was that it directed one's thoughts toward the shameful death of a wicked criminal. How could God's chosen simultaneously be God's cursed (Gal 3:13)? Paul tried to remove the obstacle by means of connecting Christ's crucifixion with the tradition of God's suffering servant (Isa 53). Indeed, "for our sake he [God] made him [Messiah] to be sin who knew no sin, so that in him we might become the righteousness of God" (2 Cor 5:21).

Perhaps the most foolish and objectionable aspect of the message of the cross was that weakness and suffering should count as a demonstration of power. For Paul, Christ manifested God's power through his self-sacrifice, thus proving that love is stronger than death, a principle rooted in God's enigmatic wisdom from "before time" that no eye has seen, no ear has heard, and no human imagined. The principle is so "unworldly" that this world's powers did not understand what they were actually doing when they crucified the Lord of glory (1 Cor 2:8).

While affirming the uniqueness of Jesus's death on the cross, Paul also sees it as a principle of life for all who believe in the Messiah. With his self-humiliation Jesus had taken the first steps in a victory march that would continue until all enemies are defeated (1 Cor 15:26). To understand the cross as something that Christ has done "for us" is one thing, but to accept it as an inner light on how the Christ-like life should be lived is wisdom that only the spiritually mature could fathom. To make the foolishness of Christ a rule for one's life is burdensome (1 Cor 4:9–16).

For Paul, imitating the crucified Christ was first of all a challenge for himself. To the Corinthians he writes that he stands before death every day and emphasizes the value of having fought beasts in Ephesus. He wishes to carry in his body the same death that Jesus was made to endure and believes that Jesus's life will then become visible in him (1 Cor 15:31; 2 Cor 4:10). He describes himself as crucified with Christ and as one who does not boast of anything but "the cross of our Lord Jesus Christ, by which the world has been crucified to me, and I to the world." Therefore, he can also say that he carries the marks of Jesus (*stigmata tou Iēsou*) on his body (Gal 2:19; 6:14, 17). It seems that Paul would have objected to the notion that this was "only" a spiritual struggle.

The conviction reaches a climax in the so-called Philippian hymn that begins with the challenging words "Let the same mind be in you that was in Christ Jesus." The challenge is then exemplified by a description of Jesus taking on the role of a servant, humbling himself and obeying God's will even unto death on the cross. This obedience led to God exalting him above everything else and giving him "the name that is above every name, so that at the name of Jesus every knee should bow, in heaven and on earth and under the earth, and every tongue should confess that Jesus Christ is Lord, to the glory of God the Father" (Phil 2:5–11). Jesus's exaltation is dependent on his obedience and humiliation, and so is Paul's: "I want to know Christ and the power of his resurrection and the sharing of his sufferings by becoming like him in his death, if somehow I may attain the resurrection from the dead" (Phil 3:10–11).

Furthermore, the call to share in Christ's mind applies to all who wish to proclaim Jesus as Lord. In the First Letter to the Thessalonians, perhaps the earliest of Paul's preserved letters, he praises the addressees for being "imitators of us and of the Lord, for in spite of persecution you received the word with joy inspired by the Holy Spirit" (1 Thess 1:6). He praises the grace that has been given the believers in Philippi, to suffer for Christ and have "the same struggle that you saw I had and now hear that I still have" (Phil 1:30; cf. 2:1). However much Paul may adapt his message to different contexts—we shall note a few of those adaptations—with regard to the call to imitate the crucified Christ, he seems to be rather consistent.

The End of This Age Is Near

Paul's radical view of suffering with Christ ties in well with his conviction that the world drama's final act has been initiated. The time between Christ's death and resurrection and his return would be very short. Paul passes on the early Aramaic prayer *Maranatha*, "Our Lord, come!" (1 Cor 16:22), as an expression of his sincere expectation. He suggests that the unmarried should not marry because of "the impending crisis" (1 Cor 7:26), that "the appointed time has grown short," and that "the present form of this world is passing away" (1 Cor 7:29, 31)! He predicts that "salvation is nearer to us now than when we became believers" and that "the God of peace will shortly crush Satan under your feet" (Rom 13:11–12; 16:20). Paul's worldview is thoroughly apocalyptic. Unlike the author of the book of Revelation, however, Paul is not a speculative apocalyptic. Apart from the Second Letter to the Thessalonians (which is of disputed origin; see the section "Second Letter to the Thessalonians," p. 315), we find no timetable or heavenly topography in the Pauline letters through which one could see into the future and determine when the Lord would return. It is possible that questions to that effect had been posed in Thessalonica, to which Paul, however, only gave the oblique answer: "the day of the Lord will come like a thief in the night" (1 Thess 5:1–11). As certain as he is to come "from heaven . . . —Jesus, who rescues us from the wrath that is coming," so will his return be sudden and unexpected (1 Thess 1:9–10). Currently living and already departed disciples of Christ will together meet him in the heavens to participate in his triumphal procession over the earth. The description is reminiscent of a city ruler who meets a delegation of leading citizens outside the city walls in order to be escorted into the city. The inclusive pronouns in the expressions "*we* who are alive" and "so *we* will be with the Lord forever" (1 Thess 4:15, 17) indicate that (the early) Paul expected Christ's return within his own lifetime. There is no timetable or exact prediction, but there is a strong sense of urgency. In fact, what was said above about Paul's readiness, even desire, to share the sufferings of Christ is rooted in an apocalyptic theology of martyrdom, that is, the assurance that tribulation and suffering belong to the end times.[10]

Paul's assertion of the Lord's impending and sudden return was meant to prompt alertness and sobriety in the believers in Thessalonica (1 Thess 5:6–8). Instead, it seems to have prompted speculations and prophecies to the effect that the Lord's day had already come (2 Thess 2:1–2). Confusion and discord arose in the assembly, causing some to become gossipers and busybodies, prone to idleness and abuse of others' generosity, no longer working for their daily needs (2 Thess 3:6–12). The author of 2 Thessalonians counters these deficiencies with proposing a timetable, according to which certain events had to occur before the return of the Lord. The pattern is known from apocalyptic literature (cf. Mark 13), stipulating, for example, that "that day will not come, unless the rebellion comes first, and the man of lawlessness is revealed, the son of perdition [*ho anthrōpos tēs anomias*]" (2 Thess 2:3 RSV). The proposal seems incompatible with Paul's assertions concerning the coming of the Lord in 1 Thessalonians; therefore, many scholars have argued that someone other than Paul must have written 2 Thessalonians.

On the other hand, one should not necessarily expect systematic coherence in Paul's thinking and writing, as he was not a systematic theologian. Paul's main ambition seems to have been contextual coherence and pastoral concern. For instance, only a few years after he had written 1 Thessalonians, he addresses in Rom 9–11 (see also below) the question of how non-Jews can be part of the eschatological people of God and why, in the present, there is an enmity of Jews toward the gospel. There he "reveals" to his addressees the mystery that the full number of gentiles will be reached *before* the liberator will come from Zion and take away all sin from Jacob (Rom 11:25–26). The completion of the mission to the gentiles is thus a precondition for the salvation of all Israel (*pas Israēl*), which will be initiated by the coming of the deliverer from Zion. This comes very close to asserting an eschatological time sequence. Also, Paul's experiences of persecution and prison cells may have affected his expectation of the proximity of Christ's return. To the Philippians he writes that he would gladly "depart and be with Christ" but had chosen to "remain in the flesh" for their sake (Phil 1:19–24). He retains his conviction that the Lord is near (Phil 4:5) but has come to accept that that day may occur after his death.

Finally, Paul's assertions about the new life in and with Christ presume what

10. See Beker, *Paul the Apostle*, 135–38.

seems a rationally irreconcilable, yet, some would argue, existentially coherent duality that is sometimes labeled as Paul's "no longer/not yet" or his "already/not yet" eschatology. Paul asserts that believers in Christ have been "declared righteous by faith" (Rom 5:1 NET) but that they also "eagerly wait for the hope of righteousness" (Gal 5:5). He affirms that "if anyone is in Christ, there is a new creation: the old has passed away [*ta archaia parēlthen*], behold, the new has come" (2 Cor 5:17), yet appeals to believers in Christ "to present your bodies as a living sacrifice, holy and acceptable to God" (Rom 12:1). He even admonishes them to "put on the Lord Jesus Christ" (Rom 13:14). Indicative and imperative, affirmation and admonition go hand in hand.

Scholars disagree on whether the subject "I" of Rom 7 should be taken as autobiographical or rhetorical. Whichever one prefers, Paul here asserts an "already/not yet" duality of experience, where one and the same "I" serves the law of God with the mind, and the law of sin with the flesh. It longs for liberation from "this body of death" and thanks God through Jesus Christ our Lord for both as well as in anticipation of eschatological deliverance (Rom 7:24–25). For Martin Luther, this duality marks the point of departure for his famous dictum: *simul iustus et peccator*. For Rudolf Bultmann, this "no longer/not yet" duality, as he calls it, is the existence in faith where hope and fear belong together as correlatives. "The man of faith utterly surrenders to God's care and power, waiving all care or power of his own and all security that might be at his disposal." [11]

In a different context, Paul embraces a more dynamic understanding of that same tension. Speaking of the power of Christ's resurrection and participation in his sufferings, he states, "Not that I have already obtained this or have already reached the goal; but I press on to make it my own. Beloved, I do not consider that I have made it my own; but one thing I do, forgetting what lies behind and straining forward to what lies ahead" (Phil 3:12–13). One could argue, then, that those who favor a dynamic or progressive understanding of the life-in-Christ experience (*Become who you are!*) can also find support in Paul.

Israel, Gentiles, and God's Inscrutable Ways

The Letter to the Romans stands out from the rest of Paul's correspondence as the only letter to an assembly that he has not founded himself (Rom 1:13). Especially chapters 1–8 have often been taken as Paul's timeless message to a universal audience, independent of particular concerns or contextually determined responses. While Romans is indeed more systematically structured and less involved in overt situational concerns than, for instance, 1 Corinthians is, it has been increasingly recognized that this letter also, in fact, addresses the particular situation in Rome. In chapters 9–11

11. Bultmann, *Theology*, 1:322.

Paul turns his direct attention to the place of Israel in God's plan of salvation, and to the responsibility of gentile Christians toward members of the people of Israel. It is not, however, a salvation-historical excursus that stands in contrast to the letter's otherwise timeless message of the justification of "the ungodly" (*ho asebēs*; Rom 4:5; 5:6), but rather a continuation of the argument of chapters 1–8, now specifically applied to the correlation between the people of Israel and gentile followers of Christ. Thus, in these chapters, Paul is not using the word "Jew" (*Ioudaios*), except when stating that God's concern is for both "Jews and Greeks" in 9:24 and 10:12. Instead, his focus shifts to Israel and Israelites (thirteen references) and "people" (*laos*, six references), terms that he does not use at all in chapters 1–8.

Having argued in the earlier chapters the sinfulness of all humankind ("Jews and Greeks") as well as the personal responsibility of every human being (*pasan psychēn anthrōpou*, Rom 2:9), justification by faith, and participation in the life of Christ through baptism for all, Paul now undergirds his assessment by querying causes and reasons with specific questions. *Why* do some Israelites not believe in Christ? *Why* are gentiles (Greeks and other non-Jews) part of God's overall plan of salvation, and why should they be? *How* does this divine design affect the coexistence of Jewish and gentile believers in a Jewish Messiah, and how does it affect the respect for Jews who do not believe Jesus to be the Messiah?

Nowhere does Paul express his personal sorrow as openly as when he describes his kinsmen's incapability to accept the gospel. He writes, "I am speaking the truth in Christ—I am not lying; my conscience confirms it by the Holy Spirit—I have great sorrow and unceasing anguish in my heart. For I could wish that I myself were accursed and cut off from Christ for the sake of my own people, my kindred according to the flesh" (Rom 9:1–3; cf. 10:1). Paul then provides a list of qualities that show the unique nature, blessedness, and standing of Israel before God: "They are Israelites, and to them belong the adoption, the glory, the covenants, the giving of the law, the worship, and the promises; to them belong the patriarchs, and from them, according to the flesh, comes the Messiah, who is over all, God blessed forever. Amen" (Rom 9:4–5).

And yet the majority of Israelites did not recognize the salvation that God had prepared through Jesus the Messiah. How can that be? Can God's chosen people share in so many blessings yet be blind to what God is doing through his Messiah? Has God rejected his people? Or is God simply unjust? For Paul, these questions are naught but rhetorical and deserve one response only: a resounding *mē genoito*—certainly not (Rom 9:14)! God's righteousness is not up in the heavens, not an inaccessible ideal, no aloof notion. It is the basis for a relationship; it guarantees the fulfillment of promises given. God's righteousness expresses itself as faithful love that never fails, as a helping power that never wavers (cf., e.g., Isa 51:5–8).

Paul begins to explicate what seems to be an enigma by referring to God's sovereignty in his dealings with Abraham's and Jacob's offspring (Rom 9:6–13), and with Moses and Pharaoh (9:14–18). He discards any rational objections from his interlocutor with a categorical rebuke: "Who indeed are you, a human being, to argue with God?" (9:20). He then compares God to a potter and humans (Jews and gentiles, 9:24) to pottery, made into objects of wrath or objects of glory (9:19–26). The logical contradiction remains: humans are responsible for their actions but have no choice. God is merciful in all his actions but chooses to harden whomever he wishes!

As though not entirely content with his own conclusions and searching for an alternative response, Paul introduces the distinction between the people and *the remnant*, quoting from the prophet Isaiah twice: "Though the number of the children of Israel were like the sand of the sea, only a *remnant* of them will be saved; for the Lord will execute his sentence on the earth quickly and decisively," and "If the Lord of hosts had not left survivors to us, we would have fared like Sodom and been made like Gomorrah" (Rom 9:27–29, quoting Isa 10:22–23 and 1:9). Looking back on the history of the people of Israel, there is a pattern of the people falling short of God's expectation. Yet, now God's sovereignty of choice is tempered by the unconditional promise that God will never completely abandon his people. God is immutable in his faithfulness to the people of the covenant, and God's mercy toward the people (*laos*) is unconditional. Israel's children may be reduced to a few, but never will God revoke his eternal covenant with his people; never will his righteousness falter. Always will there be a remnant (*leimma*), "chosen by grace" (*kat' eklogēn charitos*, 11:5). Paul reaches the conclusion that God's distribution of mercy is inscrutable but based on God's promises that are valid independent of human merit. God simply will never "allow" the entirety of Israel to fall away; he will always retain a remnant for himself.

Having argued God's sovereignty and unfailing commitment to the people, at least as a remnant of Israel (Rom 9:6–29), Paul now turns to the question of *why* only a remnant and not all of Israel (thus far!) attained to the goal set out by the law of righteousness (*nomon dikaiosynēs*). Paul's response is, again, enigmatic. On the one hand, Israel's striving for righteousness was misguided ("they did not succeed in fulfilling that law" [*eis nomon ouk ephthasen*]) because they did not fathom that God's righteousness also included the gentiles (the stumbling block, 9:31–32). Their zeal for God was not enlightened (*ou kata epignōsin*), so they did not recognize that the Messiah would provide righteousness for everyone who believes. They did not realize that the *telos* (goal/fulfillment/end) of the law is the salvation of all who have faith (10:1–4). On the other hand, the misguidedness is *caused by God*, who "gave them a spirit of stupor" (11:8 RSV). Moreover, those who did submit to God's righteousness, the remnant, did not do so by themselves but were kept by God and chosen by grace (11:5–6). This is the only time in Rom 9–11 that Paul uses the word "grace" (*charis*), leaving no doubt that both faith and stumbling are entirely God's work.

The enigma clearly necessitates an answer to the most difficult question: "Have they stumbled *so as to fall*?" (11:11). Would God choose a people for himself, only to condemn the majority of it to ignorance and perdition? Are God's dealings with Israel simply mirroring the choice of Pharaoh as a vessel of wrath made for destruction (9:23), endured by God until the appropriate time? Paul's response is a clear and emphatic *mē genoito*—certainly not!

From this point on in the argument, Paul makes no further attempts at solving the enigma, but instead shoulders the mantel of the prophet and reveals a secret (*mystērion*): "a hardening has come upon part of Israel, until the full number of the gentiles has come in. And so all Israel will be saved" (Rom 11:25–26). Paul distinguishes two kinds of hardening, the sclerosis (Gk. *sklērotēs*) of Pharaoh's heart, and Israel's hardening, for which he uses the Greek word *pōrōsis* (see also Rom 11:7), which is often used as a medical term to denote a callus. A callus can be a good thing, Mark Nanos reminds us, that promotes healing as it covers and protects a wounded area.[12] Moreover, with regard to Israel, the callus is a blessing for the gentiles, a salvation-historical necessity for them, and ultimately also for Israel. Through Israel's "hardening" the gates of salvation have been thrown open to embrace the nations of the world: "through their stumbling salvation has come to the Gentiles" (11:11). However painful now, the story has a good ending, since the salvation of the gentiles will incite Israel (11:11), so that eventually all Israel will be saved (11:26). Ipso facto, the mission to gentiles is in the best interests of the people of Israel.

What can we learn from this about the situation in Rome? To begin with, the rhetorical questions in 11:1 and 11:11 indicate that there were tensions between Jews and gentile Christ followers in Rome. The latter seem to have come to reject the former and their standing before God. They may have come to believe that Israel's time was over for good, that God's promises to Israel have been revoked. In response, Paul does his utmost to demonstrate that if God's promises to Israel cannot be trusted, then God's promises in Christ cannot be trusted either. Doubts about God's faithfulness to Israel lead by necessity to doubts concerning the trustworthiness of the gospel, for "in it [the gospel] the righteousness of God is revealed" (Rom 1:17).

Paul returns to his initial concern regarding Israel's privileges before God (Rom 9:4–5), now focusing his attention on the congregational life in Rome. To this end he uses the olive tree metaphor as an illustration (11:17–24). Paul is clearly not interested in horticultural accuracy but has branches from a wild olive tree, contrary to what is natural (*para physin*), grafted into a cultivated olive tree (*kallielaion*)—the point being that gentile believers, wild branches as they are, share the richness of the Israelites, the natural (*kata physin*) branches, by being attached to the root. Natural branches that have been broken remain natural and holy because of the root from which they stem (11:16). That they are hardened is integral to God's plan of salvation for a predetermined purpose and for a limited time period (11:25–26). It seems that the totality of original olive branches represents Israel, and the other branches the nations alongside the Israelites (cf. Jer 11:16; Hos 14:6), whereas the root symbolizes the patriarchal ancestry, before, beyond, and including Israel, although this is not clearly stated.

12. Nanos, *Reading Romans*, 193.

The message to the gentile believers in Rome is "Do not become proud, but stand in awe" (Rom 11:20). Ripples on the surface can temporarily obscure the view into the depths of reality, but they cannot revoke it. "As regards the gospel they are enemies for your sake; but as regards election they are beloved, for the sake of their ancestors" (11:28). Israel has a special place in God's heart, notwithstanding that "there is no distinction between Jew and Greek; the same Lord is Lord of all and bestows his riches upon all who call upon him" (10:12 RSV).[13] In the end, the important thing is that everything works together to accomplish the one thing that bears any significance: "God has imprisoned all in disobedience so that he may be merciful to all" (11:32).

The focus toward the end of Rom 9–11 is exclusively on the God of Israel and his dealings with all humankind. Paul never mentions Christ in all of chapter 11 and lets his reasoning culminate in a doxology of God, which also contains no reference to Christ, the only such doxology in his letters! "O the depth of the riches and wisdom and knowledge of God! How unsearchable are his judgements and how inscrutable his ways!" (Rom 11:33).

An ancient olive tree in Jerusalem, where Paul studied in his youth. Photo by Anders Runesson.

Enigmatic and paradoxical reasoning appears to be typical for much of Paul's style of communication. He molds his theological assertions and arguments as he responds to problems and needs that arise in different assemblies of believers. He makes systematic coherence subservient to a contextual concern for the community to which he writes. His main objective is to respond in a manner that benefits a pastoral purpose.

One Body with Many Members

While still pondering the meaning of the olive tree metaphor, the attentive audience in Rome is challenged by yet another mental image that features their self-understanding and community ideals, the body metaphor (Rom 12:3–5). Whereas

13. Nanos, *Reading Romans*, 137–38: "Paul confronts his listeners for harboring a presumptuous attitude as well as demonstrating indifference to the suffering experience of the other who does not share their confession. These Israelites are also in covenant partnership with God, although they are presently suffering discipline."

the olive tree metaphor underscores how Christ-following non-Jews should behave in relation to Jews in general, the body metaphor focuses on the relationship *within* the assembly of Christ followers. Whereas the olive tree metaphor highlights the historical necessity and meaning of difference, the body metaphor demonstrates the organic necessity and meaning of unity. All members originate from and belong to the same body; the difference is found in their functions: "For as in one body we have many members, and not all the members have the same function, so we, who are many, are *one body in Christ*, and individually we are members one of another" (12:4–5).

A list of different kinds of gifts of grace by which everyone enriches all accentuates the unity (Rom 12:6–8). The count culminates in a section on love and compassion for all people and ends with citations from Prov 25:21: "If your enemies are hungry, feed them; if they are thirsty, give them something to drink" (Rom 12:20). The implications are proverbial, yet an allusion to the "enemy" mentioned in the previous chapter (Rom 11:28) seems likely, meaning that the specific admonishment of gentile Christ followers in Rome continues.

A similar yet more detailed description of the body metaphor is found in 1 Cor 12. There the emphasis is on *God as the initiator* ("For in the one Spirit we were all baptized into one body—Jews or Greeks, slaves or free—and we were all made to drink of one Spirit," 1 Cor 12:13; cf. Gal 3:26–28) and on *equating* the community of believers with the body of Christ ("you *are* the body *of* Christ" (1 Cor 12:27).

Ancient writers have often used the body metaphor to illustrate unity and belonging, usually of a city or a state, at times of an association. Similar to the Stoics, Paul does not delimit the togetherness in one body geographically or ethnically but includes human beings of all kinds (1 Cor 12:13 and Gal 3:26–28). Neither does he (or the Stoics) distinguish natural from supernatural reality, as his reasoning about the resurrection of the body in 1 Cor 15:35–49 amply demonstrates. The modern "enlightened" mind tends to consign suggestive expressions such as "you are the body of Christ" to figurative speech. For Paul and the Stoics, however, there is deeper meaning, as the physical does not oppose the spiritual but rather presupposes it (1 Cor 15:44). Earthly and heavenly bodies, although different, are part of one reality. Some are perishable, some imperishable, and reality is organized according to hierarchies and qualities, but it is always one reality.[14] The physical unity of man and woman in intercourse is "the same" as the unity of members in the body of Christ (1 Cor 6:15); the consumption of bread and wine in the Eucharist is "the same" as fellowship with the body and blood of Christ (1 Cor 10:16–17). Similarly, Paul can assert that Christ "will transform the body of our humiliation that it may be conformed to the body of his glory, by the power that also enables him to make all things subject to himself" (Phil 3:21).

Symptomatic for such organic reasoning is the distribution of gifts of grace (*cha-*

14. Martin, *The Corinthian Body*, 9–15, 127–29.

rismata). The assembly is a charismatic community that manifests God's grace in words and actions, missions and tasks. As a body, the assembly is more than a gathering of people called by God to unity and care for one other. The body is God's work, held together by God and manifesting itself in an organized array of miracles (*energēmata*), gifts of grace (*charismata*), functions (*praxeis*), and services (*diakoniai*) (1 Cor 12:6–10; Rom 12:4–7).

Paul refers to members of the Christ communities as "called to belong to Jesus Christ" (Rom 1:6); "baptized into Christ" (Rom 6:3); "joint heirs with Christ" (Rom 8:17); "one body in Christ" (Rom 12:5); "the body of Christ" (1 Cor 12:27); and "in Christ Jesus . . . children of God through faith" (Gal 3:26). This affinity to Christ is true even beyond the grave, so that "the dead in Christ" (1 Thess 4:16) have a special place at Christ's second coming.

Jewishness, Circumcision, and the Law

We noted earlier how Paul traveled from place to place along the northern Mediterranean and preached that people from any ethnic or religious background could join the Christ movement and become partakers in the promises and blessings that God has given to the people of Israel. Moreover, circumcision and/or formal conversion to Judaism was not a requirement; indeed, it was prohibited, the main rationale being Paul's conviction that, by faith in Christ, Jews and non-Jews were to be united in one eschatological community. However, unity was not to be understood as uniformity. Christ-following Jews and gentiles were equal in Christ, yes, but they were also interdependent in their difference. The eschatological vision includes Jews *and* gentiles, which is grounded for Paul in his monotheistic faith: God is one and therefore the God of Jews *and* gentiles. As such, God "will justify the circumcised on the ground of faith and the uncircumcised through that same faith" (Rom 3:29–30).

Since faith in Christ has its origins in Judaism and is rooted in the Hebrew Bible, the Law and the Prophets, the question of how gentile Christ followers should relate to Judaism demanded a response even in assemblies that only, or mostly, consisted of believers with non-Jewish backgrounds (such as probably in Thessalonica). How should gentiles who had decided to believe in the God of Israel and in a Jewish Messiah conduct themselves in everyday life in relation to the synagogue community (see the section "Jewish Christ Followers and the Emergence of Christianity and Judaism," p. 365), their own families of origin, and Greco-Roman society at large?

The letters of Paul testify to the fact that there was an urgent need for clarification and advice on a number of issues. Disagreements had led to fighting and undermined relations, especially since not even the apostles seemed to see eye to eye on some of the subject matter (Gal 2:11–15). Many must have requested unequivocal and universal guidance on practical issues, such as meal fellowship, conduct at worship, marital relations, burials, and business partnerships. How should gentiles as followers of Christ relate to Jews and Jewish cultural norms, on the one hand, and to their native families and society, on the other? We shall focus at this point on Paul's advice to gentiles concerning Jewishness, circumcision, and the law in the letters to the churches in Galatia, Rome, and Corinth. It is in these letters that these topics are most prominent.

To begin with we should listen to Paul's own understanding of and approach to the task of reaching out to gentiles. In 1 Cor 9:19–27 Paul compares his missionary activity with an athletic competition for a prize, stating that his preaching and conduct are driven and operated by a single maxim: "I have become all things to all people, that I might by all means save some" (v. 22). It would appear that Paul, in his own mind, was a pragmatist, contextually sensitive to each particular situation, always outcome oriented. Yet some would argue that this fits the style and character of Paul's letters badly. In the Second Letter to the Corinthians, Paul himself admits to a widespread opinion among the saints in Achaia: "For they say, 'His letters are weighty and strong, but his bodily presence is weak, and his speech contemptible'" (2 Cor 10:10). Apparently, the members of his Christ groups had enjoyed his humble appearance and demeanor in personal encounters (see also Gal 4:12–14) but were quite perplexed by his letters, as they included polemical rhetoric, upsetting admonitions, and ironic reproach. Does this mean that the pragmatic and lenient touch in 1 Cor 9:22 applies only to Paul's personal encounters and that there was a change of strategy and approach when the preacher became a letter writer? Do the letters in fact convey a one-sided impression to the distant reader of who this man was?

We shall start with the question of what it means for a gentile to become a Jew, and compare Paul's argument in the letters to the Galatians and Romans. In the Letter to the Galatians, Paul firmly emphasizes that in Christ there is no discrimination of status between Jews and "Greeks" and that all who are baptized are *one* in Christ (Gal 3:27–28). He polemicizes against the Galatian addressees' desire to assimilate to Jewish culture, declares proselytism a yoke of slavery (4:31–5:1), and warns them that if they do convert, they are excluded from Christ and have become alienated from grace (5:3–4). The general tenor here implies, so it seems, a depreciation of proselyte conversion, a depreciation that does not apply to Jews by birth (2:17), such as Paul himself.

In Romans, the situational context is opposite to the one in Galatia, and Paul's tone is quite different. In Rome, gentile Christ followers are not interested in becoming Jews but rather exalt themselves over against their Jewish fellow citizens, whom they may share the synagogue with. Thus, Paul emphasizes the priority of Jews in all of God's dealings with humanity ("to the Jew first and also to the Greek," beginning in Rom 1:16). He also underscores that Israelites have a privileged and unceasingly valid standing before God. They play a vital role in God's plan even to the end, however it may seem at the present time, whereas gentile Christ followers will never possess the same natural quality as Israelites (Rom 11).

The impression of contextualized theology is corroborated by how Paul deals with the specific value and function of circumcision. In Galatians, Paul tells non-Jews who believe in Christ that being circumcised after having received faith amounts to a betrayal of God's plan for the world in Christ, and thus constitutes a threat to their salvation. In Romans, on the other hand, Paul puts Abraham forward as one who received circumcision as a sign (*sēmeion*) of and a seal (*sphragis*) on the righteousness of faith that he had before he was circumcised. Abraham was circumcised by faith and thus became the father of both the circumcised who believe and "all who believe without being circumcised and who thus have righteousness reckoned to them" (Rom 4:11). Paul's argument in Romans is about timing and sequence, in which the former is seen to be greater than the latter. Abraham believed first and was circumcised afterward; thus, faith has priority over circumcision. However, Abraham's faith was "sealed," authenticated, by his circumcision. By implication, then, Paul asserts that it is a good thing to be circumcised by faith and that circumcision after and by faith is not an annulment of faith but rather the authentication of faith. One can easily imagine how the Galatians would have responded: "But that's exactly what we want!" For obvious reasons, this line of argumentation would be counterproductive in the Galatian context. So Paul simply avoids mentioning that, or when, Abraham was circumcised, even as he specifically addresses the faith of Abraham in Gal 3:6–10.

Turning to what Paul has to say about circumcision in 1 Corinthians, the context is quite different again. Paul's main concern in this letter is unity, love, and interdependence, most elegantly argued in chapters 12–14. He had received reports of social and spiritual inequality, competition, even oppression among members of the assembly. Motivated by these concerns, he apparently decided to treat the difference between Jews and Greeks as something to be appreciated as part and parcel of a variety of societal differences, such as slaves and free, men and women. In Corinth, Paul does not emphasize his opposition to circumcision of gentiles at all, as clearly it played only a marginal role. There were both those who contemplated circumcision and those who wanted to restore their foreskin (1 Cor 7:18), and the motivations on both sides were social rather than theological.

The Corinthian assembly appears to have consisted mainly of uneducated, socially and economically exposed members ("what is foolish in the world . . . , what is weak . . . , what is low and despised in the world, things that are not," 1 Cor 1:27–28). Although they do not seem to have been as poor as the believers in Macedonia (cf. 2 Cor 8:2), some in fact depended for their daily bread on the common meal (1 Cor 11:22). A few powerful and prominent church members (1:26), whose responsibility it should have been to share their abundance with others ("discerning the body," 11:29), "humiliate[d] those who had nothing" (*kataischynete tous mē echontas*, 11:22). Under these circumstances and for social or economic reasons (as with regard to slavery, 7:21–22), some considered altering their ethnic/religious identity.

Quite different from his approach in Galatians, Paul seems somewhat undecided, even empathizing with some of the arguments for change from slavery to freedom (7:21). But then he states the guiding principle: "in whatever condition you were called, brothers and sisters, there remain with God" (1 Cor 7:24; see also 7:17, 18, 20). Paul's concern in Corinth is clearly not about soteriology (as in Galatians), or about gentile Christian pride (as in Romans), but about stabilizing a confused and imbalanced situation. Seen from this angle, combining what have been described as contradictory claims may actually make sense: (1) "Circumcision is nothing, and uncircumcision [foreskin] is nothing"; (2) "but obeying the commandments of God is everything" (1 Cor 7:19).

Turning now to the meaning and purpose of the law in Paul's letters, it has often been claimed that Paul contradicts himself not only between letters but also within one and the same letter. As already noted, in both Galatians and Romans Paul presents Abraham's faith with a focus on time and sequence. In Galatians he does not, however, mention Abraham's circumcision, though the value and meaning of circumcision is the letter's primary concern. Instead, Paul focuses on the contrast between promise (*epangelia*) and law (*nomos*). The promise was made by God to Abraham and to his seed (*sperma*, Gal 3:16). By using a rabbinic exegetical technique and capitalizing on the fact that the word *sperma* is singular in form (although he accepts it as a collective plural in 3:29), Paul claims that Abraham's offspring, to whom the promise is given, is Christ and no other. To this he adds that the promise was made 430 years before the law came (3:17), thus "proving" that the law is secondary and incidental compared to the promise through which the inheritance was given (3:18). Next, Paul asserts the superiority of the promise by claiming that it was declared by God himself, whereas the law was issued by angels and through a mediator (3:19).

The reason for driving this wedge between law and promise is that the two were intended, according to Scripture, for different functions and purposes: the promise, to give righteousness and life to those who believe; the law, to condemn and kill anyone who does not abide by it (Gal 3:10, quoting Deut 27:26). The assertion that the law cannot measure up to the promise is not based on an inference drawn from human experience, or Paul's own experience, but on the recognition of divine design and scriptural foresight. In the context of Galatians, not abiding by the law may entail encouraging non-Jews to identify with the law through circumcision.

Moving on to Romans, we note, first, that Paul asserts that the law is given by God as a guide to right living. Its basic principles, to do what is good and avoid evil, are written on *everyone's* hearts, wherefore God will judge and reward all people, without distinction, according to their works (Rom 2:2, 6, 11, 15). Non-Jews who fulfill the law by nature get praise, and Jews, the hearers of the law, are reminded that the privilege of having access to the law entails specific responsibilities (2:17–27). The utter human failure of compliance with the law is highlighted in the third chapter of Romans, where Paul argues that all people, "Jews and Greeks," are under the power of sin, that *no one* is righteous before God. The function of the law is to hold all humans accountable before God (3:20) and to induce wrath (4:15). Later on in the letter (esp. ch. 7) Paul elaborates the human dilemma further and makes it abundantly clear that the problem is not the purpose or the direction of the law but the overwhelming power of temptation and sin over human nature.

At this point, however, Paul introduces a distinction between the law of works (*nomos tōn ergōn*) and the law of faith (*nomos tou pisteōs*) (Rom 3:27). He seems to have the same law in mind for both phrases, but with two different modalities or faces. As the law of works, the law condemns by revealing God's will and making human fallibility visible (2:12–3:20). As the law of faith, it gives life and manifests itself as "the righteousness of God through the faith of Christ [*dikaiosynē theou dia pisteōs Iēsou Christou*]" (3:22; for "faith *of* Christ" see below). On the basis of this equation, Paul can answer his own rhetorical question "Do we then overthrow the law by this faith?" with a ringing "By no means [*mē genoito*]! On the contrary, we uphold [*histanomen*] the law" (3:31).

In Corinth, there clearly is not much debate over the role or function of the law, nor is there any dissent concerning the value of the law in relation to faith. The law (*nomos*) is referred to a few times (1 Cor 9:8–9, 20; 14:21, 34; 15:56), mostly to show cause for ethical instructions. People are expected to respect and accept guidance from the law of Moses (1 Cor 9:8).

In sum, the differences between Paul's argumentation on becoming a Jew, circumcision, and the law in these three letters are apparent. In Galatians, where gentile Christ followers desire to be circumcised, becoming a Jew amounts to submitting to a yoke of slavery, circumcision amounts to falling away from grace (5:4), and the law is portrayed to them as being opposed to faith (3:12) and with a purpose to condemn (3:10–12, 19–22). In Romans, where gentile Christ followers treat Jews with disrespect, the privileges of being an Israelite are praised, circumcision stands out as a seal of righteousness by faith (4:11), and the law is portrayed as being fulfilled in Christ (10:4). In 1 Corinthians, where the focus is on roles and honor in society, the distinction between circumcised and uncircumcised members of the community has no apparent value, and keeping the commandments of God is put above all else (7:19).[15] The phrase "neither circumcision nor uncircumcision [*oute peritomē . . . oute akrobystia*] counts for anything" appears with slight variations in both Gal 5:6; 6:15 and 1 Cor 7:19. Yet, as we have seen, the implications are different in the two letters.

Returning to the question of whether Paul's pragmatism and adaptability is lim-

15. For a convenient overview of how Paul's concept of law oscillates, see Räisänen, *Paul and the Law*, 16–41. Räisänen argues that Paul was "not conscious of his actual oscillation" (28), yet that he was "first and foremost a missionary, a man of practical religion who develops a line of thought to make a practical point, to influence the conduct of his readers" (267).

ited to his personal encounters, we may now conclude that his letter writing was in fact guided by a similar concern. Maybe the confrontational aspect was not as palpable in personal encounters as it is at times in the letters. But assessing the variety of argumentation on the three topics of Jewishness, circumcision, and the law in three different letters has shown that Paul was in fact using the rhetorical means at his disposal to "become all things to all people, that [he] might by all means save some" (1 Cor 9:22).

Justification by Faith and Participation in Christ

Up to the 1970s, most interpreters of Paul agreed that the most important concern in Paul's letters was the affirmation of faith versus works, and that Paul was arguing, with great fervor and against firm Jewish opposition, that unconditional salvation was offered to all humankind, solely by the mercy of God in Christ. "Justification by faith" was held to connote unmerited *acquittal* from guilt, wherefore Gal 2:16 was read as an affirmation that whoever believes in Christ is declared righteous and forgiven, apart from any effort of one's own. In traditional Protestant thinking, Paul's plight naturally coincided with Martin Luther's intense plight for a gracious God; Luther's law-free gospel provided the answer to the universal quest of every human being: "How can I find peace with God?" Luther jubilantly joined Paul's triumphant exclamation in Rom 8:1, "There is therefore now no condemnation for those who are in Christ Jesus," and Rom 8:33–34, "Who will bring any charge against God's elect? It is God who justifies. Who is to condemn? It is Christ Jesus, who died, yes, who was raised, who is at the right hand of God, who indeed intercedes for us." There seemed to be no doubt that Paul's main objective was to fight against legalistic works-righteousness, and for *sola gratia*, and that his churches suffered from the same fear of the final judgment as the Western church in the late Middle Ages.

Developments toward the end of the first century seemed to validate the traditional understanding of Paul's struggle. In assemblies who saw themselves as heirs of Paul, the conviction that faith stood in contrast to deeds, that salvation was by grace through faith and without regard to works (e.g., Eph 2:8–9; Titus 3:4–5; 2 Tim 1:9), was held up high. In its critical dissociation, the Letter of James confirms the same development when it claims that "faith by itself, if it has no works, is dead" (Jas 2:17), that "our ancestor Abraham was justified by works" (Jas 2:21), and concludes that "a person is justified by works and not by faith only [*ouk ek pisteōs monon*]" (Jas 2:24). The works mentioned in the Letter of James are works such as giving clothes and food to those who are in need.

The chain of reasoning seemed solid, although there have always been objections to painting Paul and James as polar opposites. In fact, from one angle Paul and James seemed to be on the same side. Even in the Letter to the Galatians, which more than any other appears to reject the validity of the law, Paul reaches the conclusion that the only thing that counts is faith working through love (5:6), that the whole law is summed up in the commandment of love (5:14), and that those living in the flesh and doing the works of the flesh (*erga tēs sarkos*) shall not inherit the kingdom of God (5:19–21).

Step by step for the last fifty odd years, every aspect of the traditional understanding of Paul has been called into question, so that in 1983 James D. G. Dunn fittingly coined the phrase "the new perspective on Paul."[16] Almost from the start there were, of course, not one but several new perspectives on Paul. Yet the assertion that unites them all, and the springboard, is the recognition that Second Temple Judaism was *not* a legalistic religion, and that Paul was fighting for something else than faith apart from works. The claim had been made before, but it was E. P. Sanders who broke the mold in his 1977 publication *Paul and Palestinian Judaism*. Sanders argued with great vigor that the Jewish literature of the Second Temple period proves beyond doubt that Palestinian Judaism at the time of Jesus and Paul was not legalistic and not concerned with earning salvation by means of meritorious works. The common denominator that emerged, instead, was a pattern of religion that Sanders labeled *covenantal nomism*. The pattern is firmly grounded in the notion of *unconditional election* and revolves around the two key aspects of "getting in" by grace and "staying in" by works of law. Works cannot earn salvation; they are, however, the condition of remaining "in." A few texts from the time seem to promote meritorious works for those who are "in," but the great bulk of the Jewish literature of the Second Temple period does not. In fact, in Sanders's view, election by grace is so fundamental that the rabbis often presuppose it without discussing it (see also the section "A General Summary of Pauline Research," p. 19).

Sanders's reappraisal of Second Temple Judaism led Dunn to propose a major reinterpretation of the conflict in Galatia and of Gal 2:16 in particular, the key feature being that "works of the law" concern the status of gentiles in the first Christian communities rather than the doing of good works. There is a particular set of laws and customs that functioned as ethno-religious identity markers for Jews. These "works of the law" were circumcision and purity and Sabbath regulations. Thus, when Paul opposed the works of the law, he did not stand up against works-righteousness but against national exclusivism.[17] Consequently, Paul was dealing not with a universal problem of human religiosity but with a specific historical concern. Against his opponents who argued that only Jews could be full members of the people of God, Paul asserted that all who believe in Christ are also children of Abraham.

The third major contribution to the new perspective on Paul, which actually preceded and contributed to the other two, came through Krister Stendahl's article "The Apostle Paul and the Introspective Conscience of the West." In this article Stendahl

16. Dunn, "The New Perspective on Paul," 89–110.
17. Dunn, "The New Perspective on Paul," 105–10.

claims that there is no evidence in the Pauline epistles that Paul's conscience was particularly delicate or introspective (as was Luther's). Instead, Paul's conscience can be characterized as robust. Neither was Paul particularly concerned with Augustine's and the Reformers' plight for a gracious God. Instead, Paul's main concern regarding justification by faith and not by works was "the place of the Gentiles in the church and in the plan of God."[18]

The fourth contribution to the new perspective on Paul also comes out of the 1977 publication by Sanders, albeit a reappraisal of Albert Schweitzer's *Mysticism of Paul the Apostle*. Sanders asserts that "the main theme of Paul's theology is found in his participationist language rather than in the theme of righteousness by faith."[19] Paul's soteriology does not center on juridical conceptions of atonement but on themes of union with Christ. Shifting the main theme of Paul's theology from "justification by faith" to "participation in Christ" has ramifications for how covenantal nomism converges with Paul's understanding of "staying in" for Christ followers. Participation in Christ entails the experience of "a transfer of lordship and the beginning of a transformation which will be completed with the coming of the Lord."[20] Thus, freedom from sinning and the performance of good works happen as a natural outflow of being in Christ; it is a matter of the Spirit producing its fruit, or the power of God revealing the righteousness of God through faith for faith (Rom 1:17).

Recently, John M. G. Barclay has put forward a theory of grace (*charis*) that seems to put "justification by faith" firmly within the participationist paradigm. Barclay argues that from the social and theological domain of *charis* as "gift" in an ancient Mediterranean context, even the best of gifts entails expectations or obligations. "The notion that gifts are in principle 'purer' by expecting nothing in return is a peculiar modern conception that has almost no counterpart in antiquity. . . . And like all gifts, the divine gift carries expectations and obligations (the connection between *Gabe* and *Aufgabe* was self-evident in antiquity)." The unique part is that the gift was given to *unfitting* recipients, but since it is the Christ gift, it "will finally be completed (as gift) in the full transformation of fitting recipients."[21]

From another angle of ancient thought, the participationist paradigm has been shown to corroborate the notion that Paul and his contemporaries did not distinguish natural from supernatural reality, which his reasoning about the resurrection of the body in 1 Cor 15:35–49 amply demonstrates (as does his reasoning about the body of Christ; see the section "One Body with Many Members," p. 411). Like the Stoics, Paul presupposes that the physical does not oppose the spiritual, but rather presupposes it, as the two belong to the same *reality*. Now, for Paul, similar to being united

18. Stendahl, "Apostle Paul and the Introspective Conscience of the West," 204.
19. Sanders, *Paul and Palestinian Judaism*, esp. 419–28.
20. Sanders, *Paul and Palestinian Judaism*, 549.
21. Barclay, "Believers and the 'Last Judgment' in Paul," 208.

and intertwined in "one spiritual body" with Christ, humans are also intertwined with their ancestor Adam, by means of being of the same "dust" (1 Cor 15:47–49). And they are intertwined with Abraham and Christ by means of sharing the same divine *pneuma* (not a person, obviously, but the vital component of knowing the mind of God; see 1 Cor 2:11–15; Rom 8:16). "Gentiles who come to share the *pneuma* of Christ in baptism share in this contiguity back to Abraham and are thus seed of Abraham and coheirs as they participate in the stuff of Christ."[22] Insights on ancient metaphysics connect back to Schweitzer, who had defined the character of Paul's soteriology as a mystical and natural (*mystisch-naturhafte*) union with Christ.

The last component in the reassessment of Paul's main theme concerns the genitive construction "Christ's faith" (*pistis Christou*), which occurs several times in Paul's letters. A growing number of interpreters have come to prefer a subjective rather than an objective rendering of this genitive and translate the phrase as "faith of Christ" rather than "faith in Christ," the significance being that the emphasis shifts from anthropology to Christology. "Christ's faith" denotes not the faith that humans have in Christ (objective genitive) but Christ's own faith (subjective genitive). Given the semantic spectrum of the word *pistis*, which includes faith, faithfulness, and trust, *pistis Christou* may even be rendered as "faithfulness of Christ." Thus, as Abraham believed/trusted the calling and promises of God and hence was justified (Gen 15:16, quoted in Gal 3:6), so also Christ, "that in Christ Jesus the blessings of Abraham might come upon the Gentiles" (Gal 3:14 RSV). A subjective rendering of "Christ's faith" (*pistis Christou*) seems to square also with Rom 5:19 ("Just as by one man's disobedience many were made sinners, so by one man's obedience many will be made upright" [RSV]) and Gal 3:9 ("Those who believe are blessed with Abraham who believed"). An additional benefit of the subjective rendering is that the extensions "even we have believed in Christ" in Gal 2:16 (RSV) and "for all who believe" in Rom 3:22 no longer come across as redundant repetitions of the preceding phrases, but instead point out that believing in Christ is counted by God as justification on account of the faith(fulness) of Christ. Needless to say, the subjective genitive fits nicely with the participationist theme.

Lately, a number of New Testament scholars (Mark D. Nanos, Paula Fredriksen, Pamela Eisenbaum, Magnus Zetterholm, and others), have begun to reach beyond the new perspective on Paul, convinced that Paul should be interpreted *within* first-century Judaism rather than next to or somehow opposed to. These scholars reject the "new perspective" inasmuch as it shares the traditional point of departure that Paul must have found *something principally wrong* with Judaism. They embrace Sanders's finding regarding covenantal nomism but do not concur with Dunn and others that Paul opposed Judaism's commitment to ethnic identity, variously described as "ethnocentrism," "badges of identity," "particularism," or "nationalism." They ask

22. Stowers, "What Is 'Pauline Participation in Christ'?," 359.

why Paul would oppose "particularism" when at the same time creating new assemblies that are set apart by way of faith in/of Christ? They also ask why Christian interpreters would affirm the formation of a Christian identity yet object to similar measures regarding Jewishness? Some in the "Paul within Judaism" group embrace the so-called Sonderweg trajectory (proposed by Lloyd Gaston, John G. Gager, and Stanley Stowers), which detects in Paul's letters a "special way" to salvation for non-Jews through Christ, alongside the path of salvation in the Sinai covenant for Jews. But others do not, asserting basically that Paul believed that the Messiah had come and that gentiles should be invited to convert to Judaism without circumcision.

In sum, Paul remained a Torah-observant representative of Second Temple Judaism also after his change of conviction about Jesus being the Messiah. His letters were written and intended for non-Jews. The assemblies that he founded were subgroups of Judaism, new Jewish "sects" or "reform movements" that practiced a Jewish cultural way of life but remained non-Jews.[23] (For more details, see the section "New Perspectives on Paul," p. 28.)

The Scope of Salvation

We have noted how Paul contextualizes his theological convictions from letter to letter. However, on the question of the time (past, present, or future) of salvation, Paul seems completely consistent in all of his letters. He never speaks of salvation (*sōtēria*) or "to be saved" (*sōzomai*) as something that *has been done*, but always as something that *is happening*, the completion of which is still in the future. Aspects of salvation, such as justification, are a reality *now* through Christ's death and prove the certainty of complete salvation to come (Rom 5:9). As to participation in the death and resurrection of Christ, while baptism seems to include both, Paul divides carefully between having been (*gegonamen*) united with him in a death like his and going to be (*esometha*) united with him in a resurrection like his (Rom 6:5). Full salvation from sin and "flesh" has to wait until the resurrection at the end of this age (Rom 13:11; 1 Cor 1:18; 5:5; 2 Cor 2:15; 1 Thess 5:8; cf. Eph 2:5, 8). In tune with this, when Paul speaks of being saved from danger or from an emergency in this life, he uses another verb (*rhyomai*; see Rom 15:31; 2 Cor 1:10).

Regarding the question *to whom* salvation from sin and death applies—all humankind or only those who believe in Christ (universal or particular salvation)—the most explicit affirmations support a universalist conviction. Like a crescendo preparing for the doxology that praises God's inscrutable wisdom (Rom 11:33–36), Paul exclaims that "God has imprisoned *all* [*ta panta*] in disobedience so that [*hina*] he may be merciful to *all* [*ta panta*]" (Rom 11:32), thus affirming the ultimate salvation not only of all Israel but of all of humanity. The assertion is not new, as already in

23. See Nanos and Zetterholm, *Paul within Judaism*, 2–3, 10.

Rom 5:18 Paul assures his readers that "just as one man's trespass led to condemnation for *all*, so one man's act of righteousness leads to justification and life for *all*." Similarly, in 1 Cor 15:22 Paul states, beyond doubt, that "as *all* die in Adam, so *all* will be made alive in Christ"; in 15:25 he asserts that "he must reign until he has put *all* his enemies under his feet" and in 15:28 that "when *all* things are subjected to him, then the Son himself will also be subjected to the one who put *all* things in subjection under him, so that God may be *all in all* [*panta en pasin*]." According to 2 Cor 5:19, "in Christ God was reconciling *the world* to himself," and in Phil 2:9–11 Paul asserts that "God also highly exalted him and gave him the name that is above *every* name, so that at the name of Jesus *every* knee should bend, in heaven and on earth and under the earth, and *every* tongue should confess that Jesus Christ is Lord, to the glory of God the Father."

If we add the passages from the disputed letters to this survey, the evidence for universal salvation in the Pauline corpus seems overwhelming. Especially Col 1:19–20 asserts in no uncertain terms that "for in him *all* the fullness of God was pleased to dwell, and through him God was pleased to reconcile to himself *all things* [*ta panta*], whether on earth or in heaven, by making peace through the blood of his cross" (cf. Eph 1:22–23).

Next to these strong affirmations of God's ultimate cosmic triumph through and in Christ, when everything will be taken up in God's glory, and when there will be no more space for evil or resistance, there are, however, other passages in those same Pauline letters that suggest a final judgment when individuals will perish (1 Thess 1:10; 1 Cor 3:17; 9:22; Rom 10:1). In 1 Cor 1:18 Paul states the distinction: "For the word of the cross is folly to those who are perishing, but to us who are being saved it is the power of God" (RSV). Even in Colossians we read that "the wrath of God is coming on those who are disobedient" (3:6) and that "the wrongdoer will be paid back for whatever wrong has been done, and there is no partiality" (3:25). Members of the body of Christ, whom Paul assured that there is no condemnation (Rom 8:1), would have to appear before God's tribunal (Rom 14:12), could fall away from grace (Gal 5:4), and would reap destruction if they sowed to the flesh (Gal 6:6–9). Challenge and promise go hand in hand in exhortations to keep spirit and soul and body sound and blameless until the coming of our Lord Jesus Christ (1 Thess 3:13; 5:23; 1 Cor 1:8).

What to make of this diversity? Some scholars have argued that Paul's thought is developing and that the later Paul (Romans, Colossians, Ephesians) consistently affirmed the ultimate salvation of all creation, including all human beings.[24] Others, the majority in fact, hold that Paul subordinated the universalistic passages to the particularistic ones, and that his emphasis on faith as a condition requires him to assert that only believers are finally saved. Here we find E. P. Sanders, who emphasizes throughout his works that participation in Christ is paramount for all of Paul's

24. For an early proponent, see Dodd, "Mind of Paul: III."

soteriology. A third group opts for the opposite order of subordination and sees the universalistic passages standing out as Paul's main emphasis.[25] Fourth, there are those who find that Paul's conceptual clarity is wanting. Among them is J. C. Beker, who finds from a structuralist perspective that in the "deep" structure, the "coherent core," Paul's thought is corporate and universalistic; *there* the apocalyptic victory of God dominates. However, "his thrust cannot be logically pressed, because the context decides at every turn Paul's argumentative stance." Thus, for Beker, Paul's hermeneutic is characterized by the deliberate use of a "mixed language" that ultimately defies logical precision.[26]

Eugene Boring finds that Paul's soteriological assertions, instead of being analyzed as propositions, should be recognized as determined by the demands of central encompassing images: the imagery "God as a judge" presupposes conditional ("by faith") salvation; the imagery "God as king" presupposes unconditional ("by grace") salvation. Neither of the two should be subordinated to the other, since without the God-the-judge image, universal salvation would seem like fate and evangelism would lose its urgency, and without the God-the-king image, affirming limited salvation would amount to affirming a frustrated God who could not bring his creation to completion. Boring concludes that "Paul affirms *both* limited salvation *and* universal salvation. . . . As propositions, they can only contradict each other. As pictures, they can both be held up, either alternatively or, occasionally, together, as pointers to the God whose grace and judgment both resist capture in a system, or in a single picture."[27]

Assemblies and Society

Assemblies

We have painted a rough picture of Paul's conception of how his assemblies related to him and to each other, and how he defined their purpose, future, and relation to the Jewish diaspora communities and to the people of Israel. At this point our focus turns to how the assemblies related to Greco-Roman society (see also the section "Greco-Roman Religions and Philosophies," p. 84).

When Paul in his letters addresses believers in different cities, he uses the word *ekklēsia*. In Greek society, this word was used in various ways, most commonly to describe a gathering of citizens in a city-state who were eligible to vote (*ekklētoi*). Less specified, the word could also describe a spontaneous gathering of people (see

25. See, e.g., Best, *First and Second Epistles to the Thessalonians*, 368–69.
26. Beker, *Paul the Apostle*, 193–94.
27. Boring, "Language of Universal Salvation in Paul," 292.

Acts 19:32, 39–40). The Septuagint (LXX, the Greek translation of the Hebrew Bible) translates the Hebrew word *qahal* with the Greek words *synagōgē* (e.g., Ezek 38:4) or *ekklēsia* (e.g., Ps 26:23). At times both words occur together (*en mesō ekklēsias kai synagōgēs*, Prov 5:14), which may be translated as "in the assembled congregation." In the Hebrew Bible the words are *qahal* and *edah*, translated by the NRSV as "the public assembly." This indicates that in the LXX *ekklēsia* and *synagōgē* were taken as practically synonymous. The word *ekklēsia* occurs in Paul's letters with or without attributes, in plural and singular. Modern English translations most commonly use "church," but some use "congregation" (notably Tyndale 1534; also Jubilee Bible 2000), some use "assembly" (World English Bible [WEB]). German translations translate *ekklēsia* as "Gemeinde" (Luther Bible [LB], Unity Translation [EÜ]) or "Versammlung" (Elberfelder [ELB]). In this book we have chosen to use "assembly."

In Greco-Roman society *ekklēsia* is one of many words used for associations, where people of different social classes meet to uphold social, religious, or professional relations; consume communal meals; and revere earthly and supernatural benefactors (see the section "Associations: Men and Women as Leaders and Members," p. 155). When a whole household had become Christ followers, the family gathered in the atrium for worship, prophesying, singing, and celebrating the Eucharist. The atrium, usually the first room as one entered the Roman house and facing the street, contained the house altar (*lararium*), and was the natural place for religious cult activities in the home. Paul seems to assume that the gate of the house was open, so that visitors could come and go, when he writes, "If, therefore, the whole church comes together and all speak in tongues, and outsiders or unbelievers enter, will they not say that you are out of your mind?" (1 Cor 14:23). An interesting detail has been preserved in the legend of Paul and Thecla, where we can read that Thecla sat in the neighboring house's window day and night listening to Paul preaching in Onesiphorus's house.

An inscription found in Corinth in 1929, according to which Erastus financed street paving in exchange for being named vice mayor. Perhaps this is the same Erastus who sends greetings to Rome (Rom 16:23). If such is the case, we have yet more indication that Paul managed to reach wealthy and influential individuals in Corinth. Photo by Dieter Mitternacht.

Earlier we referenced a visit from Chloe's people to Paul in Ephesus. Perhaps Chloe was a fairly wealthy woman with business contacts in Ephesus; perhaps she was a *mater familias* who led her "Christian" household as a widow. Aside from Chloe's people, the household of Stephanas is mentioned as the first gathering of converts in Achaia, and we hear of the assembly meeting in Priscilla and Aquila's house (1 Cor 16:15, 19; Rom 16:3–5) and also of the assembly in Nympha's house (Col 4:15). Regarding Stephanas's household, we learn that they were devoted to the service of the saints (1 Cor 16:15). As a tentmaker (Acts 18:3), Paul belonged to the lower classes of society and likely succeeded best in reaching out to people from those classes (cf. 1 Cor 1:26). This of course does not disprove the possibility that he also succeeded to persuade some of a higher status.

It may reasonably be assumed that house assemblies consisted of up to forty people. As numbers increased, they would also gather in larger groups, maybe in a club house or a synagogue building, so that the same people sometimes met in smaller, sometimes in larger units. Paul, for example, sends greetings to the assembly in Corinth (singular) but refers to Chloe's people and Stephanas's households as groups within the assembly in the same city. Whether or not Chloe's and Stephanas's functions as congregational leaders were dependent on charismatic qualities is not mentioned, but it is evident that their social roles as heads of household were among their merits. That women led three of the four households that are mentioned should not come as a surprise, as it corresponds with archaeological finds from Pompeii, where women were frequently named as the heads of large households and owned houses of considerable sizes.

New Creation and Marginalization

The great variety of associations and cults indicates that the authorities in Greco-Roman society tolerated plurality. However, tolerance ended abruptly when such plurality went against the law, order, or the interests of the empire. Some scholars have argued that the public profession of Jesus Christ as Son of God and Savior (see box 5.3) and the confession that "Jesus is Lord" (1 Cor 12:3) were interpreted as an affront to the emperor, since these titles belonged to the emperor.

On the other hand, explicit statements against the Roman Empire or the emperor are conspicuously absent from Paul's letter. Also, Paul's frequent references to the cross were unlikely to provoke the authorities of the empire. But this does not mean that Paul was unpolitical or quietist. Instead, his social criticism seems to have been more fundamental, and his talk of the cross nothing less than an attack on "the rulers of this age [*hoi archontes tou aiōnos*]" (1 Cor 2:8). From this fundamental point of view, a kingdom or an emperor seems but a superficial ripple on the surface of world history, a God-ordained authority accountable to the divine judge and appointed to protect the good and punish the wicked (Rom 13:1–5). Such authorities may or may not be servants of God; however, "the rulers of this age" are essentially evil, the source of sin, flesh, and death. Against that, only an equally fundamental counter-power will do, and for Paul that is "the new creation." It began, subversively and violently, in Christ's death on the cross and can be compared to a bridgehead set up in hostile territory. The violence of this "invasion" is, however, inverted and of a kind that "none of the rulers of this age understood" (1 Cor 2:8). Instead of exerting violence, Christ let the violence of the powers kill him, and so overcame violence and evil with innocent suffering and death.

Box 5.3
ICHTHYS

ICHTHYS is Greek for "fish" and was used as an acronym for *Iēsous CHristos THeou Yios Sōtēr* (Jesus Christ, Son of God, Savior). The acronym and the fish as a symbol occur in Roman catacombs. It is not clear when it first came into usage by the Christ followers, but the middle of the second century seems likely. An interesting reference in this regard is found in Tertullian (155–230 CE), who, when writing about baptism, expresses himself in the following way: "But we, little fishes, according to the model of our *Ichthys* Jesus Christ, have been born in water."

It was clear to Paul that through baptism all believers were partakers of the death of Christ and had died to sin (Rom 6:2–3). They were no longer subject to the divisions of the old age; distinguishing circumcision from uncircumcision has lost its significance as a measure for membership ranking (Gal 6:14–15). In the new creation, there was to be no more discrimination based on human standards (*kata sarka*, 2 Cor 5:16–17). The faith of these believers was exclusive; there was no room for the emperor cult or any other cult. Anything but the worship of the God of Israel was *eidōlolatria*. Christ followers were to part with the power structures and values of the old aeon.

For Jews who had come to believe in Christ/the Messiah, the relation to the surrounding community did not change much. Many of their fellow Jews opposed them, but they still belonged to the Jewish community as they continued, like Paul, to worship the God of Israel in the local synagogue. Their identity was that they were part of the chosen people and abided by the covenant and its obligations.

Proselytes to Judaism joined a functioning social, economic, and religious network and were included in the regulations for and privileges granted to Jews in Greco-Roman society, such as exemption from military service and cultural obligations that are contrary to Jewish law. They could establish new family ties, marry Jewish partners, and conduct their business, economic, and cultural relations according to well-established rules and safeguards. In a society where everything was connected, including earthly and spiritual affairs, religious conversion was a tricky business; everything was affected if someone ceased to fulfill his or her duties.

For gentiles who had come to believe in Christ, the situation was different. Many of them had previous affiliations to Judaism as so-called God-fearers and were accustomed to alternating between their native family and community obligations (including cultic obligations) and associating with the synagogue community and worship. As uncircumcised Christ followers, they were, however, facing marginalization from two sides. They had broken with their family obligations, disengaged from their inherited social and cultural duties, on account of their exclusive commitment to Christ. Thus, they were identified, sometimes ostracized, as deserters of family and ancestry. Unlike proselytes, they had no new social and religious community that was ready to receive them into its net of basic provisions and protection, and Paul's claim that in Christ there is neither Jew nor Greek had not had much resonance in the synagogues. One can easily imagine the social and religious homelessness experienced by uncircumcised Christ followers, especially once the initial enthusiasm was fading. Considering the alternatives, conversion to Judaism must have seemed like a reasonable way out of a rather vulnerable situation, since, after all, all they wanted was to become what Paul was, a circumcised follower of Christ.

The effects, gravity, and consequences would have differed from city to city. Much would have been dependent on whether a social network for the Christ-following

The prison cell in Philippi in which, according to tradition, Paul and Silas were held. Photo by Dieter Mitternacht.

community could be established in a short period of time. Also, the severity of marginalization was probably more acute in rural than in metropolitan contexts, so that the consequences outlined here may be more applicable to Galatia than, for instance, to Corinth. Galatia, of course, is of particular interest, as it is in the Letter to the Galatians that Paul makes the most controversial claims about Judaism, the law, and circumcision. There, marginalization had become acute, so that some felt that they had to choose between returning to the religion of their ancestors (Gal 4:8–11) or becoming Jews through circumcision.

In Corinth the transition appears to have been quite smooth, as from the beginning there were several households where believers could become part of a functioning family network. Maybe some synagogue associations in a city were willing to integrate non-Jewish Christ followers as full members or subgroups into their community. In Philippi the hardships were great from the very beginning, and the assembly did its utmost to embrace its calling; the struggle was hard and despair widespread. Paul challenges them to be of the mind as Christ who submitted to obedience unto death and was rewarded beyond measure (Phil 2:6–11). "Rejoice in the Lord always; again I will say, Rejoice" (Phil 4:4), Paul exclaims, trying to turn their focus away from the earthly, to stop living like "enemies of the cross of Christ," and to accept, instead, that "our citizenship is in heaven, and it is from there that we are expecting a Savior, the Lord Jesus Christ" (Phil 3:18, 20).

With Spirit and Power

Conflict and confrontation followed Paul wherever he went. Many of his own kinsmen rejected him, yet he succeeded in place after place to win gentiles over to his gospel. What was the appeal? What made people trust his preaching, despite opposition, and share his way of life, which he himself described as being crucified with Christ? Why would they be willing to refrain from founding a family and, instead, prepare for departure from this world?

For Paul, the success of his gospel was without a doubt due to God's direct intervention. He had experienced how God revealed his Son to him and knew that the Spirit of God's active intervention was decisive for understanding "the thoughts of Christ." He reminds the Corinthians that what happened with them was due not to any persuasive ability of his but rather to a manifestation of the Spirit and power (1 Cor 2:4, 16; cf. 1:17). In the Letter to the Galatians, he emphasizes that their faith brought about the giving of the Spirit and miracles (Gal 3:2–5); and to the Thessalonians he writes, "Our message of the gospel came to you not in word only, but also in power and in the Holy Spirit and with full conviction; just as you know what kind of people we proved to be among you for your sake" (1 Thess 1:5). Paul's trademark, if you will, was the manifestation of the Holy Spirit in response to his preaching. His charisma created an atmosphere and experience of the presence of God's power.

From his first visit to Galatia he recounts that the people there thought him to be an angel from God, or even Christ himself, despite his weakness (Gal 4:14–15). Similar impressions can be gathered from Acts, where Luke tells of how the people in Lystra mistook Paul and Barnabas for the gods Zeus and Hermes, who had descended from heaven (Acts 14; see also 13:4–12).

For Paul, the Spirit of God was crucial for everything—for understanding the gospel, for the experience of God, and also for living the new life in Christ. "Live by the Spirit, I say, and do not gratify the desires of the flesh. For what the flesh desires is opposed to the Spirit, and what the Spirit desires is opposed to the flesh; for these are opposed to each other, to prevent you from doing what you want." Paul promises that if one opens one's heart to the Spirit, one will receive fruits and gifts and be able to live a life in accordance with the law, summarized as "You shall love your neighbour as yourself" (Gal 5:14–17). In the seventh chapter of Romans, Paul summarizes the human dilemma with the famous words "For I do not do the good I want, but the evil I do not want is what I do. Now if I do what I do not want, it is no longer I that do it, but sin that dwells within me" (Rom 7:19–20). It has often been said that Paul spells *sin* with a capitalized *S* since for him it is a personified and evil power inside humankind, the outcome being that instructions that are meant as guides to a good life instigate temptations, so that what is good accomplishes that which is evil. But at the same time, he seems utterly convinced that if the Spirit that awakened Christ from the dead replaces sin in humankind, dead bodies will come alive (Rom 8:11).

Manifesting the conviction in real life is, of course, a bit more complicated than writing about it. Reality is more difficult to handle than the ideal, as Paul's repeated admonitions to the Christ groups amply confirm. As the return of Christ appeared delayed and the crises within the assemblies and with the society surrounding them kept increasing, the message of the crucified Christ was more difficult to live by than many had estimated under the impression of Paul's charisma. Disappointment with the (lack of) impact of the Spirit, or the new creation, paired with the delay of Christ's return, may have been additional reasons that the non-Jewish Christ followers in Galatia wished to be circumcised and integrated into the local Jewish community. Without Paul's inspiring presence, his vision and radical thought had little chance of succeeding.

Successors of Paul

The end of the 60s entailed huge changes for the assemblies in Jerusalem, Antioch, Ephesus, Corinth, and Rome. Paul and Peter died as martyrs in Rome, and James "the brother of the Lord" met the same fate in Jerusalem. Of the known "apostles," only John remained. According to tradition, John lived in Ephesus up until the time of Emperor Trajan. He is presented as the companion of Peter (Acts 3:1; 4:13; 8:14;

Gal 2:9), a bearer of tradition, and the teacher of Polycarp, but in terms of being a regional leader he seems to have played an inconspicuous role. A new generation of leaders had to face fairly sudden and difficult challenges.

Who would continue the dynamic work of Paul? Who would hold together the networks that he had built? Who would take the lead and show the way in times of crisis? The will to continue the dynamic and at times overwhelming legacy of Paul was there, but there was also a need for peace and for building respect and acknowledgment in society (Titus 1:8; cf. Acts 9:31). At least three trajectories of tradition, or successions of Paul, may be traced in the New Testament. They are represented by (1) the First and Second Letters to Timothy and the Letter to Titus, (2) the Gospel of Luke and Acts, and (3) the Letter to the Colossians and the Letter to the Ephesians. As compared to the Johannine tradition, especially the letters of John, which testify to deep inner schisms, the Pauline tradition is remarkably cohesive. The network that Paul and his coworkers had built appears to continue to function; successors try their best to adjust Paul's central ideas to new situations and contexts. We will here introduce a few trajectories in the Pastoral Letters. Acts has already appeared several times in our analysis, and a related question from the Letter to the Ephesians will be highlighted in the section "'One New Humanity' (Eph 2:15), a Pauline Tradition and Its Reception History," p. 566. For dating of the texts, see the section "Letters Likely Not Formulated by Paul Himself," p. 324.

To Matter in Society

"As for me, I am already being poured out as a libation, and the time of my departure has come. I have fought the good fight, I have finished the race, I have kept the faith. From now on there is reserved for me the crown of righteousness" (2 Tim 4:6–8). The author of the Second Letter to Timothy presents himself as the aging Paul who looks back on his life with satisfaction and gives his younger coworker guidance on how the assemblies are to find and secure their place in society. The detailed instructions given in 1 Timothy and Titus seem to suggest that the letter genre is only a pretense; in reality these texts constitute congregational guidelines in the form of letters. Second Timothy is very personal, the only really "private" letter among the Pauline letters.

Typical for the Pastoral Letters is the great emphasis on the assemblies "lead[ing] a quiet and peaceable life in all godliness and dignity." Praying for kings and people with power is seen as an important task; the assembly is "the pillar and bulwark of the truth" and "the word that is trustworthy," a treasure to safeguard (1 Tim 2:1–4; 3:15; Titus 1:9). The apostle's disciple is the link to the next generation and the guarantor of the tradition's trustworthiness (2 Tim 2:2). The focus on spreading the gospel, confrontations with power holders, and the message concerning God's Messiah who put an end to this evil time have taken a back seat and pushed into the limelight the care of the Lord for his flock and directions for congregational structures, respectable leadership, and sound education. The proclamation of the word, kerygma, has been toned down in favor of the duty to safeguard "the good treasure [*tēn kalēn parathēkēn*]" (2 Tim 1:14).

Box 5.4
The Pastoral Letters

The collective term "Pastoral Letters," coined in the eighteenth century, is used as a designation for the First and Second Letters to Timothy and the Letter to Titus. *Pastor* is Latin and means "shepherd, leader." In the Canon Muratori (see p. 213), these letters are said to regulate the ecclesiastical discipline (*in ordinatione ecclesiasticae disciplinae*).

Both Titus and Timothy contain detailed instructions on which are the "right" qualities and way of life for an overseer (Gk. *episkopos*, from which *bishop* is derived, 1 Tim 3:2; Titus 1:7) and a helper (Gk. *diakonos*, from which *deacon* is derived, 1 Tim 3:8, 12). Instructions for elders (Gk. *presbyteroi*) and overseers overlap. Both should be blameless and take responsibility for God's church by preaching the word and teaching (1 Tim 3:5; 5:17; Titus 1:6–7). The overseer should have a "firm grasp of the word that is trustworthy" and be able to "refute those who contradict [the word]" (Titus 1:9). Neither the Eucharist nor baptism are mentioned in association with this description of tasks.

Whether there were at this time generally accepted practices for how to appoint or elect elders or overseers cannot be said for certain. According to Titus 1:5, the messenger of the apostles is commissioned to appoint elders; according to Didache 15.1, the assemblies appoint their bishops. It is unclear whether an assembly should have only *one* bishop. Around the year 100, Ignatius of Antioch claims and instructs that there should be *one*. The Pastoral Letters may corroborate this by implication as they refer to the overseer only in the singular (1 Tim 3:1–2; Titus 1:6–7; but cf. Phil 1:1).

The roles of leadership provided by the Pastoral Letters may have had their "predecessors" exclusively within contemporary Judaism, as "elder" and the "council of elders" (*presbyterion*, 1 Tim 4:14) are well-known terms from the synagogue, but there are no traces of the word *presbyterion* in Greek literature. At the same time, there were usually no overseers in the synagogue, although the Dead Sea Scrolls indicate that the Essenes had both elders and overseers, who were also supposed to be shepherds of the flock (cf. Acts 20:28–29).

Solidifying Structures and Leadership

A direct occasion of the Letter to Titus seems to have been the lack of official and tried leadership. Titus is given the mission of journeying to each city on Crete and to appoint elders (Titus 1:5). This indicates that Paul and others with him had not seen the need to prepare the assemblies for the transition to the next generation. The situation in Corinth indicates that there was a sort of charismatic leadership (1 Cor 12:28), as well as implicit agreements that those who organized gatherings in their house would also be accepted as seniors (1 Cor 16:15–19; see also Phlm 1–3, 21–22). But there were no appointed leaders with formally recognized authority (1 Cor 6:5–6). The statement in Acts that Paul and Barnabas appointed elders in each assembly (Acts 14:23) seems to have been a Lukan ideal with limited backing in reality. In the seven letters authored by Paul himself, Paul never mentions any elders, and the term *episkopoi* (plural) occurs only once in a greeting (Phil 1:1). Nor does Paul ever legitimize any leadership roles with theological arguments, and he appears to view them only as functions.

As we have seen earlier, Paul's letters refer to several household associations with both male and female leaders whose authority is connected to their social role as "owner" of the house (Chloe and Stephanas in Corinth, for example). We have also seen that a household can function as an association in which the *pater/mater familias* acted as the head (see the section "Associations: Men and Women as Leaders and Members," p. 155). Indeed, it seems a small step to eventually start using the term *episkopos* for this person, who already functions as the shepherd of the group, is responsible for the household, is already used to performing ritual actions, such as praying before meals, and who has the means of offering hospitality and accepting the weak into the community (cf. Stephanas in Corinth, 1 Cor 16:15).

It has been suggested that the absence of elders in the early household assemblies was because elders were only needed when several groups in the same city had to be coordinated. Until that point, each assembly had one *episkopos*. As the need for coordination increased, presbyteries were formed, and at times would consist of the same people who were overseers of the individual assemblies. Another explanation would be that there was no need for presbyteries as long as the early assemblies identified themselves as part of the larger synagogue community, which was usually run by a council of elders. However, because of the increasing departure of Christ groups from the synagogue community, not least because non-Jewish Christ followers began to organize and lead the assemblies, a growing need for separate institutional structures developed (see the section "Jewish Christ Followers and the Emergence of Christianity and Judaism," p. 365). From this angle there was, in fact, never a time without a "church" council, and no original one-man rule. Instead, leaders of household assemblies were always part of or subordinate to a leadership collegium.

In a later phase (sometime during the second century) we see a development that one member of the presbytery is appointed to be the *episkopos* for all. The fact that this was a disputed practice that could lead to abuse of power is indicated in the First Letter of Clement (dated to around the year 95). In that letter the presbyter collegium in Corinth is being defended against an autocratic bishop who would prohibit household assembly leaders from celebrating the Eucharist in their houses. In fact, the only mention of *episkopos* in the singular is in reference to God (1 Clem. 59:3).

The Change of Relations

The Pastoral Letters exemplify how the relationship between assemblies and society at large changed, and how that affected the ambition and structure of assemblies. Whereas in the pioneering phase the relationship was often one of conflict and tension, now the concern became increasingly to exhibit a respectable leadership and community structure. The delayed *parousia* quite certainly played a part in this development, as did the conviction that prophetic leadership needed to be reconciled with a structurally organized continuity (1 Tim 4:14; 5:23).

Some early Christ groups had begun to identify themselves as non-Jewish communities, so that around the year 100 Ignatius of Antioch would state rather bluntly in his letter to the Magnesians, "It is outlandish to proclaim Jesus Christ and practice Judaism, for Christianity did not believe in Judaism but Judaism in Christianity—in which every tongue that believes in God has been gathered together" (Ign. *Magn.* 10.3).[28] The undifferentiated way in which Tit 1:14 refers to "Jewish myths or to commandments of those who reject the truth" or 1 Tim 1:4 to "myths and endless genealogies that promote speculations" indicates that these letters belong to the time of Ignatius. Defining apostasy from the faith as "abstinence from foods, which God created to be received with thanksgiving by those who believe and know the truth" (1 Tim 4:3) points in the same direction. For Paul, these were matters of dispute over right practice in light of the mission to the gentiles, but not even in the heat of battle would he have called Peter an apostate. That it would be a sign of apostasy to forbid marriage (1 Tim 4:3) is exceptionally difficult to swallow considering Paul's recommendations to the unmarried in Corinth (1 Cor 7:8–9). In fact, the way false teachings are rejected is entirely different from Paul's own context. Instead of presenting counterarguments, the authors of these letters are content with simple references to that which "has been entrusted to you" (1 Tim 4:1; 6:20; 2 Tim 1:14; 2:2; Titus 3:10–11).

The leadership ideals that are provided are meant to help the assemblies find their place in society as respectable associations. Contemporary social norms therefore become guiding posts for what is to be accepted as proper and important. An overseer (*episkopos*) ought to be a good *pater familias* with a good reputation. He should not have been married more than once, have faithful and well-mannered children, not

28. Ehrman, *Apostolic Fathers*, vol. 1.

be a recent convert, be able to handle money, and not be fond of alcohol. This ideal of choosing leaders from among the quiet and self-controlled makes one wonder whether Paul himself would have made it through the first screening of applications (Titus 1:6–9; 1 Tim 3:4; cf., e.g., Gal 3:1; 5:12). Raymond Brown puts it succinctly: "Rough vitality and a willingness to fight bare-knuckled for the Gospel is part of what made Paul a great missionary, but such characteristics might have made him a poor residential community supervisor."[29]

The lists that define a poor lifestyle and warn against dangerous leaders, name characteristics that anybody might agree should be condemned. Such people are "boasters, arrogant, abusive, . . . lovers of pleasure rather than lovers of God" (see 2 Tim 3:1–9). The admonition to "avoid them" (v. 5) seems superfluous. The vilification of "weak women who will listen to anybody and can never arrive at a knowledge of truth," who apparently cannot resist these infiltrators (v. 6), makes one wonder about the reliability of labels and descriptions. How easy it is to dismiss critical voices through character assassination. Lifestyle norms are applied also to women, children, and slaves. Society's respect is won when all behave "as they ought." Slaves should not take advantage of their Christ-following master, but rather serve even more willingly (1 Tim 6:2). Women should accept their place in the home and be quiet in public spaces (1 Tim 2:9–15; 3:11; see also the section "Men, Women, and Power in Ancient Society and the Early Jesus Movement," p. 147).

By presenting Paul and his turbulent life as "an example to those who would come to believe" (1 Tim 1:12–17), the authors of the Pastoral Letters affirm the memory of a charismatic leader. But as to the tenor of the letters, there is very limited interest for unpolished individuals who stir up commotion. The rough pioneer type complicates a respectable establishment in society and may even hinder the institutionalization of the church. We are reminded of how much even structural and organizational instructions are bound by time and setting. The Pastoral Letters succeeded in uniting a respectful memory of the charismatic and provocative apostle Paul with instructions for a stable institutional church structure, thereby preserving for future generations of Christ followers the possibility of embracing both: maintenance of what has been tried and tested, openness toward the new and unexpected. The Pastorals also testify to a reduction, even repression, of the diversity and plurality of people, views, and community life, as compared to the days of Paul.

Further Reading

Barclay, John M. G. *Paul and the Gift*. Grand Rapids: Eerdmans, 2017.

———. *Pauline Churches and Diaspora Jews*. Grand Rapids: Eerdmans, 2011.

29. Brown, *Churches the Apostles Left Behind*, 35.

Beker, J. Christiaan. *Paul the Apostle: The Triumph of God in Life and Thought*. Philadelphia: Fortress, 1980.

Brown, Raymond E. *The Churches the Apostles Left Behind*. New York: Paulist Press, 1984.

Cameron, Ron, and Merrill P. Miller, eds. *Redescribing Paul and the Corinthians*. Atlanta: Society of Biblical Literature, 2011.

Fredriksen, Paula. *Paul: The Pagans' Apostle*. New Haven: Yale University Press, 2017.

Gager, John. *Who Made Early Christianity? The Jewish Lives of the Apostle Paul*. New York: Columbia University Press, 2015.

Harland, Philip A. *Associations, Synagogues, and Congregations: Claiming a Place in Ancient Mediterranean Society*. Minneapolis: Fortress, 2003.

Harrill, J. Albert. *Paul the Apostle: His Life and Legacy in Their Roman Context*. Cambridge: Cambridge University Press, 2012.

Hays, Richard B. *The Faith of Jesus Christ: The Narrative Substructure of Galatians 3:1–4:11*. Grand Rapids: Eerdmans, 2001.

Korner, Ralph J. *The Origin and Meaning of* Ekklēsia *in the Early Jesus Movement*. Leiden: Brill, 2017.

Langton, Daniel R. *The Apostle Paul in the Jewish Imagination: A Study in Modern Jewish-Christian Relations*. Cambridge: Cambridge University Press, 2010.

Lopez, Davina C. *Apostle to the Conquered: Reimagining Paul's Mission*. Philadelphia: Fortress, 2010.

Martin, Dale B. *The Corinthian Body*. New Haven: Yale University Press, 1995.

Nanos, Mark D. *Reading Romans within Judaism*. Eugene, OR: Cascade Books, 2018.

Nanos, Mark D., and Magnus Zetterholm, eds. *Paul within Judaism: Restoring the First-Century Context to the Apostle*. Minneapolis: Fortress, 2015.

Räisänen, Heikki. *Paul and the Law*. Philadelphia: Fortress, 1986.

Sanders, E. P. *Paul and Palestinian Judaism: A Comparison of Patterns of Religion*. Philadelphia: Fortress, 1977.

Stendahl, Krister. *Paul among Jews and Gentiles, and Other Essays*. Philaelphia: Fortress, 1976.

Stowers, Stanley K. "What Is 'Pauline Participation in Christ'?" Pages 352–71 in *Redefining First-Century Jewish and Christian Identities: Essays in Honor of Ed Parish Sanders*. Edited by Fabian E. Udoh. Notre Dame, IN: University of Notre Dame Press, 2008.

Thiessen, Matthew. *Paul and the Gentile Problem*. Oxford: Oxford University Press, 2016.

Udoh, Fabian E., Susannah Heschel, Mark A. Chancey, and Gregory Tatum, eds. *Redefining First-Century Jewish and Christian Identities: Essays in Honor of Ed Parish Sanders*. Notre Dame, IN: University of Notre Dame Press, 2008.

Watson, Francis. *Paul, Judaism, and the Gentiles: Beyond the New Perspective*. Grand Rapids: Eerdmans, 2007.

Wendel, Susan J., and David Miller, eds. *Torah Ethics and Early Christian Identity*. Grand Rapids: Eerdmans, 2016.

Westerholm, Stephen. *Perspectives Old and New on Paul: The "Lutheran" Paul and His Critics*. Grand Rapids: Eerdmans, 2004.
Winter, Bruce W. *Seek the Welfare of the City: Christians as Benefactors and Citizens*. Grand Rapids: Eerdmans, 1994.
Zetterholm, Magnus. *Approaches to Paul: A Student's Guide to Recent Scholarship*. Minneapolis: Fortress, 2009.
Zetterholm, Magnus, and Samuel Byrskog, eds. *The Making of Christianity: Conflicts, Contacts, and Constructions; Essays in Honor of Bengt Holmberg*. Winona Lake, IN: Eisenbrauns, 2012.

Johannine Christ Followers

The Gospel of John presents a clearly structured account of what occurred on Golgotha, summarized in five scenes (John 19:16b–37)—a five-part altarpiece (*Pentaptychon*) for reflection and meditation, if you will. The scenes are as follows:

1. The Inscription: Jesus as King (vv. 16b–22)
2. The Seamless Tunic: Jesus as Priest? (vv. 23–25a)
3. Jesus's Mother and the Beloved Disciple (vv. 25b–27)
4. Jesus's Cry of Thirst and the Handing Over of the Spirit (vv. 28–30)
5. The Flow of Blood and Water (vv. 31–37)

This series of images from the last day of Jesus's life, the sixth day of the week, when the sun had passed its zenith, must have been quite important for the gospel writers. The central scene logically receives the most attention: On the cross Jesus sees his mother and the disciple whom he loves. To his mother he says, "Woman, here is your son," and to the disciple he says, "Here is your mother." Through these five scenes the author wants to convey what happened, but perhaps even more to give the reader a deeper understanding of the actual event. These kinds of presentations of the accounts of Jesus are quite frequent in the Gospel of John. They mediate a message to the readers in the context of the readers. It is a message that has varied during the different stages of the history of the text.

The central scene in the Gospel of John's *Pentaptychon*—it does not exist in the other gospels—has been interpreted in various ways. Perhaps most important is what is implied in Jesus's words that make "the disciple whom he loves" the son of Jesus's mother, and thus a brother of Jesus. This is the meaning and outcome of Jesus's death. A new family is born; Jesus leaves behind a brother in the world. From a Johannine perspective, this brother is *all* of Jesus's disciples, present at the cross, as the disciple Jesus loved. Indeed, two days later they are called the brothers of Jesus (20:17; cf.

21:23), and Jesus's mother is accordingly afforded a home among them (19:27). The two (or three) other women who were present at the cross serve as a reminder to us that among the "brothers" there were also prominent women: a new community of siblings is born with Jesus's death. This is the message of the central scene in the Gospel of John's *Pentaptychon* for those who viewed it in the later part of the first century, people who later came to be known as "Johannine Christ followers." They might as well have been called "Johannine Jews," as they were with the greatest of likelihood Jews or adherents of Judaism.

These people are present already in the overture to the gospel, John 1:1–18, a gateway that opens toward the widest possible setting: the time before the beginning of all things, God and the Word with God, also God, and their activities in the world. The field of activities is gradually reduced: the Word in creation and with humans, the Word in its own and among its own (in the context of the Gospel of John primarily the land of Israel, especially Jerusalem, and the people of Israel), and finally in those who accept him, "who believe in his name" (1:12–17). They are born of God; they are God's children. With all their might they sing, "From his fullness we have all received, grace upon grace" (1:16). In the Gospel of John, these Johannine Christ followers identify themselves as the disciples who come to believe in Jesus as Messiah, Son of God, and hold fast to this belief.

Beyond the Gospel of John, we have four other Johannine texts in the New Testament—the three letters of John and the book of Revelation—that in the second century and later were attributed to Jesus's disciple John, son of Zebedee. They are themselves anonymous, save for the book of Revelation (or The Revelation of John, as it is called in the manuscripts). The author's manner of describing the apostles and himself does, however, indicate that he may in fact not be one of Jesus's twelve disciples. He presents himself as a servant of God, as a prophet among prophets, as a brother among brothers. The book of Revelation received the name it bears today at the same time as the other Johannine texts—that is, in the 90s or around the year 100. Together they constitute almost a fifth of the New Testament. A first attempt at describing the Johannine Christ followers might thus be as messianic Jews who have produced, accepted, and used the Johannine texts and their antecedents during the latter part of the first century. It is evident that several authors are behind the Johannine texts.

The Gospel of John and the three letters of John are connected for many reasons. One can refer to diction, sentence structure, style, ideological content, structural patterns, and so on. They often speak of the Father and the Son, of God's Son who became human, of light and darkness, truth and lies, God and Satan, being born of God, having an origin in God or belonging to God, being God's child, knowing God, remaining in God, keeping the commandments, loving one another, and so on. The first letter connects closely with the Gospel of John, especially its beginning and end and the section that is normally referred to as the Farewell Discourse (John 13–17). Fernando F. Segovia even claims that John 16 is written in the same context and with the same purpose as 1 John. The second letter is about the same issues as the first. It is at the same time very similar in form to the third letter and has the same sender. They are in fact so similar that some have wanted to see one as an imitation of the other. These four writings can thus for good reasons be combined under an overarching category that we traditionally call the Johannine texts.

It is with reference to these texts that we will here discuss the Johannine Christ followers. The Gospel of John has clearly been written over a longer period of time within a particular community, at least by a group of "authors" who were close to each other. The use of the word "we" can sometimes be interpreted as a reference to this "Johannine school" (John 21:24; 1 John 1:1–4; 3 John 9–12). The letters also indicate that some groups of messianic Jews were connected to one of these Johannine teachers, who is called "the Presbyter" ("the elder") in the two short letters. We can thus speak of a group of messianic Jews in the early church who adhered to the language and message of Jesus that we find in the Johannine texts. We can obtain a fairly good picture of them in 2 John, at the end of the first century.

This fragment of the Gospel of John, called P^{52}, is the oldest preserved manuscript from the New Testament. The fragment, the front of which contains 18:31–32, and the backside 18:37–38, was found in Egypt and is dated to around 120–150 CE. The University of Manchester Library.

The Family of Truth and Love

The Christ followers in the letters of John are described mostly in relational terms: they are children, loved ones, brothers, siblings, and friends; they know, love, remain in, and so on. This idea of community is seen especially in the short second letter, which is quite similar to the first. It is addressed to "the elect lady and her children" (2 John 1), and the final verse sends greetings from "the children of [her] elect sister" (2 John 12). These formulations are unique but have certain similarities in the contemporary setting. A group of people in antiquity, such as a city, could be addressed as "lady," which in Greek is *kyria*. The connection to the Old Testament and Jewish traditions is, however, more important. God's people on earth, or parts of it, are called "daughter Zion" (Zeph 3:14) or "virgin Israel" (Jer 31:21). Samaria is called the sister of Jerusalem (Ezek 16:46; 23:4). The people are God's bride, a picture that recurs in the New Testament—for example, in John 3:29, where everybody who joins Jesus is seen as a bride—and the covenant between God and his people is described as a marriage (Hos 1–3; Ezek 16). Seeing how many terms in the introduction of the letter are associated with a kind of covenant thinking, this background with its female imagery is probably the closest comparison.

We should perhaps also mention the book of Revelation, not for its use of the bride metaphor, but for the concept of the woman and her child in Rev 12. Just before that chapter, the ark of the covenant in the heavenly temple becomes visible to the prophet (11:19), and that which is revealed in chapter 12 is actually the history of the people of the covenant. The woman represents the people of God in its entirety, both in its Old Testament and New Testament forms; "her seed" is also a reference to the people of God, the church. Just as "the woman and her seed" in Revelation is a reference to the church, "the elect lady and her children" in 2 John may be referring to a local Christian community.

The "elect lady" in 2 John is thus with great likelihood a way of speaking about God's people on earth: a specific Johannine assembly, probably a house church or an association synagogue. The closest parallel to this may be found at the end of 1 Peter, where the "sister church in Babylon" (5:13)—that is, an assembly in Rome—sends greetings to the "chosen," who are addressed at the beginning of the letter (1:1). Also, 1 Peter is dominated by the concept of God's people. Second John addresses the target assembly as "dear lady" (v. 5), and the individual members of said assembly are thus referred to as "her children." The recipients of the letter are addressed as "you" (singular) in verses 4, 5, 13 and as "you" (plural) in verses 6, 8, 10, 12, a variation that is best explained by a collective meaning of the word "lady." That Kyria would be an individual woman is less likely.

The collective aspect, the local (house) assembly as a unit and a whole, is expressed through this biblical use of language. The fact that both verse 1 and verse 13 speak of the "elect lady"/"elect sister" confirms the same impression, as also the word "elect" is frequently used both for the people of God in its entirety and for individual members of this people (1 Pet 1:1; Rom 8:33; Col 3:12). The assembly is chosen by God and therefore in a special way connected to him. Introductory associations with family and marriage, perhaps also to *Kyrios*, "the Lord," strongly emphasize the solidarity of the group, as well as the collective aspects of singular terms. A local Johannine community is not only a number of individuals but a very well-connected entity, a flock of God with God/Jesus as the shepherd, or, to take a parallel from the Gospel of John, a vine of God—that is, Jesus himself with his disciples as branches (John 10; 15). Thus, the people presented at the beginning and end of 2 John form a community of love based on the truth (the words "love" and "truth" are repeated in the text)—a family of God that can partake in the common joy of meeting one another (v. 12), a complete joy because it has its source in God and is anchored in eternity. Alas, under evident pressure from outside, this intimate divine communion of siblings is torn apart toward the end of the first century. According to 1 John 2:19, for example, the consequences were quite severe. Some hate their "brothers," and others love them.

An Intra-Jewish Perspective

Seeing the Johannine Christ followers as Jews who came to believe in Jesus as Messiah, the Son of God, seems most fitting. Some features in the Gospel of John, such as the explanations of Semitic words, may indicate that the gospel in its final form was also meant to be read by non-Jews. Also, the short letters seem to conflate Jewish, Greek, and Johannine characteristics. Such conflations, however, may very well have existed within a Jewish context, and the gospel displays consistently a very strong Jewish ambiance. There are therefore good reasons to view the Johannine texts and the Johannine Christ followers from an intra-Jewish perspective, a perspective that may indeed have a universal range: "for God so loved the world" (John 3:16); "this is truly the Savior of the world" (John 4:42); "he is the atoning sacrifice for our sins, and not for ours only but also for the sins of the whole world" (1 John 2:2).

The description of the Johannine Christ followers in 2 John can be understood in general terms; it does, however, display a clear connection to the Old Testament's way of speaking of the covenant between God and Israel. It seems as though the concept of a new covenant contributed to the Johannine Christ followers' self-perception and identity from early on. They saw themselves as true Jews who, through the arrival of the Messiah, lived in a renewed covenant. Something similar can be said to some degree of other movements within Judaism before the Common Era; what was special to the Johannine Christ followers, however, was that they saw Jesus of Nazareth as the awaited Messiah, he who would come.

There are several references in the first letter to that which the addressees heard from the beginning—that is, the message that reached them when they came to believe in Jesus as Messiah. To hold fast to this message is necessary in order to be united with God here and now and thereby obtain eternal life. It is reasonable to assume that some central thoughts in this early teaching have left traces in the letter. In the final few lines, it is written, for instance, "And we know that the Son of God has come and has given us understanding so that we may know him who is true" (1 John 5:20). This formulation is a clear allusion to Jer 31:31–34 and the new covenant: God is to write his law in their hearts (the Greek translation, LXX, translates "minds") so that they no longer need to teach each other. All will know God. All sins will be forgiven. According to a parallel in Ezek 36, God is to give the people both his law and spirit so that they can do that which God wills. The set of concepts that belongs to the new covenant (forgiveness of sins; knowing God; obtaining God's law inwardly; no need of a teacher; new proximity to God, which results in a new form of obedience to the law; new and close communion with God, etc.) in many ways dominates 1 John. Speaking of God's faithfulness and righteousness as the basis for forgiveness (1 John 1:9) also has its source in the central covenant formula in Exod 34:6–7, with parallels both elsewhere in the Hebrew Bible and in Qumran texts.

Now, if the Messiah, God's Son, had come down to the world, the new covenant ought to be in place with its heavenly blessings. A close affiliation with God (knowing God, being in God, being born of God, having God's *sperma* [Gk. for "seed"] within oneself, having eternal life, etc.) had become reality for the Johannine Christ followers through Jesus Christ, God's Son, "the true God and eternal life" (5:20). These Christ followers would surely not classify themselves as "Johannine" but would perhaps see themselves as the people of Nathanael, or the "Nathanaelites," after Nathanael in John 1:45–51, who was a "true Israelite" with the full confession, "Rabbi, you are the Son of God! You are the King of Israel!" As God's gift to Jesus—Nathanael means "God's gift"—he represents the true disciple. The Johannine Christ followers surely saw themselves as true Israelites within the large Jewish community, as had many small groups in Israel's history before them (the holy remnant in the Hebrew Bible or in texts from Qumran).

These messianic Jews in the early church surely had their own history during the first century, even though we know little about them today. Their numbers varied and they lived in various places—a community of several generations. Some teachers and conveyors of Jesus stories—the "Johannine school"—had prominent positions and characterized the different communities. The Jewish revolt against the Romans in the 60s surely influenced them, as must have the changes within Judaism and the Roman Empire after the destruction of Jerusalem and its temple in the year 70. One phenomenon recurs in *all* Johannine texts, and that is conflicts of different types. Jesus's appearance and preaching about him led to "partings," "schisms" (Gk. *schismata*), within the Jewish communities. Thus, in one sense, these Johannine writings can be described as crisis literature.

The conflicts are described in various ways. In the gospel, they originate in different reactions to Jesus, what he says and does; in other words, it is a question of belief or unbelief. The conflicts also include disagreements between groups and individuals within Judaism that have different views on Jesus. The first letter describes a fateful division of the Johannine community (1 John 2:18–19), which, according to the dominant Christian interpretation, was due to a conflict about different forms of Christ belief. Those who left the assembly were influenced by gnostic teachers and had fallen away from the true Christ faith and conduct (*apostasy hypothesis*). Or, according to scholars from the latter half of the twentieth century, they developed their own Johannine way of thinking and living, which led to their exclusion from the Johannine Christ followers (*progression hypothesis*). The opponents were either gnostics or ultra-Johannine Christ followers. In the second letter, false teachers who have left the teachings of the Messiah are referred to in a similar way. The third letter encourages Gaius to accept brothers, likely wandering Jewish Christ-following prophets and teachers who did not belong to the Johannine Christ followers, and equip them for further travels, because Diotrephes refused to accept them. Diotrephes thus also distanced himself from the Presbyter and the Johannine Christ followers.

Is there a third alternative? Yes, many of them may be interpreted as returns to, and a remaining in, a Jewish faith that did not profess Jesus as Messiah (*regression hypothesis*). Any clear reasons behind this relapse are not given, but the gospel mentions a fear of Jewish leaders who had decided that any who acknowledged Jesus as Messiah would be excommunicated from the synagogue (9:22–23). Many who had come to believe in Jesus, even members of the Great Council, did not wish to openly admit it because of the Pharisees, as they did not want to be excommunicated from the synagogue (12:42–43). And according to Jesus's farewell speech (16:2–3), disciples of Jesus would in the future be excommunicated from the synagogue and killed, something that became a reality during the end of the first century.

These statements indicate that the Johannine Christ followers belonged within the public Jewish synagogue or were groups within association synagogues. As Jews, they were exempted from Roman conscription into the military, they did not have to worship the Roman emperor, and they could keep their own religious customs and festivities. Excommunication from the synagogue, however, meant that they would no longer hold these privileges. In addition to this, the introduction of a special Jewish tax by the Roman state made clear who was a Jew and who was not. The book of Revelation testifies to an increased demand on the Christ followers to worship the emperor. It is therefore historically likely that during the 80s and 90s Johannine Christ followers were heavily pressured by both Jews and Romans to abandon their messianic faith. Those who, according to the first letter, had left the Johannine community—the ones called antichrists and false prophets—are, from this perspective, those Johannine Christ followers who had left their messianic faith and returned to their old non-messianic Jewish faith. It seems as though the Johannine Christ-following groups disbanded around the turn of the first century. Some returned to their earlier communities, others sought more general Christian groups, and yet others felt more at home in gnostic-influenced assemblies. The Johannine Christ followers began to scatter just when the final editions of the Johannine writings were completed and came into use outside the Johannine community.

Eternal Life? Belief and Unbelief?

With this background, the terms "belief" and "unbelief" take center stage in the Johannine writings. To have eternal life, now and through faith, is the absolutely decisive concern. This is still the case after the texts are finalized. John 1–20 concludes with the statement: "so that you may come to believe that Jesus is the Messiah, the Son of God, and that through believing you may have life in his name" (John 20:31). Similarly, the first letter states: "I write these things to you who believe in the name of the Son of God, so that you may know that you have eternal life" (1 John 5:13). Both statements are naturally interpreted as encouragements to the addressees to hold fast to their messianic belief and be immersed in it, thereby gaining eternal life. In other words, the statements would seem to signify that both documents serve the purpose of edification for the community. However, from very early on, John 20:31 came to be read as an invitation *to come to* faith in Jesus, and the gospel, therefore, as a document for mission.

The Gospel of John uses the verb "to believe" (*pisteuein*) more than any other text in the New Testament (ninety-nine times), and the word is paralleled by other relational words, such as "see," "hear," "feel," "love," and "remain in." The word is often paired with a preposition (*pisteuein eis*) such that the meaning shifts more toward "rely entirely on," "bind oneself to," or "unite with." Unification between the Son and his own (the disciples who did not abandon him), and thus the Father, is described through these relational words as well as through images of the new community as a flock of sheep or a vine (John 10; John 15).

Of special interest in this context are the stories of Jews who came to believe in Jesus and later chose to abandon him. This occurred in the synagogue of Capernaum according to John 6. Those who had been present at the bread miracle on the other side of the Sea of Galilee followed Jesus, and in Capernaum's synagogue he speaks of himself as the manna and as the bread of life. The more Jesus speaks of himself, especially the words about eating his flesh and drinking his blood, the more critical the people in the synagogue become. Even many of his disciples react negatively and no longer wish to follow him. At the end of the story, the only ones remaining are the twelve apostles, who profess their faith in Jesus as the mediator of eternal life. But among the twelve there was also a traitor, a constant reminder of the risk of apostasy within the group of disciples.

Even in the temple's courtyards in John 8:31–59—a scene that has several expressions in common with the first letter's talk of antichrists—a development of faith is palpable. Jesus turns to "the Jews who had believed in him." His first response indicates that they were not truly willing to remain in Jesus's word—that is, accept the revelation of his relationship with God, of the Son and the Father. This leads to the harshest conversation we have between Jesus and other Jews in the gospel. These Jews who had once believed now took up rocks to throw at him. The conflict continues in John 9–10. A new division (*schisma*) occurred among the Jews that heard him (10:19–21) for the same reasons as earlier—that is, Jesus's statements about his unity with the Father. Here, too, it is a question of life, and life in abundance. "My sheep hear my voice," Jesus says. "I know them, and they follow me. I give them eternal life" (10:27–28). In true Johannine fashion, the division is amplified by the usage of dualistic language, opposites such as light/darkness, truth/lies, life/death.

Guidance in the Whole Truth

Similar to the lengthy faith process of many Johannine stories, which surely had analogies among the Johannine Christ followers and their surroundings, we find an interpretative process that left clear traces in the Johannine texts: brief commentaries; interpretative minor details; structural patterns; a series of typically Johannine words like "signs," "glory," "works," "time," "testify," "believe," in addition to other relational words mentioned above. The whole Johannine production is infused with the notion of the Helper or Paraclete (from Gk. *paraklētos*), a built-in elucidation program (John 14:15–17, 26; 15:26–27; 16:7–15) that encouraged renewal of different kinds. The Paraclete teaches and convinces—that is his main purpose. Indeed, Jesus says, "He will take what is mine and declare it to you" (John 16:14). This will happen after Jesus's time (death and resurrection) in the community that eventually takes shape in the Johannine Christ followers.

A Different Gospel

The Johannine texts are different, and so are the Johannine Christ followers. When Augustine expounded the Gospel of John in the beginning of the fifth century, he wrote, "The church knows two lives . . . one in the effort of action, the other in the reward of contemplation. . . . This [first life] has been signified by the apostle Peter, that other by John" (*Tractate on John* 124.5 [Rettig]). Clement of Alexandria had already two hundred years earlier characterized the gospel as "a spiritual gospel." Insights into the Johannine conceptual world and the uniqueness of the production are evidently quite old.

This uniqueness has its explanation primarily in the nature of the people and community that produced and lived with the writings—that is, the Johannine Christ followers. The Spirit, the Paraclete, led them to this deeper understanding of Jesus's teachings and their consequences. Johannine Christ followers lived in a particular Jewish environment; they had their own history. This strong anchoring in a historical setting is important for understanding how the Johannine texts have been interpreted later in history. The enemies could be Johannine Christ followers who had left their belief in Jesus as Messiah, the Son of God, or Christ followers who had been influenced by gnostic thoughts, or Jews in general. Generalizing the message of the Johannine texts or readdressing them carries unmistakable risks.

Further Reading

Ashton, John. *The Gospel of John and Christian Origins*. Minneapolis: Fortress, 2014.

Augustine of Hippo. *Tractates on the Gospel of John 112–124*. Translated by John W. Rettig. Pages 1–94 in *The Fathers of the Church*, vol. 5. Washington, DC: Catholic University of America Press, 1995.

Belle, Gilbert van, Jan G. van der Watt, and P. Maritz, eds. *Theology and Christology in the Fourth Gospel: Essays by the Members of the SNTS Johannine Writings Seminar*. Leuven: Leuven University Press, 2005.

Bernier, Jonathan. *John and Judaism: A Contested Relationship in Context*. RBS 87. Atlanta: SBL Press, 2017.

Brown, Raymond E. *An Introduction to the Gospel of John*. New Haven: Yale University Press, 2003.

Hanson, Anthony T. *The Prophetic Gospel: A Study of John and the Old Testament*. Edinburgh: T&T Clark, 1993.

Minear, Paul S. *John: The Martyr's Gospel*. New York: Pilgrim Press, 2003.

Moloney, Francis J. *Belief in the Word: Reading John 1–4*. Minneapolis: Fortress, 1993.

Olsson, Birger. *A Commentary on the Letters of John: An Intra-Jewish Approach*. Eugene, OR: Pickwick, 2013.

Reinhartz, Adele. *Befriending the Beloved Disciple: A Jewish Reading of the Gospel of John*. London: T&T Clark, 2002.

Schneiders, Sandra Marie. *Written That You May Believe: Encountering Jesus in the Fourth Gospel*. New York: Crossroad, 2003.

Non-Rabbinic Jews and Varieties of Judaism

In contrast to the earlier scholarly view that described the rabbinic movement as strong and influential already in the immediate aftermath of the destruction of the Second Temple, more recent scholarship suggests that the rabbinic movement remained a loose-knit network throughout the second century, beginning to gain influence only in the third or even fourth century. Rather than the swift ascent to power that scholars had earlier envisioned, the rabbinic movement seems to have emerged at a slow pace and to have been one of several groups that was competing for leadership. This understanding is largely the result of a more critical reading of rabbinic sources that takes into account the fact that they reflect the perspective and concerns of a religious elite, that rabbinic stories are literary creations with a didactic purpose and not intended to record historical events, as well as the role that later redactors had in reworking earlier material. The insight that the rabbinic movement did not dominate Jewish life in the way previously held raises the possibility that a variety of Jewish groups and ideologies continued to exist after the destruction of the Second Temple. An increasing number of scholars now maintain that Judaism post-70 was as diverse as it had been before.

The existence of non-rabbinic groups or individuals is indicated in rabbinic literature itself, although it is difficult to know what to make of the rather vague references to them. Rabbinic sources mention the *ame ha-aretz*, whom they describe as impious and unlearned. This is probably an example of the attitude of the elite toward ordinary people, but the depiction may also reflect polemics against a group or groups of Jews who simply did not share rabbinic interests and concerns. We also find rabbinic statements about Sadducees, sometimes portrayed as accepting Scripture only but rejecting oral tradition, and about individual priests and charismatics who appear to have retained pre-rabbinic models of religious authority. In addition, rabbinic literature mentions the *minim* ("sectarians" or "heretics"), the rabbinic generic term denoting non-rabbinic Jews of various stripes. It is clear from the sources that some *minim* were Jesus followers, but the term is broad and used to refer to other non-rabbinic groups and individuals as well.

The synagogue has been suggested as a possible setting for the preservation and/or development of non-rabbinic forms of Judaism. Archaeological remains, mainly from the Galilee, as well as early rabbinic sources seem to indicate that the synagogues were subject to a non-rabbinic leadership that did not always agree with rabbinic ideas and customs, while the rabbis and their disciples preferred the study house (*bet midrash*). The targums, the Aramaic translations and interpretations of the Hebrew Bible, which are generally believed to have originated in a synagogue setting, likewise reveal traces of a non-rabbinic origin. As the rabbinic movement gradually strengthened its position, the rabbis also gained more influence over the synagogues and the targums, but in spite of their rabbinization at some point in time, traces remain of their origins outside a sphere of direct rabbinic influence.

In pursuit of first-hand evidence for a post-70 diversity within Judaism, some scholars have explored the possibility that certain texts preserved in the collections of writings known as the Pseudepigrapha may provide traces of non-rabbinic forms of Judaism. These texts were preserved by Christians, and nearly all of them are the result of a long process of formation. Most of them were originally composed in Greek, although a Hebrew or Aramaic original is presumed for some of them. In cases where references or allusions to Jesus or New Testament texts appear, scholars are divided over the question of whether an originally Jewish work was later reworked by Christians, or whether it was entirely composed by Christians. Scholars in the first camp tend to see such texts as essentially Jewish with negligible Christian interpolations, while those in the other camp see them as Christian. The tacit assumption underlying the discussion is that "Christian" means gentile Christian, but another possibility is that Jews who had embraced Jesus interpreted the texts in light of the Jesus event, expanding and adding to them. This position is an outcome of the insight that Jewish self-identity in antiquity seems to have allowed for adherence to Jesus as an option *within* Judaism. Some recent scholarship has suggested that the groups behind these writings were "continuous communities," that is, Jewish groups who at some point in time incorporated Jesus into their worldview and worship, while retaining a Jewish self-identification.

However, we must also take into consideration that many Jesus followers already during the early centuries CE were gentiles, and hence some of these "continuous communities" likely also included gentile adherents to Jesus. In view of the attraction that Judaism seems to have held for non-Jews in the immediate centuries before and after the beginning of the common era, the presence of gentiles in Jewish groups was probably very common and did not distinguish Jesus-oriented groups from other Jewish groups. These gentiles likely had varying attachments to Jews and Judaism, but many of them seem to have adopted parts of a Jewish worldview and some even a semi-Jewish lifestyle. Since in most cases we cannot determine the ethnicity of ancient authors and addressees, we may want to at least consider texts that were likely produced by groups that were made up of a mix of Jesus-oriented Jews and gentiles as potential witnesses to a diversity within Judaism.

Although by no means exhaustive, the survey below provides a brief overview of texts from the Pseudepigrapha that may reveal traces of non-rabbinic forms of Judaism, preserved by Jesus-oriented groups of Jews and gentiles. They comprise a variety of different genres, including apocalypses, retellings of history, heavenly ascents and revelations, and deathbed speeches (testaments).

God's Justice and the Destruction of the Temple

Fourth Ezra, 2 Baruch, the Apocalypse of Abraham, and Liber antiquitatum biblicarum (L.A.B.) were probably written in Palestine sometime in the late first or early second century in response to the fall of Jerusalem and the destruction of the Second Temple. Fourth Ezra struggles with the question of God's justice in the wake of

Israel's fate at the hands of the Romans and doubts the viability of his covenant with Israel. The emphasis is on the sinfulness of humanity and judgment; only a remnant of the people will be saved (12:34). Second Baruch does not doubt the justice of God and emphasizes that those who observe the law will be protected. The destruction of the temple is a punishment for transgression, but God is merciful to those who repent and keep the law. Both 4 Ezra and 2 Baruch have a strong interest in the Messiah, and both draw on traditions that are close to rabbinic sources.

The Apocalypse of Abraham struggles with the problem of evil, especially in the form of idolatry, and ponders the question of what role the chosen people—Abraham's descendants—plays in the world. The work includes mystical and dualistic ideas, which have parallels in the Qumran literature, and it constitutes a link between early apocalyptic traditions and later *hekhalot* literature. It seems to contain allusions to Jesus, but there is no scholarly consensus on this. The Liber antiquitatum biblicarum is an early example of the genre known as rewritten Bible. It recounts the biblical narrative from Adam to David, revising and expanding the story as the author sees fit. It is one of the earliest works of midrash and shares some traditions with later rabbinic midrash. Like the works mentioned above, it seems to have been written not long after the destruction of the Second Temple and to derive from a similar social and cultural context. It emphasizes that God will never abandon his people no matter how hopeless their situation appears and no matter how much they suffer. However long it takes, they will be saved in the end.

The Law of Moses and Ethical Norms for All

A number of Jewish texts from the late first or second centuries focus on the ethical commandments of the Torah and seem to posit a universal pattern of piety incumbent on Jews and gentiles alike. The fourth and fifth books of the Sibylline Oracles, dated to the late first century, urge gentiles to abandon idolatry, turn to the worship of the one God, and observe a set of basic moral standards. Humankind is divided into two groups—the pious and the impious—but while the pious are closely associated with Israel, piety is defined in terms that make no reference to Israel's covenantal relationship to God. The oracle is addressed to gentiles who are urged to convert to a pattern of piety that is identified with Israel but not explicitly linked to the law of Moses. Piety involves rejection of idolatry, worship of the one God, and abstention from murder, dishonesty, adultery, and male homosexual relations (4:25–34; cf. 5:429–31). The fifth book of the Sibylline Oracles expresses outrage with the gentile nations in general and with Rome in particular, whereas the fourth book sees the destruction of the temple as a punishment for sins.

The first- or second-century Testament of Abraham is an account of events leading up to Abraham's death, including a cosmic journey, characterized by Terence

Other texts, which may constitute evidence of the continued existence of a variety of forms of Judaism preserved by Jesus-oriented groups of Jews and gentiles, are the Lives of the Prophets, 3 and 4 Baruch, and the Odes of Solomon. Many of these writings indicate an active interest in prophetic and priestly traditions, and it is possible that some segments of the Jewish population continued to adhere to such models of authority. Or, perhaps the first century witnessed a revival of prophetic activity because of the widespread belief that the end of time was near.

Adherence to Jesus in Continuity with Judaism

Another group of texts that has recently been explored as potential evidence for non-rabbinic forms of Judaism is found in the Christian apocrypha. A handful of these texts combine adherence to Jesus with a Jewish self-identity and/or display a generally favorable attitude to Judaism and Jewish law and were likely composed by Jesus-oriented Jews and/or gentiles during the early centuries CE. Reading such texts as evidence of a diversity of Jewish religiosity, rather than as expressions of a heretical Christianity ("Jewish Christianity"), is the result of the insight that Jewish identity in antiquity was flexible enough to accommodate Jesus-oriented Jews. However, as noted above, many if not most Jesus adherents already during the early centuries CE were likely gentiles, and there is often no way of determining whether a given text was composed by a Jesus-oriented Jew or a gentile. Rather than focusing on the question of ethnicity, it may be more fruitful to focus on particular traits of the texts, which may seem to indicate a Jewish, or partly Jewish, social context. One could reasonably argue that texts that see adherence to Jesus as being in continuity with Judaism stand in radical continuity with Second Temple Jewish traditions, display more "Jewish" features than we usually associate with Christian texts, and adopt a Jewish self-identity and/or seem to have been shaped in part by contact with non-Jesus-oriented Jews,[31] evolved in a Jewish milieu, and could thus potentially reveal traces of non-rabbinic forms of Judaism. This holds true even if some, or even most, of the members of the groups behind such texts were gentiles. Texts displaying some of these traits include the Apocalypse of Peter, the Gospel of Nicodemus, the Protevangelium of James, and some of the Pseudo-Clementine writings.

A text that seems to have functioned in a Jewish milieu and been authored by a Jesus-oriented Jew is *Recognitions* 1.27–71, a distinct source preserved in the Pseudo-Clementine writings. Dated to circa 200 CE, it was written by an author who believed that Jesus was the Messiah and who saw his advent as the goal and fulfillment of Israel's history. Most scholars agree on the Jewish character of this source, citing the author's concern for Jerusalem and the land of Israel, the sympathetic attitude to non-Jesus-

31. Characteristics identified by Reed, "'Jewish Christian Apocrypha,'" 113.

oriented Jews, the portrayal of Jesus adherents as a group within Judaism, the praise of Hebrew as the original tongue of humankind, and the absence of anti-Jewish polemic common in contemporaneous gentile Christian texts. The author is concerned to convince his fellow Jews that Jesus is the Messiah and emphasizes the continuity between Jesus's teachings and those of Moses. Jesus is seen as the prophet predicted by Moses (Deut 18:15–18; Acts 3:22–23), but as both prophet and Messiah he is even greater than Moses (*Rec.* 1.59.2–3). He is said to have abolished the sacrifices, in their stead instituting immersion in water "for the forgiveness of sins" (1.39.1–2). Apart from the innovation of baptism, Jewish practices seem to remain the same. The author even states explicitly that adherence to Jesus is the only difference between the Jesus followers and "those among our people who do not believe" (1.43.2; cf. 1.50.5). The author's focus is solely on Jews. The mission to the gentiles is mentioned only a few times in passing and is said to have come about only because all Jews have not embraced Jesus (1.42.1).

In contrast to *Rec.* 1.27–71, the *Homilies* (or *Klementia*), one of the two main texts that make up the Pseudo-Clementine writings, is mainly concerned with the mission to the gentiles but nevertheless displays signs of having been shaped by a Jewish milieu. The early fourth-century *Homilies* is believed to rely on a no-longer-extant early third-century source that likewise focuses on gentiles, prescribing for them a slightly expanded version of the Apostolic Decree (Acts 15:19, 21). Jesus is seen as the latest incarnation of the Prophet of Truth, whose teachings for gentiles stand in continuity with Moses's teachings for Jews. In the case of the *Homilies*, it does not seem possible to determine whether the author(s)/redactor(s) was a Jesus-oriented Jew or a gentile, but the work presents its instructions as Jewish teachings for non-Jews, and a number of traits in the text might seem to indicate that the author and his addressees were at home in a social milieu that also included non-Jesus-oriented Jews.

For instance, the author is sympathetic to non-Jesus-oriented Jews and insists that they remain part of God's people and have their own path to salvation through Moses (*Hom.* 8.5–7). Moreover, he is familiar with specifically rabbinic ideas (2.38.1; 3.47.1) and accepts rabbinic claims to authority, presenting prophetic truth as being conveyed in two equivalent ways; through the oral interpretative tradition passed on from Moses and through the teachings of Jesus transmitted via Peter and his followers (3.4.1; 16.14.4–5; cf. 3.70.2). He envisions his assemblies of Christ as being closely aligned with Jews and Judaism, while marking a certain distance from gentile forms of Christianity. It is noteworthy that he does not use the word "Christian," instead referring to the worshipers of the only God as *theosebeis* (God-fearers or God-worshipers), a term that includes non-Jesus-oriented Jews as well as Jesus-oriented gentiles. Possibly, this terminological choice signals both a connection to Judaism and a protest against the separation of Jesus followers from Jews and Judaism within other Christian groups.

According to the *Homilies*, baptism transforms "pagans" into righteous gentiles and gives them the same status as Jews without turning them into Jews. Both Jewish and gentile *theosebeis* must observe God's law, but the commandments for the latter seem to be fewer than those incumbent upon Jews. Since the *Homilies* is concerned with law observance for gentile adherents to Jesus, we cannot draw any certain conclusions regarding Torah observance for Jews who had embraced Jesus, but the high regard in which the author holds "God's law," along with the fact that Jesus is seen primarily as a teacher of gentiles and that Jews are generally held up as a model of behavior, would seem to indicate that he did not envision any change in their lifestyle. With the Jesus event, the people of God has been reconfigured along purity lines rather than ethnicity, but Jewish law and Jewish values constitute the standard by which baptized gentiles are expected to live.

The *Epistula Petri* and *Contestatio* (or *Adjuration/Diamartyria*), two introductory writings attached to the Greek codices of the *Homilies*, also deserve to be mentioned, although their unclear date and relation to the *Homilies* make this evidence difficult to assess. Here, Torah transmission among the followers of Moses is presented as the model for the transmission of Peter's teachings (*Ep. Pet.* 1.1–2; 3.1–2), and against "some from among the gentiles" who have rejected his legal teachings and distorted his words in order to achieve the "dissolution of the law," Peter asserts the eternal continuance of "the law of God, which was spoken by Moses and affirmed by our Lord" (2.2–4). According to the *Contestatio*, Peter's teachings should be safeguarded only by those who are circumcised and faithful (*Cont.* 1.1), possibly reflecting a Jewish milieu, or at the very least a wish to present Jesus's teachings as belonging in a Jewish context.

The problem we face when trying to recover non-rabbinic forms of Judaism is that rabbinic Judaism has become the sole criterion by which Jewishness is determined. Thus, whatever does not conform to rabbinic standards is deemed non-Jewish, creating a vicious circle that prevents us from discerning a potential diversity within post-70 Judaism. Conversely, texts that include references to Jesus are automatically considered Christian, and hence non-Jewish. However, we must keep in mind that in the early centuries of the common era, Judaism and Christianity were not yet established as clearly separate entities, and many ordinary Jews and Jesus followers do not seem to have considered Jesus-centeredness and Torah-centeredness as mutually exclusive. Organized around voluntary associations, which based membership on a common occupation and residence in the same neighborhood as well as cult, ancient Greco-Roman society would have seen a constant interaction among "pagans," Jews (Jesus-oriented and non-Jesus-oriented), and Jesus-oriented gentiles. Such daily contacts would have included an exchange of ideas as well as polemics. Many ideas that would eventually be defined as "Christian" and "Jewish" respectively were established in a process of identity formation whereby some notions prevalent in first-century Judaism were appropriated by groups of Jesus followers and, as a result, were de-emphasized or even rejected by non-Jesus-oriented Jewish groups. The latter, who over time would form the nucleus of rabbinic Judaism, emphasized different aspects of Second Temple Judaism and invented new literary genres, locating God's presence in law rather than in history. Many of the texts preserved in the Pseudepigrapha seem to have undergone a similar process. Jesus-oriented groups appropriated them, and as these groups became increasingly gentile, the texts were disowned by Jews.

Further Reading

Collins, John J. *The Apocalyptic Imagination: An Introduction to Jewish Apocalyptic Literature.* 2nd ed. Grand Rapids: Eerdmans, 1998.

Donaldson, Terence L. *Judaism and the Gentiles: Jewish Patterns of Universalism (to 135 CE).* Waco: Baylor University Press, 2007.

Feldman, Louis H., James L. Kugel, and Lawrence H. Schiffman, eds. *Outside the Bible: Ancient Jewish Writings Related to Scripture.* 3 vols. Philadelphia: Jewish Publication Society, 2013.

Frankfurter, David. "Beyond 'Jewish Christianity': Continuing Religious Sub-Cultures of the Second and Third Centuries and Their Documents." In *The Ways That Never Parted: Jews and Christians in Late Antiquity and the Early Middle Ages.* Edited by Adam H. Becker and Annette Yoshiko Reed. Minneapolis: Fortress, 2007.

Himmelfarb, Martha. "The Partings of the Ways Reconsidered: Diversity in Judaism and Jewish-Christian Relations in the Roman Empire; 'A Jewish Perspective.'" In *Interwoven Destinies: Jews and Christians through the Ages.* Edited by Eugene J. Fisher. Mahwah, NJ: Paulist Press, 1993.

Jones, F. Stanley. *An Ancient Jewish Christian Source on the History of Christianity: Pseudo-Clementine Recognitions 1.27–71.* Atlanta: Scholars Press, 1995.

Reed, Annette Yoshiko. "'Jewish-Christian' Apocrypha and the History of Jewish/Christian Relations." In *Rediscovering the Apocryphal Continent: New Perspectives on Early Christian and Late Antique Apocryphal Texts and Traditions.* Edited by Pierluigi Piovanelli and Tony Burke. Tübingen: Mohr Siebeck, 2015.

———. "Rabbis, 'Jewish Christians,' and Other Late Antique Jews: Reflections on the Fate of Judaism(s) After 70 C.E." In *The Changing Face of Judaism, Christianity, and Other Greco-Roman Religions in Antiquity.* Edited by Ian H. Henderson and Gerbern S. Oegema. Gütersloh: Gütersloher Verlagshaus, 2006.

Zetterholm, Karin Hedner, "Jewish Teachings for Gentiles in the Pseudo-Clementine *Homilies*: A Reception of Ideas in Paul and Acts Shaped by a Jewish Milieu?" *Journal of the Jesus Movement in Its Jewish Setting* 6 (2019): 68–87.

Gnosticism and "the Gnostics"

The term "Gnosticism" is derived from the Greek word *gnōsis*, which means "knowledge," especially in the sense of theoretical knowledge or insight. The term is customarily used for systems of thought prevalent in the early Christian period that (1) emphasized the spiritual knowledge about human beings' true, divine origin and (2) regarded the visible world and the human body as created, not by the supreme God, but by an inferior creator-God.

The term "Gnosticism" itself is a late invention, coined in the seventeenth century. There were, however, in the second century people who designated themselves as "gnostics" (*gnōstikoi*)—that is, "those in the know." They preferred myth as the venue to address the present state of affairs in the world, the human condition, and the ultimate goal of humankind. The information we have of the teaching of these people is related to their elaborate views about the divine realm and their story of how our world came into being. In this story, a female divine being, called Wisdom (*sophia*), disturbed the tranquility of the divine realm. She reached outside the boundaries of the divine world to find herself a consort. The result of Wisdom's ill-advised action was the inferior creator-God, who created a universe of his own, with heavens, angels, the visible world, and humans (Irenaeus, *Against Heresies* 1.29).

This myth builds on, but also dramatically subverts, the Jewish tradition in which God's wisdom had been described as God's first creation and companion assisting God in the creation of the world (Prov 8:22–31). The myth is also indebted to the Platonic philosophical tradition, in which it was held that a creator-God (called the demiurge, "craftsman") observed the preexisting world of ideas and used it as a model for the creation of our world. The negative picture drawn of the creator-God in the gnostics' myth, however, made their teaching distinct from the philosophical mainstream.

Some scholars propose that we should speak of "gnostics" only in connection with these people who designated themselves as such.[32] There were, however, other early Christian groups who taught myths similar to that of the gnostics but did not call themselves gnostics. This raises the question of whether *we* can call them gnostics (because their teaching was in part similar with that of the "original" gnostics) or not (because they didn't use "gnostic" as a self-designation).

The issue is even more complicated for two reasons. First, other kinds of Christians also used the term "gnostic" to refer to a right kind of Christian. Clement of Alexandria (ca. 150–215) described as "the gnostic" the ideal Christian, who always knows and chooses the right course of action in different situations. Clement distinguished not between "faith" and "knowledge" but between two kinds of knowledge, "true" and "false." This distinction entitled him to appropriate the term "gnostic" and to reject other Christians who claimed this term for themselves.[33] Second, the scholarly usage of "Gnosticism" can be misleading. More often than not, the impression is created that "Gnosticism" formed a front different from, and opposed to,

32. Brakke, *Gnostics*.

33. Marjanen, *Was There a Gnostic Religion?*, 14–15.

true Christianity.[34] This usage blurs the fact that most of those people who are now lumped together as "gnostics" understood themselves as Christians. Would Clement have been able to identify them as a different front?

Gnostic Ideas behind New Testament Texts?

Gnosticism is an especially fuzzy concept in the academic study of New Testament texts. It used to be connected with views that were *rejected* by New Testament authors, and it used to be assumed that Paul's opponents in 1 Corinthians, who taught that "all things are lawful for me" (1 Cor 6:12), were Christians of gnostic variety.

The contradicting statements about sin and sinlessness in 1 John are sometimes explained in a similar manner. The author of 1 John insists that those born of God do not and even cannot sin (1 John 2:4–10), but he also instructs the readers that they should *not* say "we have no sin" but that they should confess their sins instead (1 John 1:8–9). One explanation of the contradiction between these two views is that the author embraced sinlessness as an ideal, but condemned Christians who saw in this ideal an excuse for immoral behavior. The opposed teaching in this case would be that those in the know are sinless by nature and therefore remain sinless no matter what they do.

Even though the author of 1 John does not describe his opponents' moral errors in detail, scholars have been eager to posit a link between these opponents and the gnostic teaching, which allegedly permitted immorality for some people. The problems with this explanation are twofold: we can't be at all sure what the author's opponents taught, and the image of gnostics as approving of and practicing immoral behavior is based on malevolent rumors coming from polemical texts written much later than 1 John.

On the other hand, it has been suggested that some New Testament authors, including Paul and the author of John's Gospel, borrowed some ideas from gnostic thought, such as the portrayal of Christ as the "man of heaven" (thus Paul, 1 Cor 15:48) and the heavenly revealer descending from and ascending back to God (thus John's Gospel). It used to be assumed that both teachings presuppose a more elaborate myth of God's messenger on earth, and that this myth was in some way "gnostic."

The Nag Hammadi Library

Such theories about the gnostic background of New Testament texts have become outdated since they are based on views about Gnosticism that were preva-

34. King, *What Is Gnosticism?*

lent in scholarship prior to the discovery of the Nag Hammadi Library in Egypt in 1945. This collection comprises thirteen volumes of firsthand sources—that is, texts written by people whose views were previously known from their opponents' polemical works.

The Nag Hammadi Library was put together in the late fourth century CE, and all texts in it are in the Coptic language (the last form of Egyptian). Nevertheless, it can be assumed that many texts in this collection were originally composed in Greek, some already in the second and the third centuries CE. In some cases, this can be proven beyond doubt: there are earlier Greek fragments for some texts included in the Nag Hammadi Library, some others contain grammatical infelicities that can only be due to a Greek original, and some are mentioned or referred to in texts composed much earlier than the Nag Hammadi Library. For example, Irenaeus in the 180s knew a work that was identical with, or very similar to, the Secret Book of John.

The Nag Hammadi Library is *not* a collection of gnostic texts only, although it is often described as such. There are a number of texts in which cosmic myths similar to those taught by the aforementioned gnostics are related, but there are also many texts in which such myths play no role whatsoever. Most texts in the library are *Christian* in the sense that in them Jesus is the main character as the revealer of things divine, and his disciples frequently appear as recipients and transmitters of this revelation. The most common form of such texts is revelation dialogue, in which Jesus's teaching is interrupted by the disciples' short questions. In addition, there are many other types of texts, such as treatises, myths, prayers, and liturgical instructions.

A large majority of the texts in the library were previously unknown. The library contains no copies of biblical texts, but they are quoted and explained in some of the library's texts. There are also some non-Christian texts in this collection. One volume (NHC VI) features an excerpt from Plato's *Republic* and passages from Hermetic texts. In addition, there are other texts in this library where neither Christ nor the disciples are mentioned at all. It is debated whether their authors were Christians or not.

One of these texts, Eugnostos the Blessed, is an especially intriguing case: someone found it necessary to "Christianize" this text by turning it into a dialogue between Jesus and the disciples; the resulting text is called the Wisdom of Jesus Christ. It is striking that the latter text did not replace the former; both texts are placed back to back in one volume of the Nag Hammadi Library (NHC III).

It is important to note that the Nag Hammadi Library is not the only existing collection of this sort. There are other, smaller collections of Coptic texts with similar tenets. The most famous of them are the Berlin Gnostic Codex (Berlinus Gnosticus, BG) and the Codex Tchacos (CT). The publication of the latter collection in 2006 made headlines since it contains the Gospel of Judas. In this text, Jesus harshly condemns the apostles and their form of Christianity, and conducts private discussions with Judas the Betrayer. These collections show that such texts must have enjoyed great popularity in Egypt in the early centuries CE.

Major Strands of Christian Gnostics

Two major strands of early Christianity represented in the Nag Hammadi Library are the so-called Sethians and the school of Valentinus. While the latter group was well known already, prior to the library, from other sources, one of the most important results of Nag Hammadi studies has been the discovery of Sethian theology and its vast importance. At least eleven texts in the Nag Hammadi Library represent this current (Secret Book of John, Nature of the Rulers, Gospel of the Egyptians, Revelation of Adam, Three Steles of Seth, Zostrianos, Melchizedek, Thought of Norea, Marsanes, Allogenes the Stranger, and Three Forms of First Thought). Some of these texts show remarkably close similarities with the mythic theology of the aforementioned gnostics.

Sethians

The group of people now called "Sethians" did not use this name for themselves, but they called themselves (or sometimes all humans) "the seed of Seth." Seth is the third son of Adam and Eve in the biblical creation story (Gen 4:25). In Sethian mythology, Seth transmits to humankind the secret revelation Adam received from the supreme God.

Divinity is described in Sethian mythology as a trinity consisting of Father, Mother, and Son. "Mother" is another name for the Father's first thought, which set the creation of the divine world in motion. It is emphasized in Sethian texts that the Father of all cannot be grasped with human reasoning:

> The One is not corporeal and it is not incorporeal.
> The One is not large and is not small.
> It is impossible to say,
> How much is it?
> What [kind is it]?
> For no one can understand it.
> (Secret Book of John, NHC II, 3)[35]

The inferior creator-God is in Sethian texts called Yaldabaoth. While it is unclear what this Semitic name means ("a child of chaos" or "the father of Sabaoth"?), this

35. Trans. Meyer, *Nag Hammadi Scriptures*, 109.

god is identified with the Jewish God described in the Hebrew Bible. The Sethian picture of this god is a very negative one. Just like God in the Hebrew Bible, Yaldabaoth claims to be the only god: "I am a jealous god and there is no other god beside me" (Secret Book of John, NHC II, 13; cf. Isa 45:5–6; 46:9). Yet unlike in the Hebrew Bible, this self-acclamation is presented as empty boasting, only due to Yaldabaoth's ignorance of the higher God: "For if there were no other god, of whom would he be jealous?" (Secret Book of John 13).

Yet another characteristic feature of Yaldabaoth and his angelic minions, who assisted him in the creation of the world, is unrestricted sexual desire. When the true God sent Eve to Adam to instruct him, Yaldabaoth "defiled" her image by having intercourse with her. As a result, the whole of humankind was infected with obsessive sexual lust (Secret Book of John 24). Sexual desire, however, was only one of several things by which Yaldabaoth and other evil angels sought to lull humankind into the state of forgetfulness; luxury items ("gold, silver, gifts, copper, iron, metal and all sorts of things") were also introduced for this purpose (Secret Book of John 29).

Although the present state of humankind in this world is described in dark colors in Sethian texts, the texts also show a way out of this state. Christ is described as the heavenly revealer who comes down to "the realm of darkness" and raises humans up from their ignorance:

> I said, Let whoever hears arise from deep sleep.
> A person wept and shed tears. Bitter tears the person wept away, and said, "Who is calling my name? From where has my hope come as I dwell in the bondage of prison." (Secret Book of John 31)[36]

The conversion described here is not merely an intellectual one; it also involved a baptism, which is portrayed as a seal bestowed on the awakened person. Some other Sethian texts are very much focused on this ritual, envisaging a number of baptisms to be performed at different levels of one's spiritual progress (one example: Zostrianos, NHC VIII).

The origins of Sethian thought and mythology cannot be traced with certainty. The use of Semitic names for key characters in the Sethian myth suggests that its roots lie in some form of ancient Judaism. In addition, some Sethian authors seem to have been familiar with nonbiblical Jewish apocalypses and share with them the tendency to rewrite and expand the biblical creation stories. It is, however, difficult to explain against this background why Sethian thought became so clearly adverse to key Jewish beliefs. For the most part, the evidence for Sethians shows Christian features (such as the crucial role ascribed to Christ as the heavenly revealer), but there are some Sethian texts where Christian traits are less clearly visible or entirely

36. Meyer, *Nag Hammadi Scriptures*, 131.

absent. It has been proposed on the basis of such texts that Sethian thought gradually became less Christian and more aligned with non-Christian philosophy.[37]

The School of Valentinus

Valentinus was an early Christian teacher who moved from Egypt to Rome circa 130 CE. He is considered the founder of an early Christian group that became quite popular in different parts of the Roman Empire. Valentinus's own views are poorly known; less than a dozen brief passages from his works survive in his opponents' works. Valentinus, however, had a few prominent followers whose views were more fully described in writings of early Christian heresy-hunters.

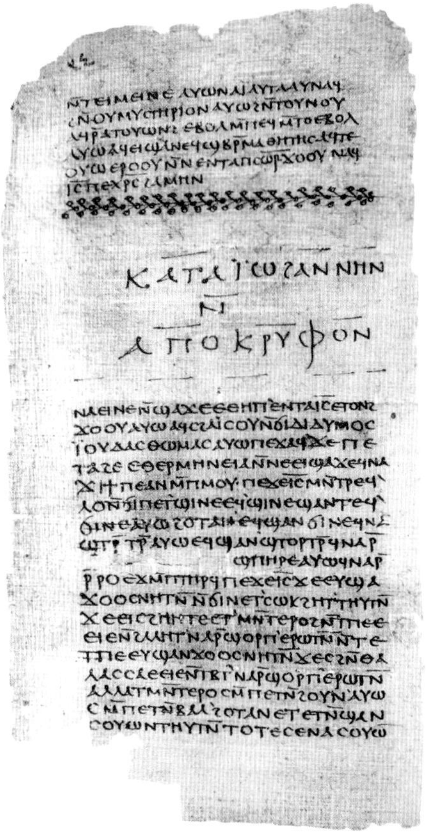

The Nag Hammadi Library confirms the importance of the school of Valentinus. At least eight of the library's texts come from people linked with this group (Prayer of the Apostle Paul, Gospel of Truth, Treatise on the Resurrection, Tripartite Tractate, Gospel of Philip, First Revelation of James, Interpretation of Knowledge, Valentinian Exposition with Liturgical Readings).

Apocryphon of John at Nag Hammadi. Coptic Museum, Cairo, Egypt.

Some members in the school of Valentinus were as keen mythmakers as Sethians. Valentinians shared with Sethians the myth of Wisdom's error that resulted in the emergence of the creator-God and the creation of our world, but Valentinians were much less extreme in their interpretations of this myth. They didn't identify the creator-God with the devil, as Sethians did. In the Valentinian myth, the creator-God is ignorant of the truly divine realm but benevolent toward humankind. In addition, Valentinians taught that the divine Wisdom constantly supervised the creator-God's work. This must mean that Valentinians didn't consider the present world an awfully bad place to live in.

Valentinians stood closer than Sethians to the forms of Christianity that won the day in history. In fact, the opponents complained that it was often difficult to tell a Valentinian from an "ordinary" Christian (Irenaeus, *Against Heresies* 1, preface; 3.15.2).

37. Turner, *Sethian Gnosticism and the Platonic Tradition.*

Valentinians did compose new texts about Jesus, but they also worked on New Testament gospels. One Valentinian teacher, Heracleon, wrote the first known commentary on John's Gospel, and another one, Ptolemaeus, wrote a study on the Old Testament law (*Letter to Flora*), in which he supported his arguments with the teachings of Jesus and Paul. Valentinians even partially recognized the value of the Hebrew Bible: it contains the divine Wisdom's true revelation—but also parts stemming from the creator-God and other parts stemming from humans (such as Moses).

The opponents described Valentinians as elitist Christians who thought more highly of themselves than of others. According to the opponents, Valentinians were inspired by Paul's division between "spiritual" and "soul-endowed" (NRSV: "natural") Christians. For instance, Paul had said that "those who are spiritual discern all things, and they are themselves subject to no one else's scrutiny" (1 Cor 2:15). The opponents said that Valentinians considered themselves spiritual Christians but placed all other Christians into the inferior class of soul-endowed people. Moreover, the opponents claimed that Valentinians regarded membership in these classes as natural-born qualities, so it was impossible to be promoted from the inferior to the superior class.

The opponents accused Valentinians, as self-styled spiritual Christians, of giving themselves license to do whatever they wanted, while they demanded strict moral discipline from others. The moral errors of Valentinians included seducing married women, eating meat offered to idols, and visiting gladiator shows. Such accusations were probably rumors rather than facts. Claims about opponents' uncontrolled sexual lives were commonplace in ancient polemics against any kind of group of people, including those of different nationality and those who held different convictions.

The Valentinian texts in the Nag Hammadi Library confirm that many Valentinians were interested in expressing their theology in the form of cosmic myth, but these texts give a quite different picture of Valentinian morality. Valentinian authors encouraged their readers to show good deeds to others: "Steady the feet of those who stumble and extend your hands to the sick. Feed the hungry and give rest to the weary. Awaken those who wish to arise and arouse those who sleep, for you embody vigorous understanding" (Gospel of Truth, NHC I, 33).[38]

One Valentinian text, however, shows that at least some Valentinians approved of the distinction between more and less mature Christians. In the Interpretation of Knowledge (NHC XI, 1) those lacking the spiritual gift are included into a Christian community, but they are not entitled to speak in the community's meetings

While the opponents described Valentinians as misbehaving elitists, a closer look shows that Valentinians were interested in the cultivation of the soul in a way that made it turn away from matter and material things and toward spiritual realities. Even in the Valentinian myth, much attention was paid to mental disturbance

38. Trans. Meyer, *Nag Hammadi Scriptures*, 33.

brought about by wrong kinds of emotions, and Valentinians promoted Christ as the healer of such emotions. This links the Valentinian teaching closely with the philosophers of their time who often styled themselves as doctors of the soul.[39]

Secret Gospels: Thomas, Mary, and Judas

The newly discovered Coptic texts also contain a number of writings that are called "gospels" already in the original manuscripts. The best-known examples of such texts are the Gospels of Thomas, Mary, and Judas. Only the Gospel of Thomas comes from the Nag Hammadi Library. The Gospel of Mary is included in the Berlin Gnostic Codex, and the Gospel of Judas in the Codex Tchacos.

All these gospels are different, each in their own way, from New Testament gospels, for they offer no consistent narrative from Jesus's baptism to his death and resurrection. The Gospel of Thomas comprises 114 sayings of Jesus; only a few of them contain short dialogues between Jesus and his disciples. The Gospel of Mary offers an account of Mary's vision, in which Jesus imparted her privileged information that Mary now, after the resurrection, transmits to other disciples. The Gospel of Judas is an account of Jesus's discussions with his disciples in the week preceding his death.

"Gospel," thus, was not yet a fixed literary genre when these texts were written. The gospels of Mary and Judas are in many respects similar to other texts that are variously titled "revelation" (*apokalypsis*) or "secret book" (*apocryphon*), and even some later "acts" of individual apostles contain similar elements.

The Gospel of Thomas was put together in the end of the first century or in the beginning of the second. There are a few Greek fragments of this gospel, the earliest of which is from around 200 CE. The fragments show that the Greek version of this gospel was in circulation already in the second century. Some sayings in the gospel may be dependent on the Synoptic Gospels, but there are no clear signs that its author(s) knew John's Gospel. Most scholars agree that the Gospel of Thomas does not offer much new information about the historical Jesus's teaching. (The Jesus Seminar, which is sometimes accused of being too friendly with the Gospel of Thomas, lists only one saying in this gospel that has no synoptic parallel as possibly going back to Jesus!)

The Gospel of Thomas is more valuable as a witness to a form of non-apocalyptic early Christianity in which Jesus's role as a teacher of spiritual insight was emphasized. The Gospel of Thomas, however, is not a gnostic gospel. It neither contains cosmic myths similar to "gnostics," nor does it embrace the idea of an inferior creator God.

39. Dunderberg, *Beyond Gnosticism*, 111–18.

The Gospel of Thomas encourages the reader to reflect on the teaching stored in it: "Whoever discovers the interpretation of these sayings will not taste death" (Gos. Thom. 1). The apocalyptic expectation of an otherworldly kingdom is ridiculed and replaced with the idea of self-knowledge: "If your leaders say to you, 'Look, the kingdom is in heaven,' then the birds of heaven will precede you. . . . When you know yourselves, you will be known and you will understand that you are children of the living Father" (Gos. Thom. 3; cf. 113).[40]

The self-knowledge is based on the recognition of one's divine origin: "We have come from the light, from the place where the light came into being by itself, established [itself] and appeared in their image" (Gos. Thom. 50). The true self is one's inner human being. The Gospel of Thomas does not propagate a real hatred of body, but it is concerned with the soul that clings to "the flesh" (Gos. Thom. 112), and it sees in the visible world a carcass (Gos. Thom. 56).

The Gospel of Thomas is very critical of traditional Jewish practices, such as circumcision, fasting, and even prayer. Still, the gospel illustrates the original state, to which all humans should return, with images referring to the biblical account of the paradise: "For there are five trees in paradise for you; they do not change, summer or winter, and their leaves do not fall. Whoever knows them will not taste death" (Gos. Thom. 19). The idea of paradise also forms the background to the view that God's kingdom is realized when the distinction between male and female disappears (Gos. Thom. 22). This teaching reflects a Jewish tradition that the very first human comprised both sexes, and that the sexual difference came about only when Eve was created; the Gospel of Thomas teaches the return to the most original state of humankind, in which this difference didn't yet exist.

The Gospel of Mary was composed sometime in the second century. The Coptic version of this gospel is not complete; a number of its pages have disappeared. Two short Greek fragments (from the third century) show that the text was originally composed in Greek. Just like the Gospel of Thomas, the Gospel of Mary is not a gnostic gospel: cosmic myth plays little role in it, and the inferior creator-God is entirely absent. The Gospel of Mary, however, shows clearer signs than the Gospel of Thomas of being dependent on New Testament gospels.

The Gospel of Mary portrays Mary of Magdala as the closest follower of Jesus who after his departure encouraged other disciples: "Do not weep and be distressed nor let your hearts be irresolute. For his grace will be with you and will shelter you" (Gos. Mary 9). What is striking in this gospel is that it addresses the value of women's teaching. Peter first compliments Mary as one whom the Savior loved "more than all other women" and asks her to "tell us the words of the Savior" (Gos. Mary 10). Yet after having heard Mary's account of how the soul defeats its adversaries, Peter

40. Trans. Meyer, *Nag Hammadi Scriptures*, 139. For the critical stance toward "your leaders" in Thomas, see Uro, *Thomas*, 80–105.

(together with other disciples) is not at all pleased but heaps scorn at Mary because she is a woman: "Did (the Savior) . . . speak with a woman without our knowing about it?" (Gos. Mary 17). Mary must defend herself, and Levi (Matthew) joins her: "Assuredly the Savior's knowledge of her is completely reliable. That is why he loved her more than us" (Gos. Mary 18).

Such features in the Gospel of Mary may be understood as a critical response to the policy recommended in the Pastoral Epistles that women should remain silent in the meetings of Christians: "Let a woman learn in silence with full submission. I permit no woman to teach or to have authority over a man; she is to keep silent" (1 Tim 2:11–12). It should be noted that the Gospel of Mary does not portray Mary as Jesus's wife or lover; she is instead depicted as his most perceptive disciple.

The Gospel of Judas became known only when the Codex Tchacos (named after the owner of this collection) was published in 2006. The gospel was marketed as revealing that Judas was Jesus's star disciple, but nobody considers this text a historically reliable account of the relationship between Jesus and Judas. This gospel was composed in the second century, for Irenaeus, bishop of Lyon, knew of it already around 180 CE.

The Gospel of Judas is closely linked with the Sethian theology described above; a major part of it is dedicated to a cosmic myth of Sethian bent. But why does this gospel single out Judas as Jesus's confidant? Judas was chosen for this role because the gospel's author was very unhappy with the form of Christianity that had claimed apostolic authority. The choice of Judas served to ridicule that authority: even the betrayer understood Jesus better than the apostles.

The gospel's point, thus, was not so much to rehabilitate Judas as it was to lay bare the errors of one kind of Christianity. One of the issues was probably martyrdom. We know from other sources that many Christian teachers urged their audiences to be ready to die for their faith. In the Gospel of Judas, the martyrs' zeal is turned into a horrific vision of men, women, and children waiting to be slaughtered on an altar, where the disciples perform as priests. Human sacrifice is considered, in an apocalyptic fashion, as one sign that the last day is near (Gos. Jud. 38–41).

Judas himself is an ambiguous figure in the gospel bearing his name. On the one hand, he is the only disciple who understands Jesus and whom Jesus teaches in private. On the other hand, this gospel agrees with New Testament gospels that Judas betrayed Jesus and handed him over to authorities for money (Gos. Jud. 58). In this gospel, stars are presented as misleading all humans, including other disciples. Judas is also subject to astral deception, and Jesus denies him the access to the divine realm. Judas thus seems to belong somewhere between the completely ignorant disciples and the ideal followers of Jesus. The ambiguity has led to a long scholarly debate about whether Judas is in this gospel a bad guy or a good guy.

Conclusion

A closer look at groups designated as "gnostics" shows considerable diversity among them; some groups stood closer than others to the form of Christianity that won the day in the fourth century and is for this reason best known to us.

As regards Gnosticism and the New Testament, it is very difficult to trace any reliable links between the mythic teachings described above and the theology (or polemics) of Paul and John. The only case where such connections can be seriously considered is that of the Pastoral Epistles, which may have been written no earlier than the beginning of the second century.

The opponents described in 1 Timothy had clearly marketed their teaching as "knowledge," since the author of this epistle combats this claim in speaking of "the profane chatter and contradictions of what is *falsely called knowledge* [*gnōsis*]" (1 Tim 6:20). The author's other comments on the opponents suggest that they were myth-makers: the readers are warned against those teaching "myths and endless genealogies" (1 Tim 1:4; "myths" are also mentioned in connection with rejected opinions in 1 Tim 4:7; 2 Tim 4:3–4). Such comments would make good sense in connection with the gnostic Christians described above. Yet even here the evidence remains spurious.[41] We are not informed more closely what kind of myths the opponents taught. One particular problem is the claim in 1 Timothy that the opponents "demand abstinence from foods" (1 Tim. 4:3); this detail would fit better with Christians who had adopted a Jewish lifestyle, as there is little evidence for such instructions among the gnostics.

Further Reading

Brakke, David. *The Gnostics: Myth, Ritual, and Diversity in Early Christianity.* Cambridge, MA: Harvard University Press, 2010.

Dunderberg, Ismo. *Beyond Gnosticism: Myth, Lifestyle, and Society in the School of Valentinus.* New York: Columbia University Press, 2008.

Kasser, Rodolphe, Marvin Meyer, and Gregor Wurst, eds. *The Gospel of Judas: Together with the Letter of Philip, James, and a Book of Allogenes from Codex Tchacos.* Washington, DC: National Geographic, 2007.

King, Karen L. *What Is Gnosticism?* Cambridge, MA: Harvard University Press, 2003.

Layton, Bentley. *The Gnostic Scriptures: A New Translation with Annotations.* New Haven: Yale University Press, 1987.

Marjanen, Antti. *Was There a Gnostic Religion?* Publications of the Finnish Exegetical Society 87. Göttingen: Vandenhoeck & Ruprecht, 2005.

41. Marjanen, *Was There a Gnostic Religion?*, 5–9.

Marjanen, Antti, and Petri Luomanen, eds. *A Companion to Second-Century Christian "Heretics."* Leiden: Brill, 2005.
Meyer, Marvin. *The Nag Hammadi Scriptures: The Revised and Updated Translation of Sacred Gnostic Texts.* New York: HarperOne, 2007.
Tuckett, Christopher, ed. *The Gospel of Mary.* Oxford: Oxford University Press, 2007.
Turner, John Douglas. *Sethian Gnosticism and the Platonic Tradition.* Quebec: Les Presses de l'Université Laval, 2001.
Uro, Risto. *Thomas: Seeking the Historical Context of the Gospel of Thomas.* Edinburgh: T&T Clark, 2003.
Williams, Michael A. *Rethinking "Gnosticism": An Argument for Dismantling a Dubious Category.* Princeton: Princeton University Press, 1996.

Diversity and the Struggle for Unity

As we have already witnessed, New Testament texts reflect a great deal of diversity. The four evangelists tell the same story but from different perspectives, using different interpretative tools to describe the same events. The Pauline letters are based on specific congregations and reflect the needs and situations in these local contexts. The Acts of the Apostles describes only one history of early mission, and the book of Revelation, whose apostolic origins have long been questioned, reveals the vision of early Christians. The experiences shared by Jesus's disciples were interpreted differently in different milieus, and when different narratives spread to different regions and served as the basis for the formation of new congregations, they were expressed according to ethnic, social, ideological, and political circumstances. On the basis of the preserved texts, it is possible to distinguish between several groups within the Christ-following world, such as the above-mentioned Christ-following Jews, the Pauline Christ groups, the Johannine Christ followers, and the various gnostic groups. It is clear that there were other groups in addition to these, some that are not easily described since the lines between groups were often blurred. As always when it comes to historical research, we must expect the picture to be broader than merely what the surviving texts describe. This is in part because the texts in question were often written with the aim of making the lines between groups clearer and deal with conflict, and also because they make up only a very small section of the entirety of texts from this period, and thus reflect only a small section of that society.

The fact that a group with a communal experience of a prophetic figure within only a generation or two could exhibit such a degree of diversity may seem strange to the general observer. The reasons behind this diversity are many, and the most important ones become clear if one compares the process to the emergence of Islam. First, unlike Muhammad, Jesus never created an organized group of individuals and did not leave any revelations with clear instructions as to what the future would look like organizationally. Second, a variety of texts attributed either to Jesus's disciples or to individual revelation (Paul) were soon in circulation; these texts presented their own interpretations of Jesus's words and actions, and sometimes they even contradicted each other (unlike in Islam, where the Qur'an was compiled already by the first Rashidun caliphs). Third, unlike Muhammad, who vigorously opposed the polytheistic religious practices of his society, Jesus and his disciples did not differentiate themselves from Judaism; rather, they claimed to have the most valid interpretation of it. In addition, other contemporary concepts and ideologies also influenced Jesus's followers. Thus, as a rule, early Christ-following communities had access to only some of the texts that would eventually form the New Testament, and they were left with the decision as to how their belief in their Messiah would be affected by their surrounding religious and cultural traditions. This degree of openness meant that belief in Christ was highly adaptable to different contexts. However, it also meant that the interpretation of who Jesus was and what his life meant was not normative; it differed depending on context and community.

To better understand this context, let us for a moment engage in a small thought experiment. Let us imagine that a group of Christ followers from different parts of the world convened in Jerusalem in the year 100. Among them are a Jewish teacher from Alexandria, a freed slave from Rome, a philosopher from Athens, a carpenter from Ephesus, a farmer from Edessa, a merchant from Cyprus, and a scribe from Nazareth. Soon they would discover that not only do they have different perceptions about what has occurred, different texts, and different interpretations, but also they worship in different ways, are organized according to different structures, and have differing ideas about how a "good Christ follower" should live. Some of them had access to the Gospel of Mark, others the Gospel of Matthew, while still others kept strictly to Paul or the traditions of the Gospel of John; some may even have access to all or none of these texts. One of them would be an actively practicing Jew, one had abandoned his Jewish heritage, while another barely had any knowledge of the Jewish tradition, and still another saw himself as incorporated into the Jewish people. While some saw Jesus as the prophet who was to usher in the end of the ages, others viewed him as God in human form. For some, his death was an atoning sacrifice; for others, a victory over death. Several of them believed that it was essential to follow the law, some believed that only certain commandments were to be held, while others believed that all divine law had now ceased to be relevant. We could continue the experiment until we are faced with the realization that there were very few common denominators among the first Christ followers—so few, in fact, that common labels such as "Christian faith" or "Christianity" appear quite problematic.

During the first three hundred years, however, there emerges from the previous diversity a Christian tradition with a shared collection of texts, a more normative worship and congregational structure, and a common, generalized perception/interpretation of what the Christian faith means and how it should be organized.

In the remainder of this chapter, we shall explore how this was possible, focusing especially on the emergence of a normative congregational structure and a shared view of holy texts and traditions. However, before we immerse ourselves in this, it may be wise to first discuss the conditions that made this move from diversity to unity at all possible.

The Impetus for Unification

There is a popular perception that Christian unity was something forced onto the tradition by power-hungry church leaders, especially the pope, who molded Christianity by removing those with different ideas, kept the truth hidden, discredited alternative traditions, and persecuted those who opposed him. However, this perception is extremely anachronistic and does not correspond with what we know about the time period at hand. The emergence of papal authority is a historical *result* of Christian unity, not a *condition* of it. We cannot speak of a central ecclesial power behind the struggle for unity until the time of Emperor Constantine (306–337 CE), and even after Constantine the struggle for unity emerges more as an imperial struggle than an ecclesial initiative. It was the emperor who organized the councils and urged the creation of a more unified ecclesial structure and doctrine. The bishops and church leaders who were called to this council were in fact more interested in preserving their own independence and theological interpretations than they were in a unified church. It was the politicization and legalization of the role of bishop that eventually led to a more unified church structure within the Roman Empire.

Of course, this does not exclude the existence of other, more deeply rooted driving forces that paved the path in different ways for the political process that Constantine began after his accession to power in 306. Without an early and intense struggle for unity, the church would not have had the strength and impact that led to political recognition during the 300s. It was not the numerical superiority of the Christian faith (generally scholars agree that only around 10 percent of the population was Christian in the year 300) but rather the strong unity and the refusal to compromise in questions of faith that made the church an important factor in stabilizing the empire. When Constantine invited bishops from all over the empire to Nicaea in Asia Minor in 325 CE, they were not complete strangers to each other, despite coming from different political, social, and ethnic contexts and despite representing different traditions. Unlike earlier periods, they now read the same holy texts and told similar stories about the apostles, prophets, and martyrs; and in general they all demanded that whoever was to be baptized must believe in the Trinity. They shared a similar view about how the congregation should be organized and led, where the line should be drawn against "pagans" (that is, those who were neither Jews nor Christ followers). They had similar rules regarding the manner in which members should live, and similar sanctions against those who failed to live up to these rules. None of these common factors were a given at the conception of the Christ-following tradition, and none of them were forced on the community by a higher power.

Historically, we can distinguish at least three driving forces behind the emerging unity. First, there was a great deal of communication between different Christ groups. As becomes apparent already in the oldest New Testament texts, early Christ followers, teachers, and leaders were constantly traveling. Already in the first century, most bishops and Christian leaders seem to have traveled. Some early figures, such as Justin Martyr and Origen, taught in different cities; others, such as Clement of Alexandria and Cyprian, fled persecution. Still others, including Ignatius of Antioch, were taken away as prisoners. In one of the oldest texts, the Didache, there is a section that gives advice on how traveling teachers should be treated, and in apocryphal descriptions of the acts of the apostles and other early texts, the motif of travel is central. The Pauline letters are only the beginning of an extensive correspondence in which Christ-following assemblies discuss central issues with each other. Just as the Pauline letters would soon be sent around as a collection, so too other texts came

Rome, view from the Colosseum with the Arch of Constantine to the left and the Arch of Titus on the far right. The time span between the reign of these two emperors from the first and third centuries CE corresponds with the time period dealt with in this book. The religious and political reorientation that occurred during these three hundred years "between the two Arches of Triumph" contributed decisively to the emergence of Christendom. One must not forget, however, that during this period there were also other factors that contributed to the process of unification. Photo by Dieter Mitternacht.

into circulation. A good example is the Letter of Clement, which was written by the bishop of Rome in order to contribute to the solution of a conflict in the congregation in Corinth; however, the text was later circulated among many other congregations as well. Somewhat later, Ignatius of Antioch encourages Christian unity in a number of letters to different congregations. Eusebius of Caesarea records a long list of later attempts to solve conflicts or inform about local traditions via letter correspondences in his *Ecclesiastical History*, written around 320 CE. The letters created a greater solidarity and fellowship among congregations around the Mediterranean, which was only increased by their wide circulation. It was also common for acknowledged authorities on the Christian faith and tradition—for example, Origen—to be invited to speak in different congregations; sometimes they were even invited to settle local arguments. Toward the end of the third century, it had already become common for bishops to convene in order to solve certain more difficult issues—the so-called local synods.

Second, conflicts and schisms between congregations were taken very seriously. This is evident already in the Pauline letters and certain gospels, especially John. In fact, the majority of the material we have access to from the third and fourth centuries revolves around conflicts and local arguments. Conflict solution generated much textual deliberation. One important reason for all these conflicts was the diversity of beliefs. In an attempt to legitimize and justify different beliefs and practices and the interests of specific groups, tensions arose between congregations such that Christian unity was threatened to a point where the survival of the movement itself was unsure. It was clearly in the interest of the movement itself to achieve a higher level of unity by developing arguments for certain viewpoints and seeking widespread support for them. The process of legitimizing and seeking support for standard viewpoints led to an extensive correspondence between Christ groups, and also a growing circulation of religious texts and textual interpretations. In this way, Christ groups became more and more dependent on each other, which eventually led to the formation of common interpretative traditions, foundational texts, and practices. This came at the cost of specific traditions that did not enjoy a wider acceptance, so that interpretations that were more profiled and strongly colored by local tradition were left behind and marginalized. Consequently, to establish which texts and traditions were the most commonly known, communal, or catholic (in the word's original sense) became one of the decisive factors in the struggle toward unity. In the chapter concerned with the formation of the canon, we have already observed how this objective affected which texts were included in the New Testament. The canonization process was not governed, as many assume, by the desire to create a unidirectional narrative (something Marcion attempted) but rather by the desire to include texts that reflected the parts of the diversity that were most commonly known and adhered to. It is therefore natural that the lists of approved texts differed on lesser points between groups for a long time (see the section "The Origins and Transmission of the Texts," p. 202).

Third, the early Jesus movement lived in constant debate, both with the Jewish tradition and with contemporary popular philosophy—a debate that necessitated well-thought-out arguments for faith and praxis as well as theological reflections. It soon became apparent that the New Testament texts did not provide any unified guidelines as to how the Jewish heritage should be treated, or how congregations should deal with non-Jews wishing to join them. Nor were there any ready-made answers for all the questions Christ followers were asked when they were forced to explain and justify their faith to contemporary critics. Instead, Christ followers had to look to the ancient Scriptures for support of their faith and praxis, and then express it in ways that could be understood outside a Jewish context. We shall return to the issue of Christian scriptural interpretation below. As to the second part, the reformulation of scriptural support in non-Jewish terms, there is a common misconception that the unification of the Christian faith occurred purely within a hellenizing context. This theory was advocated for by the German historian Adolf von Harnack more than a century ago. It stated that the meeting with Hellenistic culture and Greek philosophy changed the originally Jewish and biblical Christian proclamation of faith into something completely different.

This chronological theory about the transformation from diversity to unity is, however, a misconception. First, Judaism in the time of Jesus was already firmly integrated in Hellenistic culture, and many New Testament texts, especially the Pauline letters, were evidently at home in Greek thought. Thus, there never was a tradition that was not part of the Hellenistic world. Second, it is impossible to prove that the theologians of the fourth century were more influenced by Greek philosophy than those of the first century. Rather, the unifying process meant that the earlier diversity of traditions that attempted to relate Christian faith to different contexts and expressions gradually gave way to a more comprehensive adaptation of the ancient heritage. While teachers of the first century focused more on connecting points between the Christ-following tradition and its Hellenistic surroundings, the theologians of the fourth century were more concerned with reinterpreting Greek traditions and making them accessible to Christian reflection. Thus, one might even speak of a dehellenizing process as Christian reflection intensified.

As we have seen, different texts, letters, theological explanations, Bible commentaries, and other teaching materials played an important role in the process of unifying a diverse Christianity. Some of these texts were more widely circulated and read than others, albeit yet without being granted any special status or authority. Some were written by private Christian teachers, others by bishops. The authors of these letters are commonly divided into two categories: the apostolic fathers and the apologists. There are some important exceptions to these categories, including *The Apostolic Tradition*, attributed to the presbyter Hippolytus, who was active in Rome around the year 200. While the works of the apostolic fathers, written around 100–150 CE, are less comprehensive than the New Testament, the works of the apologists, a larger group of authors, roughly spanning the years 150–250, make up around one hundred texts. Naturally, the texts are very different, but they have in common that they would all be included in the unified tradition. Thus, their spread constitutes a part of the actual process from diversity to unity, and the frames of interpretation and tradition they create can also be seen as the frames for the emerging tradition.

Box 5.5 ***Apostolic Fathers and Apologists***

The Writings of the Apostolic Fathers

The oldest Christian texts next to the NT and its Apocrypha are called the Apostolic Fathers, the assumption being that these texts were written by disciples of the apostles. They include the following texts:

- Didache (end of first century CE)
- First Letter of Clement (ca. 100 CE)
- Letters of Ignatius of Antioch (ca. 110 CE)
- The Papias fragments (ca. 120 CE)
- Shepherd of Hermas (ca. 150 CE)
- Martyrdom of Polycarp (ca. 160 CE)
- Letter of Barnabas (mid-second century CE)
- Second Letter of Clement (mid-second century CE)
- Letter of Diognetus (ca. 200 CE)

Apologists

The apologists were early Christian writers during the second and third centuries CE, who wrote texts in defense of the Christian faith against representatives of Greco-Roman culture and religions, gnostics, and Jews. The most important among them are the following:

- Justin Martyr (ca. 100–165 CE)
- Aristides of Athens (mid-second century CE)
- Tatian (mid-second century CE)
- Athenagoras (second half of second century CE)
- Theophilus of Antioch (second half of second century CE)
- Clement of Alexandria (ca. 150–215 CE)
- Tertullian (ca. 160–225 CE)
- Minucius Felix (early third century CE)
- Origen (ca. 185–254 CE)

Worship and Congregational Structure

Communal worship stood at the center of the struggle toward a greater degree of unity. As a collective and communal act, worshiping together implies a form of unity: a shared order, a shared way of viewing this order, and the distribution of different tasks and rules for who can participate. Already in the New Testament texts, we find examples about conflicts concerning communal worship. In the Acts of the Apostles, we can read about the difficulties when trying to carry out communal worship with both Jews and non-Jews, and Paul mentions the order of worship and who should lead it on several occasions. In the oldest texts outside the New Testament, there are various examples of conflict about worship as well as detailed descriptions of how it should be carried out. In the Didache, written around the year 100, we have not only descriptions about how worship should be carried out but also general rules for how one should pray. In the letters of Ignatius, we find a set of rules as to how the congregation should be organized in terms of structure and leadership. In addition to the issues of how worship should be carried out, who should be allowed to participate, and who should lead, there was the problem of *when* the worship should happen, which was especially relevant where the celebration of religious holidays was concerned, especially Easter. It is not surprising that the road to a communal order was not easy, and that it took a long time before it was reached.

The point of departure for Christian worship was Jewish worship. Jesus partook in the religious life of the synagogues and of the temple, and it was to these very locations that the author of the Acts of the Apostles ties the early Jesus movement. It is also obvious that the oldest Christian worship traditions, such as Scripture reading, prayers, hymns, and eventually music, build first and foremost on the Jewish synagogues. We are, however, not that well informed about synagogue worship in New Testament times. Beginning with the third century, the sources abound, but still we cannot be absolutely sure that the similarities that appear between Jewish and Christian worship are based on common roots, as similarities may be due to reciprocal influences. Even though the temple in Jerusalem was destroyed, we can say with certainty that temple worship also played a role in shaping early Christ worship, which is evident especially in the interpretation of worship as a communal offering and how this should be embodied. Apart from the influence of the synagogue and the temple, the Jewish rituals that took place in the home, especially the Sabbath meal, were important for the formation of Christ groups and thus for shaping of the communal worship.

Apart from the Jewish setting, Christ worship also reflects other religious and social influences, especially in congregations where the concrete link to the Jewish heritage may not have been as strong as in others. For example, the worshiping of Christ as Lord and king led many Christians to direct aspects of emperor worship toward Christ instead of the emperor. In other areas, clear Jewish archetypes were missing, such as with baptism as a renewal in Christ and an initiation into the mystery, and thus other traditions from different contexts were used to explain the phenomenon (see the section "Greco-Roman Religions and Philosophies," p. 84). In some areas, like architecture, it is impossible to distinguish between Jewish and Hellenistic influences since Judaism had at this point already appropriated large parts of Hellenistic culture.

In the New Testament texts, it is clear that communal meals were at the center of the worship of the first Christ groups. The meal served as a reminder to the community that Christ himself was tangibly present. In the Acts of the Apostles, these meals are referred to throughout as "breaking bread," and Paul speaks of "the Lord's supper." Soon, however, the word "Eucharist," from the Greek word meaning "thanksgiving," was used to denote the communal meal, which in Jewish tradition and in, for example, the Gospels and Paul has a strong tie to the thanksgiving said during the communal meal. In the Gospels, the communal meals are linked to Jesus's last supper with his disciples. In 1 Cor 11, Paul makes a similar link. According to the Synoptic Gospels, this meal was a Passover meal, while John states that the Passover lamb was sacrificed the same day Jesus was crucified. Despite this, there is no clear link to the Passover meal in early Christian liturgy. Rather, it is the Jewish Sabbath meal that is used as inspiration for the formation of the meal. It is also clear that other, very different traditions were linked by some early communities to the celebration of the Eucharist. In several of the early Eucharist prayers, and in the traditional Roman Eucharist prayer, the celebrant says, "Jesus lifted his gaze toward heaven and thanked God," which is an obvious reflection of the story of the two loaves and five fish (Matt 14; Mark 6; Luke 9). That the feeding miracle describes the meaning of the Eucharist is also a well-known theme among the early Christ-following authors (cf. John 6).

The descriptions of the Gospels and of Paul indicate that the communal meal was originally a full meal that, in accordance with Jewish tradition, began with the breaking of bread and ended with a prayer of thanksgiving over the cup. Soon these two rituals (the breaking of the bread and the prayer of thanksgiving over the cup) became one ritual, occurring at the same place in the chronology of the meal. The strong connection to bread and wine that the Gospels and Paul bear witness to is a theme found throughout early Christian traditions. The meal also seems to have been a specific ritual act, separate from the worship involving prayers and the reading of Scripture. Neither the Gospels nor Paul nor the Didache connects the communal meal to the reading of Scripture or prayer. Around the year 100, the governor of Bithynia, Pliny the Younger, describes how the Christians gather at dawn to sing hymns and swear a collective confession and afterward meet for a shared meal. Justin Martyr, writing around 150 CE, is the first to tell us of a Christian worship that includes reading from the Scriptures, preaching, and having a meal together.

Just because we are better informed about the history of the emergence of the communal meal does not mean that reading of the Scriptures, prayers, and hymns played a subordinate role in early Christ groups. The synagogue worship style was in all likelihood the basis, but because we have a limited amount of information concerning synagogue worship around this time, it is difficult to ascertain exactly what structure early Christ worship followed. We can be certain that there were readings from the Septuagint, perhaps with an emphasis on the Pentateuch and the Prophets. However, it is still uncertain as to whether there were readings from the Psalms in synagogue worship, and there is no evidence for the singing or reading of hymns in Christian worship until the fourth century. Where the New Testament is concerned, the Pauline letters were in all likelihood read even during Paul's own lifetime, in the congregations they were sent to, as well as in others. The emergence of the Gospels is likely linked to the reading of texts during communal worship, but there is no mention of this until Justin Martyr describes how congregations read from the "memorandum of the Apostles." In his description of worship, Justin also connects these readings to some sort of preaching, an encouragement to live in accordance with the texts. Despite the fact that we remain uncertain as to which and how many texts the early congregations read, there is enough evidence to suggest that very early on a tradition formed in which the gospel texts were read last, preceded by readings from the Septuagint and Paul.

Apart from the Eucharist meal and the readings, prayer and communal song also played a role in early Christ worship. The Jewish heritage most likely played an important role in influencing worship. In the Didache, the custom of praying three times a day is mentioned to have occurred at the third, the seventh, and the ninth hour of the day—times that echo the passion story, Acts of the Apostles, and Dan 6:10. The custom of praying together in the morning and in the evening is also mentioned in early sources from Christ groups as well as in Jewish sources, and so is getting up at specific times in the night to pray. However, these customs are not officially structured in a regulated format until the emergence of monasticism, and eventually they entered the spiritual life of the bigger churches. A decisive factor for the emergence of a shared order for these prayers and other liturgical customs was the emergence of pilgrimages in the fourth century. The traditions that developed in the monasteries of the east and west strongly influenced worship in Jerusalem and spread throughout the Christian world through the pilgrims.

The issue of leadership and whom one should listen to was, of course, decisive in the question of a greater Christian unity. We have already seen examples of how the Pauline letters and the Johannine texts attempt to solve this issue. One problem that the early Jesus movement ran into was the relationship between local congregations and traveling preachers. How were congregations supposed to meet these individuals and judge who was speaking the truth, who was a "false prophet," and who created division? The Didache provides some insight to this topic in its description of how congregations should receive traveling apostles, prophets, and local religious leaders. It states that traveling preachers should be received and provided with housing and food for a maximum of two days. If they stay longer than this period, and if they ask for money, they are considered false prophets. But if a true preacher decides to settle with the congregation, he should be given a befitting salary. Decisive factors are whether the preaching is in accordance with established teaching and the preacher's lifestyle. The tension between local congregations and traveling preachers is a recurring theme in early Christian texts. In some cases, the texts are about movements led by traveling prophets like the Montanists (active from the end of the second century to the beginning of the third) rather than individual charismatics. This tension reached its height with the creation of the monastic movement during the second half of the fourth century.

Regarding the organization of Christ groups, bishops, presbyters, and deacons were present already in New Testament congregations. In the writings of Ignatius of Antioch we find the first developed reflections about the office of congregational leadership and its importance both for the individual congregation and for the relationship between congregations. According to Ignatius, unity is manifested through adherence to the bishops, without whom the Eucharist cannot be celebrated. The bishops were also the only ones allowed to baptize or officiate agape meals. As Christ is one, the cup is one, and the bishop, presbyters, and deacons are one. Behind this statement, one can sense an experience of division and competition between congregational leaders. The tradition that each congregation has its own bishop seems to have been widely acknowledged and practiced since New Testament times. It was not until later, when more than one congregation formed in large cities like Rome, or when congregations started forming in remote villages, that the system changed so that presbyters or deacons and bishops of one congregation were responsible for a larger area. As the church expanded substantially during the third century, the prestige and responsibilities linked to the office of bishop increased. With this increase came the need to regulate elections, appointments, and geographic responsibilities of the office, a topic that came to be central in the first large church councils of the fourth century.

Box 5.6
Excerpts from Ignatius

For when you are subject to the bishop as to Jesus Christ, you appear to me to live not in a human way but according to Jesus Christ, who died for us that you may escape dying by believing in his death. And so—as is already the case—you must not engage in any activity apart from the bishop, but be subject also to the presbytery as to the apostles of Jesus Christ, our hope. If we live in him, we will be found in him. And those who are deacons of the mysteries of Jesus Christ must also be pleasing in every way to all people. For they are not deacons dealing with food and drink; they are servants of the church of God. And so they must guard themselves against accusations and against fire. So too let everyone respect the deacons like Jesus Christ, and also the bishop, who is the image of the Father; and let them respect the presbyters like the council of God and the band of the apostles. Apart from these a gathering cannot be called a church. (*To the Trallians* 2.1–3.1 [Ehrman, LCL])

And so, just as the Lord did nothing apart from the Father—being united with him—neither on his own nor through the apostles, so too you should do nothing apart from the bishop and the presbyters. Do not try to maintain that it is reasonable for you to do something among yourselves in private; instead, for the common purpose, let there be one prayer, one petition, one mind, one hope in love and in blameless joy, which is Jesus Christ. Nothing is superior to him. You should all run together, as into one temple, as upon one altar, upon one Jesus Christ, who came forth from one Father and was with the one [*Or: and was with him*] and returned to the one. (*To the Magnesians* 7 [Ehrman, LCL])

Around the year 200, Hippolytus, the presbyter of Rome, authored a text with the title *The Apostolic Tradition*. In this text, he lays out how congregations should be structured and how they should worship according to established tradition. The fact that this text, written in Greek, was circulated with such speed, was translated into all of ancient Christianity's languages, and became the basis for all later liturgical orders indicates that its content was generally accepted. Thus, *The Apostolic Tradition* can be viewed as both an expression of the common factors of early Christianity and an important contributor to the process of unity. The text does not provide an account of an ordinary Sunday mass—maybe this was viewed as unnecessary—but the celebration of the Eucharist is described twice, first in connection with the ordination of a bishop, and later in connection with baptism. Unity in individual congregations is strongly emphasized, and, as in the Didache and the account of Justin Martyr, reconciliation between members of a congregation, embodied in the kiss of friendship, is listed as a condition for celebration of the Eucharist.

The question of unity in early Christian tradition is naturally connected with the question of separation from outsiders. The borderline between insiders and outsiders can already be seen in New Testament texts related to baptism. In both the Didache and Justin Martyr, baptism is clearly defined as a prerequisite for participation in the celebration of the Eucharist. It seems clear that baptism of children was being practiced at this time, although we cannot know how widespread this practice was. It is not until the year 200 CE that we encounter voices who are negative toward the baptism of children, as well as a defense of child baptism. With the expansion of the church toward the end of the third century and especially during the fourth century, a tradition of waiting for baptism until adulthood, or even until one's deathbed, becomes popular. A decisive factor for the emergence of this tradition seems to have been the heavy emphasis on the fact that a baptized person had to live a sin-free life. Augustine was the foremost voice against this view and advocated the importance of baptizing everyone, even infants. The conflicts about baptism that emerged in the early church were not about the necessity of baptism, or the age of the individuals baptized. Rather, they were about who was allowed to baptize, and how one could identify a baptism as theologically valid. Because baptism implied participation in the inner workings of the congregation and the eucharistic agape meal, it was important to know which individuals were actually baptized and could then be trusted. This became even more important during times of persecution, and many of the baptism conflicts erupted over accusations of betrayal. The fact that the traditions that were the most stringent concerning the requirements for baptism and who could baptize eventually disappeared bears witness to the fact that it was not the groups requiring the strictest unity that won the day, but rather those who accepted a certain diversity.

Another important aspect of the development toward unity and the creation of communal worship norms was the establishment of a shared time for worship and for the celebration of religious holidays. Communal worship necessitates that participants are in the same place at the same time, and a communal celebration of, for example, the death and resurrection of Christ necessitates an agreement between congregations as to when it should be celebrated. Specific times and dates for worship were important identity markers. There does not seem to have been any larger conflict concerning the decision to celebrate the Eucharist on Sundays. Already in the New Testament texts, there appears a special emphasis on the first day of the week (Sunday); and in the Didache, the letters of Pliny the Younger, and other texts concerning worship, Sunday is identified as the day of Christian worship. The designation of Sunday as a day of worship, in contrast to the Jewish Sabbath, has a parallel in the Didache, which states that Christians, in contrast to the "hypocrites," should fast on Wednesdays and Fridays instead of Mondays and Thursdays.

Agreeing on a date for the celebration of Easter was more challenging. Certain congregations, the so-called quartodecimans, refused to abandon the practice of celebrating Easter in accordance with the Jewish Passover festival, since this corresponded to the New Testament Easter. This meant that Easter was celebrated on a specific date, the fourteenth of Nisan, and thus could fall on any day of the week. Others wanted to celebrate the resurrection on a Sunday, a day symbolic of new life, regardless of the specific date. As long as there was little contact between congregations, this did not constitute a problem. However, as more and more Christ followers started moving around, especially to Rome, and the exchange between congregations increased, these differences became problematic. Was it enough to agree locally on a day for the celebration of the holiday, or was it, for the sake of unity, important that all believers celebrated Easter on the same day? While the bishop of Rome in the mid-second century agreed with the latter, others, such as Irenaeus of Lyon, argued that the enforcement of such a unity came at a price that was too high. However, the need for unity was very strong, and during the third century an order that established a common day for celebrating Easter was composed in Alexandria and distributed to local congregations. A common formula for the calculation of the right day was later established at the Council of Nicaea in 325 CE.

Finally, despite the apparent diversity, texts from very different contexts seem to suggest that, nonetheless, a common kernel of traditions about worship and congregational structure had emerged. While we encounter a great deal of diversity in other areas of Christian life, the Eucharist celebration and the structure of leadership within congregations seem to have been rather similar for most congregations. Even the prayers we find in early apocryphal texts, such as the texts associated with John and Thomas, reflect the same praxis and basic ideas. The leader of the congregation led the Eucharist celebration together with the elders (presbyters) and the deacons. Worshipers met on Sundays to read from the Scriptures, both the Hebrew Bible and the New Testament, and to share a meal in which only the baptized could participate. Unity, coexistence, and reconciliation between congregation members is strongly emphasized in the texts, as is the connection to Christ during worship. Worship revolved around thanksgiving, which, like the bread and wine, was called a sacrifice, and everyone was expected to live a morally acceptable life.

Box 5.7
Excerpts from Justin Martyr's Apology

After thus baptizing the one who has believed and given his assent, we escort him to the place where are assembled those whom we call brethren, to offer up sincere prayers in common for ourselves, for the baptized person, and for all other persons wherever they may be, in order that, since we have found the truth, we may be deemed fit through our actions to be esteemed as good citizens and observers of the law, and thus attain eternal salvation. At the conclusion of the prayers we greet one another with a kiss. Then, bread and a chalice containing wine mixed with water are presented to the one presiding over the brethren. He takes them and offers praise and glory to the Father of all, through the name of the Son and of the Holy Spirit, and he recites lengthy prayers of thanksgiving to God in the name of those to whom He granted such favors. At the end of these prayers and thanksgiving, all present express their approval by saying "Amen." This Hebrew word, "Amen," means "So be it." And when he who presides has celebrated the Eucharist, they whom we call deacons permit each one present to partake of the Eucharistic bread, and wine and water; and they carry it also to the absentees. (*First Apology* 65 [Falls])

On the day which is called Sunday we have a common assembly of all who live in the cities or in the outlying districts, and the memoirs of the apostles or

> the writings of the Prophets are read, as long as there is time. Then, when the reader has finished, the president of the assembly verbally admonishes and invites all to imitate examples of virtue. Then we all stand up together and offer up our prayers, and, as we said before, after we finish our prayers, bread and wine and water are presented. He who presides likewise offers up prayers and thanksgivings, to the best of his ability, and the people express their approval by saying "Amen." The Eucharistic elements are distributed and consumed by those present, and to those who are absent they are sent through the deacons. (*First Apology* 67 [Falls])

Scripture and Tradition

The common denominator of diversity in the early Jesus movement were the Scriptures—that is, the Hebrew Bible. With the exception of some of the shorter letters (Titus, Jude, and 2–3 John), all New Testament texts refer either explicitly or implicitly to the Hebrew Bible, as do the Apostolic Fathers. It is natural, therefore, that questions concerning how the Hebrew Bible should be used and interpreted were central in the emergence of a unified Christian church. But already in the New Testament, two authoritative voices on this subject appear: the words of Jesus and the teachings of the apostles. As is clear in the Pauline letters, the latter was an important argument for Paul in his attempt to halt the fragmentation of the early congregations. To agree on which texts accurately described the apostolic tradition and relayed Jesus's own teaching was therefore crucial, not in the least because of the many texts produced and circulated during the second and third century that claimed to reproduce Jesus's teaching (often in the form of a farewell speech after the resurrection) and the apostle's experiences and revelations. The common usage of the terms "secrets," "the hidden," and "spiritual wisdom," which are even used in New Testament texts, bears witness to the belief in the early congregations that the truth was not to be found "in the letter" but rather hidden behind it, and thus it was better communicated via oral tradition. That such oral traditions were written down much later does not make them less valuable.

Perhaps the biggest challenge for the earliest congregations was how they should relate to the collection of Jewish texts, later named by Christians the Old Testament. For non-Jewish Christ followers, the majority of the texts from the Hebrew Bible must have been almost impossible to understand, at first glance even irrelevant, and not something that would easily interest non-Christian neighbors. At the same time, these texts were the basis of the gospels about Jesus, and they also laid the foundations for Paul's theology. Drawn to its logical extreme, the question was how one could assert that the Hebrew Bible was the word of God, on the one hand, and ignore most of its commandments, on the other hand.

It is therefore natural that we meet a multitude of attempts in the New Testament at dealing with the Hebrew Bible. As we have seen in the chapter about the history of the Christian canon (chapter 4), there was a rather significant group of people under the leadership of Marcion who argued that the Hebrew Bible was irrelevant, superseded by the revelation of Christ. Others, primarily gnostic groups, tried to interpret the Hebrew Bible as an allegorical reflection on humanity and its relationship with God in an attempt to remove the texts from their Jewish historical setting. Still others tried to preserve the strong bond between the Jesus movement and Jewish history and argued that only the ritual specifications in the Mosaic law had been superseded by Christ. Between these viewpoints was a continuum of varying interpretations.

The relationship between the Jesus movement and contemporary Jewish groups and their interpretations of the Scriptures was essential for the Christ-following interpretation of the Hebrew Bible. It can be said without doubt that it was in discussion with contemporary Jewish groups and by means of Jewish interpretative tools that the early church managed to establish a communal approach to the Hebrew Bible. This was partly because in a Jewish context Christ followers were completely dependent on the Hebrew Bible for explaining and justifying their faith, and partly because there were several Jewish interpretative models that gave the texts a more universal meaning, relevant also for non-Jews. The textual interpretation of Philo of Alexandria (ca. 20 BCE–50 CE) played a fundamental role in influencing the theology of Origen, who in turn helped shape Christian biblical interpretation. Similarly, the rabbinic interpretative traditions created a background for the emergence of the biblical interpretation of the Syrian church, which then helped shape Greek Bible usage, especially during worship.

During the third century, the question of whether there was any continuity between the Jewish tradition and the Gospels constituted the main source of conflict between different Christ groups. Eventually, the view that the prophesies of the Hebrew Bible verified the Gospels and their message, an approach advocated by Justin Martyr among others, triumphed over those who believed that the God of the Hebrew Bible was not the same as the one revealed through Christ. Anchoring the new movement historically in its Jewish heritage turned out to be more tenable and convincing than attempting to create a brand-new tradition based only on the New Testament. During the fourth century, it therefore became important to provide Christian biblical interpretation that was firmly grounded both in its historical heritage and the new Christ-group traditions. This became especially important when the Christian faith started to become relevant in philosophically educated circles.

The lifelong and vastly comprehensive interpretative work of Origen (ca. 185–254 CE), a theologian schooled in Alexandria, had a decisive effect on the development of Christian biblical interpretation. By distinguishing between different levels within a text, he could do justice to the different meanings it contained: historical, moral, and spiritual meanings. Although Origen's methodology, as well as his commentaries on almost every book of the Bible, came to have a great impact on and to form the basis for Christian biblical interpretation, he was not without critics. Certain rhetorically schooled Christ followers, mostly tied to the school in Antioch, argued that Origen's emphasis on the spiritual meaning of texts based on allegorical readings opened up for arbitrary interpretations that lacked a historical basis. Instead, they suggested a typological reading where the biblical narratives were seen as models for faith, the church, and the pattern of Christian life.

The relationship between the early church and the New Testament texts has already been treated in the section on the canonization process. It is striking that, as far as we can see, there were no major conflicts about the usage and interpretation of these texts. Apart from Marcion's reductions of the collection, and rare arguments questioning the authority of Paul within certain gnostic and Jewish Christ groups, the early church was basically in agreement about what should be read and, at least until the fourth century, was open to different traditions being practiced in different congregations. From the words of the church fathers, we know that several apocryphal gospel texts and apostle narratives were in circulation without their usage being questioned. The same was the case with various childhood gospels and the Acts of Paul and the Thomas texts. The interpretation of these texts did not create the same problems as did the interpretation of the Hebrew Bible texts. Indeed, Origen's deep and often original philological and allegorical interpretation of the Gospel of John did not have any major impact.

More interesting than the question of interpretation is how the Bible itself was used. It is intriguing to note that the Bible was not commonly used to justify certain points or actions. Rather, people read it as a pattern in which they could view themselves, their own questions and experiences. Many early Christian texts are characterized by a sort of recycling of New Testament material in a collage of quotes, biblical connections, and personal reflections, all expressed in New Testament diction. Often we find that single biblical events or wordings are injected without commentary into contemporary contexts and attributed new meaning. In this way, the meanings of texts are enriched, and by means of a common biblical diction and thought world, diverse positions are joined together in one common frame of reference.

One reason that the interpretation of New Testament texts was not a central problem in the early church was that, in all likelihood, they were not viewed as helpful in solving the conflicts that dominated large sections of early Christianity. These problems mainly revolved around Christian praxis in a non-Christian world and how a Christian should live, as well as around which congregations actually counted as Christians, how they should be led and structured, and what was to be done with those who were baptized but did not live up to their baptism. The New Testament texts do not provide any clear, unified answers to these questions; rather, one could accuse the texts of sometimes contradicting each other on these topics.

Thus, instead of biblical texts, two other factors grew in importance over time:

(1) the rule of faith and the creed, and (2) the apostolic succession. The creed echoed the Trinitarian confession said during baptism and summarized the Christian faith: the belief in the Father as creator, Jesus Christ as Savior, and the Spirit as life-giver. This seems to have been enough to serve as a communal doctrine. It was not until the fourth century that the battles about what the creed actually meant erupted. It was therefore the apostolic succession, and the mutual recognition of each other, that was used to solve conflicts. Already in the letters of Paul we find exhortations not to divide but to adhere to the traditions transmitted by the leaders appointed by the apostle, who received them from Christ himself. References to received traditions and rightly appointed leaders return continually in the majority of conflicts and become decisive for the development toward unity. By arguing that the congregation had remained true to the teachings of their first leader, who was appointed by an apostle, and by pointing out that the present bishop stood in an unbroken succession of bishops going back to the apostle, congregations could justify and defend their praxis and interpretations.

This referencing of tradition and succession necessitated mutual acknowledgment. Therefore, it became important that a local bishop was approved and acknowledged by other bishops in the region and, later on, by the bishop in the center of the province. However, the argument of tradition ran deeper than the question of rightful and church-approved leadership. The most decisive factor was whether the congregation's praxis and traditions could be traced to those of the apostles. Because most of the available texts did not provide any answers to questions of tradition, references were instead made to oral traditions and to praxis that had been passed down in tradition. For example, the ways in which baptisms and worship were carried out could not be defended using arguments taken from the Bible or from a developed theology. Instead, praxis was defended by arguing that it stemmed from the apostolic time.

The central significance of the tradition in the early church, visible still in the Catholic and Orthodox traditions today, can thus be traced back to attempts made during the formative years to unify the Christian movement in a time of great diversity and rapid spread. Without the help of an established canon and an ideologically elaborate theology, the early followers of Christ appealed to tradition as a building block in the process of growing together and demonstrating that they shared a common heritage. The relationship between text and tradition was not actualized until the fourth century, when the Christian community had the economic, social, and political resources required for a thorough reflection on pressing theological inconsistencies. In this context, Basil of Caesarea (ca. 330–379 CE) refers to the distinction Aristotle made between the ways in which people learn: via teaching (*mathein*) and via experience (*pathein*).

In the church, teaching happens through the readings of texts, and experience through the praxis of the church, in worship, prayer, and fasting. The first happens openly and is open to everyone. The second happens on a personal level and necessitates initiation via baptism. The deeper meaning of faith in the words of the confession is hidden. It is not written down in the Scriptures; it is transmitted via tradition. It is a revelation, like the meaning behind the parables in the Gospels, and it is revealed only to those who are part of the community of believers, since it necessitates initiation. Therefore, the interpretation of the Bible in the early church is always subjected to association with the community in which the Bible is handed down.

Further Reading

Bradshaw, Paul F. *The Apostolic Tradition: A Commentary*. Hermeneia. Minneapolis: Fortress, 2002.

Brown, Peter. *Power and Persuasion in Late Antiquity: Towards a Christian Empire*. Curti Lecture Series. Madison: University of Wisconsin Press, 1992.

Brox, Norbert. *A History of the Early Church*. London: SCM, 1994.

Chadwick, Henry. *The Church in Ancient Society: From Galilee to Gregory the Great*. Oxford: Oxford University Press, 2003.

Esler, Philip F., ed. *The Early Christian World*. 2nd ed. London: Routledge, 2017.

Freyne, Sean. *The Jesus Movement and Its Expansion: Meaning and Mission*. Grand Rapids: Eerdmans, 2014.

Holmes, Michael W., ed. *The Apostolic Fathers: Greek Texts and English Translations*. 3rd ed. Grand Rapids: Baker Academic, 2007.

Kelly, J. N. D. *Early Christian Creeds*. Harlow: Longman, 1981.

Limor, Ora, and Guy G. Stroumsa, eds. *Christians and Christianity in the Holy Land: From the Origins to the Latin Kingdoms*. Turnhout: Brepols, 2006.

Maier, Paul L. *Eusebius: The Church History*. Grand Rapids: Kregel, 2007.

Miller, Patricia Cox. *Women in Early Christianity: Translations from Greek Texts*. Washington, DC: Catholic University of America Press, 2005.

Nasrallah, Laura. *Christian Responses to Roman Art and Architecture: The Second-Century Church amid the Spaces of Empire*. Cambridge: Cambridge University Press, 2010.

Rousseau, Philip. *The Early Christian Centuries*. London: Longman, 2002.

Bíblia

Readings

In the previous chapters the emphasis was on presenting the outcomes of scholarly research. Through comparisons and interpretations of various sources, we have moved in a chronological fashion from past historical and religious settings, to reasonable reconstructions of the historical Jesus, to the content and main ideas of New Testament texts. We have learned about the formation of the texts; how they were used and collected; how people, groups, and settings related to each other; and how a diversity of communities that go, in hindsight, under the label "early Christianity" contributed to a tradition with a common textual collection as well as similar worship and congregational practices.

Historians and exegetes examine sources of different kinds and construct historical contexts and relationships in order to reach plausible results; they assess a formation process, contexts of communication, and where a text (in its final form) belongs ideologically at the time; they determine the theology that took shape in a certain time and context. Preunderstandings and interests (conscious and unconscious) are bound to influence the interpretative work one way or another.

The purpose of this chapter is to describe and exemplify the hermeneutics of reading and the process of examination. We will present perspectives and theories concerning texts, contexts, and readers and suggest a basic step-by-step procedure for how to interpret a New Testament text that is followed by two example interpretations that elaborate the procedure. You will soon discover that there is not *one* interpretation, not *one* perspective, and certainly not *one* meaning. There are many approaches to the "worlds of the texts," riddled with caves and paths that invite exploration, not least of oneself as a reader—how one's perceptions, interests, aims, and purposes play into the reading and interpreting process. A historical text-oriented method seeks to alert the interpreter to subjective perspectives and toward identifying the text's first meaning and communicative context. Yet this method is also bound to time and preunderstandings. Following certain basic steps—a kind of interpretative template—is useful and guards against making basic mistakes, without asserting that it would safeguard the interpreter entirely. But a basic methodology still requires an awareness of reading processes and textual theories, of perspectives and presuppositions.

The two example interpretations are followed by a number of readings of specific New Testament passages that apply specific methods, approaches, or perspectives, such as narrative and rhetorical, hermeneutical, ideological, and postcolonial. An interest in historical circumstances is combined with elaborations of a text's argumentation structure and relevance for different readers. The purpose of presenting these readings is to demonstrate how perspectives, methods, and interests yield a variety of results, as well as to exemplify the creative subjectivity of all interpretation.

To state that interpretations are unavoidably subjective is, however, *not* the same as stating that all interpretations are equally legitimate or plausible. Reading texts in translation, for example, can never be equal to reading them in their language of origin, since translations in themselves are interpretations that inevitably create a distance between reader and text. Similarly, interpreting an isolated sentence or phrase cannot do justice to the entire text to which it belongs. To interpret a sentence or passage in context gives more reliable access to its meaning.

A common way of signposting where different methods locate meaning is with *the world behind the text*, *the world in the text*, and *the world in front of the text*. The signposts seem to separate the different interpretative endeavors diachronically. At the same time it is rather difficult, if not impossible—especially today when the historical-critical method has lost its defining character—to pin any particular method to a diachronic or a synchronic level of interpretation. Nevertheless, as a way of visualizing the locations of meaning, the distinction can be helpful.

Method and perspective cannot be separated; theory and practice go hand in hand. That we still divide method and theory in this manner can be likened to learning how to drive. One must first master driving a car on a straight and wide road before attempting to tackle the intricacies of city traffic, where it is necessary to make fast and complex decisions.

Approaches to the Text

The most important tool in interpreting texts, including biblical ones, is you, the reader. You are the one who reads the texts, and you are the one who interprets them. Without your commitment, there is no understanding. A toolbox for interpreting biblical texts must focus as much on the interpreter as on the text.

All understanding of texts is dependent on knowledge, experiences, and the reading capacity of the reader. These, together with the text in question, construct understanding of meaning. Thus, understanding varies from one reader to another, even when studying the same text. Texts offer multiple paths, and readers make choices based on their tradition and setting. If the reader lacks interest in the text—if the reader has no questions at the outset—the result will be meager. One of the purposes of exegetical training is to practice and maintain the ability to read and interpret texts.

Listening to a piano concerto by Mozart can be a pleasurable musical experience, even if the listener knows nothing about the music in advance and cannot explain the experience. It just is. Experienced listeners of music will have different reactions than those who seldom listen. One who plays the piano pays attention to certain details; one who knows how a piano concerto is typically composed and what to expect in the first movement, or is familiar with Viennese classicism, can hear things that the one who lacks musical training or experience will not be able to notice.

Reading comprehension can be compared to the above example. It varies depending on the reader's knowledge, experiences, and interpretative abilities. This is especially the case when reading biblical texts, where you have to justify your reading and compare it with others' views. One begins to reflect on one's interpretation, and on how to motivate a particular reading. The process awakens a kind of hermeneutical awareness; that is, the reader begins to critically analyze what interpretation is, and how interpretations come about.

In this section, we will describe some of that which we know happens when reading a text, and present in a simplified manner the three most common approaches to texts in the history of biblical interpretation. Since linguistic theories and textual theories are the basis of every interpretation, a few examples of such theories will be presented, and thereafter some guidelines for exegesis. Finally, we will consider different interpretative variables in the context of an interpretative process, the plethora of interpretative approaches existent today, and some attempts at presenting methodological syntheses for the interpretation of biblical texts.

Do You Understand How You Read?

We expect that one who has studied exegesis and biblical interpretation is able to answer questions such as "What does the text say? Do you understand *what* you are reading?" Equally important for an exegete, however, is the ability to answer questions like "Do you understand *how* you read?" and "Do you understand *why* you read?" These three questions (what, how, and why) are interconnected. Since the Bible is accessible to many kinds of readers in different times and cultures, the number of interpretations will inevitably be astronomical. This statement becomes obvious when one considers all the traces that the Bible has left in the history of the church, in art, music, literature, laws, social structures, language, ideas, beliefs, and so on—or if one were to collect all the interpretations of a specific biblical text today. The goal of a completely objective interpretation or absolute truth can never be attained. An important task, then, for hermeneutics (the art of interpretation) is to find a balance between the notion that there is only one right interpretation and the perception that a text can be interpreted in whichever way the reader wants.

Readers of the Bible in Western cultures may not be very numerous; they are, however, quite diverse. People can read a biblical text with entirely different interests, including the following:

- to obtain guidance in their own life
- to help others live
- to lead people to faith in Jesus Christ
- to enjoy an ancient, holy text
- to reconstruct a historical process
- to attain a clearer historical meaning in the text
- to build a Christian theology
- to find reasons for their own convictions
- to describe the translucent shroud that is inevitably cast over a translated work
- to see patterns of rhetoric or narration in the text
- to gain an increased understanding for their own culture

The above list could be much longer. The question "Why?" has many answers yet is relatively easy compared to the question "How?" Our lives are a constant process of interpretation, and textual interpretation is an important part of that process. Reality exists only in a mediated form, in interpretative conceptions. Because language has an essential role in this process of life, texts also become important. Exegetical craftsmanship is a hermeneutical activity.

A General Reading Model

The theoretical aspects of this presentation may be illustrated with what, according to modern research, is known today about the reading process.[1] It can be described by the model in figure 6.1. According to this model, we never meet a text empty-handed. When we read, prior knowledge and experiences are activated and structured by our "preunderstanding," a vital part of the entire reading process.

While reading the text, the eye registers letters, words, and phrases. But we do not read everything, since our brain registers only a minimum number of characteristics and focuses on how to fill in the blanks with what seems necessary to obtain the

1. Sundblad et al., *LUS: En bok om läsutveckling.*

whole. This whole is dependent on our preunderstanding, because our brains select contextually appropriate characteristics. Already at the first reading, preunderstanding and reading cooperate in ways that we often are not aware of.

The correlation of reading and preunderstanding results in a reading comprehension that can be either conscious or not. It is limited in scope: from parts of words to shorter passages. These units of reading comprehension continuously influence our preunderstanding and provide the constituents for a perception of content; that is, the brain constructs also here a whole, based on the information available. The perception of content develops gradually, and we obtain a progressively better picture of the whole. Also, this is influenced by preunderstanding while reading.

The perception of content—that is, the result of a reading—is often associated with what we already know. Processing the content can be more or less creative and usually depends on our interests while reading ("attention-demanding activity" in figure 6.1). We may note especially (1) the relationship between perception of content and prior knowledge, (2) the perception of content, (3) reading comprehension, or (4) reading. This leads to revised perceptions of the text's form, content, and function.

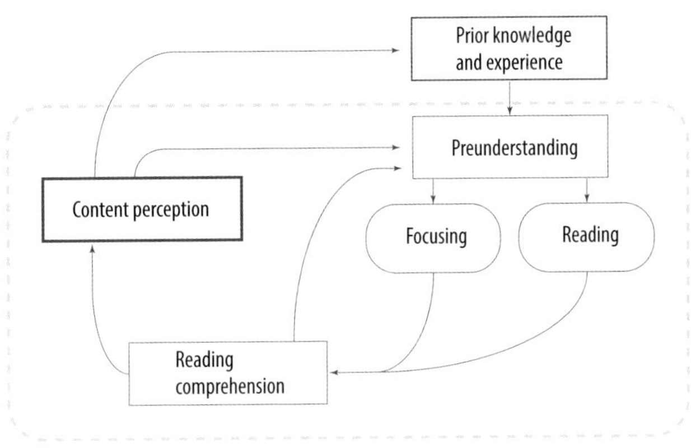

Figure 6.1 The reading process.

Remember that this is simply a model of the reading process, not the process itself. What the model does not show is that all its parts function concurrently, that conscious and subconscious processes are blended, and that attention may be directed toward different elements. From this reading model, we may draw several conclusions regarding the mechanisms of biblical interpretation; for our purposes, however, it may suffice to note two points:

- There are better and worse readers, and as a result, different perceptions of content are bound to arise. Pay attention to, for example, which parts and features in a text (a whole text document) have been included in an interpretation. Attention-demanding activities must become conscious and be practiced.
- In every interpretation there is preunderstanding. A perception of content is the product of both the text and the reader's prior knowledge and experiences. How can these preunderstandings that all biblical scholars have be made conscious and explicit?

What is said here of the reading process can also be applied to the concept of understanding in general. As soon as we attempt to understand, we activate prior knowledge, experiences, and feelings in our brain. It may be compared with understanding a movie: it consists of a limited number of fragments (scenes), yet we can leave the cinema with a feeling of having watched and understood a whole course of events. All the disparate pieces of information are connected in the brain and supplemented with other information, and thus we process everything into an understanding of the larger context, and finally of the whole movie. Understanding, as reading, is a creative, interactive process for the individual, with varying results. The greater and more complicated a phenomenon is, the greater the variation.

Three Main Approaches to the Texts

Allowing for some simplification, the history of biblical interpretation purports three main approaches to texts: a religious, a historical, and a linguistic-literary approach.

1. *The Bible is read as a religious document, as Holy Scripture*. The texts are relevant and more or less normative for people today. Like other religious texts, the Bible deals with important life questions: life and death, guilt and punishment, God, evil, and so on. For a great number of Bible readers, the Bible is Holy Scripture—the word of God—a divine revelation of God, our fellow humans, the world, and ourselves. Often, the biblical texts function as God's immediate and direct communication with humans. The texts deal with human beings here and now.

2. *The Bible is read as a historical document*. Such a reading seeks to reconstruct a historical situation or process; it sheds light on past relationships, explains past events and actions, and so on. How did the movement of Christ followers come into existence? What was the relationship like between them and their surrounding society during the first century? How does the picture of Christ change in the New Testament texts? These are typical questions for the historical reader. The Bible texts are primarily seen as historical data. The central focus lies not on the text itself but rather on something that was contemporary to the text's writing, or "something" responsible for the text's creation: the context of communication, the author's intention, individual actions and events, psychological and social behavior, and so on.

3. *The Bible is read as a literary document*. For this kind of reading, the focus in on that which is said in the text, how it is said, and how it works in different settings, sentences, images, patterns, greater structures, and so on. The Bible is read like any other text might be. From such a perspective, translation becomes part of a linguistic history, and the text's reception history additionally becomes a chapter of its own. The texts themselves, read not as God's word, and less so as historical sources, have left many traces. In many interpretations, analyses of textual structure, textual genre, intertextuality, and the text's symbolic universe are typically literary.

Throughout history, these three basic perspectives have worked together, albeit in varying proportions. They may be compared with three lanes on the same highway leading toward interpretations of biblical texts with a rich array of opportunities to switch lanes.

Academic and Ecclesial Interpretation Practices

Is an exegetical interpretation the same as a Christian interpretation or a theological interpretation? What do they have in common, and what sets them apart? In the book *Tolkning för livet* (Interpretation for life) from 2004, Ola Sigurdson suggests that for theology the actual "text" is the context in which the Bible takes shape, not the biblical text in itself. Sigurdson thus refers to Christian usage of the Bible as characteristic of a Christian interpretation. Therefore, when aiming at a Christian interpretation, one needs to be educated in the church's hermeneutical strategies.[2] It is the life of the community of faith, its activity and organization that is the fundamental means of the Christian church of interpreting the Bible as Scripture. Interpretative processes are embodied primarily in the Christian worship service with its contextualizing of individual episodes in the Bible, which may happen in a social setting, in the delivering of the sermon, or in the mystery of the Eucharist.

In that same book, another theologian, Cristina Grenholm, argues that the interpretative processes within academia and church ought to be basically the same, as all biblical interpretation has three dimensions: the textual, the contextual, and the theological. Grenholm's "scriptural criticism," formulated together with Daniel Patte, can be compared to a triangle with three interpretative points: critical theology, critical biblical analysis, and critical contextual analysis (see fig. 6.2). Every corner of the triangle corresponds to one of these points. Critical biblical analysis is directed toward the text, critical theology toward the conceptual content in Christian faith, and critical contextual analysis toward the setting in which the interpretation takes place. How these three points characterize academic practice is, however, not taken up. Potentially, her perception may be interpreted as indicating that even if the text is the main object within academia, one must, as in all hermeneutical work, also take into account traditions and contexts of the interpretative process and setting.

In this form of scriptural interpretation lies, according to Grenholm, a threefold challenge. "Bible scholars often only consider the text. In dialogue with Bible scholars, systematic theologians view the process as twofold. Feminist theologians, liberation theologians, postcolonial critics, and even practical theologians who all focus on the function of biblical interpretation face another problem. They have accepted the threefold challenge but meet with difficulties in the discussions with Bible scholars and

2. Ola Sigurdson, "Bibeln som Skrift: Om bibelns anspråk på aktualitet och auktoritet i den kristna kyrkan," in Bengtsson and Eriksson, *Tolkning för livet*, 230–31.

The semantic dimension is dealt with in dictionaries, where the meanings of different words are determined on the basis of the context in which they are used. Words can refer to the real things, such as *chair, land, house, Peter*; to various attributes, such as *elegant, evil, beauty*; to actions and states of being, such as *to run, to be pleased, to lie down*. They can also mark the relationship between different elements in a text, such as *and, therefore, when, through, on*. A word's syntactic form does not always correspond to its semantic meaning: at his coming = when he comes; the kingdom of God = God rules/has a kingdom; the forgiveness of sins = God forgives those who have sinned; her humiliation = she has been humiliated/is humiliated; her strength = she is strong; and so on.

The pragmatic dimension is important as it marks how language is always anchored in an extratextual, interpersonal dimension. Language is always bound to certain settings and persons. Which meanings does the sender imbue his or her words with? How does the receiver understand them? How much knowledge and experience do the sender and the receiver have in common as the basis for their communication? What ability does the sender have to express him- or herself? How familiar is the receiver with the rhetorical patterns that the sender makes use of? How large is the risk of misunderstanding? In which situation were the words uttered? Are both sender and receiver familiar with that which is written in the text? For questions like these, it is not enough to simply know the linguistic system. The language users are also included in the interpretation of a language-based document.

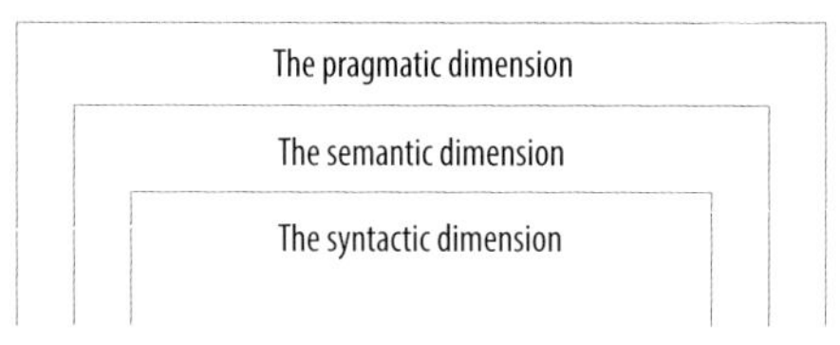

Figure 6.4 The three dimensions of linguistic signs.

It has long been discussed how the relation between these three dimensions ought to be described. It is probably best to speak of it as an inclusive relationship. Figure 6.4 illustrates how the three dimensions are dependent on one another, and how all texts, through the pragmatic dimension in language, are bound in time. As this also applies to interpretations of texts, it is therefore not enough to simply refer to grammar or to a dictionary. The textual document as a whole, the relationship between the constituent parts and this whole, and the document's function in a specific setting all determine to a high degree how we will understand the text. However, it is not always easy to determine the historical setting of a particular biblical text. Generally the information is too scarce. Sometimes parts of a text from many different contexts are gathered into one textual document, such as texts regarding the law in the Hebrew Bible. Sometimes we simply need to accept a very general historical setting, as is the case for temple liturgy or synagogue piety in the diaspora in some of the psalms. We therefore often have no choice but to deal solely with the syntactic and semantic dimensions. As a result, we can do no more than construct several settings with several interpretations for a text.

A historical reading that focuses on the actual textual communication is, however, only one means of interpretation. We can analyze only the textual world, or we can use the text as a source for a historical reconstruction, or we can place the text in other contexts. The recontextualization of texts—that is, the use of texts in new contexts—occurs already in the Bible (e.g., through the insertion of quotations from the Hebrew Bible in the New Testament). This is very common in the history of biblical interpretation.

Theory of Texts: Communication and Social Embedding

The basis for interpretation lies not only in theories of what language is but also in theories of what a text is. When linguists around 1970 began to show an interest in the phenomenon of "text," many attempts were made at presenting various definitions and textual models. As examples, the work of Dressler and of Gülich and Raible (see Olsson) may be mentioned.[4] Hellspong and Ledin, adherents of Michael Halliday's socio-semiotic textual theory and his emphasis on text's social embedding, suggest seven characteristics of a text.[5]

A text communicates. Through a specific use of signs, a text wants to convey something. It works as a means of expression, a form of address from a sender to a receiver. The text assumes that there is a receiver that can interpret its many signs. Some speak of the text's *signaling function* when it addresses the receiver; its *diagnostic function* when it expresses that which the sender thinks and feels; and its *symbolic function* when it points toward the world outside the text. These functions can be mixed in very different ways in a text. When we communicate with signs, we always construct a *perception of reality* and not *reality itself.*

A text is intentional. It has some kind of objective. It is supposed to have certain effects, the very least of which is to be received and understood. "Where is the text headed? What is the author looking for?" We generally tie the intention of the text to one author, but it can also be associated with multiple individuals in more collective works. Even genres can have their own intentions: a tale wishes to entertain, a myth wishes to convey a truth about the human being and her existence, a law wishes to promote a certain kind of organization in society, and so on.

A text is verbal. That which has thus far been said of a text can also be applied to a painting or a sculpture. Unique to a text, however, is that it is language-based—it consists of words. A word has meaning (it provides an expression with certain qualities); it has a reference (it points to a certain phenomenon). Words can have a primary meaning (denotation) as well as secondary meanings (connotation). Together, the words form a kind of fabric or texture; one of the meanings of the Latin

4. Dressler, *Einführung in die Textlinguistik*; Gülich and Raible, *Linguistische Textmodelle*; Olsson, "Decade of Text-Linguistic Analyses."

5. Hellspong and Ledin, *Vägar genom texten.*

word *textum* is "fabric." A word in a text must be understood in relation to the words that come just before and just after it (syntagmatic relations), but a word also is given meaning from its usage in different parts of a textual document (paradigmatic relations)—for example, the word "righteousness" in the Letter to the Romans.

A text is stable. It differs from oral communication. It can be used and reused. Much material in the Bible was at first, with all the flexibility it entails, oral tradition. When an oral tradition is recorded in text, a certain objectification occurs, separating what is said from its direct affiliation with the sender, and the text begins to live its own life. A text may be seen as both time bound and autonomous.

A text is coherent. Its constituents remain connected in some manner. As readers, we constantly search for that which ties different words, phrases, and sentences together. We want to perceive a whole. We want to find some kind of overarching theme (thematic coherence). A story contains events that are spatially, temporally, or even logically related to each other. A letter can compile arguments that will compel the recipient to adhere to the wishes of the sender. Hellspong and Ledin subsume cohesion (the syntactic ties in the text) under coherence. Coherence does not always demand cohesion. In fact, many texts display a structure in which coherence is built in hierarchical levels that successively overarch one another. In such cases, one can generally reduce the content to a summary clause or sentence.

A text is conventional. It must follow certain accepted norms and rules, or else readers cannot understand it. Good texts always have a good balance between old information and new information. Good texts always follow patterns of texts that we know of, even if these do not exist in written or conscious form. We call them genres or text types. All texts build in some manner on earlier texts; sometimes these texts are especially distinct through citations or associations (so-called intertexts).

A text is creative. With this, Hellspong and Ledin mean to convey that there must always be something in a text that deviates from the conventional. Different genres allow for different measures of creativity and innovation. Creativity is primarily the domain of the author, but also the receiver contributes with independent readings of a text.

As a basis for their analysis of texts, Hellspong and Ledin simplify their text model to five components: "A text comes into existence as one (1) in a certain setting, *the context*, (2) uses words, *the textual*, (3) in order to convey something, *the ideational*, (4) to somebody, *the interpersonal*, (5) in a certain way, *the style*."[6] The broad and in many ways difficult term "style" is here used to represent many characteristics of a text: genre, structure, rhetorical aspects, argumentation, grammatical peculiarities, usage of certain words, phrases and thematic words, and so on.

For the analysis of an entire text, context refers to the setting of the text and its

6. Hellspong and Ledin, *Vägar genom texten*, 47.

intertextual context. As we analyze biblical texts, we are often dealing with parts of a textual document, and "context" normally entails only the part's relation to the whole document. We thus expose the textual, ideational, and interpersonal structure. Style is determined by the interaction that exists between these three structures for the purpose of making an impression on the reader.

Variables of the Interpretative Process

Text interpretation entails two major components: text and interpretation. There are, however, as already mentioned, several other components that contribute to the interpretative process. The most important components may be extracted from the following formula:

I interprets *Y* as *Z* for *U* aiming for *V*

I represents the one who is interpreting, *Y* the text that is interpreted, *Z* the type of result, *U* the receiver of the text, and *V* the aim of interpretation.

I always interpret a text for somebody—for myself or for others. Will interpretations differ if we change the variable *U*? Will the interpretation differ if we interpret for an exegetical colleague, for one who has just begun theological studies, for a gathering of elementary school teachers, for priests in training, or for specialists of Near Eastern history? There's no question that the manner of presentation will differ, but what of the actual interpretative process? Experience shows that even this can vary, since different receivers of the interpretation trigger different aspects and aims; that is, *U* is connected with *Z* and *V*. The variable *V*, the aim of interpretation, has already been dealt with when we listed different interests in the interpretative process, such as "to reconstruct a historical process" or "to build a Christian theology" (see the beginning of this section). We could add more aims to that list. The variable *Z* gives the type of results one wishes to reach in the interpretative work:

- A *translation*, where *Z* ought to be, as much as possible, equivalent with *Y*
- An *explanation*, where *Y* is seen as an expression of, or the cause of, *Z*
- An *application*, where *Y* is applied to the situation of, or the case of, *Z*
- A *demythologizing*, where *Y* is interpreted as the non-mythological message *Z*

As we continue to reflect on the interpretative process, we are alerted to its fluctuating and complex nature, even when we limit ourselves to historical-literary interpretations of biblical texts.

For analytically aware forms of textual interpretation, we can expand the formula by introducing the method (M):

I interprets *Y* through *M* as *Z* for *U* aiming for *V*

We note that the term "biblical interpretation" can designate many kinds of activities depending on how we determine these variables in the interpretative process. We can never simply "read *as* it is written."

As we continue to consider the variable *I*, the interpreter in the process, a formula suggested by the sociologist Lindholm can be helpful.[7] It reads:

> A phenomenon *F*—seen from perspective *P* in a context (field, setting) *C*—has the meaning *X* for a person (interpreter) *I*.

This definition is illustrated in figure 6.5.

Applied to the process of biblical interpretation, *F* is the text to be interpreted, and *I* is the interpreter, who can choose to analyze a text from different perspectives *P*: literary categories, feministic readings with gender and power as interpretative categories, the text's symbolic world, text-critical or source-critical categories, and so on. Changing perspectives should be a basic exercise in exegetical education. The interpreter is part of a larger context *C* and belongs to a particular culture, society, group, setting (i.e., the interpreter has his or her own "history"). However, the interpreter can modify *C* to some degree (not as much as *P* though). Also, *F* belongs in a way to the same context as *I*. Consequently, every interpretation of a text, and this includes biblical texts, is both historically and culturally bound.

Lindholm's model complicates the notion of speaking of just two major components (text and meaning, *F* and *X*, which in the natural sciences might correspond to data and theories. In a misdirected zeal for clarity, *I* was removed and *P* and *C* were turned into absolutes. Biblical research may be said to have originated thence. The strength of Lindholm's definition lies in the fact that it once more focuses attention on the researcher, on different perspectives, and on how different contexts affect interpretations. Lindholm does not relate his categories and the relationships between them to biblical scholarship; nevertheless, there are important insights to be gained.

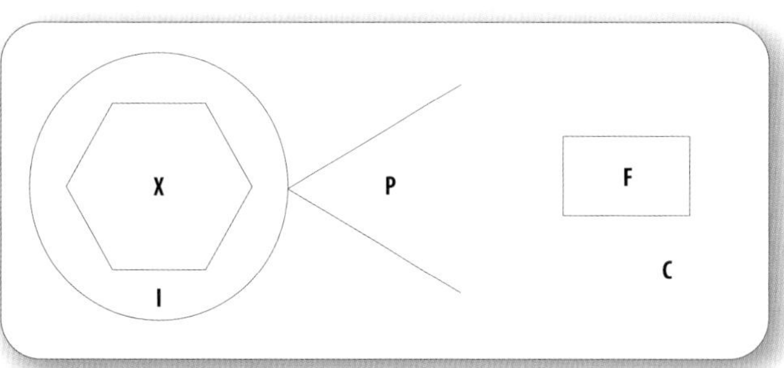

Figure 6.5 The interpreter in the interpretative process.

7. Lindholm, *Vetenskap, verklighet och paradigm.*

The components of the interpretative process surface very clearly as we analyze the reception history of the Bible. A variety of processes of interpretation inspire new possibilities for interpretation, which then can be tested against the text. Furthermore, we gain rich insight into other times and cultures, as well as the life and livelihood of various individuals and groups. In this field of research, much remains to be investigated.

Translations of the Bible

When interpreting the Bible, multiple languages will always be involved. The texts are written in Hebrew, Aramaic, or Greek, and the language that is used in presenting the results of an interpretation is generally different from those mentioned. Most people read biblical texts in translation. Every translation is but an approximation of the original, and most certainly not semantically identical to it. This means that there are good reasons to make use of more than one translation, preferably ones that differ from each other in type and interpretation. It is always an obstacle not to have access to the original text.

Disregarding works that retell the stories of biblical texts, such as *The Living Bible, Paraphrased* (1971), or perhaps the multitude of translations available for children, translations of the Bible may be roughly divided into four groups.

- *Type A*—literal translations that try to represent the original as precisely as possible, such as the American Standard Version (1904). A so-called interlinear edition, where every word of the Hebrew, Aramaic, or Greek original, if possible, is linked to an English counterpart, can replace this type of translation.
- *Type B*—translations that preserve tradition and liturgical variants and are often text-critically and philologically meticulous. They often translate the original using traditional biblical language. A typical example of this class is the Revised Standard Version (1952), a revision of a revision of the classical English translation, the King James Version (1611). The Revised Standard Version has been revised again, now as the New Revised Standard Version (1989), written with a focus on inclusive language. The Swedish Bible of 1917, as well as many other revised church bibles, also belongs to this group. Especially with regard to interpretation of the original, Svenska Folkbibeln (Swedish People's Bible, 1998) should also be counted as type B.
- *Type C*—translations that retell a Bible text according to scientific research, reconstructing both the content and the style of the original in modern English. These translations are often equipped with detailed notes and explanations. Some of these are the New English Bible (1961, 1970), the New

American Bible (1970), La Bible de Jérusalem (1956, translated into many languages), and La Traduction Oecuménique de la Bible (1972, 1975). To this category belongs also Bibel 2000.

- *Type D*—common language translations that try to convey the original content in a language that is common to the majority of people. The best known of these is Today's English Version (1966, 1976), also known as the Good News Bible. It has counterparts in many languages: Die Gute Nachricht (1971), Bonnes Nouvelles Aujourd'hui (1971), and so on. To this category may also be counted the Contemporary English Version (1995), which takes into special consideration the oral performance of texts.

Differences between various translations depend primarily on the following characteristics:

1. *Text-critical differences*. The manuscripts differ from each other, and different readings have been chosen, so-called text-critical variants.
2. *Philological differences*. Words, phrases, clauses, and sentences in the original text can be interpreted in different ways.
3. *Translation-related differences*. These consist of different principles of language use (older or modern language, formal or common language, biblical language or language known by all, etc.) and principles for how a translator wants to portray the content, form, and style of the original (direct the conveyed content at the reader; reflect formal qualities of the original, such as diction—e.g., an important word in Greek should always be translated with the same word in English—word order, clause formulation, sentence structure, etc.; find stylistic counterparts to the style that a certain biblical text exhibits). Different principles lead to different kinds of translations.

Every translation is an interpretation of the original. This becomes clear not only in the text itself and its structure but also in other material that is normally present in Bible editions: introductions of various kinds, chapter summaries or headings, certain notes, references to parallels, word explanations at the beginning or end, tables of contents, indexes, maps, and various illustrations. All of this can contribute to an understanding of the text. Some wish to remove such material from Bible editions in the belief that they can arrive uninfluenced and without preconceptions at a text. This is not possible. Knowledge and experiences are always necessary for good readings to be made. This supplementary material ought thus to be viewed as a commentary on the text, and as such ought to be read with a critical eye. A comparison between different translations may be found abundantly useful in upholding this critical approach.

Types of Interpretation

In 1993 the Pontifical Biblical Commission produced a document for the fifty-year anniversary of the papal decree that opened the door to modern biblical scholarship within the Roman Catholic Church. The document summarized modern interpretative methods and models of reading. It is called *The Interpretation of the Bible in the Church* (1994), and the presentation below follows the layout found in this document. Methods are presented in summary fashion, the purpose of which is to give an orientation. In the readings that follow, some of the methods presented here, or aspects of them, will then be applied to certain texts. Every reading is introduced by a short description of the interpretative type that is used.[8]

1 *The historical-critical method*—text criticism, literary (source) criticism, form criticism, and redaction criticism. In its traditional form it is a method for historical reconstructions, rather than for interpreting the meaning of a biblical text. It primarily wants to describe the historical process that led to the final edition of texts. In more modern scholarship, this diachronic, genetic approach has supplemented the literary analyses with synchronic analyses that view the text as contemporary with a certain communication setting. This method also includes basic text-critical and philological criticism. Nowadays, its purpose is to highlight meaning embedded in texts based on editors' and authors' perspectives. It is an important part of the scientific study of biblical texts.

2 *Rhetorical analysis*, like the next two forms of analysis, belongs to a group of literary methods that make the text—not its formation process or its historical reference—the focal point of interpretation. Analytical categories from biblical literature that is rooted in Semitic culture, from classical rhetoric, and from the so-called new rhetoric are used to describe the texts and their effects on recipients. Of the literary readings, the rhetorical is most closely related to historical analyses, as it is often combined with a reconstruction of the text's context of communication.

3 *Narrative analyses* focus even more on the text itself—especially stories—as a self-contained textual, literary world. A story evokes in the reader an image of an author, the so-called *implied author*, and an image of the recipient, the so-called *implied reader*. By identifying with the recipient implied in the text, a modern reader can entertain the story's message and meaning. A narrative analysis focuses on the interplay between these two implied components, as well as on spatial and temporal patterns in the text, the text's *point of view*, and its *plot*.

8. See also Gerdmar and Syreeni, *Vägar till Nya Testamentet*.

4 *The semiotic method* has much in common with the narrative approach but is more focused on the deep structure of texts. It has its foundation in Russian formalism, a literary theory quite different from that which underlies narrative analysis. On the narrative level, semiotics studies those transformations that occur during the development of a story. On the so-called discursive level, there is a focus on how different significant elements (people, places, times, etc.) develop in the text. This facilitates a determination of which values and which ideology the text builds on.

5 *Canonical perspectives*, like the following two perspectives, place the biblical texts within a specific tradition. Primarily Old Testament scholars have supported the thesis that texts should be read in the context of the Bible as whole—that is, in the context of a Christian canon that was first completed in the fourth century. The biblical writings should be treated not as a collection of different and independent texts but as an expression of an inherited tradition. Every text should be interpreted in light of the canon or as part of a canonical process within which interpretative criteria coincide with those of the church's later history. This holistic view of the Bible characterizes several biblical theologies as well.

6 *A Jewish perspective* of biblical interpretation is based on the fact that the Hebrew writings in the Hebrew Bible were first interpreted in Jewish communities long before the Common Era. Here we find the Septuagint, the Targumim, and a large amount of noncanonical texts. It is from this broad interpretative tradition that the Christian church and the early New Testament texts are born. The Jewish tradition of interpretation continues even after the New Testament up to the present day and is a resource for today's exegetes (perhaps more for historical and theological investigations than for presentations of individual texts).

7 *A reception history perspective* includes the entire history of the texts in various media. It takes into account all the traces that the Bible has left in academia, the ways the church has interpreted biblical texts, and the Bible's significance within art, music, literature, film, laws, political systems, ideas and concepts, and so on. The reception process has a reciprocal character: biblical texts, structures, themes, motifs, and metaphors influence societies, groups, and individuals (sometimes described as the Bible's Wirkungsgeschichte, or history of influence); and people, both men and women, use and interpret biblical material for different purposes and in different settings (reception history in a limited sense). An analysis can begin in the Bible or in material that has made use of the Bible, either knowingly or unknowingly. Reception analysis contributes to hermeneutics itself, as well as to the history of hermeneutics.

8 *Sociological reading*, like the next two methods, makes use especially of re-

sults and methods from other scientific fields. Sociology is largely significant for historical reconstructions (institutionalizing, authority, the church-sect relationships, etc.) and content-related descriptions (e.g., the text's symbolic world). Thus, it contributes to the interpretation of individual texts.

9 *Cultural-anthropological, socio-anthropological reading* is similar to sociological reading. It focuses especially on that which characterizes different groups and types of people, as well as their cultural setting: the Mediterranean individual, honor and shame, family relations, the holy and the profane, rites, taboos, magic, and so on. For more on this, see "Method Syntheses" below.

10 *Psychological, psychoanalytical reading* builds on theories from psychology or psychoanalysis (models from Freud or Jung, cognitive psychology, personality theories, developmental psychology, social psychology, psychology of religion, etc.). The inclusion of psychology enriches reading, as texts are also expressions of life experiences and behavioral norms. It can shed light on cultic rites, sacrifices, prohibitions, imagery, and apocalyptic views.

11 *Liberation theological interpretation*, like *feminist* interpretation and *postcolonial* interpretation, situates interpretation programmatically and consistently within contexts of contemporary society. Therefore, it incorporates a clear political dimension. These approaches can be combined with several of the other methods. The point of departure for liberation theologians is the idea that God is present in people's history and wants their salvation. God is the God of the poor and cannot accept injustice and oppression. An exegesis of biblical texts can therefore not be neutral but leads to liberating action. Postcolonial interpretation is associated with a criticism of Western aspirations to objectivity and claims of universal validity for interpretative paradigms. This perspective is discussed in more detail in the readings on pp. 580–99.

12 *Feminist interpretations* first and foremost maximize power and gender as interpretative categories in biblical analyses. In an early phase, the analyses' primary objective was to make women visible in biblical texts. In later phases they concentrated more on the androcentric and patriarchal qualities of the Bible. Texts and interpretations are always marked by different interests, and this ought to surface in every investigation. Today, there is a great interest in the ideological effects when reading biblical texts. A feminist perspective promotes ideological criticism of both biblical texts and Bible scholars; therefore, it has a clear place in any ethical criticism of the Bible.

The papal document introduces the above types of interpretation as acceptable for reading and analyzing biblical texts. However, it forcefully speaks against fundamentalist interpretations that "invite people into a sort of intellectual suicide." Fundamentalists interact with biblical texts as if they had been dictated word by word by God, and claim, quite unreasonably, that the texts are somehow infallible. They reject all historical-critical analysis; deny any development of the traditions concerning, for example, Jesus; and read texts regarding the creation of the world as literal facts. They advocate a reading of the Bible that rejects all critical questioning and analysis. According to the papal document, such an approach is directly in denial of the historical qualities of biblical revelation and does not fully acknowledge the reality of the incarnation. The Bible is Holy Scripture but also a document written by humans.

It ought to be noted that these forms of interpretation do not share the same properties. Some have the character of fully developed methods (e.g., rhetorical or semiotic analysis), others can be used in combination with different kinds of methods (e.g., feminist interpretations), and yet others function mainly as overarching concepts within which one can interpret texts (canonical interpretations).

All interpretative approaches do not lead to the same goal; an echo will reproduce the distinct character of its source. There are, however, good reasons to combine some methods, such as sociological and historical-critical analysis. Results may at times be carefully compared: Do they strengthen or contradict each other? However that may be, the above summary illustrates the diversity of possibilities within the field of modern biblical interpretation.

Method Syntheses

Many have wished to construct a universal method uniting all that should be done when interpreting a text. The historical-critical method has long laid claim to being the only "true" method, "Die exegetische Methode." Also in the modern age of interpretative pluralism, there are those who have presented more general method syntheses that integrate several—if possible all—methods; among them is Vernon K. Robbins, who has long labored to produce an integrated interpretative method that he calls "socio-rhetorical interpretation."[9] As the name implies, the theoretical framework is rhetorical and sociological. Texts are primarily seen as means and forms of communication. They are like a thick tapestry or texture that is intricately structured in a number of ways. Robbins divides his analysis into five parts:

1. *Inner texture.* This part studies the linguistic features exhibited by the text—the text's internal world. Robbins especially emphasizes repetition, development of themes, narrative patterns, beginning-middle-end, argumentation, and the involvement of aesthetical and sensory characteristics of the text.
2. *Intertexture.* This part studies how the text interacts with phenomena outside the text, such as historical events, texts, customs, values, media, and institu-

9. Robbins, *Exploring the Texture of Texts.*

tions. The analysis is directed toward different uses of external textual material and toward text-related cultural, social, and historical relationships.

3 *Social and cultural texture.* This part, using sociological and anthropological theories, studies the social and cultural world that the text expresses or creates—that is, the text's symbolic world. This applies to different ways of speaking about the world, honor and shame, different personality types, agreements between individuals, challenges and answers, and so on. By studying these characteristics of the text and its time, the interpreter's ties to his or her own culture (ethnocentrism) and time (anachronism) are reduced.

4 *Ideological texture.* This part studies individuals who are involved in the interpretative process—their cultural, social, and ideological positions. This includes the interpreter and those that the interpreter speaks to, other interpreters of the text (such as writers of commentaries), and even the text itself, as well as the people in text, who function as dialogue partners in the interpretative process. Which interests are at work in the interpretative process, and how are they related to each other?

5 *Sacred texture.* This last part recognizes students who want to know how these texts relate to their everyday Christian lives, focusing especially on what the text says about God, Jesus, and other holy persons, about the Spirit and spiritual beings, about God's salvation history and the salvation of humankind, about how humans respond to God's calling, and about different forms of religious community life.

As a whole, this synthesis of methods is fairly complex but claims a wide range of applicability of results from other fields related to human and social sciences. It also poses many questions that sharpen the attention of the reader and increases the reader's hermeneutical awareness.

Kari Syreeni's hermeneutical three-world model also unites several methods in a collective design.[10] It distinguishes three synchronic (see figure 1.1, p. 37) levels of interpretation and analysis: the textual world, the symbolic world, and the concrete world. The *textual world* partially corresponds to the first point on Robbins's list above and has been the object of many analytical forms over the past few decades. The *symbolic world* approaches Robbins's third point, while the *concrete world* designates the outer relationships that the text in different ways refers to. Through Syreeni's model, a text-oriented method that normally distinguishes between reality and text (e.g., a literary, textual-linguistic, rhetorical, or narrative reading) is combined with a sociological interpretation that is dominated by the difference between ideology and reality. Behind the term "symbolic world" lies the expression "symbolic universe"

10. Syreeni, "Wonderlands."

coined in Berger and Luckman's sociology of knowledge.[11] It is the ideological superstructure that organizes our understanding and interpretation of life and reality. The three-world model does justice to our construction of reality, both textually and ideologically. Indeed, the textual world must be related to both the concrete world and its symbolic representation. This model is more manageable than that of Robbins. Its strength lies in the fact that it includes and focuses on the symbolic world. Thus, it makes possible a distancing from the texts that facilitates criticism of content, something that is particularly difficult to obtain in analyses that are solely text-oriented.

Proximity and Distance

Many interpretative exercises foster primarily a hermeneutics of proximity, or as it is sometimes called, a hermeneutics of empathy—a listening, accepting attitude toward the text. Such an approach involves evoking and amplifying the meaning of a text. The interpreter accepts the conditions suggested in the text and reads it from what might best be described as "the inside." As much as possible, this interpreter is in agreement with the text: the textual world constitutes the center. When the symbolic world and the text's historical ties to extratextual phenomena are added, the road opens up toward distanced hermeneutics, or a hermeneutics of suspicion. The interpreter can now question the uncritical acceptance of the truth of the text and view it from other positions than that of the text. Such a critically analytical step is essential to interpretation as it allows for the recognition that a text's claims are conditional on whoever wrote it. The interpreter can compare, contrast, and reflect on his or her own context, or other contexts. In feminist, liberation, or postcolonial readings, these text-external positions of the interpreter are especially prominent, thus opening up for ideological criticism that can be applied to both the biblical text and the reader. No interpretation is innocent; it will always be, to varying degrees, imbued with aspects of the interpreter's interests. Such interests may have to do with anything from race and ethnicity to gender and sexuality to nationalism and postcolonialism. Biblical research thus strives to cross the border between exegesis and cultural-scientific disciplines. Indeed, this form of hermeneutical, ideology-critical investigation has become increasingly common in today's world. Every scholar must take the interpretative role seriously and take responsibility for his or her interpretation of the biblical texts.

Further Reading

Black, David Alan. *Linguistics for Students of the New Testament: A Survey of Basic Concepts and Applications*. Grand Rapids: Baker, 1995.

11. Berger and Luckmann, *The Social Construction of Reality*, 95.

Beaugrande, Robert de, and Wolfgang Dressler. *Introduction to Text Linguistics.* London: Longman, 1981.
Douglas, J. D., ed. *The New Greek-English Interlinear New Testament.* Wheaton: Tyndale, 1993.
Green, Joel B., ed. *Hearing the New Testament: Strategies for Interpretation.* 2nd ed. Grand Rapids: Eerdmans, 2010.
Halliday, Fred, and Jonathan Webster. *Text Linguistics: The How and Why of Meaning.* London: Equinox, 2014.
Jeanrond, Werner. *Theological Hermeneutics: Development and Significance.* New York: Crossroad, 1991.
Lindholm, Stig. *Vetenskap, verklighet och paradigm.* Stockholm: Almqvist & Wiksell, 1980.
Olsson, Birger. "A Decade of Text-Linguistic Analyses of Biblical Texts at Uppsala." *ST* 39 (1985): 107–26.
Pontifical Biblical Commission. *The Interpretation of the Bible in the Church.* Boston: Pauline Books & Media, 1996.
Robbins, Vernon K. *Exploring the Texture of Texts: A Guide to Socio-Rhetorical Interpretation.* Valley Forge, PA: Trinity Press International, 1996.
Syreeni, Kari. "Wonderlands: A Beginner's Guide to Three Worlds," *SEÅ* (1999): 33–36.
Sundblad, Bo, Kerstin Dominković, Birgita Allard, and Nina Dominkovic. *LUS: En bok om läsutveckling.* Stockholm: Almquist Wiksell, 1983.

How to Do a Historical, Text-Oriented Interpretation of a New Testament Text Passage

What was said in the previous section about processes of understanding, language and text theories, variables and methods of interpretation, and worlds of the text makes clear that text and interpretation include many different aspects. Besides Syreeni's hermeneutical three-world model, which distinguishes three synchronic levels of interpretation and analysis (the textual, the symbolic, and the concrete world; see the section "Method Syntheses," p. 506), another, more widespread three-world model locates the meaning of a text in the world behind the text, the world in the text, and the world in front of the text. The models intersect and overlap at times within a method, and the diversity of hermeneutical insights can be a challenge to anyone. We shall here provide a simplified guide on how to conduct a historical, text-oriented interpretation of a New Testament text.

The label "text-oriented" indicates that the focus is on the *final form* of the text. New Testament texts, especially the gospels, evolved from the time of Jesus's ministry (around 30 CE) until their form was finalized, four or more decades later. During this time, sources, editions, and revisions were woven together into one text. The special task of the historical-critical method (text-, source-, form-, and redaction-criticism) is to analyze the history of the text diachronically, to shed light on its prehistory, and to determine a text's historically valid meaning. Chapter 3, "The Historical Jesus," exemplifies this kind of approach (see also the section "Paths to the Past: On Sources and Methods," p. 31). This historical, text-oriented interpretation guide, however, approaches the text primarily from a synchronic perspective and in its final form.

Regarding the world *behind* the text, the focus is on the symbolic world and historical circumstances that may be surmised from the text in its final form. Regarding the world *in* the text, we analyze the literary context and structure of the text passage, genre and function, the qualities of words and expressions, and intertexts. Regarding the world *in front of* the text, the interpreter is asked to consider, in addition to the stipulated perspective (more on this in the next paragraph), other perspectives that are pertinent to the content of the text passage.

For this exercise, the parameters of the interpretation formula (*I interprets Y through M as Z for U aiming for V*), described in the previous section, are defined as follows: the interpreter (*I*) is a student, the text (*Y*) is a New Testament passage, the type of result (Z) is an interpretation paper for a course in New Testament studies. The receiver (*U*) is the examiner and fellow students; the aim of the interpretation (*V*) is to identify what the text in question may have communicated to its first addressees in their specific cultural and historical setting. The method (*M*) outlines the interpretative steps or road signs of a basic historical-literary interpretation. In order to achieve the aim (*V*), the language, content, and form of the text are examined and that which is hinted at or implied is made explicit. The text is seen as an expression of a communicative event. As we get toward the end of the exercise, the interpreter (*I*) will have the opportunity to consider his or her position and role in the interpretation process (see figure 6.5, p. 500) and reflect consciously on how a historical-text-oriented analysis of the text resonates with one's own presuppositions and interests (*C*). At this point the challenge is to identify analogies and hermeneutical reflections for meaning (*X*) of the phenomenon/text (*F* = *Y*).

The order in which the interpretative steps are presented suggests how the analytical procedure should be conducted (*via inventionis*). For the presentation of the results (the actual paper), the order may be changed in accordance with what appears most suitable (*via expositionis*). Two sample interpretations ("A Historical, Text-Oriented Reading of Matt 8:14–17" and "A Historical-Analogical Reading of Matt 5:3–10," pp. 517 and 531) illustrate how a paper that uses this approach may turn out.

Initial Examination of the Text Passage

Begin by carefully reading the passage that you are going to interpret. Compare different translations with each other and, if possible, consult the Greek text. Get as much help as you can from dictionaries and commentaries. To improve your attentiveness to detail, read through box 6.1, "Some Exercises for Reading and Writing," p. 515. Make notes on variations and on how connotations shift between translations. Make some preliminary decisions on what seems important to return to and discuss in more detail. You may need to reconsider your initial choices later in the process, so make notes.

The Literary Context of the Text Passage

Examining the literary context of the text means recording everything you observe about how the text fits in with what comes both before and after it in the document of which it is a part. Distinguish between the broad and the immediate literary context.

The *broad* literary context concerns that which is characteristic for the whole document. Here you may ask questions such as: Can the document be divided into main parts? If yes, what is characteristic of each part? To which main part does the passage you are interpreting belong? Is the passage part of the beginning, the middle, or the end of the document?

The *immediate* literary context concerns the relationship between the verses before and after the passage in question. Are there, for example, keywords that create connections between different parts of the text? Are there common themes that occur in and around the passage? What is specific to this passage? How does it correspond with or differ from the immediate context? Is the delimitation of the passage marked by anything in particular (either formally or with respect to content)?

The Structure of the Text Passage

Having considered the literary context, you can turn to the analysis of the text passage itself. Such an analysis can be performed in many ways. One way of getting started is to divide the text into smaller segments and describe how they relate to each other. The divisions may be based on content or theme, on narrative markers or progression of argument. Sometimes a chiastic pattern may catch your attention, and sometimes repetitions or framings will become apparent.

In a text with a complex structure, you may notice shifts of genre and function, or you may identify "subgenres" such as teaching and admonishment (see the next section). In letters, epistolary formulas may function as division markers; if the text follows a rhetorical composition, ancient speech patterns may be used as a guide.

In short, look for kinds of sentences, content units, thematic words, arguments, and temporal, logical, rhetorical, stylistic, and numerical patterns. Consider choice of words, repetition, train of thought, narrative pattern, overall impression of the text (which senses it appeals to), and so on. Mark words or expressions that seem to structure the text; construct a mind map, or use colored pens to make the structure explicit.

Genre and Function

Like members of a family, many texts have certain characteristics in common, thus evoking similar responses and expectations in readers. This is because texts usually belong to particular types or genres. Sometimes specific markers in the text indicate a specific genre. If a text begins with the phrase "Once upon a time . . . ," "Recipe," or "Sostratus to Zenon. Greetings!," a reader will know what to expect. Other ways of recognizing the genre of a text is by content (a story, an argument), or how the content is constructed (a poem).

Sometimes a text can be divided into subgenres. A letter of Paul, for instance, may contain admonishments (e.g., Rom 12:1–3), theological arguments (e.g., Rom 6:1–11), a midrash (i.e., an interpretation of a text from the Hebrew Bible, e.g., Gal 4:21–5:1), hymns (e.g., Phil 2:5–11), and/or lists of virtues (e.g., Gal 5:19–21 and 5:22–23). The Gospels contain parables, miracle narratives, and so on. Sometimes repetition, rhythm, and choice of words make the reader aware that a text shifts from prose to poetry and back to prose (e.g., 1 Cor 13). Sometimes translations make the poetic structure of some passages visible in the layout (see, e.g., the Beatitudes in Matt 5:3–10, or the Magnificat in Luke 1:46–55).

External form and conventions—the social context—can signify a text's function. The purpose of a text may be to solve a specific problem, or to give general advice. It may be to describe how one should view Jesus and the early church, or to paint a vision of the future with the help of imagery and complex symbols.

Different types of texts and contexts, then, evoke different kinds of readings, which in turn encourage different perceptions of meaning. A poem cannot be read the same way as a newspaper; a historical account is different from a novel, a story from an argument, a parable from a description. A letter elicits different associations than a gospel; an apocalyptic text like Revelation is read differently from a historical account like Acts; and so on.

Based on these considerations, try to determine the genre and function of your text passage as well as its relation to the whole document of which it is a part.

Words and Expressions

As you analyze the structure of the text, you will likely encounter certain words and expressions that require further attention. Investigate those that seem *most important* and determine the meaning for your understanding of the text. Examining well-known words and expressions, like "blessed," "faith," "Christ," or "Pharisees," may prove especially rewarding. Some words and expressions may require historical and social investigations—for example, "Galilee," "Romans," "fishermen," "barley loaves," "Sadducees," "crucifixion," "Corinth," "Cephas," and "circumcision"; or formulations like "In those days a decree went out from Emperor Augustus that all the world should be registered" (Luke 2:1); others presuppose a particular religious or cultural context—for example, when Paul speaks of a person who was "caught up to the third heaven" (2 Cor 12:2)—or suggest that the addressees of the letter possibly have been bewitched (Gal 3:1).

Investigate *what* the text says and *how* it is said. Examine whether the thought processes in your passage are reminiscent of other thought processes in the whole document, or in documents that the passage in question has a clear relation to. For instance, you may find that a text is inspired by Jewish piety or Stoic ethics. In such cases it may be of interest to illuminate words and expression from documents that belong to those traditions. It is here that you can make good use of concordances, encyclopedias, and commentaries, where you can find information regarding content or references to sources that you may need to consult.

Intertexts

If there is a quote from or an allusion to another text (most often the Hebrew Bible), you need to examine the intertextual relationship. How does the quote support the argument (e.g., Gal 3:10–12)? If your passage is from one of the Synoptic Gospels, there may be parallels in the other two. Do the similarities and differences shed light on the understanding of your passage? Paul seems to be quoting an early Christian tradition in 1 Cor 15:3–7. How does that contribute to his argument? More intricately, there seems to be a connection between the Gospel of John and the First Letter of John. Somehow, the texts seem to illuminate each other, perhaps even to the degree that one text wishes to correct unsound readings of (maybe earlier versions of) the other.

In all these cases it is important to compare the texts and investigate the relationship between them. Contrasts and comparisons enrich the reader's ability to see that which is particular to every text.

The Symbolic World of the Text

The text's symbolic world encompasses the broad cultural, religious, or political conditions to which a text belongs. It is about roles and power structures, customs and values that are presupposed by or woven into an argument or a story. In biblical texts, these conditions belong to another time and may need explication in order to highlight aspects that may otherwise be overlooked.

For example, how did the Mediterranean culture in which honor and shame are of central importance affect conversion or changes in loyalty? How did early followers of Christ, Jew or gentile, relate to contexts where solidarity with synagogue associations was the norm? What effect did the destruction of the temple and the banishment of Jews from their homeland have on the relationship between Jews and gentiles in Antioch? What may have been the impact of the proclamation of Christ as king and savior in a world where Caesar was praised as king and savior? A text may articulate a cultural convention or phenomenon that needs to be investigated in order to clarify circumstances and meaning. For instance, what does it mean that the Samaritan woman has had five husbands and is now living with another man (John 4:16–19)? A close examination of the symbolic world may reveal that the presumption of her immoral character is very unlikely.

Be alert to what the text can convey in terms of social values, cultural norms, living standards, authority structures, and so on, that determined people's thoughts and actions.

The Historical Circumstances of the Text

A historical, text-oriented interpretation asks questions regarding the historical circumstances and communication situation of the text, such as: What geographical, political, social, and religious settings, conditions, and concerns are being articulated in the text? What seems to be the overarching purpose? What can be known from within the text about the relationship between sender and receiver? Who is writing to whom? What does it mean, for instance, for our reading of the Letter to the Romans to find out that Paul had never visited the city (Rom 1:13) yet knew a great number of people there (Rom 16)? How does the unique crucifixion narrative of the Gospel of Luke ("Father forgive them . . . ," Luke 23:34, etc.) impact our view of the recipient(s) for whom the gospel was written?

Inferences regarding a document's entire historical context require the analysis of the entire document. For this you should consult the different sections of chapter 4, "The Texts," as well as commentaries on individual books of the Bible.

Conclusions concerning Your Text Passage

Having reached the end of the methodological procedure, it is now time to summarize the findings that you have accumulated. The purpose of a summary is not to write something "new" or different from the methodological analysis but to present its results and main insights. Use your findings and describe how you perceive the main argument/point/message of the text passage.

Some Analogies and Hermeneutical Reflections

The methodological procedure proposed here is devised to focus on historical and text-oriented questions. It calls you to refrain from engaging too quickly in analogies (biblical or other) or hermeneutical reflections about the meaning of the text for you, the interpreter, the church, society, humanity, or the world as you know it from your own experience. This does not mean that looking for analogies or reflection should be neglected. Rather, forcing oneself to look for answers to historical and text-oriented questions tends to generate new and unexpected insights that enrich hermeneutical reflection (see, for instance, "A Historical-Analogical Reading of Matt 5:3–10," p. 531).

Your personal concerns, cultural context, and inherited presuppositions will always affect your interpretation, as has been argued already (see figure 6.5, p. 500). No one is an island. A preference for historical, text-oriented aspects of a text is born out of presuppositions. Some may even find neither of these two methods satisfactory and prefer to approach the Bible as literary fiction, as a book of oracles, or as a philosophical or theological handbook.

This last step, then, serves the purpose of reflecting on analogies between your text and other texts in the Bible thematically, ethically, or in other ways. You may have become aware of issues and concerns in society and church that seem to be analogous to your findings in the text. There may be aspects of your own life circumstances and experiences that seem to resound in the text. Or you may decide to write a sermon outline or a Bible lesson.

Finally, you may want to reflect on what you have covered in your analysis and what you have not, and how your own perception of the text or concepts in the text, or of Jesus, faith, being a Christian, or the Bible, may have changed. You may also want to share how you would continue the analysis if given the opportunity.

Box 6.1
Some Exercises for Reading and Writing

Various reading and writing exercises can improve one's attentiveness to detail in a text and increase reading skills. It is essential to take note of *what is said* and *what is not said* in a text—what is expressed directly and what may be implied only. Gaps in an argument or narrative, just like pauses in music, can be very important in the process of interpretation. The following suggestions may function as complements to the methodological analysis:

- *Retelling.* Write a summary of the narrative or argument. Retell the text while changing who is speaking (choose among those that are mentioned in the text), and do so with varying attitudes to the content (positive, negative, critical, etc.). Change the genre of the text, or retell it in a different setting.

- *Segmenting the text.* Divide the text into simple clauses with one main piece of information in each. Underline, for example, all the verbs in the text, and make a clause with each verb. Determine, if possible, the content in each clause, and describe the relationships between the clauses. Reconstruct the text, and put the clauses in chronological or logical order, or into an order that conveys the message most clearly.
- *Changing the media.* Turn the text into a drama, or an act in a drama. Create a picture or a series of images that describe the content of the text. This will make explicit which parts of the text provide the most pertinent information, and which parts require contextual filling-in of the blanks.
- *Comparisons.* Compare different translations, and note major lexical or syntactical differences. Compare different accounts of the same event in, for example, the Gospels. Compare with texts of the same genre, such as miracle stories, or texts with the same themes, or similar argumentative or rhetorical structures or content, such as letters, or parts of letters (introductions, exhortations, ethical instructions, household codes, etc.).
- *Attentive readings.* Focus on the actors in the text: main character(s), side character(s), and personal relationships. Pay attention to the action in the text: What has happened, is happening, will happen? Wherein lies the core of the action? Observe temporal, spatial, and logical points and patterns in the text. Focus on the argumentation's character and structure: What type of argumentation is it? Which rhetorical aspects does the text exhibit? Examine the beginning and end, thematic words, contrasts, and the climax of the text.
- *Observe the narrative context.* Who is telling what to whom, how, and for what purpose? Search for images, metaphors, and intertexts (quotes from or allusions to other texts), and note how they are used.

Further Reading

Aune, David E. *The New Testament in Its Literary Environment*. LEC. Philadelphia: Westminster John Knox, 1987.

Carter, Warren, and Amy-Jill Levine. *The New Testament: Methods and Meanings*. Nashville: Abingdon, 2013.

Green, Joel B., ed. *Hearing the New Testament: Strategies for Interpretation*. 2nd ed. Grand Rapids: Eerdmans, 2010.

Hartman, Lars. *Approaching New Testament Texts and Contexts*. WUNT 311. Tübingen: Mohr Siebeck, 2013.

Hayes, John R., and Carl R. Holladay. *Biblical Exegesis: A Beginner's Handbook*. 3rd ed. Louisville: Westminster John Knox, 2007.

Hull, Robert F. *The Story of the New Testament Text: Movers, Materials, Motives, Methods, and Models*. Atlanta: Society of Biblical Literature, 2010.

A Historical, Text-Oriented Reading of Matt 8:14–17

The interpretation of Matt 8:14–17 presented here as a pedagogical example serves the purpose of highlighting a number of interpretative approaches/methodologies. The interpretation is oriented toward the textual dimension of the text and thus deals with the fundamental questions regarding language and the definition of a text. They are fundamental in that they recur in many types of interpretations. In addition, this approach views the texts from a communicative perspective and attempts to delve into the situation within the text as much as possible. Thus, what follows is a text-oriented, historical reading of Matt 8:14–17—a methodological, analytic exercise that focuses on one issue at a time. The task should be viewed as an exercise in dialogue that engages in a conversation with the text and with others about the text, and that critically examines all the material stored within the text.

The Text

As the point of departure for the interpretative process, I have selected three translations. One is literal, the King James Version, and two more recent translations are modern, the New Revised Standard Version and the Contemporary English Version.

> And when Jesus was come into Peter's house, he saw his wife's mother laid, and sick of a fever. And he touched her hand, and the fever left her: and she arose, and ministered unto them. When the even was come, they brought unto him many that were possessed with devils: and he cast out the spirits with *his* word and healed all that were sick: That it might be fulfilled which was spoken by Esaias [Isaiah] the prophet, saying, Himself took our infirmities, and bare *our* sicknesses. (KJV)

> When Jesus entered Peter's house, he saw his mother-in-law lying in bed with a fever; he touched her hand, and the fever left her, and she got up and began to serve him. That evening they brought to him many who were possessed with demons; and he cast out the spirits with a word, and cured all who were sick. This was to fulfill what had been spoken through the prophet Isaiah, "He took our infirmities and bore our diseases." (NRSV)

> Jesus went to the home of Peter, where he found that Peter's mother-in-law was sick in bed with fever. He took her by the hand, and the fever left her. Then she got up and served Jesus a meal. That evening many people with demons in them were brought to Jesus. And with only a word he forced out the evil spirits and healed everyone who was sick. So God's promise came true, just as the prophet Isaiah had said, "He healed our diseases and made us well." (CEV)

The Literary Context

Task: The first task is to determine how these verses fit into the gospel as a whole, how they relate to their immediate context, and how we can view these verses as an entity separate from the text surrounding it.

Tools: The tools include reading of the entire document, the translations (paying attention to the way the text has been organized—for example, layout and subtitle), and commentaries (the division of the whole text into smaller sections and descriptions of the context).

Interpretation: The material in Matthew is to a large degree organized according to thematic blocks. With the exception of the beginning and the end (chs. 1–2 and 26–28), there are five longer speeches surrounded by narrative sections. The speeches often begin with a short scene and end with a comment like the one in 7:28–29. The first speech, in chapters 5–7, portrays Jesus as the great Teacher, and the section that follows, chapters 8–9, portrays him as the great Miracle Worker. The words of the people in 9:33b function as a culminating chorus to the whole section, with some deviating voices in 9:34. The effect of Jesus's actions is twofold. The scene in 9:35–38 introduces the speech in chapter 10.

In Matt 8–9 there are three sections in which Jesus performs miracles, three in each section: 8:1–17; 8:18–9:8; and 9:18–33a. Since two miracles are tied to each other in the beginning of the third section, there are ten miracles in all. The miracles are presented as showcases of Jesus's power. Matthew 5–9 serves as an overarching presentation of Jesus, his words, his actions, and their effects. Like Moses, Jesus teaches from a mountain, and, again like Moses, Jesus performs ten miracles (see Exod 4 to Num 10:10).

In the first section, Jesus cures people from diseases. He heals a man with leprosy (8:1–4), cures a lame man (8:5–13), and frees an individual from a fever (8:14–15). The section concludes with Jesus healing many possessed and sick individuals, which the evangelist comments on with a citation from Isaiah (8:16–17). Thus, 8:1–17 is an easily defined entity within a larger framework. The second section concerns itself more with Jesus's power over the sea, demons, and sin. In the third section, Jesus intervenes so that people regain their ability to live, talk, and see. Between the three sections, there are scenes with differing content that explain what is needed if one wants to be a follower of Jesus: to believe in Jesus. The word "follow" occurs in 8:1, 10, 19, 22, 23; 9:9, 27, and the words "belief/disbelief" occur in 8:10, 13, 26; 9:22, 28, 29.

Our verses, 8:14–17, are separated from the previous verses via a change in place, time, and person in verse 14. The day is rounded off by what is said in verse 16. The citation in verse 17 is a commentary on everything that has happened in the first section, and therefore fulfills the function of sectioning it off. In verse 18 we see the emergence of a new theme. Summaries of Jesus's healing activities are common in Matthew (see, e.g., 4:23–25; 8:16; 9:35; 12:15–16; 14:13–14, 35–36; 15:29–31; 19:1–2; 21:14).

Thus, in the gospel as a whole, Jesus is portrayed as one who expels evil spirits and heals the sick. Matthew 8–9 revolves around what happens when Jesus comes into contact with people in need and what it means to follow Jesus. The word "follow" occurs a great deal, as do expressions for belief and disbelief. Jesus's powerful actions in Matt 8–9 seem to have a meaning beyond simply healing individuals.

Structure

Task: The next task is to determine how the text, in our case Matt 8:14–17, is structured. What smaller subsections can it be broken into, and how do these relate to each other? Here one can focus on different elements within the text—for example, different kinds of sentences, content units, thematic words, arguments, and distinctive genre characteristics, as well as different temporal, logical, rhetorical, stylistic, and numerical patterns. It is clear that the author of the gospel possessed a keen interest in patterns, which may be seen in the family tree in Matt 1, which has three sections of fourteen generations, something specifically noted in the text. It is possible to construct a text in a myriad of ways. Describe the structure or structures that you find to be significant for your understanding of the text.

Tools: The tools include reading of the text, translations (typography), commentaries (discussions of structure), and literature specifically dealing with textual structures.

Interpretation: A cursory reading of the text reveals that it is made up of two distinct sections, 8:14–15 and 8:16–17, or perhaps even three, if one wishes to take verse 17 as a separate entity. Verse 17 has somewhat different content and says something about the other verses, thus occupying a level above them in terms of importance and structural role. Simultaneously, verse 17 is usually translated as a subordinate clause to the previous verses. There is, however, reason to translate it as a separate clause, as the CEV does. The evangelist's comments often take the form "(this happened) so that . . . ," where "this happened" is not present in the original text.

If we shift our focus to the more literal translation (KJV), the clauses in the story of the healing of Peter's mother-in-law become clearer. The story contains first a short subclause followed by five main clauses, all beginning with "and." This simple syntax form, which translations tend to change because of linguistic patterns in the receptor language, makes it easy to memorize the text, to remember the story. The first main clause is somewhat more complex than the others because of the phrase "lying in bed with a fever" (which consists of two verbs in the original text, *beblēmenēn kai pyressousan*).

If we focus on the content of the text, the following pattern emerges:

1 Jesus enters Peter's house.
2 Jesus sees Peter's mother-in-law.
3 She is lying in bed.
4 She is sick with a fever.
5 Jesus touches her hand.
6 The fever leaves her.
7 She gets up.
8 She begins to serve Jesus.

Clause 1 sets the scene for what is about to take place. The rest of the clauses give a very symmetrical impression. Clauses 2, 5, and 8 describe the relationship between Jesus and the woman, and describe an exchange in which the woman becomes the subject in clause 8. The rest of the clauses are statements about the woman. The content of clauses 3 and 4 is turned on its head in clause 6 and 7, respectively. Such a simple pattern is not common in texts, but all texts are "patterned." Thus, the existence of the semantic structure is a fact, but what can it say about the story, and how can it aid us in its interpretation? It is reminiscent of a circular construction of texts that is not uncommon in the Bible, the *chiasm*, which in this case consists of seven clauses:

A
    B
        C
            D
        C'
    B'
A'

Even the four basic elements of a miracle story are arranged in a semantic pattern:

- Meeting between two individuals
- Description of illness
- The actual healing
- The effect of the healing

For more detail on miracle stories, see the section "Intertexts," p. 525 below, where three versions of such stories are explored.

The continuation of the day, described in verse 16, is simply and succinctly told. After the time is indicated, in the same way as in verse 14, two main clauses are introduced: Jesus expelling demons from the possessed and healing the sick. The quotation from the Hebrew Bible in verse 17 is a good example of a Hebrew parallelism (saying the same thing twice).

Thus, in terms of presentation, the text is short and stylized. Both the syntactic and the semantic structure indicate that it was used as teaching material in the early Jesus movement. The content of the narrative seems to tell us more than simply that Jesus healed a sick individual. Jesus sees the person, Jesus touches the person, and the person gets up and starts to serve him. Jesus's touch fundamentally changes the individual. According to the evangelist, Jesus's healing is the fulfillment of what Isaiah said: Jesus heals so that the Scripture may be fulfilled.

Genre and Function

Task: Here the task is to determine the genre, the general literary category of the text, or both. What can this genre say about the content and function of the text in question?

Tools: The tools include a thorough reading of the text in question, texts belonging to the same genre, translations (titles, notes, index), commentaries (discussions of genre, text categorization, and style), dictionaries/lexicons (for words such as "gospel," "wonder," "miracle," and "miracle narratives"), and works specifically dedicated to the discussion of different genres, in this case Gerhardsson and others.[12]

Interpretation: Matthew 8:14–17 is a small section of a larger context: the gospel. The Gospels are similar in genre to ancient narratives of great men and miracle workers but are characterized by their purpose of proclaiming Jesus as the Messiah of the Jews and the Savior of the entire world. They highlight Jesus's uniqueness and want to inspire their audiences to believe in him. In 8:14–15 we find a miracle narrative with all the characteristics of the genre: Jesus encounters an individual, her

12. Gerhardsson, *Mighty Acts*, 11–19.

sickness is described, Jesus heals her, and the effects of Jesus's miraculous healing are described. The initiative here lies with Jesus: he "sees" Peter's mother-in-law. The following elements of the narrative could not be expressed any clearer: she was lying in bed with a fever; Jesus touched her hand; the fever left her; she got up and began to serve him. We shall return to the difference in wordings in the next section.

A miracle narrative can be read and understood in many different ways. It can be read as a sign that Jesus is the soteriological figure promised in the Hebrew Bible. The quotation in verse 17 puts Jesus in the role of the Lord's servant in Isa 40–55. The same is true for Matt 12:15–21. One could also choose to understand the texts as proof that Jesus has the same power as God (cf. the end chorus in Matt 9:33). One could read the text as a sign that the kingdom of God is near, as an expression of Jesus's compassion and love for humanity, or as part of the struggle against evil in the world, since Jesus expels evil spirits and demons. The specific pattern of the narrative in combination with the context also opens up for a more paradigmatic reading of the text. The text teaches a lesson about something more general, about what happens in the encounter between Jesus and people. The quotation in verse 17 revolves around Jesus's person and his actions.

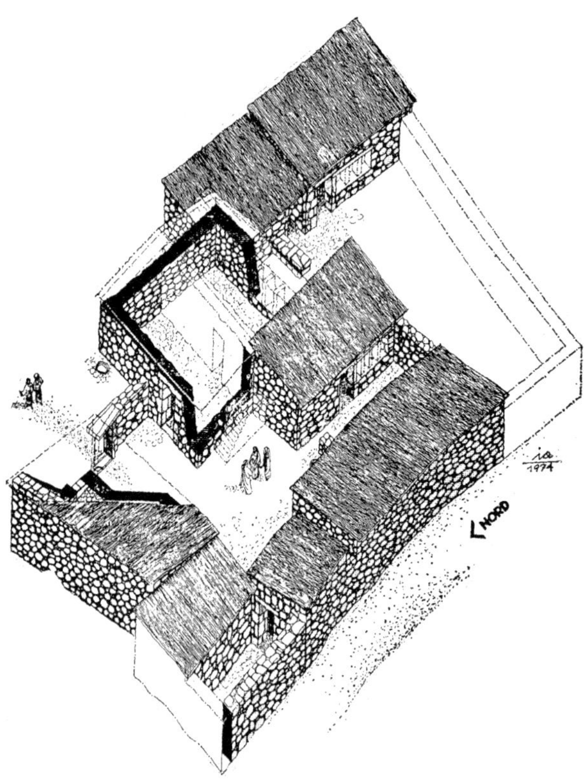

Reconstruction of Peter's house in Capernaum. There are indications in the archaeological remains suggesting that followers of Jesus may have used one of the rooms for communal gatherings as early as the late first century. The house was later rebuilt as a so-called *domus ecclesiae* (house church; late fourth century). In the second half of the fifth century, the *domus ecclesiae* was torn down and replaced by an octagonal structure, which had its center located exactly above the room used for communal gatherings in the late first century. From Stanislao Loffreda, *Recovering Capharnaum*, 2nd edition (Jerusalem: Franciscan Printing Press, 1993).

Birger Gerhardsson has described the differences between therapeutic miracles (the healing of sicknesses) and nontherapeutic miracles in Matthew.[13] In the latter category, the problematic faith of the disciples is highlighted. The focus is on the faith of the miracle worker rather than on those witnessing the event. The calming of the storm in Matt 8–9 is an example of this. The nontherapeutic miracles are often characterized by symbolic acts. As a rule, Jesus takes the initiative. The story of the healing of Peter's mother-in-law can

13. Gerhardsson, *Mighty Acts*, 38–67.

be firmly categorized as a therapeutic miracle, like all the miracles in Matt 8–9. At the same time, the story has a paradigmatic function: it teaches a general lesson about what ensues when Jesus takes the initiative in the encounter with people.

Thus, the text is a very short and stylized miracle narrative, combined with a summary describing how Jesus healed many sick, and with a reference to Scripture that places Jesus in the role of the Lord's servant in Isa 53. The first two verses share the literary characteristics of other healing miracles in Matthew, but the actual telling of the story points to the larger themes of faith and persecution. The text thus assumes a paradigmatic and pedagogical function when it describes the encounter between Jesus and people. The summarizing note describing how Jesus drove out many evil spirits and healed many becomes a presentation of Jesus as an individual, perhaps *the* individual, with the power of healing.

Words and Expression

Task: The task now is to clarify the meaning of individual words and expressions. When in doubt, you must choose between different possible meanings. If necessary, you must choose between different readings that affect the interpretation of the text. You also must describe historical and contextual details when necessary for the understanding of the text.

Tools: These include reading of the text, different translations (including the notes), commentaries, concordances, and dictionaries. A concordance of the New Testament lists the passages in which individual words are used. Greek dictionaries and grammars, which are a natural part of this task, cannot be used in a study based on translation, but some more general dictionaries and encyclopedias explain the importance of significant words and expressions.

Interpretation: Certain words and expressions are explained in different parts of the analysis. In this example, we will deal with the remaining words according to the order they occur in the text (according to the KJV), adding some comparisons with Mark and Luke, in anticipation of the next point.

- *Peter's house.* Peter is the name given to the disciple Simon, a fisherman from Bethsaida who later settled in Capernaum, by Jesus when he spoke about his *ekklēsia* in Matt 16:13–20. In the New Testament he is often presented as the leader of the twelve disciples, and in Matthew he is described as the guarantor for the teaching coming from Jesus. In the Gospel of Mark we learn about the house of Simon and Andrew; in Luke it is described as Simon's house. The choice of the name Peter leads one's thoughts to the global congregation of Jesus. In excavations in Capernaum, archaeologists discovered a housing complex that may have belonged to Peter and Andrew, situated along the main road, not far from the synagogue. Via a gate from the street, one enters a courtyard where the majority of household tasks would have been carried out. Adjacent to the courtyard are a number of small rooms, where the different families would have kept their belongings and had their sleeping areas. Peter's mother-in-law was mostly likely lying in one of these rooms. Those visiting the housing complex in the evening could very well have been gathered by the gate or in the communal courtyard. To use the translation "home" here, as CEV does, is not optimal.

- *Lying in bed.* The word used in the Greek is not the most common word for sleeping. It rather means "fettered" or "bound to the bed." The same word is used in Matt 8:6 and 9:2.
- *Fever.* Here the usual word for fever is employed. Luke makes a differentiation between large and small fevers. (The diagnosis system was not very well evolved at this time.)
- *Touched.* This word choice differs from Mark, where "grabbed" is employed. In Luke, Jesus leans over the woman and speaks sternly to the fever.
- *Left.* This expression indicates that the fever was understood as something that possessed the woman. Similarities with demon expulsion are most obvious in Luke.
- *Stood up.* This word is the same as the one used to describe Jesus's resurrection: he was revived, resurrected. Luke uses a more general term, the same as is employed in the beginning of the story: "he stood up and walked." Mark uses the same verb as Matthew, but in a way that means "get up" or "rise." The expression used in Matthew is associated with resurrected and new life.
- *Served them.* When Mark and Luke write that Peter's mother-in-law "served them," it can in all likelihood be assumed that she gave them something to eat: she waited on them. However, the word in the Greek text (*diakoneō*) is also the most common Greek word for general service. Because Jesus is the only object in the sentence, and keeping the context and structure of the story in mind, we suggest that "serve" should be used in translations of Matthew. "Serve" can be associated with the terms "follow" and "faith," concepts that are integral to the larger context of the narrative.
- *Evening.* This word literally means "when the sun sets" and thus, according to Jewish custom, indicates the time when the day ends and the next one begins. In Luke and Mark the day is a Sabbath, and thus the sun setting indicates that the Sabbath has ended. In Matthew there is no indication that the day is a Sabbath.
- *With (his) word.* The translations "with his word" and "with only a word" infuse meaning into this expression. See Matt 8:8 and compare the role Jesus's word has in these miracle narratives. Jesus carries out his miraculous actions through what he says.

- *That.* "So that", "in order that." The Greek word normally indicates purpose. CEV has chosen a more open connection to the previous section. Because verse 17 is so clearly speaking about what occurred previously in the narrative, it becomes natural to view this clause as an ellipsis. This means that we need to insert an expression meaning "this happened" prior to it. Such reflexive citations are common in Matthew (e.g., 1:22; 2:15, 17, 23). Verse 17 has no parallel in Mark or Luke.
- *Fulfilled.* To fulfill or make come true what it says in the Hebrew Bible can mean one of three things: (1) to fulfill what has been promised, (2) to fill the prophecies with new meaning, or (3) to end, annul, or destroy what has been said. In this context, the first interpretation seems best suited. This has been made explicit in CEV, which mentions both God and God's promises. God has promised certain things through his prophets, which are now coming true.
- The quotation from Isaiah will be commented on in the section below.

In sum, a number of the words used in Matthew (e.g., "fettered/bound to," "stand up," "served," and perhaps even "Peter's house") carry specific associations in their New Testament context, associations that often differ from those in Mark and Luke. These literary aspects only grow in significance when one reads the story as an illustration of what happens when Jesus encounters humanity.

Intertexts

Task: The task is to analyze quotations from other texts or clear references to other texts written prior to our text; and to compare parallels with other gospels in order to be able to describe and interpret the text in a clearer manner. There are also a number of thematically related texts that need to be taken into consideration, including parallel passages (see below).

Tools: The tools include reading of the text of the Hebrew Bible and other intertexts, and reading of notes in translations, commentaries, synopses, and works especially focused on this topic. When reading the Hebrew Bible, it is often necessary to read a translation both of the Hebrew text and of its Greek translation, the Septuagint. They can be found in commentaries such as Brachter's.[14] In a synopsis of the Gospels, the parallel texts are organized in columns on the same page to ease the comparative process.

Interpretation: For the analysis of Matt 8:14–17, there is reason to work with the quotation in verse 17 and with the parallels in Mark 1:29–34 and Luke 4:38–41. Isa-

14. Brachter, *Old Testament Quotations.*

iah 53:4 is translated as follows in the CEV: "He suffered and endured great pain for us"; the NRSV translates it as "Surely he has borne our infirmities, and carried our diseases." In Isaiah, the verse is part of a description of "the Lord's suffering servant," a weak and defeated individual who suffers in the place of the people, sacrificing himself for their sins. In the New Testament, the text is used to describe Jesus's mission and soteriological acts (see Mark 1:11 par.; 10:45; 14:24; Luke 22:37; John 1:29, 36; Acts 8:30–35; 1 Pet 2:22–25). In Matt 8–9, it describes a strong man who is carrying out miraculous works. He is not sick; rather, he heals the sick. He removes people's sicknesses—here Matthew uses a word that often means "weaknesses"—by healing them. The word "carry" in the second line in all likelihood means "carry away," "lift off." Instead of the word "pains" in the second line, Matthew employs a common word for sickness. The author seems to have translated the Hebrew verse himself and formulated it in a way best suited to his purposes in Matt 8. The usage of Isa 53 could, however, join Jesus's healing activities to his soteriological acts. The miracles in Matt 9:1–8 illustrate how Jesus heals the sick and forgives sins.

In order to compare the three narratives of how Jesus healed Peter's mother-in-law, we shall present the parallels in Mark and Luke in the same way that we previously presented Matthew's version. In Mark and Luke, the story is part of a description of a Sabbath in Capernaum, in the beginning of Jesus's ministry.

Mark

1 They leave the synagogue.
2 They soon reach Simon and Andrew's house.
3 James and John are with them.
4 Simon's mother-in-law is lying in bed.
5 She has a fever.
6 The disciples talk to Jesus about her.
7 Jesus approaches her.
8 He grabs hold of her arm/hand.
9 He helps her stand up.
10 The fever leaves her.
11 She begins to wait on them.

Luke

1 Jesus leaves the synagogue.
2 He goes to Simon's house.
3 Simon's mother-in-law is plagued by a fever.
4 The fever is serious (large).
5 They pray to him for her.
6 He leans over her.

7 He rebukes the fever.
8 The fever leaves her.
9 She immediately gets up.
10 She waits on them.

We have already commented on some of the differences in diction. The Markan version is the longest of the three, with many named characters. The presentation is simple. The flow of information would perhaps have gone smoother had the author told the story from a "we" perspective: "We went from the synagogue and arrived at our house . . . ," as if Peter were telling the story. The occurrence would become a family event in Peter's life, without any interpretative undertones. The focus of the Lukan version is on Jesus, as indicated by its introduction. We are not told who the others are who are following along. The sickness is described in more detail, and the healing is reminiscent of an exorcism with immediate effects. More so than in Mark, Jesus is presented in Luke as the great physician. In both cases, people other than Jesus take the initiative, as is the norm in miracle narratives. Here the Matthean version deviates, as Jesus is the one taking the initiative.

In sum, the unique usage of Isa 53:4 in Matt 8 brings together healing and forgiveness of sins in Jesus's ministry. A comparative reading of the Markan and Lukan versions illustrates that Matthew's context, structure, usage of Isa 53, and carefully picked diction are unique to the gospel. The same event can undoubtedly be interpreted in many ways.

The Symbolic World of the Text

Task: To which symbolic world does the text belong? What are the social, cultural, and ideological dimensions present in the text? For this task, the perspective must be widened to include the gospel in its entirety and its place in its contemporary thought world, as well as in Jewish and early Christ-believing faith (see Robbins's model in the section "Method Syntheses," p. 506). Because one small section of a larger text cannot, as a rule, provide us with much information concerning its symbolic world, it is necessary to limit this exercise to a very basic textual analysis. The symbolic world of the text could provide the theme for a larger, specialized investigation.

Tools: These include reading of the entire document (gospel) and the document's contemporary texts; sociological and feminist commentaries, dictionaries, and specialized sociological, anthropological, and ideological studies may also be helpful.[15]

15. E.g., Malina, *New Testament World*; Pilch and Malina, *Biblical Social Values and Their Meaning*.

Interpretation: The four verses in Matt 8:14–17 and their context raise questions about the anthropology of the text (how the text views people), the construction of the figure of Jesus and his actions, as well as about God and God's plan, as indicated by the quotation from Isaiah.

The stories in Matt 8–9 focus on individuals (with the exception of the fourth miracle, 8:23–27, where a specific group, Jesus's twelve disciples, are in a boat on a stormy sea). The individuals are sick and in need of healing. At the time of the gospels, sicknesses were often described as evil spirits possessing a person. These persons are thus prisoners in need of liberation, sinners in need of forgiveness, blind in need of sight, mute in need of a voice, dead in need of life. The descriptions of the people's handicaps and needs are mixed so that a correlation is made between physical sicknesses or handicaps and sin. This combination can be found in the Hebrew Bible and in other Jewish texts; see Isa 33:24 for an example. Often sicknesses were interpreted as God's punishment for the sins of a person.

Jesus heals the sick people through his word or through his touch. This is the main point in Matt 8–9. In our text, Jesus even takes the initiative. He "sees" the suffering person, and he has the power to make her well. Indirectly, he is presented as the Lord's servant in Isa 53, but not as the weak and defeated man, but rather more along the lines of how God is presented earlier in Isaiah, as the figure who will one day heal his people and give them salvation (Isa 29:18; par. Matt 11:2–6). The miracles can thus be seen as part of God's kingdom. Jesus's miracles become a sign that the kingdom of God is on its way. As the agent of God, he fights the evil that saturates human existence. Because of this, a Jewish reader of the text would associate Jesus with the Messiah, God's anointed, who was to bring salvation to his people and take away their sins (Matt 1:21). They could call him Emmanuel, God with us (Matt 1:23). Through him, God was supposed to renew the covenant with Israel.

God is indirectly present in this description of Jesus's ministry. God's dominion on earth—the "kingdom of heaven" according to Matthew, where heaven is simply a way of referring to God—is made real according to the promises given in the Hebrew Bible. This is indicated through the citation from Isaiah in verse 17. The first Christ followers interpreted Jesus, his person and actions, using the Hebrew Bible as the point of departure. The fulfilling of the promises in the Hebrew Bible could also mean that they were given new meaning or a different significance. This is a natural consequence of moving texts from their historical context into new situations. The majority of the early Jesus movement interpreted Jesus according to the Hebrew Bible, not the Hebrew Bible according to Jesus. However, in Matthew, Jesus seems to carry out certain actions necessary to fulfill what God has promised according to the covenant.

In sum, within our text is embedded an anthropology that paints individual people as weak, sick, and sinful. Through Jesus's healing, their situations are changed. His miracles become signs of God's kingdom in their midst, which becomes a fulfillment of what God has promised in the Hebrew Bible.

The Historical Circumstances of the Text

Task: The task here is to paint, in large strokes, the historical circumstances in which the text was first understood. This is somewhat easier where letters are concerned. For the Gospels, one needs first and foremost to consider the context of the authors rather than that of Jesus, which in Matthew's case puts us somewhere in the 80s CE. However, the material usually has a long redaction history from around the year 30 until the final editing of the gospel. It is the result of a long line of shifting communication situations, which cannot be discussed in detail in this section. Historical investigations of texts tend to expand into specialized studies.

Tools: The tools include reading of the entire document, introductions to individual Bible books in translation, commentaries, dictionaries, and isagogic presentations.

Interpretation: Matthew was completed in its final form around the year 80 CE. The author is unknown but was in all likelihood a Jew and a scribe, learned in both Hebrew and Greek. He was not an eyewitness. The author used Mark as a source and perhaps one other source as well, which can also be found in Luke (although this is debated by scholars). The document most likely originated from Antioch or Galilee. The audience was first and foremost Jews who believed in Christ. Matthew includes more of Jesus's teaching and more on the structure and organization of the church than the other Synoptic Gospels do. Jesus is presented as the great Teacher. The story about Peter's mother-in-law may very well have been told and used in early worship and teaching of the followers of Christ, and later acquired a literary form that portrayed a meeting with Jesus.

In sum, the story has most likely been molded within the context of worship and teaching and was seen by Jewish followers of Jesus as an important part of the message about Jesus Christ. The connection to the covenant in the Hebrew Bible is of the utmost importance in the context of the gospel. The editing of the gospel was most likely finalized around the year 80 CE in the eastern part of the Roman Empire.

Conclusion

Task: The task is to conclude the results of your analysis. The so-called pragmatic research question should serve as a guideline: Who is telling what to whom, and for what purpose? The emphasis lies on "what" and "for what purpose."

Interpretation: The author of Matthew wants to portray Jesus's actions of power in this part of the narrative (Matt 8–9) in order to encourage or deepen faith in Jesus Christ as Israel's Messiah. Jesus meets people in need and heals them. This results in some coming to faith in him and others dismissing him. The way in which the healing of Peter's mother-in-law is told has its own contextual, structural, and stylistic characteristics, something that becomes even clearer when the story is compared with its two parallels. Some of these characteristics include a careful choice of details, a symmetrical semantic structure, and a quotation from Isa 53 that helps the reader interpret what is happening. The story has most likely acquired its current form over a period of time, in the context of Christian worship and teaching. The story clearly wants to transmit to its audience more than just the healing of Peter's mother-in-law. The peculiarities of the text can be explained if the story is interpreted as a generalizing application for human beings. Jesus sees them in their suffering, bound by illness/sin; Jesus touches them, and they rise up to a new life of serving him. They become Jesus followers. Therefore, the text is interpreted both as a miracle story and as a paradigm. Are there other explanations for the author's way of telling the story? The usage of Isa 53 and the description of the sick, especially in Matt 9:1–8, create a connection between sin and sickness, healing and forgiveness. In accordance with the promises in the Hebrew Bible, Jesus is portrayed as the servant of God, raising a sign of God's kingdom on earth. According to the evangelist, Jews should thus recognize Jesus as the Messiah promised in the Hebrew Bible, who renews the covenant between God and God's people.

Hermeneutical Reflections

Task: This is the place to reflect on what you have covered in your analysis and what you have not covered. For example, are there perceptions in the text about God, Jesus, humanity, or the world that do not match your own perceptions? Have your own perception of these concepts changed during the course of your analysis? How would you like to continue the analysis if given the opportunity?

Example: I would like to continue the analysis of the anthropology presented in the text. How do you relate the Matthean view of humanity and sin with the anthropology that people in your context identify with today? What is the meaning of sin and forgiveness (Matt 6:9–15)? Matthew is the only one who includes the phrase "for the forgiveness of sins" in the description of the Last Supper. Other authors in the New Testament, with the exception of Luke, almost never bring up the concept.

I would also like to study the portrayal of Jesus further. How much of Matthew is determined by a Jewish audience? What effect would a change in audience have on the text? The result of my textual analysis could be interpreted as traditional. Jesus not only takes away the sin of humanity; he also liberates them and turns them into who they are meant to be. Has my Christian background made me blind to other readings of the text? The interpretation of the Hebrew Bible raises a number of questions. Who owns the interpretative privilege? Jews? Christians? Scholars of literature? Does Jesus do certain things just because they are described in the Hebrew Bible, or does Matthew add such stories in order to show who Jesus is and convince his Jewish audience that he is Israel's Messiah?

Further Reading

Aland, Kurt, ed. *Synopsis of the Four Gospels: Greek-English Edition of the Synopsis Quattuor Evangeliorum*. 12th ed. Stuttgart: UBS, 2001.

Bratcher, R. G. *Old Testament Quotations in the New Testament*. London: UBS, 1967.

Gerhardsson, B. *The Mighty Acts of Jesus according to Matthew*. Eugene, OR: Wipf and Stock, 2016 (first published 1979).

Malina, Bruce. *The New Testament World: Insights from Cultural Anthropology*. Atlanta: John Knox, 1981.

Pilch, John J., and Bruce Malina, eds. *Biblical Social Values and Their Meaning: A Handbook*. Peabody, MA: Hendrickson, 1993.

A Historical-Analogical Reading of Matt 5:3–10

A historical-analogical reading of a text consists of an elementary text-oriented analysis of the text and a comparison with other texts from different times that are written with the same theme or belong to the same genre. One of the beatitudes in Matt 5 deals with peace and will here first be examined in its own setting. We thereby obtain a voice of peace that is, according to the gospel text, the voice of Jesus himself. This voice is then compared to other voices of peace, first a biblical chorus of voices (to the degree that such a chorus can be accurately reconstructed), and then a voice from our own time. This type of analysis helps us understand better what Jesus says in this passage with regard to peace work, as well as what can even be meant by "peace work."

Searching exclusively for biblical analogies is reminiscent of an attempt at formulating a biblical theology—that is, a systematic presentation of what the Bible says about a certain subject. This is, however, not the purpose here. Our point of departure is that the Bible contains a multitude of voices that cannot be reduced thematically, most times, to a single voice. Biblical texts do not offer a uniform theology but can contribute to a systematic reflection on different topics such as God, the world, and humankind. Thus, a historical-analogical reading is a methodically mindful expansion of the hermeneutical reflection that can occur last in an interpretative process (see above) and opens the way to ideological criticism of the biblical accounts.

The Literary Context

The Gospel of Matthew is built around five speeches (chs. 5–7, 10, 13, 18, and 24–25). Our text, Matt 5:3–10, introduces the first and longest speech, known as the Sermon on the Mount. Given their position both in chapters 5–7 and in the gospel as a whole, these verses are imbued with special significance. The speech is about heaven and especially the way of life that belongs to the kingdom of heaven (see fig. 6.6).

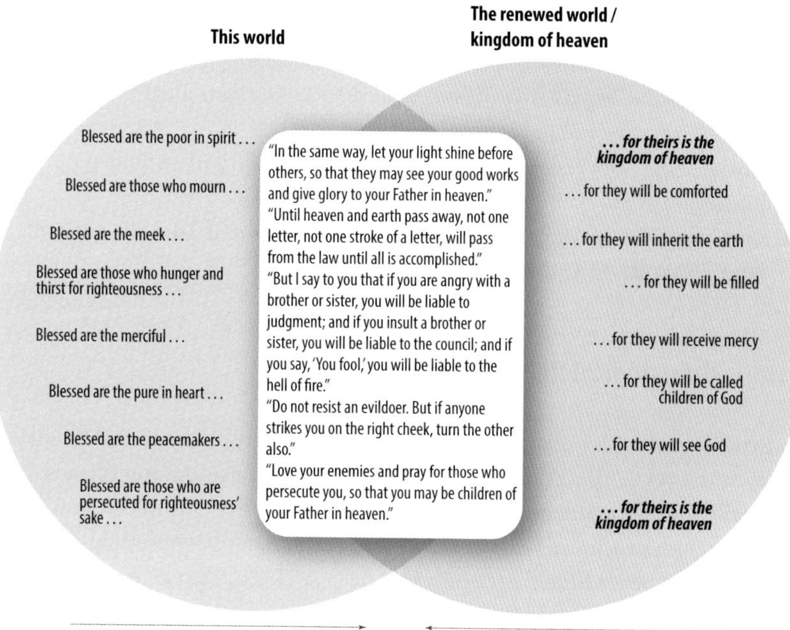

Figure 6.6 The Sermon on the Mount and the Gospel of Matthew's (theological) worldview.

As a gateway into the entire Sermon on the Mount, the text is well delimited from the scene description that is given just before: Jesus is on the mountain as Moses once was on Sinai; large numbers of people are around him and the disciples closest to Jesus. As a teacher of the time, he is sitting as he presents the law from the perspective of heaven.

The delimitation to that which follows, however, is nowhere near as clear. We have another two beatitudes in verses 11 and 12, but these have a different form (changing of person from "they" and "those" to "you" and "mine"). The structure of verses 3–10 (see below) clearly indicates that we can understand each of the first eight beatitudes as a unit in itself. Verses 11 and 12 function more like an expansion and explanation of the eighth beatitude and therefore of the persecution that the people addressed by the Beatitudes were suffering.

The Structure of the Text Passage

The text passage consists of eight parts, each of which contains three components: (1) the word "blessed," (2) a description of certain people, and (3) an explaining/motivating statement.

1 Blessed are the poor in spirit,
for theirs is the kingdom of heaven.
2 Blessed are those who mourn,
for they will be comforted.
3 Blessed are the meek,
for they will inherit the earth.
4 Blessed are those who hunger and thirst for righteousness,
for they will be filled.
5 Blessed are the merciful,
for they will receive mercy.
6 Blessed are the pure in heart,
for they will see God.
7 Blessed are the peacemakers,
for they will be called children of God.
8 Blessed are those who are persecuted for righteousness' sake,
for theirs is the kingdom of heaven.

The first and last motivations are exactly the same and thus frame the eight verses as a whole. In numbers 4 and 8, we are met with the central word of the Sermon on the Mount: righteousness. In a sense, this word divides the text into two parts, numbers 1–4 and numbers 5–8. In verse 11, the words "for righteousness' sake" are replaced with Jesus pointing at himself and become "on my account." Is this text a description of eight categories of people or eight descriptions of a single group of people? The structure of the text, the monotone repetition, and the occasional difficulty of distinguishing the descriptions speak for the latter. That which characterizes these people, among other things, is the upholding of peace. Thus, we have a very well-structured text that emphasizes a central meaning.

Genre and Function

The repetitions, rhythm, and the biblical diction (see below) give the text a poetic character. It is reminiscent of the rhythmic parallelism that characterizes Hebrew poetry. These eight beatitudes are also presented in poetic form (as above) in some Bible editions. They are to be read slowly with much reflection, and preferably memorized. Poetry in the Bible often has an educational purpose. Like the setting of the scene in Matt 5:1–2, the form emphasizes the text's educational character and gives weight to that which is said (cf. Mao's Little Red Book). We can enjoy the Beatitudes' fine formulation, but they primarily wish to teach us something.

Even the genre *beatitudes* belongs within the domain of teaching. This type of text is most common in wisdom literature of different kinds (e.g., Ps 1:1; Sir 25:8–9; 26:1), which are usually introduced with the words "Blessed/fortunate is the one who . . ." We also have a collection of beatitudes among the poetic wisdom literature from Qumran (4Q525). In general, this type of text has an admonishing or proclaiming function. Theologically, beatitudes can be seen as part of a code of ethics, or as part of the gospel's preaching, or as both of these.

We can formulate the Beatitudes in three alternative ways, here exemplified with the first beatitude:

1 Blessed are the poor.
2 The poor are blessed.
3 Blessed be the poor!

The second alternative is functionally the most clear: a statement that says something about the poor (informative function). The first alternative may be interpreted in the same way as the second alternative, but with a stronger emphasis on "blessed." These two alternatives might even be taken as an indirect appeal: be poor and you will be blessed (prescriptive function). The third alternative has the form of an exclamation and may be compared with so-called performative clauses like "congratulations," "I bless you," or "I baptize you." As we say the words, we also perform an action, meaning that in this case we cannot view the words as simply informative. With these words, Jesus also does something with the poor: he wishes them blessedness; he proclaims them blessed. The word "blessed" in different settings resonates to the English ear with happiness, something unreal, or death; in the biblical ear, however, it resonates with salvation, gift, joy, eternity, and God. With his teachings on the kingdom of heaven, Jesus distributes salvation and joy.

Given Matthew's presentation of the kingdom of heaven, the Beatitudes' function can be interpreted primarily as performative and secondarily as prescriptive. The gospel comes first, and ethics come later; there is no reason to expect a solely informative function.

Words and Expressions

The text contains a series of loaded biblical words that need to be explained. As always, there are many interpretations for everything in a text, and we have to select the alternatives that seem to be the most plausible (the reader may want to compare what is presented here to other translations, annotations, and references to parallels):

1 *The poor in spirit* are those who are poor in *their own* spirit, not poor in regard to God's spirit. Their entire being is poor before God; facing severe difficulties (economic, social, political), they learn not to rely on anything but God's help and intervention. The language used is common in the Psalms and Isaiah (Ps 34:19; 37:14; Isa 61:1; Luke 4:18–19; Matt 11:5), as well as in Qumran texts (same phrase as in 1QM XIV, 7). The German *Die Gute Nachricht* captures it well. The poor are "those who stand with empty hands before God."

2 *Those who mourn* are not those who have lost something/someone or weep for their own sin, but those people who weep for the world's current state; they are people who are waiting for God's intervention. Compare this with Isa 40:1–11; 61:2–3; Luke 2:25.

3 *The meek* are those on whom external circumstances have imposed a particular situation in life and who are dedicated to God. Being meek is more about a relationship to God than a relationship to other people. See also Ps 37:3–7 and 37:11: those who trust God/leave their future in his hands are still (calm, settled) before God and trust him (cf. Matt 11:29; 21:5). The word resembles the meaning of the word "poor" (see above) very closely. It certainly does not simply circumscribe a personality trait or temperament (still, mild, kind).

4 *Those who hunger and thirst for (the) righteousness* are people who, as indicated by the double "hunger and thirst," are in extreme need and thus eagerly await change. Many interpret "righteousness" as people's righteous action. But the definite article in the original (*the* righteousness) indicates, rather, a longing for God's righteousness—that is, for God's sovereign intervention resulting in judgment and salvation. Such language is found in the Psalms, the book that seems to have supplied many expressions and phrases to the Beatitudes. See, for example, Ps 40:1–10, especially verse 10, which refers to God's victory and liberation.

We note that the first four descriptions address mainly the relationship with God, and only secondarily the relationship with other humans.

5 *The merciful* are those who practice mercy, who care for other humans, just as God accepts not only the pious but also the sinners. The term is about compassion that comes to expression in concrete action that helps people (cf. Luke 10:25–37). Jesus's contemporaries spoke of "works of mercy" that largely correspond to the list in Matt 25:35–40.

6 *The pure in heart* are those whose will, thought, and feelings are pure. The emphasis lies not on having a clean conscience but on being pure and honest in relationships with other people and with God (see Ps 24:4; 51:12). James 4:8 places the pure in heart in contrast to people who are double-minded. The pure in heart, then, are undivided and wholeheartedly one in word and action (Matt 6:22–24).

7 *The peacemakers.* Older translations sometimes preferred "the peaceful." The Greek text has a word that combines "peace" with "do" (*eirēnopoioi*), thereby indicating an activity that can hardly be reflected by the word "peaceful." Instead, this Semitic word combination lands somewhere in the middle between active and passive: to practice peacefulness, keep the peace, create peace around oneself. Translations use "peacemakers," "make peace," "work for peace," "*Frieden schaffen*," or "*faire oeuvre de paix*."

8 *Those who are persecuted for righteousness' sake.* The phrase "for righteousness' sake" connects to number 4 above. In verse 11, this phrasing is replaced with Jesus's reference to himself ("on my account"). With him the kingdom of heaven is there, and it is people's involvement with the kingdom of heaven and its righteousness that leads to their persecution. This last beatitude (which is developed in verses 11–12) shows that the addressees of the text do not live in quiet isolation, even though the first four beatitudes could have the reader thinking something to that effect. As a whole, however, the passage demonstrates that the battle under the banners of mercy and peace—good versus evil—leads to hatred, slander, and suffering.

An Initial Summary

The inferences are varied and not without tension; the people described are weak and oddly passive. In times of economic and social hardship, they learned that help comes from God. In themselves they are poor, standing before God with empty hands. Their trust is in God. Therefore, they humble themselves and face adversities. Especially the first four beatitudes make this very clear. They mourn for the world and eagerly await God's intervention. We can assume that their lives, most certainly, were not peaceful or tranquil. Further, they are pure in heart; they have turned themselves entirely to God, serving him with undivided and dedicated hearts. Because their center of gravity is in God, they can stand strong no matter what comes at them.

A divinely anchored passiveness is perhaps what emerges most clearly from the descriptions of people in the Beatitudes. However, the same people are also active and strong; they are merciful, they care, and they work in different ways toward creating peace in their environment. The people of the Beatitudes are peacemakers.

The eight "for" clauses of the Beatitudes somehow seem to articulate Jesus's own motivation, the main reason being expressed in numbers 1 and 8: "theirs is the kingdom of heaven." The kingdom of heaven is the same as the kingdom of God. God's dominion or rule emerges from Jesus's words and actions. In Judaism the phrase "the Heavens" is a term that circumscribes God. The reason for Jesus's actions is therefore not found in the qualities of these people, but rather in God himself. From a Jewish perspective, even the passive constructions ("be comforted," etc.) are paraphrasing

God's actions: God will comfort them, God will satisfy them, God will show them mercy, God will call them his children/sons. Inheriting the earth is the same as inheriting the kingdom of heaven. In the transition to a new age, these people are, by their association to Jesus, drawn into God's work on earth. The Beatitudes should be read through a Christocentric, eschatological, and cosmic lens.

The Text's Intertexts

The Sermon on the Mount in Matthew and the Sermon on the Plain in Luke (6:17–49) have several things in common. Many, but notably not all, believe that the two evangelists made use of the same source in their writing: the so-called Q source. Assuming such a single source existed, the fact that the two gospels exhibit many differences cannot be overlooked. In Luke, there are a number of disciples and a large gathering of people, and Jesus both speaks and heals. The speech begins with four beatitudes and four corresponding lamentations. You who are poor / you who are rich; you who are hungry / you who are full; you who weep / you who are laughing; and the hated and excluded / those who are spoken well of. This corresponds well to numbers 1, 4, 2, and 8 and their expansion in Matthew. According to Luke, Jesus directs his attention to the many disciples and speaks to them directly with the words "blessed are you who are poor," and so on. It is clear that Jesus speaks to the physically poor, hungry, and weeping disciples. The dual relationship between God and human beings that we find in Matthew through the usage of language from (among other texts) the Psalms and Isaiah has here largely been reduced to the latter (see above). The people we meet in Matthew belong to an *anavim*-piety (Heb. *anavim* = poor) that developed within Judaism before the Common Era. In Luke we meet them in chapters 1–2 and partially also in 4:14–20, but definitely not as clearly in "his" beatitudes. Both ways of using the word "poor" may have their roots in Jesus.

The Symbolic World of the Text

The Beatitudes ought to be placed into the conceptual world of Matthew as a whole, a world that is also inhabited by contemporary Jewish, Christian, Greek, and Roman texts. What kinds of people exist in this symbolic universe? Are they mainly poor and excluded? Are they simple people? What do they know of the political situation in the contemporary known world? How do they distinguish between the divine and the earthly spheres? How did they see themselves in relation to other people? Questions of this kind are very important for those who wish to use this text about peace. Biblical texts about violence and peace are considered below, but these points unfortunately cannot be explored in any greater depth here owing to space limitations.

The Historical Circumstances of the Text

We will treat this section very briefly as well, referring back to the detailed description of Matthew's historical context in chapter 4. Regarding the Beatitudes, we may add that varying numbers and combinations of beatitudes most likely existed in several contexts from Jesus's own time up to the 80s, when the gospel was finalized. Toward the end of this time period, it seems that the Beatitudes were included in a body of teachings to guide and comfort a group of Jewish followers of Christ (and also some of non-Jewish origin) who, after a period of conflict, had left the Jewish community they had been part of. They saw themselves as the true people of God, as the result of a renewed covenant, and as Jesus's own congregation on earth.

Analogies: Biblical Voices on Peace Work

The interpretation of the Beatitudes presented in this section has hitherto followed the standard procedure of an elementary historical analysis in order to obtain a picture of the peace workers referred to in the text. Now we shall expand the analysis to include other texts on peace, partially from the Bible as a whole and partially from our own time. Biblical voices contribute to the symbolic world and the life philosophy of audiences during Jesus's time as well as the time of the gospel text. A voice from our own time can provide alternative perspectives and heighten our sensitivity to what may be the meaning of "peacemaking" in Matt 5.

According to the Bible, humans are both good and evil. Thus violence becomes, on both a large and a small scale, one of humankind's central problems. Together, humans must find ways to decrease violence and to create peace in their surroundings. At the risk of misunderstanding and oversimplification, I will combine biblical voices about peacemaking and sketch a threefold path: the path of power and strength, the path of law and order, and the path of love and self-giving.

The path of power and strength. The Hebrew Bible—that is, three-fourths of the Christian Bible—has a reputation of being full of violence and intolerance: the constant bloodshed, the conquest of Canaan, holy wars, condemnation of other peoples, and so on. No question, we are faced with dark images from the history of humankind. "The earth was filled with violence" (Gen 6:11). The Bible speaks more often of discord than peace.

In the Hebrew Bible, violence is often opposed with violence, thus exemplifying the path of power and strength. However, it is important to note that the Hebrew Bible never glorifies violence. We may note as well that the Hebrew Bible openly addresses (e.g., Hos 4:1–2) and interacts with the problem of violence. When violence is detected, people look for ways to overcome it. Blood revenge is, no matter how strange it may sound, an early method of fighting violence: it achieves a certain protection for the individual by means of limiting retribution. The same can be said for "eye for eye, tooth for tooth" (Exod 21:24–27). Violence is opposed with violence, but in a regulated way. The Hebrew Bible also contains visions of a world without violence and injustices. These visions become stronger and stronger the further in time we progress. God will visit his people and establish his dominion over the entire world. Swords will be forged into ploughshares, spears into pruning-hooks (Mic 4:2–4). God shall give humankind a new heart—indeed, a piece of God himself (Jer 31:33–34; Ezek 36:26)—and a new world will emerge.

In the New Testament, the path of power and strength is greatly reduced, but it is still present (and not just in Revelation). According to Paul, "the God of peace will shortly crush Satan under your feet" (Rom 16:20) and "rulers do not bear the sword for no reason" (Rom 13 NIV). Even Jesus took a whip in his hand and drove away all who sold and bought in the temple of Jerusalem (Mark 11:15–17). The path of power and strength therefore still exists in the New Testament, but the great battle belongs to the future.

The path of law and order. This is, in a way, reason's path to peace. In order that we may live together in peace, we *need* regulations and rules. Through laws and agreements, the lust for violence is suppressed, and discord is kept under control. Diplomacy is the primary means to respond to terrorism. The Hebrew Bible with its many laws is a manifestation of this kind of thinking. This hardly needs to be exemplified, as the word for "law" is literally part of its name (Tanak, see box 1.2, p. 9). Turning to the New Testament, we can cite 1 Cor 14:33: "God is a God not of disorder but of peace." The Bible's main passage, however, must be Gen 2:15. Humankind has as its mission the management of God's creation, which in itself includes the common task of forming a society in which peace and justice prevail. In a biblical perspective, the path of law and order is an utterly essential part of the path to peace. All people—Christians and non-Christians—can unite in walking this path, with the shared aim of shaping human existence together.

The path of love and self-giving. The further we come in the Bible, the broader this path becomes. To give instead of taking revenge, to reward evil with good, to turn the other cheek, to voluntarily suffer in the place of others, to love the enemy, indeed to meet violence with nonviolence and good deeds—that is what characterizes this main path, judging by the Bible's presentation of reality. This remarkable approach to violence emerges from the piety we see, for example, in Pss 37 and 7. In the Hebrew Bible, the clearest representation is found in the Lord's suffering servant (Isa 40–53, esp. Isa 53).

The path of self-giving, humility, and suffering dominates the New Testament. This applies primarily to the central figure of these texts. Jesus walks the way of peace that is described in Isa 53: to suffer voluntarily, to give of oneself, to give one's life for the benefit of others, although impeccable himself. As a servant, he washed his disciples' feet—that is, purified humans in anticipation of their new communion with God and each other. Peace was proclaimed on Christmas Eve by the choir of angels simply because it could now be found on earth as a new opportunity through the child in the manger. Christ is the peace of the world. For many reasons, this is the most important statement about peace in the New Testament. Christ has forever shaped the path to peace that is presented in the Bible, and Christ is and remains a source of power for all who work for peace.

Walking the path of suffering and giving is typical not only of Jesus; he is accompanied by his followers (see Matt 5:38–48; 1 Pet 2:21–25). Jesus is the great model, the template that his followers hope to adhere to in their own lives. They embody Christ in their surroundings.

The path of love and self-giving is not the way of reason, however. It may rather be described as the way of miracles, requiring patience and humility and, not least, complete rest and trust in God, made possible through unification with Jesus Christ. Only as a part of God's construction on earth, the cornerstone of which is Christ, is this path fully navigable. If anybody wishes to discover the uniqueness of the Bible's road to peace, it may be found on this lane.

The biblical voices on peace have here been depicted as a threefold path toward greater peace on earth. The path of suffering and giving is clearly the most central to the New Testament, embodied by Jesus himself. If we now return to the peacemakers in Jesus's Sermon on the Mount, we find that they belong to the third path. The most peculiar thing about them is the unification of weakness and strength, of passiveness and activeness. We meet the simple workers for peace, who in their secure ties to God can do that which is good, can fight for peace in their surroundings and take on suffering for the sake of righteousness—that is, for their involvement in God's peace work on earth. The Bible presents multiple ways of battling against evil; the peace workers that Jesus praises and blesses in the beginning of the Sermon on the Mount belong to those who have chosen to walk the path of love and self-giving.

Analogies: A Voice from Our Own Time

A number of organizations in today's world have declared it their mission to work for peace. One such organization is the Swedish Peace and Arbitration Society (SPAS). One of the main objectives of the organization is to bring about political change that benefits peace and disarmament, both nationally and internationally. It asserts that "a lasting and sustainable peace can best be achieved without the use of armed violence and we work from the assumption that humans both want and can live in peace. We are convinced that a world without war is possible."

SPAS declares that a sustainable peace requires "a relationship between two or more states or groups that is characterized by an absence of military buildups and preparations for war. When sustainable peace prevails, the parties have a shared conviction that an armed conflict between them is unthinkable and that future conflicts will be resolved through cooperation by peaceful means."

SPAS's peace work includes factors such as

- democratization and respect for human rights;
- international cooperation;
- the development of methods for conflict management; and
- strong international laws and disarmament.

SPAS states that the growth of sustainable peaceful relations and democratic development is prevented by poverty, environmental destruction, improvident use of natural resources, and large economic disparities within states and regions. It therefore supports "initiatives that will lead to ecologically sustainable development and improved living conditions for the world's poor."[16]

Perhaps the differences between this text and the Beatitudes will be noted first. SPAS works with relations between states, nations, and ethnic groups. Is that perspective generally included in Matt 5? Or does Jesus speak only to those who have no influence on the political arena? Is he not interested in this level of peace work, focusing only on individuals and their immediate surroundings? SPAS also provides a number of concrete examples of how peace work will be carried out. In relation to this, the words in Matt 5:9 may appear general and vague. Jesus only binds together peace work with other qualities of these people: mercy, honesty, and uprightness.

In Matt 5, all peace work is rooted in a relationship with God and his future intervention. SPAS assumes that people can and want to live in peace, whereas Matt 5 seems to have a more pessimistic view of humankind. Ultimately, an intervention from God is required. Confidence exists in both peace texts—a trust in humankind and a trust in God. Without such confidence, there can be no functioning peace work.

SPAS and Matt 5 have in common the rejection of violence as a solution to the problem of violence. But while SPAS is investing most in the path of justice and order, the foolish peace workers in Matt 5 wander in the way of love and self-sacrifice. The biblical text clearly has its strength, but it also has clear limits as to what peace work can mean.

Some Hermeneutical Questions for Further Reflection

I ask myself: Is this way of interpreting the Beatitudes dependent on my own ideological perceptions? What do I consider to be a good form of peace work? Do my answers to this regulate how I interpret biblical and other texts on peace? Are there other important voices regarding peace work that ought to be considered in an anal-

16. Quotations translated from the idea program of the Swedish Peace and Arbitration Society, accessed December 27, 2019, https://www.svenskafreds.se/foreningsinformation/ideprogram/.

ysis such as this? Is Jesus's approach in Matt 5 a realistic perception of peace work? Is Matt 5 relevant only to those who believe in Jesus? Is peace work as described by Matt 5 possible only for followers of Christ? These questions only scrape the surface of what can be considered. Comparing analogies of texts about peace brings up scores of new questions and contributes to a clearer view of what defines a biblical text.

Further Readings

Luz, Ulrich. *Matthew 1–7: A Commentary.* Rev. ed. Hermeneia. Minneapolis: Fortress, 2007.

Swartley, Willard M. *Covenant of Peace: The Missing Peace in New Testament Theology and Ethics.* Grand Rapids: Eerdmans, 2006.

World Council of Churches. *Just Peace Companion.* Geneva: WCC Publications, 2012.

How Are Good Deeds Motivated? An Argumentation Analysis of 1 Pet 1:17–19

Human communication is complex. Judging from everything from everyday discussions to juridical or political arguments, one can state that communication is never only about applying formal logical rules. Humans intuitively know that persuasion can be achieved only when the logical is combined with and amplified by other rhetorical means. Aside from the receiver's logical agreement, her feelings and trust also need to be awakened and won over. Further, every argument includes a number of unspecified premises and conclusions, and it is often these that decide whether the addressee will be convinced or not. An important part of argumentation analysis therefore consists of making "hidden" thoughts and motives visible.

In order to clarify what is happening under the surface of an argument, analytical tools have been developed since the 1950s.[17] These tools can be applied also to an analysis of biblical texts, as readers of these texts also attempt to understand what an argument is all about.[18]

Toulmin's Descriptive Model

Many methods are descriptive; that is, they describe the explicit and implicit argumentation in a text and leave the conclusions about the argument's factual quality for

17. Toulmin, *Uses of Argument*; Perelman, *The New Rhetoric.*

18. Thurén, *Rhetoric and Argumentation.*

the reader. Others—such as Van Eemeren's modern pragma-dialectic method—are normative; that is, they can be used to evaluate the argument's factual quality.[19] An already classic way of analyzing the thought process of a text is Toulmin's descriptive model.[20] It offers rules that expose unmentioned premises and rules, and therefore is very suitable for analyses of the ideological or theological content of a text. In this model, a specific function is identified for each part of the argument—independent of whether it is explicit or implicit. The following three elements occur in every argument:

Claim (*C*) gives the results that are based on the argumentation.
Data (*D*) describes the specific facts on which the argumentation rests.
Warrant (*W*) describes how one gets from *D* to *C*. Contrary to *D*, *W* is a general rule.

The argumentation can also contain different elements:

Backing (*B*) describes that which supports *W*'s validity and why *W* suits this argumentation. *B* contains general information, such as statistics.
Rebuttal (*R*) describes under which circumstances *C* is valid.
Qualifier (*Q*) describes how reliable the argumentation is.

It is important to carefully identify each individual statement's actual function, because it is common, for example, for *D* and *B* to be confused with each other. One of Toulmin's examples from 1958 assumes a Swedish situation (see ill. A).

Illustration A

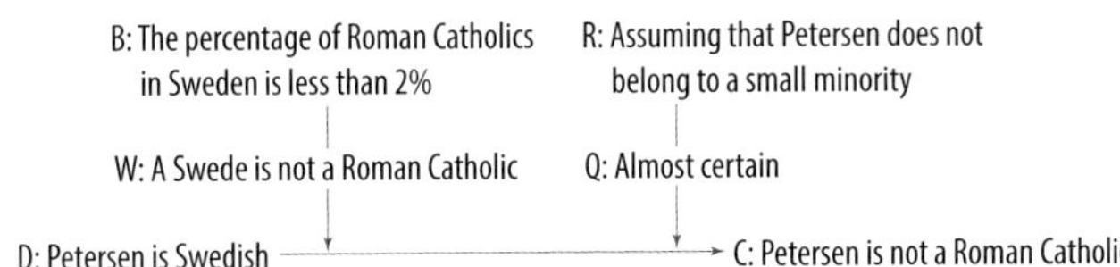

The weak point of an argumentation analysis is often how expressions are presented in the text. They need to be modified in some way, which invites singular interpretation. In the following presentation, implicit expressions are presented in *italics*.

19. Van Eemeren et al., *Handbook of Argumentation Theory*.
20. Toulmin, *Introduction to Reasoning*.

Analysis of 1 Pet 1:17–19

The admonishment in 1 Pet 1:17 may be used to illustrate how complicated thought processes can be in a single verse. This presentation will be an overview.[21]

> If you invoke as Father the one who judges all people impartially according to their deeds, live in fear during the time of your exile.

Claim (*C*)—that is, that which the sender wishes the addressees to believe—is found at the end: they shall live in fear. What this means is not explained here. *Data* (*D*)—that is, the specific facts that the author assumes the addressees unquestioningly accept—is found in the beginning: "you invoke [God] as Father." Further, it is mentioned that (D^1) God is an impartial judge. But how do we get from $D + D^1$ to C? What is implied? Where is the implicit and universally valid rule (*W*) that creates a bridge between *D* and *C*?

The rule (*W*) that can best be applied to this situation may be summarized as follows: "One ought to be afraid of a sharp-sighted and impartial judge" or "One ought to be afraid of a person who cannot be resisted." The general experience of people with judges is the *Backing* (*B*). *W*'s effectiveness assumes in this case that the addressee does not feel entirely innocent (see ill. B).

Illustration B

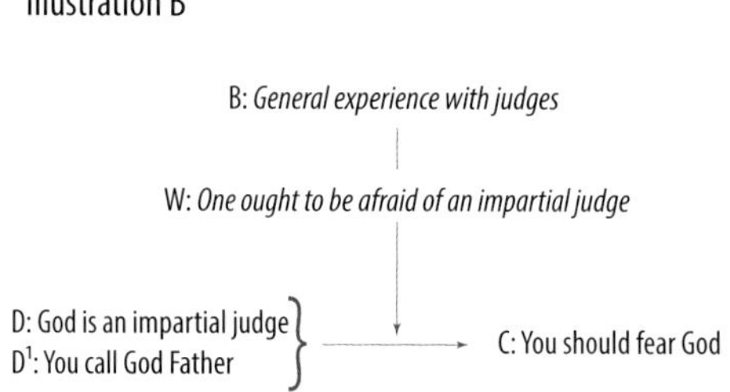

D^1, however, fits poorly with the situation at hand. Something is missing. The thought process assumes that the receiver fills it with his or her own additions. For example, you invoke him as Father (*D*), and therefore you live in close contact with him (implicit C^1/D^2), meaning in turn that he knows all your faults (implicit C^2/D^3). This makes it especially important for the addressees to fear God. Between every *D* and *C*, we can glimpse another *W*.

As opposed to formal logic, this type of open-endedness, or boundlessness, belongs to the qualities of human argumentation: one can always continue to question into infinity, "How do we know that?" or "What does this have to do with the situa-

21. See further Thurén, *Argument and Theology in 1 Peter*, 111–16.

tion at hand?" Conscious of the fact that the process needs to be interrupted at some point, we will ask but a few more questions.

The receiver can also read the text in a different way. That he or she can call the judge "Father" actually disqualifies him from being a judge, which then becomes a *Rebuttal* (*R*). If necessary, its relation to the argument may be explained by an additional *Warrant* (*W*) (see ill. C).

Illustration C

R: Except when you call God Father
B: General experience with judges
W: A father is a partial judge
W: One ought to be afraid of an impartial judge
D: God is an impartial judge
C: You ought to fear God

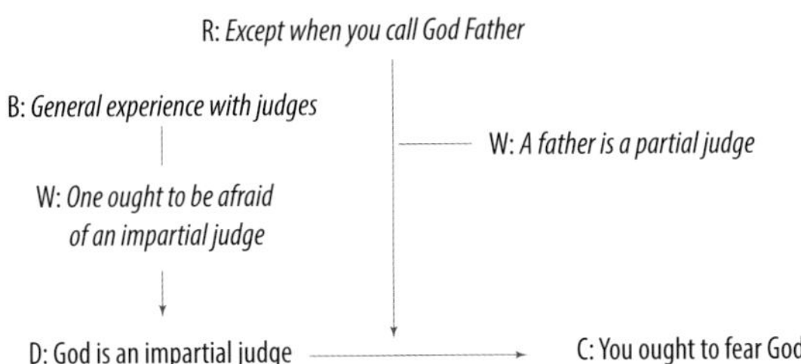

The fact that the Father is disqualified as judge because of his benevolence fits rather poorly with the instruction to fear God. However, if the Greek word *phobos* is interpreted not as fear, but in the more positive sense of "God-fearing" or "trembling/ trepidation before the holy," we have two new interpretative alternatives (presented in ill. D in a somewhat simplified manner).

Illustration D

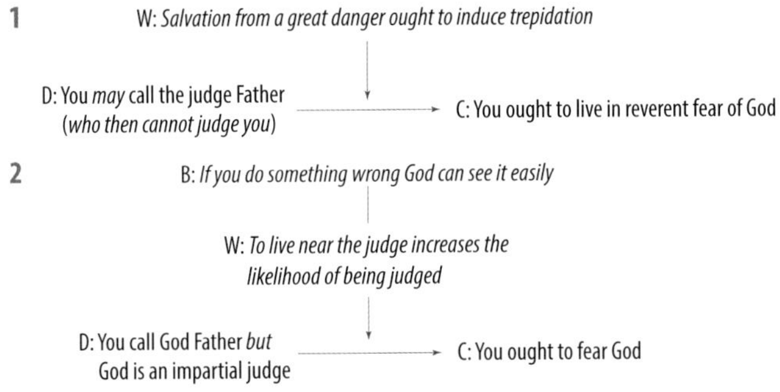

1
W: Salvation from a great danger ought to induce trepidation
D: You may call the judge Father (who then cannot judge you)
C: You ought to live in reverent fear of God
2
B: If you do something wrong God can see it easily
W: To live near the judge increases the likelihood of being judged
D: You call God Father but God is an impartial judge
C: You ought to fear God

Which alternative is to be preferred: number 1 or 2? One method by which to answer this is to attempt to analyze the literary context. Thus, we need to examine 1 Pet 1:18–19, in which the exhortation is motivated with a participle construction that exists in a "grounds-conclusion" relationship to said exhortation.

> You know that you were ransomed from the futile ways inherited from your ancestors, not with perishable things like silver or gold, but with the precious blood of Christ, like that of a lamb without defect or blemish.

Reading this, we can see an emphasis on the value of salvation and the good situation in which the addressees now find themselves. This, then, would support alternative 1 (see ill. E).

Illustration E

D: You have been ransomed with Christ's precious blood → C: You ought to live in reverent fear of God

However, how do we get from *D* to *C*? The answer is not as straightforward as it should be, as *W* ought to be simply a general rule, not containing any specific information. In all likelihood, we are confronted with an argumentative chain, where not all the parts are explicit, and the receiver(s) ought to come up with some of the elements on their own. For example, the following elements (*D* or *C*) could potentially occur (see ill. F).

Illustration F

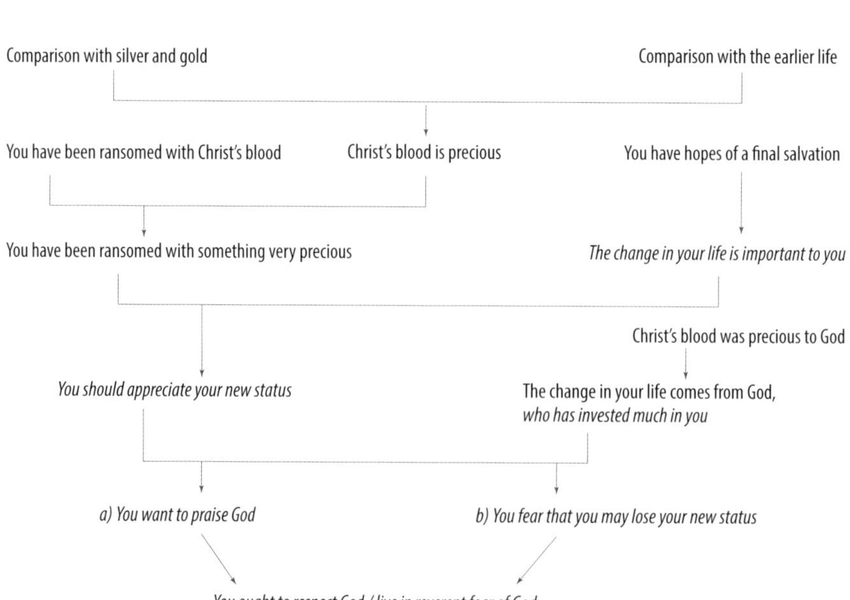

Between these elements the reader would, of course, need to identify more adequate *W*s and other elements as needed.

The analysis answers a theological question: How does the author motivate good deeds? What constitutes the foundation of Christian ethics? The argumentation analysis penetrates and makes visible two almost equally plausible alternatives of a thought process, drawing from both verse 17 and verses 18–19. Either the addressees' new situation ought to induce their desire to praise and give thanks to God, which logically entails that they wish to live in accordance with his will. Or they should be aware of the risk that they may lose this new situation—thus motivating them to not go against God's will.

When the whole text is then analyzed with the same method, we find that both alternatives occur throughout the entirety. The "positive" motivation is dominant, albeit the "negative" motivation is still present.

Further Readings

Eemeren, F. H. van, et al. *Handbook of Argumentation Theory*. Dordrecht: Springer, 2014.

Perelman, Chaim H., and Lucie Olbrechts-Tyteca. *The New Rhetoric: A Treatise on Argumentation*. Notre Dame, IN: University of Notre Dame, 1969.

Thurén, Lauri. *Argument and Theology in 1 Peter*. Sheffield: Sheffield Academic Press, 1995.

———. "On Studying Ethical Argumentation and Persuasion in the New Testament." Pages 464–78 in *Rhetoric and the New Testament*. Sheffield: JSOT Press, 1993.

———. *Rhetoric and Argumentation in the Letters of Paul*. Oxford Handbook of Pauline Studies. Oxford: Oxford University Press, 2019.

Toulmin, Stephen E. *An Introduction to Reasoning*. 2nd ed. New York: Macmillan, 1984.

———. *The Uses of Argument*. Cambridge: Cambridge University Press, 1958.

"Am I Now Seeking Human Approval?" A Rhetorical-Epistolary Reading of Gal 1:10

The task before us is to identify the rhetorical function of Paul's questions in Gal 1:10: "Am I now seeking human approval, or God's approval? Or am I trying to please people?" Since the questions are preceded by a double curse, many commentators have found the questions bewildering. What is the point of emphasizing that cursing people must not be mistaken for pleasing people, especially when the letter's addressees seem to be on friendly terms with those who are being cursed? Whichever way one looks at the communication dynamics here, the questions in 1:10 seem unwarranted.

The editors of NA[28] (a text-critical edition of the Greek NT) somehow acknowledge the problem by separating verse 10 from the preceding verses and formatting it as part of the next paragraph. Some translations (e.g., NRSV) leave the bewilderment unresolved and put the verse in its own paragraph.

We will argue, in turn, that Paul's response should be viewed as an ironic rebuttal of suspicions by the addressees that he is inconsistent and indecisive. From this perspective the connection between verses 8–9 and verse 10 appears appropriate. The irony, however, is not easily recognized, since the suspicions to which it corresponds are based on personal encounters in Galatia between Paul and the addressees. Hints to this effect can be found in Gal 4:12–18 and in the persistent rumors mentioned in Gal 5:11.

We will approach the task first by considering the pragmatic dimension of texts, especially letters, which remind us of the lack of information that can lead a secondary letter reader astray. We will also consider what is or should be typical of ancient letter introductions, according to ancient writers on epistolary theory. In addition, we will take into account an intertext in the Pauline corpus that may shed further light on suspicions concerning Paul's singlemindedness and decisiveness. The intertext also sheds light on Paul's rhetorical wit and ability to rebut such suspicions.

Rhetorical and Epistolary Text Analyses

Rhetorical and epistolary text analyses focus on the text's pragmatic dimension—that is, how the text employs expressions and strategies as means of communication between sender and receiver.[22] The path from sender to receiver is not straight, and the relation between a sender's intention and the actual impact on a receiver depends on many factors (see the section "Variables of the Interpretative Process," p. 499). Moreover, while an ancient letter may contain a performative utterance such as a command, an instruction, a praise, or a reprimand that aims directly at the situation of the addressees, the effect or outcome of the performative in that specific context is known only to the one who is part of the actual communication event. The sender's anticipations may be signified in the text, but a contextually and historically distant analysis can only ever at best approximate the impact in the original communication.[23]

Turning to Galatians, we note that Gal 3:1 ("You foolish Galatians! Who has bewitched you?") is undoubtedly a reprimand. What effect this reprimand had on

22. For the distinction between the syntactic, semantic, and pragmatic dimensions of texts, see the section "Theory of Language: The Three Dimensions of Signs," p. 497.

23. For a discussion of passages with direct situational pertinence, and anticipated persuasion in Galatians, see Mitternacht, "Foolish Galatians."

the original addressees, however, is less than apparent. This is particularly pertinent to ancient letters, since a true letter is but "one of the two sides of a dialogue" (Demetrius, *On Style* 223 [Innes, LCL]). Only the original addressees, who represent the other side of the dialogue, would have known the entire dialogue. The distant reader can only read between the lines. What personal relations and experiences are hidden in the background? What was the normal tone in exchanges like this? How do expressions and rhetorical strategies come across and relate to expectations?

A particular feature of contextual epistolary analysis is found in Gal 1:6: "I am astonished that you are so quickly deserting the one who called you." The Greek word *thaumazō* (here translated as "astonished") basically means "surprised." Investigations of ancient letters have, however, revealed that the phrase "I am very surprised that . . ." is a standard formulation in so-called ironic rebuke letters and that the phrase signals not only surprise but also irritation and dislike. The reader who is not accustomed to this epistolary convention may easily miss the actual impact of the signal.

In a third example that highlights the disadvantage of the distant reader, we find a categorical blaming of a third party: "It is those who want to make a good showing in the flesh that try to compel you to be circumcised—only that they may not be persecuted for the cross of Christ. Even the circumcised do not themselves obey the law, but they want you to be circumcised so that they may boast about your flesh" (Gal 6:12–13). Against such selfish action, of which the addressees apparently have to be made aware, Paul presents his own resolve: "May I never boast of anything except the cross of our Lord Jesus Christ, by which the world has been crucified to me, and I to the world" (v. 14). The first addressees may or may not have been perplexed by Paul's comparison, but they could base their arbitration on their own personal experiences. The distant reader, however, would need to hear the third party's response, at least, before assessing the situation. In any event, Paul's judgment is but *one of several* possible assessments, and not all the addressees may have agreed with him. The question is also how the ironic rebuke in 1:6, which assumes their appreciation of the "third party," squares with this accusation.

We also need to remind ourselves that ancient letters were primarily written for the ear; the overlap between speech and letter is undeniable. The Greek word *epistolē* (epistle) was originally used to denote something that was presented orally by a messenger. In part, this was a practical necessity. According to some calculations, only two of every hundred grown men—and far fewer women—in Greco-Roman society were literate. For many of the addressees, the only way to access the content of the letter was to hear it read out loud. However, the ancient "mailman" would often have been given instructions on how the letter should be presented with regard to tone of voice, gestures, rhythmic expressions, and so on, so that even for the recipient who *could* read, the oral reception of a letter was crucial. Quiet reading for oneself appears to have become common practice first in the tenth century. When, for example, Augustine (354–430 CE) in his *Confessions* points out that Ambrose (ca. 339–397, bishop of Milan) would read his letters *quietly*, he does so to indicate how irregular that was at the time.[24]

Furthermore, oral communication is appraised differently from the written word; in oral communication a thought process should be straightforward, with a new statement preferably building on the statement just prior. The listener should be able to follow the reasoning easily, which means that complex arguments should be avoided. In other words, demands for a sound oral argument are lower than for a written text, which can be revisited over and over. This should be taken into account, for instance, when considering Paul's Scripture references in the third chapter of Galatians, where the logical argumentation does not seem to stand scrutiny.[25] In an oral performance, the argument may well have been persuasive enough.

Finally there is the question of rhetorical genre and means. Ancient rhetoricians (primarily Aristotle, Cicero, and Quintilian) suggested that any public speech belonged to one of three types (genres), each with its own rhetorical structure. The first and most important was the speech in the courtroom (the judicial speech), where something in the past had to be examined and evidence was presented to convince the court of what is right and what is wrong. The second type of speech is related to the political arena (the deliberative speech), where a speaker would try to generate support for a proposed course of action or a political decision. The third type of speech (the epideictic or demonstrative speech) was delivered at festivities of various kinds or other public gatherings, often for the purpose of praising, but at times blaming, somebody or something.

A number of attempts have been made to assess the rhetoric of Paul's letters in terms of one of these types of speeches, and often analyses cannot agree. Galatians, for example, has been analyzed as an apologetic speech, a political speech, and a praising/blaming speech. Each analysis has provided insights into possible rhetorical strategies and potential persuasive effects. Attempts to apply a speech genre to a letter have shown, however, that the rules of composition are not as strict for letters as they are for speeches. Indeed, ancient letter theoreticians count many more types of letters than types of speeches. One of these theoreticians lists twenty-one types of letters and adds, "Possibly time will produce even more than these, as time is a very skilled inventor of competences and theories."[26] Aside from the multitude of letter situations, letter writers employed a number of so-called standard formulations that functioned as letter-specific communication signals.[27]

In other words, letters are not the same as speeches and cannot be expected to

24. Augustine, *Confessions* 6.3 (LCL, p. 273).
25. Hietanen, *Paul's Argumentation in Galatians*.
26. Pseudo-Demetrius, "Epistolary Types," in Malherbe, *Ancient Epistolary Theorists*, 30–41.
27. Dahl, "Paul's Letter to the Galatians"; R. Longenecker, *Galatians*.

comply with the same structures that speeches do. Yet rhetorical analyses can still give many important insights into letters. This is especially true for the fundamental rhetorical means, *ethos*, *logos*, and *pathos*. Independent of the medium utilized, it is always important to win the trust of the addressee (*ethos*), seek the right balance of factual arguments (*logos*), and appeal to the addressees' feelings and emotions (*pathos*). The rhetorical manuals available to us give a great deal of good advice for how to acquire this art of persuasion.

Paul and Eloquence

In his first letter to the Corinthians, Paul asserts that his preaching did not occur "with eloquent wisdom," and adds emphatically: "so that the cross of Christ might not be emptied of its power" (1 Cor 1:17). The expression "eloquent wisdom" suggests the ability to use fine language to influence philosophical, religious, and ethical beliefs. One cannot but wonder how this emphatic distancing from eloquence relates to the fact that in the same letter Paul employs a number of rhetorical devices. Indeed, even the distancing statement in 1 Cor 1:17 itself is formulated like a rhetorical antithesis. Other rhetorical devices found in 1 Corinthians are anaphora and litotes (1:26), antistrophe (1:26–28), accumulation (2:1–5), and enthymeme (2:10).

What, then, could the purpose of the distancing have been? Did Paul position himself against skilled orators like Apollos of Antioch, who was also active in Corinth (1 Cor 1:12)? Or did he want to distance himself from *empty* rhetoric ("empty words"), something that already Plato and Aristotle had criticized the sophists for. If one proclaims the wisdom of God, there is no need for added rhetorical effects.

Perhaps the key to why Paul dissociated himself from eloquence of speech can be found in 2 Cor 10:10, where he recounts what his critics seem to think of him: "For they say, 'His letters are weighty and strong, but his bodily presence is weak, and his speech contemptible.'" Paul seems to accept their judgment in general, although with different connotations. He had behaved meekly while present in Corinth, in the hope that it would be interpreted as "the meekness and gentleness of Christ" (2 Cor 10:1–2; cf. Gal 4:13–15). Some, however, had deemed that Paul need not be taken seriously.

These observations generate new questions: How did those who actually knew Paul read his letters? How did those who remembered him as a meek and gentle preacher interpret his at times brusque and decisive style of letter writing, and his use of irony and sarcasm? And what can the modern reader of Paul's letters learn from this? In order to answer these questions, we will now examine the introduction to Galatians, which concludes with the rhetorical inquiry "Am I now seeking human approval?" together with an assurance that this would be entirely incompatible with being a servant of Christ (Gal 1:10).

A Successful Introduction?

The purpose of an introduction, which in rhetorical terms is called an *exordium*, is to establish contact, attract attention, and above all to get into "the good graces of [one's] hearers" (*captatio benevolentiae*). On this topic Cicero writes, "An exordium is an address bringing the mind of the hearer into a suitable state to receive the rest of the speech; and that will be effected if it has rendered him well disposed towards the speaker, attentive, and willing to receive information" (*On Invention* 1.15 [Hubbell, LCL]). Only when the speaker is absolutely assured of the addressees' affection for what is being said can they proceed to the issue at hand. If the subject matter is controversial, Cicero writes, then the introduction ought to be constructed with great care. One ought to attempt to capture the good graces of the listeners and master their emotions—if necessary by means of evasive and disguised strategies (*On Invention* 1.15), rhetorically termed *insinuatio*. In another rhetorical manual, we find the advice that if an audience appears convinced of the contrary, the speaker ought to carefully attempt to win the goodwill of the listener, or make them attentive, or responsive, through masked wordings (*Rhetoric to Herennius* 1.4.6).

How does Galatians relate to these instructions? The letter commences with the greeting: "Paul an apostle . . . to the churches of Galatia: Grace to you and peace from God" (1:1–3). This greeting is composed in accordance with conventions of letter writing in antiquity. However, while the Greek greeting normally uses *chairein* (greetings), Paul mixes Greek and Jewish in his: *charis kai eirēnē* (grace and peace).

The greeting phrase is elongated by two extensions, the first of which consists of a dissociation: "sent neither by human commission nor from human authorities," combined with a confession: "but through Jesus Christ and God the Father" (1:1). The dissociation appears, rhetorically speaking, rather early on in the letter, albeit the target remains undetermined, securing attention as well as letting causes remain hidden. Not until later does Paul tell of the disputes and confrontations in Jerusalem and Antioch, at which time the reader may begin to suspect what the unspecified marker at the beginning was meant to imply.

In a second expansion of the greeting phrase, it is said that Jesus Christ "gave himself for our sins to set us free from the present evil age" (1:4). The expression "Christ died for our sins" is very well known and likely originates in a pre-Pauline tradition (cf. 1 Cor 15:3). However, the addition of purpose (set us free from the present evil age) is previously unknown and does not occur in any of Paul's other letters. Something known is welded to something new. Rhetorically, this is in agreement with Aristotle's instructions to prove one's thesis through that about which there is consent (Aristotle, *Topics* 1.1.22–24; cf. *Rhetoric to Herennius* 1.69). Once more, attention is attracted while the purpose is left unclear and open. Further on in the letter, and especially in the letter's personal conclusion, it turns out that the connection between

Christ's sacrificial death and being set free from the present evil age is the nucleus of the letter's most controversial concern.[28]

A letter written on papyrus.
The Metropolitan Museum of Art, New York.

The transition from the letter's greeting to the main body in 1:6 is made, as we have already noted, through an ironically expressed rebuke ("I am astonished that . . ."), the reason for which is slightly cryptically formulated: ". . . you are so quickly deserting the one who called you in the grace of Christ and are turning to a different gospel—not that there is another gospel, but there are some who are confusing you and want to pervert the gospel of Christ" (1:6–7). A certain sincerity begins to surface, yet it is still far from the stern warning in 5:4: "You . . . have cut yourselves off from Christ; you have fallen away from grace."

We can infer that the mixture of known and new, ironic and serious, vague and critical corresponds to a rhetorical situation that, on the one hand, requires argumentation belonging to the category *insinuatio* (as resistance is to be expected) and, on the other hand, counts on the goodwill of the addressees. The sober address "to the churches," as compared to "the church *of God*" in 2 Cor 1:1 or "the saints in Christ" in Phil 1:1, as well as the absence of the otherwise typical thanksgiving in Paul's letters, indicates a calculated sternness by the sender. No doubt, the addressees noted right from the beginning that Paul was not trying to flatter them.

In what follows, the initial restraint is discharged almost entirely: "But even if we or an angel from heaven should proclaim to you a gospel contrary to what we proclaimed to you, let that one be accursed! As we have said before, so now I repeat, if anyone proclaims to you a gospel contrary to what you received, let that one be accursed!" (1:8–9). Including curses in the introduction of a letter is, rhetorically speaking, surprising, to say the least. Betz has attempted to explain the unexpected by means of a comparison with Demosthenes's *On the Crown* (one of the masterpieces of Greek rhetoric), in which a curse is added at the conclusion (*peroratio*). He then suggests that since introduction and conclusion "were considered intimately related, the difference is insignificant."[29] This, however, hardly solves the problem at hand, as the introduction's specific function was to act as a *captatio benevolentiae*, and, in an oral performance, the temporal space between introduction and conclusion is real.

Is there any other explanation? First of all, we may note that Paul still exercises a certain restraint in that he formulates the curses as conditional clauses: "If . . . let that one . . ." Further on in the letter, this conditionality disappears entirely and is replaced with a categorical affirmation: "But whoever it is that is confusing you will pay the

28. Mitternacht, "Foolish Galatians," 411–12.
29. Betz, *Galatians*, 46.

penalty" (5:10). To this is attached a sarcastic joke that gives some insight into the author's feelings regarding the subject: "I wish those who unsettle you would castrate themselves!" (5:12). Second, the curses must be read together with the questions that follow them (1:10), to which we shall now turn.

Unmotivated Questions?

Directly after the curses, we find two questions that seem uncalled for, to say the least: "Am I now seeking human approval, or God's approval? Or am I trying to please people?" (1:10). The Greek words that translate "seeking . . . approval" (*peithein*) and "to please" (*areskein*) are often used to describe cunning rhetoricians, sophists who fool their audience with fine words and flattery. Further, the word *arti* (meaning "just now, at this moment") in the first question indicates that the questions ought to be read in direct relation to the curses. But how does this all fit together? Betz laments in his commentary on Galatians, "In verse 10 Paul raises and answers two different questions which have kept commentators puzzling."[30]

Once more we are reminded that a letter is but one side of a dialogue. For the modern reader, it seems natural to ask: Who could suspect Paul to be pleasing people by cursing them? But what if Paul's intention was quite different, and what if the first addressees were quite alert to Paul's intention, thinking, "Alright, we admit that Paul can be firm and take the bull by the horns. We *now* understand that being a servant of Christ does not mean being weak and without a backbone. Paul can also be categorical and resolute." If this was the case, for the Galatian addressees the rhetorical effect of the curses in 1:8–9 was completely different. They would have perceived the curses not as part of an angry confrontation but rather as an attempt to correct a widespread view that Paul was inconsistent and indecisive. And, most significantly, from this angle the questions in verse 10 are no longer baffling but connect well with verses 8–9.

Viewing verse 10 as focusing on Paul's character is further supported by the ensuing narrative (1:13–2:15), which serves the purpose of establishing the author's credibility and perseverance (*ethos*) against possible suspicions (nota bene) of being subservient (1:20). Paul recounts in several episodes his irreproachable eagerness in the face of the supreme revelation that he received from Christ himself, and his tenacity in defending that revelation. Others, especially Peter, may have deviated from the true path and betrayed the gospel because of the fear of "false brothers" or reprisals (2:14–15). Paul, however, held fast to the truth of the gospel at all times. Rhetorically speaking, this is an appropriate move, since "the orator persuades by moral character when his speech is delivered in such a manner as to render him worthy of confidence; . . . moral character, so to say, constitutes the most effective means

30. Betz, *Galatians*, 54.

of proof" (Aristotle, *The Art of Rhetoric* 1.2.4 [Freese, LCL]). Paul's main rhetorical purpose in the introduction to Galatians may thus have been to show proof of his personal trustworthiness, unwavering character, and perseverance in order to neutralize doubts that he might be trying to please people. In that case, we need to take seriously what we suspected from 2 Cor 10:10. The addressees knew Paul as a different person than the one who seems to surface in his letters.[31] Did they perhaps have legitimate cause to suspect that Paul was incalculable, wanting to please? There may have been uncertainty in Galatia as to whether or not Paul was unequivocal in his position, even regarding circumcision. Why else would he ask in 5:11, "But my friends, why am I still being persecuted if I am still preaching circumcision?" (yet another question that has confounded scholars).

In sum, the rhetorical aim of this letter introduction may have been to counteract a nagging suspicion. The addressees may have been surprised, even entertained, but in the end they cannot but agree: a servant of Christ may appear frail and indecisive when he or she chooses to follow in the master's footsteps, but this must not be mistaken for trying to please people.

Statue of Paul at the Basilica of Saint Paul outside the Walls, Rome, Italy. According to tradition, the basilica was built on Paul's tomb. The statue shows a man with a stern face and a sword. The sword symbolizes the martyrdom of Paul as well as the *spiritus gladius*, the sword of the Spirit, of which Paul writes in his letters. Photo by Dieter Mitternacht.

Concluding Thoughts

Paul seems to have had reason, more than once, to defend himself against the suspicion that he might be an insecure and meek person. He does so by demonstrating in his writing his readiness and tenacity to face the suspicion of indecisiveness. During his visit to Galatia, his aim had been to resemble the crucified Christ. This

31. Mitternacht, "'Forceful and Demanding,'" 375–90.

had attracted the goodwill of the believers, but it had also awakened, from Paul's perspective, an incorrect grasp of the gospel's claim to truth. Can the harsh and intolerant tone, offensive to the modern reader who knows Paul only through his letters, have been a rhetorical device, a means, at times ironic, of combatting the suspicion of indecisiveness by those who knew him from personal encounters?

Galatians contains several parallel themes, one of which concerns Christ-like suffering. Through the proclamation of the self-sacrificing Christ (1:4) the introduction signals the theme, which is made explicit in the affirmation "I have been crucified with Christ" (2:19), generalized by the request, "Friends, I beg you, become as I am, for I also have become as you are" (4:12), and accentuated in the conclusion of the letter ("I carry the marks of Jesus branded on my body," 6:17). With the construction of 1:8–10 Paul attempts to show with rhetorical finesse that he rejects flawed weakness and that he propagates a Christ-like weakness instead. The addressees were to understand that life with Christ does not entail docility, but rather a determination against all odds to hold fast to the calling to suffer in the image of the crucified.

Unfortunately, history remains silent on whether Paul was successful in the end. But what has been passed down through generations of theologians and artists for two thousand years is the image of a stern and decisive apostle—a picture that may have to be revised. Questions and doubts concerning the consistency of Paul's argumentation, oral or written, whether his contingent affirmations have a coherent core, and what he aspired to with his claim to "become all things to all people, that [he] might by all means save some" (1 Cor 9:22) continue to be a matter of dispute among modern readers and interpreters of his letters. (See the section "Paul, His Assemblies, and His Successors," p. 399.)

Further Reading

Aune, David E. *The New Testament in Its Literary Environment*. LEC. Philadelphia: Westminster John Knox, 1987.

Carter, Warren, and Amy-Jill Levine. *The New Testament: Methods and Meanings*. Nashville: Abingdon, 2013.

Green, Joel B., ed. *Hearing the New Testament: Strategies for Interpretation*. 2nd ed. Grand Rapids: Eerdmans, 2010.

Hartman, Lars. *Approaching New Testament Texts and Contexts*. WUNT 311. Tübingen: Mohr Siebeck, 2013.

Hayes, John R., and Carl R. Holladay. *Biblical Exegesis: A Beginner's Handbook*. 3rd ed. Louisville: Westminster John Knox, 2007.

Hull, Robert F. *The Story of the New Testament Text: Movers, Materials, Motives, Methods, and Models*. Atlanta: Society of Biblical Literature, 2010.

Mitternacht, D. "'Forceful and Demanding': On Paul as Letter Writer." *Theology and Life* 36 (2013): 375–90.
Nanos, Mark, ed. *The Galatians Debate: Contemporary Issues in Rhetorical and Historical Interpretation.* Peabody, MA: Hendrickson, 2002.

Lost and Found: A Narrative-Critical Reading of Luke 15

A Brief Introduction to Narrative Criticism

In order to take seriously that the gospels and Acts are each cast in narrative form, interpreters have looked for resources and tools within studies of literary theory. A spoken or written account of connected events, real or imaginary, presented in a sequence of written or spoken words, is often called a story or a narrative. How do we deal with the fact that narrative texts have a built-in polyphony in that they allow for, and even may include, several contradictory voices? In biblical studies, the constellation of interest and variety of practices in the study of narratives has been consolidated under the heading *narrative criticism*.[32]

In the late 1970s interpreters began to challenge the dominant historical-critical approach within the field and asked: So what? What is the meaning of the text as a whole? What is the overall message of, for example, the Gospel of Luke? What is the plot or the story line? What does this have to do with us as readers? In addition, interpreters of the Gospel of John started asking questions about meaning on a different level, with the groundbreaking work of Alan Culpepper as a remarkable starting point.[33] The interest in biblical texts as historical or theological documents was met by an approach that read them as literary texts, with a narrative focus.

Whereas a historical-critical approach asks questions such as what kind of political system was at work in the Mediterranean region at the time of Jesus, or what kind of ship Paul might have used on his missionary travels, narrative approaches are instead concerned with the deeper meaning of the story. The main idea is that readers of the gospels should read the narratives and relate to them as they present themselves in their final form. The work aims at involving and engaging the reader, as well as inviting the reader to share in the text's point of view, attitudes, and values.

Narrative criticism invites the reader to assess the work as a whole and to note stylistic characteristics that resemble those of other narratives, such as a novel or a film. Repetitions, inconsistencies, or gaps in a narrative are treated not as signs of diverse sources or flawed editing but as tools of communication, indications of an overall plot. Although at times this approach contests prominent opinions, the focus

32. Green, *Methods for Luke*, 74.
33. Culpepper, *Anatomy of the Fourth Gospel.*

of narrative criticism is always on the final form of the text, not on any earlier layers or on the role of a potential editor.

Readers are seen as active, as opposed to passive, recipients of an open text, since there is no single meaning of a biblical text. The responses of readers vary; the place from where a text is read influences which voices from the narrative polyphony resound the strongest.

According to Joel B. Green, who has contributed significantly to the study of narrative approaches to the New Testament, "the list of literary devices to which narrative critics might attend is practically endless." The main purpose, as he sees it, is to develop "literary sensibilities" and "a close reading of the text."[34] Nevertheless, a few elements may be considered central to narrative criticism of biblical texts:

1. *Staging*. Here we ask for a whole set of issues related to where, when, and how the scene is staged. The reader can be imagined as holding a camera. Who, then, is in the center of the scene? What is in focus? Is anyone or anything zoomed in? Furthermore, what about geography or architecture? Paying attention to what artifacts, tools, or animals frame the scene is also important. Where are the objects or characters located in relation to each other? How is time and place changing from scene to scene?
2. *Characters and characterization*. Narratives give us insights about characters either by *telling* or *showing*. For example, Lazarus was a poor man, we are told in Luke's Gospel (16:20), and the rich man from the same story is shown as arrogant by his behavior toward Lazarus (16:24, 27). A character's insights, words, and responses contribute to our understanding of him or her either as a sympathetic character, such as Jesus or the Virgin Mary, or as an antihero, such as Judas. Main characters are surrounded by minor characters, some of which are named and some of which remain anonymous. All characters, however, can develop and change as the narrative progresses. Ambiguous characters, such as the apostle Peter, behave according to, or in contradiction of, the gospel's point of view, depending on which scene and what events are being reported. What kinds of actions and events are the characters involved in?
3. *Plot*. The outline of events in a narrative, or the structure of the action, or the final end toward which everything in the work leads, directly or indirectly, is called the plot. In the gospels as a whole the plot can be said to be the evangelist's interpretation of the story. But how is the story developing—how does it start and how does it end? The plot of Luke's Gospel in narrative terms might consist of showing that Jesus, who was sent from God, was the Messiah and brought salvation to the world. Smaller sections relate to this overall plot, although these can also contain subplots of their own.

34. Green, *Methods for Luke*, 98.

Looking for such elements in texts gives readers a necessary sensibility. Narrative criticism hopefully makes the text more interesting and meaningful; it is used not merely as a method of reconstructing history or finding one isolated theological message. More than just reporting long lists documenting which narrative elements may be found in a story or a work, narrative criticism invites readers to meet the text with a certain attitude or expectation. A list of narrative elements can function as a starting point for critical discussions. Like the reader of a novel or the audience of a play or a movie, stories from the Bible *expect* involvement. The reader can identify or recognize parts of his or her own life in narratives, and stories therefore contribute to the reader's understanding of the world.

A Narrative Approach to Luke 15

Scholars have applied narrative-criticism approaches to the whole Gospel of Luke or on Luke-Acts as a literary unit. Robert Tannehill's *The Narrative Unity of Luke-Acts: A Literary Interpretation* is one example of a work treating the entire body of texts together. Also, smaller sections can be read with a special focus on various narrative elements.

In the following we will look at Luke 15, a compact collection of three parables on being lost and found. Because of its central theological message and influential reception in history and art, some interpreters call this chapter *the heart* of Luke's Gospel. Staging, characters, and plot are central analytical categories.

The Opening Scene and Its Characters

Luke 15 starts with a small frame narrative, which introduces the three stories and gives some important narrative information: "Now all the tax collectors and sinners were coming near to listen to him [Jesus]. And the Pharisees and the scribes were grumbling and saying, 'This fellow welcomes sinners and eats with them.' So he told them this parable . . ." (vv. 1–3)

If we look at the staging here, two groups of characters are surrounding the main character (Jesus): first we have the tax collectors and the sinners (as a collective group), who are moving and coming near Jesus to listen to him. They are sympathetic to the main character and show the ideal attitude of the narrative: they are coming near in order to listen. Indeed, we are shown, through their actions and attitudes, what kind of characters they are, even though no words or thoughts are reported on their part in this scene.

The second group of characters, however, the Pharisees and the scribes, are grumbling. They show a skeptical attitude to the main character. They do not come close, and instead increase the distance, as demonstrated by their critical words. They also characterize both the main character ("this fellow") and the group who are close to Jesus ("sinners") by the use of negative terms. Two aspects of Jesus's actions are criticized: he both welcomes sinners *and* eats with them. But the reader's sympathy is not supposed to be influenced by the Pharisees and the scribes' attitude. Their point of view is reported, but neither their actions nor their words belong to the narrative's ideal universe or worldview.

The overall plot of Luke's Gospel is intended to show that Jesus is the Savior of the whole world. In chapter 15 it is clearly demonstrated that tax collectors and sinners, too, are included in this "whole world." Jesus's welcoming them and eating with them are concrete events showing what kind of character he is. Luke places Jesus together with them, without fearing that their low status might influence the main character negatively. The presence of these characters (tax collectors and sinners) in this scene contributes a great deal to the overall plot of the gospel.

The Many Levels of Plot

As an answer to the Pharisees and the scribes' accusation, the main character (Jesus) tells three stories, three parables: the first about a man (a "shepherd") who leaves the ninety-nine sheep to search for the single one that is lost; the second about a woman who loses one coin, who lights a lamp, and searches carefully until she finds it; and the last about a man who has two sons, the youngest of which asks for his share of the property, squanders it abroad, and finally comes home again. The last scene of each of the three stories includes some sort of celebration and joy. It is suggested that the reader carefully review Luke 15:4–32 in order to fully follow and understand the rest of this section.

As part of Luke's overall plot, these parables can be grouped together with other stories of being lost and being found. Already in Luke 2, the twelve-year-old Jesus is lost from his parents on their way home from Jerusalem, but after three days he is found in the temple, his Father's house (Luke 2:41–52). At the end of the gospel, Jesus is lost in the darkness of death, but after three days he is found and comes back as the risen Lord (Luke 23:44–24:12). The three parables also deal with being lost and found as the central plot. But if we read the text with literary sensibility and pay attention to the polyphony, what kind of narrative universe are we invited into in Luke 15?

To state that these three stories are "parallel" will not suffice for the purposes of narrative criticism. If the message is the same, why are three parables in a row included in the narrative? If the point is that God searches for those lost, why bother presenting all three stories? Seen from a narrative point of view, a text's message is not wrapped in arbitrary narrative frames. The narrative elements all contribute in order to construct meaning in a story. More detail and nuances are needed. From a narrative perspective, it matters a great deal that the parables manifest in different narrative worlds, with differences in staging and characters.

As we have seen, we can talk about plot on many different levels. Obviously, the gospel as such has an overall plot. In addition, a small narrative can also have a separate subplot. In summary, there are a great deal of interpretative possibilities that follow from this approach: we can look for the overall plot within chapter 15, argue that the three stories share the same plot as other stories of being lost and found that occur in the gospel, or posit that each of the three parables has its own subplot. All of these plots or structures of action can then, of course, overlap and intersect in a variety of ways.

Claudia Carolina Coréa Ortíz, *A Path to Follow*. Jim Elfström / IKON Church of Sweden Picture Archive.

Questioning the Main Characters

Obtaining tools that help in studying characters and characterization is one of the great benefits that come with narrative criticism. Let us first look for the main characters, which are all anonymous. In the first parable it is obviously the shepherd (or, rather, a man), in the second the woman, and in the third the youngest son (or maybe his brother or the father?). The shepherd and the woman are presented as fairly simple characters, doing their one task, with no time to develop or change during the narrative. In the last story, the youngest son seems to go from being a decent and proper young man to being an outcast who hangs around day workers, slaves, and prostitutes, only to once more return to being a proper son of the household.

The ninety-nine plus one sheep can perhaps be called characters—they are living animals—although they do not initiate any action but are rather *acted on* in the story. The nine plus one coins can hardly be called characters, but function more like artifacts, objects, or tools. The one plus one sons are indeed characters, main or perhaps minor.

The third story, with its many characters and development, is fruitful for discussing potential different plots. Depending on how the story is read, both brothers, as well as their father, can be the main character. If we read this story as the third one in a sequence that is written with the theme of losing and finding, it is the father who can be listed with the shepherd and the woman. He has lost his son and then finds him again. If the focus, however, is on which character gets most attention, the youngest son definitely has the most time in the spotlight. And what about the oldest son? Is the story perhaps about him and how hard it is to stay at home and take care of everything, trying to be loyal and faithful?

In addition to these three characters, several minor, simple characters, doing their task and then leaving, populate the story: the man that the son hired himself to in order to earn a living in the foreign country (v. 15); the people (coworkers?) he talks to in his need when he comes to himself (v. 17); the father's slaves (v. 22); another slave talking to the older brother (v. 26); the older brother's friends (v. 29); and the prostitutes in the foreign country (v. 30). Without these characters and their small tasks, we would not be reading the same narrative.

In contrast to the first two narratives, the third one has an intricate plotline and a whole gallery of main and minor characters, whose roles can be questioned and discussed. Some interpreters have also used narrative criticism and argued that one character is missing from this last story: in this household with a father, sons, and slaves, there is a marked absence of a mother.

Staging the Scenes

The characters of the three stories are set in places that are typical for their roles and related to geography and architecture: in the wilderness, in the household setting, or in a foreign country. The shepherd moves around alone. He leaves the ninety-nine sheep out there in the wilderness and looks for the one that is lost. It is easy to imagine, although not specifically mentioned in the text, a setting in which the shepherd wanders around in the mountains for a very long time, becoming more and more desperate as it gradually gets darker and the sheep he loves is still nowhere to be found. And when he finds the lost sheep, the poor animal is shivering, very afraid. The text tells us that the shepherd rejoices and carries the lost one back to the ninety-nine on his shoulders. And then he celebrates with others.

The woman, on the other hand, remains in the house but is also on her own. She loses one of her ten coins and starts searching for it. The house must have been dark, since she needed a lamp. She sweeps the house and finally finds it. She too celebrates with others.

The last story, with its more complex storyline, moves with the youngest son from place to place in the various scenes, from the father's house to a foreign country, to the field of pigs, to the way home, to the homecoming party. Several scenes are presented. The oldest son is in the fields and returns home, stopping on his way to talk with a slave messenger, and then remains outside the place of celebration, where he accuses his father. Almost comically, the celebration seems to go on, without the oldest son.

The time aspect also differs: looking for a sheep may take the whole day, while finding a coin inside a house probably takes less time. The third story has a much longer time span; it might take weeks, months, or years before the lost son comes home.

The Last Scene: A Happy Ending

Another narrative element borrowed from film and fiction deals with how the story develops, how the plot ends. Do these stoires have happy endings?

In the first story, the shepherd leaves the ninety-nine sheep to look for the one that is lost. A reader or listener from antiquity—or others with experience or competence in sheep holding—would perhaps have thought this act irresponsible and stupid: leaving them in the wilderness means some of them risk being killed by wild animals, or perhaps they might run away. To risk ninety-nine for one introduces a scale of value into the narrative's worldview, signaling that the shepherd cares more about the one sheep. This impression is strengthened by the comment given by Jesus after the parable: "Just so, I tell you, there will be more joy in heaven over one sinner who repents than over ninety-nine righteous persons who need no repentance" (v. 7). The impression that Jesus is less concerned about the majority is articulated in a comparison: the single lost sheep is the sinner whom Jesus speaks of, and his repentance is more worthy of celebration than that of ninety-nine righteous persons (or sheep). A celebration indicates a happy ending to the story, yes, but some disharmony and conflict are introduced in the ending as well. Some are apparently not worth celebrating, since they are not repentant sinners.

In the last story, a similar conflict is spelled out in more detail. The oldest brother feels excluded from the party. He expresses his dissatisfaction and confronts his father, and in his anger refuses to enter. He finds the celebration unfair.

In both of these stories, the party is not for everyone. Some of the characters are excluded from it. In the second story, however, where the woman finds her lost coin, there is a happy ending for all. "When she has found it, she calls together her friends and neighbors, saying, 'Rejoice with me, for I have found the coin that I had lost.' Just so, I tell you, there is joy in the presence of the angels of God over one sinner who repents" (vv. 9–10). Indeed, nobody is here excluded from rejoicing, neither when women friends and neighbors are invited (the friends and neighbors are female in the Greek text) nor in Jesus's commentary.

How does the narrative element of a "happy ending" influence the plot of the different stories? One might say that the second story works best as a narrative of joy. Neighbors and friends are invited to share in the joy when what was lost is found. In the first and the last story, the joy is incomplete. The story of the woman and the coin is unambiguous in communicating a message of joy when something is found. Thus, the plot of the final celebrations in chapter 15 moves from incomplete to complete to incomplete. The staging of the second story with its female characters is complete, with no exceptions. The second story has a unique interpretative potential: the female community appears as the most complete model for celebrating joy.

The Narrative World and Its Reception

It is beyond doubt that the first and last narratives of Luke 15 have enjoyed the most influential reception. As stories, they are rich, complex, and easy to remember. The shepherd has become a favorite image of the Lord, building on Old Testament/Hebrew Bible stories of the Good Shepherd. Painters and other artists have presented the sheep in the wilderness, found in church art and most children's Bibles. Also, the lost and found son has become something of an archetype: when he is in the deepest darkness and desperation, far away from his father's house, he comes to himself and returns. The motif of the running and welcoming father is among the most painted biblical scenes. The shepherd and the father are well-integrated images of God in Christian thought.

But why are there so few depictions of the second parable and its characters? This small narrative consists of only three verses and has not had the same reception. The reason for this may be found, first, in that the two parables work better as narratives. A lost sheep in the wilderness or a lost son in a foreign country is easier to identify with than a lifeless lost coin inside a dark house. At first glance, the plots are richer and are staged in a more complex manner in these stories. They are more interesting to depict in art as well. Second, and perhaps more important, the way each story lets certain characters portray God must be considered. Shepherd and father seem acceptable, but what about a woman? How can she be an image of the divine? And whereas the shepherd invites his fellow friends and neighbors to celebrate with him, and the father holds a party with his household, it is the *female* neighbors and friends who represent "the angels of God" in the second story.

The female presence at the center of the stage, with a woman doing female tasks and the celebration as an event for female friends and neighbors, has probably contributed to the story's limited influence in reception and interpretation within a tradition that favors the male subject position for humans and God. The narrative world of this story has been too dangerous or too trivial to be given a prominent position in the reception history.

Reading with a "literary sensibility," a close narrative reading of the text nevertheless reveals a potential for the second parable. It has its own specific plot. It includes a happy ending that overcomes the divided joy of what was lost but now found. The female characters do not have objections; they do not say no to a party. The celebration is for everyone, and all are invited—not only those of the household but neighbors and friends as well. And nobody complains, just like the angels of God.

Concluding Remarks

Narrative criticism offers tools that help readers to see biblical stories as narratives; they are stories told to involve and engage readers. Paying attention to narrative elements helps interpreters see how these texts participate in complex communication processes. Narrative criticism in all its variety, with its specific vocabulary borrowed from literary studies, offers terms and concepts to talk about narrative observations in a more nuanced way. The special foci suggested here—on plot, characters, and staging—contribute to distinguish certain streams in the polyphony of New Testament stories. Various characters and events contribute to convince the readers of the story's plot.

The position from which a text is read contributes to the reading and the construction of meaning. Different narrative worlds may appeal to different readers. For example, in a context where different kinds of women in the global world are active Bible interpreters, stories such as the second parable in Luke 15 with its specific plot, characters, and staging have potential to gain new relevance. In addition, in a context of conflict and disagreement, this story with its happy ending, where all are invited to the celebration, can be a more relevant narrative than those including elements of struggle and objection. The story about good neighbors who share moments of joy with each other has the potential to be a collective metanarrative of coexistence in a divided world.

Narrative criticism contributes to opening up interpretative potential and invites the readers to be active participants, to be involved in the production of meaning. The three stories of Luke 15 should therefore not be reduced to "parallels"—as simply repeating the same message over again—because they have different narrative worlds, characters, and staging. Each of them has a unique narrative meaning. Here, literary sensibility and curiosity work as tools for close reading.

These are some of the contributions that narrative criticism can provide in the process of interpreting biblical texts. But there are also other questions to be asked. For example, what do we know about the Pharisees and the scribes at the time of Jesus? Who are the characters in Luke 15 that complain about the celebration supposed to represent? What is a parable? How can a shepherd, who is dirty, living around animals far away from civilization, be an ideal image of God? How can a woman performing everyday female tasks, celebrating with her neighbors and friends, represent God? Why is it only Luke among the Synoptics who includes the two last parables? These are indeed important questions, although not the main focus of narrative criticism. Although not primarily interested in the historical circumstances of the text, such as the text's prehistory, narrative analyses of the final form of biblical texts can benefit from considerations of the symbolic world of the text in its own time.

In order to initiate reflection on these questions, we need to combine narrative criticism with other approaches from the interdisciplinary field of biblical exegesis. Narrative criticism may offer answers to some interpretative questions, but will inevitably raise new ones in so doing.

Further Reading

Green, Joel B. *Methods for Luke*. Cambridge: Cambridge University Press, 2010.

Tannehill, Robert C. *The Narrative Unity of Luke-Acts: A Literary Interpretation*. 2 vols. Minneapolis: Fortress, 1990–1994.

Thatcher, Tom, and Stephen D. Moore, eds. *Anatomies of Narrative Criticism: The Past, Present, and Futures of the Fourth Gospel as Literature*. Atlanta: Society of Biblical Literature, 2008.

"One New Humanity" (Eph 2:15): A Pauline Tradition and Its Reception History

According to Eph 2:14–15, Jesus has abolished the law and torn down the wall dividing Jews and non-Jews so that "he might create in himself one new humanity in place of the two, thus making peace." Later in the same letter (4:24), the author adds an imperative: "clothe yourselves with the new self, created according to the likeness of God in true righteousness and holiness."

The concept of the new human being has generated a number of varying interpretations and theories among scholars. A modern Nicaraguan preacher interprets the text as presenting a method by which to achieve peace among the Abrahamic religions: "All of us—Jews, Christians, Muslims—need to hear this gospel of peace, preached by the Jewish prophets, Christian apostles, and the Muslim prophet from Mecca: that God means to create a new human being, a new generation of people, in order to forge peace and put an end to enmity." Other interpreters have come to the surprising conclusion that Jesus, the new human being, wasn't Jewish at all, or that his Jewishness is of no relevance to Christian identity. In terms of the history of ideas, the Marxist utopia concept is linked to this text as well, since it advocates a new society devoid of class differences and conflicts. All the examples discussed so far are examples of the text's modern reception history. We shall, however, attempt to trace an earlier reception history, where Ephesians itself exemplifies the reception of Paul's undisputed letters. One result of this innovative reception of Paul is the concept of the new human being.

Ephesians is one of the disputed Pauline letters and was most likely written approximately a decade after Paul's death. Several scholars believe that the author of the letter had access to and made use of Colossians, which is one of the earliest of the disputed letters. This hypothesis is not without its faults. On the one hand, there are serious scholars who continue to assert that at least Colossians and possibly Ephesians should be attributed to Paul. On the other hand, one cannot ignore the fact that the seven undisputed letters may have been edited later (a common hypothesis), or that some of them actually belong among the disputed letters (a more rare assertion). Despite these issues, one can say with confidence that Ephesians belongs to the Pauline tradition, in which the thoughts of the apostle were expanded on in new situations.

Paul did not coin the phrase "one new human being" (*hena kainon anthrōpon*), but the thoughts behind the concept can be found in the genuine letters. According to Ephesians, the "one new human being" refers in part to Jesus, who has created it in his own being, and in part to Christians, who are supposed to "clothe themselves" in it. These two aspects are connected already in Paul. Paul was convinced that Christ represented something radically new, and that those who were "in Christ" represented a new creation. Indeed, Paul saw the Christian community as the body of Christ. Thus, these thoughts are all genuinely Pauline, expressed in Ephesians as "the new humanity," a new race even, that is different from Jews and non-Jews. We shall here consider three aspects—Christology, ecclesiology, and anthropology—found first in Paul, then in Colossians, and lastly in Ephesians, in order to find out how the author of Ephesians builds on and develops Paul's theology.

Christ as the New Adam: A Pauline Christology

Especially in his letter to the Romans, Paul elaborates on the incompatibility of Adam and Christ. According to Rom 5:12–20, sin, and thus death, came into the world through the actions of the first human. But Adam is also Christ's counterpart, wherefore Paul introduces a *typological* interpretation. Christ is at once the counterpart and opposite of Adam. This typological interpretation resurfaces in 1 Cor 15:45–49, where he interprets the story of creation and states that "the first man, Adam, became a living being," arguing that "the first man was from the earth, a man of dust; the second man is from heaven." Thus, Adam was an earthly creature, in contrast to Christ, who was from heaven. Thanks to Christ, we now have the possibility of becoming the true image of God: "Just as we have borne the image of the man of dust, we will also bear the image of the man of heaven."

The concept of two separate figures, Adam and Christ, may seem like a rather liberal interpretation of the story of creation, despite the fact that it is in part based on Genesis, which includes two creation stories. According to the first story, God says,

Ato Matewos Legesse, *Exile*. Jim Elfström / IKON Church of Sweden Picture Archive.

"Let us make humankind in our image, according to our likeness," and then continues to create humankind "in his image, in the image of God he created them; male and female he created them" (Gen 1:26–27). The other story, described in Gen 2:7, states, "God formed man from the dust of the ground, and breathed into his nostrils the breath of life; and the man became a living being." After this, God creates Eve from Adam's rib bone. Only the first story explicitly states that humankind was created in the likeness of God.

Thus, the creation story lends itself to speculations as to the existence of a second angelic or holy human being in heaven. The Jewish philosopher Philo of Alexandria interpreted the text in Platonic fashion, arguing that the perfect human being, the true image of God, was only a thought in God's head. Within the gnostic tradition, the story of creation and the first sin yielded a complicated mythology, which explained the creation of the visible world and outlined the way back to the heavenly origins of humanity. However, the fully developed gnostic system did not come into use until the second century CE. Rather, Paul's Adam/Christ typology is apocalyptically oriented, focusing on God's recreation of the world through Christ. In Romans, Paul expresses his hope that all of creation will be recreated at the end of time, while upholding that the most important thing will be the coming glory of Christ followers: "For the creation waits with eager longing for the revealing of the children of God; for the creation was subjected to futility, not of its own will but by the will of the one who subjected it, in hope that the creation itself will be set free from its bondage to decay and will obtain the freedom of the glory of the children of God" (Rom 8:19–21). The glory that Paul speaks of is a pure spiritual existence, one that Christ has already achieved. In 2 Corinthians, Paul compares Jesus with Moses. In this comparison, everything in the past, including the law, fades away and ends up becoming impermanent. The new spiritual existence will also be shared by believers in Christ: "And all of us, with unveiled faces, seeing the glory of the Lord as though reflected in a mirror, are being transformed into the same image from one degree of glory to another; for this comes from the Lord, the Spirit" (2 Cor 3:18).

The Old and the New Man: A Pauline Concept of Human Beings

Paul realized that the full glory of his vision for the future was not yet consummated. Followers of Christ, however, were given a foretaste by means of the Holy Spirit of what is to come. In addition, Paul was convinced that believers did experience a real transformation through their communion with Christ: "So if anyone is in Christ, there is a new creation: everything old has passed away; see, everything has become new!" (2 Cor 5:17). In Gal 6:15, Paul speaks of this "new creation" again. Indeed, for Paul, in baptism the believer "died" with the crucified Christ and was "buried" with him, in order to be resurrected to a new life with him (Rom 6:1–14). Thus, in accordance with the ritual of baptism, it makes sense when Paul says, "As many of you as were baptized into Christ have clothed yourselves with Christ" (Gal 3:27).

However, while Paul asserts that baptism brings about a "new creation," he also thinks that "the old man" from before repentance and baptism has not completely vanished. Paul's terminology is somewhat confusing, since he also speaks about the "outer" and "inner" natures: "So we do not lose heart. Even though our outer nature is wasting away, our inner nature is being renewed day by day" (2 Cor 4:16). The renewal of an individual involves a constant struggle of striving toward doing God's will and controlling one's sinful impulses. "Do not be conformed to this world but be transformed by the renewing of your minds, so that you may discern what is the will of God—what is good and acceptable and perfect" (Rom 12:2).

The Assembly as the Body of Christ: Paul's View of the Church

Paul's baptismal theology encompassed a community aspect, since an individual who was baptized and renewed in the name of Christ became a member of the assembly. The new community was meant to unite everyone "in Christ" so that previous differences between human beings were erased: "There is no longer Jew or Greek, there is no longer slave or free, there is no longer male and female; for all of you are one in Christ Jesus" (Gal 3:28). Of these contrasting identities, the difference between Jews and non-Jews (Greeks, gentiles) was most pertinent to Paul (cf. Rom 10:12). Most important, the law of Moses must not be a barrier between Jews and non-Jews *in terms of salvation* (see also the section "Paul, His Assemblies, and His Successors," p. 418).

In 1 Cor 12, Paul applies to the Christian community a well-known political metaphor about society as a body with many different functions. The thought recurs in Rom 12:4–5: "For as in one body we have many members, and not all the members have the same function, so we, who are many, are one body in Christ, and individually we are members one of another." Paul does not bond the idea of the *ekklēsia* as the body of Christ with the typology about Jesus as the last Adam. There is, however, an important association between them as both are *collective* models. Christ and Adam represent all of humanity in one single individual, and the *ekklēsia* as the body of Christ is an entity composed of many members. Since both models describe Christ as a collective person, further associations between them developed in the Pauline school.

"The Old and New Man" in Colossians

All these Pauline concepts may be found behind Col 3:9–11 when it refers to "the old self" and "the new self": "Do not lie to one another, seeing that you have stripped off the old self with its practices and have clothed yourselves with the new self, which is being renewed in knowledge according to the image of its creator. In that renewal there is no longer Greek and Jew, circumcised and uncircumcised, barbarian, Scythian, slave and free; but Christ is all and in all!" In this exhortation, the Pauline terminology is slightly expanded as it urges followers of Christ to "strip off the old self" and "clothe yourself with the new self." Reminiscent of Gal 3:27, this new existence erases the barrier between Jews and non-Jews, a distinction that seems less pertinent in Colossians, since it adds "barbarian" and "Scythian" as it encourages the supersession of national and ethnic boundaries. The pair "male and female" is not mentioned at all, which is not surprising when one considers Col 3:18: "Wives, be subject to your husbands, as is fitting in the Lord." However, the pair "slave and free" remains despite Col 3:22: "Slaves, obey your earthly masters in everything, not only while being watched and in order to please them, but wholeheartedly, fearing the Lord." The idea of Christ as the new Adam is implicitly present in the encouragement to become the image of the Creator. Colossians 1:15–20 recites a hymn that affirms Christ as the "image of the invisible God, the firstborn of all creation" (v. 15). Thus, to become the image of God means becoming like Christ. Despite this being a logical necessity, it is not very prominent in Colossians, likely because the letter as a whole propagates a hierarchical view of society, the church, and the Christian family. Paul's idea of the church as the body of Christ is developed hierarchically so that Christ now is "the head" of the body (Col 1:18).

"The New Man" in the Letter to the Ephesians

In contrast to Colossians, "the new man" in Ephesians is a direct reference to Christ, who in his person has created a single, new human being. One may wonder whether this concept implies that Jesus was not a Jew. However, obviously the reference is not to the earthly Jesus but to the heavenly Christ. Paul had no interest in Jesus's earthly life other than his being "born of a woman, born under the law" (Gal 4:4). For Paul, the crucified Christ was a symbol of the end of the last epoch of time before the salvation of the world, and as such also the end of the "old human," who stands under the law of sin and must be kept "dead" (Rom 6:10–11). The risen Christ, who is the last Adam, is part of the new creation, the new order of humanity.

In Ephesians, this Pauline tradition is developed and expanded beyond Paul's own writings. That Jesus's death on the cross overturned the law is an idea that Paul would not confirm; his emphasis was on the believers' removal from under the law, and in Rom 3:31 he argues that the law itself was not at all superseded by faith in Christ. However, Ephesians clearly states that the Mosaic law, which was seen as a barrier between Jews and non-Jews, has been overturned, so that Jews and non-Jews can unite in the new spiritual human, Christ. Also new in Ephesians is the strong emphasis on the reconciliation between Jews and non-Jews. From this perspective, Ephesians stands in contrast to Paul, who spoke bitterly of an irreconcilable enmity between the old and new covenants in Gal 4:21–31—yet Paul himself seems to take back most of that in Rom 9–11.

As in Colossians, Christ is the "head" of the body (*ekklēsia*), yet, at the same time, all Christians should unite in him (Eph 4:15). In Eph 5:25–33 this unification is expressed as a secret, a mystery, and is compared to the union between a man and his wife. The individual believer is initiated in this new body through the purifying waters of baptism (v. 26). Thus the assembly becomes the bride of Christ: "so as to present the church to himself in splendor, without a spot or wrinkle or anything of the kind—yes, so that she may be holy and without blemish. In the same way, husbands should love their wives as they do their own bodies" (vv. 27–28). In order to understand the marriage metaphor, one needs to keep the second story of creation in mind, where the first woman is created from Adam's rib bone. "Therefore a man leaves his father and his mother and clings to his wife, and they become one flesh" (Gen 2:24). Christ and his *ekklēsia* become one creature, where Christ is responsible for spiritual perfection, and the assembly for the visible and physical (cleansed by the purifying waters of baptism) part.

While Colossians still looks forward toward the imminent return of Christ (see Col 3:1–4), Ephesians speaks instead of a constant process, where the "entire body"—that is, the *ekklēsia*—grows and expands in love (Eph 4:16). The assembly is compared to a temple, a holy building that is "built upon the foundation of the apostles and prophets, with Christ Jesus himself as the cornerstone" (Eph 2:20). Paul is, of course, counted as one of the apostles. The author of Ephesians, writing after the death of his teacher (Paul), knows that the *ekklēsia* is here to stay.

The Third Race: From Ephesians to the Church Fathers

The idea of the "new human being" presented in Ephesians bears witness to a growing self-awareness among Christians toward the end of the first century. From originally being a Jewish movement, they came to view themselves as something new in a predominantly gentile context. Paul and his successors are one source of this development. During the second century, Paul was appealed to by Marcion, who drew the radical conclusion that the God of Christianity is different from the God of Judaism and the old covenant. Other non-Jewish Christians saw greater continuity yet believed that the Christian *ekklēsia* had taken Israel's place as the chosen people of God. This so-called replacement theology proved extremely destructive and is still all too common a perception.

Ephesians' vision of reconciliation between Jews and non-Jews in the new human being, Christ, is more accommodating regarding the affiliation with Judaism. It represents a much-needed alternative to the sense of bitterness and enmity between the two covenants as it is expressed in Paul's convoluted allegory in Gal 4. It has often been assumed that the author of Ephesians was a Christian Jew, who reminds the Pauline *ekklēsia* of its Jewish roots. This, however, is uncertain, since both Colossians and Ephesians are targeting a non-Jewish audience: according to both, the Mosaic law represents the old, superseded religion.

Resounding the spirit of Ephesians, Christians during the fourth century were often referred to as "the third race" (*tertium genus hominum*), different from both Jews and non-Jews. However, traces of replacement theology may be found behind this terminology, since the idea of God's people, the chosen representatives for all of humanity, is transferred from the Jewish people to non-Jewish Christianity. It is also misleading to assume that Ephesians proclaims the universality of Christianity over a nationalistically determined Judaism. The Christian movement had deep roots in Judaism. The lawless gospel for non-Jews was proclaimed by Paul, a Jew, whose utopia of a new creation was inspired by an interpretation of the creation story in the Hebrew Bible.

Further Reading

Harrill, J. Albert. "Ethnic Fluidity in Ephesians." *NTS* 60 (2014): 379–402.
Lüdemann, Gerd. *Heretics: The Other Side of Early Christianity*. Louisville: Westminster John Knox, 1996.
Ziesler, J. A. *Pauline Christianity*. Oxford: Oxford University Press, 1990.

Living in the Time after Jesus: A Hermeneutical Analysis of the Johannine Farewell Discourse in John 13–17

The lengthy farewell speech in John 13–17 has sometimes been called Jesus's "last will." It is a passage that invites the reader to hermeneutical reflections. Hermeneutical exegesis focuses on problems in the text that are relevant to Bible readers and interpreters here and now. The farewell speech is unique to the Gospel of John, and it reflects the faith and life of the community behind the gospel. Therefore, we must pay close attention to the specific literary and historical context of the text. Yet the problems articulated were common to all early followers of Christ. How were they supposed to live their lives in the time *after* Jesus, and in which ways was he still present and active? The answers to these questions given in the farewell speech resurface in many variations in the writings of all Christian groups—both then and now.

The Farewell Speech in the Gospel of John: Literary and Editorial Observations

The Gospel of John can be divided into either two or three main parts, depending on whether chapters 13–17 (the farewell speech) are seen as part of the passion narrative (chs. 18–21), or as a separate part. Chapters 1–12 are about Jesus's public ministry to the Jews, while chapter 13 together with 12:37–50 marks a decisive turning point in the gospel. Jesus bids his disciples farewell (chs. 13–17), is crucified and resurrected (chs. 18–21), and then returns to the Father. The parting scene between Jesus and his disciples, composed of the Last Supper and the farewell speech, forms the center of the gospel, both summarizing Jesus's earthly ministry and providing insights for the time after Jesus. The farewell speech with its narrative frame can be divided into the following sections:

The Last Supper (13:1–30): Jesus washes the feet of his disciples and points out who will betray him

The First Farewell Speech (13:31–14:3)

a. Introduction/transition from the passion narrative to farewell speech (13:31–38)

b. "Do not be afraid": Jesus bids farewell (14:1–31)

The Second Farewell Speech (15:1–16:33)

a. "Remain in me": the vine and the branches, etc. (15:1–16:4a)

b. "I have much to tell you": about the time to come (16:4b–33)

Jesus's Prayer to the Father (17:1–26)

The Last Supper sets the scene for both the farewell speech and the passion story. The Johannine passion narrative agrees in general with the Synoptic Gospels. However, noteworthy deviations include the introduction of the beloved disciple, who lies next to Jesus during the supper (13:23), and the detailed description of how Jesus washes his disciples' feet. The farewell speech may have been recited and transmitted orally at first, probably during gatherings and agape meals. With time it was linked to a written passion narrative that was similar to Mark's. The first speech ends with the words "Rise, let us be on our way" (14:31; cf. Mark 14:42). The reader expects the passion narrative to begin (compare 18:1–2 with Mark 14:23), but instead yet another speech follows. The second farewell speech (chs. 15–16) and the concluding prayer (ch. 17) may include older oral traditions, but theses chapters were probably added after the narrative frames of the story were already established.

The majority of the second farewell speech builds on and develops themes introduced in the first speech. However, the parable of the vine (15:1–6) at the beginning of the second speech introduces a new theme, while at the same time connecting with the washing of the disciples' feet and exploring what participation in Christ entails (13:7). Structurally, it should be noted that the first part of the second farewell speech (15:1–16:4a) stands in the middle of the whole farewell scene. However, one can hardly assert that the farewell speech is the outcome of minute literary planning. Many themes, such as the promise of the Helper (the Paraclete), are repeated with small variations several times. These repetitions together with the many thematic offshoots and contradictions indicate that the text has emerged as the result of successive additions and reinterpretations.

In contrast to the Synoptic Gospels, John does not narrate the Last Supper as a Passover meal or a eucharistic meal. The bread and wine are not equated with the body and blood of Christ (see, however, John 6:51–59). Instead, John emphasizes that Jesus himself is the Lamb of God (1:29), and that he died on the cross while the Passover lambs were slaughtered (19:26), a tradition that Paul also seems to have been aware of (1 Cor 5:7). Instead of a eucharistic meal, John introduces

Alphonso Doss, *Foot Washing*. Jim Elfström / IKON Church of Sweden Picture Archive.

another ritual act with symbolic meaning—namely, the washing of the feet of his disciples and two explanations for why he did it. The two explanations (13:6–11 and 13:12–17) differ from each other, which would indicate that the washing of the disciples' feet attracted theological and practical interest, perhaps even dispute, in the Johannine community.

John does not reproduce the Gethsemane scene in Mark 14:32–42, which is no coincidence. Rather, the farewell speech can be interpreted as a correction of the synoptic Gethsemane tradition, whose image of a weak Jesus stands in stark contrast to Johannine Christology. The Johannine Jesus does not implore the Father to "remove this cup from me" (Mark 14:36). Instead, this prayer is rejected in John 12:27: "And what should I say—'Father, save me from this hour'? No, it is for this reason that I have come to this hour." And when Peter draws his sword upon Jesus's capture, Jesus tells him, "Put your sword back into its sheath. Am I not to drink the cup that the Father has given me?" (18:11). Unlike Mark, John emphasizes that the *disciples* were worried about Jesus's capture. Thus, the farewell speech is ecclesiologically oriented: Christ's assembly stands in the center. Consequently, the first farewell speech begins with these comforting words: "Little children, I am with you only a little longer. . . . Do not let your hearts be troubled. Believe in God, believe also in me" (13:33; 14:1).

The Literary Genre of the Farewell Speech: Last Will or Revelatory Dialogue?

John 14–17 has the general function of a farewell speech given by someone who is about to leave his or her closest friends or family. That the individual who is leaving wants to address his or her loved ones one last time before the imminent separation is a well-known behavioral pattern in various cultures and accentuates a patriarchal society—for example, at the deathbed of the family head. In the Hebrew Bible and in early Jewish texts, this general pattern became a literary type or genre. Many of the structural elements and much of the typical content of a literary last will are already present in Gen 47:29–49:33. The dying patriarch Jacob gathers Joseph and his other sons around him, blesses them, promises that God will watch over them, proclaims what will happen to them in days to come, and instructs them concerning his burial. Deuteronomy 31–34, the entire book of Deuteronomy in fact, is a farewell speech. It provides a summarized history of the people, visions for the future, the law, and further ethical rules with blessings and curses. The Testaments of the Twelve Patriarchs is likely a Jewish document, reworked by Christian editors, with the farewell speech as an overarching genre.

In the New Testament, Paul's farewell speech in Acts 20:17–36 provides an interesting comparison. The author of Acts has stylized it like a literary testament. Paul gathers the elders of Ephesus and holds a speech, in which he first reminds them of his previous work as an apostle and claims to have fulfilled his duty. Then he predicts that this is the last time the elders will see him, and that chains and suffering await him at the end of his journey. Paul foretells that false prophets will emerge from among the Christ followers themselves, exhorts them to remain alert, and points to his own impeccable life in the service of the gospel. Not surprisingly, Luke is the synoptic author who comes closest to presenting the Last Supper as a farewell speech (Luke 22:14–38).

A number of factors point to the possibility of John 13–17 also employing this genre. The text refers to the life works of the departing individual (Jesus) and provides ethical guidelines for those he is leaving behind, as well as words of comfort, encouragement, and warnings about a worrisome future. Many aspects of the text, such as Jesus calling his disciples "my children" (13:33), the question about Jesus's successor or representative (the Helper or Paraclete, 14:16), and the accounting motif (17:4, 6, 14) can be explained by and better understood against the background of the traditional pattern of the farewell speech.[35]

At the same time, John 13–17 is not the farewell of an individual who is dying (Jesus's burial is not mentioned in these chapters); instead, it could also be seen as the resurrected Christ addressing his church. The concluding prayer is traditionally known as a "high priestly prayer," reminiscent of the Letter to the Hebrews' description of the risen Christ as a heavenly high priest. This is somewhat misleading, since John's Jesus does

35. See the detailed study of M. Winter, *Das Vermächtnis Jesu und die Abschiedsworte der Väter.*

not have the function of a high priest. It is noteworthy, however, that Jesus is almost portrayed as a heavenly creature in chapter 17: "I am no longer in the world . . ." (John 17:11). Similarly, the beginning of the second half of the second farewell speech presents a Jesus who seems to have already left the temporal world: "I did not say these things to you from the beginning, because I *was* with you" (16:4b; a similar statement can be found in Luke 24:44, spoken by the risen Christ). The texts from Nag Hammadi present us with a comparison in the form of a genre called *revelation dialogues* or *dialogue gospels*.[36] In these mostly gnostic texts, the risen Christ answers the questions of his disciples as an expansion of his earthly teaching. These texts were written later than John, but it is plausible that the evangelist was familiar with earlier revelation dialogues that have not been preserved. The possibility of the risen Christ giving further instructions to his disciples was also known to Luke: Acts 1:1–11 describes how Jesus instructed and taught his disciples for forty days *after* his resurrection.

It is remarkable that John's Jesus never gives the disciples additional or secret instructions after his resurrection. That the final words of Jesus appear in the form of a farewell speech at the Last Supper *before* the crucifixion is a deliberate choice made by the author. The one responsible for guiding the church with "the whole truth" is not a risen or heavenly Christ but rather the Holy Spirit (John 16:13). Simultaneously, the aspects of the text that reflect a revelation dialogue cannot be ignored. The ambiguous literary format reflects a *hermeneutical* problem, as Ernst Käsemann observed in his classic study of John 17.[37] How can it be that the evangelist, who so strongly emphasizes that Jesus was resurrected and is alive (11:25), still attests a testament to him?

The Presence of the Departed One: The Vision of Christian Community in the Farewell Discourse

The farewell speech wrestles with a problem common to all of early Christianity as well as modern Bible readers: What exactly is the relationship between the departed Jesus and the community of believers now living in the world? The different ways in which this relationship is described in John 13–17 can be divided into three generalized hermeneutical categories. They all have a multifaceted cultic, social, and practical basis in the history of the Johannine community.

Jesus's Presence as His Return According to the first farewell speech (13:31–14:31), Jesus is returning to the Father and "preparing a place" for his disciples, but he is coming back to retrieve them so that "where I am, there you may be also" (14:2–3). This asser-

36. See Dettwiler, *Die Gegenwart des Erhöhten*, 21–27.
37. Käsemann, *The Testament of Jesus*, 1.

tion presupposes the apocalyptic expectation that Jesus shall return sometime in the near future, perhaps in connection with some transformative cosmic event, in which the faithful will be taken up to heaven (cf. Paul in 1 Thess 4:17). However, the Farewell Discourse reinterprets this idea as a reunification in the opposite direction, where Jesus and the Father are the ones who come to those who believe (John 14:23). In addition, John 14:19 explains that Jesus is invisible to the world but can be seen by his disciples. These different explanations of Jesus's presence indicate intense reflection on Jesus's departure and return. It seems as though, at first, the Johannine community embraced the apocalyptic expectation, but began to reconsider the options as the return did not seem to occur. With the passing of time, a hermeneutical void arose that demanded a different explanation, the result of which was a positive reinterpretation of the waiting period as a time of Jesus's presence among his disciples.

Continuous Presence In the parable of the vine and the branches found in the beginning of the second speech, the hermeneutical reflection explores partly new paths. Here the focus is on "remaining" in Jesus. In the center of this thinking stands the question of the church's and the individual believer's faithfulness. The metaphor can be compared to Paul's idea that the church was the body of Christ (e.g., see Rom 12:4–5). The fact that the parable accentuates the threat of being cut from the vine (John 15:2, 6) may reflect divisions in the Johannine community, something that becomes clearer in the Johannine letters. This community-oriented or ecclesiological concept comes from the belief in Jesus's *continuous presence* at communal meals and meetings. Parallel to this cultic presence, the commandment of love is emphasized. Unlike the double commandment of love in the Synoptics (Mark 12:28–34 par.), it is presented as Jesus's "new commandment" and includes only love between Christ followers (John 13:34–35). Besides the commandment to love, the Farewell Discourse inculcates general instructions from Jesus (see, e.g., John 14:23; 15:10).

Presence through Successors and Representatives A third hermeneutical path within the Farewell Discourse is that the church and the believers *continue* Jesus's ministry on earth. The idea of a testament makes special sense in this context. The Christian community is supposed to administer and continue the traditions and beliefs that Jesus revealed and left behind as an inheritance. The concept of inheritance can be used to sum up this way of interpreting Jesus's presence: his teachings and commandments constitute part of the inheritance he endowed his disciples with. Simultaneously, the idea that Jesus's disciples are his successors also says a lot about the group's visions for the future: "Very truly, I tell you, the one who believes in me will also do the works that I do and, in fact, will do greater works than these, because I am going to the Father" (John 14:12). Christ followers were coming to terms with the fact that they were living in the time *after* Jesus. Jesus had returned to the Father, and to balance out this fact, emphasis was placed on the Holy Spirit and its presence among Jesus's followers as a "Helper." In his classic commentary on John, Raymond E. Brown cleverly remarks, "The Paraclete is the presence of Jesus when Jesus is absent."[38]

Thus, the three main hermeneutic strands in John 13–17 interpret Jesus's presence (*parousia*) as return, continuous cultic presence, or, indirectly, as deputized ministry. Despite the fact that the editorial history of the Farewell Discourse is shrouded in relative mystery, the development of the ideas has most likely gone in this direction, that is, from a futuristic aspiration to a more contemporaneous emphasis, where questions regarding the role of the emerging assembly in the world are more prominent. Despite this, the original apocalyptic expectation seems to remain to a certain degree. John 16:16–24 can be interpreted as the promise of a reunion sometime in the near future, and in 1 John (3:9) this aspiration is even more clearly defined. Thus, new interpretations do not necessarily supersede or replace previously held beliefs: the early belief systems of the Jesus movement included several seemingly contradictory concepts.

All of these three main strands, as well as a similar development, can also be found in the Synoptic Gospels. Mark, the oldest gospel, is futuristically oriented and expects to reunite soon with Jesus—who is absent for the moment. At the end of the gospel (Mark 16:8), there is no description of a meeting between the risen Christ and his disciples, only a promise that it would occur. Matthew, written somewhat later, is more oriented toward the present and has a greater interest in ecclesiology. In chapter 18, the community of believers in Christ is addressed directly by Jesus. The gospel ends with an image of the risen Christ who remains with his disciples, saying, "And remember, I am with you always, to the end of the age" (Matt 28:20). However, in Luke and Acts the risen Christ bids his disciples farewell, and they in their turn continue his ministry after the Pentecost. There is, however, an expectation of Jesus's return (Acts 1:11), an affirmation that would soon become a permanent part of the church's creed.

Giving Space to Interpretation as a Duty of New Testament Hermeneutics

Hermeneutical exegesis strives to achieve an understanding of the texts as a whole, where the "now" of the interpreter meets head to head with the "then" of the text, in an exegetically responsible way. The analysis above has focused on problems that unite the past and present audiences of the text. In this way, hermeneutical exegesis creates a space for the continued interpretation of the text, since it is dependent on the interests and aims of the interpreter. The *primary hermeneutical* question concerns the "now"—that is to say, the context of the interpreter and his or her response to the text. Situations where this primary hermeneutical interest dominates are, for

38. Brown, *Gospel according to John*, 2:1141.

example, personal Bible reading or preaching. The *secondary hermeneutical* approach focuses on the "then" of the text. Hermeneutical exegesis is therefore located *between* the *object* of interpretation—the text and its original context—and the interpreting *subject*. It is also possible to deepen the hermeneutical exegesis by introducing further approaches to the texts that meaningfully bring together the historical and the present, thus structuring the interpretative space between "then" and "now." Such integrative approaches can be found, for instance, in sociological and psychological exegesis. One may wish, for instance, to apply modern theories of bereavement processes in order to better understand the Gospels' progressive reflections about Jesus's departure. Such analyses highlight how early Christ followers went through many of the same problems that people today struggle with. Hermeneutical exegesis does not provide any direct answers to our existential questions, but, with the help of different methodologies, it can open up the interpretative space where answers can be found.

Further Reading

Brown, Raymond E. *The Gospel according to John*. 2 vols. AYBC 29. Garden City, NY: Doubleday, 1966–1970.

Dettwiler, Andreas. *Die Gegenwart des Erhöhten: Eine exegetische Studie zu den johanneischen Abschiedsreden (Joh 13,31–16,33) unter besonderer Berücksichtigung ihres Relecture-Characters*. FRLANT 169. Göttingen: Vandenhoeck & Ruprecht, 1995.

Käsemann, Ernst. *The Testament of Jesus: A Study of the Gospel of John in the Light of Chapter 17*. London: SCM, 1978.

Syreeni, Kari. "In Memory of Jesus: Grief Work in the Gospels." *BibInt* 12 (2002): 175–97.

Winter, Martin. *Das Vermächtnis Jesu und die Abschiedsworte der Väter: Gattungsgeschichtliche Untersuchung der Vermächtnisrede im Blick auf Joh. 13–17*. FRLANT 161. Göttingen: Vandenhoeck & Ruprecht, 1994.

Who Is Part of the Future? A Feminist Analysis of Rev 17:1–19:10

In the poem "Apocalypse" (1965), the Nicaraguan priest and poet Ernesto Cardenal, known for his work with the Sandinista movement, rewrites parts of Revelation in light of his own time. The world is divided into two power blocks that represent the enemies of the Lamb. The United States of America—signifying the unequal economic world order—is the "great Babylon," whose fall will pave the way for a new world. In the desert, where the devil is carrying out atomic bomb tests, the "great female prostitute" sits on "a scarlet beast full of blasphemous slogans." In one of her hands she holds the signs of capitalism—bonds, shares—and in the other the symbols of dictatorship: a cup filled to the brim with the blood of the opposition, the tortured, the executed, and the martyrs of Christ. She is drunk on the blood, singing "like a whore in a nightclub," laughingly showing her gold teeth and lipstick of blood.

In the midst of Cardenal's social critique we find, without critical assessment, the image of the "the happy whore," standing in stark contrast to the reality of Latin American women. One of the oppressed is fashioned as an image of oppression. In order to describe the inequalities of the world, Cardenal employs the contempt felt against "the whore." The poem conveys a widespread misogyny, which teenage girls in many parts of the world recognize, as they are called "slut" when they refuse to conform to strict traditional norms for female behavior. The following textual analysis deals with a Bible text that uses the oppressed as a symbol for an arrogant, greedy, and oppressive empire condemned by God.

A Feminist Exegetical Reading of Rev 17:1–19:10

The feminist exegetical analysis that will be presented here critically approaches traditional interpretation and historical usage of the text. It also perceives the text within its social and historical reality of gender-related power structures. Gender will be used as an analytical tool: What hidden meanings of the text can be uncovered if we take seriously the perception of gender—the perception of "masculine" and "feminine"—in the culture that produced the text? The text is understood with the help of gender, and the way that gender is used in a text can shed some light on gender perceptions of the cultural environment of the text. As is often the case, Rev 17:1–19:10 closely affiliates the concept of gender with the concept of sexuality, and—in a manner characteristic of society at the time—gender and sexuality are closely connected to notions of "pure and impure," "shame and honor."

"Feminist analysis" does not comprise a particular methodology, but rather a perspective. The analysis that follows has its foundations in traditional exegetical work focusing on the structure of Rev 17:1–19:10 and on placing this particular passage in its literary and historical context. The theories used to understand "pure and impure," "shame and honor" are informed by cultural anthropology.

We are working with three main presuppositions. First, the biblical texts are thoroughly androcentric, meaning that men figure as the center and norm while women are relegated to the periphery as the other—the deviant. Second, the texts are written in a society in which female subordination to male authority was the norm. Third, gender is an ever-changing historical and cultural construction in which the biological, social, and symbolic dimensions of "gender" cannot be separated. We can separate them in theory, but in praxis they are constantly intertwined.

When working with a biblical text, the symbolic dimension is often clearly in focus, but it should be kept in mind that the "woman," "female prostitute," and "bride waiting for her groom" presented in the text are connected to the circumstances of real women. Therefore the text can also be assumed to affect these circumstances, even if this effect may be difficult to track and measure.

Similarly, when the text asserts that the great prostitute will be murdered because of her sexual pursuits—in a way that may be termed misogynistic—there is no need to assume that the author was driven by excessive personal hatred of women. He may have been a raging misogynist, but he may just as well have been a decent fellow who had a healthy relationship with his Christian sisters—at least those who shared his interpretation of the Christian religion. We will never know the answers to these personal inquiries, and for that reason they have little bearing on our discussion. What this analysis wants to show instead is that certain culturally conditioned understandings of women and femininity, including those which can certainly be described as misogynic, are used in Revelation to communicate a certain message.

Revelation's usage of these images and symbols transmitted certain messages to the readers, even though the readers probably did not explicitly recognize them as part of a gender perception in the same way we will throughout this analysis. Using the category "gender" for the analysis is thus useful for a historical analysis.

The perception of women presented in Revelation can also be found in modern sources and attitudes, making it relevant to today as well. After all, this is not about whether a long-since buried prophet had a problematic view of women; it is about understanding our culture so that we can properly criticize and change it.

This analysis thus aims at making visible the subordination of women in these texts and in their interpretation, with the expressed agenda of promoting social change. The analysis will deal with both that which is familiar and that which is foreign, letting the text itself produce questions relevant even in our own time.

The Structure and Place of the Passage in the Book of Revelation

A detailed discussion of the structure of Revelation and the mixing of genres in 17:1–19:10 appears in chapter 4. The passage is held together by the theme "Babylon." The text is clearly delimited by a new beginning: in 17:1 a new subject introduces a new vision to the narrator/seer with the words: "Come, I will show you the judgment of the great whore." The "judgment of the great whore" is also one of the main themes of 17:1–19:10. In order to render the judgment understandable, the whore needs to be presented and the reason behind the judgment explained. In 18:4–19:5 different reactions to the judgment are presented; in 19:6–8 the salvation the judgment results in are discussed; and 19:9–10 contains some commentaries on 17:1–19:8.

The end of the section at 19:11 is also clearly indicated through the introduction of a new character (a white horse with a rider). The section as an entity ties back to the bowl series in chapter 16 (see 17:1) and comprehensively describes the judgment mentioned in 16:17–21, especially 16:19. For further connections to previous verses, see also Rev 14:8. Our section is thus well anchored in Revelation as a whole and is extremely significant, which is indicated by the fact that the judgment of Babylon is foreshadowed in 14:8 and 16:19. It is a decisive moment in the events that Revelation describes, since it represents God's long-awaited victory and the circumstances surrounding the coming of the new world. The fact that the fall of Babylon, which has previously been designated a fact (14:8 and 16:19), is here described in detail, as well as the fact that the same event has come up many times, using many different symbols, emphasizes the centrality of the section.

The section is structured using both changes of subjects and focus. Where the subject is concerned, there is an "I" who throughout the text sees, hears, is taken away, and reacts to what he sees and hears: 17:1; 18:1, 4, 21; 19:1, 5, 6, and 9 (possibly the same angel as in 17:1). A number of other characters speak to the angel and carry out a variety of actions: new subjects are introduced in 17:1; 18:1, 4, 21; 19:1, 4, 5, 6, and 9. Where the focus is concerned, it shifts from heaven to earth. In chapters 17–18 the text describes occurrences on earth, whereas in 19:1–8 the reaction to these occurrences in heaven are described. Revelation 19:9–10 could be interpreted as being told from a perspective that has returned to the earth. Thus, 17:1–19:10 includes a shifting heaven-earth perspective, as is characteristic of Revelation (see the section "Catholic Letters, the Letter to the Hebrews, and the Book of Revelation," p. 352).

In 17:1–19:10 there are four different images of Babylon, which can be summarized in the following way:

17:1–17	a female prostitute who will eventually be violated and killed
18:2–3	an abandoned city
18:8–19	a burning city
18:21	a large stone that is thrown into the ocean

The dominating images are the ones of the prostitute and the city. Sometimes this imagery becomes unclear. The literary convention of personifying cities as women can explain this confusion. Revelation 18:1–2 is about a city, 18:3 is about a prostitute, 18:4 is again about a city, and 18:5–7 about a prostitute. In several places both are used—for example, in 18:16 and 19:3 (both cities and women can burn). The connection between the woman and the city is explicitly stated in 17:5, 18.

The image of the female prostitute is the most commonly occurring symbol for Babylon. It dominates the passage and is clearly meant as a link to what is to come (the bride, the wife of the Lamb, in 21:9–10). When the imagery is first employed in 17:1–6, 18, the "whore" is used without explicitly stating that she is identical to Babylon. Also, in 18:3 and 18:7–8 she is described as a woman, but in such a way as to lead the reader's thoughts to the prostitute in chapter 17 and 19:2–3.

A table of contents for the section could look something like this:

17:1–18	A vision of Babylon
18:1–3	The fall of Babylon proclaimed
18:4–24	The judgment over Babylon, described in more detail, and four reactions to its fall: kings of the earth who weep (18:9–10); merchants of the earth who grieve (18:11–17a); seamen and sailors of the earth who grieve and complain (17b–19); a heavenly voice encouraging people to jubilate (18:20). The first three reactions are from a human or worldly perspective, and thus not correct, whereas the fourth reaction is from a heavenly perspective, and thus correct.
19:1–18	A change in place and narrator (v. 1) suggests the introduction of a new section. At the same time, the section could be seen as another reaction to the fall of Babylon. It directs its speech explicitly at the reader. Verse 8 emphasizes the importance of unswerving loyalty to God, and of choosing the side of God in the last battle.

Backgrounds in Older Texts

Like the entire book of Revelation, this section weaves together older material, without ever quoting explicitly. From the many themes and images that have been borrowed from other texts, I have here chosen to analyze two: Babylon and the prostitute.

Babylon was a city in modern-day Iraq, the center of the Babylonian Empire, which captured and colonized Judea and destroyed the temple in 587 BCE. In the wake of this catastrophe, they took many people into exile. Consequently, many texts in the Hebrew Bible speak of the desire for God's debilitating judgment to come over Babylon (e.g., Jer 50–51; Ps 137:8–9; Isa 47). Revelation 17:1–19:10 is a continuation of this tradition of demonizing Babylon. In Revelation, "Babylon" has, however, come to signify another empire: Rome (see 17:18). It is not an illogical choice, since Babylon and Rome had destroyed the First and the Second Jewish Temple, respectively. By using the name "Babylon," the author means to insinuate much more than a mere pseudonym. Instead, the usage of the name results in a collection of memories of another empire that persecuted and attempted to destroy the people of God. By doing this, the text invokes associations with older texts, making Rome, alias Babylon, into a mythical "evil empire" by describing Babylon as an enemy of God.

Many of the texts describing Babylon make it obvious that the concern is with Rome. This is most clear in 17:18. There are, however, other options; 17:1 may be referring to the water in the Tiber, but Babylon also had a river running through it, the

Euphrates, something mentioned in Jer 51:13. "Many waters" in Hebrew literature can be a symbolic reference to a people or armies (e.g., Jer 47:3; Isa 7:12; 8:7–8). "Waters" can be images for chaos and evil powers (e.g., Ps 32:6). There is, then, an ambiguity in the text, with three possible associations, which does not necessarily have to be solved: a city known to some members of the audience (= Rome), biblical texts about Babylon, and biblical images of evil.

In addition, the "seven hills" described in 17:9 could be a reference to the seven hills of Rome. That the kings of the world had whored around with Babylon (17:2; 18:3, 9) could be an image for the many kingdoms that traded and had political alliances with Rome. That she drinks blood could be a reference to the violence that accompanied Roman governance. Revelation 17:9–12 seems to be a direct reference to an emperor, although it is unclear which one. Since seven is the number of completeness and head is a symbol for power, the "seven heads" could be an image for "complete power," thus referencing the power an emperor enjoys. Revelation 17:12 is in all likelihood a reference to Roman vassal kingdoms, although it is unclear which ones. Since ten stands for "totality" and horns are a symbol for power, the "seven horns" could be a collective reference to the vassal kingdoms. When the whore and the beast from 17:3 are found in the desert, all the imagery for Rome has receded into the background. In the Hebrew Bible, the desert is a common hiding place for demons.

The image of Babylon as a prostitute could be understood as a negative caricature of Roma, the goddess who personified the city of Rome. The author of Revelation could have been making a connection with the various female representations on coins, or the personification Roma. The Roma cult came into being in association with several other cults, which began to form around emperors and powerful, charitable men around the eastern Mediterranean during the Hellenistic era. Smyrna (cf. Rev 2:8–11) is said to be the place where the goddess Roma was first worshiped, and the cult was well established in the cities that hosted the communities to whom the author of Revelation is writing in the book (Rev 2–3). According to the revelation John receives, the personification of Rome is repellent and contemptible: an overconfident prostitute drunk on human blood. Normal political and economic life is depicted as unacceptable sexual activity, which draws down God's judgment on the sexually active woman. When Rome, in the form of Roma, becomes the object for cultic worship, it represents for John a sort of anti-God power, which is trying to encroach on that which belongs only to God.

Personifications of cities as women are a well-known concept in the Hebrew Bible (e.g., Isa 1:21; 23:15–18; 66:7–11; Nah 3:4–7; Jer 50:8–18; Ezek 16, 23). A city can be stereotyped as a "good woman" (Isa 66:7–11) or a "bad woman." In Ezek 16 Jerusalem (also Samaria in Ezek 23) is described as an unfaithful wife and a promiscuous woman. In both passages, contemporary politics are compared to a sexual orgy (see Ezek 16:33–34). When the imagery is used about the people of Israel or Jerusalem, the underlying thought is that there is a covenant between the people and God, which the people have broken. Marital infidelity and promiscuity thus become relevant images for such covenant breaks. When the image is used to describe *other* peoples, like those in Babylon and Rome, the logic begins to halt. Perhaps this is why many prophetic texts speak about merchandise (Isa 23 about Tyre) or political alliances as prostitution (see also Nah 3). Prostitution does not imply that a contract has been broken, but rather it indicates an economic transaction and a sort of loosely defined relationship—like merchandise and political alliances. Prostitutes were also depicted and understood as shameful. Revelation and the sources it relies on reflect a double standard for men and women: it is the prostituted woman, rather than her customer, who is punished for her immorality (17:2; 18:3, 9).

We can also note that the whore in 17:3b–6 is clothed in luxurious clothing, almost like an aristocrat or a queen (cf. 18:7; purple is a royal color). This image fits well with other contemporary texts that depict prostitutes as rich and well-dressed and as incarnations of sin: greed, lust, love of flattery. The luxury clothing of the whore is a contrast to the bride's shining white linen in 19:8.

Women, Sexuality, and Purity

In the Roman Empire, prostitution was regulated by law. Female prostitutes had varying status and living conditions depending on their circumstances. For example, if they were officially registered, they held a higher social status than those who were not; if they worked within the bounds of a brothel, they had more security than those who did not. Prostitution was seen as a necessary evil, and accordingly prostitutes (despite variations in this category) were generally people with low status who were looked down on.

The honor-and-shame cultural sphere within which Revelation was written resented female prostitutes, because they did not adhere to the social demands placed on women. They did not uphold sexual exclusiveness and lived in a permanent state of shamelessness. "A prostituted woman" could thus function as a symbol of chaos that breaks the proper order of things and therefore becomes something evil. In addition, for people versed in the Hebrew Bible, there was an established form of language in which "a shameless woman who has unacceptable sex" became an image of betrayal toward God or a symbol for hostile political powers.

Thus, "a prostituted woman" as a metaphor for Rome, alias Babylon, is indeed a term of contempt and distancing. The power that, according to official society's views, bore civilization, peace, order, and all human social life is described as the most shameful and contemptuous of things. Such language is semantically entirely dependent on the social contempt for prostitutes. The picture of Rome as the whore of Babylon can be understood as John wanting readers to take action in the conflict

Emmanuel Garibay, *Emmaus*. Jim Elfström / IKON Church of Sweden Picture Archive. Just as the feminist interpretation of Revelation 17–19 in this section responds to historical circumstances of a biblical text that have epitomized women prostitutes as evil, the painting is a parable on eyes being opened to truth and prejudice today. It depicts a Christ event occurring in a most adverse and unexpected manner, challenging the observer to consider the radical nature of Jesus's ministry as a friend of sinners and tax collectors.

that for him exists between God and Satan, between followers of Christ and contemporary culture. To accomplish this, the picture plays on feelings and attitudes long cemented deep within the readers, perhaps so deep that the readers even lacked the capacity to fully formulate them—attitudes that arose like a kind of natural order. As is still widespread in the modern day, in those times there was no distinct line between the views on prostituted women and the views on other women. The views on prostitutes are simply amplified aspects of the views on women in general.

One of the many antitheses in Revelation is that between Babylon and Jerusalem. They represent two realms and are thus described as the whore (17:1–19:3) over against the bride of the Lamb (19:7–8; 21:1–2, 9). Despite all the differences between antiquity and today, we can still speak of a certain historical continuity. In the symbolic dimension of the construction of gender roles in today's society, we find a prominent contrasting of different kinds of women: bad women and good women or, in the language of today, "sluts and good girls." These two poles of contrast are interestingly dependent on each other for their definition. We may also describe the contrast between the whore and the bride as analogous to that between the woman who breaks the demands of honor and the one who upholds them.

Revelation clearly presents us with these contrasts (17:1–2; 21:9–10), and modern translations mirror the Greek text as well. The clothing of the whore and that of the bride contrast each other (17:4; 19:8), but we also find more complex presentations in Revelation. For example, the woman clothed with the sun (ch. 12) is a multifaceted image. A possible explanation as to her nature might be "the people of God." Her glory makes possible an understanding of her as a clear contrast to the splendor of Babylon, which she exceeds in magnificence. At the same time, however, she does not entirely fit into the contrast we find in Revelation, which ultimately makes her appear as a more central figure that stands out from the rest.

Images of women are not only metaphorical plays with contrasts; they are also used in analogies. In the letter to the assembly in Thyatira (Rev 2:18–29), we meet Jezebel, who becomes an analogy for the whore Babylon. The passage may refer to an actual leader in the assembly who stood in opposition to John or in any case appeared opposite to his views on what followers of Christ should be like. Jezebel is likely not her real name but is used for polemical purposes in order to awaken parallels to the queen in 1 Kgs 16, 18, 19, and 21 and 2 Kgs 9. Jezebel is associated with cults of gods other than the god of Israel and has become a picture of the strong, God-opposing woman. Here we can once again observe how John tries to persuade his audience to agree with him, and it is hard to measure the historical reliability of the polemics. Whether immorality and meat eating in Rev 2:20 are meant to be symbolic or concrete is difficult to establish, especially since the eating of sacrificial meat could be a reference to the praxis described by Paul in 1 Cor 10:27–31, and because "immorality" is a rather capricious term. The entire description of this woman, the names given to her, and the actions attributed to her awakens a natural connection to the older texts about all that the prophets opposed. Her immorality also makes her analogous to the whore of Babylon: she is on the local scale what the whore of Babylon is on the cosmic scale. The great, cosmic conflict is thus applied to the assembly's everyday life.

Even the fornicators (*pornoi*) among those excluded in 21:8 and 22:15 seem analogous to the prostituted woman (*pornē*). The same word is used, although in different genders.

Who, then, is analogous to the bride—the opposite of the whore? One option is the woman clothed with the sun. Another option is the 144,000 male virgins in 14:1–5. The context of verse 4 clearly suggests that these "virgins" are males (the Greek *parthenos* can have either feminine or masculine grammatical gender). This may be due to the author's intention to contrast the 144,000 with women such as Jezebel and Babylon. Their virginity is reminiscent of the cultural ideal for the woman, who guards the family's honor by protecting her virginity. In the world created by the author, they differentiate themselves from those men who have had sex with Jezebel and Babylon, and from the male whores described in 21:8, who are excluded from the new Jerusalem, since the male virgins have never been "tainted" by sexual relations with any women.

But the ideal Christians are men. Revelation describes ethics and loyalty toward God as the author understands God. In other words, obedience is crucial, since living according to God's will means living in a divinely ordained order without causing rebellion or chaos. In this image of the ideal, the "good woman" of the honor culture is a good representative. At the same time, the culture is deeply androcentric, and the norm is male. Thus, in the construction of the ideal Christian identity in Revelation, the subjects are males painted in the same light as the cultural ideal of the "good women." Ergo, these ideal men have the same relationship to God as an honorable woman had to her sovereign husband.

We cannot know for sure what exactly the image of Christ followers as a collective of male virgins entailed practically—other than a demand for loyalty toward a certain interpretation of Christ belief. There is not enough evidence to establish whether the ideal remained a kind of symbolic self-image or whether it actually resulted in a community of celibates. If such a community existed, we may assume that it could also have contained women. There is, however, no conclusive evidence about this either.

That the 144,000 had kept away from all women, not only "bad women," can be seen as an extension of the female imagery in, for instance, Jewish wisdom literature. With time, these images get more brutal and general. It becomes difficult to tell whether the "bad women" are a particular group, or whether the characterization applies to women in general. In Rev 14:1–5, "women" represent that which can pull the faithful away from God.

In the description of the 144,000 in 14:1–5, we encounter the same language of purity that so markedly characterizes the book of Revelation as a whole. In the conceptual world of the Bible, of which Revelation was a part, "purity" is connected to temple and cult. Revelation makes it clear that that which has no place in the New Jerusalem is that which has no place in the temple cult: the abominations, the unclean. If we engage Mary Douglas's understanding of clean and unclean as a language for order, where what is "clean" is in its right place in the world order, and what is "unclean" is in the "wrong" place, then categories of purity become a way of organizing the world. The distinction between clean and unclean is also a basic aspect of how Revelation structures a world and a symbolic universe.

Terms for impurity gather around the Babylon images in 17:1–19:10. In 17:4–5 impurity and sexuality seem deeply connected. In this way, Babylon is the opposite of the new Jerusalem. Revelation 21–22 indicates that those who want to have a place in the new Jerusalem must fulfill the requirements for purity that are prescribed for priests during their temple duty; however, there is no temple, since God is their temple and lives there. This proximity to God requires strict adherence to purity rules.

In 21:5–8 God speaks directly about who is included and who is excluded from the walls of the new Jerusalem. The author implies the highest authority, since the words are put into God's own mouth. Many of those who are excluded are described in terms of impurity or sexual immorality. The unfaithful, in addition to magicians and idolaters, are also excluded, as well as the "liars," whose lies consist of calling God that which God is not (e.g., Roma or the emperor). There is a similar list in 22:15. That the "impure" are excluded becomes very clear in 21:27, where the text states that "nothing unclean will enter it [the new Jerusalem], nor anyone who practices abomination or falsehood."

Purity language and cultic purity terms are used abundantly in Revelation about the Christ followers. Sixteen times they are called "the holy." In 22:11 especially, "the one who does wrong . . . and the one who is impure" are put into stark contrast with "the righteous . . . the holy" (see also 18:20; 19:8). Followers of Christ are priests (1:6; 5:10; 20:6) or soldiers, or both, in the holy war. Priestly duty and holy wars require purity (Deut 23:9–11) and temporary abstinence from sex. In Revelation, those who are saved will, in the future, always participate in worship services, and they should always be ready for the holy war. Logically, they must be in a constant state of purity through abstention from sex, as the 144,000 have. Again, the author strengthens the contrast between Babylon and Jerusalem, and those listening to the apocalypse of John would have been forced to pick a side.

Concluding Remarks

In this analysis of Rev 17:1–19:10, I have attempted to show how a "prostituted woman" became an image for an ungodly world power. Revelation makes ample use of female and sexual imagery, as well as purity imagery, in all likelihood to influence the followers of Christ with regard to choices and actions, self-image, and their understanding of the world. They should view the mighty empire, for them the entire world, as a despicable whore, who would soon be murdered and burned. They should view themselves as virgin men (perhaps also women), always prepared to go out and fight the holy war and to serve as priests of God. They should understand their distancing themselves from society as keeping themselves uncontaminated by women, and so remain untouched by the "great whore" and all other whores on earth. They should thus wait for a new world, unsullied, just as they were unsullied, where they would rule as priests and kings. They were to live in obedience, like a good woman, in the order that God has ordained. How many retained this message and what it meant in practice to live as John wanted them to live can never be known; we can only guess. And exegetes tend to guess quite differently.

All these possible meanings surface in a feminist analysis that recognizes the unreasonable identification of a prostitute with an evil empire. Within the framework of its culture, it may have seemed reasonable, and—as Cardenal's poem showcases—can still seem so today. From a feminist perspective, the apparent reasonability is the most unreasonable aspect of the imagery. Revelation is an ambivalent text. It has inspired visions of terminating an unfair world order, like that of Cardenal's poem and other liberation theologians. But it is also, from a feminist point of view, *part* of an unfair world order.

Further Reading

Aune, David. E. *Revelation*. 3 vols. WBC. Waco: Word, 1997–1998.

Huber, Lynn. "Revelation." In *The Oxford Handbook of New Testament, Gender, and Sexuality*. Edited by Benjamin H. Dunning. Oxford: Oxford University Press, 2019.

Levine, Amy-Jill, ed. *A Feminist Companion to the Apocalypse of John*. Feminist Companion to the New Testament and Early Christian Writings 13. London: T&T Clark, 2009.

Pippin, Tina. "The Revelation to John." Pages 109–30 in *Searching the Scriptures*. Vol. 2 of *A Feminist Commentary*. Edited by Elisabeth Schüssler Fiorenza. New York: Crossroad, 1994.

Schüssler Fiorenza, Elisabeth. *Revelation: Vision of a Just World*. Proclamation Commentaries. Minneapolis: Fortress, 1991.

———, ed. *Feminist Biblical Studies in the Twentieth Century*. The Bible and Women 9. Atlanta: SBL Press, 2014.

Stenström, Hanna. *The Book of Revelation: A Vision of the Ultimate Liberation or the Ultimate Backlash? A Study in 20th Century Interpretations of Rev 14:1–5, with Special Emphasis on Feminist Exegesis*. Doctoral diss., Uppsala University, 1999.

Stichele, C. van der. "Just a Whore: The Annihilation of Babylon according to Revelation 17:6." *Lectio Difficilior* (European Web-Journal for Feminist Exegesis). www.lectio.unibe.ch 1/2000.

"Legion Is My Name, for We Are Many": A Postcolonial Reading of Mark 5:1–20

A Postcolonial World

We live in a postcolonial world. That means that we live in the wake of the colonial era, when the colonial powers of Europe (England, Portugal, Spain, France, the Netherlands, and Germany) ruled 80 percent of the world. This colonial era began in the middle of the sixteenth century and lasted until the first half of the twentieth century. At a cursory glance, the withdrawal of the colonial powers could be seen as

Francisco Sanchez Flores, *Crucified among the People*. Jim Elfström / IKON Church of Sweden Picture Archive. The painting contextualizes Jesus's suffering through an identification with the suffering of the poor.

a liberation. Former colonies were given sovereignty, and the power of shaping the new nations lay in the hands of its actual inhabitants. Unfortunately, this image is far too simplified to represent what actually transpired. Despite the fact that many countries gained independence, the colonial relationship between the West (that is, North America, Western Europe, and to a certain extent Australia and New Zealand) and the rest of the world remains.

Many postcolonial scholars today call this new situation *neocolonialism* (neo = new). This term indicates that the West in many ways still constitutes the center around which the other regions of the world (periphery) have to revolve. This is evident in areas such as culture, economy, world trade, and academia.

The neocolonial situation is part of the larger umbrella concept of *postcoloniality*. As a concept, postcoloniality includes *all* reactions to and consequences of colonization. This involves everything from drinking coffee manufactured in a previously colonized country to the economic ties that many of the former colonies of the world have with the West today. In other words, postcoloniality is what happens in the meeting between the colonial power and the colonized nation, starting from the beginning of the colonization and stretching to long after the colonization ends, and the effects this has on the world. The prefix "post" in postcoloniality should therefore not be interpreted as indicating a condition appearing *after* the definitive end of colonization. Postcoloniality does not begin when the colonization ends. This is the very situation in which we find ourselves today. The vast majority of colonies have gained independence, but the effects of their colonization have not died out but rather continue to make themselves felt in a different neocolonial form.

Postcoloniality should not be confused with *postcolonialism*. Postcoloniality is a phenomenon, a reality in which we all live in our world today, since modern colonization has come to define much of the prevailing world order. Postcolonialism, on the other hand, refers to theories about postcoloniality. Postcolonial scholars have taken it upon themselves to analyze postcoloniality, neocolonial structures, and their basis in the modern colonial era. The relationship between postcoloniality and postcolonialism can be illustrated in the form of a chart (see fig. 6.7).

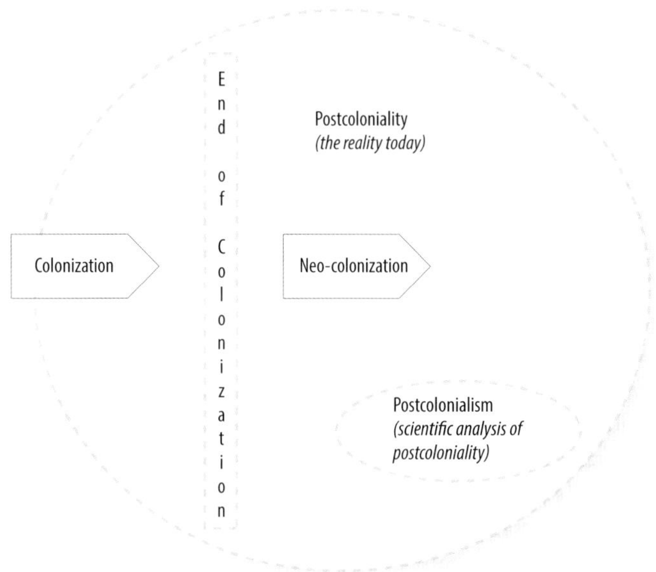

Figure 6.7 The relationship between postcoloniality and postcolonialism.

The Emergence of Postcolonialism as an Academic Discipline and Its Place in Biblical Studies

Postcolonialism originated as a concept in the 1980s within the study of literature. Postcolonialism may be defined as an academic response to the postcolonial world we live in. Pioneers in the development of postcolonial theory include Edward Said, Homi Bhabha, and Gayatri Spivak. Postcolonial research quickly diffused across the traditional boundaries of academic disciplines and should today be considered an interdisciplinary subject. Biblical studies is one of many subjects where postcolonial analysis has had an impact. Fernando Segovia, Kwok Pui-lan, and R. S. Sugirtharajah are among the best-known postcolonial biblical scholars today.

One way of applying postcolonialism to biblical studies is to read the biblical narrative from a historical perspective of colonialism and postcoloniality. Another way is to focus on the critique of Western exegetical methods as springing from En-

View over the ruins of the Byzantine monastery at Kursi, looking northwest; Lake Tiberias is visible in the background. According to Christian tradition, it is the site of the miracle of the swine, where Jesus commanded the demons to enter a herd of swine, which then rushed into the lake and perished (Mark 5:1–20). Photo by Anders Runesson.

of Mark was written for a group of people who found themselves at the peripheries of society, marginalized and persecuted.

As mentioned, the event described in Mark 5:1–20 takes place in the Decapolis area. This part of Galilee had a complicated history, since various rulers believed they had claims to it. In the beginning of the first century CE, the area was strongly influenced by Greek (Hellenistic) culture and religion. The population was composed of various ethnic groups. At the time of Mark, the Decapolis was controlled by Rome and was important to the Romans for military and economic reasons. The area functioned as a military buffer zone around Palestine, and it was home to various trade routes to South Arabia and India. For the people living in the Decapolis, Roman presence brought with it a certain level of stability and security, and it is very likely that many did not see Roman colonial rule in a solely negative light. Cities that had been razed to the ground during the power struggle between the Maccabees and the Seleucids were rebuilt, and the region was annexed to the Syrian province. Thus, when the author writes that Jesus left Galilee and went to the Decapolis, this was the political and colonial milieu that he entered, and this is the context in which he expelled the demons from the man in Gerasa.

In a postcolonial reading of the Markan text at hand, the word "legion" is central. The word is used four times in the Gospels, twice in Mark (5:9, 15), once in Luke (8:30, a parallel text to Mark), and once in Matthew when Jesus is arrested (Matt 26:53). In Rome, "legion" (which originally meant "to gather together") referred to a group of soldiers consisting of six thousand foot soldiers and 120 cavalry.

Mark's usage of the word "legion" in the story about the possessed man in Gerasa has been interpreted in a variety of ways. More traditional exegetes argue that it simply indicates that the man was possessed with a large multitude of unclean spirits, and that Jesus's power was strong enough to expel even such a large number of demons. Others, among them postcolonial exegetes, argue that Mark's usage of the term "legion" actually refers to the Romans. From this perspective, the text takes on a whole new meaning. Not only is Jesus more powerful than the colonial power; he also puts himself into direct opposition to their presence in the region. This becomes especially tangible when one considers the fact that he expels the demons from the man and lets them enter a herd of swine, which consequently run over the edge of a cliff and drown. The Roman presence in Decapolis came in the form of the Tenth Legion, *Legio X Fretensis*, whose emblem included a wild boar—a swine. Thus, the text alludes to the Roman presence twice, once by using the word "legion," and once by emphasizing the herd of swine. The fact that Jews considered swine unclean makes the parallel even more forceful, not in the least since later rabbinic literature often equates the Romans with swine.

A postcolonial reading of the text takes different colonial situations on different levels seriously: both the situation of Mark's author and audience and Jesus's own political context are considered. A reading that interprets "legion" as referring only to the sheer amount of unclean spirits Jesus expelled ignores the contexts of the text and the implications they have for both the narrative and history.

So, who exactly was the possessed man portrayed in the text, and how should we interpret the "sickness" that Mark describes? The text tells us that a man from Gerasa was possessed by unclean spirits (summarized by the word "legion"), and that they caused him to scratch himself until he bled, to live among the graves, and to be so strong that no one could restrain him. Because there is nothing wrong with the man physically, one could interpret him as suffering from a serious mental ailment. The question is why Mark portrays the man as mentally ill.

From a postcolonial perspective, the answer to this question may be found in the context in which the text places the possessed man. Sugirtharajah, in an attempt to answer the question contextually, describes how Roman occupation used forced recruitment of locals for the army as a colonial strategy. This meant that locals were forced to leave their homes. Sugirtharajah links this to modern psychological studies that exhibit a clear connection between similar conditions (as forced recruitment) and increased mental illness among the local population. One way of referring to or interpreting mental illness during the first century was to say that unclean spirits possessed the person in question. The reason that Mark mentions the physical strength of the man could be that it presents him as a likely recruit for the Roman army. Thus, the behavior and mental illness of the man are interpreted by some postcolonial scholars as a result of the colonial power's occupation strategies.[40]

When Jesus asks for the man's name, the answer itself becomes a reference to what ails him—*legion*: the Roman army and its forced recruitment. Jesus's healing of the man consists of his expelling the demons from the man and letting them (re)enter a herd of swine, which consequently run off a cliff and drown. The man did not calm down until *legion* had completely vanished. Mark's description of people's reaction to the healing of the possessed man may seem strange on first appraisal. They ask Jesus to leave (Mark 5:17). However, once again the answer can be found in the colonial context of the narrative. Seen from the perspective of the members of the local population, which thrived on the presence of the colonial power, it is a natural reaction. When occupying an area, the Romans allied themselves to powerful members of the local population—for example, important merchants or landowners. The description of the group of people who arrive on the scene of the healing to see what transpired and ask Jesus to leave could be a description of the reaction of people who benefited from the occupation. If Jesus's healing of the man is described as an act of anticolonialism, it would be natural for these people to oppose him.

The task that Jesus gives the healed man is that he should stay in the Decapolis and witness about his healing (Mark 5:19–20). If the postcolonial reading of this text is factual from a historical perspective, it means that the man was instructed to tell the inhabitants of the Decapolis that the days of the Roman occupation were almost over: the Messiah's arrival brought with it political liberation. In this way, Mark's Jesus has clear political contours, and thus the focus of the narrative is not missiological, as some traditional interpretations would have it, but rather on advocating the anticolonial views and actions of Jesus.

We do not know how the gospel's first audience in Rome viewed this text, but given the text's usage of military terminology, it is historically likely that they understood the text as anticolonial, not in the least because of their own oppression

40. Sugirtharajah, "Colonial Trauma and Madness: The Case of the Gerasene Demoniac," in *Postcolonial Criticism and Biblical Interpretation*, 91–94.

by a colonial power. Thus, the postcolonial exegesis of the text, which is inspired by modern (post)colonial conditions, may in fact be more historically plausible than the more traditional interpretation. This illustrates that all interpretations are contextually dependent, something postcolonial scholars have been asserting since the birth of the discipline.

Further Reading

Ashcroft, Bill, Gareth Griffiths, and Helen Tiffin. *The Empire Writes Back: Theory and Practice in Post-Colonial Literatures*. London: Routledge, 1989.

Dube, Musa W., and Jeffrey Lloyd Staley, eds. *John and Postcolonialism: Travel, Space and Power.* The Bible and Postcolonialism 7. London: Sheffield Academic Press, 2002.

Moore, Stephen D., and Fernando F. Segovia, eds. *Postcolonial Biblical Criticism: Interdisciplinary Intersections*. London: T&T Clark, 2005.

Runesson, Anna. *Exegesis in the Making: Postcolonialism and New Testament Studies.* Leiden: Brill, 2011.

Segovia, Fernando F. "Mapping the Postcolonial Optic in Biblical Criticism: Meaning and Scope." Pages 23–78 in *Postcolonial Biblical Criticism: Interdisciplinary Intersections*. Edited by Stephen D. Moore and Fernando F. Segovia. London: T&T Clark, 2005.

Segovia, Fernando F., and R. S. Sugirtharajah, eds. *A Postcolonial Commentary on the New Testament Writings*. London: T&T Clark, 2009.

Sugirtharajah, R. S. *Postcolonial Criticism and Biblical Interpretation*. New York: Oxford University Press, 2002.

Ukpong, Justin S. *Reading the Bible in the Global Village: Cape Town*. Global Perspectives on Biblical Scholarship. Atlanta: Society of Biblical Literature, 2002.

Appendix 1
Nonbiblical Sources

When studying the New Testament, Jesus, and the early Christ movement, scholars make use of a great number of texts that were written at either approximately the same time as the New Testament or a few hundred years before or after. These texts can, with some simplification, be divided into three main groups: Christian noncanonical texts, Jewish noncanonical texts, and Greco-Roman texts. It is important to remember that many of the "Christian" texts were authored by Jewish followers of Jesus and are therefore in a sense both Christian and Jewish (see the section "Jewish Christ Followers and the Emergence of Christianity and Judaism," p. 365). It is also important to note that some of the Jewish non-canonical texts may have been authored by followers of Jesus (see James Davila, *The Provenance of the Pseudepigrapha: Jewish, Christian, or Other?* [Leiden: Brill, 2005]). Furthermore, all texts are situated, from a more general contextual perspective, in the surrounding Greco-Roman political and cultural setting.

Thus, when for pedagogical purposes we divide the texts into three categories, the category "Christian noncanonical texts" designates texts that were written by Jewish and non-Jewish Christ followers. The category "noncanonical Jewish texts" designates texts that were written by Jews who were likely not among the followers of Jesus. Finally, "Greco-Roman texts" designates texts that were written by non-Jews who were not followers of Jesus.

This source material has been translated and collected in a range of publications. In the following sample, several texts are suitable for readers who are new to the field, but there is also material here for those who wish to continue with further study.

An often-forgotten group contemporary with the Jesus movement is the Samaritans. The reason why their texts are usually not listed in source collections is that most of their preserved texts are of a late date. Before we continue with our three categories below, however, we would like to highlight a recent translation into English of the Samaritan Pentateuch, as this version presents us with important comparative material: B. Tsedaka and S. Sullivan, eds., *The Israelite Samaritan Version of the Torah: First English Translation Compared with the Masoretic Version*, trans. B. Tsedaka (Grand Rapids: Eerdmans, 2013).

Christian Noncanonical Texts

A selection of Christian noncanonical texts can be found in the following publications: T. Burke and B. Landau, eds., *New Testament Apocrypha: More Noncanonical Scriptures*, vols. 1 and 2 (Grand Rapids: Eerdmans, 2016, 2020); B. Ehrman, *Lost Scriptures: Books That Did Not Make It into the New Testament* (Oxford: Oxford University Press, 2003) and *Lost Christianities: The Battles for Scripture and the Faiths We Never Knew* (Oxford: Oxford University Press, 2003); J. K. Elliott, *The Apocryphal New Testament: A Collection of Apocryphal Christian Literature in an English Translation Based on M. R. James* (Oxford: Oxford University Press, 1993); H.-J. Klauck, *Apocryphal Gospels: An Introduction*, trans. B. McNeil (London: T&T Clark, 2003); J. A. Robinson, ed., *The Nag Hammadi Library in English*, 3rd rev. ed. (San Francisco: HarperCollins, 1990); W. Schneemelcher and R. M. Wilson, ed., *New Testament Apocrypha*, 2 vols., 2nd rev. ed. (Louisville: Westminster John Knox, 1991–1992).

Q is a special case (see the section "Q as a Source and Historical Background," p. 238), as this hypothetical source can be seen (if it exists) only through the material that Matthew and Luke have in common. If one accepts the hypothesis that this material has its origins in a written gospel (Q) that was used by both Matthew and Luke, this gospel must be deemed noncanonical. There are critical editions in which Q has been reconstructed, an easily accessible version of which is the one by J. M. Robinson et al., *The Sayings Gospel Q in Greek and English: With Parallels from the Gospels of Mark and Thomas* (Minneapolis: Fortress, 2002).

With regard to the patristic literature, there is an essential introduction available that covers the time period from the second century to Pope Leo the Great (440–461 CE) in J. Quasten, *Patrology*, 3 vols. (Brussels: Spectrum, 1950–1960). English translations are available online: see the Early Church Fathers series at Christian Classics Ethereal Library (http://www.ccel.org/fathers2/). There are also sourcebooks focusing on women in early Christianity, among which is P. C. Miller, *Women in Early Christianity: Translations from Greek Texts* (Washington, DC: Catholic University of America Press, 2005).

Jewish Noncanonical Texts

For the Old Testament Pseudepigrapha, see J. H. Charlesworth, ed., *The Old Testament Pseudepigrapha*, vol. 1, *Apocalyptic Literature and Testaments*, and vol. 2,

Expansions of the "Old Testament" and Legends, Wisdom and Philosophical Literature, Prayers, Psalms and Odes, Fragments of Lost Judeo-Hellenistic Works (New York: Doubleday, 1983–1985); R. J. Bauckham, J. R. Davila, and A. Panayotov, eds., *Old Testament Pseudepigrapha: More Noncanonical Scriptures*, vol. 1 (Grand Rapids: Eerdmans, 2013). See also D. M. Gurtner, *Introducing the Pseudepigrapha of Second Temple Judaism: Message, Context, and Significance* (Grand Rapids: Baker Academic, 2020).

Philo and Josephus are available both in Greek and in English translation in the Loeb Classical Library. Philo (10 vols. and 2 supplements) is translated by F. H. Colson and G. H. Whitaker; the supplements are available not in the original Greek but in translation from Armenian by R. Marcus. Josephus's works (10 vols.) are translated by H. St. J. Thackeray, R. Marcus, A. Wikgren, and L. H. Feldman. A new multivolume translation and commentary of Josephus's works is being published by Brill Academic. The most recent volume is by P. Spilsbury, *Judean Antiquities*, vol. 11 (2016). Also, Philo of Alexandria's works are currently being translated anew by Brill, the latest volume published being A. C. Geljon and D. T. Runia, *On Cultivation*, vol. 4 (2012).

The Dead Sea Scrolls have been translated into English, and there are several editions, one of which is G. Vermes, *The Complete Dead Sea Scrolls in English* (New York: Penguin Press, 1997). If the reader wishes to have both the Hebrew text and an English translation, there are also several choices. A thematically organized presentation of the Qumran texts in two comprehensive volumes has been edited by D. W. Parry and E. Tov, in association with G. I. Clements, *The Dead Sea Scrolls Reader*, 2 vols., 2nd rev. ed. (Leiden: Brill, 2014). Another edition is that of F. García Martínez and E. J. C. Tigchelaar, eds., *The Dead Sea Scrolls Study Edition*, 2 vols. (Leiden: Brill, 2000). M. Abegg, P. Flint, and A. Ulrich, in *The Dead Sea Scrolls: The Oldest Known Bible Translated for the First Time into English* (San Francisco: HarperSanFrancisco, 1999), have compiled the Qumran fragments that contain biblical texts, thus giving a version of the Hebrew Bible from Jesus's time. An introduction to Jewish literature from this time may be found in G. W. E. Nickelsburg, *Jewish Literature between the Bible and the Mishnah: A Historical and Literary Introduction* (Philadelphia: Fortress, 1981).

Rabbinic literature is dated later than the New Testament but may contain traditions that go back to the late first century. The oldest rabbinic collection of texts, the Mishnah (ca. 200 CE), is found in English translation by H. Danby from 1933 (Oxford: Clarendon). A good annotated version with both Hebrew text and English translation, as well as an index (in both languages), is found in P. Blackman, ed., *Mishnayot: Pointed Hebrew Text, English Translation, Introductions, Notes, Supplement, Appendix, Indexes, Addenda, Corrigenda*, 7 vols., 2nd rev. ed. (New York: Judaica Press, 1963–1964). The Tosefta, which is often dated somewhat later than the Mishnah, has been translated by J. Neusner, *The Tosefta: Translated from the Hebrew* (New York: Ktav, 1977–1986). A translation of the Jerusalem Talmud (Talmud

Yerushalmi; ca. 400 CE) into German is available in M. Hengel, *Übersetzung des Talmud Yerushalmi* (Tübingen: Mohr Siebeck, 1980). A new English translation is under way, and a number of tractates have already been published in the series Studia Judaica (Berlin: de Gruyter, 2000–); the editor is H. W. Guggenheimer. The Babylonian Talmud (Talmud Bavli; ca. 500 CE) is translated into English by I. Epstein, *The Babylonian Talmud, Translated into English with Notes, Glossary, and Indices* (London: Soncino Press, 1961). Soncino has also published an edition with both Hebrew text (Vilna edition) and an English translation (1960; 32 vols., also available digitally). The rabbinic literature is very extensive, and one ought to have access to introductory literature upon commencing one's studies in this field; a good introduction is that of G. Stemberger, *Introduction to the Talmud and Midrash* (Edinburgh: T&T Clark, 1996).

For understanding texts in institutional settings, ancient synagogues emerge as important contexts. Sources from the beginnings of these institutions until 200 CE are collected in A. Runesson, D. D. Binder, and B. Olsson, *The Ancient Synagogue from Its Origins to 200 CE: A Source Book* (Leiden: Brill, 2010).

Greco-Roman Authors and Texts

The Loeb Classical Library, providing both the original text and English translation, is the best resource that includes all of the most important authors (see the third list, "Greco-Roman Sources," below for some examples of texts and authors that are relevant to the study of the New Testament). It is important to know not only what these texts say of Greco-Roman culture, religion, and politics, but also what their authors thought about Jews and (Jewish and non-Jewish) followers of Jesus. An indispensable research tool in this regard is the work of M. Stern, *Greek and Latin Authors on Jews and Judaism*, 3 vols. (Jerusalem: Israel Academy of Sciences and Humanities, 1974–1984). For Christ groups, see J. G. Cook, *Roman Attitudes toward the Christians: From Claudius to Hadrian* (Tübingen: Mohr Siebeck, 2010). See also discussion in R. L. Wilken, *The Christians as the Romans Saw Them* (New Haven: Yale University Press, 1984). Roman law that relates to Jews is collected in the important volume by A. Linder, *The Jews in Roman Imperial Legislation* (Jerusalem: Israel Academy of Sciences and Humanities, 1987).

Beyond the sources and introductions mentioned so far, different collections of sources cover texts and inscriptions from all three categories. L. H. Feldman, *Jew and Gentile in the Ancient World* (Princeton: Princeton University Press, 1993), is a thematically organized discussion by subject, containing headings such as "Contacts between Jews and Non-Jews in the Land of Israel," "Popular Prejudice against Jews," and "The Success of Proselytism by Jews in the Hellenistic and Early Roman Periods."

A good companion to this book is L. H. Feldman and M. Reinhold, eds. *Jewish Life and Thought among Greeks and Romans: Primary Readings* (Minneapolis: Fortress, 1996). This collection of sources includes both Jewish and Greco-Roman authors, all speaking to issues where Jewish and Greco-Roman life intersected and led to various reactions, from conflict to cooperation and conversion. C. K. Barrett, *The New Testament Background: Selected Documents*, rev. ed. (London: SPCK, 1987), is also thematically organized, covering other sources. Here we find material on Roman emperors; papyri and inscriptions are organized by subject (e.g., magic and religion, socioeconomic relationships); philosophers and poets are given a chapter of their own, as are gnosis and mystery religions. A more recent and extensive collection of sources is found in C. A. Evans, *Ancient Texts for New Testament Study: A Guide to the Background Literature* (Peabody, MA: Hendrickson, 2005). This collection covers all three of the text groups noted above but also includes Samaritan sources. An added benefit is that it covers a great deal of inscriptions, coins, and ostraca, which is unusual for collections of this kind. However, a weakness of this collection is that its chapters on the Greco-Roman literature are very short (they are treated in more detail in Barrett, above).

There are a number of source books that focus on women in antiquity. Among these, the following may be mentioned: M. R. Lefkowitz and M. B. Fant, *Women's Life in Greece and Rome: A Source Book in Translation*, 3rd ed. (Baltimore: Johns Hopkins University Press, 2005); J. Rowlandson, *Women and Society in Greek and Roman Egypt: A Sourcebook* (Cambridge: Cambridge University Press, 1998).

Christ groups, whether Jewish or not, as well as other Jews often organized themselves into associations. Knowing more about Greco-Roman and Jewish associations is therefore essential. Specialized sourcebooks have recently been published by J. S. Kloppenborg, R. Ascough, and P. Harland. For students, R. Ascough, P. Harland, and J. S. Kloppenborg, eds., *Associations in the Greco-Roman World: A Sourcebook* (Waco: Baylor University Press, 2012), is recommended.

Finally, there is also a different kind of source collection, which has the layout of a commentary to the New Testament texts. This means that it goes through the New Testament texts "verse by verse," from the Gospel of Matthew to the book of Revelation, and gives, for each section of text, examples of non-Christian and later patristic source material that illuminates the passage in question. A good example of such a commentary is that of M. E. Boring, K. Berger, and C. Colpe, *Hellenistic Commentary to the New Testament* (Nashville: Abingdon, 1995).

Below we present three lists of texts or authors that are important in the study of the New Testament. The dates given in the second column are approximate. You can find the texts in which you are interested in some of the text collections and translations mentioned above. Several of these authors and texts are discussed elsewhere in this book.

Christian Noncanonical Sources

Gospels

Title and description	Approximate date
Gospel of the Nazarenes (similar to the Gospel of Matthew, authored in Aramaic [using either Matthew or Matthean tradition]; an expression of Christ-centered Judaism)	Early second century CE
Gospel of the Ebionites (emphasizes Jesus's human nature and the abolishing of sacrificial rituals; vegetarian tendencies; expression of Christ-centered Judaism)	Early second century CE
Gospel of the Hebrews (describes important events in Jesus's life; gnosticizing tendencies; expression of Christ-centered Judaism)	Early second century CE
Gospel of the Egyptians (Jesus speaks with Salome; ascetic message)	Early second century to fourth century CE
Gospel of Thomas (consists of Jesus sayings; lacks a narrative structure)	Early second century CE
Gospel of Peter (about Jesus's death and resurrection; markedly anti-Jewish)	Early second century CE
Gospel of Mary (Mary Magdalene is presented as Jesus's most-loved disciple; Jesus gives her special information that she then conveys to the others)	Second century CE
Gospel of Truth (text about the saving knowledge that is passed down through Jesus)	Second to fourth centuries CE
The Protevangelium of James (about the childhood and raising of Mary, Jesus's mother, in the temple; emphasizes the virgin birth)	Mid-second century CE
Gospel of Philip (a collection of mystical reflections, possibly consisting of excerpts from other works)	Second to fourth centuries CE
Gospel of Judas (presents Judas as Jesus's closest disciple; Judas betrays Jesus because Jesus asks him to do so)	Third to fourth centuries CE
The Secret Gospel of Mark (Jesus raises a dead man; said to be a more spiritual version of the Gospel of Mark; discovered by Morton Smith; authenticity of this document is much debated)	58? 1758? 1958?

Acts of Apostles

Title and description	Approximate date
Acts of John (about John, son of Zebedee, and his mission; among other things John raises persons from the dead)	Second half of second century CE
Acts of Paul (tells of Paul's martyrdom and how he, after his death, shows himself to Emperor Nero)	Late second century CE
Acts of Thecla (about Thecla's conversion, how she travels with Paul and shares in his mission)	Late second century CE
Acts of Peter (about Peter's adventures as a missionary, especially his confrontation with Simon Magus)	Late second century CE
Acts of Thomas (describes how the disciple Thomas, who is claimed to be Jesus's twin brother ["Toma" in Aramaic, meaning "twin"], travels to India and there spreads Christianity)	Second century CE

Letters and Similar Texts

Title and description	Approximate date
First Letter of Clement (from congregation in Rome to congregation in Corinth; contains Jesus sayings and cites Paul)	ca. 96
Didache (contains instructions on ethics, rites, and community organization)	ca. 100
Letter of Barnabas (included by certain authorities in the canon; treats the relationship between [non-Jewish] Christianity and Judaism, and sees Judaism as a false religion)	ca. 130
Second Letter of Clement (was part of the canon in certain churches; is not a letter but a sermon treating the importance of living a life of high morals before judgment comes; could contain material from the Gospel of Thomas)	Mid-second century CE
Third Letter to the Corinthians (accepted as canon by some churches; is incorporated in the Acts of Paul [see above]; anti-gnostic)	Mid-second or late second century CE

Paul's letter to the Laodiceans (included in the New Testament by some churches; consists of a compilation of different parts of Pauline theology)	Late second century CE
Pseudo-Clementine literature (*Homilies* and *Recognitions*; an expression of Christ-centered Judaism; presents two paths to salvation: Moses for Jews who do not believe in Jesus, and Jesus for all others; those who affiliate with both Moses and Jesus have achieved the best life.)	Third century
Pseudo-Titus (claims ascetic ideals and sexual abstinence also for those who are married)	Fifth century

Apocalyptic Literature

Title and description	Approximate date
The Shepherd of Hermas (focus on Christian ethics and the possibility of regretting sin and repenting also after having been baptized)	Mid-second century CE
Apocalypse of Peter (part of the canon in some churches; about the final judgment and its consequences for the evil and the good; Christ followers are given a share of the kingdom's eternal blessings)	Mid-second century CE
Apocalypse of Paul (describes Paul's vision during a journey through the heavens [cf. 2 Cor 12]; heaven and hell; reward and punishment)	Fourth century

Other Texts

Title and description	Approximate date
Odes of Solomon (there is a discussion on whether this text is "Christian" or "Jewish"; it is often listed together with Jewish texts in source collections [cf. Charlesworth, *Old Testament Pseudepigrapha*, vol. 2]; it is likely that this text originally expressed a Christ-centered Judaism)	ca. 100 CE

Jewish Sources

Apocrypha and Pseudepigrapha

Title and description	Approximate date
Tobit (story of the pious Tobit, who lived in Nineveh with his family, and whose son married a Jewish girl in Media; God helps his own; emphasizes the cohesion of family and certain rules for life)	200–100 BCE
Letter of Aristeas (about the translation of the five books of Moses [Genesis, Exodus, Leviticus, Numbers, Deuteronomy] into Greek in Alexandria)	ca. 170 BCE
Wisdom of Jesus, Son of Sirach (reminiscent of Proverbs; divine wisdom at the center; contains rules for life)	ca. 190 BCE
Sibylline Oracles, book 3 (treats the final days; condemns "idolatry" and sexual behavior that is deemed sinful; presents the importance of the temple of Jerusalem: non-Jews who send sacrifices to the temple will be saved)	163–145 BCE
Book of Jubilees (revision of stories from Genesis and Exodus)	100s BCE
Testaments of the Twelve Patriarchs (God is holy and merciful, but there is a focus on judgment; Torah and ethics at the core; ideals reminiscent of certain thoughts within Stoicism)	100s BCE
Book of Judith (tells of how the Jewish people were saved by Judith when the city Bethulia is besieged; significance of prayer and God's intervention are at the core of this story)	ca. 100 BCE
1 Maccabees (portrayal of the Jewish revolt against the Seleucid king Antiochus IV Epiphanes; the Maccabean family at the center, the same family that then ruled Israel until Rome's conquest in 63 BCE; the book covers the time span between 175 and 135 BCE)	ca. 100 BCE
Wisdom of Solomon (belongs to the genre of wisdom literature, likely written in Alexandria; about the persecution of Jews but also about God's salvation; certain aspects are reminiscent of Philo's writings)	ca. second to first century BCE

1 Enoch (consists of five separate texts that are dated differently; a heavenly messiah is mentioned in chapters 45–57)	ca. second to first century BCE
2 Maccabees (describes largely the same events as 1 Maccabees but is independent of this text)	first century BCE (before 63 BCE)
3 Maccabees (describes events that are said to have taken place in the Hasmonean period; Israel's God saves his people)	Early first century BCE in Egypt
Psalms of Solomon (three groups are portrayed: righteous, sinners [both categories within the Jewish people], and gentiles [potentially the Roman invaders]; the problem of evil is treated in multiple places)	First century BCE (likely between 70 and 40 BCE)
Testament of Job (some scholars view this text as being written by the Therapeutae, but this is impossible to prove; God is described as "Father"; women have a prominent place, and, among other things, Job's daughters inherit spiritually more important things than his sons)	First century BCE to first century CE
Joseph and Aseneth (further develops Genesis; deals with conversion to Judaism)	First century BCE to first century CE
Pseudo-Philo (Torah is the light of the world, but the text implies punishment for the ungodly; Israel cannot be destroyed as long as it does not sin; the concept of the covenant is the frame for the theological material)	First century CE, likely before 70
Testament of Moses (Moses's speech to his successor Joshua, predicting Israel's history from the conquering of Canaan to the end of time; the temple's destruction is mentioned; evil is defeated at the end)	First century CE
4 Maccabees (philosophical framework; emphasizes the triumph of reason over emotions; detailed descriptions of martyrs: rather keep the law [which is rational] and be killed than escape alive and break the law; contains connections to both Platonic thinking and Stoicism)	First century CE
4 Ezra (apocalyptic text; seeks a solution to the situation after the fall of the temple in 70 CE; strong emphasis on law and the significance of keeping it in its entirety)	ca. 90 CE–100 CE

2 Baruch (apocalyptic text; likely written in Israel, wishes to support Jews both there and in the diaspora; the temple's destruction was a punishment for Israel's sins, but God has not abandoned his people; non-Jewish nations will be destroyed in the end times, but some will be saved)	Early second century CE
Letters of Bar Kokhba (letters authored at the time of the Bar Kokhba rebellion, some of which were written by Bar Kokhba himself)	132–135 CE

Philo and Josephus

Author/title and description	**Approximate date**
Philo, *On the Contemplative Life* (an apologetic text describing Jewish sects in a positive light; especially well-known for its depiction of the Therapeutae)	First half of first century CE
Philo, *Against Flaccus* (defense against an attack on the Jews and Judaism in Alexandria)	First half of first century CE
Philo, *On the Embassy to Gaius* (defense against an attack on the Jews and Judaism in Alexandria; Philo protests before the emperor)	First half of first century CE
Josephus, *Jewish War* (seven books; Josephus blames the rebellion/war on Jewish fanatics)	Late 70s CE
Josephus, ***Jewish Antiquities*** (from creation onward, redescribed; twenty books)	ca. 94 CE
Josephus, *The Life* (autobiography)	Second half of the 90s CE
Josephus, *Against Apion* (defense of Judaism against accusations from non-Jews; two books)	ca. 96 CE

Qumran (see box 2.9, "The Qumran Literature," on p. 138)

Rabbinic Literature

Title and description	**Approximate date**
Mishnah Avot (describes, among other things, how oral Torah was conveyed through the centuries from Moses to the Pharisees; rich in ethical teachings)	ca. 200 CE (date debated), but contains earlier traditions

Mishnah Yomah (treats the Day of Atonement and the temple cult in relation to this festival)	ca. 200 CE, but contains earlier traditions
Mishnah Megillah (describes, among other things, synagogue liturgy)	ca. 200 CE, but contains earlier traditions

Greco-Roman Sources

Author and description	Approximate date
Zeno (taught in Athens; founder of Stoicism)	ca. 336–263 BCE
Cicero (politically active orator and philosopher at the time of the Roman Republic's decline and fall)	106–43 BCE
Seneca (politically active Roman philosopher [Stoic] and author of dramas)	4 BCE–65 CE
Epictetus (freed slave, Stoic philosopher; teachings preserved in the *Enchiridion* [handbook], or *The Art of Living*)	ca. 55–ca. 135 CE
Pliny the Elder (wrote *Natural History* [37 vols.]; mentions the Essenes, who, he says, lived west of the Dead Sea)	23 CE–79 CE
Dio Chrysostom (Greek orator who recorded Roman history)	ca. 40–ca. 120 CE
Plutarch (wrote biographies of eminent Romans and Greeks; also described how the Egyptian gods Isis and Osiris were worshiped [*Moralia*])	ca. 46–ca. 125 CE
Pliny the Younger (Roman senator; wrote as governor of Pontus to the Roman emperor Trajan with, among other things, questions as to how he ought to deal with [non-Jewish] Christ followers)	ca. 61–ca. 112 CE
Tacitus (Roman historian; mentions Jesus as crucified by Pilate)	ca. 56–after 118 CE
Juvenal (wrote satires; complained, among other things, of people who became Jews and thus, according to him, abandoned Roman law [*Satires* 14.100–101])	ca. 60/70–ca. 135 CE

Suetonius (wrote biographies of Roman emperors; mentions the banishment of Jews from Rome under Emperor Claudius [cf. Acts 18:2] as well as Nero's punishment of Christ followers, an incident that is also mentioned by Tacitus)	ca. 123–ca. 175 CE
Apuleius (portrayed, among other things, the Isis mysteries; in the novel *Metamorphosis*, or *The Golden Ass*, there is an excellent example of *interpretatio Romana* [11.1–5] [see also the section "Mystery Religions," p. 101])	ca. 124–170 CE
Marcus Aurelius (emperor, Stoic; represents late Stoicism; wrote *Meditations*)	121–180 CE (emperor 161–181 CE)
Dio Cassius (grandson to Dio Chrysostom; recorded Roman history)	ca. 165–after 229 CE

Appendix 2
Jewish History: A Chronological Overview

The years in the lists are approximate, and some of the dates are debated. Some information has not been included, and the lists are not complete.

Judah/Yehud under Persian Rule (ca. 539–330 BCE)

Year	Persian king	Governor of Judah/ Yehud	Source
539–530	Cyrus II (the Great)	Sheshbazzar (538)	Ezra 1:8; 5:14
530–522	Cambyses		
522–486	Darius I	Zerubbabel (515)	Hag 1:4, 14
		Elnathan (510)	Seals
		Yehoeser (490)	Ceramic seal
486–465	Xerxes	Ahsai (470)	Ceramic seal
465–424	Artaxerxes I	Nehemiah (445–432)	Neh 5:14; 12:26
423–405	Darius II	Bagavahya (407)	Papyrus
404–359	Artaxerxes II		
359–338	Artaxerxes III		
338–336	Arses (Artaxerxes IV)		
336–330	Darius III		
		Yeheskia (330)	Coins

Israel under Ptolemaic Rule (Egypt) (ca. 304–198 BCE)

Year	Ptolemaic king	Jewish high priest
304–283	Ptolemy I	Onias I (ca. 300)
283–246	Ptolemy II	Simon I (ca. 270)
246–221	Ptolemy III	Onias II (ca. 250)
221–204	Ptolemy IV	Simon II (ca. 219–190)
204–180	Ptolemy V	

Israel under Seleucid Rule (Syria) (ca. 198–167 BCE)

Year	Seleucid king	Jewish high priest
223–187	Antiochus III Megas (the Great)	
187–175	Seleucus IV Philopater	
175–164	Antiochus IV Epiphanes	Onias III (?–175; the last high priest appointed in the traditional way)
		Jason (175–172)
		Menelaus (172–162)

The Maccabean Period (167–63 BCE)

(The Maccabean Revolt begins in 167; Hasmonean state is formed in 142)

Year	Seleucid king	Jewish ruler
166–160	Antiochus IV Epiphanes (175–164)	Judas Maccabeus
	Antiochus V Eupator (164–162) (minor; regent: Lysias)	Alcimus, high priest (162–159)
160–142	Demetrius I Soter (162–150)	Jonathan Maccabeus, governor (*stratēgos*) and high priest
	Alexander I Balas (150–145)	
	Demetrius II Nicator (145–140)	
	Antiochus VI Epiphanes (145–142) (minor; regent: Diodotus Trypho)	No high priest (159–152?)
142–134	Diodotus Trypho (142–139/138)	Simon Maccabeus, governor (*stratēgos*) and high priest
	Antiochus VII Sidetes (139/138–129)	

134–104	Demetrius II Nicator (129–126/125)	John Hyrcanus, high priest
	Cleopatra Thea ("goddess") (126/125–123) Antiochus VIII Grypus (126/125–96) Seleucus V (126) *Divided kingdom* Antiochus IX Philopater Cyzicenus (114/113–95)	
104–103		Aristobulus I, king and high priest
103–76	Civil War	Alexander Jannaeus, king and high priest
	Seleucus VI (95) Antiochus X Eusebes (95) Demetrius III Philopater Soter (95–88; in Damascus) Antiochus XI Epiphanes (95; in Cilicia) Philip I (95–84/83; in Cilicia) Antiochus XII Dionysus (87; in Damascus) Philip II (84/3) Armenian occupation of Syria under Tigranes of Armenia (83–69)	
76–67	Roman General Lucullus conquers Syria (69); appoints Antiochus XIII Philadelphus as vassal king (69–63)	Salome Alexandra, queen Hyrcanus II, high priest
67–63	Pompey annexes Syria into the Roman Empire (63) and abolishes the monarchy	Aristobulus II (d. 49), king and high priest; power struggle against Hyrcanus II (who is supported by Antipater)
63	Roman general Pompey conquers Jerusalem (63)	Hyrcanus II, high priest (63–40; d. 30)

Israel under Roman Rule (from 63 BCE)

		ROMAN AND JEWISH LEADERS IN ISRAEL	
Year	**Roman ruler**	**Judea and Samaria**	**Galilee and the northeastern regions**
60–42 BCE	First triumvirate (60–48): coalition between Julius Caesar, Crassus, and Pompey	Antipater, governor of Judea (63–43 BCE) Hyrcanus II, ethnarch (47–40 BCE) without any real power	
	Julius Caesar, ruler (47–44)	Fasael, governor of Jerusalem (47–40)	Herod the Great, governor of Galilee (47–40)
	Civil war (44–42)		
42–4 BCE	Second triumvirate: alliance between Octavian, Lepidus, and Mark Antony	Partial occupation of Israel (40–38) Antigonus, high priest (40–37) Herod made king (40), rules over all Israel (37–4 BCE)	
4 BCE–41 CE	Octavian Augustus, emperor (27 BCE–14 CE) Tiberius (14–37) Gaius Caligula (37–41)	Archelaus, ethnarch over Judea, Samaria, and Idumea (4 BCE–6 CE) Judea is ruled by Roman governors: Coponius (6–9) Ambivius (9–12) Annius Rufus (12–15) Valerius Gratus (15–26) Pontius Pilate (26–36) Marcellus (36–37) after which Agrippa I	Herod Antipas, tetrarch over Galilee and Transjordan (Perea) (4 BCE–39 CE, after which Agrippa I); Philip, tetrarch over Iturea and Trachonitis (4 BCE–34 CE, after which Agrippa I)

41–54	Claudius (41–54)	King Herod Agrippa I rules over all Israel, the same area that Herod I controlled (41–44). Roman procurators rule over all Israel: Fadus (44–46), Tiberius Alexander (46–48), Cumanus (48–52).	
54–117	Nero (54–68)	Felix (52–60) Festus (60–62) Albinus (62–64) Florus (64–66)	King Agrippa II (53–ca. 100) rules over Chalcis in 50; from 53 instead over the areas that Philip had ruled; from ca. 55 also over parts of Galilee and Perea.
	Galba/Otho/Vitellius (68–69)	Jewish rebellion 66–70. Vespasian leads the Roman forces until 69, when Titus takes over. Jerusalem's temple is destroyed year 70. Masada falls ca. 74. After the war, Judea becomes a Roman province.	
	Vespasian (69–79)	Cerialis (70–71) Bassus (71–73)	
	Titus (79–81) Domitian (81–96) Nerva (96–98) Trajan (98–117)	Silva (73–81)	
117–	Hadrian (117–138)	Upon Agrippa II's death ca. 100, all of Israel is added to the province Judea. Governor: Lusius Quietus (ca. 117). Bar Kokhba revolt (132–135). Governors: Tineius Rufus (139), Julius Severus (135). Hadrian rebuilds Jerusalem as Aelia Capitolina, a Roman military colony with temples to Jupiter. The province is given a new name: Syria Palestina.	

Appendix 3
Maps

Israel under the Maccabees
Judea before the uprising, 166 BCE
Maccabean domain at maximum extent
Mediterranean Sea
PHOENICIA
Tyre
Mt. Hermon
Litani R.
Pharpar R.
Panias
Cadasa (Kedesh)
Asor (Hazor)
Seleucia
Ptolemais (Acco)
GAULANITIS
Carnaim
Sea of Galilee
Arbela
Gamala
Mt. Carmel
Sepphoris
GALILEE
Hippos
Dion
Geba
Mt. Tabor
Philoteria (Beth-Yerah)
Yarmuk R.
Abila
Gadara
Edrei
Dora
GALADITIS
Strato's Tower
Scythopolis (Beth-shan)
Pella
Narbata
SAMARIA
Samaria
Mt. Ebal
Ragaba
Gerasa (Jerash)
Mt. Gerizim
Shechem
Amathus
Apollonia
Capharsaba
Pharathon
Jordan R.
Jabbok R.
Yarkon R.
Alexandrium
Joppa
Ramathaim
Gedor
Beth-dagon
Adida
Timnah
Gophna
TOBIADS
Lydda
Modin
Apherema
Bethel
Philadelphia (Amman)
Jamnia (Jabneh)
Beth-horon
Elasa
Mizpah
Dok
Gazara (Gezer)
Caphar-salama
Michmash
Jericho
Adasa
Azotus (Ashdod)
Kidron
Emmaus
Jerusalem
Heshbon
Mt. Nebo
Samaga
Beth-haccherem
JUDEA
Qumran
PHILISTIA
Bethlehem
Hyrcania
Ascalon (Ashkelon)
Beth-zacharias
Beth-basi
Medeba
Marisa (Mareshah)
Adullam
Tekoa
Beth-zur
Machaerus
Hebron
Dead Sea
Anthedon
Gaza
Adora (Adoraim)
En-gedi
Arnon R.
IDUMEA
Masada
Raphia
N. Besor
Arad
Beer-sheba
NABATEA
Zoar
AKRABATTENE
Zered R.
0 10 20 30 miles
0 10 20 30 40 kilometers

Israel in New Testament Times
Extent of Herod's kingdom
Herodian fortress city
Decapolis city (time of Herod)
Other city
Territory given to Herod Philip
Territory given to Archelaus; Roman province of Judea since 6 CE
Territory given to Herod Antipas
Decapolis
Mediterranean Sea
Sidon
Abila
ABILENE
ITUREA
Abana R.
Damascus
SYRIA
Mt. Hermon
Pharpar R.
Leontes R.
Tyre
PHOENICIA
Caesarea Philippi
GAULANITIS
TRACHONITIS
Raphana
L. Huleh
J. Jarmuk
Hazor
GALILEE
TETRARCHY OF PHILIP
Ptolemais (Acco)
Chorazin
Capernaum
Gennesaret
Bethsaida
Gergesa
Sea of Galilee
BATANEA
Mt. Carmel
Kishon R.
Cana
Magdala
Hippos
Sepphoris
Tiberias
Yarmuk R.
Nazareth
Mt. Tabor
Abila
AURANITIS
Nain
Gadara
Dor
Megiddo
Caesarea (Strato's Tower)
Scythopolis
Pella
Dion
SAMARIA
DECAPOLIS
Sebaste (Samaria)
Salim?
Gerasa
Mt. Ebal
Amathus
Mt. Gerizim
Sychar
Jordan R.
Jabbok R.
Me Jarkon
Antipatris (Aphek)
Alexandrium
Joppa
PEREA
(SEMI-INDEPENDENT MUNICIPALITY)
Philadelphia (Amman)
Jamnia
Jericho
Azotus (Ashdod)
Emmaus
Cyprus
Mt. Olivet
Esbus (Heshbon)
Jerusalem
Bethany
Bethany beyond Jordan
Medeba
Bethlehem
Hyrcania
Ashkelon
JUDEA
Herodium
Machaerus
Hebron
Adora
Gaza
Dead Sea
Arnon R.
Raphia
Besor Br.
IDUMEA
Masada
Arad
Beer-sheba
Malatha
NABATEA
Zered Br.
0 10 20 30 miles
0 10 20 30 kilometers

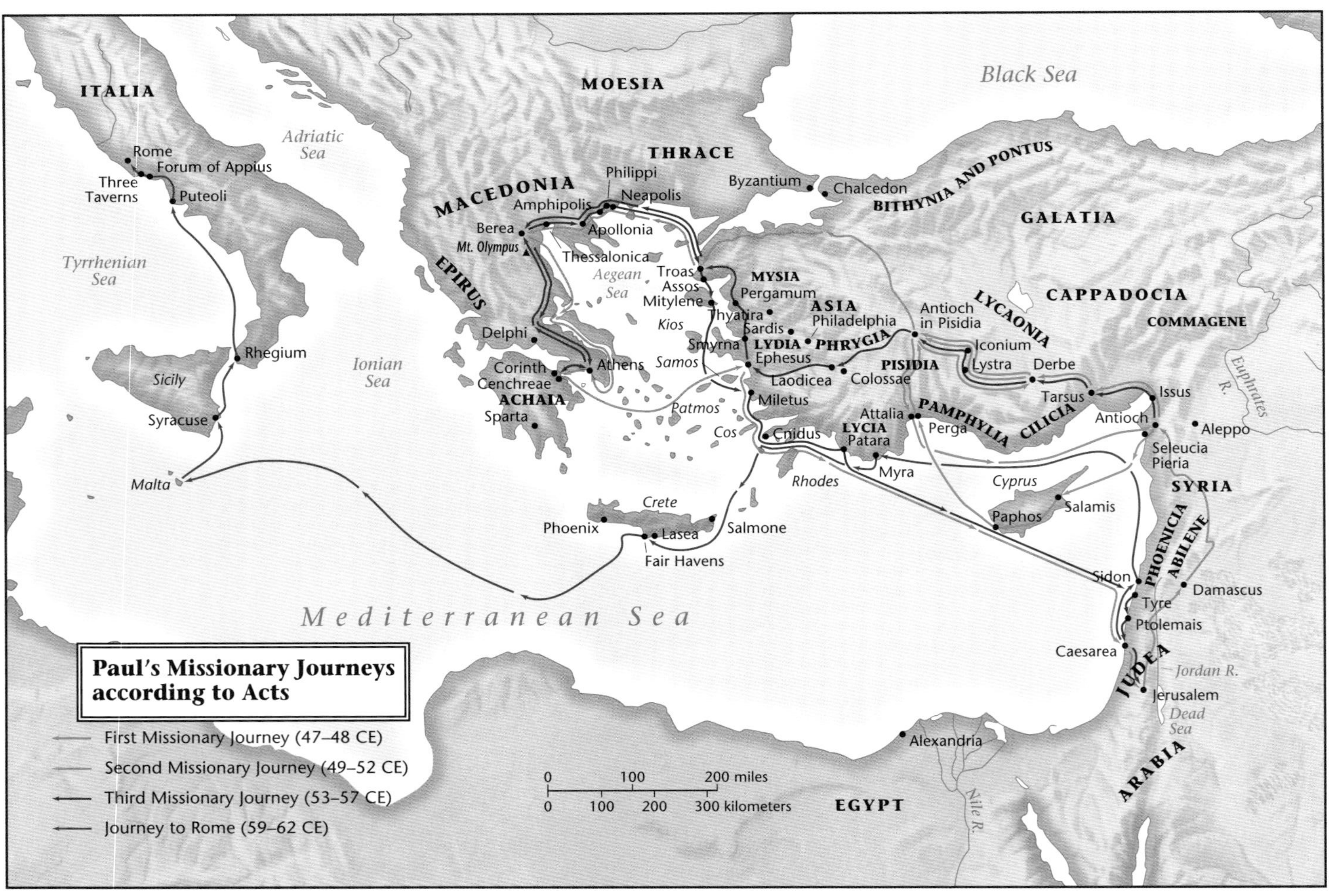
Paul's Missionary Journeys according to Acts
First Missionary Journey (47–48 CE)
Second Missionary Journey (49–52 CE)
Third Missionary Journey (53–57 CE)
Journey to Rome (59–62 CE)
0 100 200 miles
0 100 200 300 kilometers
Black Sea
Mediterranean Sea
Aegean Sea
Ionian Sea
Adriatic Sea
Tyrrhenian Sea
Dead Sea
Euphrates R.
Jordan R.
Nile R.
ITALIA
MOESIA
THRACE
MACEDONIA
EPIRUS
ACHAIA
MYSIA
LYDIA
ASIA
PHRYGIA
PISIDIA
LYCIA
PAMPHYLIA
CILICIA
LYCAONIA
GALATIA
CAPPADOCIA
COMMAGENE
BITHYNIA AND PONTUS
SYRIA
ABILENE
PHOENICIA
JUDEA
ARABIA
EGYPT
Rome
Three Taverns
Forum of Appius
Puteoli
Rhegium
Sicily
Syracuse
Malta
Mt. Olympus
Berea
Amphipolis
Apollonia
Thessalonica
Philippi
Neapolis
Delphi
Corinth
Cenchreae
Sparta
Athens
Troas
Assos
Mitylene
Kios
Samos
Patmos
Cos
Rhodes
Crete
Phoenix
Lasea
Fair Havens
Salmone
Byzantium
Chalcedon
Pergamum
Thyatira
Smyrna
Sardis
Philadelphia
Ephesus
Miletus
Cnidus
Laodicea
Colossae
Antioch in Pisidia
Iconium
Lystra
Derbe
Perga
Attalia
Patara
Myra
Tarsus
Issus
Antioch
Seleucia Pieria
Aleppo
Cyprus
Salamis
Paphos
Sidon
Tyre
Ptolemais
Caesarea
Jerusalem
Damascus
Alexandria

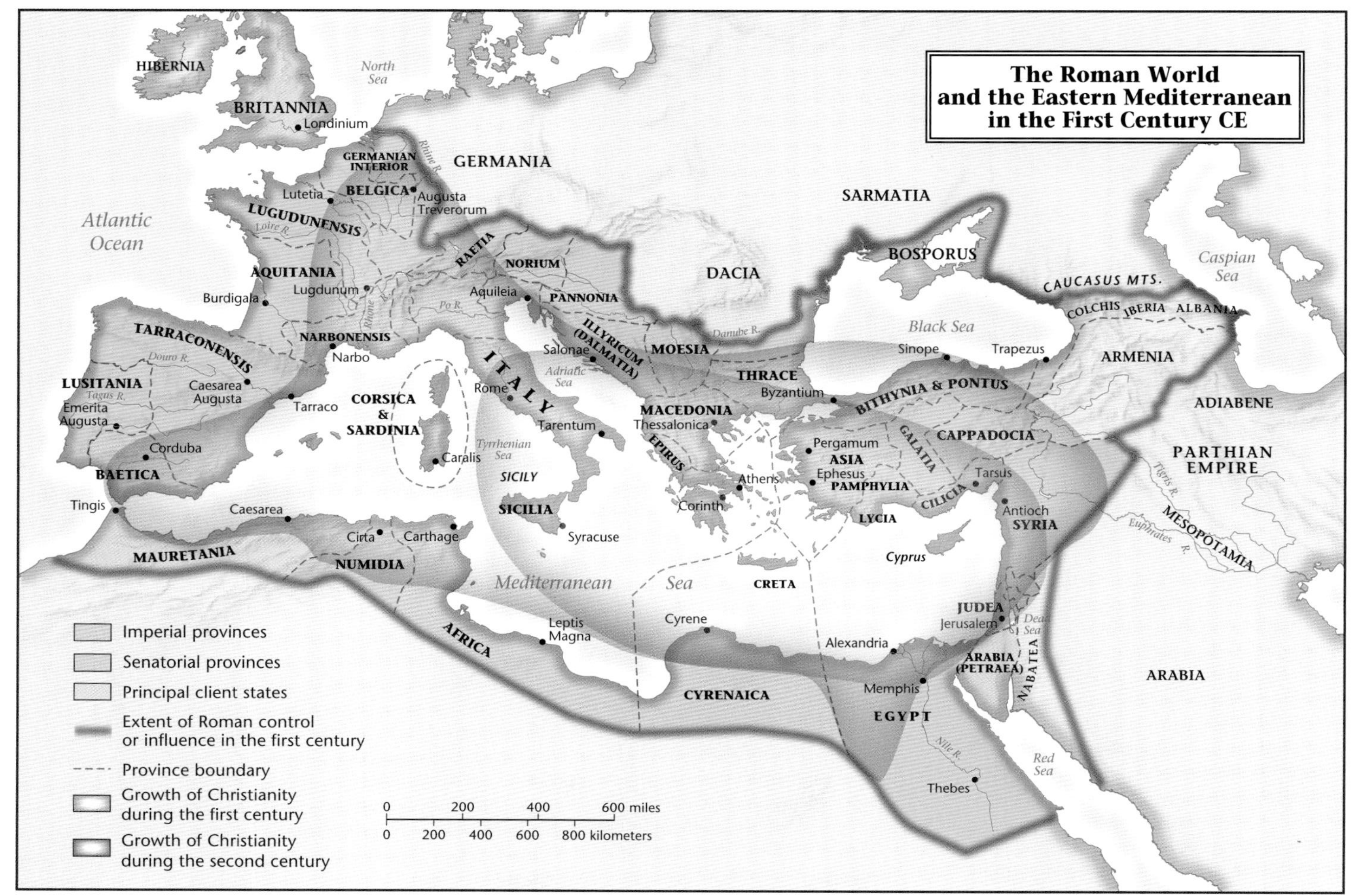
The Roman World
and the Eastern Mediterranean
in the First Century CE
HIBERNIA
North Sea
BRITANNIA
Londinium
GERMANIAN INTERIOR
GERMANIA
Rhine R.
Lutetia
BELGICA
Augusta Treverorum
SARMATIA
Atlantic Ocean
LUGUDUNENSIS
Loire R.
RAETIA
NORIUM
BOSPORUS
DACIA
Caspian Sea
CAUCASUS MTS.
AQUITANIA
Lugdunum
Aquileia
PANNONIA
Burdigala
Rhone R.
Po R.
COLCHIS
IBERIA
ALBANIA
Black Sea
Danube R.
TARRACONENSIS
NARBONENSIS
Narbo
ILLYRICUM (DALMATIA)
Salonae
MOESIA
Sinope
Trapezus
ARMENIA
Douro R.
ITALY
Adriatic Sea
THRACE
Byzantium
LUSITANIA
Tagus R.
Caesarea Augusta
CORSICA & SARDINIA
Rome
BITHYNIA & PONTUS
ADIABENE
Emerita Augusta
Tarraco
MACEDONIA
Thessalonica
Tarentum
CAPPADOCIA
Corduba
Tyrrhenian Sea
Pergamum
ASIA
GALATIA
PARTHIAN EMPIRE
Caralis
EPIRUS
Ephesus
Tarsus
BAETICA
SICILY
Athens
PAMPHYLIA
Tigris R.
Tingis
Caesarea
SICILIA
Corinth
CILICIA
Antioch
SYRIA
LYCIA
MESOPOTAMIA
Euphrates R.
Cirta
Carthage
Syracuse
MAURETANIA
NUMIDIA
Cyprus
Mediterranean
Sea
CRETA
JUDEA
Jerusalem
Dead Sea
Cyrene
Leptis Magna
Alexandria
AFRICA
ARABIA (PETRAEA)
NABATEA
ARABIA
Memphis
CYRENAICA
EGYPT
Nile R.
Red Sea
Thebes
Imperial provinces
Senatorial provinces
Principal client states
Extent of Roman control or influence in the first century
Province boundary
Growth of Christianity during the first century
Growth of Christianity during the second century
0 200 400 600 miles
0 200 400 600 800 kilometers

Glossary

Abraham (Abram) The first of Israel's three patriarchs (Gen 12–25). He emigrated from Mesopotamia to Canaan and entered into a covenant with God, the sign of which was circumcision (Gen 17:10). He obeyed God's commandment to sacrifice his son Isaac but was stopped by an angel of the Lord just before the act. Instead, he sacrificed a ram (Gen 22). The place of this sacrifice was later identified as Jerusalem.

Achaia A Roman province that covered the south of Greece, with Corinth as its capital.

Adam According to Gen 2, he was the first human being. He is compared in 1 Cor 15 and Rom 5 with Christ. Adam came from earth and was given physical life; Christ, the last Adam, came from heaven and is the Spirit that gives life. Through Adam's disobedience, sin was introduced to the world; Christ's obedience gives life and righteousness to all.

Alexander the Great (356–323 BCE) A Macedonian ruler who through his conquest spread Greek culture throughout the entirety of the eastern Mediterranean regions, as well as into regions near (modern) India's borders. With him, Hellenism was born. His teacher was the philosopher Aristotle.

Alexandria The name of a great number of cities that were founded by Alexander the Great. The most renowned is Alexandria at the Nile Delta in Egypt. Alexandrian theology emerged from the end of the second century and is characterized by an allegorical interpretation of the Bible (Clement of Alexandria, Origen).

antichrist (Gk. for "against Christ") Enemy of Christ and his followers (e.g., 1 John 2:18; cf. 1 Thess 2:3; Rev 13:5).

Antioch in Galatia/Pisidia Originally a Phrygian city that was founded by Seleucus I Nicator. From 43 CE, the city is included in the Roman province of Galatia. Antioch was located near the border to Pisidia, which gave rise to the expression "Antioch in Pisidia" (*Antiocheian tēn Pisidian*) in Acts 13:14.

Antioch on the Orontes Ancient and medieval city in Syria, now called Antakya and located in Turkey. According to Acts 11:26, this city housed the first Christ groups outside Israel.

Antiochus Epiphanes (ca. 204–164 BCE) A Syrian monarch who attempted to hellenize the Jews and replace the worship of Israel's God in the temple of Jerusalem with that of Zeus, leading to the Maccabean Revolt.

apocalypse (Gk. *apokalypsis*, "revealing, revelation") The word is used for texts that claim to reveal something, a secret, that has been hidden. This gave rise to the name of the book of Revelation, the last book of the New Testament.

apocalyptic A kind of worldview and body of literature characterized by revelations about the end of the world through visions and journeys to heaven. An initiated soothsayer, often writing under a pseudonym, is shown divine secrets and uses these to predict the future.

Apocrypha (Gk. *apokryphos*, "hidden" or "difficult to understand") Apocryphal texts claim authority but often lack general recognition as legitimate parts of the Bible. There are New Testament as well as Old Testament Apocrypha; among the New Testament Apocrypha we find, for example, the Gospel of Thomas. Many of these texts contain teachings that go against mainstream Christian tradition. *See also* Nag Hammadi; pseudepigrapha; Septuagint.

Apostolic Fathers Designates a collection of Christian writings from around 100–150 CE: Didache, the First Letter of Clement, the seven letters of Ignatius, the letter of Polycarp and Polycarp's martyrdom, the Letter of Barnabas, the so-called Second Letter of Clement, the Shepherd of Hermas, the Letter to Diognetus, and the fragments of Papias. The authors of these texts are considered by tradition to have been disciples of the apostles.

***aposynagōgos* (Gk. for "excluded from the synagogue")** The word is found in the New Testament only in John 9:22; 12:42; and 16:2.

Aramaic A Semitic language that originated in the central Euphrates region and spread to Syria and Mesopotamia around the years 800–600 BCE. The books of Ezra and Daniel in the Hebrew Bible contain Aramaic sections. Jesus would have spoken an Aramaic dialect when he addressed the crowds.

Aristotle (384–322 BCE) A Greek philosopher and natural scientist. He began studies at Plato's academy in Athens at age seventeen, became the teacher and mentor of the thirteen-year-old prince Alexander of Macedonia (who became "the Great") in 343 BCE, and taught from 355 BCE in the Lyceum in Athens. Among his many writings are *Physics*, *Metaphysics*, *On the Heavens*, *Nicomachean Ethics*, *Politics*, *Rhetoric*, and *Poetics*.

ark of the covenant A holy chest for the Israelites that represented God's presence.

It was placed in the "holy of holies," the inner room, first in the tabernacle and later in the temple of Jerusalem (Exod 25:19–22; 1 Sam 1–6; 2 Sam 6; 1 Kgs 8).

Armageddon According to Rev 16:16, the location of the final battle. Likely the name is referring to the plains of Megiddo and the ancient city Megiddo, near Mount Carmel. The city was an important strategic stronghold.

Asia Minor Ancient designation of Anatolia, a peninsula between the Black Sea and the Mediterranean basin, which today constitutes the main part of Turkey's Asian regions. The border to the east is unclear but is sometimes defined as the upper reaches of the Euphrates. In antiquity, Asia Minor was divided into the following: Cappadocia, Pontus, Paphlagonia, Bythinia, Galatia, Phrygia, Mysia, Troas, Aeolis, Lydia, Caria, Lycia, Milyas, Cabalia, Pamphylia, Pisidia, Lycaonia, Isauria, and Cilicia.

Athanasius (ca. 295–373 CE) Bishop of Alexandria. He authored a text to the "entire" church in the year 367 CE, wherein the twenty-seven books that today constitute the New Testament are counted as writings recognized by the church.

Augustine of Hippo (354–430 CE) Theologian from Tagaste in North Africa who was of great importance to Roman and Reformation theology. His best-known work, *Confessions*, contains the famous words, "You have made us for yourself, and our hearts are restless until they rest in you."

Augustus (63 BCE–14 CE) Roman statesman and emperor (31 BCE–14 CE). His original name was Gaius Octavian, but he was later adopted by Julius Caesar, shortly before Caesar's death. As son and heir, he swore to avenge Caesar's murder.

Babylon Capital of Babylonia, founded by Hammurabi (1792–1750 BCE), capital of the Neo-Babylonian Empire (625–539 BCE). Alexander the Great wanted to make the city the center of his vast empire, but instead its significance diminished over time. In 1 Pet 5:13 the author greets the addressees from the church in "Babylon," which in contemporary Jewish and Christian literature was a code name for Rome (cf. Rev 14:8; 18:2).

Balaam Diviner from Petor on the Euphrates who was persuaded by Balak, king of the Moabites, to curse Israel but was instead forced by God to bless the people three times (Num 22–24). Balaam then attempted to get the people to reject God by tempting them to participate in cultic prostitution (Num 31:16). In the New Testament, Balaam symbolizes seductive false teachers who lead good Christians into sinful behavior and idolatry for personal gain (Jude 11; 2 Pet 2; Rev 2:14).

Bar Kokhba (d. 135 CE) Born Simon ben Kosiba, he was the leader of the Jewish revolt against the Romans in 132–135 CE. Bar Kokhba means "son of the star," and many thought him to be the messiah. The revolt was violently crushed, Bar Kokhba fell, and Jerusalem was destroyed and replaced by a Roman city (Aelia Capitolina), to which no Jew had access.

Barabbas Jewish man who was arrested by the Romans for committing murder and other crimes, mentioned in connection with Jesus's trial.

Barnabas Coworker of Paul, mentioned in the Pauline letters (e.g., Gal 2:11–15) and in Acts. Barnabas was a Levite from Cyprus and was originally called Joseph. According to tradition, he founded the church on Cyprus and is buried there.

Barnabas, Letter of A Christian writing from around 130 CE that is included in the collection Apostolic Fathers.

Beroea Name of a city in southern Macedonia, located at the foot of Mount Bermios, where Paul arrived on his second missionary journey and founded a church. Paul's coworker Sopater was from Beroea.

Bethesda ("the house of mercy") Name of a dual pool in ancient Jerusalem with five porticoes. Its water was believed to have miraculous powers (cf. John 5).

Bethlehem ("house of bread") The city where Jesus was born (Matt 2:1; Luke 2:4), located in Judea near Jerusalem. As King David was from Bethlehem, it was believed that the messiah would also be born there. *See also* Nazareth.

Birkat Haminim The twelfth prayer in the second part of the daily prayers of the mornings and evenings in the synagogue. Birkat Haminim is a prayer against false teachers.

bishop (Gk. *episkopos*, "overseer") In New Testament times, the term was not clearly distinguished from "elder" (Gk. *presbyteros*). In Acts 20 the elders of the congregation in Ephesus (v. 17) are also called overseers (v. 28). The plural for overseers (*episkopoi*) in one congregation is also found in Phil 1:1. Instructions concerning the qualities and way of life of a bishop are given in 1 Tim 3:1–7 and Titus 1:7–9.

Bodmer papyri Very old papyrus texts that are now curated by the Bibliotheca Bodmeriana in Cologny, outside Geneva. Together with the Chester Beatty papyri, they contain, except for a few small fragments, the oldest manuscripts of the New Testament (the oldest of which is from ca. 200 CE). *See also* papyri.

Caesar, Julius (100–44 BCE) Roman commander, statesman, and ruler who came from the patrician house of the Julii.

Caesarea Ancient city name that was given to cities in honor of the Roman emperors Augustus and Tiberius; among them are Caesarea Philippi and Caesarea Maritima.

Caesarea Maritima ("by the sea") Also called Qesarya (Hebrew transcription), a city on the coast of Israel between Haifa and Tel Aviv. Named by Herod the Great. *See also* Caesarea.

Caesarea Philippi City on the source of the Jordan River, named by the tetrarch Philip. *See also* Caesarea.

Caiaphas High priest in Jerusalem during the years 18–36 CE and chairman of the Sanhedrin during the trial of Jesus.

Canaan (possibly Heb. for "lowlands") Designation of the region that God, according to Gen 12:5, gave to Abraham and his descendants. The people living in the lands before the Israelites conquered it were called Canaanites.

canon (Lat. *canon*, from Gk. *kanōn*). The word has a number of related meanings: "straight bar/rod," "yardstick," "precept," "rule," "pattern," "table," etc. It was used in religious contexts to describe an authoritative text or collection of texts.

Canon Muratori A manuscript fragment found in 1740 by the librarian L. A. Muratori in Milan. The text originated in Rome ca. year 180 and contains a canon list (list of Holy Scriptures). In the fragment, criteria are given of what may be accepted as canonical texts. See the section "Which Texts Belong to the New Testament?" on p. 211.

Capernaum Small city off the northern beaches of the Sea of Galilee, founded in the second century BCE, and a center of Jesus's activities.

Catholic Letters (Gk. *katholikos*, "general") General letters in the New Testament addressed to a broad audience: 1–2 Peter, 1–3 John, James, and Jude. In a strict sense, only 2 Peter and Jude fulfill this criterion.

Cephas (Aramaic for Gk. *petros*, "the rock") Byname of Jesus's disciple Simon (John 1:42), a fisherman from Capernaum. He is portrayed as the foremost of "the twelve" and is included, together with John and James, in an inner circle around Jesus. According to the Gospel of Matthew, he was chosen by Jesus as the "rock" (Aramaic *kefa*, Gk. *petra*) on which the church would be built (Matt 16:17–19). Paul speaks of Cephas in, for example, Gal 2:11.

Chester Beatty papyri Biblical manuscripts from the third century CE currently curated by the Chester Beatty museum in Dublin. *See also* Bodmer papyri; papyri.

Chloe Rich woman from Corinth who is mentioned in 1 Corinthians. She was probably a house-church leader.

Christ (Gk. *christos*, "the anointed," from Heb. *mashiakh*, "messiah") The Jewish title "messiah" can be used for several Jewish savior figures, while Christians use the title "Christ" only for Jesus of Nazareth. Among Greek-speaking Christ groups, the title became fixed to Jesus's name very early on and was no longer translated.

Christology Study of Christ. Titles and statements from the New Testament about the man Jesus from Nazareth are systematized and related to faith in his divinity.

Cicero (106–43 BCE) Roman orator and author who, after studies in Greece, became a politician and attained the highest political office (consul) in the year 63 BCE. He first attempted to mediate the conflict between Caesar and Pompey, then sided with Pompey, but reconciled with Caesar after Pompey's defeat at Pharsalus in the year 48 BCE. Cicero wrote several books on the art of speaking, as well as many letters.

Clement of Alexandria (ca. 150–215 CE) Christian theologian and author, leader of the Catechetical School of Alexandria.

Clement of Rome (ca. 91–101 CE) Bishop of Rome and author of the First Letter of Clement, specified by the list of popes as Peter's third successor.

Clement, First Letter of Included in the collection Apostolic Fathers. *See also* Clement of Rome.

codex (Lat. for "wooden block" or "trunk") Began to be used for wax-covered wooden tablets on which one could write; later the meaning shifted to "manuscript" (cf. the word "book," which has a similar history). Later, terms like *codex membranaceus* (parchment manuscripts) and *codex chartaceus* (paper manuscript) emerged. In late antiquity the book format eventually replaced the scroll.

Codex Alexandrinus, A (02) Originated in Egypt in the fifth century CE. It contains almost all of LXX and the New Testament (lacking parts of John, 2 Corinthians, and most of Matthew) as well as the first and second letters of Clement. It is now curated by the British Museum.

Codex Bezae Cantabrigiensis, D1 (05) A bilingual Greek-Latin codex that originates in the fourth to the sixth centuries CE in the west (uncertain location). It contains the Gospels and Acts and is curated by Cambridge University Library.

Codex Claramontanus, D (06) Greek-Latin codex from the sixth century CE that contains the Pauline letters and is curated by Bibliothèque Nationale in Paris.

Codex Ephraemi Rescriptus, C (04) Originated in the fifth century CE and contains the New Testament (except Revelation). It is curated by Bibliothèque Nationale in Paris.

Codex Sinaiticus, א (01) Originated in Egypt or Palestine in the mid-fourth century CE. It contains the second half of LXX, all of the New Testament, the Letter of Barnabas, and the Shepherd of Hermas. It has been curated since 1933 by the British Museum.

Codex Vaticanus, B (03) Originated in Egypt in the beginning of the fourth century CE and contains the majority of LXX and the New Testament (except Hebrews, the Pastorals, Philemon, and Revelation). Since the end of the fifteenth century it has been curated by the Vatican Library.

Colossae Ancient city in Phrygia, near modern Honaz in western Turkey. Colossae lost much of its significance when the nearby Laodicea was founded in the third century BCE.

Corinth City on the Peloponnesus in southern Greece, where Paul founded a church ca. 49–50 CE. Archaeological remains of a Doric Apollo temple from ca. 540 BCE and a Roman forum, as well as the Nymphaeum built around the Pirene (Gk. *peirēnē*, nymph who turned into a fountain), are found at ancient Corinth. Modern Corinth lies approximately five kilometers southwest of the ancient city.

cosmology Study of the universe. In theological contexts, it can refer to different theories of the world's origins, meaning, and purpose.

covenantal nomism Term coined by the biblical scholar E. P. Sanders, referring to the Jewish theological idea that God's free and merciful election of the Jewish people as his people entails both promises and obligations stated in the Torah.

Dead Sea Scrolls Collective term for the manuscripts discovered near Qumran on the Dead Sea's northwestern side. The find was made in 1947 by a Bedouin boy who discovered, by chance, a few scrolls inside a pot in a cave. Further finds were made in ten caves in the surrounding region. The texts likely belonged to a group of Essenes that had chosen an eremitical life in the desert. Among them is a complete copy of the book of Isaiah and large or small fragments of all the biblical books except for the book of Esther. See box 2.9, "The Qumran Literature," p. 138.

deuterocanonical texts Writings belonging to a later phase of the canon. It is a Catholic term used for texts that were included in the Septuagint and the Christian Bible. These texts were excluded from the Hebrew Bible (Tanak) by Palestinian Jews. In the Protestant tradition, the same texts are collectively called "apocryphal writings." They are in turn distinguished from other texts that also originated within a Jewish setting but were never included in the Septuagint. These latter texts are called "apocrypha" in a Catholic context and "pseudepigrapha" in a Protestant context. Within Judaism, they are usually labeled as *sefarim chitzonim* (outside texts).

Diatessaron (Gk. *dia*, "through," *tessarōn*, "four") Designation for a gospel harmony that was put together by Tatian ca. 170. A gospel harmony is a synthesis of the four canonical gospels into a single account of Jesus's life. Only an Arabic translation and some allusions are preserved. It is unclear whether the original language was Greek or Syrian.

diaspora ("scattering, dispersion") Designates a scattered population that originates from a particular geographic location, often because of involuntary mass dispersion, such as the expulsion of Jews from Judea or Greeks from Constantinople. In the New Testament, it usually designates groups of Jews that have settled somewhere around the Mediterranean.

diatribe A literary genre that came into existence in the fourth century BCE among wandering Cynic philosophers. The genre corresponds to a kind of sermon with additions of anecdotes, satire, and fictional conversations, sometimes exhibiting a polemical character.

Didache Also known as "The Teaching of the Twelve Apostles," a Christian text in Greek from ca. 100 CE, which is included in the collection Apostolic Fathers.

Didymus of Alexandria (ca. 313–398 CE) Alexandrian theologian within the tradition of Origen. He is also called Didymus the Blind, because he was blind from age five.

docetism The body of teachings that claims Christ lacked a physical human body and thus only appeared (Gk. *dokeō*) to have one. This entailed that neither his suffering, his death, nor his resurrection was considered real.

Domitian (51–96 CE) Son of Vespasian and Flavia Domitilla, a Roman emperor who succeeded his brother Titus and died in the year 81 CE. He is known for his persecution and exiling of Christians and philosophers. He became gradually more despotic, came into conflict with the senate, and fell victim to a conspiracy that, apparently, even his wife Domitia participated in.

doxa The opinion that others have of one: estimation, view, reputation, credit, honor, glory.

doxology (Gk. for "glorification, praise") Within Judaism, prayers and songs are concluded with doxologies to God. Christianity's doxologies are often directed toward the Trinity (Father, Son, and Holy Spirit).

Easter *See* Passover.

Ebionites, Gospel of the *See* Hebrews, Gospel of the.

ecclesiology The study of the Christian church.

Elijah One of the prophets of Israel, active during the ninth century BCE. According to 2 Kgs 2, he was taken up to heaven in a chariot of flames. In later Jewish tradition, and even in the New Testament, Elijah is mentioned as the forerunner of the messiah, perhaps in the figure of John the Baptist. Elijah appears on the Mount of Transfiguration together with Moses (Matt 17:1–13).

Enoch Son of Jared and Noah's great-grandfather who according to Gen 5:24 while "walking" with God was taken up to heaven. There are three pseudepigraphical books with apocalyptic content that bear his name. When a text refers to the book of Enoch with no further specification, it would generally signify the first book of Enoch. *See also* deuterocanonical texts.

Epaphras Coworker of Paul who founded the church in Colossae.

Epaphroditus Member of the church in Philippi who brought a monetary gift with him from this congregation to Paul. In the Letter to the Philippians, Paul tells the congregation that Epaphroditus, who had been ill, is now well.

Ephesus Ancient city on the west coast of Asia Minor by the river Kaystros, the center of Paul's mission. The city was known for its Temple of Artemis, which was counted among the seven wonders of the ancient world. According to tradition, Jesus's mother, Mary, lived in Ephesus.

Epicureans Followers of the Greek philosopher Epicurus (341–270 BCE), who taught that happiness consisted of enjoying life in the company of good friends. See the section "Popular Philosophies," p. 104.

epistle (Gk. *epistolē*, "something transmitted") The word is often used as a genre designator of letters and letter-like writings in the New Testament.

eschatology (Gk. for "the study of the last things") The part of theology that deals with what occurs at the end of time, such as the destruction of the world, Jesus's return, the general resurrection, and the final judgment.

Essenes (Aramaic; etymology uncertain, maybe "the pious ones," "the silent ones," or "the healers") One of the Jewish religious factions in the time of Jesus. They appear to have lived separated from the rest of society, with high morals and a strong belief in fate. *See also* Qumran.

Eucharist (Gk. *eucharistia*, "thanksgiving, gratefulness") Term used for the symbolic meal of bread and wine in communion with Christ.

Eusebius of Caesarea (ca. 263–340 CE) Bishop of Caesarea Maritima who wrote the first "church history" from ca. 313 CE.

Ezra A priest who, together with Nehemiah, returned from the Babylonian exile to lead the rebuilding of the temple and the land, beginning in 538 BCE. Ezra handled primarily the religious reform work, while Nehemiah was in charge of political and social concerns. Ezra and Nehemiah have lent their names to one book each in the Hebrew Bible. In the Septuagint, the books are called First and Second Ezra, and in the Tanak they form a single text (Ezra-Nehemiah). There is also a Third and Fourth Ezra, the latter of which belongs to apocalyptic literature.

Fourth Ezra *See* Ezra.

Galatia Designates either the Roman province Galatia in central Asia Minor, which was created in the year 25 BCE, or a smaller region in the north of this province, from which the name of the entire province stemmed. The regions in the north were invaded in the third century BCE by Celtic tribes (Gk. *galatai*).

Galilee Region in the north of Israel. It contains the Sea of Galilee (also called Lake Tiberias), the cities Nazareth and Capernaum, and Mount Tabor (588 meters above sea level). In the New Testament, Galilee had a fairly poor reputation among certain groups in Judea/Jerusalem (John 7:52) and was seen as a political trouble area. Most of Jesus's activities occurred here. After the fall of the temple in 70 CE and Jerusalem's destruction around year 135, many Jews moved to Galilee. With time the region became a center of Jewish learning with several rabbinical schools.

Gamaliel the Elder An important Pharisaic teacher of the law during the first century CE, potentially related to the great Hillel; according to Acts 5:34–39, he was a respected member of the Sanhedrin. According to Acts 22:3, Paul had sat "at the feet of Gamaliel"—that is, studied under him.

Gnosticism Religious movement with a dualistic worldview. Spiritual insight or knowledge (Gk. *gnōsis*) was seen as the premise for liberation from the material, evil world, and thus for salvation.

gnostics *See* Gnosticism.

gospel (Gk. *euangelion*, "good news") First used to describe Jesus's message of the kingdom of God (Mark 1:14), later also for stories about Jesus, the gospels.

Hadrian (76–138 CE) Roman emperor from 117 CE. Hadrian founded the colony Aelia Capitolina where Jerusalem had been located before it was destroyed in the year 70. This triggered the Jewish Great Revolt under the leadership of Bar Kokhba, 132–135.

***hapax legomenon* (Gk. for "once said")** Term used for words or expressions that occur only once in a language's written sources from a certain time period, a certain author, or a certain body of text. The meaning of these words and expressions can be difficult to determine.

Hasmoneans Descendants of Hasmon, the Maccabean patriarch. This designation is especially used for rulers of the Jews during the first century CE. Many of these rulers were also high priests.

Hebrew Bible *See* box 1.2, p. 9.

Hebrews (Gk. *hebraious*) Term used in Acts 6:1 for Jews whose primary language of communication was Hebrew or Aramaic.

Hebrews, Gospel of the Variant of, or related to, the Gospel of Matthew.

Hegesippus (ca. 110–180 CE) Greek Christian author. From his five books, called the "Memoirs," nine citations are preserved by Eusebius.

Hellenism (Gk. *Hellēnismos*; cf. 2 Macc 4:13) Classification of the period of time in antiquity that began with Alexander the Great's death in 323 BCE. Ethnic Greeks (*Hellēnes*) spread their culture over a large geographical area, from the western Mediterranean all the way to Afghanistan.

Hellenist (Gk. *Hellēnistēs*) Designation for non-Greeks in antiquity who had acquired the Greek language and Greek culture, including Greek-speaking Jews. The population of Alexandria in Egypt (founded by Alexander the Great) originally consisted of a significant portion of Jews who spoke Greek. Under Ptolemy's rule (after 323 CE), the Hebrew Bible was translated in Egypt into Greek (the Septuagint). According to Acts 6, the first congregation in Jerusalem consisted of Hellenists and Hebrews.

Hermas, Shepherd of The most comprehensive text in the collection Apostolic Fathers.

Herod Antipas Ruled Galilee and Perea as a tetrarch after his father's, Herod the Great's, death, from 4 BCE until 39 CE. Ordered the execution of John the Baptist.

Herod the Great (ca. 73–4 BCE) Jewish king in Israel and tetrarch of Judea. He was named king of Judea in 40 BCE by the Roman senate. He is known for his merciless extermination of real and imagined enemies, as well as his colossal building projects, including the expansion of the temple in Jerusalem.

heterodox (Gk. *heteros*, "other," and *doxa*, "estimation/view") That which deviates from the orthodox.

Hierapolis City in Phrygia, near the hot springs in modern Turkey's Pamukkale. It was founded ca. 190 BCE by Eumenes II of Pergamum. It is said that the apostle Philip was active in Hierapolis and was ultimately both crucified and stoned there.

high priest (Gk. *archiereus*) This term is used in several religions. In Judaism, the office of the high priest was the highest religio-political position attainable, closely tied to the temple in Jerusalem. Only high priests were allowed to enter the holy of holies, the inner room in Jerusalem's temple, once a year. On that occasion they would present sacrifices and prayers for the people's atonement; cf. Heb 7–9.

Ignatius of Antioch (d. ca. 110 CE) Bishop of Antioch in Syria who was brought as a prisoner to Rome, where he was presumably executed. On the journey to Rome, he wrote the seven so-called Letters of Ignatius. *See also* Apostolic Fathers.

imitatio Christi Expresses the idea of taking Jesus as a model for one's own way of life. Paul speaks of a life "in Christ," a close communion with him and an imitation of his way of life. In the history of the Church, the ideal of imitation has been seen as an ascetic way of life, but also as something that can be realized in everyday life.

Irenaeus (d. ca. 202 CE) Bishop of Lugdunum (Lyon), a disciple of Polycarp of Smyrna in Asia Minor, who spoke against the gnostics in *Adversus Haereses* (*Against Heresies*). He is the first Christian author who refers to the four gospels.

Isaac Son of Abraham and Sarah, younger half-brother of Ishmael, married to Rebecca and father of Jacob and Esau.

Israel (Heb. for "God struggles" or "struggle with God," Gen 32:28; Hos 12:4) A name for Jacob that later became the name of an entire people and its land (Heb. *Eretz Israel*); cf. Matt 2:20–21. *See also* Palestine.

itacism (after the Greek letter *iota*) A change in the pronunciation of ancient Greek, which meant that the letter *ē* (*ēta*) and some diphthongs began to be pronounced like an *i* (*iota*). Phoebe (Gk. *Phoibē*), for example, was pronounced Phibi. Itacism began in classical times and abounded during the Hellenistic era.

Jacob Son of Isaac and younger twin brother of Esau, married to Laban's daughters Leah and Rachel. According to Gen 32:28, Jacob received the byname Israel. His twelve sons are seen as the fathers of Israel's twelve tribes.

James, "brother of the Lord" Leader of the church in Jerusalem (Acts 12:17; Gal 2:9), mentioned as one of Jesus's brothers in Mark 6:3. He was highly respected for his piety and, according to Acts 15:13–21, had a decisive voice at the meeting of apostles in Jerusalem in 49 CE. The James referred to in the Letter of James is in all likelihood this one, the "brother of the Lord." Josephus recounts that the high priest Ananias ordered James to be stoned to death ca. 62 CE.

James, son of Zebedee Brother of John (Matt 4:21).

Jerusalem (Heb. *Yerushalayim*) City 689–800 meters above sea level, surrounded by three deep valleys: Hinnom, Tyropoion, and Kidron. Jerusalem was conquered in 990 BCE by King David and his son, King Solomon, who ordered the construction of the temple that would later become the center of Jewish faith and identity. When the kingdom was divided after the death of Solomon, Jerusalem became the capital of Judea, later to become the capital of all of Israel. During Roman times Jerusalem was the most important Jewish city until 70 CE, when it was conquered by the Romans (Vespasian, Titus). The city was more or less in ruins until Emperor Hadrian destroyed it entirely in order to replace it with a Roman city by the name of Aelia Capitolina (*see also* Bar Kokhba). Not until the fourth century CE, when Emperor Constantine and his mother built significant churches in the city (as well as at other locations), did Jerusalem get back its original name. The church meeting in Nicaea (year 325) named Jerusalem Christianity's fourth most important place, and at the church meeting in Chalcedon (year 451), the city was named an independent patriarchate. At that time, many Jews had also reestablished themselves in their holy city.

John the Baptist Jewish judgment-prophet and healer/preacher at the end of the 20s

CE. According to Luke 1, his father was a priest and his mother was related to Jesus's mother, Mary. He lived as an ascetic in the desert, preached of the proximity of judgment and the need for radical repentance, and offered a baptism for the forgiveness of sins. Some of Jesus's foremost disciples had originally been disciples of John (John 1), and most likely Jesus too was one of John's disciples before he initiated his own movement. *See also* Mandaeans.

John the presbyter According to information from Papias in Eusebius's *Ecclesiastical History*, there were two Christian leaders in Asia Minor toward the end of the first century with the name John. One was the disciple John, son of Zebedee, and the other John the presbyter. Probably, different "Johns" authored the Johannine writings.

John, son of Zebedee One of Jesus's disciples who, together with his brother James and Simon Peter, formed an inner circle around Jesus. According to Christian tradition, he is the author of the Gospel of John and the letters of John and is said to have written the book of Revelation during his imprisonment on the island of Patmos (cf. John the presbyter). In art, he is usually depicted as a young man, and his gospel symbol is the eagle.

Joseph of Arimathea Member of the Sanhedrin in Jerusalem who according to the New Testament was given permission to take care of Jesus's dead body and bury him (Mark 15:42–47).

Josephus (Flavius Josephus, ca. 37–100 CE) Jewish historian of a priestly family from Jerusalem, and a Pharisee. He predicted the ascent of the Roman general Vespasian to emperor and was rewarded by being named the Flavian dynasty's protégé (hence the byname Flavius). Josephus authored four works: *War of the Jews*; *Antiquities of the Jews*; *Against Apion*; and the autobiography *The Life of Flavius Josephus*. These works contain important information about Jewish movements, traditions, and customs.

Judah Name of Jacob's fourth son with Leah (Gen 29:35), and father of one of Israel's twelve tribes. The Davidic dynasty belonged to the tribe of Judah. It was originally a designation for the tribe's land to the south of Jerusalem, and after 926 BCE for the entire Southern Kingdom (up until 587 BCE) with Jerusalem as its capital. During Persian times, it was called Yehud. When the Jews returned from their exile, the regions around Jerusalem were once more named Judah. The name occurs in Ezra-Nehemiah. *See also* Judea.

Judas One of Jesus's disciples with the byname Iscariot (Luke 6:16; Acts 1:13). Judas betrayed Jesus and surrendered him to the Sanhedrin. It is possible that his byname indicates a "man from Cariot."

Judas, "brother of the Lord" (Mark 6:3) According to Christian tradition, this Judas was the one who authored the Letter of Judas.

Judas, Gospel of Mentioned by Irenaeus in his text against false teachers and must therefore have originated before 180 CE. A Coptic translation of the gospel was discovered in Egypt in the twentieth century. It "surfaced" in Geneva in the 1970s but was not made public until 2006.

Judea The area around Jerusalem as well as the lowlands by the coast—that is, the land that previously constituted the region of the tribe of Judah. It was invaded in 63 BCE by the Romans, who subsequently left its rule to the Idumean prince Herod (thus making him king). His successor, Archelaus, came to power in 4 BCE, but ten years later the Romans converted Judea, Samaria, and Idumea to the single Roman province Judea, part of the greater administrative unit of Syria. The province was now ruled by a Roman *praefectus* (26–36 CE by Pontius Pilate). When the Romans had crushed the Bar Kokhba rebellion in 135 CE, the province's name was changed to Palestine.

Junia Female apostle according to Rom 16:7.

Justin Martyr (d. ca. 165 CE) A Greek from Flavia Neapolis in Samaria (modern Nablus). Justin Martyr suffered, as indicated by his name, the death of a martyr in Rome. He describes Christianity as the true philosophy.

Laodicea Name of several ancient cities, among which figures Laodicea on the Lycus (a tributary to the Meander River near modern Denizli in Turkey), a flourishing city with wool as the primary trading product. One of the seven addressed messages of Revelation (3:14–22) is to Laodicea; in it the church members are reproached for their lukewarm nature.

legalism A pejorative term indicating that a religion's inner core consists of laws and requirements that must be followed, so that salvation is by works rather than by faith. Compare to covenantal nomism.

Levites In the Bible they are descendants of Levi, father of one of Israel's twelve tribes. Levites did service in the temple of Jerusalem and had no land territory of their own; their livelihood came from their service in the temple.

LXX The Septuagint.

Lystra City in Lycaonia, the province designating the plains north of the Taurus Mountains (Acts 14:6, 11).

Maccabean Revolt *See* Maccabees.

Maccabees The name originates from the freedom fighter Judas Maccabeus and became a collective designation for the family that led the so-called Maccabean Revolt during the second century BCE. The revolt won independence for the Jewish people from the Seleucid ruler Antiochus IV Epiphanes. The Maccabee Simon's descendants were also called Hasmoneans.

Mandaeans (also Nasoreans) A group of people from primarily southeastern Iraq and southwestern Iran. The Mandaean language of literature is a form of eastern Aramaic. Mandaean religion has its origins in late antiquity and contains Jewish, Christian, Babylonian, and Iranian elements. John the Baptist is a central figure, and the most important sacrament is baptism, which can be experienced several times.

Marcion (d. ca. 160 CE) Ship owner from Pontus in Asia Minor who lived in Rome between 139 and 144 CE and then returned to Asia Minor as a church leader. The Marcionite church spread throughout the East and existed into the fifth century.

Melchizedek According to Gen 14, Melchizedek was a priest-king in Jerusalem in the time of Abraham, perhaps a pre-Israelite king. According to Heb 4:14–5:10, he was an impeccable high priest and a "type" of Jesus. In the gnostic text *Melchizedek* from Nag Hammadi, Melchizedek is identified with Jesus, and in Qumranite texts he is portrayed as a divine figure.

Mesopotamia ("between the rivers") The region around the Euphrates and Tigris (modern Iraq).

Messiah *See* Christ.

midrash (Heb. for "interpretation, translation") Jewish exposition of the Bible and designation for rabbinical collections of such expositions. The oldest are Mekhilta, Sifra, and Sifre to Genesis, Exodus, Leviticus, Numbers, and Deuteronomy, respectively. For examples of midrash in the New Testament, see 1 Cor 10:1–4; Gal 3:15–18.

Miletus City in Asia Minor near the mouth of the river Meander (Menderes), where Paul, according to Acts 20:17, met with the elders of the church in Ephesus. During archaic times (ca. 700–480 BCE), Miletus was a significant trading city. It was destroyed during the Ionian revolt (494 BCE), but flourished once more in the second century CE.

Mishnah (Heb. for "repetition," "teach") Judaism's oldest collection of oral Torah, divided into six main parts ("orders") with a total of sixty-three tractates, recorded ca. 200 CE under the leadership of Rabbi Yehuda ha-Nasi. *See also* Torah, Talmud.

Nag Hammadi City in central Egypt that became world famous overnight in 1945 with the discovery of the so-called Nag Hammadi texts, which comprise fifty-two mostly gnostic writings, most of them in Coptic, written on papyrus.

Nazarenes, Gospel of the *See* Hebrews, Gospel of the.

Nazareth City in Galilee where Jesus grew up.

Nehemiah *See* Ezra.

Nero (37–68 CE) Roman emperor from 54 CE, the last ruler of the Julio-Claudian dynasty. In 62 CE, Nero's first wife, Octavia, was exiled and murdered, and he married Poppaea in her stead. Nero is remembered in Christian tradition for scapegoating Christians for the Great Fire of Rome in 64 CE.

Nicodemus Pharisee and member of the Jewish Sanhedrin who visited Jesus in secret (John 3:1–12) and participated in Jesus's burial (John 19:39–42).

Nicopolis City by the Adriatic Sea, located south of Corfu (Corcyra), mentioned in the letter to Titus.

Octavian *See* Augustus.

Onesimus One of Philemon's slaves who was sent back to him by Paul.

Origen (ca. 185–254 CE) Theologian and apologist from Alexandria, disciple of Clement of Alexandria and his successor as leader of the Catechetical School from ca. 203 CE. He was ordained in 230 CE in Caesarea Maritima and is one of the ancient church's greatest biblical scholars with many extensive Bible commentaries; often his writings are characterized by allegorical interpretations of the Bible, which are likely an inheritance from Philo. According to Origen, the human soul is preexistent and determined to return to God (Gk. *apokatastasis*).

orthodox (Gk. *ortho*, "straight," and *doxa*, "estimation/view") Means accepted/approved/correct teaching; also a label for the eastern churches that adhere strictly to the teachings of the ecumenical councils.

Our Father A prayer from Jesus that has been recorded in different versions in Matt 6:9–13 and Luke 11:2–4.

Palestine (Gk. *Palaistinē*, of Heb. *Pleshet*) Originally a name for Philistia, a coastal area in southern Phoenicia. In the fifth century BCE, Herodotus used the term "Palestinian Syria" (*Syriē hē palaistinē*). The majority of Jewish and non-Jewish sources, however, call the same area (or parts of it) Judah/Yehud/Judea, the last of which was also used by the Romans on coins minted after their victory over Jerusalem in the year 70 CE (IVDEA CAPTA). After the Bar Kokhba rebellion in 135 CE, Emperor Hadrian officially changed the name of the region to Palestine. The word "Palestine" does not appear in the New Testament. *See also* Judea, Israel.

Papias (d. ca. 150 CE) Bishop of Hierapolis, a city in Asia Minor near Laodicea.

papyri The earliest textual testimonies of the New Testament are written on sheets of papyrus. They are numbered as P^1, P^2 . . . The oldest hitherto known New Testament papyrus is P^{52} from around 125 CE. It contains fragments of John 18 and is curated by the John Ryland's University in Manchester. Other important and early papyri are P^{45} from the third century, which contains parts of the Gospels and Acts; P^{46} from around 200 CE, which contains parts of the Pauline letters (not the Pastoral Letters) and Hebrews; P^{47} from the third century, which contains Rev 9:10–17:2; P^{66} from around 200 CE, which contains the majority of the Gospel of John; and P^{75} from the end of the second century, which contains the majority of the Gospel of Luke and about half of the Gospel of John. *See also* Chester Beatty papyri, Bodmer papyri.

papyrus Material on which to write that was produced from the third millennium BCE using stalks of the papyrus plant in Egypt. Wide strips were laid out in two intersecting layers, pressed together, and hit with a hammer, after which the surface was polished. *See also* papyri, parchment.

parchment Animal hides that have been processed so that one can write on them; the process was refined in Pergamum (cf. "Pergament"). *See also* papyrus.

paraenesis Exhorting/admonishing section of a text or sermon.

parousia (Gk. *parousia*, "presence, arrival") Term used for Christ's return in the end times. There was a widespread expectation of an imminent parousia among the early followers of Jesus.

Passover (Heb. *Pesach*) Together with the Feast of Booths (*Sukkot*) and Pentecost (*Shavuot*), the Feast of Passover is one of the great Jewish festivals, where the exodus from slavery in Egypt is celebrated along with the birth of the Jewish people. Passover occurs on the fifteenth of Nisan (between March 15 and April 30). In the Christian church year, Easter or Pascha, closely linked to the Passover, concludes the Holy Week and is celebrated in remembrance of Christ's resurrection.

Pastoral Letters A designation for three Pauline letters that are addressed to coworkers of Paul: 1 and 2 Timothy and Titus.

Pauline letters Of the thirteen letters of the New Testament that claim Paul as the sender, seven are counted as being actually authored by him (Romans, 1 and 2 Corinthians, Galatians, Philippians, 1 Thessalonians, Philemon). The authorship for three of the letters is disputed (Ephesians, Colossians, 2 Thessalonians). For the final three, it seems safe to assume that Paul was not the author (1 and 2 Timothy, Titus).

pedagogue (Gk. *paidagōgos*) A slave in ancient Greece who led children to and from school, and sometimes even taught them in the home (cf. Gal 4:1–3). Later, the word came to include various teachers and instructors.

Pentateuch (Gk. *penta-teuchos*, "scroll-of-five") A name for the five books attributed to Moses (Genesis, Exodus, Leviticus, Numbers, Deuteronomy).

Pergamum (Gk. *Pergamon* or *Pergamos*) Turkish Bergama, ancient city in Mysia that is mentioned in sources from ca. 400 BCE. The city had a significant library. Victories over the Galatians led to, among other things, the creation of the Altar of Zeus (Altar of Pergamum). One of the seven letters in Rev 2 and 3 is written to Pergamum (Rev 2:12–17). *See also* parchment.

Pesach *See* Passover.

pesher commentaries (Heb. *pesher*, "interpretation, solution") Among the Dead Sea Scrolls, a great number of texts were found in which biblical books—especially books of prophets and psalms—are interpreted verse by verse. A verse is cited and followed by "and its pesher is . . ." The interpretations aim to demonstrate that the "true" meaning of the text actually relates to the Qumran community and its history. Early followers of Christ used this interpretative method for the purpose of identifying allusions to Jesus in the prophetic books (e.g., Matt 1:15).

Peshitta (Syriac for "the simple/easy") Early Syrian translation of the Bible from around 380 CE.

Peter *See* Cephas.

Pharisees (probably "the separated") Religious and political party that was in stark conflict with the priestly party known as the Sadducees. They emphasized the importance of the entire people interpreting the Torah as they did. The idea of separation refers to the Pharisees' strong emphasis on ritual purity. Interpretation of the Scriptures was adapted to new situations and contexts. Two known Pharisees from the first century are Hillel and Shammai. According to the Gospels, Jesus criticized the Pharisees for their view on ritual laws. In many regards, however, Jesus was close to the Pharisees, and many of his early followers were in fact Pharisees (e.g., Paul). It is important to note that the criticism comes from *within Judaism*, not from any outside party.

Philadelphia (Gk. for "sibling love") One of the seven letters in Rev 2 and 3 is to a church in the city Philadelphia in Lydia, modern-day western Turkey (Rev 3:7–13).

Philemon A Christ-believing slave owner, likely from Colossae (Phrygia), to whom Paul wrote the Letter to Philemon.

Philippi Ancient city in northern Greece that was founded in 356 BCE by Philip II of Macedonia. This city was significant also in Roman times. Paul founded the first Christian church in Europe in Philippi (Acts 16; Letter to the Philippians).

Philo of Alexandria (also Philo Judaeus, ca. 25 BCE–40 CE) Jewish philosopher who wished to unite Platonism, Stoicism, and Jewish theology. He often interpreted the biblical texts allegorically. Philo identified the Logos (the Word) with divine reason and spoke of it as God's firstborn son. That the Logos would become flesh (John 1:14) was irreconcilable with Philo's philosophy. *See also* Origen.

Phoebe Deacon in the church of Cenchreae who delivered Paul's letter to Rome (Rom 16:1–2).

Phoenicia A collection of city-states located in the southeastern Mediterranean regions. *See also* Palestine.

Pilate, Pontius (likely d. 39 CE) Prefect of Judea (*praefectus Iudaeae*), 26–36 CE, who had multiple bloody conflicts with the populace. He gave the death sentence to Jesus and was later removed from power by the emperor because of misrule.

pneumatology Study of (the Holy) Spirit.

Polycarp (d. ca. 156 CE) Bishop of Smyrna in Asia Minor. According to tradition, he was a disciple of the apostle John in Ephesus. His letters to the church in Philippi are preserved. Polycarp's *Martyrdom* is the oldest-known Christian text on martyrdom.

Praetorium Name for both a Roman prefect's residence and for the Imperial Guard's accommodation in Rome.

preexistence A term for Jesus's existence before the creation of the world. Belief in Jesus's preexistence may be implied in John 1:1–14 and Phil 2:6–7.

presbyter (from Gk. *presbyteros*, "older person," "elder") In many early societies and religious communities elders played a distinctive and well-known leadership role (Gen 50:7; Exod 12:21; Num 20:7; Ezra 6:7). Elders are mentioned frequently as members of the Sanhedrin (e.g., Matt 21:23; Mark 15:4; Luke 20:5; Acts 4:5). The first congregation of Christ followers in Jerusalem was led by the (twelve?) apostles and elders (Acts 11:30; 15:4, 22). James, "the brother of Jesus," seems to have had a decisive voice among the elders (Acts 15:19). Decisions, however, were made with "the consent of the whole congregation" (Acts 15:22).

priest (Gk. *hiereus*) In the Hebrew Bible, as well as in the New Testament, priests are ministers of the temple cult (e.g., Matt 8:4). When Jesus is called "a priest for ever" (Heb 7:21) or a "high priest" (Heb 7:26), the connection with the temple cult is apparent. The designations "holy priesthood" (*hierateuma hagion*) in 1 Pet 2:5 and "priests" (*hiereis*) in Rev 1:6; 5:10; and 20:6 comprise *all* believers. As to church leadership, the New Testament mentions only bishops, presbyters, and deacons. Christian denominations with priests as leaders emphasize that "priest" is etymologically derived from the Greek word *presbys*, "old man."

pseudepigrapha (from Gk. for "untrue signature") Designating texts that are written under pseudonyms. Anonymous authors use the name of an ancient person with great authority to gain the attention of their audience. The designations "pseudepigrapha" and "apocrypha" are closely related but are used differently in Catholic and Protestant traditions (deuterocanonical). *See also* Apocrypha, deuterocanonical texts.

Q source ("Q" from the German *Quelle*) A source containing words attributed to Jesus that many scholars argue was used in the Gospels according to Matthew and Luke.

Quintilian (ca. 35–100 CE) Roman teacher of rhetoric; classical rhetorician with Cicero as his model. His twelve-volume *Institutio oratoria* contains instructions on rhetoric and moral stance.

Quirinius (d. 21 CE) Roman politician and prefect of Syria, 6–7 CE, who ordered a census of Judea. In Luke 2:2 this census is mistakenly associated with the birth of Jesus.

Qumran Community to the northwest of the Dead Sea, where archaeologists have excavated a compound that had been inhabited from ca. 135 BCE to 68 CE. The group living there placed great weight on ritual purity and communal meals. *See also* Essenes.

rabbi Teacher of Torah in Judaism.

rabbinic According to rabbinic theology, Torah represents God's presence (*shekhinah*). Therefore, study of the Torah is one of the most important tasks humans can have. The rabbi's role is to apply the Torah and its laws to different situations, taking changes in context into account. The rabbinic period stretches from 70 CE to the Arabian conquest in the beginning of the seventh century.

Sadducees A religious conservative party in Israel that primarily consisted of aristocrats and the upper ranks of the priesthood in Jerusalem.

Samaritans People who trace their origins back to before the Jewish exile and claim to be heirs to the old Israelite traditions. Samaritans rejected the temple in Jerusalem and saw their own temple on Mount Gerizim as the original center of worship of Israel's God (cf. John 4).

Sanhedrin (Heb. loanword from Gk. *synedrion*, "gathering") The highest Jewish juridical body in Judea, led by the high priest.

Sardis The capital of the Kingdom of Lydia (modern Turkish Sart), where the rich king Croesus reigned. During Roman times, the area was part of Asia Minor.

One of the seven authored messages in Rev 2 and 3 is to the Christ followers in Sardis (Rev 3:1–6).

Sea of Galilee Also called Lake Tiberias. According to the synoptics, it was at the shores of this lake that Jesus called his first disciples, Peter, Andrew, James, and John, who were fishermen.

Septuagint (from the Latin for "seventy," abbreviated with the Roman numerals LXX) A translation of the Jewish Scriptures to Greek. According to the Letter of Aristeas (second century BCE), seventy-two Jewish teachers, six from each tribe, came from Jerusalem, on the request of the Pharaoh Ptolemy II Philadelphus (285–247 BCE), to Alexandria and independently translated each of the five books of the Pentateuch from Hebrew to Greek, and their texts were found to be entirely in agreement. The other texts in the Hebrew Bible and some other Jewish texts were translated later. The Septuagint has a larger scope than the Hebrew canon, including texts that have later been labeled deuterocanonical or Old Testament apocrypha.

Sermon on the Mount Compilation of Jesus's words in Matt 5–7. This compilation includes the Beatitudes, the Lord's Prayer, and well-known sayings like "Love your enemies and pray for those who persecute you" (5:44), "Ask, and it will be given to you; search, and you will find . . ." (7:7), and "Do to others as you would have them do to you" (7:12).

Silvanus (or Silas) Leader among the Christ followers of Jerusalem who was sent out with Paul and Barnabas to Antioch in order to deliver the final decision of the Jerusalem Conference. He became one of Paul's companions (Acts 15) and is listed as one of the senders of 1 Peter (5:12).

Simon *See* Cephas.

Smyrna Rich Greek trade city on Asia Minor's west coast (cf. Rev 2:8–11).

Sodom and Gomorrah Significant cities in the Valley of Siddim by the Dead Sea that are judged and destroyed, according to Gen 19, through fire from heaven because of their sinfulness. They become a symbol of God's punishing judgment (Matt 10:15; 11:23).

Son of Man (Gk. *ho huios tou anthrōpou*) Jesus's self-description in the Gospels that elsewhere in the New Testament occurs only in Acts 7:56. The meaning of the expression is unclear, but it appears to be original, as it was not taken up by Jesus's followers as a christological title and does not figure in any creeds.

Sosthenes Head of the synagogue in Corinth and spokesman in the accusation of Paul before the Roman governor Gallio (Acts 18:17).

Stephen One of the seven men who were chosen to organize the distribution of food among the widows in Jerusalem's congregation. Stephen was stoned to death after a speech before the Sanhedrin and is counted as the first Christian martyr (Acts 6–8). Among his opponents are the men from the "synagogue of the Freedmen" (Acts 6:9).

Stoicism A school within Greek and Roman philosophy with an emphasis on personal ethics that was founded by Zeno of Citium in the fourth century BCE. Zeno taught in a portico, the *Stoa* in Athens, hence the name.

Suetonius (ca. 70–130 CE) Roman author who wrote *De Vita Duodecim Caesarum* (Lives of the Twelve Caesars). He wrote detailed and partially indiscrete portraits of Roman rulers from Caesar to Domitian.

synagogue (from Gk. *synagōgē*, "gathering, house of gathering") In the land of Israel, there were communal (public) synagogues with social, political, and religious functions, as well as association synagogues with a common religious interest (e.g., the synagogues of the Essenes) or common specific societal group (e.g., "the synagogue of the Freedmen," Acts 6:9). In the diaspora, Jewish gatherings and gathering houses were seen as a kind of *collegia*—that is, associations among others.

syncretism (Gk., literally "together as the Cretans") The term is used to designate a mixing of views/beliefs from two or more religions—for example, when Greek and oriental views were intertwined with a mystery cult. Many scholars consider the term problematic.

tabernacle The portable sanctuary that the Israelites carried with them during the forty-year desert wandering (Exod 25–27). Acacia wood made up the tabernacle's frame, with bindings of flax yarn. The ark of the covenant was kept in the tent's inner room, the holy of holies, which was separated from the previous room by a valuable curtain called *paroket*.

Tacitus (ca. 56 to after 118 CE) Senator and historian of the Roman Empire.

Talmud Judaism's foremost collection of oral Torah in which Mishnah is expanded with rabbinic discussions. Talmud exists in two versions: the younger Babylonian Talmud (Talmud Bavli), which was completed ca. 500 CE, and the older and shorter collection, the Palestinian or Jerusalemite Talmud (Talmud Yerushalmi) from ca. 400 CE. Like the Mishnah, both Talmudim are divided into orders (*sedarim*) and tractates (*massekhot*) with primarily juridical (halakic) and narrative (haggadic) materials.

Tanak An acronym that is constructed of the first letters in Torah (Law), Nevi'im (Prophets), and Ketuvim (Writings). Tanak contains twenty-four books, whereas the Christian Old Testament, owing to another way of assembling the same texts, contains thirty-nine books. The difference with regard to content is negligible.

Tertullian (d. after 220 CE) Church father active in Carthage who wrote apologetics and polemics against Jews and heathens and against Marcion (*Adversus Marcionem*). He sided with Montanism and broke away from the mainstream church ca. 207 CE (according to Jerome's *De viris illustribus* [On famous men] 53).

Thecla Legendary coworker of Paul, known through the Acts of Paul and Thecla from the end of the second century CE.

Theophilus (Gk. for "loved by God") Addressee of both the Gospel of Luke and Acts. The honorary attribute "most excellent" (Luke 1:3) speaks for the addressee being a real person, perhaps a Roman official (cf. Acts 23:26 and 24:2 where the governor Felix is addressed in the same way).

Thessalonica One of ancient Macedonia's most important cities, founded in 315 BCE and named after the sister of Alexander the Great. The strategic location along the Via Egnatia and the ideal port opening facilitated the city's growth and development into a military and commercial center. In 146 BCE the Romans made the city the capital of all of Macedonia. To this day, the Via Egnatia leads straight through the city and past the remains of Emperor Galerius's Triumphal Arch (Kamara) from 305 CE (which signifies Roman victory over the Persians in 297 CE).

Thomas, Gospel of Collection of 114 Jesus sayings that was found in Nag Hammadi in a Coptic manuscript. The original language was likely Greek, and the text originated at the latest in the second century CE. Many of the Jesus sayings are also known from or reminiscent of sayings in the Synoptic Gospels, especially Matthew, while others are unique, such as number 77b: "Cleave a (piece of) wood; I am there. Raise up a stone, and you will find me there" (translation by Blatz).

Timothy Coworker of Paul from Asia Minor (mentioned in, e.g., 1 Thess 1:1).

Titus (39–81 CE) Son of Vespasian, completed the campaign against Judea and succeeded his father as Roman emperor in the year 79 CE. *See also* Domitian.

Titus Coworker of Paul (cf. Gal 2:1) and, according to Titus 1:4, the addressee of the Letter to Titus.

Torah (Heb. for "teaching") In a narrow sense, a designation for the five books of Moses (Genesis, Exodus, Leviticus, Numbers, Deuteronomy), but also a general designation of that which is seen as God's teachings to his people. In rabbinic tradition, it is normal to distinguish between written and oral Torah. The latter was recorded in the Talmud, the core of which is the Mishnah.

Trajan (53–117 CE) Roman emperor from 98 CE.

Twelve, the In Matt 10, Luke 6, and Acts 1, the Twelve are listed by name: "first, Simon, also known as Peter, and his brother Andrew; James son of Zebedee, and his brother John; Philip and Bartholomew; Thomas and Matthew the tax collector; James son of Alphaeus, and Thaddaeus; Simon the Cananaean, and Judas Iscariot" (Matt 10:2–4). The number twelve is a symbol of Israel's twelve tribes, and these twelve disciples therefore are thought to represent the foundation of the renewed people of God.

two-source hypothesis A theory that claims that the Gospels according to Matthew and Luke build to a great degree on two written sources: the Gospel of Mark and an oral source, which is designated as Q. *See also* Q source.

Tychicus Coworker of Paul according to, for example, Acts 20:4 and Eph 6:21.

Vespasian (Titus Flavius Vespasian, 9–79 CE) Roman emperor from 69 CE and founder of the Flavian dynasty; father of Titus and Domitian. He was the general of an army of four legions that was sent out to quell rebellious Judea at the end of the 60s. Vespasian began construction of the Coliseum in Rome.

Via Egnatia Roman military and commercial road from around 150 BCE. The Via Egnatia created a link between Asia Minor and Europe, between the Bosporus strait and the Adriatic Sea.

Vulgate (Lat. *Vulgata*, "the common translation") A revision of Latin translations of the New Testament and a new translation of the Old Testament from Hebrew to Latin, made by Jerome (Hieronymus) around 400 CE. During medieval times, the Vulgate became the official Bible of the Roman Catholic Church.

Zealots (from Gk. *zēlōtēs*, "eager supporter") A religiously motivated resistance movement against Roman occupation of Israel, which shared many ideals with the Pharisees.

Contributors

Håkan Bengtsson (ThD, Uppsala University), associate professor of religious studies, Department of Theology, Uppsala University, Sweden

Samuel Byrskog (ThD, Lund University), professor of New Testament, Center for Theology and Religious Studies, Lund University, Sweden

Ismo Dunderberg (ThD, University of Helsinki), professor of New Testament, Faculty of Theology, University of Helsinki, Finland

Bengt Holmberg (ThD, Lund University), professor emeritus of New Testament, Center for Theology and Religious Studies, Lund University, Sweden

Jonas Holmstrand (ThD, Uppsala University), associate professor of New Testament exegesis, Department of Theology, Uppsala University, Sweden

Marianne Bjelland Kartzow (ThD, University of Oslo), professor of New Testament, Faculty of Theology, University of Oslo, Norway

Thomas Kazen (ThD, Uppsala University), professor of biblical studies, Stockholm School of Theology, University College Stockholm, Sweden

Dieter Mitternacht (ThD, Lund University), professor of New Testament and early Christianity (retired), Lutheran Theological Seminary, Hong Kong, China; Church of Sweden Liaison Officer for Theological Education in Asia

Birger Olsson (ThD, Uppsala University), professor emeritus of New Testament, Center for Theology and Religious Studies, Lund University, Sweden

Samuel Rubenson (ThD, Lund University), professor of church history, Center for Theology and Religious Studies, Lund University, Sweden; senior professor of Eastern Christian studies, Sankt Ignatios College, Stockholm School of Theology

Anders Runesson (PhD, Lund University), professor of New Testament, Faculty of Theology, University of Oslo, Norway; adjunct professor of early Christianity and early Judaism, Department of Religious Studies, McMaster University, Canada

Anna Runesson (Ph.Lic., Lund University), university chaplain, University of Oslo, Norway

Hanna Stenström (ThD, Uppsala University), associate professor of New Testament, Stockholm School of Theology, University College Stockholm, Sweden

Kari Syreeni (ThD, University of Helsinki), professor emeritus of New Testament, Åbo Akademi University, Finland

Mikael Tellbe (ThD, Lund University), associate professor of New Testament, Örebro School of Theology, Sweden

Lauri Thurén (ThD, Åbo Akademi University), professor of biblical studies, School of Theology, Philosophical Faculty, University of Eastern Finland

Håkan Ulfgard (ThD, Lund University), professor emeritus of religious studies, Department of Culture and Society (IKOS), Linköping University, Sweden

Cecilia Wassén (PhD, McMaster University, Canada), associate professor of New Testament Exegesis, Department of Theology, Uppsala University, Sweden

Tommy Wasserman (PhD, Lund University), professor of New Testament, Ansgar University College and Theological Seminary, Norway

Mikael Winninge (ThD, Uppsala University), director of translation, Swedish Bible Society, Uppsala, Sweden; associate professor of New Testament exegesis, Department of Historical, Philosophical, and Religious Studies, Umeå University, Sweden

Karin Hedner Zetterholm (PhD, Lund University), associate professor of Jewish studies, Center for Theology and Religious Studies, Lund University, Sweden

Magnus Zetterholm (PhD, Lund University), associate professor of New Testament, Center for Theology and Religious Studies, Lund University, Sweden

Who Wrote What?

Håkan Bengtsson
"Beliefs and Practices in Second Temple Judaism"

Samuel Byrskog
"A History of New Testament Research"

Ismo Dunderberg
"Gnosticism and 'the Gnostics'"

Bengt Holmberg
"The Historical Jesus"

Jonas Holmstrand
"The Pauline Letters"

Marianne Bjelland Kartzow
"Lost and Found: A Narrative-Critical Reading of Luke 15"

Thomas Kazen
"The Origins and Transmission of the Texts" (except for "Reconstructing the New Testament Texts")

Dieter Mitternacht
"Beginnings" (together with Anders Runesson); "Paul, His Assemblies, and His Successors"; "How to Do a Historical, Text-Oriented Interpretation of a New Testament Text Passage"; "'Am I Now Seeking Human Approval?' A Rhetorical-Epistolary Reading of Gal 1:10"; the glossary; all chapter introductions and picture captions (together with Anders Runesson)

Birger Olsson
"Johannine Christ Followers"; "Approaches to the Text"; "A Historical, Text-Oriented Reading of Matt 8:14–17"; "A Historical-Analogical Reading of Matt 5:3–10"

Samuel Rubenson
"Diversity and the Struggle for Unity"

Anders Runesson
"Beginnings" (together with Dieter Mitternacht); "Paths to the Past: On Sources and Methods"; "Men, Women, and Power in Ancient Society and the Early Jesus Movement"; "Jewish Christ Followers and the Emergence of Christianity and Judaism"; Appendix 1; all chapter introductions and picture captions (together with Dieter Mitternacht); Box 2.4 "The Synagogue"

Anna Runesson
"'Legion Is My Name, for We Are Many': A Postcolonial Reading of Mark 5:1–20"

Hanna Stenström
"Who Is Part of the Future? A Feminist Analysis of Rev 17:1–19:10"

Kari Syreeni
"'One New Humanity' (Eph 2:15): A Pauline Tradition and Its Reception History"; "Living in the Time after Jesus: A Hermeneutical Analysis of the Johannine Farewell Discourse in John 13–17"

Mikael Tellbe
"Greco-Roman Religions and Philosophies"

Lauri Thurén
"How Are Good Deeds Motivated? An Argumentation Analysis of 1 Pet 1:17–19"

Håkan Ulfgard
"Catholic Letters, the Letter to the Hebrews, and the Book of Revelation"

Cecilia Wassén
"From Persians to Romans"; Appendix 2

Tommy Wasserman
"Reconstructing the New Testament Texts"

Mikael Winninge
"The Gospels and the Acts of the Apostles"

Karin Hedner Zetterholm
"Non-Rabbinic Jews and Varieties of Judaism"

Magnus Zetterholm
"The Peculiar Case of Pauline Scholarship and Judaism"

Rebecca Runesson and Noah Runesson
translated all of chapters 2–4, the appendices, and the glossary. For chapters 1, 5, and 6 they translated "A History of New Testament Research"; "Paths to the Past: On Sources and Methods"; "Jewish Christ Followers and the Emergence of Christianity and Judaism"; "Johannine Christ Followers"; "Diversity and the Struggle for Unity"; "Approaches to the Text"; "A Historical, Text-Oriented Reading of Matt 8:14–17"; "A Historical-Analogical Reading of Matt 5:3–10"; "How Are Good Deeds Motivated? An Argumentation Analysis of 1 Pet 1:17–19"; "'One New Humanity' (Eph 2:15): A Pauline Tradition and Its Reception History"; "Living in the Time after Jesus: A Hermeneutical Analysis of the Johannine Farewell Discourse in John 13–17"; "Who Is Part of the Future? A Feminist Analysis of Rev 17:1–19:10"; "'Legion Is My Name, for We Are Many': A Postcolonial Reading of Mark 5:1–20." The remaining sections were submitted to the editors in English.

Bibliography

Achtemeier, Paul D. *1 Peter*. Hermeneia. Minneapolis: Fortress, 1996.

Aland, Kurt, ed. *Synopsis of the Four Gospels: Greek-English Edition of the Synopsis Quattuor Evangeliorum*. 12th ed. Stuttgart: United Bible Societies, 2001.

Albertz, Rainer. *From the Exile to the Maccabees*. Vol. 2 of *A History of Israelite Religion in the Old Testament Period*. London: SCM, 1994.

Allison, Dale C. *A Critical and Exegetical Commentary on the Epistle of James*. ICC. London. Bloomsbury, 2013.

———. *The Historical Christ and the Theological Jesus*. Grand Rapids: Eerdmans, 2009.

Anderson, Paul N. *The Riddles of the Fourth Gospel: An Introduction to John*. Minneapolis: Fortress, 2011.

Anderson, Robert T., and Terry Giles. *The Keepers: An Introduction to the History and Culture of the Samaritans*. Peabody, MA: Hendrickson, 2002.

Apuleius. *The Golden Ass*. Translated by Sarah Ruden. New Haven: Yale University Press, 2011.

Aristotle. *The Art of Rhetoric*. Translated by John H. Freese. Loeb Classical Library 193. Cambridge, MA: Harvard University Press, 1926.

Ashcroft, Bill, Gareth Griffiths, and Helen Tiffin. *The Empire Writes Back: Theory and Practice in Post-Colonial Literatures*. London: Routledge, 1989.

Ashton, John. *The Gospel of John and Christian Origins*. Minneapolis: Fortress, 2014.

Attridge, Harold W. *Hebrews: A Commentary on the Epistle to the Hebrews*. Hermeneia. Philadelphia: Fortress, 1989.

Augustine of Hippo. *Tractates on the Gospel of John 112–124*. Translated by John W. Rettig. Pages 1–94 in *The Fathers of the Church*, vol. 5. Washington, DC: Catholic University of America Press, 1995.

Aune, David E. *The New Testament in Its Literary Environment*. LEC. Philadelphia: Westminster John Knox, 1987.

———. *Revelation*. 3 vols. WBC. Waco: Word, 1997–1998.

Baird, William. "Biblical Criticism: New Testament Criticism." Pages 730–36 in *Anchor Bible Dictionary*. Vol. 1. Edited by David Noel Freedman. New York: Doubleday, 1992.

———. *History of New Testament Research*. 3 vols. Minneapolis: Fortress, 1992–2013.

Barclay, John M. G. "Believers and the 'Last Judgment' in Paul: Rethinking Grace and Recompense." Pages 195–208 in *Eschatologie–Eschatology*. Edited by Hans-Joachim Eckstein. WUNT 272. Tübingen: Mohr Siebeck, 2011.

———. *Jews in the Mediterranean Diaspora: From Alexander to Trajan (323 BCE–117 CE)*. Berkeley: University of California Press, 1996.

———. *Paul and the Gift*. Grand Rapids: Eerdmans, 2017.

———. *Pauline Churches and Diaspora Jews*. Grand Rapids: Eerdmans, 2011.

Barth, Markus. *Ephesians: A New Translation with Introduction and Commentary*. 2 vols. AYBC 34–34A. New Haven: Yale University Press, 1974.

Barth, Markus, and Helmut Blanke. *Colossians: A New Translation with Introduction and Commentary*. AYBC 34B. New Haven: Yale University Press, 2005.

Barton, Stephen C., ed. *The Cambridge Companion to the Gospels*. Cambridge: Cambridge University Press, 2006.

Batten, Alicia J., and John S. Kloppenborg, eds. *James, 1–2 Peter, and Early Jesus Traditions*. London: Bloomsbury, 2014.

Bauckham, Richard. *The Climax of Prophecy: Studies on the Book of Revelation*. Edinburgh: T&T Clark, 1993.

———. *Jesus and the Eyewitnesses: The Gospels as Eyewitness Testimony*. 2nd ed. Grand Rapids: Eerdmans, 2017.

———. *Jude–2 Peter*. WBC 50. Grand Rapids: Zondervan, 2014.

———. *The Theology of the Book of Revelation*. Cambridge: Cambridge University Press, 1993.

Bauckham, Richard, Alexander Panayotov, and James R. Davila, eds. *Old Testament Pseudepigrapha: More Noncanonical Scriptures*. Vol. 1. Grand Rapids: Eerdmans, 2013.

Bauks, Michaela Bauks, Wayne Horowitz, and Armin Lange. *Between Text and Text: The Hermeneutics of Intertextuality in Ancient Cultures and Their Afterlife in Medieval and Modern Times*. Göttingen: Vandenhoeck & Ruprecht, 2013.

Baur, Ferdinand C. *The Church History of the First Three Centuries*. London: Williams and Norgate, 1878.

Beard, Mary, John North, and Simon Price. *Religions of Rome*. 2 vols. Cambridge: Cambridge University Press, 1998.

Beaugrande, Robert de, and Wolfgang Dressler. *Introduction to Text Linguistics*. London: Longman, 1981.

Becker, Adam H., and Annette Yoshiko Reed, eds. *The Ways That Never Parted: Jews and Christians in Late Antiquity and the Early Middle Ages*. Minneapolis: Fortress, 2007.

Becker, Eve-Marie. *The Birth of Christian History: Memory and Time from Mark to Luke-Acts*. New Haven: Yale University Press, 2017.

Beker, J. C. *Paul the Apostle: The Triumph of God in Life and Thought*. Philadelphia: Fortress, 1980.

Belle, Gilbert van, Jan G. van der Watt, and P. Maritz, eds. *Theology and Christology in the Fourth Gospel: Essays by the Members of the SNTS Johannine Writings Seminar*. Leuven: Leuven University Press, 2005.

Bengtsson, Håkan, and Anne-Louise Eriksson. *Tolkning för livet: åtta teologer om Bibelns auktoritet*. Enskede: TPB, 2004.

Berger, P. L., and T. Luckmann. *The Social Construction of Reality: A Treatise in the Sociology of Knowledge*. Garden City, NY: Anchor Books, 1966.

Bernier, Jonathan. Aposynagōgos *and the Historical Jesus in John: Rethinking the Historicity of the Johannine Expulsion Passages*. Leiden: Brill, 2013.

———. *An Introduction to the Gospel of John*. New Haven: Yale University Press, 2003.

———. *John and Judaism: A Contested Relationship in Context*. RBS 87. Atlanta: SBL Press, 2017.

———. *The Quest for the Historical Jesus after the Demise of Authenticity: Toward a Critical-Realist Philosophy of History in Jesus Studies*. London: Bloomsbury, 2016.

Berquist, Jon L. *Judaism in Persia's Shadow: A Social and Historical Approach*. Minneapolis: Fortress, 1995.

Best, Ernest. *The First and Second Epistles to the Thessalonians*. Harper's New Testament Commentaries. New York: Harper & Row, 1972.

Betz, Hans Dieter. *Galatians: A Commentary on Paul's Letter to the Church in Galatia*. Hermeneia. Philadelphia: Fortress, 1988.

Bieringer, Reimund, Didier Pollefeyt, and Frederique Vandecasteele-Vanneuville. *Anti-Judaism and the Fourth Gospel*. Louisville: Westminster John Knox, 2001.

Bilde, Per. *En religion bliver til: en undersøgelse af kristendommens forudsætninger og tilblivelse indtil år 110*. Copenhagen: Anis, 2001.

Black, David A. *Linguistics for Students of the New Testament: A Survey of Basic Concepts and Applications*. Grand Rapids: Baker, 1995.

———. *New Testament Textual Criticism: A Concise Guide*. Grand Rapids: Baker, 1994.

Bockmuehl, Markus, and Donald A. Hagner, eds. *The Written Gospel*. Cambridge: Cambridge University Press, 2005.

Bond, Helen K. *The Historical Jesus: A Guide for the Perplexed*. London: T&T Clark, 2012.

Boring, M. Eugene. "The Language of Universal Salvation in Paul." *JBL* 105, no. 2 (1986): 269–92.

Bovon, François. *Luke*. 3 vols. Hermeneia. Minneapolis: Fortress, 2002–2013.

Bradshaw, Paul F. *The Apostolic Tradition: A Commentary*. Hermeneia. Minneapolis: Fortress, 2002.

Brakke, David. *The Gnostics: Myth, Ritual, and Diversity in Early Christianity.* Cambridge, MA: Harvard University Press, 2010.

Bratcher, R. G. *Old Testament Quotations in the New Testament.* London: United Bible Societies, 1967.

Brodd, Jeffrey, and Jonathan L. Reed. *Rome and Religion: A Cross-Disciplinary Dialogue on the Imperial Cult.* Atlanta: Society of Biblical Literature, 2011.

Brooke, George J. *Reading the Dead Sea Scrolls: Essays in Method.* EJL 39. Atlanta: Society of Biblical Literature, 2013.

Brooten, Bernadette J. *Women Leaders in the Ancient Synagogue: Inscriptional Evidence and Background Issues.* Chico, CA: Scholars Press, 1982.

Brown, Peter. *Power and Persuasion in Late Antiquity: Towards a Christian Empire.* Curti Lecture Series. Madison: University of Wisconsin Press, 1992.

Brown, Raymond E. *The Birth of the Messiah: A Commentary on the Infancy Narratives in the Gospels of Matthew and Luke.* AYBRL. New York: Doubleday, 1993.

———. *The Churches the Apostles Left Behind.* New York: Paulist Press, 1984.

———. *The Community of the Beloved Disciple.* New York: Paulist Press, 1979.

———. *The Death of the Messiah: From Gethsemane to the Grave; A Commentary on the Passion Narratives in the Four Gospels.* AYBRL. 2 vols. New York: Doubleday, 1994.

———. *The Epistles of John: A New Translation with Introduction and Commentary.* AYBC. New Haven: Yale University Press, 1995.

———. *The Gospel according to John: A New Translation with Introduction and Commentary.* AYBC 29. Garden City, NY: Doubleday, 1966–1970.

Brox, Norbert. *A History of the Early Church.* London: SCM, 1994.

Bultmann, Rudolf. *Theology of the New Testament.* 2 vols. Waco: Baylor University Press, 2007 (first published: vol. 1, 1951, and vol. 2, 1955).

Burkert, Walter. *Greek Religion.* Translated by John Raffan. Cambridge, MA: Harvard University Press, 1985.

Burkett, Delbert. *Rethinking the Gospel Sources: From Proto-Mark to Mark.* London: T&T Clark, 2004.

Burns, Joshua Ezra. *The Christian Schism in Jewish History and Jewish Memory.* Cambridge: Cambridge University Press, 2016.

Burridge, Richard. *What Are the Gospels? A Comparison with Graeco-Roman Biography.* 2nd ed. Grand Rapids: Eerdmans, 2004.

Burrus, Virginia, ed. *Late Ancient Christianity.* A People's History of Christianity. Minneapolis: Fortress, 2010.

Byrskog, Samuel. *Story as History—History as Story: The Gospel Tradition in the Context of Ancient Oral History.* Leiden: Brill, 2002.

Cameron, Ron, and Merrill P. Miller, eds. *Redescribing Paul and the Corinthians.* Atlanta: Society of Biblical Literature, 2011.

Campbell, William S. *The Nations in the Divine Economy: Paul's Covenantal Hermeneu-*

tics and Participation in Christ. Lanham, MD: Lexington Books/Fortress Academic, 2018.

Carleton-Paget, James. "Jewish Christianity." Pages 731–75 in *The Early Roman Period*. Vol. 3 of *The Cambridge History of Judaism*. Cambridge: Cambridge University Press, 1999.

Carter, Warren, and Amy-Jill Levine. *The New Testament: Methods and Meanings*. Nashville: Abingdon, 2013.

Chadwick, Henry. *The Church in Ancient Society: From Galilee to Gregory the Great*. Oxford: Oxford University Press, 2003.

Charlesworth, James H., ed. *The Old Testament Pseudepigrapha*. 2 vols. New York: Doubleday, 1983–1985.

Chester, Andrew, and Ralph P. Martin. *The Theology of the Letters of James, Peter, and Jude*. Cambridge: Cambridge University Press, 1994.

Cicero. *On Invention; The Best Kind of Orator; Topics*. Translated by H. M. Hubbell. Loeb Classical Library 386. Cambridge, MA: Harvard University Press, 1949.

Clark, Gillian. *Christianity and Roman Society*. Cambridge: Cambridge University Press, 2004.

Cockerill, Gareth L. *The Epistle to the Hebrews*. NICNT. Grand Rapids: Eerdmans, 2012.

Cohen, Shaye J. D. *The Beginnings of Jewishness: Boundaries, Varieties, Uncertainties*. Berkeley: University of California Press, 1999.

———. *From the Maccabees to the Mishnah*. Philadelphia: Westminster, 1987.

Cohn, Norman. *Cosmos, Chaos and the World to Come: The Ancient Roots of Apocalyptic Faith*. New Haven: Yale University Press, 1993.

Collins, Adela Yarbro. *Crisis and Catharsis: The Power of the Apocalypse*. Philadelphia: Westminster John Knox, 1984.

———. *Mark: A Commentary*. Hermeneia. Minneapolis: Fortress, 2007.

Collins, John J. *The Apocalyptic Imagination: An Introduction to the Jewish Matrix of Christianity*. 3rd ed. Grand Rapids: Eerdmans, 2016.

———. *Historical Criticism in a Postmodern Age*. Grand Rapids: Eerdmans, 2005.

———. *The Invention of Judaism: Torah and Jewish Identity from Deuteronomy to Paul*. Oakland: University of California Press, 2017.

Collins, John J., and Daniel C. Harlow, eds. *The Eerdmans Dictionary of Early Judaism*. Grand Rapids: Eerdmans, 2010.

Conzelmann, Hans. *Die Mitte der Zeit: Studien zur Theologie des Lukas*. Tübingen: Mohr Siebeck, 1953.

———. *The Theology of St. Luke*. Minneapolis: Fortress, 1964.

Coogan, Michael D., ed. *The Oxford Encyclopedia of the Books of the Bible*. 2 vols. Oxford: Oxford University Press, 2011.

Cook, John Granger. *Roman Attitudes toward the Christians: From Claudius to Hadrian*. WUNT 261. Tübingen: Mohr Siebeck, 2010.

Cotter, Wendy J. *The Christ of the Miracle Stories: Portraits through Encounter*. Grand Rapids: Baker Academic, 2010.

Cranfield, C. E. B. *A Critical and Exegetical Commentary on the Epistle to the Romans*. 2 vols. Edinburgh: T&T Clark, 1979.

Crossan, John Dominic. *Who Killed Jesus? Exposing the Roots of Anti-Semitism in the Gospel Story of the Death of Jesus*. San Francisco: HarperSanFrancisco, 1995.

Crossley, James G. *The New Testament and Jewish Law: A Guide for the Perplexed*. London: T&T Clark, 2010.

Culpepper, R. Alan. *Anatomy of the Fourth Gospel: A Study in Literary Design*. Minneapolis: Fortress, 1983.

Dahl, Nils A. "Paul's Letter to the Galatians: Epistolary Genre, Content and Structure." Pages 117–42 in *The Galatians Debate: Contemporary Issues in Rhetorical and Historical Interpretation*. Edited by Mark D. Nanos. Peabody, MA: Hendrickson, 2002.

Davies, W. D., and Dale C. Allison. *Matthew*. 3 vols. ICC. London: T&T Clark, 2004.

Davila, James. *The Provenance of the Pseudepigrapha: Jewish, Christian, or Other?* Supplements to the Journal for the Study of Judaism 105. Leiden: Brill, 2005.

Dawes, Gregory W. *The Historical Jesus Quest: Landmarks in the Search for the Jesus of History*. Louisville: Westminster John Knox, 2000.

Demetrius. *On Style*. Translated by Doreen C. Innes. LCL 199. Cambridge, MA: Harvard University Press, 1995.

deSilva, David A. *Perseverance in Gratitude: A Socio-Rhetorical Commentary on the Epistle to the Hebrews*. Grand Rapids: Eerdmans, 2000.

Dettwiler, Andreas. *Die Gegenwart des Erhöhten: eine exegetische Studie zu den johanneischen Abschiedsreden (Joh 13,31–16,33) unter besonderer Berücksichtigung ihres Relecture-Characters*. FRLANT 169. Göttingen: Vandenhoeck & Ruprecht, 1995.

Dillon, Matthew, and Lynda Garland. *Ancient Greece: Social and Historical Documents from Archaic Times to the Death of Alexander the Great*. 3rd ed. London: Routledge, 2010.

Dodd, C. H. "The Mind of Paul: III." Pages 118–26 in *New Testament Studies*. Manchester: Manchester University Press, 1953.

Donaldson, Terence L. *Gentile Christian Identity from Cornelius to Constantine: The Nations, the Parting of the Ways, and Roman Imperial Ideology*. Grand Rapids: Eerdmans, 2020.

———. *Judaism and the Gentiles: Jewish Patterns of Universalism (to 135 CE)*. Waco: Baylor University Press, 2007.

Douglas, J. D., ed. *The New Greek-English Interlinear New Testament*. Wheaton: Tyndale, 1993.

Dowden, Ken. *Religions and the Romans*. London: Duckworth, 1998.

Dressler, Wolfgang. *Einführung in die Textlinguistik*. Tübingen: Niemeyer, 1972.

Drijvers, Han. "Syrian Christianity and Judaism." Pages 124–46 in *The Jews among Pagans and Christians*. Edited by Judith Lieu, John A. North, and Tessa Rajak. London: Routledge, 1992.

Dube, Musa W., and Jeffrey Lloyd Staley, eds. *John and Postcolonialism: Travel, Space and Power*. The Bible and Postcolonialism 7. London: Sheffield Academic Press, 2002.

Dunderberg, Ismo. *Beyond Gnosticism: Myth, Lifestyle, and Society in the School of Valentinus*. New York: Columbia University Press, 2008.

Dunn, James D. G. *The Cambridge Companion to St. Paul*. Cambridge: Cambridge University Press, 2003.

———. *The Epistles to the Colossians and to Philemon*. NIGTC. Grand Rapids: Eerdmans, 2014.

———. *Jesus Remembered*. Vol. 1 of *Christianity in the Making*. Grand Rapids: Eerdmans, 2003.

———. *A New Perspective on Jesus: What the Quest for the Historical Jesus Missed*. Grand Rapids: Baker Academic, 2005.

———. "The New Perspective on Paul." Pages 89–110 in *The New Perspective on Paul: Collected Essays*. WUNT 185. Tubingen: Mohr Siebeck, 2005.

Dunn, James D. G., ed. *Jews and Christians: The Partings of the Ways A.D. 70 to 135*. Grand Rapids: Eerdmans, 1999.

Dunning, Benjamin H., ed. *Oxford Handbook on New Testament, Gender, and Sexuality*. Oxford: Oxford University Press, 2019.

Eemeren, Frans H. van, et al. *Fundamentals of Argumentation Theory: A Handbook of Historical Backgrounds and Contemporary Developments*. Mahwah, NJ: Erlbaum, 1996.

———, et al. *Handbook of Argumentation Theory*. Dordrecht: Springer, 2014.

Ehrman, Bart D. "The Text as Window: New Testament Manuscripts and the Social History of Early Christianity." Pages 803–30 in *The Text of the New Testament in Contemporary Research: Essays on the Status Quaestionis*. Edited by Bart D. Ehrman and Michael W. Holmes. 2nd ed. Leiden: Brill, 2013.

Ehrman, Bart D., ed. and trans. *The Apostolic Fathers*. 2 vols. LCL 24–25. Cambridge, MA: Harvard University Press, 2003.

Ehrman, Bart D., and Michael W. Holmes, eds. *The Text of the New Testament in Contemporary Research: Essays on the Status Quaestionis*. 2nd ed. Leiden: Brill, 2013.

Eidinow, Esther, and Julia Kindt, eds. *The Oxford Handbook of Greek Religion*. Reprint edition. Oxford: Oxford University Press, 2017.

Eisenbaum, Pamela. *Paul Was Not a Christian: The Original Message of a Misunderstood Apostle*. New York: Harper One, 2009.

Elliott, John H. *A Home for the Homeless: A Sociological Exegesis of 1 Peter, Its Situation, and Strategy*. Philadelphia: Fortress, 1981.

———. *1 Peter: A New Translation with Introduction and Commentary*. AYBC 37B. New Haven: Yale University Press, 2001.

———. *What Is Social-Scientific Criticism?* Guides to Biblical Scholarship, New Testament Series. Minneapolis: Fortress, 1993.

Epictetus. *Discourses, Fragments, Handbook*. Translated by Robin Hard. Oxford World's Classics. Oxford: Oxford University Press, 2014.

Epp, Eldon J. *Junia: The First Woman Apostle*. Minneapolis: Fortress, 2005.

———. "The Multivalence of the Term 'Original Text' in New Testament Textual Criticism." *Harvard Theological Review* 92 (1999): 245–81.

Eshel, Hanan. *The Dead Sea Scrolls and the Hasmonean State*. Jerusalem: Yad Ben-Zvi Press, 2008.

Esler, Philip F., ed. *The Early Christian World*. 2nd ed. London: Routledge, 2017.

Eusebius. *The Church History*. Translated by Paul L. Maier. Grand Rapids: Kregel, 2007.

Fiensy, David A., and James Riley Strange, eds. *Galilee in the Late Second Temple and Mishnaic Periods*. 2 vols. Minneapolis: Fortress, 2014–2015.

Fisher, Eugene J., ed. *Interwoven Destinies: Jews and Christians through the Ages*. New York: Paulist Press, 1993.

Fishwick, Duncan. *The Imperial Cult in the Latin West*. Vol. III:1–4, *Provincial Cult*. Leiden: Brill, 2002–2005.

Fitzmyer, Joseph A. *The Acts of the Apostles: A New Translation with Introduction and Commentary*. AYBC 31. New Haven: Yale University Press, 1998.

———. *First Corinthians: A New Translation with Introduction and Commentary*. AYBC 32. New Haven: Yale University Press, 2008.

———. *The Gospel according to Luke: A New Translation with Introduction and Commentary*. 2 vols. AYBC 28–28A. New Haven: Yale University Press, 1985.

Fonrobert, Charlotte Elisheva. "The Didascalia Apostolorum: A Mishnah for the Disciples of Jesus." *JECS* 9, no. 4 (2001): 483–509.

Fredriksen, Paula. *Augustine and the Jews: A Christian Defense of Jews and Judaism*. New Haven: Yale University Press, 2008.

———. *Paul: The Pagans' Apostle*. New Haven: Yale University Press, 2017.

———. *When Christians Were Jews: The First Generation*. New Haven: Yale University Press, 2018.

Freyne, Sean. *Jesus, a Jewish Galilean: A New Reading of the Jesus Story*. London: T&T Clark, 2004.

———. *The Jesus Movement and Its Expansion: Meaning and Mission*. Grand Rapids: Eerdmans, 2014.

Friesen, Steven J. *Imperial Cult and the Apocalypse of John: Reading Revelation in the Ruins*. Oxford: Oxford University Press, 2001.

Gager, John G. *The Origins of Anti-Semitism: Attitudes toward Judaism in Pagan and Christian Antiquity*. Oxford: Oxford University Press, 1983.

———. *Reinventing Paul*. Oxford: Oxford University Press, 2000.

———. *Who Made Early Christianity? The Jewish Lives of the Apostle Paul*. New York: Columbia University Press, 2015.

Garland, Robert. *Religions and the Greek.* London: Duckworth, 1995.

Gaston, Lloyd. *Paul and the Torah.* Vancouver: University of British Columbia Press, 1987.

Gaventa, Beverly Roberts, and Richard B. Hays, eds. *Seeking the Identity of Jesus: A Pilgrimage.* Grand Rapids: Eerdmans, 2008.

Gerdmar, Anders, and Kari Syreeni. *Vägar till Nya Testamentet: metoder, tekniker och verktyg för nytestamentlig exegetik.* Lund: Studentlitteratur, 2006.

Gerhardsson, Birger. *Memory and Manuscript: Oral Tradition and Written Transmission in Rabbinic Judaism and Early Christianity, with Tradition and Transmission in Early Christianity.* Grand Rapids: Eerdmans, 1998.

Gillingham, Susan E. *One Bible, Many Voices: Different Approaches to Biblical Studies.* Grand Rapids: Eerdmans, 1999.

———. *The Mighty Acts of Jesus according to Matthew.* Eugene, OR: Wipf and Stock, 2016 (first published 1979).

Goodacre, Mark S. *The Synoptic Problem: A Way through the Maze.* Biblical Seminar 80. Sheffield: Sheffield Academic Press, 2001.

Grabbe, Lester, L. *A History of the Jews and Judaism in the Second Temple Period.* 2 vols. Edinburgh: T&T Clark, 2004.

———. *An Introduction to First Century Judaism: Jewish Religion and History in the Second Temple Period.* Edinburgh: T&T Clark, 1996.

———. *An Introduction to Second Temple Judaism: History and Religion of the Jews in the Time of Nehemiah, the Maccabees, Hillel, and Jesus.* London: T&T Clark, 2010.

Green, Joel B., ed. *Hearing the New Testament: Strategies for Interpretation.* 2nd ed. Grand Rapids: Eerdmans, 2010.

———. *Methods for Luke.* Cambridge: Cambridge University Press, 2010.

———. *The Theology of the Gospel of Luke.* Cambridge: Cambridge University Press, 1995.

Gregg, Steve. *Revelation: Four Views; A Parallel Commentary.* Rev. ed. Nashville: Thomas Nelson, 2013.

Gülich, Elisabeth, and Wolfgang Raible. *Linguistische Textmodelle: Grundlagen und Möglichkeiten.* Munich: Fink, 1977.

Gurtner, Daniel M. *Introducing the Pseudepigrapha of Second Temple Judaism: Message, Context, and Significance.* Grand Rapids: Baker Academic, 2020.

Gurtner, Daniel M., and John Nolland, eds. *Built upon the Rock: Studies in the Gospel of Matthew.* Grand Rapids: Eerdmans, 2008.

Haines-Eitzen, Kim. *Guardians of Letters: Literacy, Power, and the Transmitters of Early Christian Literature.* Oxford: Oxford University Press, 2000.

Halliday, Fred, and Jonathan Webster. *Text Linguistics: The How and Why of Meaning.* London: Equinox, 2014.

Hamilton, Catherine Sider. *The Death of Jesus in Matthew: Innocent Blood and the End of Exile.* SNTSMS 167. Cambridge: Cambridge University Press, 2017.

Hanson, Anthony T. *The Prophetic Gospel: A Study of John and the Old Testament.* Edinburgh: T&T Clark, 1993.

Harland, Philip A. *Associations, Synagogues, and Congregations: Claiming a Place in Ancient Mediterranean Society.* Minneapolis: Fortress, 2003.

Harrill, J. Albert. "Ethnic Fluidity in Ephesians." *NTS* 60 (2014): 379–402.

———. *Paul the Apostle: His Life and Legacy in Their Roman Context.* Cambridge: Cambridge University Press, 2012.

Hartman, Lars. *Approaching New Testament Texts and Contexts.* WUNT 311. Tübingen: Mohr Siebeck, 2013.

Hawthorne, Gerald F. *Philippians.* WBC 43. Nashville: Thomas Nelson, 1987.

Hayes, John R., and Carl R. Holladay. *Biblical Exegesis: A Beginner's Handbook.* 3rd ed. Louisville: Westminster John Knox, 2007.

Hellspong, Lennart, and Per Ledin. *Vägar genom texten: Handbok i brukstextanalys.* Lund: Studentlitteratur, 1997.

Henderson, Ian H., and Gerbern S. Oegma, eds. *The Changing Face of Judaism, Christianity, and Other Greco-Roman Religions in Antiquity.* Gütersloh: Gütersloher Verlagshaus, 2006.

Hietanen, Mika. *Paul's Argumentation in Galatians: A Pragma-Dialectical Analysis.* LNTS 344. London: T&T Clark, 2007.

Hilhorst, Anton, ed. *The Apostolic Age in Patristic Thought.* Leiden: Brill, 2004.

Hill, Charles E., and Michael J. Kruger, eds. *The Early Text of the New Testament.* New York: Oxford University Press, 2012.

Hoglund, Kenneth G. *Achaemenid Imperial Administration in Syria-Palestine and the Missions of Ezra and Nehemiah.* SBLDS 125. Atlanta: Scholars Press, 1992.

Holmberg, Bengt. *Sociology and the New Testament: An Appraisal.* Minneapolis: Fortress, 1990.

Holmén, Tom, and Stanley E. Porter. *Handbook for the Study of the Historical Jesus.* 4 vols. Leiden: Brill, 2011.

Holmes, Michael W. "From 'Original Text' to 'Initial Text': The Traditional Goal of New Testament Textual Criticism in Contemporary Discussion." Pages 637–88 in *The Text of the New Testament in Contemporary Research: Essays on the Status Quaestionis.* Edited by Bart D. Ehrman and Michael W. Holmes. 2nd ed. Leiden: Brill, 2013.

Holmes, Michael W., ed. *The Apostolic Fathers: Greek Texts and English Translations.* 3rd ed. Grand Rapids: Baker Academic, 2007.

Hull, Robert F. *The Story of the New Testament Text: Movers, Materials, Motives, Methods, and Models.* Atlanta: Society of Biblical Literature, 2010.

Hurtado, Larry W. *The Earliest Christian Artifacts.* Grand Rapids: Eerdmans, 2006.

Jeanrond, Werner. *Theological Hermeneutics: Development and Significance.* New York: Crossroad, 1991.

Jervell, Jacob. *The Theology of the Acts of the Apostles.* Cambridge: Cambridge University Press, 1996.

Jewett, Robert. *Romans: A Commentary.* Hermeneia. Minneapolis: Fortress, 2006.

Johnson, Luke Timothy. *Among the Gentiles: Greco-Roman Religion and Christianity*. New Haven: Yale University Press, 2009.

———. *The Letter of James: A New Translation with Introduction and Commentary*. AYBC 37A. New Haven: Yale University Press, 2005.

———. "The New Testament's Anti-Jewish Slander and the Conventions of Ancient Polemic." *JBL* 108 (1989): 419–41.

———. *The Real Jesus: The Misguided Quest for the Historical Jesus and the Truth of the Traditional Gospels*. San Francisco: HarperSanFrancisco, 1996.

Johnston, Sarah Iles, ed. *Religions of the Ancient World: A Guide*. Cambridge, MA: Harvard University Press, 2004.

Josephus. *Jewish Antiquities, Books XVIII–XIX*. Translated by Louis H. Feldman. LCL 433. Cambridge, MA: Harvard University Press, 1965.

Justin Martyr. *The First Apology, The Second Apology, Dialogue with Trypho, Exhortation to the Greeks, Discourse to the Greeks, The Monarchy of the Rule of God*. Translated by Thomas B. Falls. Washington, DC: Catholic University of America Press, 1948.

Kähler, Martin. *Der sogenannte historische Jesus und der biblische, geschichtliche Christus*. Leipzig: Deichert'sche Verlagsbuchhandlung, 1892.

Kant, Larry H. "Jewish Inscriptions in Greek and Latin." *ANRW* 20.2:671–713. Part 2, *Principat*, 20.2. Edited by H. Temporini and W. Haase. Berlin: de Gruyter, 1987.

Käsemann, Ernst. *The Testament of Jesus: A Study of the Gospel of John in the Light of Chapter 17*. London: SCM, 1978.

Kasser, Rodolphe, Marvin Meyer, and Gregor Wurst, eds. *The Gospel of Judas: Together with the Letter of Philip, James, and a Book of Allogenes from Codex Tchacos*. Washington, DC: National Geographic, 2007.

Kazen, Thomas. *Jesus and Purity* Halakhah*: Was Jesus Indifferent to Impurity?* Rev. ed. ConBNT 38. Winona Lake, IN: Eisenbrauns, 2010 (originally published 2002).

———. "Sectarian Gospels for Some Christians? Intention and Mirror Reading in the Light of Extra-Canonical Texts." *NTS* 51 (2005): 561–78.

Keith, Chris. *Jesus against the Scribal Elite: The Origins of the Conflict*. Grand Rapids: Baker Academic, 2014.

Keith, Chris, and Larry W. Hurtado. *Jesus among Friends and Enemies: A Historical and Literary Introduction to Jesus in the Gospels*. Grand Rapids: Baker Academic, 2011.

Keith, Chris, and Anthony Le Donne, eds. *Jesus, Criteria, and the Demise of Authenticity*. London: T&T Clark, 2012.

Kelber, Werner H., and Samuel Byrskog, eds. *Jesus in Memory: Traditions in Oral and Scribal Perspective*. Waco: Baylor University Press, 2009.

Kelly, J. N. D. *Early Christian Creeds*. Harlow: Longman, 1981.

King, Karen L. *What Is Gnosticism?* Cambridge, MA: Harvard University Press, 2003.

Klauck, Hans-Josef. *The Religious Context of Early Christianity: A Guide to Graeco-Roman Religions*. Minneapolis: Fortress, 2003.

Klijn, Albertus Frederik Johannes, and G. J. Reinink. *Patristic Evidence for Jewish-Christian Sects*. Leiden: Brill, 1973.

Kloppenborg, John S. *Christ's Associations: Connecting and Belonging in the Ancient City*. New Haven: Yale University Press, 2019.

———. "Memory, Performance, and the Sayings of Jesus." *JSHJ* 10 (2012): 97–132.

———. *Q, the Earliest Gospel: An Introduction to the Original Stories and Sayings of Jesus*. Louisville: Westminster John Knox, 2008.

———. *The Tenants in the Vineyard: Ideology, Economics, and Agrarian Conflict in Jewish Palestine*. WUNT 195. Tübingen: Mohr Siebeck, 2006.

Kloppenborg, John S., and John W. Marshall. *Apocalypticism, Anti-Semitism and the Historical Jesus: Subtexts in Criticism*. JSNTSup 275. London: T&T Clark, 2005.

Knibb, M. A. "Martyrdom and Ascension of Isaiah." Pages 156–57 in *Old Testament Pseudepigrapha*. Vol. 2. Edited by James H. Charlesworth. New York: Doubleday, 1985.

Knight, Jonathan. *Luke's Gospel*. New Testament Readings. London: Routledge, 1998.

Knoppers, Gary N. *Jews and Samaritans: The Origins and History of Their Early Relations*. Oxford: Oxford University Press, 2013.

Koester, Craig R. *Hebrews: A New Translation with Introduction and Commentary*. AYBC 36. New Haven: Yale University Press, 2001.

———. *Revelation: A New Translation with Introduction and Commentary*. AYBC 38A. New Haven: Yale University Press, 2014.

Korner, Ralph J. *The Origin and Meaning of* Ekklēsia *in the Early Jesus Movement*. Leiden: Brill, 2017.

Kraemer, Ross Shepherd, ed. *Women's Religion in the Greco-Roman World: A Source Book*. New York: Oxford University Press, 2004.

Langton, Daniel R. *The Apostle Paul in the Jewish Imagination: A Study in Modern Jewish-Christian Relations*. Cambridge: Cambridge University Press, 2010.

Last, Richard. *The Pauline Church and the Corinthian* Ekklēsia*: Greco-Roman Associations in Comparative Context*. SNTSMS 164. Cambridge: Cambridge University Press, 2016.

Lau, Binyamin. *From Yavneh to the Bar-Kokhba Revolt*. Vol. 2 of *The Sages: Character, Context, and Creativity*. Jerusalem: Maggid Books, 2011.

Layton, Bentley. *The Gnostic Scriptures: A New Translation with Annotations*. New Haven: Yale University Press, 1987.

Le Donne, Anthony. *The Historical Jesus: What Can We Know and How Can We Know It?* Grand Rapids: Eerdmans, 2011.

Lefkowitz, Mary R., and Maureen B. Fant. *Women's Life in Greece and Rome: A Source Book in Translation*. 3rd ed. Baltimore: Johns Hopkins University Press, 2005.

Levine, Amy-Jill. *Short Stories by Jesus: The Enigmatic Parables of a Controversial Rabbi*. Nashville: Abingdon, 2018.

———. "Visions of Kingdoms: From Pompey to the First Jewish Revolt." Pages 352–87 in

The Oxford History of the Biblical World. Edited by Michael D. Coogan. Oxford: Oxford University Press, 1998.

Levine, Amy-Jill, with Marianne Blickenstaff, eds. *A Feminist Companion to Acts*. Cleveland: Pilgrim Press, 2004.

———. *A Feminist Companion to John*. 2 vols. Cleveland: Pilgrim Press, 2003.

———. *A Feminist Companion to Luke*. Cleveland: Pilgrim Press, 2004.

———. *A Feminist Companion to Mark*. Cleveland: Pilgrim Press, 2004.

———. *A Feminist Companion to Matthew*. Cleveland: Pilgrim Press, 2004.

Levine, Lee I. *The Ancient Synagogue: The First Thousand Years*. 2nd ed. New Haven: Yale University Press, 2005.

Levinskaya, Irina. *Diaspora Setting*. Vol. 5 of *The Book of Acts in Its First-Century Setting*. Grand Rapids: Eerdmans, 1996.

Lieu, Judith M. *The Theology of the Johannine Epistles*. Cambridge: Cambridge University Press, 1991.

Lieu, Judith M., John A. North, and Tessa Rajak, eds. *The Jews among Pagans and Christians*. London: Routledge, 1992.

Limor, Ora, and Guy G. Stroumsa, eds. *Christians and Christianity in the Holy Land: From the Origins to the Latin Kingdoms*. Turnhout: Brepols, 2006.

Lincoln, A. T. *Ephesians*. WBC 42. Nashville: Thomas Nelson, 1990.

Lindars, Barnabas. *The Theology of the Letter to the Hebrews*. Cambridge: Cambridge University Press, 1991.

Lindholm, Stig. *Vetenskap, verklighet och paradigm*. Stockholm: Almqvist & Wiksell, 1980.

Longenecker, Bruce W., and Todd D. Still. *Thinking Through Paul: A Survey of His Life, Letters, and Theology*. Grand Rapids: Zondervan, 2014.

Longenecker, Richard N. *Galatians*. WBC 41. Dallas: Word, 1990.

Lopez, Davina C. *Apostle to the Conquered: Reimagining Paul's Mission*. Philadelphia: Fortress, 2010.

Lüdemann, Gerd. *Heretics: The Other Side of Early Christianity*. Louisville: Westminster John Knox, 1996.

———. *Opposition to Paul in Jewish Christianity*. Minneapolis: Fortress, 1989.

Luomanen, Petri. *Recovering Jewish-Christian Sects and Gospels*. Leiden: Brill, 2012.

Luz, Ulrich. *Matthew 1–7: A Commentary*. Rev. ed. Hermeneia. Minneapolis: Fortress, 2007.

———. *The Theology of the Gospel of Matthew*. Cambridge: Cambridge University Press, 1995.

MacDonald, Margaret Y. *The Power of Children: The Construction of Christian Families in the Greco-Roman World*. Waco: Baylor University Press, 2014.

Magness, Jodi. *The Archaeology of Qumran and the Dead Sea Scrolls*. Grand Rapids: Eerdmans, 2002.

———. *Stone and Dung, Oil and Spit: Jewish Daily Life in the Time of Jesus*. Grand Rapids: Eerdmans, 2011.

Malherbe, Abraham J. *Ancient Epistolary Theorists*. Society of Biblical Literature Sources for Biblical Study 19. Atlanta: Scholars Press, 1988.

———. *The Letters to the Thessalonians: A New Translation with Introduction and Commentary*. AYBC 32B. New Haven: Yale University Press, 2004.

Malina, Bruce. *The New Testament World: Insights from Cultural Anthropology*. Atlanta: John Knox, 1981.

Marcus, Joel. *Mark: A New Translation with Introduction and Commentary*. 2 vols. AYBC 27A–B. New Haven: Yale University Press, 2002–2009.

Marguerat, Daniel. *The First Christian Historian: Writing the Acts of the Apostles*. Cambridge: Cambridge University Press, 2004.

Marjanen, Antti. *Was There a Gnostic Religion?* Publications of the Finnish Exegetical Society 87. Göttingen: Vandenhoeck & Ruprecht, 2005.

Marjanen, Antti, and Petri Luomanen, eds. *A Companion to Second-Century Christian "Heretics."* Leiden: Brill, 2005.

Marshall, John W. *Parables of War: Reading John's Jewish Apocalypse*. Studies in Christianity and Judaism / Études sur le christianisme et le judaïsm. Waterloo: Wilfrid Laurier University Press, 2001.

Martin, Dale B. *The Corinthian Body*. New Haven: Yale University Press, 1995.

McIver, Robert K. *Memory, Jesus, and the Synoptic Gospels*. Atlanta: Society of Biblical Literature, 2011.

McKenzie, Steven L., and Stephen R. Haynes. *To Each Its Own Meaning: An Introduction to Biblical Criticisms and Their Application*. Louisville: Westminster John Knox, 1999.

McKim, Donald K., ed. *Dictionary of Major Biblical Interpreters*. 2nd ed. Downers Grove, IL: IVP Academic, 2007.

Meier, John P. *A Marginal Jew: Rethinking the Historical Jesus*. 5 vols. AYBRL. New York: Doubleday, 1991–2016.

Metzger, Bruce M. *The Canon of the New Testament: Its Origin, Development, and Significance*. Oxford: Clarendon, 1987.

Metzger, James A. *Consumption and Wealth in Luke's Gospel*. Leiden: Brill, 2007.

Meyer, Ben F. *The Aims of Jesus*. London: SCM, 1979.

Meyer, Marvin. *The Nag Hammadi Scriptures: The Revised and Updated Translation of Sacred Gnostic Texts*. New York: HarperOne, 2007.

Meyers, Carol L. "Temple, Jerusalem." Pages 350–69 in *The Anchor Yale Bible Dictionary*, vol. 6. Edited by David Noel Freedman. New York: Doubleday, 1992.

———. "Was Ancient Israel a Patriarchal Society?" *JBL* 133 (2014): 8–27.

Meyers, Eric M., ed. *Galilee through the Centuries: Confluence of Cultures*. Winona Lake, IN: Eisenbrauns, 1999.

Meyers, Eric M., and Mark A. Chancey. *Alexander to Constantine: Archaeology of the Land of the Bible*. New Haven: Yale University Press, 2012.

Michaels, J. Ramsey. *The Gospel of John*. NICNT. Grand Rapids: Eerdmans, 2010.

Miller, Patricia Cox. *Women in Early Christianity: Translations from Greek Texts*. Washington, DC: Catholic University of America Press, 2005.

Minear, Paul S. *John: The Martyr's Gospel*. New York: Pilgrim Press, 2003.

Mitchell, Margaret M. *Paul, the Corinthians and the Birth of Christian Hermeneutics*. Cambridge: Cambridge University Press, 2010.

Mitternacht, Dieter. "Foolish Galatians: A Recipient-Oriented Assessment of Paul's Letter." Pages 416–19 in *The Galatians Debate: Contemporary Issues in Rhetorical and Historical Interpretation*. Edited by Mark D. Nanos. Peabody, MA: Hendrickson, 2002.

———. "'Forceful and Demanding': On Paul as Letter Writer." *Theology and Life* 36 (2013): 375–90.

———. *Forum für Sprachlose: Eine kommunikationspsychologische und epistolär-rhetorische Untersuchung des Galaterbriefs*. ConBNT 30. Stockholm: Almqvist & Wiksell International, 1999.

Moloney, Francis J. *Belief in the Word: Reading John 1–4*. Minneapolis: Fortress, 1993.

———. *The Gospel of John*. SP 4. Collegeville, MN: Liturgical Press, 1998.

Moo, Douglas J. *Galatians*. BECNT. Grand Rapids: Baker Academic, 2013.

———. *The Letter to the Romans*. 2nd ed. NICNT. Grand Rapids: Eerdmans, 2018.

Moore, Stephen D. *The Bible in Theory: Critical and Postcritical Essays*. Atlanta: Society of Biblical Literature, 2010.

Moore, Stephen, D., and Fernando F. Segovia, eds. *Postcolonial Biblical Criticism: Interdisciplinary Intersections*. London: T&T Clark, 2005.

Moreland, Milton C. *Between Text and Artifact: Integrating Archaeology in Biblical Studies Teaching*. Atlanta: Society of Biblical Literature, 2003.

Munck, Johannes. *Paul and the Salvation of Mankind*. London: SCM, 1959.

Nanos, Mark D. *The Irony of Galatians: Paul's Letter in First-Century Context*. Minneapolis: Fortress, 2002.

———. *Reading Corinthians and Philippians within Judaism*. Eugene, OR: Cascade Books, 2017.

———. *Reading Romans within Judaism*. Eugene, OR: Cascade Books, 2018.

Nanos, Mark D., ed. *The Galatians Debate: Contemporary Issues in Rhetorical and Historical Interpretation*. Peabody, MA: Hendrickson, 2002.

Nanos, Mark D., and Magnus Zetterholm, eds. *Paul within Judaism: Restoring the First-Century Context to the Apostle*. Minneapolis: Fortress, 2015.

Nasrallah, Laura. *Christian Responses to Roman Art and Architecture: The Second-Century Church amid the Spaces of Empire*. Cambridge: Cambridge University Press, 2010.

Neusner, Jacob. *From Politics to Piety: The Emergence of Pharisaic Judaism*. 2nd ed. Eugene, OR: Wipf and Stock, 2003.

Neusner, Jacob, and Bruce D. Chilton, eds. *In Quest of the Historical Pharisees*. Waco: Baylor University Press, 2007.

Neutel, Karin B. *A Cosmopolitan Ideal: Paul's Declaration "Neither Jew nor Greek, Neither Slave nor Free, nor Male and Female" in the Context of First-Century Thought*. LNTS 513. London: Bloomsbury, 2015.

Nickelsburg, George W. E. *Jewish Literature between the Bible and the Mishnah: A Historical and Literary Introduction*. Philadelphia: Fortress, 1981.

Nolland, John. *The Gospel of Matthew*. NIGTC. Grand Rapids: Eerdmans, 2005.

———. *Luke*. 3 vols. WBC. Nashville: Thomas Nelson, 1989–1993.

Novenson, Matthew. *The Grammar of Messianism: An Ancient Jewish Political Idiom and Its Users*. Oxford: Oxford University Press, 2017.

Olsson, Birger. *A Commentary on the Letters of John: An Intra-Jewish Perspective*. Eugene, OR: Pickwick, 2013.

———. "A Decade of Text-Linguistic Analyses of Biblical Texts at Uppsala." *ST* 39 (1985): 107–26.

Olsson, Birger, and Magnus Zetterholm, eds. *The Ancient Synagogue: From Its Origins until 200 CE; Papers Presented at an International Conference at Lund University, October 14–17, 2001*. Stockholm: Almqvist & Wiksell International, 2003.

Osiek, Carolyn, and Margaret Y. MacDonald, with Janet H. Tulloch. *A Woman's Place: House Churches in Earliest Christianity*. Minneapolis: Fortress, 2006.

Parker, D. C. *The Living Text of the Gospels*. Cambridge: Cambridge University Press, 1997.

Parry, Donald W., and Emanuel Tov, in association with Geraldine I. Clements. *The Dead Sea Scrolls Reader*. 2 vols. 2nd ed., revised and expanded. Leiden: Brill, 2014.

Pearson, Birger A. *Ancient Gnosticism: Traditions and Literature*. Minneapolis: Fortress, 2007.

Perelman, Chaim H. *Self-Evidence and Proof*. Cambridge: Cambridge University Press, 1958.

Perelman, Chaim H., and Lucie Olbrechts-Tyteca. *The New Rhetoric: A Treatise on Argumentation*. Notre Dame, IN: University of Notre Dame, 1969.

Perkins, Pheme. *Gnosticism and the New Testament*. Minneapolis: Fortress, 1993.

Pilch, John J., and Bruce Malina, eds. *Biblical Social Values and Their Meaning: A Handbook*. Peabody, MA: Hendrickson, 1993.

Pippin, Tina. *Death and Desire: The Rhetoric of Gender in the Apocalypse of John*. Louisville: Westminster John Knox, 1992.

———. "The Revelation to John." Pages 109–30 in *Searching the Scriptures*. Vol 2 of *A Feminist Commentary*. Edited by Elisabeth Schüssler Fiorenza. New York: Crossroad, 1994.

Pitre, Brant. *Jesus and the Last Supper*. Grand Rapids: Eerdmans, 2015.

Pontifical Biblical Commission. *The Interpretation of the Bible in the Church*. Boston: Pauline Books & Media, 1996.

Powell, Mark Allan. *Methods for Matthew*. Cambridge: Cambridge University Press, 2009.

Price, Simon. *Religions of the Ancient Greeks*. Cambridge: Cambridge University Press, 1999.

———. *Rituals and Power: The Roman Imperial Cult in Asia Minor*. Cambridge: Cambridge University Press, 1984.

Pummer, Reinhardt. *The Samaritans: A Profile*. Grand Rapids: Eerdmans, 2016.

Räisänen, Heikki. *Paul and the Law*. Philadelphia: Fortress, 1986.

Reinhartz, Adele. *Befriending the Beloved Disciple: A Jewish Reading of the Gospel of John*. London: T&T Clark, 2002.

Reventlow, Henning Graf. *History of Biblical Interpretation*. 4 vols. Translated by Leo G. Perdue. Atlanta: Society of Biblical Literature, 2009–2010.

Riches, John. *Galatians through the Centuries*. Oxford: Blackwell, 2013.

Riches, John, and David C. Sim, eds. *The Gospel of Matthew in Its Roman Imperial Context*. London: T&T Clark, 2005.

Robbins, Vernon K. *Exploring the Texture of Texts: A Guide to Socio-Rhetorical Interpretation*. Valley Forge, PA: Trinity Press International, 1996.

Robinson, James M., Paul Hoffmann, and John S. Kloppenborg. *The Critical Edition of Q*. Hermeneia. Minneapolis: Fortress, 2000.

Roukema, Riemer. "La tradition apostolique et le canon du noveau testament." Pages 86–103 in *The Apostolic Age in Patristic Thought*. Edited by Anton Hilhorst. Leiden: Brill, 2004.

Rousseau, Philip. *The Early Christian Centuries*. London: Longman, 2002.

Rowland, Christopher. *The Open Heaven: A Study of Apocalyptic in Judaism and Early Christianity*. New York: Crossroad, 1982.

Rowlandson, Jane. *Women and Society in Greek and Roman Egypt: A Sourcebook*. Cambridge: Cambridge University Press, 1998.

Runesson, Anders. *Divine Wrath and Salvation in Matthew: The Narrative World of the First Gospel*. Minneapolis: Fortress, 2016.

———. "The Historical Jesus, the Gospels, and First-Century Jewish Society: The Importance of the Synagogue for Understanding the New Testament." Pages 265–97 in *A City Set on a Hill: Essays in Honor of James F. Strange*. Edited by Daniel Warner and Donald D. Binder. Mountain Home, AR: BorderStone, 2014.

———. "Inventing Christian Identity: Paul, Ignatius, and Theodosius I." Pages 59–92 in *Exploring Early Christian Identity*. Edited by Bengt Holmberg. Tübingen: Mohr Siebeck, 2008.

———. "Jewish and Christian Interaction from the First to the Fifth Centuries." Pages 244–64 in *The Early Christian World*. Edited by Philip F. Esler. 2nd ed. London: Routledge, 2017.

———. *The Origins of the Synagogue: A Socio-Historical Study*. ConBNT 37. Stockholm: Almqvist & Wiksell International, 2001.

Runesson, Anders, Donald D. Binder, and Birger Olsson. *The Ancient Synagogue from*

Its Origins to 200 C.E.: A Source Book. Ancient Judaism and Early Christianity 72. Leiden: Brill, 2008.

Runesson, Anna. *Exegesis in the Making: Postcolonialism and New Testament Studies*. Leiden: Brill, 2011.

Rüpke, Jörg. *Pantheon: A New History on Roman Religion*. Princeton: Princeton University Press, 2018.

———. *Religion: Antiquity and Its Legacy*. Oxford: Oxford University Press, 2013.

Ryan, Jordan. *The Role of the Synagogue in the Aims of Jesus*. Minneapolis: Fortress, 2017.

Safrai, Shmuel. "Religion in Everyday Life." Pages 793–833 in *The Jewish People in the First Century: Historical Geography, Political History, Social, Cultural and Religious Life and Institutions*. CRINT, Section One. Assen: Van Gorum, 1987.

Saldarini, A. J. *Pharisees, Scribes and Sadducees in Palestinian Society*. Edinburgh: T&T Clark, 1989.

Sanders, E. P. *The Historical Figure of Jesus*. London: Penguin Press, 1993.

———. *Jesus and Judaism*. Philadelphia: Fortress, 1985.

———. *Judaism: Practice and Belief 63 BCE–66 CE*. London: SCM, 1992.

———. *Paul and Palestinian Judaism: A Comparison of Patterns of Religion*. Philadelphia: Fortress, 1977.

Sawyer, John F. A., ed. *The Blackwell Companion to the Bible and Culture*. Oxford: Blackwell, 2006.

Schäfer, Peter. *Judeophobia: Attitudes towards the Jew in the Ancient World*. Cambridge, MA: Harvard University Press, 1997.

Schmid, U. "Scribes and Variants—Sociology and Typology." Pages 1–23 in *Textual Variation: Theological and Social Tendencies? Papers from the Fifth Birmingham Coloquium on the Textual Criticism of the New Testament*. Edited by H. A. G. Houghton and D. C. Parker. Piscataway: Gorgias Press, 2008.

Schneiders, Sandra Marie. *Written That You May Believe: Encountering Jesus in the Fourth Gospel*. New York: Crossroad, 2003.

Schröter, Jens. *Jesus of Nazareth: Jew from Galilee, Savior of the World*. Waco: Baylor University Press, 2014.

Schuller, Eileen. *The Dead Sea Scrolls: What Have We Learned 50 Years On?* London: SCM, 2006.

Schüssler Fiorenza, Elisabeth, ed. *Feminist Biblical Studies in the Twentieth Century*. The Bible and Women 9. Atlanta: SBL Press, 2014.

———. *Revelation: Vision of a Just World*. Proclamation Commentaries. Minneapolis: Fortress, 1991.

Schwartz, Seth. *Imperialism and Jewish Society, 200 B.C.E. to 640 C.E.* Princeton: Princeton University Press, 2001.

Schweitzer, Albert. *The Mysticism of Paul the Apostle*. New York: Holt, 1931.

———. *Von Reimarus zu Wrede: Eine Geschichte der Leben Jesu Forschung*. Tübingen: J. C. B. Mohr, 1906.

Segovia, Fernando F. "Mapping the Postcolonial Optic in Biblical Criticism: Meaning and Scope." Pages 23–78 in *Postcolonial Biblical Criticism: Interdisciplinary Intersections*. Edited by Stephen D. Moore and Fernando F. Segovia. London: T&T Clark, 2005.

Segovia, Fernando F., and R. S. Sugirtharajah, eds. *A Postcolonial Commentary on the New Testament Writings*. London: T&T Clark, 2009.

Sellars, John. *Hellenistic Philosophy*. Oxford: Oxford University Press, 2018.

Sim, David C. *The Gospel of Matthew and Christian Judaism: The History and Social Setting of the Matthean Community*. London: T&T Clark, 1998.

Smalley, Stephen S. *1, 2, and 3 John*. WBC 51. Grand Rapids: Zondervan, 2015.

Soulen, Richard N., and R. Kendall Soulen. *Handbook of Biblical Criticism*. Louisville: Westminster John Knox, 2001.

Starr, James M. *Sharers in Divine Nature: 2 Peter 1:4 in Its Hellenistic Context*. ConBNT 33. Stockholm: Almqvist & Wiksell, 2000.

Stegemann, Ekkehard, and Wolfgang Stegemann. *The Jesus Movement: A Social History of Its First Century*. Edinburgh: T&T Clark, 1999.

Stemberger, Gunter. *Jewish Contemporaries of Jesus: Pharisees, Sadducees, Essenes*. Minneapolis: Fortress, 1995.

Stendahl, Krister. "The Apostle Paul and the Introspective Conscience of the West." *Harvard Theological Review* 56 (1963): 199–215.

———. *Final Account: Paul's Letter to the Romans*. Minneapolis: Fortress, 1995.

———. *Paul among Jews and Gentiles, and Other Essays*. Philadelphia: Fortress, 1976.

Stenström, Hanna. "The Book of Revelation: A Vision of the Ultimate Liberation or the Ultimate Backlash? A Study in 20th Century Interpretations of Rev 14:1–5, with Special Emphasis on Feminist Exegesis." Doctoral diss., Uppsala University, 1999.

Stewart, Robert B. *The Resurrection of Jesus: John Dominic Crossan and N. T. Wright in Dialogue*. Minneapolis: Fortress, 2006.

Stewart-Sykes, Alistair C. *The Didascalia Apostolorum: An English Version with Introduction and Annotation*. Turnhout: Brepols, 2009.

Stowers, Stanley K. *A Rereading of Romans: Justice, Jews, and Gentiles*. New Haven: Yale University Press, 1997.

———. "What Is 'Pauline Participation in Christ'?" Pages 352–71 in *Redefining First-Century Jewish and Christian Identities: Essays in Honor of Ed Parish Sanders*. Edited by Fabian E. Udoh. Notre Dame, IN: University of Notre Dame Press, 2008.

Strauss, David F. *Das Leben Jesu, kritisch bearbeitet*. Tübingen: C. V. Osiander, 1835.

Stuckenbruck, Loren T., and Gabriele Boccaccini, eds. *Enoch and the Synoptic Gospels: Reminiscences, Allusions, Intertextuality*. EJL 44. Atlanta: SBL Press, 2016.

Sugirtharajah, R. S. *Postcolonial Criticism and Biblical Interpretation*. Oxford: Oxford University Press, 2002.

Sundblad, Bo, Kerstin Dominković, Birgita Allard, and Nina Dominkovic. *LUS: En bok om läsutveckling*. Stockholm: Almquist Wiksell, 1983.

Swartley, Willard M. *Covenant of Peace: The Missing Peace in New Testament Theology and Ethics*. Grand Rapids: Eerdmans, 2006.

Syreeni, Kari. "In Memory of Jesus: Grief Work in the Gospels." *BibInt* 12 (2002): 175–97.

———. "Wonderlands: A Beginner's Guide to Three Worlds." *SEÅ* (1999): 33–36.

Tacitus. *The Annals*. Translated by John Jackson. Loeb Classical Library 322. Cambridge, MA: Harvard University Press, 1962.

Talbert, Charles. *Reading Acts: A Literary and Theological Commentary*. Rev. ed. Macon, GA: Smyth & Helwys, 2013.

Tannehill, Robert C. *The Narrative Unity of Luke-Acts: A Literary Interpretation*. 2 vols. Philadelphia: Fortress, 1990–1994.

Taylor, Marion Ann, and Agnes Choi, eds. *Handbook of Women Biblical Interpreters: A Historical and Biographical Guide*. Grand Rapids: Baker Academic, 2012.

Tcherikover, Victor. *Hellenistic Civilization and the Jews*. Grand Rapids: Baker Academic, 2011.

Telford, W. R. *The Theology of the Gospel of Mark*. Cambridge: Cambridge University Press, 1999.

Thatcher, Tom, and Stephen D. Moore, eds. *Anatomies of Narrative Criticism: The Past, Present, and Futures of the Fourth Gospel as Literature*. Atlanta: Society of Biblical Literature, 2008.

Theissen, Gerd. *The Quest for the Plausible Jesus: The Question of Criteria*. Louisville: Westminster John Knox, 2002.

Thiessen, Matthew. *Paul and the Gentile Problem*. Oxford: Oxford University Press, 2016.

Thiselton, Anthony C. *Hermeneutics: An Introduction*. Grand Rapids: Eerdmans, 2009.

Thurén, Lauri. *Argument and Theology in 1 Peter*. Sheffield: Sheffield Academic Press, 1995.

———. "On Studying Ethical Argumentation and Persuasion in the New Testament." Pages 464–78 in *Rhetoric and the New Testament*. Sheffield: JSOT Press, 1993.

———. *Rhetoric and Argumentation in the Letters of Paul*. Oxford Handbook of Pauline Studies. Oxford: Oxford University Press, 2019.

Toulmin, Stephen E. *An Introduction to Reasoning*. 2nd ed. New York: Macmillan, 1984.

———. *The Uses of Argument*. Cambridge: Cambridge University Press, 1958.

Towner, Philip H. *The Letters to Timothy and Titus*. NICNT. Grand Rapids: Eerdmans, 2006.

Tuckett, Christopher, ed. *The Gospel of Mary*. Oxford: Oxford University Press, 2007.

Turner, John Douglas. *Sethian Gnosticism and the Platonic Tradition*. Quebec: Les Presses de l'Université Laval, 2001.

Übelacker, Walter. *Der Hebräerbrief als Appell: Untersuchungen zu exordium, narratio und postscriptum (Hebr 1–2 und 13, 22–25)*. Stockholm: Almqvist & Wiksell International, 1989.

Udoh, Fabian E., Susannah Heschel, Mark A. Chancey, and Gregory Tatum, eds. *Redefining First-Century Jewish and Christian Identities: Essays in Honor of Ed Parish Sanders*. Notre Dame, IN: University of Notre Dame Press, 2008.

Ukpong, Justin S. *Reading the Bible in the Global Village: Cape Town*. Global Perspectives on Biblical Scholarship. Atlanta: Society of Biblical Literature, 2002.

Uro, Risto. *Thomas: Seeking the Historical Context of the Gospel of Thomas*. Edinburgh: T&T Clark, 2003.

Uro, Risto, ed. *Thomas at the Crossroads: Essays on the Gospel of Thomas*. Edinburgh: T&T Clark, 1998.

VanderKam, James C. *An Introduction to Early Judaism*. Grand Rapids: Eerdmans, 2001.

Van Voorst, Robert E. *Jesus Outside the New Testament: An Introduction to the Ancient Evidence*. Grand Rapids: Eerdmans, 2000.

Vermes, Geza. *Who's Who in the Age of Jesus?* London: Penguin Books, 2005.

Wachtel, Klaus, and Michael W. Holmes, eds. *The Textual History of the Greek New Testament: Changing Views in Contemporary Research*. Atlanta: Society of Biblical Literature, 2011.

Wassén, Cecilia. *Women in the Damascus Document*. Leiden: Brill, 2005.

Wasserman, Tommy. "Criteria for Evaluating Readings in New Testament Textual Criticism." Pages 579–612 in *The Text of the New Testament in Contemporary Research: Essays on the Status Quaestionis*. Edited by Bart D. Ehrman and Michael W. Holmes. 2nd ed. Leiden: Brill, 2013.

Wasserman, Tommy, and Peter Gurry. *A New Approach to Textual Criticism: An Introduction to the Coherence-Based Genealogical Method*. Resources for Biblical Study 80. Atlanta: SBL Press, 2017.

Watson, Francis. *Gospel Writing: A Canonical Perspective*. Grand Rapids, Eerdmans, 2013.

———. *Paul, Judaism, and the Gentiles: Beyond the New Perspective*. Grand Rapids: Eerdmans, 2007.

Weber, Ferdinand C. *System der altsynagogalen palästinischen Theologie aus Targum, Midrash und Talmud*. Leipzig: Dörffling un Francke, 1880.

Wendel, Susan J., and David Miller, eds. *Torah Ethics and Early Christian Identity*. Grand Rapids: Eerdmans, 2016.

Wendt, Heidi. *At the Temple Gates: The Religion of Freelance Experts in the Roman Empire*. Oxford: Oxford University Press, 2016.

Westerholm, Stephen. *Perspectives Old and New on Paul: The "Lutheran" Paul and His Critics*. Grand Rapids: Eerdmans, 2004.

White, L. Michael. *From Jesus to Christianity: How Four Generations of Visionaries and Storytellers Created the New Testament and Christian Faith*. New York: HarperCollins, 2004.

Williams, Michael A. *Rethinking "Gnosticism": An Argument for Dismantling a Dubious Category*. Princeton: Princeton University Press, 1996.

Wilson, Stephen G. *Related Strangers: Jews and Christians 70–170 C.E.* Minneapolis: Fortress, 1995.

Winter, Bruce W. *Seek the Welfare of the City: Christians as Benefactors and Citizens*. Grand Rapids: Eerdmans, 1994.

Winter, Martin. *Das Vermächtnis Jesu und die Abschiedsworte der Väter: Gattungsgeschichtliche Untersuchung der Vermächtnisrede im Blick auf Joh. 13–17*. FRLANT 161. Göttingen: Vandenhoeck & Ruprecht, 1994.

Winter, Paul. *On the Trial of Jesus*. Berlin: de Gruyter, 1961.

Wire, Antoinette C. *The Corinthian Women Prophets: A Reconstruction through Paul's Rhetoric*. Minneapolis: Fortress, 1990.

Witherington, Ben, III. *Conflict and Community in Corinth*. Grand Rapids: Eerdmans, 1995.

Wrede, William. *Das Messiasgeheimnis in den Evangelien*. Göttingen: Vandenhoeck & Ruprecht, 1906.

Zetterholm, Karin Hedner. "Jewish Teachings for Gentiles in the Pseudo-Clementine Homilies: A Reception of Ideas in Paul and Acts Shaped by a Jewish Milieu?" *Journal of the Jesus Movement in Its Jewish Setting* 6 (2019): 68–87.

Zetterholm, Magnus. *Approaches to Paul: A Student's Guide to Recent Scholarship*. Minneapolis: Fortress, 2009.

———. *The Formation of Christianity in Antioch: A Social-Scientific Approach to the Separation between Judaism and Christianity*. London: Routledge, 2003.

Zetterholm, Magnus, and Samuel Byrskog, eds. *The Making of Christianity: Conflicts, Contacts, and Constructions; Essays in Honor of Bengt Holmberg*. Winona Lake, IN: Eisenbrauns, 2012.

Ziesler, J. A. *Pauline Christianity*. Oxford: Oxford University Press, 1990.

Index of Subjects

Index of Scripture and Other Ancient Texts

Mark

2 Corinthians

Deuterocanonical Works

Pseudepigrapha

Dead Sea Scrolls